"Enormously ambitious, wide-ranging and filled with insights. A marvellous and impressive book that makes you re-think how and why businesses thrive (and fail)."
Peter Frankopan, *Professor of Global History at Oxford University, author of* The Silk Roads

"There is no silver bullet for competitiveness. Many books promise quick fixes, but the wisdom in this new book by Arturo Bris is taking an ecosystem approach. This is the holistic roadmap emerging markets need to catch the next waves of productivity and globalization."
Dr. Parag Khanna, *managing partner of FutureMap and author of* Connectography

"This book by Arturo Bris, brings together the insights of the IMD World Competitiveness Centre over thirty years, as well as his personal travel and research in the last six years in Asia, the Middle East, Europe and Latin America, to understand why corporations achieve success and perform the way they do. Bris covers a broad terrain, highlighting not just corporate strategies but larger societal inputs such as education and government strategies which are crucial to competitiveness. A useful comparative blueprint for corporations and countries who wish to achieve the same success as the best in the world."
Chan Heng Chee, *Ambassador-at Large and Chair of the Lee Kuan Yew Centre for Innovative Cities, Singapore University of Technology and Design*

"Arturo Bris is the superstar of country competitiveness. Over the years we have enjoyed his annual reports and rankings on the competetiveness of nations around the globe. In this seminal book he shows us why it matters for business. A warm recommendation to anyone interested in decision-making beyond the state and survival strategies of companies."
Alexander Stubb, *Professor and Director at the European University Institute, Former Prime Minister of Finland*

The Right Place

The Right Place explains why firms succeed in one country and fail in another, irrespective of their inner drivers, and suggests potential initiatives that governments can take to help the private sector create jobs and, consequently, make their countries more prosperous.

The competitiveness race is not unlike a cycling race. If you want to ride fast, you need three things: a good bike, to be in good shape, and a smooth and fast road. In a collaborative model, you might say the business is the bicycle, the business leader is the cyclist, and the road is the government and the external environment. The responsibility of a government is to design and build the best possible road. It turns out that when the road is good, good cyclists suddenly appear and want to race on it. In this book, competition and macroeconomics expert Arturo Bris provides an analysis of countries' competitive performance based on 30 years advising countries on this topic. The typical mistakes that countries make and the pillars necessary to build a competitive economy are revealled: economic performance as a necessary condition for prosperity; government efficiency, so the public sector can create the conditions for a productive economy; business efficiency, so companies can create jobs; and infrastructure, both tangible and intangible, so businesses and individuals can operate efficiently.

With contemporary case studies throughout, the book provides an illuminating read for politicians, business leaders, and students of macroeconomics.

Arturo Bris is professor of finance at IMD and the director of the world-renowned IMD World Competitiveness Center. He works with governments all over the world assessing, measuring, and managing the competitiveness of countries. He was previously an associate professor at the Yale School of Management and is a member of the advisory board of the Wealth Management Institute in Singapore and of the Strategic Board of Debiopharm. He regularly speaks at events and conferences in Asia, Europe, the Middle East, and Latin America. He has had articles published in the *Journal of Finance, Journal of Financial Economics*, and also in the *Financial Times, The Wall Street Journal, Straits Times*, and *Handelsblatt* among many others.

The Right Place

How National Competitiveness Makes or Breaks Companies

Arturo Bris

Routledge
Taylor & Francis Group

LONDON AND NEW YORK

First published 2022
by Routledge
2 Park Square, Milton Park, Abingdon, Oxon OX14 4RN

and by Routledge
52 Vanderbilt Avenue, New York, NY 10017

Routledge is an imprint of the Taylor & Francis Group, an informa business

British Library Cataloguing-in-Publication Data
A catalogue record for this book is available from the British Library

Library of Congress Cataloging-in-Publication Data
Names: Bris, Arturo, author.
Title: The right place: how national competitiveness makes
or breaks companies / Arturo Bris.
Description: Abingdon, Oxon; New York, NY: Routledge, 2021. | Includes
bibliographical references and index. | Identifiers: LCCN 2020051604
(print) | LCCN 2020051605 (ebook) | ISBN 9780367674625 (hardback) |
ISBN 9780367674632 (paperback) | ISBN 9781003131397 (ebook)
Subjects: LCSH: Industrial policy. | Economic policy. | Economic
development. | Competition.
Classification: LCC HD3611 .B878 2021 (print) |
LCC HD3611 (ebook) | DDC 338.6/042--dc23
LC record available at https://lccn.loc.gov/2020051604
LC ebook record available at https://lccn.loc.gov/2020051605

ISBN: 978-0-367-67462-5 (hbk)
ISBN: 978-0-367-67463-2 (pbk)
ISBN: 978-1-003-13139-7 (ebk)

Typeset in Minion Pro
by Deanta Global Publishing Services, Chennai, India

Contents

Acknowledgments

This book is the result of several years of trips, projects, and research that have taken my team and I around the globe. I owe gratitude to all who have made it possible.

First and foremost, I want to thank my colleagues at the IMD World Competitiveness Center. Christos Cabolis, the chief economist of the center, has been my partner in crime and a friend for more than 20 years. Christos' ideas are behind every chapter of this book, and his devotion to the center and hard work have freed up time for me to write. Senior economist José Caballero and I have known each other since our days together at the Yale School of Management many years ago. José is a thorough researcher, and I have learned from him how to avoid flaws and ambiguities. He also proposes counterpoints to my (sometimes wrong) political arguments. Madeleine Hediger is the cornerstone of the IMD World Competitiveness Center, with her passion and knowledge, maintaining close contact with our partner institutes all over the world. William Milner has contributed to this book in many ways, and the quality of his work can be observed in several chapters. I would have been unable to complete this project without the support of Catherine Jobin, who keeps us all organized in the Swiss fashion. Finally, there are several topics in the book that were born out of joint research work with Marco Pistis and Maryam Zargari. I have learned from them immensely.

I am also grateful to former members of the team who have contributed to the book in one way or another. Anne-France Borgeaud Pierazzi introduced me to the fascinating world of competitiveness and led the team in the early days. Maelle Dessard has done a fantastic job and improved our digital capabilities. Fabian Grimm is part of the family and helped me with several chapters. Former interns Jaume Aranols, Arielle Ben-Hur, Boris Buschle Bello, Job Goddard, Max Harding, Anais Paty, Julian Raub, Luis Rodrigo Úbeda, and Alexander Stalley have brought energy and fresh knowledge.

A special thanks goes to Luchia Mallet, who has shared a few of the trips and experiences described in the book with me. From Bangkok to Lima, Tokyo, and Singapore, Luchia was always the best IMD ambassador teaching me to experience other cultures and to be a more tolerant and better person.

IMD is an amazing place with remarkable people. I am deeply grateful for the support I have received from IMD Chairman Michel Demaré, IMD President Jean-François Manzoni and Dean of Faculty and Research Anand Narasimhan. They have given me the opportunity to lead a strong team and to do my research by providing me with all the resources that I could ever need, with freedom and without constraints. In this journey, I have been inspired by my colleagues Profs. Salvatore Cantale, Didier Cossin, Shlomo Ben-Hur, Tawfik Jelassi, Stephane Garelli, Phil Rosenzweig, Sean Meehan, Omar Toulan, Dominique Turpin, Francisco Szekely, Bala Chakravarthy, and Michael Wade. Also, I would have never dared embark on this adventure without the support and enthusiasm of Richie Brito, Deniz Ozaltinordu, Andrew Sabaratnam, Melissa Bonny, Naoshi Takatsu, Simon Craft, Carlos Rivera, Nadine Hack, Shawn Fedun, Stein Jacobsen, Josep Maria Puig, Roberto Abad, Mireille Terrisse, Bruno Wirz, Ian Stewart, Drazen Raguz, Lucy Jay Kennedy, Delia Fischer, Cinthia Grande, Igor Karpachev, Katie Wiley, Thierry Maupilé, Alice Tozer, Aicha Besser, Sophie Corset, Amelia La Spada, and Anne-Sophie Diserens.

I now realize that in the pages that follow, I recount experiences and examples from 53 countries. Throughout the process of writing the book, some people have been my sounding board to exchange ideas and frustrations, and to keep the project alive. I trace the origin of the book back to a dinner with Alexander Koloshenko at Café Pushkin in Moscow. I subsequently visited Alexander a couple of times to check that I was going in the right direction. Alexander is smart and critical, and I am extremely grateful for the constant inspiration. Helio Waszyk and the late José López—both former Nestlé executives—supported some of my views on key issues. I have exchanged ideas with many friends and colleagues: Zhanna Kryuchkova and Oleg Samus in Kyiv; Stephanie Cheung in Hong Kong; Patricio Rohner, Abed Saheen, Mohammad Alkhas, and Hassan Mikail in Dubai; Adel Al-Foory and Amrou Al-Sharif in Muscat; Tamer Al Mounajem in Riyadh; Julie Wehbe in Melbourne; Jason Hsu in Taipei; Townsend and Erin Goddard in Newport; Fernanda Rodríguez in Brussels; Marina Wentzel in Basel; Anna Matevosyan and Eva Vaoutsi in Zurich; Robby Mol in Amsterdam; Tony Felton in London; Dmitry Klevzhits in Minsk; Andreas Weckherlin in Taipei; Wei-Te Chen in Taichung; Marten Kaevats in Tallinn; Tatiana Malysheva in Moscow; Sandeep Sander in Copenhagen; and Liberato Milo in Sao Paulo. I am very lucky that I am close to very imaginative scholars even if they are far away. Willem Smit, now at the Asia School of Business in Malaysia, has given me many ideas and examples. Aris Stouraitis, from Hong Kong Baptist University, is extremely smart despite his football preferences. Gerda Zigiene, from Kaunas University of Technology in Lithuania, is my friend and teacher. Eduardo Engel, from the University of Chile, is one of the smartest people I know; Ivo Welch at UCLA has always been more than a coauthor and a mentor. Here in Canton de Vaud, I am very grateful to Nick and Laura Packer, Fabian Rupprecht, Amaya Larrea, and Stéphane Doutriaux.

My work overseas has received a lot of support from our partner institutes. I am grateful to all of them, and especially to Wanweera Rachdawong and Pornkanok Wipusanawan from the Thailand Management Association; H.E. Dr Eiman Almutairi, from the National Competitiveness Center in Saudi Arabia; Jung Taik Hyun of the Korea Institute for International Economic Policy (KIEP); Carlos Arruda from Fundação Dom Cabral in Brazil; Enrique Manzur from the University of Chile; Percy Marquina from Centrum in Peru; Ramon O'Callaghan from Porto Business School in Portugal; Iryna Tykhomyrova from MIM-Kyiv in Ukraine; Melinda Ciento from the Center for Economic Development of Australia (CEDA); and Saša Mrak Hendrickson from the Managers Association of Slovenia. I owe a lot of knowledge and access to information to the Hong Kong Independent Commission Against Corruption (ICAC) and particularly to Simon Peh and Lawrence Chung.

A great deal of our success as pioneers in world competitiveness must be credited to our alumni clubs everywhere. It has been through IMD alumni that I have learned what was going on in several countries on the ground. I especially want to thank Marina Filipova and Tatiana Novikova from Moscow; Alan Kallir from Sydney; Greg Robinson from Melbourne; Frederik Strange from Copenhagen; Patrick De Schutter from Brussels; Ioana Canescu from Helsinki; Lars-Fredrik Forberg from Oslo; Alexander Zinser from Zurich; Mario Basaure, Pablo Kuhlenthal, and Mark Stengel from Santiago de Chile; Tiago Santos from Porto; Alex Guest from London; Ignacio de Benito from Barcelona; Bertrand Muller from Geneva; Gerhard Beinhauer from Frankfurt; Stefan Heitmann from Kuala Lumpur; Stephanie Fan from Hong Kong; Alfonso Navarro from Lima; Javier Pernas from Buenos Aires; and Carlos Rivera from Mexico City. Thank you all for your warm welcome.

The list of researchers who have contributed to the book is long and I have mentioned some names above. I additionally want to thank Tatiana Egorova, Thomas Hauck, Emily Kalka, Christopher Morris, Shukhrat Musinov, Amy Roberts, and Oksana Zakharova.

I grew up in a small place in Spain at a time when thinking beyond the borders of my province was considered science fiction. I left Spain for the first time when I was 18 years old and travelled outside of Europe (United States) when I was 30 years old. It is then that I ate my first mango, in Hong Kong, and only a few years before I first saw an avocado. By the time I got married, I had visited only two countries other than my own. Since then, I have been extremely lucky to live an adventurous life and to meet amazing people. I want to thank the three individuals who pushed me in the right direction whenever I needed it. Francisco Rodríguez de Coro, priest and historian, taught me how to perform and love research. Rafael Repullo, professor of economics and director of the Centro de Estudios Monetarios y Financieros (CEMFI) in Madrid, was a role model and convinced me to do a PhD abroad. Professor William N. Goetzmann from the Yale School of Management gave me the best opportunity of my life and it is my mission since I met Will to be at least 10 percent as curious as he is.

Needless to say, my family has always been extremely supportive and generous. My parents Melita and Bernardino taught me and love me. My brothers Carlos, Jorge, and Diego, and my sister Melita are my best friends and I am extremely proud of all of them. I read and write from their example.

Finally, I am the luckiest person on earth because of my son and daughter. One of our American friends said once that my wife and I may be good parents because our children cannot be more different from each other. And this is completely true—that our children are different, not that we are good parents... Felipe is a young promising political analyst who questions everything I say. This is extremely helpful because he knows much more than me: about the world, about politics, about history. Thanks to him, I try not to generalize when I speak about people and societies. Amanda is still in college but she thinks like an experienced adult and possesses the leadership skills that I lack: she is driven and smart, and thanks to her my view about the West is more caustic now than it was 20 years ago. I have learned a lot from both. The two most exciting and life-changing trips of my life were their initiative: Palestine (Felipe) and North Korea (Amanda).

Most of all, thank you to my wife Eva for her love, support, and for coping with my physical absences when travelling and my mental ones when writing. You are the best person I know and I love you.

Introduction

This is the story of two companies. In many ways, they are very similar; in fact, both are craft breweries. Both are headed by smart, hardworking people. Both create an exceptional product. Yet, as we will see, the business environments in which they operate are very different.

1. THE TAYBEH BREWING COMPANY

On a normal summer day, the temperature in the city of Taybeh, high in the West Bank overlooking the ancient city of Jericho and the valley of the River Jordan, easily

1

reaches a blistering 45°C. Originally mentioned in the Bible as Ophrah[1] and later known as Ephraim, the city can be accessed through a winding, hilly road that connects it to Ramallah, the capital of the West Bank, 12 kilometers southeast. The only Christian town left in Palestine, Taybeh boasts three gloriously preserved churches—one Roman Catholic, one Greek Orthodox, and one Melkite (Greek Catholic).

The buses that take you there (known in the West Bank as "fords" or "*sevises*") can seat eight people, not including the driver. Painted yellow, these are sometimes new/sometimes old vans donated by the German government. Despite the short distance, it takes me almost one hour to get to Taybeh from Ramallah. This is because in Ramallah, you need to wait for the *sevis* to fill up. These are buses that take passengers to the hundreds of small villages in the hills north of the city. A traveler normally hails a *sevis* as if it were a taxi and tells the driver where they are going. The driver then designs a route based solely on the destinations of the eight passengers in the bus. As passengers get off, others can get on, and the route is constantly updated based on the passengers' immediate needs. Since the population density is so sparse, it would be extremely inefficient to set up buses with regular routes to these places. Instead, using this system, the bus only stops in the eight villages to which the passengers are traveling. This also solves the secondary problem of having traffic from the small villages into cities. Since buses travel from cities to villages, once their passengers disembark, they are filled by other people moving in the opposite direction. As a whole, the system is archaic and based on improvisation, but it works remarkably well.

Consequently, after waiting about 30 minutes, I finally depart. I pay the driver in cash, as I must, and instruct him to drop me in the main square of Taybeh.

The square is a dusty, open space where the streets that take you to the three churches converge. My final destination is just 10 minutes away by foot, and the smell of urine and manure accompany me most of the way.

The Taybeh Brewing Company is the first microbrewery[2] in the Middle East, as well as the first beer company in the West Bank. Along with Shepherds Beer, located in nearby Birzeit, they are the only two beer companies in the West Bank. Taybeh was founded in 1994, right after the signing of the Oslo Accords. In 1997, it licensed a brewery in Germany.

The company produces six types of beer: Golden, Amber, Dark, White, Light, and, since 2007, a non-alcoholic beer. Founded by brothers Nadim and David Khoury, it is still run as a family business today. Nadim returned from his home in the United States to his family's town in Taybeh to start the company. He had previously received a degree in brewing from the University of California, Davis. The company was started by a USD 1.2 million investment on the Khourys' part, after banks refused to lend any money for the project.

Because of its location in a region under Israeli military occupation, Taybeh Brewing Company faces significant challenges in exporting its products. The 1993 Oslo Accords gave the Palestinian Authority (PA) jurisdiction over some cities in the West Bank. Some 35% of Taybeh is defined as Area B land, subject to joint control by Palestinian and Israeli authorities, while the remaining 65% is Area C, under full Israeli control. (Area A, which includes the capital Ramallah, is under the control of the PA.) [Image 1.1]

In order for products to leave the West Bank, the shippers must get permission from the Israeli government and military, and the goods must clear Israeli security checkpoints. The company could export through Jordan, but this would mean clearing

Image 1.1 The Author with His Son Felipe in the Taybeh Brewing Company

Jordanian customs in addition to the Israeli ones that they would still need to clear, even when moving merchandise over the Jordanian–Palestinian land border.

The laborious process of exporting beer from the town of Taybeh to international markets begins with the company requesting permits to move its individual shipments of merchandise into Israel and to use Israeli ports to ship it. This often takes several weeks: the *modus operandi* of the Israeli occupation is to backlog and delay much of the bureaucracy in Palestine, which massively slows down the West Bank economy and allows Israel to exert greater control over it. When shipping internationally, Taybeh typically uses the port of Ashdod, south of Tel Aviv. However, depending on availability, they must sometimes ship through Haifa, which is further away and thus costlier.

Once the permits are ready, a shipment of beer can leave Taybeh for one of the many checkpoints separating Israel and the West Bank. At each checkpoint, the truck will be scanned by the Israeli military. The duration of these inspections is unpredictable. Usually, the trucks are checked by dogs, but at some commercial checkpoints the trucks are electronically scanned. There is a literal wall built around parts of the West Bank that prevents Palestinians from entering Israel. This also applies to Palestinian vehicles, so once the beer truck reaches the checkpoint to cross the wall, it may go no further. Here, the beer must be unloaded from the first truck and loaded onto an Israeli truck on the other side of the wall. An Israeli forwarding agent can then transport the shipment to the port.

The entire process takes several hours and must be aborted if it cannot be completed before the checkpoint closes for the day. According to Dr Maria Khoury of the Taybeh Group, this happens quite often. Taybeh is not the only company trying to ship merchandise through the checkpoints, so prior to being scanned the trucks need to wait in a long line, causing even further delays. The checkpoints may also close arbitrarily without explanation, even if Taybeh merchandise is in line to cross. Sometimes these closures correspond to Jewish holidays or labor strikes in Israel. If the truck cannot cross the checkpoint on a given day, the beer must be transported back to Taybeh to be held in appropriate storage units overnight, otherwise it will spoil. The entire operation is restarted the following day.

The occupation adds enormous costs to the beer company because of the delays and the costly, unpredictable roads to the ports. Sometimes the beer will not make the port in time and the mechandise must wait for another ship to be available, making it very difficult for the company to expand and ship internationally because of the very unpredictable shipping schedule.

Currently, Taybeh Brewing Company somehow manages to ship to Denmark, Italy, Spain, Switzerland, Sweden, the United Kingdom, Japan, and the United States. In all these countries except the United States, the beer is shipped to individual private businesses and is not readily available in most liquor stores. For example, the only place where one can purchase Taybeh in all of Switzerland is at the Palestine Grill restaurant in Zürich. In the United States, Taybeh is more widely available at liquor markets, even though it is still limited to 24 stores in the state of Massachusetts and 1 in Rhode Island. Germany, as mentioned before, has a licensed Taybeh brewery.

As a result of the export difficulties, the majority of Taybeh's product is sold in the West Bank, where it is readily available in most shops and restaurants.

2. FULL MOON BREWWORKS

On the other side of the world from Taybeh is the beautiful island of Phuket, in Thailand. Phuket is a tropical island lying off the west coast in the Andaman Sea. Together with another 32 smaller islands, Phuket—the nation's largest island—comprises the country's second-smallest province, approximately the size of Singapore. In spite of its small size, Phuket is one of the leading holiday destinations in Southeast Asia. While the island's year-round population is about half a million people, about 20% of whom are expatriates, during the high, or dry, season between November and May, with the influx of tourists, the number swells to over a million.

More than a hundred years ago, Phuket was known as Jungceylon. Today, Jungceylon is the name of one of the island's two main shopping malls. Much like its location in the center of Patong, one of Phuket's busiest towns notoriously famous for its nightlife, Jungceylon shopping mall personifies the reputation Phuket has among tourists: it is vibrant and crowded, offering an eclectic blend of modernity and tradition.

While Phuket readily offers more serenity and exclusivity to those who look beyond the popular tourist spots, choosing Jungceylon as a location for Phuket's only microbrewery was a sensible choice for its owners.

Although it is set in the heart of a dynamic place, it takes me a bit of time to find Full Moon Brewworks. The charming brewpub is accessible through Jungceylon's open-air square that binds the two shopping mall buildings; the square is brimming with restaurant and entertainment options. The brewery is somewhat hidden behind the soaring canvas sails, one of the mall's hallmarks. I spot the Full Moon sign by chance as I walk through the crowd. The mixture of buzz, people, and aromas in the air makes me forget that I am in Thailand; the setting resembles one of the world's megalopolises. Inside the brewery, the interior is imaginative and cozy. Apart from the workers, nobody else is Thai.

Sukij Thipatima and Kamalas Pattanapaisarn, both originally from Bangkok, founded Full Moon Brewworks in 2010. Their dream to develop a distinct Thai beer had been sparked a decade earlier. The two friends met in the United States, where they were both studying. Together, they would go to a pub near their campus, where they enjoyed beers very different from the lagers and ales they had known in Thailand. The fullness of the aromas of those beers fueled a desire to make craft beer available in Thailand. At the time, no information about home distilling was available in their home country.

Today, while craft beer flavors and methodologies are far more accessible in Thailand, home brewing remains illegal. Brewing for commercial purposes within a licensed brewpub or restaurant is legal, but a beer-making license does not automatically include permission to bottle and distribute off-site. To be able to both brew and distribute beer, a brewery needs to churn out at least 10 million liters annually. Such production scale requires a significant lab technology investment, which, aside from the two conglomerates that dominate the market, smaller companies simply can't afford. In contrast, a minimum quantity for a beer-making license that enables the brewer to sell draft beer on premises is 100,000 liters a year.

Full Moon Brewworks is both a brewery and a place where customers can enjoy draft beers. Depending on the season and the number of visitors, there are typically between two and seven brews available each month. Apart from creating distinctive products and making their recipes suitable for the tropical climate, Sukij and Kamalas want to guide their customers and tease their taste buds, so their brewpub also offers a hand-picked selection of import beers.

In addition, two years ago, the company expanded its product line by launching bottled beer. Currently, the brand's three most popular draft beers each have a bottled version. Since Full Moon is not licensed to bottle the beer on premises, Sukij and his partner formed a partnership with a brewery in Australia. That is what many smaller brewers in Thailand choose to do: they send the ingredients to a brewery overseas, pay them to handle the beer production and packaging, and have the bottled beer shipped back to Thailand as taxable import goods. Full Moon Brewworks opted to partner with a brewery in Australia because of that nation's high-level technology and manufacturing; there's also a free trade agreement between Thailand and Oceania. Once made, the beer is shipped from Australia to Thailand by sea.

The free trade agreement between Thailand and Oceania means that the majority of tariffs on goods imported from Australia are eliminated, allowing Full Moon to only pay the excise (alcohol) tax and VAT instead. The current law, issued at the end of 2017, stipulates that the excise tax is calculated by working out the 40% of alcohol by volume and the retail container volume percentage, and then adding another 60% of the retail price.

Sukij tells me that prior to opening Full Moon in 2010, he and Kamalas did a lot of preparation work, and it took three years just to obtain the brewing license. Choosing the right location was one of the key factors; Phuket, Patong, and Jungceylon offer an unparalleled diversity of tourists, which was necessary to get the business going. Not only are the tourists more familiar with craft beers, but they are also the ones who can afford it: high production costs keep craft beer inaccessible to average Thais. Therefore, during the first six years, the vast majority of Full Moon customers were foreigners. Since the launch of their bottled beers, the number of Thais visiting the brewery has increased to about one quarter. Nowadays, looking at Thailand as a whole, Full Moon's body of consumers is divided between 60% Thai and 40% tourists.

Originally introduced to Thailand by European visitors, Thais have been brewing their own beers since 1933, but for decades confined their efforts to producing only lager.

The new generation has developed an interest in craft beers. In spite of the new trends, strict laws and harsh penalties for home brewing are keeping the industry at a stage of infancy. Many of the existing liquor policies are a reflection of the fact that Thailand is a Buddhist country; ensuring quality is often cited as another reason for strict regulations. I learn from Sukij that in Thailand, myriads of illegal goods are produced across various industries, making home production of alcohol dangerous. He stresses that, while the license-obtaining process can be slow and full of hurdles, setting up a brewery in Thailand legally, contrary to popular belief, is far from impossible.

Only 5% of the ingredients the company uses are from Thailand. The rest are imported. For their bottled beers, the brewery sources the ingredients directly in Australia whenever possible. The ingredients that are imported from Europe are either shipped to Thailand (for their draft beer) or to Australia (for the bottled beer).

Ultimately, the brand's long-term goal is to create a new style of beer based on local Thai ingredients, without compromising the quality and the fullness of flavor. To its owners, Full Moon Brewworks is a place of excitement, a modern laboratory-playground in which they test different recipes, get direct feedback, and interact with other beer lovers. Developing and fine-tuning the perfect flavor combinations is a process of trial and error. When the microbrewery first opened, the beers were primarily based on local ingredients. While the initial products were unique in their flavors, they weren't suitable for repeated drinking, nor on a par with other international beers.

During the business's second phase, the owners focused on making the beers more international while incorporating various parts of Thai culture and folklore—such as elements from Thai novels, or words that have a uniquely Thai character—by interpreting these elements in order to create a matching local sensory flavor. That often included using specialty malts, blending many hop varieties, playing with yeast fermentation temperatures, and incorporating Thai herbs and spices. For example, one of the company's beers, Bussaba Ex-Weisse, is the German Hefeweizen-style beer in which they used the aromas of the southern ginger flower to deliver the unique Thai floral aromas.

In the current third phase, the company has started research in partnership with Chiang Mai University in Thailand, aiming to develop the "Terrier Malt" for brewing. The idea is to advance grains native to Thailand, which are otherwise non-efficient, into brewing malt, thus increasing their value and supporting the local farmers. Unlike some other projects in which mass commercial breweries use unmalted grains to produce beer, developing this malt replacement is not about cost reduction. Sukij and Kamalas believe that such malt would help them create a distinctive Thai flavor.

Switching to local substitute ingredients in this way would significantly reduce the company's production costs. Another factor that would reduce the current overheads and make the beer more attainable to the locals would be to move the production to Thailand, and Sukij and Kamalas hope to achieve this in 2019 by partnering with one of the local breweries that already has a license. As soon as they can start making all their products in Thailand, their selling price could drop by up to 15%. It would then take another three or four years to scale the production and reduce the prices further, likely cutting them in half from their current levels.

Most of Full Moon's bottled beers are distributed within Thailand. In Bangkok, for example, they are carried in fine dining establishments and independent restaurants. Smaller quantities are exported to New Zealand, Hong Kong, and London by sea freight. The company's planning, accounting, and marketing are done from Bangkok rather than

Australia; the bottled beer is made in Australia, imported to Thailand, and then exported in small volumes, such as half a container per time. Generally speaking, the import–export process is smooth and straightforward. The company gets a fresh supply from Australia, between three to five containers, on a monthly basis. Their current staff limitations, combined with the fact that they only work with distributors with a competitive edge, keep their exports limited to a few countries for the time being.

3. THE IMPORTANCE OF THE BUSINESS ENVIRONMENT

At business school, we teach students and executives how to be successful. Companies pursue market share, stock price performance, profitability, and growth. These measures of success result from the interaction of four drivers: leadership, strategy, industry forces, and country/global factors.

Leadership refers to the decisions made by senior executives and the way they mobilize resources and inspire team members to perform.

Strategy is about choice under uncertainty, and how companies position themselves in a competitive environment.

Industry forces—whether you are in the technology space or in financial services—are a big determinant of financial results, for technology companies (for instance) grow faster than tobacco companies.

Executives and business educators spend a lot of time focusing on these "inner dimensions of performance"—leadership, strategy, and industry forces—because these are under their control. We like what we can change. Very rarely do we spend time in executive programs understanding what an election in the United States means for a company's performance, or how the foreseen water shortage in the coming years will affect the performance of a Russian bank. These factors are not under our control, and we do not like to think about what we cannot change.

In fact, the fourth driver, the country/global environment (the "outer driver of performance"), determines a big chunk of a company's success, especially when the firm operates in a regulated sector.

The difference between Taybeh Brewery in the West Bank and Full Moon Brewery in Thailand is not found in the considerable skills of their respective leaders. Nor is it found in their abilities to make choices when it comes to market positioning and pricing. It would be unfair to characterize Taybeh's strategy as inadequate because the company is struggling to grow and remain profitable. Its uphill battle to transform itself into a global player is the result of a combination of unfortunate political and historical events. In contrast, Full Moon's stellar results are clearly supported by the Thai physical infrastructure, education system, fiscal and monetary policies, the geographic position of Thailand, and several other factors that are not the result of Khun Sukij and Khun Kamala's entrepreneurial merits.

The national and global environment in which a company operates is a big factor in whether it struggles or thrives. For example, we can safely say that under the present system in North Korea we will never see the emergence of a Google or an IKEA there. But unfortunately, it is also very unlikely that corporate triumphs will see the light in today's Venezuela, Mongolia, or Tanzania.

While individual innovators are important, they are not the only key to entrepreneurial success. In fact, I have been more impressed by how companies innovate in Ukraine, the Philippines, and Peru than in Silicon Valley. Innovation, economic growth, and ultimately the stock price performance of firms result from a combination of good regulation, good infrastructure, good talent management, an efficient government, and an innovative and well-financed private sector.

Individual skills and choices are important of course, but only secondary once we take into account the environmental conditions in which entrepreneurs and companies function. Even more importantly, in a globalized world, successful leadership also depends on the extent to which those at the top understand, embrace, and use to a company's advantages the regulatory, competitive, and institutional advantages provided by the political systems in the countries where a firm operates—the non-market strategy. A strategy's success depends on the legal and economic environment provided by institutions, and on the financial, political, and economic risk upon which the company makes decisions.

This is the bottom line: All else being equal, a company in Phuket has a better chance of success and survival than an identical firm in Taybeh. Any company operating in a supportive or free environment has a competitive advantage over a similar company operating in a highly restrictive environment.

Business executives know this. However, since the institutional environment can be neither changed nor predicted by company leaders, it is usually taken for granted and considered either a constraint or a competitive advantage.

4. THE EIGHT CHARACTERISTICS OF SUCCESS

In their groundbreaking book *In Search of Excellence*, first published in 1982, Thomas J. Peters and Robert H. Waterman Jr. examined 43 of Fortune 500's top-performing companies and identified the distinguishing features relative to the other, worse-performing bunch.[3] They summarized their findings in eight characteristics that make companies successful:

1. A bias for action, active decision-making—"getting on with it." Facilitating quick decision-making and problem-solving tends to avoid bureaucratic control.
2. Close to the customer—learning from the people served by the business.
3. Autonomy and entrepreneurship—fostering innovation and nurturing "champions."
4. Productivity through people—treating rank-and-file employees as a source of quality.
5. Hands-on, value-driven—management philosophy that guides everyday practice, with management showing its commitment.
6. "Stick to the knitting"—stay with the business that you know.
7. Simple form, lean staff—some of the best companies have minimal administrative staff.
8. Simultaneous loose-tight properties—autonomy in shop-floor activities plus centralized values.

Apart from the list only characterizing successful firms *ex post*, and therefore not very helpful as a prescriptive recipe, think how dependent these key success factors are on the environment where the company operates. As this book will show, in both the private and the public sector, quick decision-making is often hindered by bureaucracy and corruption, and in some countries the political risk is so high that decisions are simply not made because one does not know the plans of the next government. Being close to the customer requires the right infrastructure; this includes not only things like roads but also digital and telecommunications networks to allow executives to "hear the voice of the customer." Additionally, innovation in the 21st century is primarily driven by entrepreneurial states,[4] and innovation ecosystems that combine access to innovation/innovators, capital availability, and business-friendly regulation.

The belief that a firm's results are greatly dependent on people's productivity should acknowledge that being productive depends on the stock of capital, the working habits and regulations, technological development, the availability of natural resources, and even a country's geographical position. It also depends on the degree of economic development of the country, which means that a worker in China, for example, is much less productive than a worker in Qatar, as we will show in the next chapter.

Management practices and organizational structure are largely country dependent. For instance, corporate boards in South Korea and Japan are male dominated and insider dominated, and function completely differently from boards in Norway (where gender quotas exist) and Switzerland (a massive attractor of foreign talent where boards are significantly more diverse).

5. THE VALUE OF COLLABORATION

This book pays attention to such an array of factors. "Competitiveness" summarizes, in one word, the combination of regulatory, political, economic, and social considerations that drive the performance of companies. We will show that, in the 21st century, governments are becoming more important than ever in order to make companies strive. We will discuss why firms succeed in one country and fail in another, irrespective of their inner drivers, and suggest potential initiatives that governments can take to help the private sector create jobs and, consequently, to make their countries more prosperous. But fundamentally we will emphasize that competitiveness—as a measure of a country's success—is less about *competing* with others than about *collaborating*. Competitiveness cannot be understood as the way countries create competitive advantage to succeed in global markets, but about how countries manage their resources, capabilities, and endowments in order to generate productivity, growth, prosperity, and fairness.

The Right Place is the result of 30 years of research at the International Institute for Management Development (IMD) World Competitiveness Center. IMD pioneered the field and has since contributed to the improvement of life conditions in many countries around the world. The work was started by my colleague Professor Stéphane Garelli, who should receive all the credit for developing the methodology that has made the IMD World Competitiveness Center the leading institution in understanding, analyzing, and assessing the competitiveness of nations. I became director of the center in January 2014 when Professor Garelli went into a very well-deserved retirement.

The competitiveness race is not unlike a cycling race. If you want to ride fast, you need three things: a good bike, to be in good shape, and a smooth and fast road. In a collaborative model, you might say the business is the bicycle, the business leader is the cyclist, and the road is the government and the external environment. The responsibility of a government is to design and build the best possible road. It turns out that when the road is good, good cyclists suddenly appear and want to race on it. I will try to provide a manual for politicians to pave the way for businesses to excel—and therefore to make an economy succeed. To do so, we will build on the best practices observed in the last decades. Unfortunately, there is no single country that does everything well, so our work is a long journey across several countries and continents, uncovering the actions, ideas, and strategies that have made countries successful in a particular aspect of the overall competitiveness journey.

6. THE IMPORTANCE OF GLOBAL FACTORS

The first part of this book spotlights how business leaders and educators tend to ignore global factors as determinants of performance. I will discuss what we know about the importance of leaders, strategy, and firm-specific characteristics in determining the fate of organizations. My premise is that leaders and leadership receive too much attention because it is usually under the control of firms and those who run them.

Unfortunately, the relationship of good leadership to performance is obscured by the halo effect, which leads us to attribute good performance to good leadership only *ex post*. For example, this is very visible when one analyzes the performance of soccer teams in the UEFA Champions League. Studying soccer coaches is a clean exercise because one can track their performance very well. Based on some interesting academic work, I show that the success of a soccer team depends much more on the money that the team receives than on the skills of the coach. The wealth of a team is a function of the institutional arrangements in every national championship. In Spain, the three top clubs receive most of the money coming from TV rights. That is why these three teams have been dominating European soccer, especially relative to teams in the UK's Premier League, where TV rights are distributed more evenly.

I extend this idea to the corporate world. Indeed, my own research will show that, when illustrating why companies fail or succeed, in explaining firms' return on invested capital and stock market performance, global factors are important. In that regard, my experience with senior executives is this:

First, that companies that understand the importance of global factors tend to promote executives with a global mindset, so good leadership becomes a consequence of culture, and not the reverse.

Second, between two companies operating in the same institutional environment, you still find that the differentiating factor is the resilience of their leaders to geopolitical uncertainty, global trends, regulatory changes, and systemic changes in customers' attitudes.

Ultimately—I will argue—the extent to which countries and international institutions shape the global environment is today the most determining lever of corporate performance. Policies do have impact.

Through the history of Giant Bicycles, the largest bicycle manufacturer in the world, I describe the importance of the Taiwanese legal and business environment in facilitating the emergence and growth of a small family business that managed to dominate the world in its industry. Finally, I discuss the experience of Russia under the international sanctions that followed its annexation of Crimea to prove that the institutional environment is much more important than individual talent.

7. DEFINING A NEW MEASURE OF SUCCESS

I subsequently move to understand what we mean by competitiveness as a measure of a nation's success. In Chapter 28, I start by questioning the focus on output and growth that has traditionally been the objective of public policy. The fact is that many governments around the world recognize today that competitiveness can be measured and managed. Far away from the original construct by Michael Porter and others, we discuss how in recent years international organizations pioneered by the IMD World Competitiveness Center have defined a new measure of success that is based on the quality of institutions, human development, quality of life, and quality of government. At the core of the competitiveness of nations is their ability to be productive, which is not necessarily a consequence of winning a competition with other countries, but rather the result of open borders, trade, investment, and infrastructure. That is why the Netherlands is a competitive country and North Korea is not.

Productivity leads to competitiveness to the extent that both the public and the private sector are able to translate productive efficiency into human development. This part of the book spends a few pages reporting productivity data across the globe in the last decades. One interesting fact is that despite technology and automation, productivity—and consequently competitiveness—has not increased much since 2008. The inability to increase productivity in Western economies has caused a reduction in real wages, which is at the root of populism, protectionism, and anti-immigration trends in the recent years. It is therefore important to assess the impact of technology on prosperity, and I will show that the priority of those policies that promote digital transformation should be the creation and preservation of jobs.

In this section, I also show how endowments and initial conditions drive and constrain the competitiveness of nations. I compare Belarus and Slovenia to illustrate that point: these are two former socialist economies with very different fates in recent years. Their competitiveness today has been greatly influenced by their different cultures, geographical positions, and political choices.

The last part of the section is devoted to describing alternatives to both competitiveness and gross domestic product (GDP). The list is long, but in summary there are two problems with any alternative to competitiveness: in most cases these metrics only capture a part of what makes a country prosperous, like the quality of the environment or social fairness. Additionally, quite a few of the alternatives to competitiveness cannot be managed; they are ideal in what they try to measure, but they do not give governments sufficient policy tools to improve them. A good example is Bhutan's Gross National Happiness Index, which is implemented through a set of value drivers that are very difficult to improve through public policies. For instance, time spent sleeping has been found to be one of the key drivers of people's happiness; it is unclear how a national government policy can influence how many hours a day a citizen sleeps.

8. WHAT IT TAKES TO BE COMPETITIVE

Part 3 describes the conditions that countries must fulfill in order to be competitive. Our objective is to provide not a way to describe and compare countries but a playbook to improvement. We consequently emphasize the reforms that successful countries have implemented in order to help their corporate sectors succeed, as well as the mistakes that lead to poverty and inequality.

The first of such conditions is the definition of a *good country strategy*. Borrowing from the corporate world, I show that many countries fail to formulate and execute strategy because they do not have a clear objective and because the political dynamics, present especially in democracies, make it impossible to commit to long-term agendas. In that context, I describe Abenomics—the economic policies advocated by Shinzō Abe since the December 2012 general election, which elected Abe to his second term as prime minister of Japan—as the poster child of a good strategy, not only in its formulation and objectives but also in its execution.

But even having a good strategy does not guarantee prosperity. A necessary condition is also the *building of national consensus*, especially when deep reforms are necessary. There are plenty of examples of reforming governments in recent years that were unable to build such consensus: Macron's France, Mexico under the presidency of Enrique Peña Nieto, and South Africa and the Zuma regime. But there are also successful cases that deserve our attention and give excellent lessons. The way Finland ended up with one of the best education systems in the world helps me show the importance of building bottom-up national consensus. The cases of Portugal and its post-2009 crisis performance, and India's reforms under President Narendra Modi, illustrate the importance of leaders and culture.

After showing the importance of strategy and stakeholder engagement in the success of public policy, I then analyze the role of *political leadership and leaders* when explaining the different competitiveness paths that nations follow. In this regard, it is key to make a clear distinction between democratic regimes and the rest. In dictatorships, building national consensus and holding leaders accountable are not an issue. Not surprisingly, in the last 20 years the countries that have performed best in our competitiveness rankings are either "good" dictators (the United Arab Emirates [UAE], Singapore, Hong Kong) or "not-so-good" dictators (China, Thailand). In democracies, leaders are challenged by the opposition, electoral processes, popular movements, and private sector institutions. In those environments, individual charisma and skills are a differentiating factor—the abilities of Winston Churchill and Franklin D. Roosevelt to transform their countries are two of the traditional examples in history. I build on the experience of Maksim Liksutov, head of the Transport Department of Moscow, who, against the opposition of virtually everybody, has managed to reduce massive traffic problems in Moscow by promoting car sharing.

I will show how the combination of personal courage, support from superiors, and professional experience coming from the private sector are key success factors. Moreover, what truly matters is that political leaders have nothing to lose, so they are able to sacrifice their personal and professional careers in achieving the public good. That is why political tenure is usually a liability: as politicians stay longer in power, if they make a decision that impacts their fortunes, they have a lot to lose, and therefore they are unwilling to implement the necessary changes. This also explains why it is often (but not always!) better to have a rich person in power than a poor one: the former has less motivation to exploit the system for personal gain.

Besides a strategy, national consensus, and political leadership, the fourth ingredient in the recipe for success is the *presence of a long-term view*—something that is a natural consequence of the previous three. Compared to many other capitals in the United States, the way the city of Boston, Massachusetts, adapted itself to the 21st century has been impressive, and it is partially the result of the progressive policies of a series of

Democratic mayors. Such long-term view is made possible by the non-partisan political process in the city (political candidates cannot be supported by a specific party), and therefore their need to commit to achieving results in order to stay in power. Unless you are a dictator, only when the political process provides the accountability coming from the electoral process do leaders show the diligence needed to pursue long-term goals. In Mexico, where as a constitutional rule the president cannot be re-elected, the chances that a political leader will embark on a program of successful reforms are meager. The sequence of try-and-fail reform policies there (and in Argentina, Chile, Colombia, Ecuador, Peru, and Venezuela) is what UCLA's economist Sebastian Edwards calls "*la fracasomania*."[5]

Finally, we often see that country strategies fail because they are never executed. This is no different from what happens in the corporate domain. Examples abound in the last years: Chile, Mexico, Italy, France, Saudi Arabia. They come up with amazing plans that die in lengthy discussions, the political process, or popular opposition, often because stakeholder management is not part of the strategy equation. I will describe how execution plans should already be included in the design of a national strategy. The poster child of such a combination of planning and execution is Tony Blair's Delivery Unit, created in the United Kingdom in 2001 during his second-term government, and put to an end in October 2010 with David Cameron. The Delivery Unit was a group established to provide direct assistance to the prime minister, originally with the intention to monitor progress on the government's capacity to deliver on its electoral promises. Subsequently, delivery units have been established in Canada, Australia, Chile, Brazil, Uganda, Senegal, and Rwanda. I devote special attention to the Performance Management and Delivery Unit (PEMANDU) in Malaysia, one of the largest and most successful delivery units in the world that has been a case study by governments and international organizations. Set up in 2009, PEMANDU's objective was to promote sustainable and inclusive socioeconomic transformation by executing policy.

9. BUSINESS CONSULTANTS

One of the most pervasive phenomena in recent years is the emergence of business consultants as designers and executers of national strategies. As we advise our executives, "strategy is the role of the leader and cannot be delegated." Yet, it is difficult for me to think of a Middle East senior politician whom I have met recently who does not show up with a consultant by their side. Such ability of consultants to penetrate public policy—and the tendency of politicians to delegate to them—is also frequent in Latin America and Southeast Asia. I think this is worth a detailed analysis, and I devote an entire chapter to show the damage that big consulting firms such as McKinsey & Company, BCG, and PwC are doing to those countries where they receive mandates to design the country's strategy. It is odd, yet it happens, that political leaders give power to for-profit organizations that do not have any skin in the game and do not suffer the consequences of the failure of a national strategy. Surprisingly enough, the use of consultants in the public sector is as frequent in dictatorships as it is in democracies. The problem to me is not the moral dilemma of whether it is advisable to help a dictator, but rather that democratic leaders should always own their strategies and their consequences—and consultants are a simple way to avoid such responsibility.

10. EDUCATION

Part 4 of the book emphasizes the ingredients of a good country strategy. First and foremost, a long-term competitiveness journey starts by focusing on the education system, since talent and the intangible infrastructure of a country are necessary conditions to generate prosperity.

The question I am interested in is not which education system is best, but rather how good education systems are designed and implemented. I describe in detail the cases of Switzerland and Singapore and point to the key success factors (skills to jobs, government funding, a focus on excellence) that have made these two systems the pioneers of educational reform worldwide.

Singapore and Switzerland base their talent competitiveness on both the quality of their respective education systems and on talent attraction and retention.

Across the world there are both net importers of talent and net exporters. Net importers of talent, such as Switzerland, the United States, and the United Arab Emirates, provide quality of life and opportunities for individual growth and success, as well as safety and urban quality. I pay attention to the personal story of Abed Shaheen, the chief executive officer (CEO) of InfoFort, a company based in Dubai, to show the factors that drive the attractiveness of an economy to foreign talent. On the other hand, net exporters of talent (India, China) suffer a lack of highly qualified human capital when they do not improve their domestic education system, fiscal rules, and provision of life quality.

11. INFRASTRUCTURE

While education represents the intangible infrastructure of a country, the physical infrastructure is obviously important as well. Very often, developing a good infrastructure is the result of several generations and takes many years. This is the case in most countries in Eastern and Western Europe. Of course, these cannot be role models for emerging economies where the urgency to develop roads, airports, access to commodities, and supply chains requires effective and fast policymaking. It is then interesting to learn from those countries that, while having everything in their favor including the economic environment, natural resources, political consensus, and strong currencies, they fail to develop their infrastructure because of corruption, a focus on other priorities, or the lack of political leadership. Brazil is the best example. I spend a few pages describing the pitiful condition of the country's roads and distribution networks, and especially the reasons why such a basic priority of the economy has been so obviously disregarded.

12. THE PRIVATE SECTOR CREATES JOBS

Another important ingredient is the realization that in a free market economy the responsibility to create jobs lies with the private sector, and the public sector must only facilitate it. This is not a political statement, only the realization that countries where the state is too big (France, China, Saudi Arabia) are not very competitive. I describe in detail how the economies of Tunisia and Oman have been operating until recently, with two systems based on keeping the population placated by subsidizing the provision of social services, from electricity to gasoline and food. For some of us in the Western world, it is surprising that such a large percentage of the national budget is spent on subsidizing the national economy, with no consideration for real investment in infrastructure, education, and economic growth.

A national strategy has to be founded in the uniqueness of the country. During a recent trip to China, I had the opportunity to attend a traditional music concert in Shanghai. A traditional Chinese orchestra plays instruments such as the *erhu*, a three-string kind of violin, and the *dizi*, a simple flute. These instruments are confined to minoritarian events such as the one I attended, while the Shanghai Symphony Orchestra naturally uses the Italian violin and the traverse flute that were first used during the Roman Empire. Unlike music instruments, institutions cannot be copied, and we made this mistake after the Asian and Latin American crises of the 1990s and the 2000s. There is an increasing need for differentiation across countries; and policy consensus (remember the Washington consensus?) and the standardization of economic recipes (which management consultants love by the way) are big mistakes.

I met Ala' Alsallal in 2009 in Amman, Jordan. Ala' is the founder and CEO of Jamalon, the Amazon of the Middle East. When I met him, he was a 21-year-old entrepreneur who had clearly bought his first suit because he was told he would meet a professor. His experience, which I recount in detail in the book, showed me that our traditional approach to innovation (promotion of talent through government investment, a favorable regulatory environment) does not help a clever kid who grows up in an illegal refugee camp with his widowed mother and his four siblings, and who still manages to create a company that is worth millions today. The Jordanian path to competitiveness must be as unique as the environment in which Ala' Alsallal has grown up, and it must be different from the one in Indonesia and Uruguay. One of the first questions that politicians therefore must ask themselves is, "What makes my country unique?" Many countries have answered this question and designed their economic policies around it. For Lithuania it was talent; for Peru it was cuisine and its monumental legacy; for Israel, its innovative capacity; for Mongolia, its natural resources.

13. THE RULE OF LAW

The uniqueness of every country is also reflected in how it preserves the rule of law. Academics and international organizations have done a lot of work showing how the rule of law is a driver of a country's stock market performance, attractiveness to foreign investment, and other economic outcomes. The rule of law requires good regulation and good enforcement, and this is no better shown than in the case of insider trading regulation in Mexico. Mexico enacted severe penalties against insider trading in the 1990s, following suit with its northern neighbor, the United States, only to see that insider trading prosecution was basically non-existent in the country until 2000. Even though an optimist could attribute the lack of cases to the effectiveness of the law, in reality what happened was that, by making insider trading more costly, Mexican regulators also increased the value of corruption among judges. It was only during the last few years, and following the publicity given to some high-profile cases, that the fight against insider trading has been successful. For the rule of law to operate it is therefore more important to have an effective judiciary than an effective legislature, so fighting corruption, for example, cannot rely just on having tough laws.

Curtailing corruption is indeed a necessary condition for a competitive economy. I devote a section in the book to describing the history of Hong Kong's Independent Commission Against Corruption (ICAC), created in 1974 when the small nation was still a British colony. During the 1980s, Hong Kong still ranked among the most corrupt nations in the IMD World Competitiveness Rankings. However, it managed to become a world example in the fight against corruption by focusing on three very important battles: good regulation, good enforcement, and good education. The latter is of particular importance, and I will show that the main driver of Hong Kong's success in its fight against corruption has been its ability to instill in the new generations the ability to differentiate between personal and social gains, between what is ethically acceptable and what is not. The Hong Kong government has developed such a mindset in the population not by advertising the benefits of compliance but by starting with children at school.

I then discuss the importance of financial markets in the success of a competitive economy. Among the BRICS (Brazil, Russia, India, China, and South Africa) countries, India best exemplifies how the lack of a mature financial market through which companies can access capital and investors, severely hinders economic development. I contrast the Indian example with China, where the banking system followed a different path. Capital attraction is only possible with good stock markets, financial and fiscal rule, corporate governance laws, and the provision of security for investors. Without funding, the private sector cannot create jobs. The financial system is therefore important, and I stress the idea that strong financial markets help develop competitive economies, even though sometimes politicians think that the causality is the reverse.

14. GOVERNMENT–INDUSTRY PARTNERSHIPS

Capitalism in the 21st century will also require a new ecosystem where governments are going to play a very important role. I think it is important to acknowledge that a sustainable world economy will need the public and the private sectors to build partnerships to improve people's lives. This goes beyond the Sustainable Development Goals that I analyze in Part 5 of the book. Here, I will show how a successful economic model requires the intervention of the state in the economy, not as a controller and regulator, but as an active agent and necessary ingredient of the ecosystem. The best example of that is China, where state-owned enterprises (SOEs) operate in between the private and the public sector, and where the government provides the license to operate that allows such companies to enjoy a monopoly power that benefits citizens. Of interest among all SOEs are Chinese banks, a good example of a subsidized financial system that makes it possible for banks such as the Agricultural Bank of China to provide financial services to poor farmers in remote areas, a business that would otherwise be unprofitable. In the Chinese banking ecosystem, the state is interested in preserving living conditions for farmers, who in turn contribute to the state with their production. The bank, that is also publicly listed, intermediates between the interest of both and makes money. Private–public partnerships in the new economy create win-win situations for everybody. There are, today, similar ecosystems in place in the Middle East, Southeast Asia, and Latin America.

15. NATIONAL CHAMPIONS, BUT ALSO SMALL AND MEDIUM ENTERPRISES

When it comes to creating jobs, it is a global phenomenon that most employment is created by small and medium enterprises (SMEs). Governmental policies of the post–World War II era, especially in Asian economies, have prioritized, however, the promotion of national champions as tools to implement industrial policies. Well known are the cases of Taiwan, Malaysia, Japan, and South Korea. I spend several pages, using the example of the South Korean *chaebols*, discussing the coexistence of both large and small companies in successful economies: on the one hand, SMEs create jobs and support the operations of the larger companies in the country; on the other hand, national champions act as a focal point in financial markets to attract capital. Alas, the main pitfall of the model is that larger companies tend to pay higher salaries, and therefore attract the best talent, which indeed exacerbates the duality of the economy. As I show in the case of South Korea, a country's industrial policy must therefore promote the emergence of national champions, but it must subsequently support SMEs so they can continue generating jobs.

16. BRANDING A NATION

Our work at the IMD World Competitiveness Center has proved that one of the best predictors of a country's future competitiveness is the image of the country abroad. Not surprisingly, many countries around the world have embarked on promotional campaigns to sell their national brand to tourists, global investors, and potential customers. It is worth learning from the best practices, and that is why I describe in detail the "Amazing Thailand" and "Brand South Africa" campaigns, two extensive political initiatives with material impact on the perception of these two countries abroad. For a much smaller country, I describe the journey of Timor-Leste from a newly born country after its independence from Indonesia in 1999 until today—in between, a great example of how to brand a nation.

17. TECHNOLOGY, INNOVATION, EDUCATION, GENDER POLICIES, AND SUSTAINABILITY

In Part 5 of the book, we look ahead to discuss the challenges of competitiveness in the 21st century. In particular, we focus on the roles of technology, innovation, education, gender policies, and sustainability.

Innovation ecosystems result from the optimal combination of three factors: talent development, financial resources, and effective regulation. I start by showing, through the example of the Lumière brothers in 19th-century France, that educational institutions and particularly universities are key to developing innovative nations. More relevant is the example of Israel, "the Startup Nation," for which I show that the amazing innovation outcomes of the country are the result of a combination of geopolitical constraints and academic excellence.

Of course, technology and digital transformation will be the pillars of the competitiveness models of the coming years. The competitive advantage created by technology is easier to achieve once a nation secures financing, talent, and good regulation. We call such ability to facilitate digital transformation, the "digital competitiveness" of a country, and I present two examples: Turkey and Estonia. With respect to Turkey, its positioning as an IT hub in between Eastern Europe and the Middle East is a consequence of focused government policies and the exploitation of its strengths vis-à-vis its neighbors. Estonia requires attention because, as a nation that achieved full self-government only in 1991, it has quickly evolved into the most developed e-government in the world. Additionally, the technology ecosystem that it has created facilitated the emergence of digital champions such as Skype, TransferWise, and Nortal.

In early 2019, a group of economists coordinated by Dani Rodrik from Harvard launched the Economics for Inclusive Prosperity (EfIP) network to promote the objectives of social justice and redistribution for our economic systems.[6] For us at the IMD World Competitiveness Center this is nothing new, as we deem the concept of national competitiveness to fully embrace both inclusiveness and prosperity. In this regard, competitiveness in the 21st century is not just about economic growth but also about gender balance, income equality, sustainability, and the ability of governments to resolve failures resulting from market dynamics.

With regard to gender balance and growth, I devote a chapter to describing the experience of Norway with its corporate governance reform that aimed to increase the number of female directors on Norwegian boards. The outcome of such legal initiative shows the importance of policies at preserving inclusiveness.

Similarly, I discuss the importance of implementing sustainable development goals by a combination of initiatives by the public and private sectors. Prosperity, and therefore sustainability, requires partnerships, and we start to see the fruits of successful initiatives between companies and governments.

To emphasize the role of public policy, I devote a chapter to the interventions needed to cope with the increasingly more frequent failures of our markets systems. The classical problem is well illustrated with the legal reform in Peru that tried to enforce the usage of seat belts in cars. By increasing penalties for non-compliance, the Peruvian authorities unwittingly made bribing police officers a more attractive choice for unbuckled drivers. This is an interesting case of the unintended consequences of regulation, and I report similar market failures in countries such as China, India, Nepal, and Mexico. The main conclusion of the chapter is that governments must put the maximization of social welfare as their priority when regulating markets.

There are two final topics that I think are worth addressing to conclude this book. One is the role that education will play in the future, and especially a discussion about which education systems will countries require to cope with a completely new world. Jobs and pay are changing fast. Technology and automation are key drivers of change, but also improvements in healthcare, with the subsequent increase in longevity, changes in habits, and generational shifts are transforming labor markets. Future generations will work in positions that do not yet exist. Because automation will replace and change the nature of many of the tasks we humans perform today, the concept of a "job" is going to change fundamentally. As a consequence, the majority of workers will no longer be able to rely on a salaried job for life and will need to redefine the nature and source of their incomes. Ultimately, this will require governments to redesign their education systems. Finland, Switzerland, and Singapore will stop being the role models unless new skills are introduced into our curriculums, and education changes from a stage in our lives that prepares us for the job market to a lifetime process where we never stop learning.

Additionally, for years we have studied the relationship between competitiveness and income inequality. Some believe that inequality is the price to pay for economic competitiveness. This notion is flawed, for economic development and competitiveness do not necessarily go hand in hand. That is why increasing fairness and removing inequalities is a necessary condition for competitiveness and shared prosperity. I share the experiences of Chile and China on this front, but also discuss in detail the minimum guaranteed income proposals and pilot programs in Switzerland and Finland, as well as fiscal reforms in other countries to protect the bottom 99%. Universal basic income schemes are, in my opinion, the only possible mechanisms for how we will cope in the future with the increasing inequalities caused by automation and the resulting loss of jobs.

18. THIS BOOK IS FOR BOTH BUSINESS AND POLITICAL STAKEHOLDERS

This book is relevant for both business executives and policymakers alike.

For policymakers, my experience during recent years shows that, very often, countries lack a unique, well-defined, and—what is even more important—well-executed strategy. Sometimes, it is the result of the political system, which makes politicians ignore long-term goals in order to focus only on the next election. This is, of course, not a problem in dictatorships, which can have and preserve a long-term vision. Indeed, this leads to a second array of problems when countries follow the wrong models. How many times during my travels have I heard the statement, "We want to be the Singapore of ____ (Africa, Eastern Europe, Latin America)." My reply is always the same: "If you want to be Singapore, you need two things: one is to be an island, the second is to have a benevolent dictator, neither of which is up to you to decide." In the last years, models have also been created by international organizations, which promoted the "one size fits all" model of macroeconomic policy. The Washington consensus, which was embraced by the International Monetary Fund (IMF) and the World Bank, failed to generate prosperity when it was the recipe that nations used in the aftermath of the 2007 Asian crisis, the 1994–1995 "Tequila Crisis," and the 2001 crisis in Argentina. Even before then, the IMD World Competitiveness Center was asserting that economies have to follow their own customized models and that institutions cannot be easily imported. That is why this book pays special attention to the concept of a country strategy, borrowing from concepts that we use extensively in business education.

Understanding competitiveness and its impact on the private sector is also relevant for policymakers because today, in the post-Covid-19 world, governments are extraordinarily important. This is ironic given that we are in a globalized world and borders are becoming more porous. However, as the corporate sector gains more power through multinationals, platform companies, and digital giants, public policy must intervene to put people first. We understand today that countries (and firms in those countries) are more innovative because the public sector invests in research and development, and not the reverse. We know that the quality of human capital in a country is in direct relationship with the dollar amount invested in education per student. At the same time, new business models (platforms, blockchain technology) will require new and innovative fiscal policies to address the resulting monopoly power in some sectors.

Finally, regulation is playing a fundamental role at generating winners and losers in fintech, insurtech, mobility platforms, hospitality companies, and the collaborative economy.

All in all, digital transformation will also come to the public sector. The rise of e-governments, the emergence of cryptocurrencies, and the new role of central banks, quantum computing, and the importance of regulating artificial intelligence (AI) to solve ethical dilemmas require that our leaders understand the dynamics of a competitive system and the complex interactions between the private and the public sectors. With these trendsetting innovations, data security and the protection of private identities become one of the major challenges of the world economy, and it cannot be left to decisions made in corporate boardrooms. We have more than enough case studies today from which government officials can learn what the best practices are.

The importance of governments results from the increasing episodes of market failure that we are witnessing since the turn of the century. Labor markets are changing, and as a result of technology, the quality of healthcare, economic development, and innovation, while we are living longer we have fewer jobs available, get paid less, and compete much more on the global scene. Therefore, citizens require policy responses to guarantee a decent quality of life for the elderly and the unemployed. We need policies to help reduce income inequalities. Only by having the guidance of wise leaders can countries cope with immigration and cultural clashes.

My approach is therefore to offer government officials the tools that we often use in business school to develop leaders. In that sense, the need for a vision, the importance of personal responsibility and individual values, the ability to surround oneself with the right team, and the central distinction between power and influence are as relevant for a politician as they are for a CEO.

Understanding the forces that allow governments to generate prosperity for their people is also relevant for corporate executives. This book is not written so business leaders just learn what is going on. Businesses operate within a certain institutional environment that constrains the choices that can be made and influences their impact. I will emphasize the importance of the established infrastructure to make projects and innovations thrive. Additionally, we need to realize the impact that education, healthcare, and scientific policies have on guaranteeing the availability of a talent pool able to cope with the challenges of the 21st century. Among private sector leaders, this should not be taken for granted. As Ben W. Heineman Jr. pointed out in a 2016 article in *Harvard Business Review*:

> The contemporary CEO must not only be expert at addressing the commercial verities of products, markets, and competitors. She must also have the experience and capability to address business-in-society issues—legislation, regulation, investigation, enforcement and litigation — that now create risk and opportunity in all dimensions of corporate activity.[7]

Speaking of the major disruptions that our societies have experienced recently, the drivers of change have not been the visionary leaders in our governments. Instead, they have been generated from the bottom up: the Arab Spring, the collaborative economy, cryptocurrencies, the rise of populism. These are all social changes started by social forces. These changes can be greatly influenced by business leaders. While the *Forbes* list of the 2018 World's Most Influential People contains only three CEOs or business leaders in the top 10—Jeff Bezos from Amazon, Bill Gates from Microsoft, and Larry Page from Google—33 out of the 75 names on the list (which includes Donald Trump and Pope Francis, among others) are CEOs of global companies.

I strongly believe that the ability of a senior leader to succeed depends on his or her knowledge and mastery of the global context. As one of my colleagues has pointed out, "If you claim that only global and country factors matter, then how can you justify that two companies subject to exactly the same environmental conditions perform differently?"

The answer is twofold.

First, companies are affected by policy and regulation differently depending on their industry, geographical focus, talent management policies, governance rules, culture, and strategy.

Second, leaders' room to maneuver internally is determined by their ability to cope with institutional challenges externally; that is, a skill that leaders (and leadership schools) should nurture is *resiliency to the environment*. In 2009, Nestlé, the largest consumer goods company in the world, appointed Antonio Helio Waszyk as CEO of Nestlé India. Before his appointment, Helio had never been responsible for any profit and loss numbers. Previously, he had headed the global foods strategic business unit and Nestlé's research and development center. During his tenure, India became a key market for Nestlé and revenues grew at spectacular rates.[8] But his appointment also revealed how the food and beverages multinational thinks: in order to succeed in a market, you need to understand it, and for that, business knowledge is less important than cultural empathy. Indeed, one of the first things that Waszyk did was to forge relationships with farmers to learn about their needs. For him, that was easy: he had grown up on a farm, and being Brazilian, he perfectly understood the social dynamics; and which country could be more similar to India than Brazil.

A significant development in the coming years will be the implementation of the Sustainable Development Goals[9] through a joint agenda agreed upon by most nations of the world. Water and sanitation, reduced inequalities, no poverty, and zero hunger are, among others, social and business objectives for 2030. As a pillar of future government strategies, these should also be embraced by private sector leaders. More importantly, Goal #17 specifies the commitment to establish "Partnerships for the Goals," and in particular the need for effective partnerships, in order to "encourage and promote effective public, public-private and civil society partnerships, building on the experience and resourcing strategies of partnerships."[10] More than ever, business executives need to collaborate with governments, to realize that the new form of capitalism includes the private sector as an essential part of the ecosystem, and that the role of the public sector includes facilitating private enterprise and job creation through public investment and regulation.

Social responsibility is not only about contributing to society, but also about co-creating with public sector institutions in order to improve world competitiveness.

NOTES

1 Book of Joshua 18:21-24: "The tribe of Benjamin, according to its clans, had the following towns: Jericho, Beth Hoglah, d Emek Keziz, Beth Arabah, Zemaraim, Bethel, Avvim, Parah, Ophrah, Kephar Ammoni, Ophni and Gebaj—twelve towns and their villages."
2 A microbrewery, by definition, is an independently owned brewery that produces no more than 1.8 million liters annually. TBC's sole factory produces 600,000 liters a year, well within range.
3 Peters and Waterman (2012).
4 Mazzucato (2015).
5 Edwards (2012).
6 Suresh Naidu, Dani Rodrik, and Gabriel Zucman. *Economics for Inclusive Prosperity: An Introduction*, Economists for Inclusive Prosperity, January 2019. Ebook available at: https://ec onfip.org/wp-content/uploads/2019/02/Economics-for-Inclusive-Prosperity.pdf.
7 Heineman (2016).
8 Anurag Prasad, "The Wind Beneath Nestle's Wings," *Fortune India*, April 5, 2012.
9 In 2015, the United Nations General Assembly unanimously adopted Resolution 70/1 "Transforming Our World: the 2030 Agenda for Sustainable Development." This agenda is a plan of action for people, planet, and prosperity. It also seeks to strengthen universal peace

and simultaneously secure a sustainable future for our people and planet. See www.undp.org/content/undp/en/home/sustainable-development-goals.html.

10 "Partnerships for the Goals," The Global Goals for Sustainable Development, www.global goals.org/17-partnerships-for-the-goals.

REFERENCES

Edwards, Sebastian (2012), *Left Behind: Latin America and the False Promise of Populism* (Chicago: University of Chicago Press).

Heineman Jr., Ben W. (2016), "The 'Business in Society' Imperative for CEOs," *Harvard Business Review*, Dec. 20.

Mazzucato, Mariana (2015), *The Entrepreneurial State: Debunking Public vs. Private Sector Myths*, Revised Edition (New York: Public Affairs).

Peters, Thomas J., and Robert H. Waterman Jr. (2012), *In Search of Excellence: Lessons from American's Best-Run Companies* (New York: Harper Business).

Part 1
The drivers of business competitiveness

19. INTRODUCTION

Measuring a company's financial success is very easy. It all starts with the key performance indicators (KPI) that the firm sets in advance. These indicators can include stock price performance, profit margin, market share, revenue growth, return on invested capital, and cash flow generation, to cite a few that are standard in the corporate world today. Very often, metrics are industry-specific, so banks will measure and manage risk-adjusted returns, as risk cannot be ignored. In other cases, investors will determine whether a company is a growth or value stock, and therefore key performance indicators have to be linked to growth and profitability, respectively. Sometimes, strategies are dependent on the business cycle, so after a financial crisis the main objectives will be to rebuild the market and grow the customer base.

The fate of a company depends on the interaction of many factors. Suppose that we were trying to explain 100 percent of a company's performance as measured by any of the metrics cited above. We could assign a figure to each of the logical dimensions of performance: leadership skills/abilities, company's strategy, industry forces, country's conditions, and finally global factors.

Normally, we take the latter, global factors, for granted—which may not be a good idea. For instance, Table 1.1 reports the best and worst companies in the Standard &

Table 1.1 Best and Worst Performing Stocks in the S&P 500

Fastest-Growing Companies in the S&P 500 (2000–2018)			Best Stocks in the S&P 500 (2000–2018)		
Rank	Company	Average Annual Sales Growth 2000–2018 (%)	Rank	Company	Annualized Return in USD 2000–2018 (%)
1	Equinix	91.33	1	Monster Beverage	44.29
2	Illumina	61.85	2	Hollyfrontier	29.36
3	Align Technologies	57.57	3	Carmax	27.90
4	Netflix	53.86	4	Nvidia	27.74
5	Akamai Technologies	43.03	5	Tractor Supply	26.63
418	Xerox	−3.43	387	AES	−5.92
419	Conagra Brands	−6.17	388	Akamai Technologies	−6.78
420	Altria Group	−6.20	389	E*Trade Financial	−6.99
421	Marathon Oil	−8.07	390	Citigroup	−7.12
422	Motorola Solutions	−8.40	391	AIG	−14.15

Source: Datastream.

Poor's 500 Index (S&P 500) over the period 2000–2018. To be clear, I have computed annualized returns and sales growth rates only for the companies that belong to the index for the entire period (for example, Alphabet Inc. is not in the list because it was included in the S&P 500 in 2014). All figures are in US dollars (USD). The first columns report average annual sales growth rates (in percent), and the right-hand side columns show the annualized stock return (including dividends). Even if not necessarily the case, the top and bottom five companies are all from the United States. Surprisingly, only some of the companies on the list are well known: Netflix, Xerox, Altria Group (Philip Morris), Citigroup. But some others are not much talked about; for example, Equinix specializes in internet connection and related services, while Illumina manufactures genetic and biological systems. A striking observation as well is that Akamai Technologies, which is among the fastest-growing companies (by revenues), also has one of the worst stock market performances.

An informal survey of business executives always concludes that, absent country considerations, the main important determinant of performance is leadership and leaders, as well as industry forces. In a 2014 article in *Forbes*,[1] Monster Beverage was listed as one of America's best-managed companies, after assessing how much its current management (and in particular its chief executive officer (CEO) Rodney Sacks) had contributed. *The Economist* ("How Netflix Became a Billion-Dollar Titan") attributed to its chief content officer the right decisions that led to the company's dominance in the streaming industry.[2]

In contrast, the disastrous performance of insurer AIG, and in particular its massive collapse and subsequent bailout, has been constantly attributed to the greed and risk-taking culture established by its then CEO Maurice "Hank" Greenberg.[3]

The influence of global factors on corporate performance is least discussed, especially outside of financial circles. But they can make a big difference. The dismal performance of Altria, Marathon Oil, Citigroup, and E*Trade Financial is perhaps more related to global trends affecting the oil, tobacco, and financial services industries. Strategy is at last the result of the combination of both industry dynamics and leadership performance.

Depending on the countries where they operate, global companies must be intuitively aware of political risks. Chinese trade policies severely impact the profit margins of firms that manufacture (or purchase inputs) in China, and who wins national elections in the United States influences stock market cycles, oil prices, interest rates, and geopolitical imbalances, and thus affects corporations worldwide. Within countries, not only different policies and regulations, but also infrastructure investment and talent attraction correlate with individual stock market returns.

Table 1.2 provides statistics for the period 2000–2018, particularly the annual stock market return (in USD) for the best and worst performing markets, among those included in the Datastream World Stock Market Index. It should not be a surprise that the "best" country is Venezuela, once you take into account the colossal devaluation of its currency. At the bottom, three of the five worst performing markets in the last 18 years are also countries that suffered the European sovereign debt crisis of 2008–2013. The United States falls in the middle (39 out of 56 countries) with an average stock market return of 5.97 percent per year. All things equal, we should expect that, during the 2000–2018 period, a company in China would have performed much better than an identical firm (in terms of industry, strategy, and leadership) based in the United States.

Table 1.2 Best and Worst Performing Stock Markets in the World (2000–2018)

Rank	Country	Annualized Return in USD 2000–2018 (%)
1	Venezuela	24.31
2	China	17.21
3	Czech Republic	14.71
4	Colombia	13.78
5	Estonia	13.21
39	**United States**	**5.97**
52	Portugal	2.28
53	Turkey	1.98
54	Japan	1.95
55	Greece	−10.26
56	Cyprus	−14.86

Source: Datastream.

Note: Returns in USD.

In 2000, Professors Randall Morck from the University of Alberta, Bernard Yeung from NYU (and currently the Dean of the National University of Singapore Business School), and Wayne Yu from the City University of Hong Kong published an impactful paper in the *Journal of Financial Economics* documenting the co-movement of stocks within a particular country.[4] They gathered data from 40 stock markets in the period between 1926 and 1995. They showed that, in some stock markets, most stocks would move up or down together in a given day. In a very efficient market, where individual firm information is the most important variable determining stock returns, you should expect that about half the stocks move up and half move down. This is the case in the United States and France, where the percentage of stocks moving together is 57.9 and 59.2 percent. In contrast, in Poland, for instance, 83 percent of all stocks move together in a given day. They estimated that in Poland, 57 percent of the performance of a stock is determined by countrywide phenomena. Mindful of the time period, they also found similar co-movement rates for China (80 percent of stocks move together), Malaysia (75 percent), Mexico (71 percent), and Finland (69 percent), to name a few.

Part 1 is an attempt to disentangle several factors that determine the performance of the corporate sector. We start by discussing a particular, sanitized, natural experiment to measure the performance of leaders—European soccer—and then discuss the evidence regarding the impact of leadership, organizational structure, strategy, and country factors on corporate performance. We conclude by providing the results of a quantitative exercise that tries to answer the question in the opening statement of the chapter: out of 100 percent, what percentage can be assigned to each of the drivers of performance? (See Figure 1.1.)

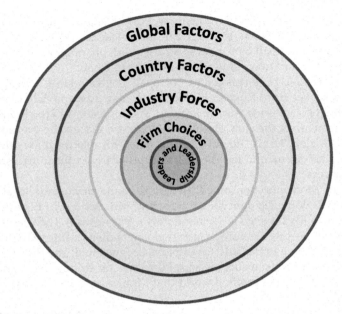

Figure 1.1 The Drivers of Performance

20. FOOTBALL: COACHES AND THE PERFORMANCE OF TEAMS

While José Mourinho, the renowned Portuguese professional football coach who most recently served as manager of English club Manchester United, is one of the most provocative figures in world football, in more recent times his prestigious past has not guaranteed victory on the field. There is no doubt that the self-proclaimed "Special One" has had success, winning the Champions League twice and capturing eight domestic league titles across Portugal, England, Italy, and Spain. Together with Carlo Ancelotti, Mourinho is the only coach to have won the Champions League with two different teams in the 21st century. However, since becoming a top manager after richly successful stints with FC Porto, Chelsea, and Inter Milan, Mourinho has faltered at top clubs Real Madrid, Manchester United, and in his return to Chelsea.

José Mourinho works his way to the top

To explain the massive success and hype around the Portuguese manager, we have to look back at his most successful period and what began his path to stardom: his time at FC Porto in his native Portugal. During Mourinho's two years at Porto, he won the league both years and started Porto's European ascent in the 2002–2003 season by winning the UEFA Cup (now known as the Europa League). The UEFA Cup was the secondary European club competition to the Champions League, the most prestigious award in club football.

In modern-day football, European Champions League football has been dominated by a small group of global giants, but a fresh Mourinho was able to break that mold with Porto in the 2003–2004 season. The Champions League is the pinnacle of European club football, and since the turn of the century, Porto has been the only team to capture Europe's top title outside of the top four European leagues (England, Germany, Italy, and Spain). As global football continues to stratify with big money concentrating on top teams, Mourinho's record may stand for many years to come.

Due to his incredible performance in Portugal, English club Chelsea, in its second season after a takeover from Russian billionaire Roman Abramovich, hired Mourinho. Mourinho brought his winning ways to London, and his team won the Premier League in his first two seasons with the club. Despite his domestic success, he was not able to fully capture European glory at his time in Chelsea. Later, his relationship with Abramovich soured, and in 2007 Mourinho left the club abruptly early in his fourth season, despite his domestic successes.

The next year, Mourinho continued his rise to managerial stardom at Inter Milan. Mourinho asserted domestic dominance early and won Serie A in his first two seasons in Milan, similar to his time at Chelsea and Porto. But it was in the Champions League that Mourinho's club wowed a European and global audience. Inter Milan beat German giant Bayern Munich to win the 2010 Champions League Final, and the Portuguese manager proved that his European success with Porto was far from a fluke. The Champions League results proved to the football world that Mourinho was a managerial force with which to be reckoned.

With so many honors in Mourinho's trophy cabinet, in 2010 he was snapped up by Real Madrid, his first attempt at managing a truly global power in football. During his first stint with Chelsea, the club was not yet a prestigious or established European contender, and Inter was suffering a 38-year European drought before Mourinho won the 2010 Champions League. But Real Madrid is known throughout the world as one of the most powerful and historical clubs in European history.

Big money does not bring big success

Compared to his previous stops, Mourinho had little success in Madrid, especially considering the financial reach, global power, and the expectations of Real. While Mourinho's meteoric rise transformed him into one of the most famous and sought-after football managers in the world, it was precisely at the moment when he became known as a world-class coach at a world-class club that his managerial career began to falter.

During his three years in Madrid, Mourinho won the Copa del Rey, Spain's top cup competition, and the league. For most coaches, this amount of success would be reason to celebrate, but Real Madrid failed to win a major trophy in his third year, and he faced multiple disappointments in European competition. Following a lackluster third season, Mourinho unceremoniously departed the Spanish giant without reaching the levels of success the Madrid faithful were expecting. In 2013, Mourinho returned to Chelsea and promised success similar to his first stint at the club. He was able to win the Premier League in the 2014–2015 season, but he stayed on top at Chelsea for a shorter time in his second go at the club. He was fired less than halfway through the following league campaign, after suffering nine losses in just 16 league games in one of the club's worst starts to a season in recent history.

Despite his rocky and controversial second stint as Chelsea manager, Manchester United was keen to make Mourinho, now a veteran presence in the industry, its manager. At the time of Mourinho's hiring, Manchester was in a tumultuous title drought since its longtime manager and club legend Sir Alex Ferguson had left his managerial post in 2013. During Ferguson's reign, Manchester United was a perennial domestic and European title challenger, winning 13 Premier League titles from 1992 to 2013. But in the three years between Ferguson and Mourinho, United fell from its top spot in England and failed to even contend for the title, finishing seventh, fourth, and fifth in the first three Premier League seasons of the post-Ferguson era.

Unfortunately for Mourinho and Manchester United, despite the wealth of resources and money at the club, Mourinho's short time there would be his worst. In Mourinho's first season, he was able to capture some silverware, winning the Europa League and bringing some hope to the United faithful. But the victory in Europe's secondary continental competition was little reason to celebrate considering United's dismal sixth-place finish in the league. In the following season, United improved and finished second in the league, but it won no trophies and was nowhere close to challenging league champions and crosstown rival Manchester City. In Mourinho's third season, United got off to a slow start, and the club fired the Portuguese manager with his team in sixth place, 19 points behind the league leaders.

Critics cite multiple reasons for Mourinho and Manchester United's fall from grace, including the manager's disagreements with star players and underperformance by backroom staff and players. Furthermore, Mourinho's adversarial attitude toward the media did not help the outspoken manager curry favor in England.

But the point stands that since becoming a well-established, world-renowned manager, Mourinho has faltered, and he enjoyed more success on his rise to the top than he has as one of the most well-known football personalities. It seems ironic that despite having greater resources at his disposal than he had during his rise to the top, Mourinho has failed to achieve the same success as he had with smaller-profile clubs. At Porto, Inter, and his first Chelsea stint, Mourinho *overachieved*. But with Real Madrid, Manchester United, and his second stint at Chelsea, he left with a record of *underachievement*.

Mourinho's story is not unique in the football industry, as many high-profile managers have experienced ebb and flow in their careers. But the importance of the high-profile football manager deserves some further exploration. Is it truly the manager who makes all the difference in world football, or are there other more important lessons to be drawn out of football that can be applied to management in a broader context?

To find the answers, let's look at how teams perform relative to their wealth.

Leadership performance in the Champions League

For every player, manager, fan, and owner in European football, the UEFA Champions League is the most important and valuable competition. Simply qualifying for the competition can be enough for some clubs to clear debts or pay for their entire budget. Revenue for continental competitions is astronomical; in 2018, UEFA announced that over EUR 2 billion will be spread among teams competing in the Champions League and UEFA's one-off UEFA Super Cup.[5] Most of this EUR 2 billion will be split among the 32 teams that qualify for the group stage of the competition.

Prize money increases as teams go further in the competition, but more than the prize money, a Champions League win solidifies the victorious club as a global power and results in valuable global sponsorships and increased brand awareness. According to UEFA, 180 million people in 200 territories watched the 2015 Champions League Final when FC Barcelona beat Juventus 3–1.[6] The chance to showcase your club on a massive global stage can translate into valuable revenue in the form of shirt sales and new sponsorships, and as football clubs are brands, it serves as incredible advertising. Therefore, clubs have an enormous incentive to perform well in the Champions League, and managers face great scrutiny for their performance in this competition.

José Mourinho received praise and fame for winning the competition with two teams that were relatively low in football's hierarchy. He also won various league titles at bigger clubs, but his underperformance in Europe often sank him despite league titles in England and Spain.

Top managers are disproportionately judged on their team's performance in the Champions League. League performance is also of great importance, but once again this is tied to the major cash cow of European football.

There are three ways to qualify for the Champions League: finishing in a "Champions League place" in your respective domestic league; winning the Champions League the previous year; or winning the secondary European competition the Europa League the previous year as well. As only two teams can qualify through winning a European competition, most teams qualify for the Champions League based on their performance in their respective domestic league.

Champions League performance can have an incredible impact on a football club's bank balance and its ability to attract fans and top players. While most professional teams will never get a whiff of the Champions League, global giants such as Real Madrid, Manchester United, Barcelona, Juventus, Bayern Munich, and Paris Saint-Germain rely on the lucrative proposition of qualifying for and doing well in the Champions League. The top global teams are a mix of historical teams and "new-money" teams bolstered by foreign investment. These two types of teams are at the top of football for different reasons; however, both have to build their continued financial success under the same restrictions. Strong Champions League performances are the best way to build a global football brand.

How important are managers?

Anticipating managerial success is very important to clubs looking to qualify for and win the Champions League. So, how does a team decide what manager will propel it to European success, and when do clubs decide when it is time to let a manager go for poor performance?

By simply looking at Champions League Finals results, measuring manager success in the competition is quite difficult. Only 3 managers in the competition's history since 1956 have won the competition three times, and 17 managers have won it twice. But multiple teams have won the competition in consecutive years while changing managers. From 1956 through 1960, Real Madrid won the European Cup (now known as the Champions League) with three different managers. Ajax and Bayern Munich have also won the competition in consecutive years with different managers.

With this said, simply evaluating the winners of the competition leaves us with an incomplete picture.

Academics and researchers have studied sports from multiple perspectives, and there are multiple studies that illuminate in more depth the role of managers in football. Some researchers have taken football as a case study to learn more about hiring effectiveness and labor markets. In general, such research attempts to evaluate how coaches and managers can be comprehensively evaluated from an economic perspective.

Risk-Averse teams fall into the inefficient hiring trap

In a study of the English football manager labor market from Tinbergen Institute, Thomas Peeters and his colleagues[7] found that clubs fall into an *inefficient hiring trap*. This means that a club is more likely to hire an experienced manager with a poor record than a young, inexperienced manager who could have the potential to be a top-level performer. The risk of insolvency is particularly high for the owners of a football club, and football is a big money sport. Therefore, clubs are more likely to "play it safe" by hiring a veteran manager with a spotty record than risk hiring a younger manager without any experience.

While the Peeters study looked specifically at English clubs, the implications of its findings can be applied to Champions League clubs as well. Despite his struggles at Chelsea, Manchester United hired Mourinho as their manager. They were likely allured by his quick results and Champions League wins with other clubs.

Another potential candidate for the role was former United player and club legend Ryan Giggs. He was relatively unknown, and the United owners seemed more likely to trust the lengthy résumé of Mourinho in spite of his recent rough patch. Former players, especially those who are a household name, are much more likely to get their first management shot at a big club. Mourinho was actually a rather unspectacular player, so he had to build up to the dizzying heights of top European football, working as an assistant manager for many years before cutting his teeth in Portugal.

Hiring a first-time manager is seen as a bigger risk than hiring a veteran, and two recent examples in the Spanish league highlight the fraught nature of hiring new managers.

First, the bad: Gary Neville's appointment at Valencia. Neville is another former United player, and after his playing days he became a popular football pundit in England. Valencia is a semi-regular Champions League team, having qualified for the group stage five times in the last decade. In December 2015, Valencia hired Neville, and it took the Englishman 10 league games to finally win his first match in Valencia. His ill-fated time with the club did not last long, and he was fired after just over four months.

Around the same time as Neville's hiring in Spain, a larger team hired one of its own former players. In early 2016, Real Madrid hired French legend Zinedine Zidane. He spent some time managing Real Madrid's second team, but this was the Frenchman's first managerial post in top-flight football and was therefore seen as a riskier hire. However, in Zidane's three seasons at the club, Real Madrid won the Champions League three times in a row.

While Real Madrid has more resources than Valencia, it must be concluded that considering Valencia's stature, Neville *underperformed*, while Zidane managed to *overachieve*, even for Real Madrid's high expectations. The cases of Neville and Zidane serve as an example of the enormous risk football clubs take in hiring new managers, and the fraught nature of judging a hire before they have performed at such a high level.

However, managers with a record can be evaluated, and from this information, it can be deciphered exactly how important a top-tier successful manager is for a Champions League club. Looking at multiple examples, this chapter will evaluate some of the trends that can be seen in the Champions League.

Follow the money

The Champions League is dominated by big money teams from the top leagues in Europe. Furthermore, the representation from these leagues in the Champions League comes from a concentrated, elite group of global superpowers. From 2008 to 2018, two Spanish teams, FC Barcelona and Real Madrid, won the Champions League a combined seven times. Even the runners-up are a "who's who" of monetary power in the game.

European club football begins to look on the surface like a financial battle for who can earn and spend the most money, rather than a matter of managers pulling off tactical master classes. However, due to the immense financial pressure of performance, top-level managers unsurprisingly command a hefty wage similar to that of world-class players. When so much money is on the line, it only makes sense for the Real Madrids of the world to throw money behind a manager they think is likely to deliver them success.

But managers might have a lesser impact than many football clubs and pundits would expect, especially in football's current stratified economic market. José Mourinho's Champions League victories with Porto and Inter came just before the latest influx of money into the sport. Mourinho's accomplishments are undeniably impressive; however, the probability of a less well-endowed team like Porto capturing European glory is becoming increasingly slim.

In Deloitte's annual ranking of football clubs by revenue, only four teams outside of the top four leagues make the top 30.[8] England dominates the list with 14 teams, thanks to the massive money generated by the Premier League's television deals. Fortunately for the rest of Europe, often only four (maximum five) English teams qualify for the Champions League, and English teams have suffered in the competition in recent years. Despite their enormous spending power, an English team has not won the competition since Chelsea in the 2011–2012 season.

So, just as choosing the best manager cannot capture all nuances of success in football, neither can money. If it were as simple as spending the most money to become successful in the Champions League, then since its big money takeover we would have expected Paris Saint-Germain to perform better in Europe.

In a study of the German Bundesliga, Gerd Muehlheusser of the University of Hamburg and his coauthors[9] evaluated managers' performances in the domestic league, and they determined that the manager makes a significant difference to their team. They argue that their findings support the hypothesis that "executives are an important factor determining organizational performance." For example, Jürgen Klopp greatly outperformed expectations during his time at Borussia Dortmund, and he has likewise gone on to do well at English side Liverpool. However, even though the overperforming German manager qualified for two Champions League Finals, he lost both, one with Dortmund and one with Liverpool.

Others are more skeptical of the impact managers have on a club's results compared to that of their players. *The Economist* published its research into this subject by using FIFA ratings from the popular video game series and player valuation data in comparison to managers' performances in their domestic leagues. Similar to the Bundesliga study, they found that some managers do regularly outperform based on the resources at their disposal. Interestingly, they found that Mourinho vastly overperformed with Chelsea in his first stint and underperformed in his time with Manchester United and his second time at Chelsea.

But, most importantly, *The Economist* found that top-level players such as Lionel Messi contribute up to twice or more to the final point total of a team than even the best manager. Most football fans would take a player of the caliber of Lionel Messi or Cristiano Ronaldo over the most decorated manager in a heartbeat, and the data may well back up that gut reaction.

Overall, the jury is still out on the importance of a high-quality manager when it comes to performance in the Champions League. But, the influence of money and the top players that come with it should not be underestimated. In the inflated market of football, managers like Klopp, Mourinho, and Zidane will only be able to achieve results at the highest level if they have the adequate financial backing to go along with their expertise in the field. If picking the right manager to lead a team to Champions League glory were easily measured, then there would not be as much employee turnover as we see in top-level football. The hypercompetitive nature of European football and the money that comes with it cause immense stress on the labor market, and it is unlikely to slow down any time soon.

A comparison of the English and Spanish domestic leagues illuminates two different outcomes for the richest teams. Spain has the two richest teams in the world, FC Barcelona and Real Madrid. This pair of Spanish teams has consistently topped the league, and in the last decade they have been the two most successful teams in the Champions League. On the other hand, England is the richest league in the world, in large part due to the massive TV deals the league has negotiated.

In Deloitte's 2019 Money League Report on football clubs' 2017–2018 revenue, nine English teams are included in the top 20. (The list does not include teams that do not participate in regular European football.) Premier League television is spread in a somewhat equal manner, thereby making the Premier League a more competitive and egalitarian league. The top English teams have to compete in their league with other clubs with deep pockets, and in part this explains the struggles of some established clubs in recent years, such as Manchester United and Arsenal.

English teams receive equal shares of some part of the television deal, but they can also receive more money based on performance and if their games are chosen for TV. The massive international deal is equally split and contributes to competitiveness in English football.

Outside of Real Madrid and FC Barcelona, the only Spanish team in the Deloitte top 20 highest revenue clubs is Atlético Madrid. Atlético has been the only Spanish club in recent years to push Barcelona and Real, and it is the third most successful Spanish club in the Champions League. In the last decade, Atlético has won the Europa League three times and reached the Champions League Final twice, in the 2013–2014 and 2015–2016 seasons. Atlético was seen as an underdog to reach the Champions League Final, but it is still one of the richest teams in European football. In fact, since Mourinho's 2003–2004 Champions League Final win over Porto, not a single finalist has been from outside of the top four leagues: England, Germany, Italy, and Spain.

Money is a much better predictor of Champions League success than any other factor, and the reasons these clubs have more money are institutional. Real Madrid and FC Barcelona are two of the most historic football clubs, and they have built international brands reflecting this success. This branding reinforces itself by feeding money back into the club's coffers, where it is then redirected to purchasing the best players to achieve success in the Champions League.

One might expect English teams to be wildly successful in the Champions League due to their massive TV deals and the league's international popularity, especially in emerging markets like Asia. However, this money is spread more evenly throughout the league, creating some level of parity. The richest clubs are still regularly the best performers, but the group of rich English clubs is quickly growing.

In total, Champions League success is broadly decided by how much money a club has and can generate on a year-to-year basis. And, among these rich clubs, there are various institutional factors, such as the TV money split and a club's history, that make some rich clubs more successful than others. Barcelona, Real Madrid, and to a lesser extent Atlético Madrid have monopolized Champions League success for Spanish clubs. But in England we would expect a larger variety of clubs to compete for a title, thus expanding the variety of English clubs competing for European glory and lowering the chances of a singular English team dominating European football.

What about other sports?

Looking beyond football, do the same trends discussed in this chapter extend to other sports such as baseball, basketball, or American football? Is management or coaching equally overvalued in these sports compared to other more important factors such as money or the structure of the national championship?

Baseball is known to be a sport highly conducive to in-depth statistical analysis. In Major League Baseball (MLB), the top league in the world, each of the 30 teams plays 162 games, so the wealth of statistical information is impressively large.

It is almost no surprise, but money may be a good indicator of MLB success. Famed statistical analysis website FiveThirtyEight discussed the prominence of analysts overvaluing the power of small-market, low-budget teams. Despite the trendiness of low payroll teams, the data shows that teams with a higher payroll still won more games. The analysts cited MLB's short, condensed playoff schedule as to why some teams with lower payrolls are able to occasionally sneak in and become world champions. If the champion were crowned over the long 162-game season, then the teams with the highest payroll would be expected to receive top honors even more than they do currently.

In America's National Football League (NFL), a handful of coaches have reached legendary status with careers at just one team, such as the New England Patriots' Bill Belichick. But many teams struggle to find their Belichick, and instead feature a revolving door of coaches. As with other American sports, professional American football has a relatively small coaching pool, so relatively successful coaches will get multiple opportunities with different teams.

Three American strategic management researchers used NFL coaches to evaluate if NFL coaches add value to their organizations.[10] They found that the most effective coaches were those who efficiently maximized the resources at their disposal. Top coaches got the best out of the All-Pro talent and turned it to wins on the field. However, most importantly, they found that these high-performing coaches could not perform if the organization did not have adequate resources.

We see the same phenomenon in teams fighting for supremacy in European football. The most successful managers have the top players at their disposal, and the winning teams have incredibly deep pockets to pursue top players. When a Champions League winning manager like Rafael Benítez was hired by Newcastle United, despite his previous pedigree he was not able to replicate that performance because Newcastle owner Mike Ashley reportedly refused to spend the necessary money to compete. As *The Guardian* reported in December 2018, "Disgruntled fans have made their feelings clear over his repeated failure to provide his managers, and in particular Rafael Benítez, with the funding to compete in the transfer market, with Ashley saying he cannot afford to do so."[11]

In October 2018, Ashley put the club up for sale.

Of course, a team in any sport cannot just throw money at their problems and expect wins to come in thick and fast, and some teams will struggle if they spend without a plan. A team with less money will occasionally pull off a major upset and dominate news headlines. But the reason these teams are so fondly remembered is that they are not the norm; rather, they are an exceptional and rare story.

Money goes a long way, and to be a Champions League–competing football club or a perennial MLB World Series contender, you have to spend money to compete with other top clubs. However, clubs will continue to battle for the top managerial talent in hopes of gaining even a slight competitive edge over their opponents. But if an outsider team wants to push into the pantheon of the elites, they will find it difficult if they do nothing but hire a veteran manager. Money spread wisely throughout the entire organization is a better measure to anticipate success.

21. THE DRIVERS OF PERFORMANCE

To be successful, companies and countries first need to determine their objectives. In the case of countries, the next chapter will address such issues in detail. We will defend that the objective of a nation is to be competitive in the sense of being able to generate prosperity through productivity in the global or regional marketplace. In the case of companies, success is measured not only by the ability to beat competitors, but also through key performance indicators such as gross margins, stock returns, or market share.

What do we know about the determinants of performance? When I approached this question for the first time, my original hypothesis was that there would be a vast amount of work and evidence showing what truly impacts firm performance. I wanted to find a study conducted by academics (or, in the worst case, by consultants) explaining first of all how the different dimensions of performance (country, industry, firm, individual leadership) contribute to and explain to what extent companies succeed or fail. A firm is a business entity that systemizes the interaction among people, machines, and materials into output. Due to the interaction among its components, many factors affect the business performance of companies, such as information technology,[12] entrepreneurial orientation,[13] strategy,[14] and leadership.

Absent such study, I decided to undertake my own. My findings are reported in Chapter 23. So I will proceed in parts.

First, I want to summarize what we know about the impact that individual leaders, firm characteristics, and industry dynamics have on performance. At the end of the day, my sport stories reveal that the success of a team is not wholly dependent on who leads the team, and that the impact of the leader depends upon other external conditions (for example, how rich the team is and subsequently which coach it can hire) that are often determined by global factors.

Among many affecting variables, in this section we are going to focus on understanding the impact of one of the factors that potentially influence the firm's performance, namely leadership. Leadership is a broad topic. It is not easy to treat leadership as an empirical variable since it is unobserved and has many personal styles such as transactional, transformational, supportive, spiritual, and so forth, which are hardly quantifiable. Also, a definition of firm performance can be elusive, ranging from employees' satisfaction to profitability. While the role of leadership in firm performance has been an interest for many academicians and practitioners, understanding the impact of leadership on firm performance can only be done on a case-by-case basis.

22. THE IMPACT OF LEADERS ON PERFORMANCE

Our first task is to clarify what we mean by "leadership."

"Leadership" is not the same as "leading."[15] The latter refers to one of several potential management functions, particularly working with people, harmonizing their relationships, and encouraging them to work and perform tasks more efficiently. Leading consists of a set of processes that direct employees toward achieving goals more efficiently.

As for "leadership," I have encountered in my research several different definitions:

> Possessing the ability to inspire and impressing followers by providing them with the purpose to fight for them.[16]
> A process of influencing employees to be motivated and encouraging their behavior to achieve the same organization goal.[17]
> A process of guiding the behavior of other individuals toward the accomplishment of some goals that have always been considered to be a postulate of an organization's success.[18]

What permeates from the latter three definitions is that leadership is a process of influencing/impressing/guiding others to fulfill an organizational objective. Therefore, "good" and "bad" leadership must be defined by the extent to which the firm objectives are achieved.[19] If leadership is effective, then those on top can make the difference between a successful strategy and a failure.[20]

Transactional and transformational leadership

Among all types, two types of leadership become the central focus for researchers in the literature—transactional leadership and transformational leadership.

Transactional leadership, better known as managerial leadership, is the type of leadership created from a working relationship. In other words, it is the leadership style based on the working relationship between leader and employee expressed as a task-oriented relationship.[21]

Transformational leadership is not based on the working environment. Instead, it is defined as a loyalty process between leader and follower, which is followed by a transformation of the value of the judgments, beliefs, and needs of its followers.[22]

The coverage of transformational leadership is broader than transactional leadership, as this type of leadership involves factors beyond the working obligation, including charisma, personal leadership, and motivational leadership.

No formal guidance rules which type of leadership is better to affect firm performance. However, one study in Nigeria pointed out that transactional leadership is more effective in small companies rather than big enterprises.[23]

Transformational leaders succeed when they possess one or some of the following traits:[24]

- **Charisma or ideal influence** describes the type of leader who influences his or her followers through the ideal figure of himself or herself such that the followers are motivated to pursue and match the standard of the leader.
- **Inspirational motivation** is the leader who influences his or her followers through inspiration in order to motivate them to catch up with the vision of the organization.

- **Intellectual stimulus** is the type of leader who stimulates his or her followers to be creative, innovative, and risk-taking to continually improve his or her performance and skills.
- **Personal appreciation** is the type of leader who leads his or her followers through understanding the followers' individual needs to achieve their potential.

Many studies focusing on transformational leadership suggest that it has a positive impact on firms' effectiveness, employee satisfaction, and employee perception.[25]

I discuss the difference between transactional and transformational because, as you will see, most of the studies that one can find focus on transformational leaders. Now we are going to investigate the core issue in this chapter, namely the impact of leadership on firm performance. Most studies focusing on this topic define leadership as transformational, but there are also a few studies that use transactional leadership. The studies in this field are also conducted through a research survey, which means the data is gathered through spreading questionnaires to group leaders, CEOs, or managers from medium- to large-scale organizations. Many factors affect leadership to effectively influence organizational performance, such as sector, location, size, and the quality of the leader.[26] These factors will determine the success of a business organization.

Let me add here that leadership is also about personal preferences for corporate policies. That is, some CEOs, despite personal characteristics and traits, will have a preference for debt over equity, dividend payments over stock buybacks, acquisitions over joint ventures, and hiring female executives over hiring male executives. Such corporate choices are not exactly leadership characteristics; however, they will be very important drivers of a company's performance and subsequently of the CEO's success.

The halo effect

The problem I have encountered in most of these studies is that they are massively biased. Let me take you through the researchers' thought process.

First, they identify a sample of companies and assess the quality of leadership, sometimes with objective measures, but mostly through surveys among employees to assess whether, for example, "My leader fosters collaboration among work groups," or "My supervisor insists on only the best performance." Afterwards, the researchers qualify and quantify the leaders' characteristics from the survey and relate these to measures of company performance.[27]

This is a big issue because opinions of leaders are *ex post* clearly influenced by performance. For example, in early 2019, Apple released disappointing news when it announced that it was cutting its expectations regarding revenues and profitability for the first quarter of the fiscal year 2019 (that is, September through December 2018). The company estimated revenues of USD 84 billion and a gross profit margin of 38 percent.[28] This compared to a higher initial estimate of USD 89–93 billion and a realized revenue of USD 88.3 billion in the same period the previous year.[29] Additionally, the update recognized a drop in profitability, down from 42 percent the previous year. The news caused the stock to drop by 10 percent, to its lowest level in the previous 18 months. Such reaction was evidence that the market perception about Apple's ability to grow had deteriorated, and the company was no longer a growth stock but rather a dividend-paying, profitable company whose value was then being delivered to its shareholders.

In times like this, it is natural to hear arguments such as, "If Steve Jobs were alive today,"[30] or "Seven years after Jobs' death, Apple starts to crumble."[31] During Steve Jobs' tenure as CEO, Apple stock went up 23.4 percent per year on average; since Tim Cook took over, it has increased by 17.5 percent on average annually. This is not new: in April 2013, when Apple plunged below USD 400 a share, a campaign with the headline "Tim Cook Should Go" ensued. Earlier, an article in TheStreet had claimed, "If Steve Jobs Were Alive, He Would Fire Tim Cook."[32]

In 2007, my colleague Phil Rosenzweig published what is, in my opinion, one of the most important books in the history of management, *The Halo Effect*. First named by psychologist Edward Thorndike in his 1920 article "A Constant Error in Psychological Ratings," it is a reference to a person being perceived as having a halo of goodness that may or may not be justified based on a limited set of facts.

Phil argued that perceptions of performance contaminate the assessments that we make about managers and leaders. He used several examples, from Lego to Cisco and ABB, to show that an individual leader's skills do *not* affect a company's performance in a significant way—instead, good performance causes us to evaluate leaders in a too positive way, inducing us to attribute stellar performance to certain leadership skills. For example, if a leader appears to be dynamic and decisive, and the company is successful, the tendency is to put a halo on the leader and attribute the success of the firm to his or her leadership. In reality, there may be many other factors or people that have made significant contributions.

The role of the mediating variable

The second difficulty when assessing the effect of leaders is that most research focuses on what I call "a mediating variable." That is, even if I do not have direct evidence of how leaders create overall value for organizations, we can test whether they have an impact on particular aspects of the company that should be naturally value-increasing. For instance, a significant number of academics have studied the impact of leaders on organizational performance, motivation, risk-taking, culture, adoption of best practices, employee satisfaction, and speed of job completion.[33]

A good assessment of the impact of leaders must be made controlling for a potential halo effect, and this can only be done if we look at leaders, not at leadership characteristics, and try to isolate the impact (positive or negative) of CEO changes. A second approach is to study changes in leadership that are completely independent of past performance. This seems impossible in principle. First, because company boards hardly say, "The CEO will be fired because he has disappointed us." Second, because the halo effect is also present *ex ante*, so when Mourinho was recruited by Real Madrid, everybody believed that his chances of winning the Champions League would be higher than his predecessors', given his curriculum.

To determine the real influence of a leader, over a period of time you would need to study the same company in the same circumstances, with the only difference being the leader. In 2010, Bennedsen, Pérez-González, and Wolfenzon (from INSEAD, Stanford University, and Columbia University, respectively) found a way to do this. They conducted a study using a sample of Danish companies where the CEO had died suddenly and unexpectedly, and was quickly replaced. They identified 6,753 deaths of CEOs and/or their family members. Furthermore, the authors meticulously sorted the tragic events into 1,015 CEO deaths, 733 spouses' deaths, 282 children's deaths, 3,061 parents' deaths, and 1,364 parents-in-law deaths. In defining firm performance, the scholars looked at operating return on asset (OROA),[34] investment, and sales growth.

Their study found that either the sudden death of the CEO or the death of the CEO's close family member was significantly related to a firm's *decline* in profitability, investment, and sales growth. (With one caveat: they found that the death of the CEO's mother-in-law generated a positive but insignificant effect on firm performance.)

A similar study was conducted by Marianne Bertrand from the University of Chicago and Antoinette Schoar from MIT. In their study titled "Managing with Style," the two professors constructed a manager–firm matched data set that allowed them to track the same top managers across different firms over time using Forbes 800 files from 1969 to 1999. In measuring corporate performance, Bertrand and Schoar utilized various financial indicators to reflect firm performance including total sales, investment, cash flow leverage, cash holding, and return on asset. There are some interesting findings from their study. First, managers matter, both economically and statistically, to the policy decisions of firms. Second, the realization of all investment, financing, and other organizational strategies systematically depends on the specific executives in charge. Third, managerial differences in corporate practices are systematically related to differences in corporate performance. Fourth, managers with higher performance receive higher compensation.

The third result is important: CEOs make a difference to results. However, the magnitude is not stellar: the authors calculate[35] that individual CEOs only contribute between 2 and 4 percent of total performance. (That is, if Apple's profit margin in 2018 was 38 percent, Tim Cook's individual decisions would be able to add, or detract, at most 1.5 percent per year.)

23. WHAT DRIVES PERFORMANCE BEYOND LEADERS?

In 2014, in partnership with Accenture Switzerland, the Institute for Management Development (IMD) World Competitiveness Center embarked on the task of analyzing the drivers of long-term success of the largest Swiss companies. The report titled *Switzerland's Top500: Sustainable success in times of change*,[36] was the first attempt to measure and assess *all* potential factors that impact the growth and profitability of companies, in order to rank and quantify them.

The report identified 36 of the 500 largest Swiss firms whose five-year growth rates in revenues and profit were above average for a period of four years (2010–2013). The companies in the study had to have their main headquarters in Switzerland, but they were not required to be publicly traded—the sample includes several cantonal and private banks.[37] Let us call these 36 companies the Swiss Growth Champions (SGC). They belong to a diverse array of industries, including banking and insurance.

Subsequently, we conducted a survey in which we received responses from 14 executives in the SGC group, as well as in another 104 non-champion firms. Our survey asked executives their perception about strategy, organizational structure, leadership, sustainability, corporate governance, and talent management, with a total of 68 questions.[38]

For example, we asked executives whether "the board is diverse in terms of gender, age, professional experience, and competencies," if "the decision-making process within your company is transparent," and whether "incentives in your company are linked to the long-term profitability of the firm." We were as picky as to ask whether "absenteeism due to illness is low within your company" or if "your company has a firm-wide digital strategy in place."

Not surprisingly, we found that the SGCs enjoyed higher return on assets (ROA) and return on equity[39] (ROE) than the rest. ROE for the SGCs was on average 7.4 percent larger than the non-Growth Champions in the period 2010–2013. ROA was 4 percent higher. They also significantly increased their employment levels over the period, posting employment growth 18.1 percent above the peer group. Finally, their stocks outperformed their peers, averaging 7.6 percent during 2010–2013.

We then conducted what in econometrics we call a *horse race*. That is, by pooling all the potential drivers of performance that we could measure, we tried to identify which ones had a stronger explanatory variable. Note that the importance of this analysis is that in a horse race we only identify significant drivers of performance *controlling for everything else*. In every industry, except financial, our results were conclusive: the Swiss Growth Champions exhibited substantially better governance, innovation practices, and talent management policies.

Specifically, *successful Swiss companies adopt more dynamic governance practices with clear accountability*. Their boards guide the actions of senior leaders by exercising their supervision and strategic roles effectively, and continuously interact and collaborate with management through an open information policy. This role of boards was much more visible in family businesses and private companies relative to listed firms.

Second, companies that encourage innovation and entrepreneurship among middle and junior executives guarantee excellence in growth and profitability. *An innovation-centric culture is key for expanding into new revenue pools*. Continuous innovation is among the factors that significantly differentiate top performers from other companies in the study. Top managers recognize the positive correlation between innovation and competitiveness and encourage employees to work on improving products and services. The encouragement of an innovative culture is, however, coupled with a limited willingness to make capital-heavy investments in times of uncertainty.

Finally, firms that develop and promote talent perform better (*"happy employees, happy company"*). *Human capital and employee engagement are crucial for sustaining growth*. The Swiss Growth Champions consider the development of talent as a key factor in sustaining growth and profitability, and the fostering of employee engagement complements the recruitment, development, and retention of talent. This focus enables companies to enjoy higher productivity, lower turnover of key positions, and lower absence rates.

More important than the significant factors were the potential drivers that we found to be irrelevant at explaining long-term success. For instance, we found that sustainability policies, organizational structure, digitalization, and industry dynamics had a second-order effect after controlling for good governance, good talent management, and innovativeness.

24. GLOBAL EFFECTS

So far, I have provided a scattered view of the different drivers of performance. But what about global effects? In this section, I explore the performance of companies considering all potential drivers. It is key to deal with the halo effect by assessing a company's performance irrespective of our perception about their leaders and their strategy. More importantly, such analysis requires a sample of companies from all over the world.

First, I will provide an illustration of my research design.

During Margaret Georgiadis' 14-month tenure as CEO of US toy manufacturer Mattel, the company went through a bumpy road. She was appointed to the job in January 2017, a few months before one of its top distributors, Toys R Us, filed for bankruptcy. At that time, Toys R Us accounted for up to 20 percent of Mattel's US sales.[40] Georgiadis had succeeded the legendary Christopher A. Sinclair, who had been chairman and CEO of Pepsi-Cola before serving as the CEO of Mattel from January 2015 to February 2017.

Sinclair's performance was unsurprisingly disappointing given the outlook of the industry and the changing habits of children, more interested now in video games than in dolls and action figures. Mattel's stock price declined from USD 30.945 when he took over the job to USD 26.21 when he resigned (a sad –15 percent return). Georgiadis had a big challenge ahead of her, but by the time she resigned in April 2018, Mattel had slipped an additional 45 percent.

Was she a good leader? Formerly a McKinsey consultant, graduate of Harvard Business School, and vice president for the Americas at Alphabet for two years, her vita is impeccable. And it would be difficult to blame her for the decline of the company. Three months after she was replaced, the company was forced to slash 20 percent of the workforce,[41] but analysts blamed Toys R Us, and not the company's changing CEOs. It could also be that Mattel had the wrong strategy, focusing on China, India, and Indonesia as growth markets for the brand besides the United States; unfortunately, these three markets never took off.

In 2015, the company implemented a misguided digital transformation with the launch of Hello Barbie, an interactive doll that could communicate with kids through a microphone in her belt buckle. Like Amazon's Alessa, it could draw upon information from the internet to reply to kids' questions. The problem was that Hello Barbie could also report anything that happened in the kids' room,[42] and additionally, it was reported that hackers could hijack the Hello Barbie and spy on children.[43] Hello Barbie quickly said "goodbye."

By year-end 2017, Mattel's sales had dropped 15 percent in one year.

That was not the end of Margaret Georgiadis' career. In April 2018, she was appointed CEO of Ancestry.com, the largest for-profit genealogy company in the world.[44] Ancestry was once a publicly traded company, having had an initial public offering (IPO) in 2009 before being taken private again three years later in a USD 1.6 billion deal. It may yet return to public ownership.[45]

Both Mattel and Ancestry.com are US companies, and even if Mattel operates internationally it is mostly affected by US institutions (bankruptcy courts, stock markets) and regulations (insider trading, IPO rules). Imagine if we could look at CEOs who change companies and countries, and even industries. Would it not be the perfect way to analyze which factors mattered most? For example, Philippe Donnet, the current CEO of Generali, the Italian insurer, was previously the CEO of AXA re (French); in the same sector, Mark Tucker, who until September 2017 was the CEO of AIA (based in Hong Kong), was previously the CEO of Prudential plc (UK).

Very few academics have tried that. In 2010, *Harvard Business Review* published a study conducted by Noam Wasserman from the University of Southern California, and Bharat Anand and Nitin Nohria from Harvard Business School, trying to identify the incremental explanatory power of individual CEOs.[46] They used a sample of 531 companies—all US firms—from 42 industries over a period of 19 years and were able to explain 49 percent of the variability in return on assets, and 67 percent of Tobin's Q—a standard metric that captures a company's growth opportunities and that is measured as the ratio of the market value of the company relative to its value in the books. Because all firms are based in the United States, the impact of global factors makes it difficult if not impossible to measure because very likely the impact of say Chinese trade policies will affect all companies in the sample in a similar way. Still, they were able to find that

Table 1.3 Explaining Performance

	Return on Assets (%)	*Tobin's Q (%)*
Year	2.6	5.2
Industry	6.3	15.5
Company	25.5	32.8
CEO	14.7	13.5
Total Explanatory Power	49.1	67.0

Source: Wasserman et al. (2010).

14.7 percent out of the 49 percent variability in return on assets, and 13.5 percent out of the 67 percent variability in Tobin's Q, are due to CEO-specific characteristics (Table 1.3).

Wasserman's article had a significant impact because, for the first time and in a thorough way, they could quantify the actual impact of CEOs on performance, and the magnitude was significant. There are two problems with this study in my opinion: by including only American companies, they are removing a lot of variation in performance that could be due to other, global effects. For instance, if 50 percent of a company's return on assets depends on global factors, then only 7.3 percent of the overall variation in that variable (14.7 percent of 50 percent of performance explained by local factors) is due to CEO decisions.

The second problem is in the econometrics. Unfortunately, the additional explanatory power of each variable depends on the order in which you run the regressions—I know this sounds cumbersome and boring, but we academics find these discussions appealing.

A recent study by Oriana Bandiera from the London School of Economics, Stephen Hansen from Oxford, Andrea Prat from Columbia, and Raffaella Sadun from Harvard has resolved both problems.[47] They studied the performance of 1,114 CEOs in six countries and were able to differentiate between "leaders" and "managers" by analyzing the day-to-day behavior of the CEO. A leader-CEO is typically more focused on externally oriented activities, time spent with C-suite executives, and internal communications, while manager-CEOs are more focused on production activities and one-on-one meetings. There are many interesting results in their study (particularly that leader-CEOs have a significantly stronger effect on corporate performance). Relevant for this chapter, they find that 17 percent of the variance in the CEO behavior index is caused by country effects. Unfortunately, they do not report the incremental impact of global factors on a company's performance overall. Besides, while the study is impressive both in its scope and detail, it includes mostly small companies (in median, firms in this study have 300 employees and USD 35 million in sales), so naturally for such firms the impact of global factors should be smaller than for the average publicly listed company, for instance.

I created the largest sample of companies that I could get with information about their current and past CEOs. My sample of companies came from two of the standard databases for international companies: Datastream and Orbis. I first obtained from Datastream accounting and stock price information from 27,147 firms from 85 countries. I then looked for the identity of their CEOs in the period 1995–2018. I could find that information for 6,310 firms and 13,507 CEOs from 71 countries. I further classified the companies into 10 industry groups.[48]

I considered two measures of performance.

The first was the annual stock price performance of the company. All the firms in the sample were publicly traded, which was obviously a problem because it restricted our conclusions to listed companies only. Returns were measured in US dollars to allow for comparability.[49]

The second performance metric was the return on invested capital (ROIC), measured as operating profit (earnings before interest, tax, depreciation, and amortization, or EBITDA), divided by the sum of debt and equity.

These two indicators provide different insights. ROIC is based on accounting data and is therefore historical. Moreover, it reflects one-shot results of a company—the profitability of investment in the given year. In contrast, stock returns are forward-looking because investors buy stocks to benefit from future returns and dividends. Moreover, stock returns reflect the future, long-term performance of the company, which is directly related both to the firm growth prospects and to the firm level of risk.

Figure 1.2 displays the median ROIC in South Korea, India, and the United States, across firms and years, and classified by industry.

Note that on the rightmost bars in the graph, India's return on capital (12 percent in median) is larger than South Korea and the United States. Additionally, within countries there is a wide variation depending on the industry. For instance, while the technology industry in India generates close to 20 percent return on capital annually between 1995 and 2018, the return on consumer goods is only 8.5 percent. Similarly, financial services in South Korea yield a meager 2 percent over the period, compared to oil and gas (12 percent).

Subsequently, I have estimated how much of the variability of each measure of performance is explained by global, country, industry, firm, and CEO-specific characteristics. Let me explain how I do it. On average, variations in performance that are similar for all companies over time are what I call "global" factors. Anything that is systematic across countries is a "country" factor. Likewise for industries. After that, any specific variation

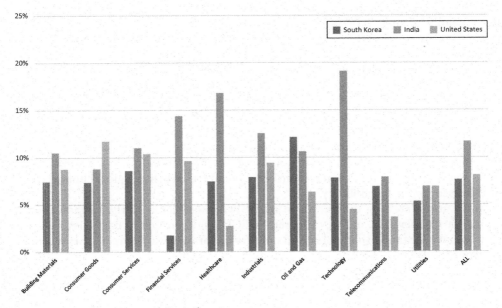

Figure 1.2 Return on Invested Capital

Table 1.4 How Much Factors Explain

	Return on Invested Capital			Stock Returns		
	All Sample	OECD	Non-OECD	All Sample	OECD	Non-OECD
Global (%)	0.2	0.2	0.7	16.7	15.2	32.6
Country (%)	2.6	1.6	6.4	8.9	5.8	11.9
Industry (%)	1.9	2.4	1.3	1.6	1.9	1.7
Firm (%)	33.1	34.6	23.9	9.4	10.5	4.7
CEO (%)	6.1	6.0	7.4	4.0	4.4	2.7
Number of Observations	53,870	41,200	12,670	82,610	66,231	16,379

in performance is either firm or CEO-specific. Since I have both companies that change CEOs, and CEOs that change companies, I can isolate the impact of the two. The results are shown in Table 1.4.

Among the factors explaining ROIC, the dominant is firm characteristics. Note that across industries there is not much difference in ROIC that is not captured by firm differences themselves. The interpretation is that Apple and Samsung display different returns on investment because of their differences in product portfolio, technology, culture, and value, and to a lesser extent because one is American and the other is South Korean. Fluctuations in ROIC are also very much independent of global and country phenomena.

For the entire sample of firms and countries, CEOs explain 6 percent of the firm's variability in ROIC. Everything else equal, this means that, on average, a CEO could have an ROIC which is 6 percent higher or lower than his or her predecessor. For an average ROIC in my sample of about 5 percent, the impact of the CEO is ±0.3 percent. Note that such impact is caused not only by personal characteristics, but also by individual choices of financial strategies, growth tools, recruitment of talent, and so on.

For stock returns, the results are somehow different. In fact, the most important determinant of stock performance is the set of global factors that impacts all companies alike. On average, 16.7 percent of the variability of a company's stock return is caused by global factors. Besides, almost 9 percent of such variability is country-specific. Only 9.4 and 4 percent are explained by firm and individual CEOs, respectively. This means that if Apple and Samsung display different stock returns, it is mostly due to the country's nationality; however, we will see as well that both companies move in a similar direction—everything else equal—in response to a global event such as a global financial crisis or the discovery of a technology.

There are interesting differences in results when one looks at the Organization for Economic Cooperation and Development (OECD) and non-OECD countries separately. In summary, I can say that global and country factors are way more important in less-developed economies. By contrast, CEOs and a firm's characteristics are more determinant of performance among OECD countries.

To explore the importance of global factors in less-developed economies, I have also split the sample depending on the country's competitiveness ranking. (I explain the ranking in the next part of the book.) Some countries, like Egypt and Kuwait, are not part of the IMD World Competitiveness Rankings, so I am losing a few observations

Table 1.5 How Much Factors Explain and Competitiveness

	Return on Invested Capital			Stock Returns		
	Top Competitiveness	Middle Competitiveness	Bottom Competitiveness	Top Competitiveness	Middle Competitiveness	Bottom Competitiveness
Global	0.3%	0.3%	0.4%	15.0%	22.1%	36.7%
Country	1.2%	2.5%	9.4%	2.6%	7.5%	12.8%
Industry	2.7%	2.5%	2.4%	2.1%	2.5%	1.8%
Firm	34.6%	29.8%	28.8%	11.3%	7.6%	4.3%
CEO	5.8%	6.7%	8.0%	4.5%	4.1%	2.4%
Number of Observations	24,211	20,456	9,203	43,585	26,538	12,487

here. However, the results in Table 1.5 confirm the same pattern: when a country is not competitive, the importance of global and country factors is huge—in total amounts to almost 50 percent of the stock price performance and 10 percent of ROIC. All in all, choices of investments and their subsequent return are very much firm-specific and not CEO-specific. As the economy becomes more competitive, global factors start losing importance. Once the country reaches the top 15 (United States, Switzerland, Germany, Singapore, Hong Kong), strategies and firm characteristics matter most. In a sense, the government becomes invisible (in total, global and country factors explain 1.5 percent in the variability of ROIC for the top 15 most competitive countries). Yet, when it comes to stock returns, even for these countries, global factors are important.

I think this makes the whole point of the book—there are thousands of articles, textbooks, and case studies that highlight the key success factors for companies based on the right choices of leadership skills and strategies. But what are the countries that—through policies—impact companies in the best possible way? Also, as the world economy develops in unison, are we creating the right conditions for the corporate sector to be profitable and sustainable, irrespective of who is in charge?

25. NATIONAL COMPETITIVENESS AND BUSINESS SUCCESS

Whether you're looking at a world-class professional football team, a toy company, or a global firm, its success will result from the ability of its leaders to navigate through a plethora of uncertainties.

Some of these uncertainties refer to the specific product market where the firm operates, and experience, resilience, and knowledge will be essential leadership skills to differentiate and excel vis-á-vis competitors.

But the ability to understand global phenomena, regulation, the institutional environment, and the constraints under which the company operates is also key. As a tool for executives, understanding what drives the success of a nation is relevant to also understanding what drives the success of the firm. As a tool for policymakers, understanding the relationship between policy and corporate performance is the first step in developing good national strategies.

The set of resources, capabilities, and factors that allows us to compare, assess, and manage countries is what we call *competitiveness*. Competitiveness is inclusive prosperity, national success, value creation for citizens, and quality of life. Why competitiveness, what makes nations competitive, and what are the potential alternatives are the objectives of the next part of the book.

Let me start by presenting two final case studies that will again highlight the importance of both the national and international contexts in impacting business success. The first case describes the history of Taiwanese company Giant, the largest bicycle manufacturer in the world. The second case describes how the international sanctions imposed on Russia after the annexation of Crimea have indeed spurred innovation to an amazing extent.

26. HOW THE NATIONAL CONTEXT MATTERS: TAIWAN AND GIANT BICYCLES

King Liu navigated a winding path to business success. Born into a merchant family in 1934, a decade before Taiwan shed Japanese colonialism, Liu's entrepreneurial spirit developed early. As a young man, the Japanese-educated engineer sought his fortune managing trucking and import companies and running factories that produced screws and wooden boxes.[50] Finding little success but amassing valuable experience, Liu even turned to eel farming. A typhoon blew away Liu's eel ponds, and the business failed. But it was an ill wind, and while Liu could not have known it then, fishing's loss was to become bicycling's gain. Low on funds, Liu in desperation convinced a few friends to pool their money to form a bicycle manufacturing business. They set up shop in 1972 in Taichung, a port city on Taiwan's west coast, with USD 130,000 in capital and three dozen employees. The company produced a meager 3,800 bikes in its first year of operation.[51] Liu optimistically and prophetically named the company Giant.

Tony Lo, a graduate of the National Taiwan University and something of a marketing wunderkind, came on board the next year. Both announced their retirements in 2018. As "one of many faceless factories vying for bike orders," Giant struggled against the island nation's reputation for low production standards and poor quality, subsisting on an anemic domestic market for steel bicycle frames, failing to obtain any orders from the big bicycle companies.[52] Still, the Liu–Lo alliance would pay off handsomely over the next 45 years. Liu not only insisted his own factory adopt Japanese-style quality standards but he also badgered Taiwan's parts suppliers into unified standards. Meanwhile Lo, the international trade expert and business negotiator, set his sights on securing an outsourcing contract that would give Giant the push it needed to start rolling as a major player in the global bicycle industry.[53]

Under founder King Liu's reign, Giant Manufacturing has steadily climbed its way to the top, like one of the company's Anthem Advanced 29 mountain bikes. By constantly reinventing the two-wheeler business to leverage markets, customer preferences, and evolving technologies, Liu and Lo have grown Giant from a minor supplier of cheap components to industry innovator and bicycling advocate.

The Schwinn deal

Giant's first big break came in 1978. After four years of hauling their bicycle prototype around the world looking for a buyer, Liu and Lo scored a coup when they signed a deal with Schwinn. The timing could not have been better. Schwinn rose to prominence with its 10-speed bike in the early 1970s. Baby boomers came of age, the environmentalist movement took hold, and the Organization of the Petroleum Exporting Countries (OPEC) oil crisis loomed, igniting the latest "bike boom" in the United States and the UK. "Everybody, it seemed in the early seventies, rushed out to buy 10-speed drop-handlebar bicycles." Schwinn sold its entire 1971 production— more than 1.2 million bicycles—before summer arrived.[54] The largest bike maker in the United States would not make the same mistake in 1972. Schwinn first turned to Japan in its search for a reliable outsource partner. But Liu's insistence on quality had begun to capture the attention of some of the world's leading bicycle makers, and in 1976, Schwinn placed a small order.[55] The orders grew. By the early 1980s, Giant was manufacturing and shipping hundreds of thousands of Schwinn World 10-speed, BMX Predators, and other bikes for its American partner, making Giant Asia's second-largest cycle producer.[56]

The bicycle industry, today

Like the market itself, bicycle demand based on bicycle type is also dispersed. Hybrids captured one-third of the market in 2017, followed by road bikes (29.4 percent of the market), mountain bikes (21.6 percent), and sport/track bikes (15.7 percent).[57] Bicycles in the track/sport category are poised to steal the market share from hybrid bikes. As the technology evolves, seasoned riders in the developed nations of North America and Europe will seek precision machines for fitness and competitive pursuits. This category will receive an additional boost as China's massive middle-class market continues to grow and spend its newfound disposable income on luxury items.

Bicycle makers are also bracing for the e-bike revolution. E-bike, or electric bike, sellers moved 35 million units in 2017, mostly in Europe and Asia. US buyers were responsible for less than 1 percent of that total. Demand in that market is expected to explode in the coming years, boosting global e-bike sales growth by 6 percent over the next five to seven years.[58]

Establishing the Giant brand

Around the same time, Giant undertook serious efforts to establish its own brand. Industry insiders appreciated Giant's quality—the Taiwanese firm was producing upwards of a million units for other "name" companies, including 80 percent of Schwinn's product line. "[The Schwinn contract] transformed us from a small company to one making over one million bicycles," Lo said. "It is fair to say that without Schwinn, there would be no Giant today."[59]

Few of those million bikes, however, carried the Giant name. Giant's original equipment manufacturer (OEM) deals with Schwinn were lucrative, but they left Giant with little room to innovate, develop manufacturing technology, or gather marketing insights. Liu and Lo seemed to sense these deficiencies and established the Taiwan Giant Sales Co. in 1981 to lay the groundwork for debuting the company's eponymous brand.[60]

Schwinn realized it had helped to create a monster that was about to transform itself from supplier to competitor. Schwinn tried to stem the tide by shifting the bulk of its outsourced supply to the China Bicycle Company in 1985. But Giant would not be denied. Liu ramped up development of the brand's foreign outposts. The Giant brand emerged onto the world stage with the launch of Giant Europe in the Netherlands in 1986. The firm took giant steps into the United States the next year, Japan in 1989, Australia and Canada in 1991, and China in 1992. Giant manufacturing never missed a step. Its export business absorbed the supply lost to Schwinn's defection. Liu's factory continued making one million-plus bicycles annually. But now, instead of "Schwinn," most carried the Giant logo. Schwinn, meanwhile, filed for bankruptcy in 1992.

Going upscale and reaching the top

As the Giant–Schwinn divorce was being finalized, Liu shifted gears to reposition his company in light of the mainland's growing hold on the lower, "Wal-Mart" end of the market. Giant carved out a niche at the higher end, while maintaining its affordable price point. Again, the timing proved advantageous. Giant's move into higher-priced, more precisely engineered bicycles took advantage of Taiwan's Industrial Technology Research Institute's (ITRI) development of carbon-fiber applications for bicycle frames.[61] The light yet rugged carbon frames obviously claimed a space among top-of-the-line road bikes. Giant upped the precision ante with computer-aided drafting and design, and was among the first to get there with the CADEX in 1987.[62] Demand followed suit. Just as Giant developed an innovative, upmarket bike, the global economy started humming and the world's citizens recommitted to physical fitness.

With a growing reputation as a manufacturer of professional-level bikes, Giant finally jumped into competitive cycling with its sponsorship of Spain's Team ONCE, beginning in 1997. Giant's aluminum alloy TCR bike made its Tour de France debut with the team that same year. With its distinctive sloping top tube, stiffer, more compact frame, and (beginning in 2003) carbon-fiber construction, the TCR was destined to change the sport forever. ONCE, and Giant-sponsored Team T-Mobile/Team Columbia won several Tour de France stages on Giant TCR TT Trinity models. More success followed for Giant-sponsored teams. Team Rabobank's Denis Menchov won the 2009 Giro d'Italia and Spain's Oscar Freire claimed the Milan San-Remo riding Giants. The company currently supplies frames, handlebars, saddles, and wheels for Team Sunweb, led by Michael Matthews and Tom Dumoulin.

Promoting an industry ...

By the turn of the millennium, Liu had firmly established his company among the industry leaders.[63] Mainland China now offered cheap labor, and the island's former OEM customers left in droves. Unwilling to sacrifice engineering and production standards, Liu decided he could not compete with China in building low-end bikes. Deciding he could not join them, Liu decided to beat them by cementing Taiwan's position as a top exporter of well-made, value-added machines.

With cooperation from Merida, Taiwan's other major bicycle manufacturer and exporter, Giant formed an association of the island's bike parts manufacturers and component makers to improve the industry. Dubbed the "A-Team," the consortium took to heart the efficient, streamlined production and supply-chain processes Toyota famously created. Giant also shared its engineering and manufacturing insights with its suppliers, helping them improve internal operations and quality control.[64] From its inception in 2003, the A-Team helped industry players reduce inventory costs, parts defects, and late deliveries and ensured Taiwan maintained its competitive advantage even as its overall bicycle production slowed. In the team's first six years, the value per bike made in Taiwan doubled, compensating for the demand lost to China.[65]

... and a lifestyle

Fitting for the head of a company called Giant, Liu has taken on a persona that is larger than life. Part cheerleader, part patron, he has worked to bring the sport to the masses. In his later years, Liu worked to boost cycling's popularity worldwide, especially in Taiwan. His efforts have paid off, and the island is now revered as a biking destination. Oddly for someone who has revolutionized the industry, Liu only seriously took up cycling when he was well into his sixties. He was further inspired by *Island Etude*, a 2007 film about a student who cycles around Taiwan, exploring its beauty and culture. Liu says he felt the film and especially the line, "With some things, if you do not do them now, you might never do them in your life," were speaking directly to him.[66] Like the film's protagonist, Liu decided to circumnavigate Taiwan on two wheels. Like most endeavors in his life, he succeeded, completing the 575-mile journey in 15 days.

> I was an old man contemplating retirement, but funnily enough, I instead discovered a brand-new me. It boosted my self-confidence, my health, and I became more willing to learn new things, to take on new challenges.[67]

Remarkably, he repeated the feat at age 80, shaving three days off his time, and thousands of his countrymen have followed his lead. Giant remains a family company. Upon King Liu and Tony Lo's retirements, the firm is now in the hands of Liu's son and new CEO, Young Liu. King Liu's niece Bonnie Tu moved from chief financial officer (CFO) to chairperson of Giant Global Group. In her previous position, she spearheaded the development of Liv Cycling, Giant's women's bike division. Like her uncle, Tu is a latecomer to cycling, but not to the business. She was a founding investor. After suffering the indignity of riding an ill-fitting bike and wearing uncomfortable riding clothes

Image 1.2 With Bonnie Tu in the Giant Headquarters

during the Tour of Taiwan, she set about creating equipment and apparel specifically made for women. Similarly, in an effort to bring bicycling to the masses, it founded its Momentum town bike line "to help you move through your life with happiness and ease."[68]

Attractive and functional, the bikes are simple to operate so casual bikers and newcomers to the sport can feel at home commuting or riding for fun. The island's bike rental platform, YouBike, grew out of Liu's desire to make bikes available to anyone who wants to ride. Despite all his commercial successes, Liu describes the public bike rental system he founded in Taiwan as the most gratifying project he has ever been a part of. YouBike started in 2012, and after a bout of fits and starts, now flourishes. Its fleet of 10,000 bright orange-and-yellow bikes is available at some 300 rental stations across Taipei. Rentals start at less than a dollar per hour.

Today, Giant also makes bicycles for every market, but its focus is on the higher-priced bikes from the "mid-premium" category (about USD 500) through professional models costing as much as USD 12,000. Even in this range, Giant has carved out a reputation for offering value for the money, thanks in part to manufacturing its own wheels and aluminum and carbon-fiber frame tubing. About a million and a half of the 5.2 million total bikes Giant factories turn out each year are made for Trek, Scott, Colnago, and other top brands under OEM contracts, making these companies customers as well as competitors.[69,70]

Institutional considerations

[Liu's] evolution from a small-town tinkerer to an industry titan reflects greater shifts of Taiwan and its economy. Once a workshop to the world, anonymously churning out bikes, cellphones (sic) and computers for big-name foreign companies, Taiwan now has firms like Giant, HTC, and Acer that have become global brands in their own right.[71]

Much of Giant's success is directly attributable to King Liu's business acumen and Tony Lo's marketing savvy. But the company has also capitalized on Taiwan's political environment, culture, and institutional factors that helped pave the way. Giant is very much a product of Taiwan's remarkable post-war transformation from a third-world nation to one of the fastest-growing economies in the world. Taiwan, of course, emerged in the aftermath of World War II as the result of the communist takeover of the mainland. Though hardly a democracy (the authoritarian Kuomintang, or KMT, ruled as a one-party state under martial law until well into the 1980s), Taiwan's geopolitical status made it an important component in the West's Cold War strategy. The United States provided the bulk of Taiwan's international assistance. Foreign aid from the White House accounted for 6.5 percent of the nascent nation's gross domestic product (GDP) from 1950 to 1965. That boost, in the form of military aid, raw materials, and industrial and statecraft intelligence, enabled Taiwan to gain a foothold that would propel its factories to global prominence.[72]

Domestic policy

In many ways, Chiang Kai-Shek's heavy-handed control over political and business institutions proved beneficial for the early development of Taiwan's manufacturing industries. The first phase in the sector's rise was an aggressive import substitution industrialization strategy the KMT adopted in late 1950. The policy's protectionism against inexpensive imports focused on subsidizing domestic producers of universal-demand products such as food, clothing, and energy. By the mid-1950s, the program was so successful that even small- and medium-sized enterprises (SMEs) could produce goods of sufficient quality and quantity to support export, primarily to the United States. This development proved advantageous to Giant, as Taiwan's reputation as a source of cheap products and reliable suppliers was widespread by the time the bicycle maker was founded.

The state assumed an even greater and more hands-on role in manufacturing as the island's industries pivoted from satisfying domestic demand to profiting from exports. The island remained poor in natural resources and private means to operate large industries. State-owned heavy industry fed smaller enterprises by supplying critical steel, aluminum, plastic, electricity, and—critical for Giant's success—carbon fiber to the country's SMEs at reasonable prices.[73] More importantly, it developed the island's labor force and technologies and advanced production processes, and laid the groundwork for entrepreneurs to enter the market.[74]

The government's favorable treatment of industrial firms and the entrepreneurs and investors that built them extended to tax policy. The Nineteen Points Program for Economic and Social Reform, announced in 1960, gave manufacturers access to the foreign and domestic investment capital they needed to expand in order to take advantage of export markets. Taipei went even further with the Statute for Encouragement of Investment, a corollary to the Nineteen Points that gave manufacturers a five-year moratorium on taxes and thereafter capped their business income tax at 18 percent, compared to 32.5 percent for distributors and retailers.[75]

Technology

Favorable tax policy and other government support assisted fledgling manufacturers in their quest to harness technology in order to improve production efficiencies, reduce costs, and streamline operations. The creation of economic processing zones (EPZs) beginning in 1966 expedited industry development. These free-trade ports not only extended tax benefits, but also exempted factories operating within them from some regulatory constraints. More importantly, they attracted firms associated with similar industries. As a result, the EPZ in Taichung developed as a hub for the bicycle industry. Not only Giant, but also Merida and several of their part and component suppliers are headquartered there. Having supply-chain partners in close proximity to one another reduced shipping costs, streamlined delivery, allowed for smaller inventories, and created other logistical advantages that Giant has deftly leveraged. Component supplier SRAM makes brake and gear components in Taichung because "it is a short distance between the suppliers and the OEM companies like Merida or Giant, so we can all pull together and work out how to shorten the lead times in material and information flow," says Jacky Lin, SRAM's factory vice-manager.

In 1973, three government research institutes merged to form the Industrial Technology Research Institute, part of Taiwan's sharpened focus on industrial technology and scientific processes as they relate to manufacturing. Giant collaborated with the ITRI in 1985 to develop the carbon-fiber technology that lifted the bicycle maker to the forefront of high-end carbon-frame bike production.[76]

Education

Dating as far back as the Japanese occupation of 1895 to 1945, Taiwanese have valued and invested in education. That commitment continued after World War II, with the KMT steadily increasing education spending—from 8.6 percent of the national budget in 1950 to 19.1 percent in 1994.[77] With few natural resources on the island, Taiwan's leaders quickly identified human capital as its most valuable asset. They worked to align secondary and higher education curricula with the skills that would prove useful in manufacturing. Along with direct aid, the United States assisted Taiwan's industrial development by educating many budding engineers, technicians, and economists at American universities.

Today, the island is experiencing some growing pains as it progresses from a manufacturing-heavy economy to a more diverse market of expanding personal and professional services and a creative economy. This is partially the result of early-2000s education reform that "upgraded" several technical colleges to universities, resulting in "a mismatch of labor supply and job market demand."[78] But that was not the case during Giant's formative and expansion years. Responding to its growing export potential, Taiwan in the 1960s and 1970s emphasized and expanded its industry-focused education, including vocational education through nine years of mandatory schooling, an extensive junior college system, and technical institutes that provided instruction on industrial engineering and innovation.[79]

The nexus of Taiwan's education and industrial policies accelerated the pace of innovation in order to stimulate export markets. More than half the country's expenditures on research and development in the 1980s came from the public sector.[80] The Industrial Policy Research Institute played a prominent part. Founded in 1973, it helped wean Taiwan industry away from a dependence on US technology. Its capacity to do so coincided with Giant's transition from low-cost vendor to American companies to manufacturer of self-branded, high-tech bikes.[81] From those humble beginnings, "Taiwan is now a supply and R&D center for the world's high-end bicycles. And no other place in the world can compete—not even close," Tony Lo proudly declared.[82]

Culture

Like many Taiwanese businesses, Giant started as an enterprise of family and friends. Undercapitalized, it followed Taiwan's family-business culture, taking little risk, remaining flexible by engaging in short-term contracts, and relying on everyone in the household to pitch in.[83] Many times, family members working in the factories were not paid for their labors. Instead, their contributions manifested in greater profits, which benefited the owner's family as a whole. Taiwanese firms today have adopted many of the West's aggressive marketing, innovation, competitive, growth-oriented traditions. But in the critical 1960s and 1970s, its business leaders were content to play the role of small, low-cost, anonymous suppliers to US and Japanese companies whose domestic labor costs were much higher. It was a strategy that suited them well. As contract manufacturers, Taiwanese firms—including Giant—were adept at conforming their plant operations to meet their customers' needs. They adjusted production and implemented the client's technologies and specifications quickly, saving the cost of marketing, retailing, and innovation.[84]

Liu established Giant at the perfect time so that when it came time to expand and hire additional workers, the company could take advantage of a large pool of motivated and cheap labor. The agriculture boom of the 1950s had run its course, and rural workers needed jobs. Taiwanese culture always valued self-sufficiency and hard work. Labor unions were slow to develop, keeping wages low. This has much to do with Taiwanese culture, specifically, Confucianism's influence on not only Taiwan, but most of East Asia that has ignited entrepreneurship and suppressed labor activism. The theory is that Confucianism's cultural emphasis on acceptance of authority and reverence of the family has translated to the working environment. "Authority" has come to include company owners and executives, who deserve loyalty. The concept of "Family" now includes co-workers, who strive together to make the business a success, even while sacrificing personal ambition and individual achievement.[85]

27. THE IMPORTANCE OF THE INTERNATIONAL CONTEXT: THE CASE OF RUSSIA

In February–March 2014, Russia annexed the Republic of Crimea—a peninsula officially recognized as part of Ukraine under international laws.[86] A large number of countries responded by imposing sanctions on Russian enterprises, state officials, and individuals. The United States imposed sanctions against more than 700 Russian individuals and companies in several rounds.[87] Presidential executive orders Nos. 13660, 13661, and 13662 issued in March 2014 authorized travel bans on certain Russian individuals and government officials, with the aim to impose the cost on those responsible for the annexation. Later in December 2014, the US sanctions were expanded to include financing restrictions imposed on six Russian banks and four energy companies. The December order also banned the supply of goods, services, and technology for deep-water and shale explorations.[88]

The sanctions were supported by other countries, including Australia, Japan, Canada, Norway, and the EU. The sanctions imposed by the EU can be broadly grouped into three categories. The first type imposes travel restrictions and asset freezes on individuals in the so-called Putin inner circle. The second type relates to restricting access to specific Russian state–owned banks as well as energy and defense companies. Third is the embargo on exports of oil exploration and production technology and equipment as well as on particular military or dual-use products.[89] In general, the so-called "economic" sanctions imposed by Western countries were primarily targeting:

- Five major state-owned Russian banks, including Bank "Rossiya," known to be the "personal bank" of senior Russian officials. Other banks on the list include Sberbank, the largest Russian bank, and Gazprombank, a member of the state-owned Gazprom group.
- Three Russian state–owned oil companies—Transneft, Rosneft, and Gazpromneft, the oil subsidiary of Gazprom.
- Three major Russian defense companies, including the famous Kalashnikov arms enterprise.
- The subsidiaries of those enterprises.

However, the sanctions do not include gas, nuclear, or space industries.[90]

In turn, Russia mirrored the Western sanctions by imposing counter-sanctions. The retaliation measures involved travel bans for a list of individuals and the import ban on agricultural products originating from the countries that imposed sanctions on Russia .[91] Other measures such as an imports ban on cars or clothes have been discussed and revisited during each new round of sanctions, but, to date, have not been implemented.

Living under sanctions

What does it feel like living under sanctions? Have they worked at all? Researchers claim that the effect of counter-sanctions was negligible for the EU and the United States as the relative share of agricultural imports to Russia was rather low and the size of the economy was big enough to compensate for the effect.[92] For the Russian economy, the outcomes were not so bright. Timewise, the sanctions happened together with a sharp and significant drop in the price of oil, which is naturally important for the Russian economy that relies heavily on extraction revenues. Consequently, the sanctions contributed to the difficulties in the macroeconomic setting the country was already facing. As a result, the country's investment attractiveness declined significantly, which resulted in capital outflow and increased pressure on the local currency (rouble). Furthermore, the state was essentially forced to support the sanctioned enterprises using several national reserve funds to finance them. Finally, the Central Bank of Russia abruptly stopped controlling the rouble exchange rate, and sharply increased the key rate, which led to the rapid depreciation of the national currency. The counter-sanctions imposed by Russia on agricultural products created short-term shortages and consequently pushed prices up, leading to higher inflation.[93] The effect was rather profound as, according to estimates, more than 60 percent of food in the shops of big cities was imported.[94] As a result, the country's real GDP in the first quarter of 2015 decreased by 2.2 percent compared to the same period in 2014.[95] Despite inhibiting economic growth and hitting mostly the middle class, the sanctions did not essentially affect Russia's fundamental economic stability.[96] Nevertheless, sanctions do create challenges (and opportunities!) for businesses of all sizes and it is interesting to take a look at the strategies employed by companies to weather them.

How do bigger companies cope?

Russia's biggest companies do not vary much industry-wise—they are either financial companies, mainly banks, or mining and extraction enterprises. At least half are either sanctioned or face increased US import tariffs on steel and aluminum. On the other hand, 26 Russian companies were on the *Forbes* Global 2000 list in 2018. It is worth mentioning that the five best-known sanctioned Russian enterprises, namely, Sberbank, VTB Bank, Gazprom, Lukoil, and Rosneft, have climbed up the rank. Rosneft is facing sectoral sanctions while its CEO is among the individuals on the personal sanctions list. Nevertheless, the company enjoys 73rd place on the *Forbes* list, climbing from 82nd in 2017. Another example—the aluminum giant United Rusal that faces both sanctions and US import tariffs. Its CEO, Oleg Deripaska, is also on the individual sanctions list. Nevertheless, the company was ranked #1,098 in 2018. So, wait a second, what is happening here? The companies banned from the largest financing sources, facing sectoral sanctions and higher import tariffs, with their heads not welcome in the largest part of the developed world, are still doing pretty well. How is it possible? Naturally, state support, loans from Chinese banks, and growing commodity prices accompanied by an expanding global economy play their roles.[97] However, those are only a part of the story.

One of the strategies still available to some of the sanctioned companies is attracting equity capital. While Exxon Mobil was forced to exit a USD 720 million joint venture with Rosneft,[98] French giant Total is enjoying the status of exclusive Western co-owner of the largest Russian natural gas projects together with Novatek (the company is on the sanctions list since July 2014). This can be partially explained by the nature of the sanctions imposed on Novatek as they do not prohibit attracting equity directly.

Another option available to the larger enterprises is technological equipment supply contracts with European suppliers guaranteed by foreign export agencies. For example, in December 2015, Sibur signed an agreement with a syndicate of European banks for a credit line for EUR 1,575 billion. The credit line was opened for contracts with Linde AG and ThyssenKrupp—supply contractors for pyrolysis and polypropylene equipment for the Zapsibneftehim complex under construction. The agreement was guaranteed by German agency Euler Hermes. In September 2015, the company raised an additional EUR 412 million in loans for the same project. The French agency COFACE was the guarantor for the deal.

Nizhnekamskneftehim (NKNH) concluded a similar deal for EUR 807 million with Deutsche Bank AG. The transaction was also guaranteed by Euler Hermes and the funds were raised for ethylene complex equipment supplied by Linde AG.

Novatek uses the same instrument for its natural gas project on Yamal. In December 2016, the company received a EUR 750 million loan from Intesa San Paolo bank guaranteed by COFACE and Italian export agency SACE and a EUR 425 million loan from Raiffeisenbank, Intesa San Paolo, and other European banks guaranteed by Euler Hermes and EKN (Sweden). According to Leonid Mikhelson, chairman of Novatek's board, those loans allowed the company not to use the total volume of loans provided by China Development Bank and China Exim Bank.

Another instrument is Eurobonds, the sale of which was prohibited for Rosneft, Transneft, and Gazprom Neft, but not for Sibur, in 2014. In September 2017, Sibur issued six-year Eurobonds for USD 500 million at 4.125 percent. By that time, one of the company shareholders, Gennady Timchenko, had been under US sanctions for three years. Sanctions-related risks affected the investment attractiveness of the securities to some extent and the funds raised turned out to be less beneficial for the company than the loan provided by the Russian National Wealth Fund in 2015. The funds of the Russian National Wealth Fund are more important than the European loans for Novatek; similarly for Sibur. Probably, this is the essence of the effect of the sanctions. While the companies have some success in finding "backdoors" to attract financing in Europe, those funds no longer play a key role for them.[99]

Besides these more conventional ways of raising funds, Russian companies also leverage more creative approaches using new technologies. For example, Sberbank successfully completed the sale of rouble-denominated corporate bonds with a total value of RUB 750 million (approximately USD 12 million) using smart contracts via the National Settlement Depository (NSD) blockchain platform. While the sanctions prohibit the supply of financing to Sberbank, the supply of technological solutions to the banking sector is not restricted.[100]

What do smaller businesses do?

While the sanctions mainly affected bigger companies, counter-sanctions hit smaller businesses and the general population harder. Or did they?

In September 2016, Deputy Chief Prosecutor of Russia Vladimir Malinovsky pointed out that, over 2015, Belorussia exported to Russia five times more apples than it produced. Later, the same "fame" reached shrimps, pineapples, and other foods exotic for Belorussia.[101] According to Sergey Lisovsky, the first deputy chairman of the Federation Council Committee on Agricultural and Food Policy and Nature Management, the sanctioned food is mainly supplied to Russia via Belorussia; however, there are also alternative channels in place.[102]

A simple web search using the most popular Russian search engine Yandex offers plenty of opportunities to buy sanctioned food items with doorstep delivery. For example, two online stores, U Augusta[103] and ItaliaNaDom,[104] offer a variety of Italian cheeses. Both companies claim to offer authentic products manufactured by small- to medium-sized Italian producers.

Besides the aforementioned, rather obvious but bordering on illegal business activities, the sanctions actually opened up avenues for numerous business activities in various fields. Probably, one of the most creative business models is exemplified by Kaappi[105] company from Saint Petersburg. The residents of Saint Petersburg and the region surrounding the city are enjoying a simplified procedure of obtaining a visa to Finland. Usually, the issued visas are long term and allow for multiple entrances upon the condition that the first entry to the Shengen zone is made in Finland. This results in the natural strategy for entering Europe widely used by the residents of the region: get a Finnish visa, enter Finland for a couple of hours, and travel elsewhere for several years. Kaappi offers free bus tours to Finland for those willing to validate their visa, with only one condition—limiting the baggage allowance to 5 kg per person. Essentially, the travelers function as "living containers" and support the second direction of Kaappi's business—joint purchases of sanctioned foods.

Russian counter-sanctions changed the lives of a famous blogger, the head of a cheese plant, an ex-showman, and a builder, who was building domes for churches. Nowadays, all of them are manufacturing cheese.

The couple that own Bebeshkino cheese farm were once a showman and a designer. Several years before the sanctions, they decided to open a cheese farm of their own, following the cheese-making technology of the 19th century. They recognize that before the sanctions, their attempts to manufacture soft cheeses similar to French ones were not much welcomed, but after the sanctions, the demand considerably exceeded their production capacity. Still, Bebeshkino is far from being alone on the market.

Farmer Oleg Sirota is well known in the Russian-speaking internet. His businesses has mushroomed because of the sanctions. He is running his cheese farm Russian Parmezan, as well as a cheese festival under the same name, and blogging about the process. Apparently, the market is still far from being saturated, so Sirota is also helping other farmers to start their cheese business. One of his followers, Vyacheslav Kovtun, co-owner of Syr&Beer, was building churches prior to the sanctions.

The embargo changed the lives not only of those who never dealt with farming before but also of already established cheese manufacturers. According to Taras Kozhanov, deputy CEO of Sernyrsky cheese plant, the demand increased threefold leading to a 2.5 increase in revenue over the first three years of sanctions being in place.[106]

While agricultural growth was somewhat obvious and expected, the boom in the services market is not so much talked about. However, the sanctions led to the rapid growth of legal and compliance services. Oleg Juice, a member of the board and the treasury head of Inteza bank, describes this in the following way:

It suffices to simply glance at current transactions on the capital markets and mergers and acquisitions, how many additional legal opinions are needed, how long the payments take, how many extra documents have to be filed, and how many investigations are to be undertaken. The number of requests exchanged by the parties when structuring a transaction and the number of services (both internal and external), that is, the number of people supporting a transaction under sanctions, has increased several times.

For example, compliance services mainly ensured that the internal documentation and procedures were in line with the regulatory demands and ensured compliance with anti-money laundering and terrorism support legislation. However, nowadays, they have to ensure that a potential contracting party will not adversely affect the transaction due to other restrictions imposed by sanctions.

Most often these restrictions relate to transborder transactions; however, essentially the US sanctions under Countering America's Adversaries Through Sanctions Act (CAATSA) cover the whole world as transactions with sanctioned enterprises are only riskless for the companies that have no assets outside of Russia. According to Juice, it is almost impossible to estimate the volume of this market, as no one would publish the revenues gained from bypassing the sanctions. However, he believes that the total volume of legal, lobbying, and intermediary services reaches dozens of USD billions.[107]

NOTES

1 Liyan Chen. "America's Best-Managed Companies," *Forbes*, Dec. 29, 2014, www.forbes.com/sites/liyanchen/2014/12/10/americas-best-managed-companies/#f99a24712766.
2 "How Netflix Became a Billion-Dollar Titan," *The Economist*, July 4, 2018, www.economist.com/graphic-detail/2018/07/04/how-netflix-became-a-billion-dollar-titan.
3 Max Ehrenfreund. "The Architects of the 2008 Financial Bailouts Have Their Day in Court," *The Washington Post*, Oct. 6, 2014, www.washingtonpost.com/news/wonk/wp/2014/10/06/the-architects-of-the-2008-financial-bailouts-have-their-day-in-court/?utm_term=.83b2d3c75670.
4 Morck et al. (2000).
5 UEFA (2018)
6 Ashby (2015)
7 Peeters et al. (2015).
8 "Deloitte Football Money League 2019," Deloitte, www2.deloitte.com/uk/en/pages/sports-business-group/articles/deloitte-football-money-league.html.
9 Muehlheusser et al. (2016).
10 Holcomb et al. (2009).
11 "Newcastle Owner Mike Ashley Looking at Four Bids in excess of £300M for Club," *The Guardian*, Dec. 5, 2018, www.theguardian.com/football/2018/dec/05/newcastle-united-owner-mike-ashley-four-bids-for-club-excess-300-million.
12 Bharadwaj (2000); Santhanam and Hartono (2003); Chae et al. (2014).
13 Wales et al. (2013); Alegre et al. (2013).
14 Leitner (2010); Pandaya (1998); Guo and Cao (2012).
15 Bach et al. (2006), as quoted in Miloloza (2018).
16 Sichone (2004).

17 Koontz et al. (1990).
18 Strukan et al. (2015).
19 Firestone ([1996]).
20 Madanchian et al. (2017).
21 Kocel (2011).
22 Bass (1990); Yildiz [et al. (2014)].
23 Obiwuru et al. (2011).
24 Bass (1990), as quoted in Strukan et al. (2017).
25 For instance, Hater and Bass (1988); Peterson et al. (1989); Bryman (1992); Yammarino et al. (1993).
26 Yildiz [et al. (2014)]; Drucker (1954); Wasserman et al. (2010).
27 For example, Wiengarten et al. ([2017]).
28 www.apple.com/newsroom/2019/01/letter-from-tim-cook-to-apple-investors/.
29 www.bloomberg.com/news/articles/2019-01-02/apple-cut-first-quarter-sales-forecast-on-weak-iphone-sales.
30 https://appleinsider.com/articles/18/04/25/defending-tim-cook-why-apple-remains-in-good-hands.
31 The quote rephrases the arguments in www.wired.com/2011/08/the-end-of-inno/.
32 www.thestreet.com/story/11722893/1/if-steve-jobs-were-alive-he-would-fire-tim-cook.html.
33 See, for example, Elenkov (2000); Zehir et al. (2014); Noruzy et al. (2013); Bass et al. ([1990], 2003); Brown (2003); Denison (1990); Cameron and Quinn ([1998]); Miloloza (2018); Northouse (2012); Yildiz et al. ([2011]); Kinicki and Kreitner (2006); Robbins and Judge (2009); Steyrer and Schiffinger ([2008]); Knies et al. (2016); Waldman et al. ([1990]); Koh et al. (1995); Wofford et al. (2001); Dvir et al. (2002); Bellé (2013); Griffith (2004); Jacobsen and Andersen (2015); Kim and Brymer (2011); Wang et al. (2011); Koech and Namusonge (2012); Steyrer and Mende (1994); Berri et al. (2009); Muchirie et al. (2012); Chae and Chang (2012); Meier and O'Toole (2013); Fenwick (2008); and Gayle (2008). See also Fuller et al. (1996) and Lowe et al. (1996) for a comment on these types of studies.
34 OROA is measured as the ratio of earnings before interest and taxes to the book value of assets. OROA is a natural measure of performance that has been previously used in the CEO turnover literature to assess the quality of operation changes around successions (Denis and Denis, 1995; Huson et al., 2004, as quoted in Bennedsen et al., 2010).
35 Bertrand and Schoar (2003).
36   www.accenture.com/t00010101T000000__w__/ch-de/_acnmedia/Accenture/Conversion-Assets/DotCom/Documents/Local/de-ch/PDF/Accenture_Study_Top500_CH_2014.pdf.
37 The sample of firms does not include firms that experienced extraordinary events such as mergers and acquisitions during the 2009–2013 period because such events influenced their results. It also excludes the real estate industry because it showed extremely volatile results, which were heavily influenced by single development projects.
38 We contacted 7,333 possible survey respondents from 289 companies. Our final results are based on a total of 660 survey responses (9 percent rate) representing 104 firms; with 69 respondents belong to 14 Growth Champions.
39 Sources used: Orbis (2014). Bureau van Dijk and Thomson One Banker (2014) Thomson Reuters.
40 www.latimes.com/business/la-fi-mattel-new-ceo-20180419-story.html.
41 http://fortune.com/2018/07/25/mattel-jobs/.
42 http://fortune.com/2015/06/03/why-google-and-mattel-are-getting-kids-and-parents-wrong/.
43 www.theguardian.com/technology/2015/nov/26/hackers-can-hijack-wi-fi-hello-barbie-to-spy-on-your-children.
44 www.ancestry.com/.
45 www.bloomberg.com/news/articles/2017-07-19/ancestry-com-is-said-to-be-close-to-hiring-banks-for-2017-ipo.
46 Wasserman [et al. (2010)].
47 Bandiera et al. (2020).
48 Industry groups are building materials, consumer goods, consumer services, financial sector, healthcare, industrials, oil and gas, technology, telecommunications, and utilities.

49 This is, in any case, not a problem since the econometric analysis controls for country-fixed and time-variant effects, so exchange rates are accounted for.
50 Ting-Fang (2016).
51 Fuchs (2017).
52 Ting-Fang (2016); Ramzy (2018); de Neef (2015).
53 Hu and Wu (2015).
54 Reid (2017), 3.
55 Hu and Wu (2015).
56 Bike Exchange, n.d.; Huang (2009).
57 Persistence (2018); Technavio (2018).
58 Market Research Future (2018).
59 Latz (2015).
60 Hu and Wu (2015).
61 Hu and Wu (2015).
62 de Neef (2015).
63 Fueled by fitness, environmental, and financial concerns, the global bicycle industry is poised for a strong showing over the coming decade. Already a USD 40 billion sector, bicycle manufacturing is projected by some analysts to reach USD 75 billion to USD 80 billion by 2026. The growing middle class in China and India offers a vast potential market, and the trend in Europe toward greater investment in bicycle lanes and other infrastructure improvements is expected to stimulate demand.

The market is quite fragmented, with the top seven manufacturers capturing only 12 percent of sales revenue. Bicycle consumers run the gamut from leisure riders and urban commuters to outdoor enthusiasts and athletes. Manufacturers have responded by offering a variety of bicycles corresponding to the performance and budgetary demands of the various target markets. Most key market participants offer brands in all these categories: road, mountain, and sport bicycles, as well as hybrids that combine characteristics of all three. For instance, Taiwan's Merida offers several models designed for road, city, and mountain riding in addition to lines built specially for women and young riders. US-based Trek is known for its outdoor adventure bikes, slotting its offerings into narrow segments to appeal to specific enthusiasts such as mountain, downhill, gravel, fitness, and triathlon. Others, like India's Hero, compete by leveraging economies of scale and a streamlined supply chain, passing production savings along to consumers. Poised to become the industry's largest producer, Hero made 5.2 million bikes in 2017, second only to Giant's 5.3 million, yet its revenue was a mere USD 360 million – less than 20 percent of Giant's turnover. Yet, Hero's net profits weighed in at fully 60 percent of Giant's (Uma, Kavitha, and Ramya, 2018; [Giant, n.d.]). Smaller manufacturers appeal to one particular niche: Pinarello for light, responsive road bikes; BMC for racing cycles; Eddy Merckx for comfortable endurance bikes.
64 *Georgia Asian Times* (2014).
65 www.bicycleretailer.com/international/2008/05/02/team-bikes-are-mission-possible#.XFR7v1Uzb8x, last consulted on January 2, 2019.
66 Ramzy (2013).
67 AFP (2016).
68 Giant Bicycles, [n.d.]
69 Fuchs (2017).
70 Several companies compete with Giant in the mid-upscale global bicycle market:
   • Trek – The biggest bike manufacturer in the United States, with USD 1.7 billion in annual revenue, Trek also produces a line for every budget and category. It enjoys a reputation for technical innovation for high quality, especially in its top-of-the-line road machines [Johnson 2008)].
   • Specialized – A pioneer and market leader in the mountain bike market, earning high marks for its S-works brand. Specialized has extended this line's success into road bikes (Johnson, 2008).
   • Cervelo – A Canadian brand now owned by a Dutch holding company, Cervelo is a leader in the premium road bike category. Its racing line emphasizes aerodynamic design and speed at all costs, often sacrificing comfort and lightness for performance (Arthurs-Brennan, 2018b).

- Pinarello – Pinarello continues the Italian tradition of building highly engineered, responsive road bikes. The Dogma line of race bikes features flattened tubes for greater stiffness. The company extends the technology to hybrid commuter bikes and endurance models (Arthurs-Brennan, 2017).
- Cannondale – Successfully incorporating racing technology and insights into affordable premium bikes for avid amateurs, Cannondale is owned by Dorel Industries, which has moved production to Taiwan. It is known for design innovation, developing new technologies for suspension forks, cranksets, and bottom brackets (eBicycles, n.d.; Arthurs-Brennan, 2018a).

71 Ramzy (2013).
72 Runde (2015).
73 Rigger (2014), p. 50.
74 Rigger (2014), pp. 48–49.
75 Kuo, Ranis, and Fei (1981).
76 Rigger (2014), p. 56.
77 Fukuyama (2001)
78 Rigger (2014).
79 MoE (2011)
80 Wade (1990)
81 Robinson (2009)
82 Huang (2009)
83 Redding (1990)
84 Rigger (2014).
85 Dore (1996)
86 BBC News (2018).
87 Meyer et al. (2018).
88 US Department of State (2019).
89 European Commission (2019).
90 BBC News (2014).
91 Gros and Di Salvo (2017)
92 Ibid.
93 Christie (2016).
94 BBC News (2014).
95 Eurostat (2019).
96 Trolanovski (2018).
97 Rapoza (2018).
98 Ibid.
99 Kipa (2018).
100 MarketScreener (2018).
101 Bocharova and Feiberg (2019).
102 Rasulov (2017).
103 www.uavgusta.ru/.
104 http://italianadom.ru/.
105 https://kaappi2.ru/.
106 Lakina (2017).
107 Bakhvalova (2018).

REFERENCES

AFP (2016), "Taiwan's Octogenarian Bike Pioneer on Pedal Power Mission," *Daily Mail*, https://www.dailymail.co.uk/wires/afp/article-3472387/Taiwans-octogenarian-bike-pioneer-pedal-power-mission.html.

Alegre, Joaquin, and Ricardo Chiva (2013), "Linking Entrepreneurial Orientation and Firm Performance: The Role of Organizational Learning Capability and Innovation Performance," *Journal of Small Business Management* 51(4): 491–507.

Arthurs-Brennan, Michelle (2017), "Pinarello Bikes 2019 Range: Know Your Dogma F10 from Your K10S," *Cycling Weekly*, https://www.cyclingweekly.com/group-tests/pinarello-bikes-350778.

Arthurs-Brennan, Michelle (2018a), "Cannondale 2019 Road Bikes: Which Model Is Right for You?" *Cycling Weekly*, https://www.cyclingweekly.com/group-tests/cannondale-bikes-351846.

Arthurs-Brennan, Michelle (2018b), "Cervelo Bikes 2019: Ultimate Guide," *Cycling Weekly*, https://www.cyclingweekly.com/group-tests/cervelo-bikes-s-series-r-series-p-series-c-series-344225.

Ashby, Kevin (2015), "Berlin final captures the world's imagination," *UEFA*, https://www.uefa.com/uefachampionsleague/news/newsid=2255318.html#/.

Bakhvalova, Milena (2018), Звездный час белорусской креветки: санкции стали прибыльным бизнесом (The Moment of Glory of Belorussian Shrimps: The Sanctions Turned to be a Profitable Business), Banki.ru.

Bandiera, Oriana, Stephen Hansen, Andrea Prat, and Raffaella Sadun (2020), "CEO Behavior and Firm Performance," *Journal of Political Economy*, Volume 128, Number 4.

Bass, Bernard M. (1990), "From Transactional to Transformational Leadership: Learning to Share the Vision," *Organizational Dynamics* 19(3): 19–31.

Bass, Bernard M., Bruce J. Avolio, Dong I. Jung, and Yair Berson (2003), "Predicting Unit Performance by Assessing Transformational and Transactional Leadership," *Journal of Applied Psychology* 88(2): 207.

BBC News (2018), "Crimea Profile."

Bellé, Nicola (2013), "Leading to Make a Difference: A Field Experiment on the Performance Effects of Transformational Leadership, Perceived Social Impact, and Public Service Motivation," *Journal of Public Administration Research and Theory* 24(1): 109–36.

Bennedsen, Morten, Francisco Pérez-González, and Daniel Wolfenzon (2010), *Do CEOs Matter?*. Columbia Business School, Columbia University.

Berri, David, Michael Leeds, Eva Marikova Leeds, and Mike Mondello (2009), "The Role of Managers in Team Performance," *International Journal of Sport Finance* 4(2): 75–93.

Bertrand, Marianne, and Antoinette Schoar (2003), "Managing with Style: The Effect of Managers on Firm Policies," *Quarterly Journal of Economics* CXVIII(4): 1169–1208.

Bharadwaj, Anandhi S. (2000), "A Resource-Based Perspective on Information Technology Capability and Firm Performance: An Empirical Investigation," *MIS Quarterly*

BikeXchange (n.d.), "Giant Bikes," https://bikexchange.com/bike-brands/giant-bikes-review.

Bocharova, Svetlana, and Anton Feiberg (2017), Россиянам запретят покупать «санкционку» из Белоруссии и Казахстана (Russians Will Not Be Allowed to Buy Sanctioned Foods from Belorussia and Kazakhstan), rbc.ru.

Bowen, Brent D. et al. (2013), "An Innovative Leadership Effectiveness Measure: Applied Analytic Indicators of High-Consequence Industry Performance," The 2nd International Conference on Leadership, Technology and Innovation Management.

Brown, Barbara S. (2003), *Employees' Organizational Commitment and Their Perception of Supervisors' Relations-Oriented and Task-Oriented Leadership Behaviors* (Doctoral dissertation, Virginia Polytechnic Institute and State University.

Bryman, Alan E. (1992), *Charisma and Leadership in Organizations* (London: SAGE Publications).

Cameron, Kim S., and Robert E. Quinn (1998), *Diagnosing and Changing Organizational Culture: Based on The Competing Values Framework* (Reading, MA: Addison-Wesley).

Chae, Ho-Chang, Chang E. Koh, and V.R. Prybutok (2014), "Information Technology Capability and Firm Performance: Contradictory Findings and Their Possible Causes," *MIS Quarterly* 38(1): 305–326.

Christie, Edward Hunter (2016), "Sanctions after Crimea: Have They Worked?" *NATO Review*.

de Neef, Matt (2015), "A Tour of Giant's Taichung Factory," *CyclingTips*, https://cyclingtips.com/2015/02/a-tour-of-giants-taichung-factory.

Deloitte (2019), "Deloitte Football Money League 2019," https://www2.deloitte.com/uk/en/pages/sports-business-group/articles/deloitte-football-money-league.html.

Denison, Daniel R. (1990), *Corporate Culture and Organizational Effectiveness* (New York: Wiley).

Dvir, Taly, Dov Eden, Bruce J. Avolio, and Boas Shamir (2002), "Impact of Transformational Leadership on Follower Development and Performance: A Field Experiment," *Academy of Management Journal* 45(4): 735–744.

Elenkov, Detelin S. (2002), "Effects of Leadership on Organizational Performance in Russian Companies," *Journal of Business Research* 55(6): 467–480.

European Commission (2019), "EU sanctions against Russia over Ukraine crisis."

Eurostat (2019), "Database – Eurostat," http://ec.europa.eu/.

Firestone, William A. (1996), "Leadership: Roles or Functions?" in Leithwood Kenneth A. et al. (eds.), *International Handbook of Educational Leadership and Administration* (The Netherlands: Kluwer Academic Publishers).

Fuchs, Chris (2017), "From Taipei Streets to the French Alps, Giant's Bikes Found Success with Reinvention," *NBCNews.com*, https://www.nbcnews.com/news/asian-america/taipei-streets-french-alps-giant-s-bikes-found-success-reinvention-n805761.

Fuller, Jerry Bryan, Coleman E.P. Patterson, Kim Hester, and Donna Y. Stringer (1996), "A Quantitative Review of Research on Charismatic Leadership," *Psychological Reports* 78(1): 271–287.

Georgia Asian Times (2014), "Taiwan's Bicycle World," https://gasiantimes.com/misc-asia/taiwans-bicycle-world.

Griffith, James (2004), "Relation of Principal Transformational Leadership to School Staff Job Satisfaction, Staff Turnover, and School Performance," *Journal of Educational Administration* 42(3): 333–356.

Gros, Daniel, and Mattia Di Salvo (2017), *Revisiting Sanctions on Russia And Counter-Sanctions on the EU: The Economic Impact Three Years Later* (Brussels, Belgium: Centre for European Policy Studies).

Guo Z.F. and Cao L., (2012), "An Analysis of The Degree of Diversification and Firm Performance," *International Journal of Business & Finance Research* 6(2): 53–58.

Hater, J.J., & Bass, B.M. (1988), "Superiors' Evaluations and Subordinates' Perceptions of Transformational and Transactional Leadership," *Journal of Applied Psychology* 73(1): 695–702.

Holcomb, Tim R., R. Michael Holmes Jr., and Brian L. Connelly (2009), "Making the Most of What You Have: Managerial Ability as a Source of Resource Value Creation," *Strategic Management Journal* 30(): 457-485.

Hu, Mei-Chih, and Ching-Yan Wu (2015), "Giant Bicycle and King Liu," in Yu Fu-Lai Tony, and Ho-Don Yan (eds.), *Handbook of East Asian Entrepreneurship* (London: Routledge).

Huang, Joyce (2009), "Taiwan's Healthy Export," *Forbes*, https://www.forbes.com/global/2009/0608/bikes-giant-king-liu-taiwans-healthy-export.html#42d4fac27698.

Jacobsen, Christian Bøtcher, and Lotte Bøgh Andersen (2015), "Is Leadership in the Eye of the Beholder? A Study of Intended and Perceived Leadership Practices and Organizational Performance," *Public Administration Review* 75(6): 829–841.

Jing, Fenwick Feng, and Gayle C. Avery (2008), "Missing Links in Understanding the Relationship Between Leadership and Organizational Performance," *International Business & Economics Research Journal* 7(5): 67–78.

Johnson, Sara (2008), "Trek Bicycle Brand Analysis," *Issuu*, https://issuu.com/aboutsara/docs/trek_brand_analysis.

Kim, W.G.; Brymer, R. A. (2011), The Effects of Ethical Leadership on Manager Job Satisfaction, Commitment, Behavioral Outcomes, and Firm Performance," *International Journal of Hospitality Management* 30(4): 1020–1026.

Kinicki, Angelo, and Robert Kreitner (2006), *Organizational Behavior: Key Concepts, Skills and Best Practices*, 2nd Edition (New York: McGraw-Hill).

Kipa, Dmitry (2018), Санкциям вопреки: как российские компании находят деньги в Европе (Despite Sanctions: How Russian Companies Find Money in Europe), Forbes.ru.

Knies, Eva, Christian Jacobsen, and Lars Tummers (2016), "Leadership and Organizational Performance: State of the Art and Research Agenda," in Storey, John et al. (eds.), *The Routledge Companion to Leadership* (London: Routledge).

Kocel, Tamer (2011), *Business Management*, 13th Edition (Istanbul: Beta Publications).

Koh, William L., Richard Steers, and James R. Terborg (1995), "The Effects of Transformational Leadership on Teacher Attitudes and Student Performance in Singapore," *Journal of Organizational Behavior* 16(4): 319–333.

Lakina, Ekaterina (2017), Пармезан от патриота: как сделать бизнес на санкциях (Parmiggiano from a Patriot: How to Make a Business on the Sanctions), http://www.forbes.ru.

Latz, Phil (2015), "Giant's Remarkable Ride," *Bicycle Trade*, http://www.bicyclingtrade.com.au/interviews/global-leaders/giant-s-remarkable-ride.

Leitner, Karl-Heinz, and Stefan Güldenberg (2010), "Generic Strategies and Firm Performances in Smes: A Longitudinal Study of Austrian SMEs," *Small Business Economics* 35(2): 169–189.

Lowe, Kevin B., K. Galen Kroeck, and Nagaraj Sivasubramaniam (1996), "Effectiveness Correlates of Transformational and Transactional Leadership: A Meta-Analytic Review," *Leadership Quarterly* 7(3): 385–425.

Madanchian, Mitra, Norashikin Husseim, N., Fauziah Noordin, F., and Hamed Taherdoost, (2017), "Leadership Effectiveness Measurement and Its Effect on Organization Outcomes," The 10th International Conference Interdisciplinary in Engineering, 2016, Tirgu Mures, Romania.

Market Research Future (2018), "Electric Bicycles Market Research Report – Forecast to 2023," https://www.marketresearchfuture.com/reports/electric-bicycles-market-4186.

MarketScreener (2018), "Sberbank CIB and MTS Issue Bonds with Settlement in Roubles Using Smart Contracts Via NSD Blockchain Platform."

Meyer, Henry, Laurence Arnold, and Olga Tanas (2018), "All about the U.S. Sanctions Aimed at Putin's Russia," Bloomberg.com.

Miloloža, Ivan (2018), "Relation of Leadership and Business Performance: Balanced Scorecard Perspective," *Interdisciplinary Management Research* XI: 159–179.

Morck, Randall, Bernard Yeung, and Wayne Yu (2000), "The Information Content of Stock Markets: Why Do Emerging Markets Have Synchronous Stock Price Movements?" *Journal of Financial Economics* 58(1): 215–260.

Muehlheusser, Gerd, Sandra Schneemann, Dirk Sliwka, and Niklas Wallmeier (2016), "The Contribution of Managers to Organizational Success," *Journal of Sports Economics* 19(6): 786–819.

Northouse, Peter G. (2012), *Leadership: Theory and Practice* (Thousand Oaks, CA: SAGE Publications).

Noruzy, Ali, Vahid Majazi Dalfard, Behnaz Azhdari, Salmam Nazari-Shirkouhi, and Aliasghar Rezazadeh (2013), "Relations Between Transformational Leadership, Organizational Learning, Knowledge Management, Organizational Innovation, and Organizational Performance: An Empirical Investigation of Manufacturing Firms," *International Journal of Advanced Manufacturing Technology* 64(5–8): 1073–1085.

Obiwuru, Timothy C., Andy T. Okwu, Victoria O. Akpa, and Idown A. Nwankwere (2011), "Effects of Leadership Style on Organizational Performance: A Survey of Selected Small Scale Enterprises in Ikosi-Ketu Council Development Area of Lagos State, Nigeria," *Australian Journal of Business and Management Research* 1(7): 100–111.

Pandaya Anil M., Narendar V. Rao, (1998), "Diversification and Firm Performance: An Empirical Evaluation," *Journal of Financial and Strategic Decisions* 11(2): 67–81.

Peeters, Thomas, Steven Salaga, and Matthew Juravich (2015), "Matching and Winning? The Impact of Upper and Middle Managers on Team Performance," Tinbergen Institute Discussion Paper 15-115/VII.

Persistence Market Research (2018), "Global Market Study on Bicycle: Sports Bicycles to Pedal Up in Terms of Sales, Hybrid Bicycles to Lose Value Share," https://www.persistencemarketresearch.com/market-research/bicycle-market.asp.

Peterson, Mark F., Robert L. Phillips, and Catherine A. Duran (1989), "A Comparison of Japanese Performance-Maintenance Measures with U.S. Leadership Scales," *Psychologia: An International Journal of Psychology in the Orient* 32(1): 58–70.

Ramzy, Austin (2013), "A Maker of Bikes Now Makes a Point of Riding Them," *New York Times*.

Rapoza, Kenneth (2018), "How Russia's Largest Companies Have Weathered Sanctions," Forbes .com.

Rasulov, Vladimir (2017), "Неявные границы Как в Россию попадают санкционные продукты (Unclear Borders. How do Sanctioned Goods Enter Russia?)," http://www.kommersant.ru.

Reid, Carlton (2017), *Bike Boom: The Unexpected Resurgence of Cycling* (Washington, DC: Island Press).

Rigger, Shelley (2014), *Why Taiwan Matters: Small Island, Global Powerhouse* (Lanham, MD: Rowman & Littlefield Publishing Group).

Robbins, S.P.; Judge, T.A. (2009). *Organizaciono Ponašanje*, 12th Edition, Zagreb: Mate d.o.o.

Rosenzweig, Phil (2014), *The Halo Effect:… and the Eight Other Business Delusions That Deceive Managers* (New York: Free Press).

Santhanam, Radhika, and Edward Hartano (2003), "Issues in Linking Information Technology Capabilities to Firm Performance," *MIS Quartely* 27(1): 125–153.

Steyrer, Johannes, Michael Schiffinger and Reinhart Lang (2008), "Organizational Commitment—A Missing Link Between Leadership Behavior and Organizational Performance?" *Scandinavian Journal of Management* 24(4): 364–374.

Strukan, Edin, Milan P. NIkolić, and Senad Sefić (2017), "Impact of Transformational Leadership on Business Performance," *Tehnički vjesnik* 24(2): 435–444.

Technavio (2018), "Global Bicycle Market 2018–2022," https://www.technavio.com/report/gl obal-bicycle-market-analysis-share-2018?utm_source=usa1&utm_medium=bw:wk34&utm _campaign=businesswire.

The Economist (2019), "Managers in Football Matter Much Less than Most Fans Think." January 19th.

Ting-Fang, Cheng (2016), "The Legendary Founder of Taiwan's Giant Cycles into the Sunset," *Nikkei Asian Review*, https://asia.nikkei.com/Business/The-legendary-founder-of-Taiwan-s -Giant-cycles-into-the-sunset.

Trolanovski, Anton (2018), "Russia Keeps Getting Hit with Sanctions. Do They Make A Difference?" *The Washington Post*.

U.S. Department of State (2019), *Ukraine and Russia Sanctions*, available at https://www.state.go v/ukraine-and-russia-sanctions/#:~:text=Executive%20Order%2013660%20%2C%20signed %20on,assets%20of%20the%20Ukrainian%20people.

European Union of Football Associations (UEFA) (2018), "How Clubs' 2018/19 UEFA Champions League Revenue Will Be Shared," https://www.uefa.com/uefachampionsleague/news/newsid =2562033.html?iv=true.

Waldman, David A., Bernard M. Bass, and Francis J. Yammarino (1990), "Adding to Contingent-Reward Behavior. The Augmenting Effect of Charismatic Leadership," *Group & Organization Management* 15(4): 381–394.

Wales, William J., Vinit Parida, and Pankaj C. Patel (2013), "Too Much of a Good Thing? Absorptive Capacity, Firm Performance, and the Moderating Role of Entrepreneurial Orientation," *Strategic Management Journal* 34(5): 622–633.

Wasserman, Noam, Nitin Nohria, and Bharat N. Anand (2010), "When Does Leadership Matter? The Contingent Opportunities View of CEO Leadership," in Nohria, Nitin, and Rakesh Khurana (eds.), *Handbook of Leadership Theory and Practice* (Boston: Harvard Business School Press).

Wiengarten, Frank, Chris K.Y. Lo, and Jessie Y.K. Lam (2017), "How Does Sustainability Leadership Affect Firm Performance? The Choices Associated with Appointing a Chief Officer of Corporate Social Responsibility," *Journal of Business Ethics* 140(3): 477–493.

Wofford, Jerry. C., J. Lee Whittington, and Vicki L. Goodwin (2001), "Follower Motive Patterns as Situational Moderators for Transformational Leadership Effectiveness," *Journal of Managerial Issues* 13(2): 196–211.

Yammarino, Francis J., William D. Spangler, and Bernard B. Bass (1993), "Transformational Leadership and Performance: A Longitudinal Investigation," *Leadership Quarterly* 4(1): 81–102.

Yildiz, Sebahattin, Faruk Bastürk, and İlknur Taştan Boz (2014), "The Effect of Leadership and Innovativeness on Business Performance," The 10th International Strategic Management Conference.

Zehir, Cemal, Öznur Gülen Ertosun, Songül Zehir, and Büsra Müceldili (2014), "The Effects of Leadership Styles an Organizational Culture over Firm Performance: Multi-National Companies in Istanbul," Procedia – Social and Behavioral Sciences 150. .

Part 2
Understanding competitiveness

28. INTRODUCTION

What should the objective of a government be? More generally, what should the goals of the public sector be? Such questions are not usually addressed in electoral campaigns and political debates. We tend to simplify political objectives when we describe ideologies and say, for instance, that the political right is interested in economic growth while the left prefers fairness and income redistribution. Such simplification is useful, but wrong. The first reason is that economic growth and income redistribution are achieved irrespective of the political sign of a government. China's growth has been impressive in the last 10 years, amidst a significant deterioration in income disparities in the country—because China is a communist country.

The second reason is that nations are always in different stages of economic development and therefore the effectiveness of policies depends on the starting point. A marginal increase in disposable income in Qatar (one of the richest countries in the world on a per capita income) is probably easier to achieve than in India, which is both larger and poorer.

The third reason is that external factors have a higher impact. The biggest declines in gross domestic product (GDP) over the 20th century happened during and around economic and political crises[1]: the two world wars and the 1929–1933 Great Depression. In the 21st century, the biggest economic recession has been caused by a global pandemic. This means not only that attributing performance to a particular government is neither fair nor appropriate, but also that managing GDP per capita or reducing income disparities is not directly at the will and power of a particular government.

Let us take a look at the evidence. Which countries excel in delivering economic growth? Table 2.1 summarizes 50 years of economic growth since 1968, where growth is measured as real GDP per capita growth, and where GDP is adjusted by purchasing power and measured in constant 2010 US dollars. In the period 1968–2017, GDP per capita growth in the average country and year is 1.7 percent. Rather than reporting the fastest- and slowest-growing countries, Table 2.1 reports the percentage of years in the period when economic growth is positive. Burundi, Congo, Jamaica, Argentina, and Liberia are the countries where GDP per capita grows the least number of years (68, 66, 66, 64, and 59 percent). This is not surprising as their economies have been in a recession for long periods in the last half century. In contrast, in 3 countries among the 264 reported in the World Bank Development Indicators, growth has been positive every single year—Egypt, Israel, and Pakistan. In Colombia, GDP per capita has grown all but one year. It would be hard to defend that these countries are successful economies.[2]

Some countries grow more frequently than others, and some countries grow faster than others. Panel B of Table 2.1 puts China, Botswana, and Singapore as the champions of growth in the last 50 years. China's growth is, however, uneven, because its economy has only exploded in the last two decades. The reverse is true for South Korea and Oman. Panel C is interesting if we take into account that the data is measured after adjusting by purchasing power: Qatar can buy 177 times as many goods and services as the inhabitants of the Central African Republic. The world is massively unequal, with a

Table 2.1 GDP per Capita 1968–2017

Panel A		Panel B		Panel C	
Country Name	Number of Years with Positive Growth (%)	Country Name	GDP per Capita CAGR (%)	Country Name	GDP per Capita 2017 (Constant USD)
Egypt	100	China	3.79	Qatar	116,936
Israel	100	Botswana	3.54	Macau	104,862
Pakistan	100	Singapore	3.10	Luxembourg	94,278
Colombia	98	South Korea	3.08	Singapore	85,535
China	96	Oman	2.97	Brunei	71,809
United States	86	United States	1.22	United States	54,225
United Kingdom	86	United Kingdom	1.01	United Kingdom	39,753
Japan	86	Japan	1.22	Japan	39,002
Mexico	86	Mexico	1.50	Mexico	17,336
Brazil	84	Brazil	1.67	Brazil	14,103
Burundi	68	Jamaica	0.61	Niger	926
DR Congo	66	Georgia	0.60	DR Congo	808
Jamaica	66	DR Congo	0.50	Liberia	753
Argentina	64	Central African Rep.	0.40	Burundi	702
Liberia	59	Liberia	−0.12	Central African Rep.	661

Note: All figures in 2010 PPP USD.

few countries producing significantly more than the average, and with a bulk of middle-class world economies and a few very poor countries. The GDP per capita of the average country is USD 18,200, and the median is USD 12,600, which means that half the countries in the world have outputs below that figure.

Which countries are more equal? Of course, it is important to distinguish between the stated objectives of a particular government and its actual goals. In many instances in democratic regimes, politicians only strive to stay in power after the next election.

If success is measured as income fairness, Table 2.2 describes income disparities in several ways. Both the Gini coefficient and the income share held by the top 10% measure income accumulation by the top and display similar results: the most equal countries are in Europe, the least in Africa and Latin America. The World Bank's Human Capital Index (HCI) is designed to capture the amount of human capital a child born today could expect to attain by age 18.[3] The figures must be interpreted in percentages. For instance,

Table 2.2 Income Disparities in the World

Panel A		Panel B		Panel C	
	Income Share Held by Top 10% (%)	Economy Name	Human Capital Index (HCI) 2017	Country Name	GINI Coefficient 2017
Slovak Republic	21	Singapore	0.88	Ukraine	25.0
Slovenia	21	South Korea	0.85	Slovenia	25.4
Kosovo	22	Japan	0.84	Czech Republic	25.9
Ukraine	22	Hong Kong	0.82	Moldova	26.3
Czech Republic	22	Finland	0.81	Kosovo	26.5
United States	NA	United States	0.76	United States	41.5
United Kingdom	25	United Kingdom	0.78	United Kingdom	33.2
Mexico	NA	Mexico	0.61	Mexico	43.4
Brazil	NA	Brazil	0.56	Brazil	NA
Japan	NA	Japan	NA	Japan	NA
Panama	39	Liberia	0.32	Brazil	51.3
Colombia	40	Mali	0.32	Mozambique	54.0
Brazil	40	Niger	0.32	Zambia	57.1
Zambia	44	South Sudan	0.30	Namibia	59.1
Namibia	47	Chad	0.29	South Africa	63.0

in a country such as Liberia the HCI of 0.32 means that if current education and health conditions in Liberia persist, a child born today will be 32 percent as productive as he or she could have been if he or she enjoyed complete education and full health. African economies rank at the bottom, and Singapore, South Korea, and Japan achieve the highest scores. These are the combination of three factors: survival, education, and health, suggesting that in these countries, children born today are going to achieve the highest levels of productivity. However, the top five countries in the HCI are very small economies, so the question remains whether large countries (India, China, but also the United States) are doomed because their policies are not scalable and inequalities and unfairness are difficult to remove from the system. Surprisingly as well, countries that perform extremely well in other metrics (such as GDP per capita) are not at the top on the HCI ranking: Qatar (0.615), Luxembourg (0.692).

In any case, I would not be the first one to put a big question mark regarding the effectiveness of GDP in measuring social welfare. In his macroeconomic textbook, Harvard economist Greg Mankiw clearly[4] mentioned that GDP is an imperfect measure for economic activity and most problematic when comparing the standard of living across countries. The core reason behind his statement is simply because GDP contains pitfalls in various aspects. Historically, it is also very interesting that even the original creator of GDP, Simon Kuznets, has warned of the potential defects on the quantitative indicator by saying that:

> The valuable capacity of the human mind to simplify a complex situation in a compact characterization becomes dangerous when not controlled in terms of definitely stated criteria. With quantitative measurements especially, the definiteness of the result suggests, often misleadingly, precision and simplicity in the outlines of the object measured. Measurements of national income are subject to this type of illusion and resulting abuse, especially since they deal with matters that are the center of conflict of opposing social groups where the effectiveness of an argument is often contingent upon oversimplifications.[5]

For many reasons, measuring prosperity through GDP is flawed:

> GDP does not measure the quality of output, and therefore the quality of life. For a GDP missionary, an Italian violin and a Chinese *erhu* are both violins, but one sounds much better than the other.
>
> GDP and hidden economic activities, such as prostitution and house care, are not included in a country's output.
>
> GDP harms the environment. A manufacturing plant that pollutes the atmosphere contributes positively to economic growth.
>
> GDP ignores fairness and redistribution because it looks at the total (average) wealth of an economy, not how it is distributed.
>
> GDP per capita level cannot be compared across economies because even after adjusting for different price levels, living in Finland is different from living in Ghana, and it might be possible to achieve a higher quality of life in Ghana with the same salary.

To summarize—based on traditional measures, the concept of country success is polysemic. When I ask in my executive classes which countries are most successful in the last years, participants usually mention China, Switzerland, Singapore, the United States, and the United Arab Emirates (UAE). These countries are not only rich, but also slow-growing, disparate in terms of income distribution, and not necessarily providing relatively better development opportunities to children than in other small economies.

29. WHAT IS COMPETITIVENESS?

The term "competitiveness" is a familiar one in our daily lives, and one that tends to define human society. When we hear the word, it is intrinsically associated with competition, or the ability of someone to compete with his or her peers. When a company beats rivals, captures market share, or gains comparative advantage, we consider it to be "competitive."[6] The way that the term was later extended to also assess the success of a country is difficult to track, but I suspect that it all started in 1990 with the publication of Michael Porter's *The Competitive Advantage of Nations*.[7] In his book, Porter borrows the term from the corporate world to stress that the success or failure of nations is relative, and therefore countries "compete" with one another in order to be more prosperous.

Note that the analogy does not imply that when Switzerland successfully competes with Austria, Switzerland is better off and Austria is worse off; only that Switzerland is more successful than Austria. This is important because when I meet government officials, they often misunderstand the concept, and consider themselves to be uncompetitive because their neighbor is a powerful economy. The danger of such confusion is to consider that, in order to be successful, a nation needs to beat others (instead of cooperating with them through trade), and particularly to be involved in more successful export. Spain had a Minister of the Economy and Competitiveness for quite a long time, yet official publications often conveyed the wrong impression on how to indeed become competitive: "The concept of competitiveness for an economy is associated with achieving larger advantages from international trade by improving terms of trade."[8] Along the same lines from the same publication: "National competitiveness is related to the ability of a country to export."[9]

Porter also introduced the main ingredient in the competitiveness equation: productivity. The term "productivity" here is strongly related to production activity, which is aligned with the ability of a particular country to produce goods and services. In subsequent research reports,[10] Porter suggested that it is mostly appropriate for competitiveness to be measured by productivity, and that productivity is the factor that most readily determines economic prosperity. Other international institutions followed suit: the Competitiveness Advisory Group (1995) defines competitiveness as "the elements of productivity, efficiency, and profitability." In a similar tone, the World Economic Forum (WEF) also associates national competitiveness with productivity, and defines competitiveness as "the set of institutions, policies, and factors that determine the level of productivity of an economy, which in turn sets the standard of prosperity that the economy can achieve."[11]

So what can we understand as "productivity"? Simply put, at the national level, productivity is the power and ability of a country to produce goods and services. However, although productivity is strongly related to the national production ability, it is not necessarily equivalent to economic growth.

A nation's standard of living depends on the capacity of its companies to achieve high levels of productivity—and to increase productivity over time. Sustained productivity growth requires that an economy continually upgrade itself. A nation's companies must relentlessly improve productivity in existing industries by raising product quality, adding desirable features, improving product technology, or boosting production efficiency.[12]

Comparative advantage is one requirement needed to ensure that production activity can turn into competitiveness. The idea raised here is that countries can be more competitive if they produce and trade specific goods or services which they are naturally well-placed to do better than others. In other words, countries which have endowments of specific resources will be able to produce goods and services more efficiently than ones that are not fortunate to possess them. For example, countries blessed with abundant gold deposits can be more competitive in the production of gold-related products, or countries with significant oil reserves are obviously better placed to produce oil-related goods or services. It should also be noted that endowed capital can help the country to minimize production costs and sell products at lower prices. By achieving this specialization, nations can become more competitive as a result.

It is important to understand that a nation's success is also primarily dependent on the objectives and direction of government (more about this later). Although comparative advantage is essential, it is not sufficient to achieve national competitiveness in the long run. In 1994, Nobel laureate Paul Krugman wrote an article with the suggestive title "Competitiveness: A Dangerous Obsession," in which he contended that successful competitiveness requires a continuous dynamic process of comparative advantage over a period of time, rather than only being comparatively advantaged on the factor of endowments.[13] The *obsession* that Krugman writes about derives, in my opinion, from +confusing competitiveness with competition. For Krugman, the fact that countries focus on competing in international markets is not only wrong but also dangerous, because it derails governments from their true objective of ensuring that people are materially better off.

Productivity is not competitiveness

Indeed, competitiveness does not neglect citizens. A country cannot be competitive if it is unable to create prosperity for its people. One of the major indicators for welfare is that citizens can expect to enjoy a healthy level of income, and one that progresses over time. As suggested by the Organization for Economic Co-operation and Development (OECD), competitiveness is

> the degree to which a nation can, under free trade and market conditions, produce goods and services which meet the test of international markets, while simultaneously maintaining and expanding the real income for its people over the long term. Such understanding brings to the core a proposition that competitiveness is embedded in the type of economic system, in this case, a free market economy.[14]

The IMD World Competitiveness Center is a pioneering organization in the study and measurement of competitiveness. We define it as "the ability of a country to facilitate an environment in which enterprises can generate sustainable value," in order to stress the difference between the public and private sectors. The public sector sets the conditions for the economy, while the private sector creates jobs. This does not contradict the idea that productivity drives competitiveness; rather, it complements this notion by adding the requirement that for a country to be competitive, it must generate prosperity for its citizens.

Productivity is therefore the result of an optimal combination of inputs: natural resources, geographical position, political choices, the enforcement of good regulation, and satisfactory health and education systems (see Figure 2.1).

However, productivity should not be considered the end of the competitiveness equation. Productivity is particularly related to prosperity and value created by enterprises, because productivity is the main determiner of salaries. People earn their productivity, and that is why football players (who are effectively marketing machines to sell T-shirts) earn so much, and lumberjacks so little. In the long run, labor wages are equal to labor productivity. Wages, in turn, determine tax revenues for a government, its ability to invest in roads, hospitals, and schools, and thereby the correlation between skills and the needs of the labor market. When an economy is productive, it attracts foreign investment, it creates jobs, it generates output, and therefore economic growth is also created. With economic growth,

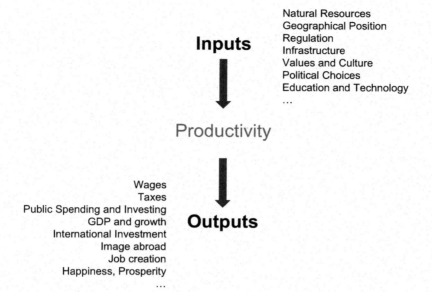

Figure 2.1 The Competitiveness Flow

the image of the country abroad improves, and ultimately talent is attracted to the country, creating a virtuous circle in which infrastructure, healthcare, and the country's education system can again improve, thus driving productivity once more.

Natural resources are not necessarily conditional to productivity. Switzerland is competitive despite its lack of natural resources and its adverse geographical position (landlocked, without access to the sea, mountainous orography) because it has developed a good regulatory environment, and because its education system is excellent, among other reasons. Institutions can sometimes replace the natural endowments of a country, but not the reverse. Indeed, institutional quality is a mandatory requirement for prosperity. Struggling countries such as Argentina, Venezuela, the Philippines, and South Africa prove that a privileged geographical position and an ample supply of natural resources do not guarantee competitiveness.

However, natural conditions and good institutions also require that a minimum quality of life, in terms of health and education standards, be preserved. The genocidal colonization and posterior abandonment of India by the British Empire may be a much maligned act historically, but the empire at least left impressive economic and social institutions behind, along with an efficient judiciary that had copied that of the metropolis, rule of law (more to come later in Part 3). The history of India is well known. A sequence of postcolonial governments, poor choices in economic policy, and an unfavorable international environment prevented the development of a satisfactory education system and a suitable infrastructure in the country, with largely disastrous consequences. Indeed, India is only recovering from these tribulations in the modern era.

The virtuous circle of competitiveness can break at any point throughout the history of a nation. Obviously, political choices (or impositions) are not exogenous by their very nature, and the competitive fate of a country is massively shaped by its political leaders.

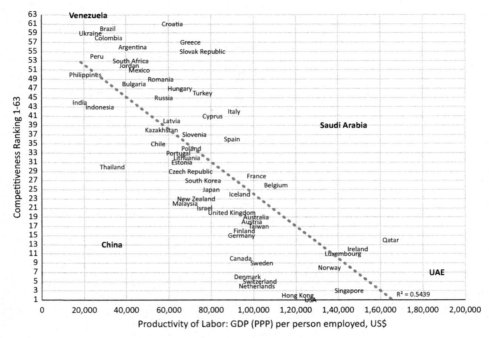

Figure 2.2 Competitiveness and Productivity

Source: IMD World Competitiveness Center.

Competitiveness as inclusive prosperity

Therefore, countries become competitive by optimizing their resources and capabilities in order to sustain a productive economy. But it cannot stop there. For productivity must translate into inclusive prosperity; that is, a fair system that distributes welfare and quality of life among citizens. In that regard, productivity is a necessary, but not a sufficient, condition for competitiveness.

To see that, look at Figure 2.2. The horizontal axis displays labor productivity in US dollars in 2017 for the 63 economies included in the IMD World Competitiveness Rankings. The next chapters will pay detailed attention to this variable, but for now it is sufficient to note that the United Arab Emirates and Qatar are the two most productive economies in the world (with an output per capita of USD 186,900 and USD 165,372, respectively), while India, the Philippines, and Venezuela are the countries with the lowest productivity (USD 18,528, USD 21,300, and USD 22,693, respectively). Productivity numbers are not adjusted by cost of living, so naturally the figures are not necessarily comparable in terms of purchasing power.

The vertical axis in Figure 2.2 represents the 2018 competitiveness ranking, with the United States #1 and Venezuela #63. The dotted line plots a fitted straight line that suggests a natural statistical relationship between competitiveness and productivity. The regression line is useful because countries on the north of the line are those for which their competitiveness ranking is lower than what their productivity level should predict. These countries are "wasting productivity"; in other words, they are not translating productivity gains into prosperity and competitiveness. Countries in this category are Italy, Argentina, and Qatar, for example.

รายงาน : ไทยตั้งเป้าติดอันดับ 20 ขีดความสามารถแข่งขันในโลก

Image 2.1 Thailand and Competitiveness. Minister Pootrakool announces on March 8, 2018, that a pillar of the new economic strategy of Thailand is to place Thailand in the top 20 countries in the IMD World Competitiveness Ranking.

Countries whose combination of productivity–competitiveness lies below the dotted line are the ones that achieve significantly higher competitiveness levels given their productivity levels. That is, countries such as the Netherlands, Indonesia, and China are more competitive in what their productivity should predict. Compare, for instance, the cases of the Netherlands and France. Both countries have very similar productivity (USD 101,950 and USD 102,188 per worker, respectively); however, the Netherlands is ranked #4 and France #28.

Why are productive countries not necessarily competitive?

As I stated earlier, productivity is important because it determines salary levels; in principle, this is true. Most times, however, *average* productivity is only linked to *average* salaries, indicating that there may be massive inequalities in income distribution. This is the case for example in the UAE and Saudi Arabia—productivity of labor is driven by the abundance of oil, but only a few have benefited from it.

Another reason is that public policies fail to invest the returns from the productive economy into the long-term pillars of prosperity, such as education, healthcare, and physical infrastructure. This may happen because the structure of the public sector does not allow for an efficient allocation of resources, either because of corruption or excessive bureaucracy. Figure 2.2 highlights the case of Venezuela in the northwest part of the graph, a country rich in natural resources but where the public sector has decimated the nation's wealth. Similar argument can be made about Greece, Hungary, Turkey, and Argentina, where state bureaucracy hinders the ability of the private sector to generate jobs and opportunities.

Sometimes, regulation allows the extraction of rents by a minority at the expense of the majority. The extracting minority may not necessarily be from the government. For example, corporate governance rules may give an advantage to capital income over labor income, thereby boosting income inequality. In some other cases, the lack of inclusive institutions, or the significant power gained by extracting elites (i.e., the army), prevents that productivity from translating into prosperity.

Finally, external conditions also matter. Ukraine's ability to develop a competitive economy is obviously made difficult by a hostile neighbor. In that regard, it is impressive how Israel, facing similar conditions, has fared.

There are also countries that manage to excel in competitiveness despite not having stellar productivity levels. The case of Switzerland, Denmark, Canada, and Sweden is noteworthy in Figure 2.4. These countries are less productive than Qatar and Luxembourg, to cite two very efficient economies. Yet, they are more competitive. Fundamentally, public policy in these countries guarantees people's prosperity and fair distribution of wealth (at least in relation to the average country). This is done through efficient investments in education and healthcare, the provision of a social safety net, efficient public sectors and investments in the long term with a clear vision to preserve the prosperity of future generations.

Competitiveness success: the Netherlands

As my colleague Stéphane Garelli interestingly points out in the foreword of the IMD World Competitiveness Yearbook in its 30th edition, competitiveness analysis should be interpreted as a snapshot at a moment in time rather than a forecasting exercise. It remains, however, a good assessment of a country's socioeconomic foundations upon which a nation can build long-term value creation, success, and prosperity for its citizens. Paying attention to the so-called "good students" in the field can therefore be helpful, as it indicates the kind of efforts countries can make to become more competitive and ultimately better off. In 2018, a country which emerges as particularly competent in providing a solid framework conducive to competitive advantages is the Netherlands!

Placing 4th out of 63 countries studied in the overall ranking, the Netherlands stands out for its incredible consistency in achieving top 10 positions in all four competitiveness factors: economic performance (6th), government efficiency (8th), business efficiency (6th), and infrastructure (9th). This high-performance stability across all four pillars of competitiveness is remarkable and the subsequent paragraphs will explain how it plays an important role in explaining why Dutch prospects for future growth are looking bright should the country continue following similar trends in the coming years. In essence, the Netherlands will be used as a case study to portray how competitiveness is measured by the IMD's World Competitiveness Center and provide some explanations as to its applicability, usefulness, and impact in a real-world business environment.

First, let's take a look at some of the indicators which comprise the economic performance pillar and break down their contribution to Dutch competitiveness. Although some weaknesses such as high gasoline or office rental prices are apparent, the Netherlands fairs extremely well in numerous areas—predominantly in the fields of international trade and investment. Indeed, the country can be considered a paradigm for economic diversification, and this has proven attractive to foreign investors as illustrated by the country's direct investment flows into the country as well as abroad. Coupled with a considerable export sector of goods and commercial services, these large investment inflows have allowed the Dutch economy to benefit from a healthy current account balance, ranking 7th in the IMD's competitiveness ranking for that indicator. Despite a high cost of living which is often associated with a booming economy through inflationary pressure, the Dutch have successfully created the conditions necessary to benefit from diversified export-led growth. As such, the Netherlands has intelligently worked toward becoming an attractive investment location by offering a wide range of quality goods and services.

Such dispositions are usually dependent on a government's ability to incorporate strong and effective legislations which respect the rule of law and reassure investors. In this regard, the Netherlands has achieved a very high standard of government efficiency, managing to move up 10 spots over the last four years by steadily improving the effectiveness of its institutional and societal frameworks. In fact, the Dutch are in the top 3 for seven of the IMD's competitiveness indicators for government efficiency! Among the country's main strengths are the spread of its interest rates, effective competition legislation, the perceived absence of threat from state ownership of enterprises (survey data), and the openness of public sector contracts to foreign investors. Justice, respect for the rule of law, and pension funding also distinguish themselves as particularly prominent. However, improvements could be achieved in the tax policy sub-factor where the country's comparatively poor performance should raise some eyebrows. Total collected tax revenues amount to nearly 40 percent of national GDP, and the extremely high effective personal income tax rate of 27.1 percent places the country in the tail-end of the ranking. With high consumption and corporate tax rates as well as consequential employee and employer security contribution rates, the Netherlands should be careful not to disincentivize its workforce further as it could risk losing potential talent to countries that offer more attractive rates.

However, concerns over non-competitive taxation policies are counteracted by the Netherlands' impressive business efficiency, which offers ideal conditions for companies and individuals to continue conducting corporate activity in the country. Interestingly, most of the indicators scoring highly under the business efficiency pillar for the Netherlands come from survey data, indicating that Dutch business executives are very satisfied with the quality and readiness of the national business infrastructure. As a whole, senior executives have expressed great levels of satisfaction with the local availability of venture capital as well as the quality, productivity, and international experience of the workforce. Additionally, small- and medium-sized enterprises are deemed to be well equipped for meeting the demanding requirements of international markets. Combined, these characteristics are extremely important as they act as major attractiveness factors for both local and foreign investors. Through the strong interdependence of the competitiveness pillars, it comes as no surprise that the country's efficient business infrastructure is therefore tied to large levels of foreign direct investment and ultimately a strong economic performance.

In the Dutch case, the three pillars mentioned above are further supported by some of the world's best physical, technological, and scientific infrastructure, which contributes greatly to the resilience of the country's economy. The education system, for instance, increasingly meets the changing needs of society and prepares young adults for their professional careers. Furthermore, basic infrastructure such as road and rail networks is of high quality, and survey respondents are convinced that the maintenance and development of such systems are adequately planned and financed. This political drive to maintaining a high standard of infrastructure may be explained by the country's demographic shift and the implicit need of continuing to attract young talent and foreign workers. Indeed, the Netherlands is currently fighting against the negative impacts of the population's slow growth (just 0.65 percent per annum) and a dependency ratio that is among the highest in the IMD's sample of countries (0.53 dependents per individual of economically active age). Investing in infrastructure is therefore one of the most effective ways to achieve this aim as it offers foreign workers and domestic talent the prospect of a dynamic and stimulating living and working environment as well as a high quality of life.

Although the costs of investing in health, education, and environmental infrastructure may appear very expensive in the short term, it produces long-run outcomes which are extremely desirable for the economy, such as a physically and mentally healthy population and a more agile and responsive workforce.

A country's ability to innovate and foster creative solutions to complex societal problems also plays a role in determining how competitive it is. Perhaps one of the most noteworthy examples of the Netherland's innovative thinking and future-driven development remains its fascinating capital city. Beyond the world-renowned canals and iconic red brick buildings which characterize it, Amsterdam also lives off a strong history of innovation. Located at the mouth of the Amstel River, the city has long been a driver of creative solutions against problems as diverse as flooding and erosion. Recently awarded the title of European Capital of Innovation in 2017 in recognition of its innovative potential, Amsterdam was one of the first cities globally to implement a smart-city strategy, back in 2009. The Dutch capital differentiates itself from other cities active in the field through the governance model it employs to define its smart strategy. After an initial phase in which the municipality played a central role in the implementation of projects, it has now moved toward a decentralized, learning-by-doing, bottom-up approach which incorporates numerous other stakeholders. Citizens, private companies, non-governmental organizations (NGOs), and other relevant actors now take an integral part in the process and play a crucial role in determining the design and implementation of smart initiatives, while the municipality has shifted its efforts to being a mere smart vision facilitator.

This approach has heightened the identification of citizens' priorities and strongly supports the active engagement of all parties to promote a more sustainable and equitable future for the city. Relating back to competitiveness, this is a major attribute for the Netherlands as promoting innovation and technological progress in this way allows for greater participation of both public and private actors. Collective solutions which address the wants and needs of the population and satisfy the economic conditions necessary for private entrepreneurs to make a profit ultimately lead to a win-win situation that elevates the national prosperity of all, hence making the country more competitive.

Fundamentally, the strong interdependence among the pillars of competitiveness helps to explain a large part of the Dutch success story. Achieving top positions in each, the country's impressive stability acts as a sort of multiplier effect which generates positive spillovers across the whole economy. This stability is much appreciated by investors, who feel confident about capitalizing on the versatility and adaptability of Dutch firms that are often leaders in their trades, ranging from the banking sector (ING group), to the petrol (Shell) and petrochemical (Akzo Nobel) industries, as well as various providers of consumer goods and services such as Unilever and KPMG. If the Netherlands continues to provide an environment as consistently stable as the one it presents today, there is little doubt that the future's bright!

When a country is not competitive: the case of North Korea

The other side of the coin is the Democratic People's Republic of Korea (DPRK). I had the chance to visit the country in 2016. Having spent the last 10 years in Switzerland, I have enjoyed the experience of living in a competitive, modern, innovative country with a superb quality of life. Even in the poorest countries in the world, one sees a bright future, although it is sure to be found at the end of a very dark, long tunnel of poverty and lack of institutions. Without a doubt, I have seen the ugliest side of world competitiveness in a country with only a sliver of hope.

The DPKR enjoys a privileged geographical position: it has access to trading routes through its eastern (Sea of Japan) and western coastlines (Yellow Sea). It shares borders with two of the world superpowers: China and Russia. Indeed, through its Russian border it can access Vladivostok, a major port city and only 684 kilometers from Pyongyang. (Of course, it is limited to the South with South Korea, a country that is 80 percent smaller but with double the population.) North Korea is rich in mineral reserves, in particular, coal, iron ore, limestone, magnesite, graphite, copper, zinc, lead, and precious metals.[15] Despite being a mountainous country, 19.5 percent of its territory is arable land and 46 percent forest.

However, the DPKR is first and foremost a failed economy. Remarkably, one of the very few low-income countries which is not in Africa, it is still recovering from a famine in the 1990s, following the collapse of the Soviet Union, that killed approximately two million people. Touristic brochures and the media will say otherwise. But even on my trip, meticulously controlled by the Korea International Travel Company, during which I could only see what they wanted me to see, there were glaring examples of depravity. Agriculture laborers still use tools and systems from before the Industrial Revolution: no mechanization, all tasks performed by hand, lack of long-term planning and product diversification, and certainly low productivity. The DPRK is a deserted landscape with no trees or vegetation and a primary sector which seems far from being self-sufficient. I had the opportunity to visit a cooperative farm in Chonsamri, which operates under the same premises as those in Mao Zedong's disastrous Great Leap Forward in China: the government imposes a production quota (usually of basic products such as rice and cabbage), and the cooperative farmers keep the surplus. Since the government controls both the quota and the price paid, the prosperity of the cooperative members is completely in the hands of the government.

Industrial equipment is obsolete: during a visit to a water bottling plant in Kangso, I could see that the machinery had been manufactured in Italy in 2002, even though the plant was inaugurated in 2012. In the Kaesong Koryo Museum, I was presented with a display of "North Korean" technology which included mining equipment by Caterpillar and robots with the Siemens logo. Buses and planes are Russian; cars are Chinese and Japanese, in addition to the Mercedes and Audis driven by party officials (which can be easily identified by the 02 and 216 plate numbers); trains are German, telephones are Chinese, coffee is Swiss. I visited a training center to experience the North Korean technological revolution, and students were working with Dell computers whose branding was carefully covered with a North Korean logo. However, all these items were ridiculously old and close to their breaking point, so one has the impression of being in an eastern European city in the 1950s.

When governments care about prosperity, the first need to satisfy is the physical infrastructure. Excluding the residential area of Pyongyang, the rest of the country is in perilous ruins. It was a nightmare to drive the 180 kilometers that separate Pyongyang from Panmunjom and the demilitarized zone (DMZ). This contrasted significantly with my drive from Seoul to the DMZ in 2004 via an impeccably smooth highway. There has been no infrastructural development in the last 20 years ever since Soviet money stopped flowing into the country. My guide explained very proudly how the road on which we were driving on our way to Mount Myohyang had been built by students who volunteered during the "Arduous March" of the 1990s. While I had reasons to believe that the students

Image 2.2 a and b: Bottling Plant in Kangso. (Namp'o Special City, South P'yŏngan Province)

had not volunteered in the strictest sense of the word, it was clear that the construction had been undertaken by amateurs who had little or no experience in constructing roads.

People suffer. I was not allowed to see it, and I was never told so. However, the signs of malnutrition, low quality of life, as well as a lack of culture, recreation, and leisure are evident. I attended a concert by the North Korea National Orchestra and saw the magnificent National Theater. However, instruments were clearly old, untuned, and low quality, overshadowing the players' skill. Supermarkets (if the dark and standardized establishments where the locals buy food can be called that) offer only the basics: rice, tomatoes, onions, potatoes, bread, tea, and coffee. In the countryside, most of the houses had no electricity or running water, so I had to shower with icy water in my "luxurious" hotel in Chongchun. In most of the public buildings (museums, exhibition centers, government departments), however luxurious they appeared from the outside, they proved to be decrepit inside, with no running water or heating. I endured a few power cuts during my stay, which are a daily occurrence for the people of North Korea.

What is the root of such a colossal failure? Certainly, the political system. The country is one of the, if not the, most grim dictatorships in the world. The population of 24 million lives under the complete control of the Workers' Party, the centralized government and its president, Kim Jong Un.

After spending time in the country, it is clear that the dictatorship's reputation as a fundamentalist, communist, kleptomaniac, nepotistic, and megalomaniac is well-deserved. Private initiative does not exist and the party dictates which school you will attend, whether you will grow up with your parents or not, where you will work and live, and whether you can move from one place to another. Police are everywhere and the army can be seen performing any number of tasks outside of their usual roles, including construction, street cleaning, traffic control, and farming. Prices are fixed across the country, and of course there are no banks, internet, social networks, trade unions, proper political parties, or places of worship. The Juche idea (Kim Il-sung's philosophy based on the proposition that men control and decide everything, so people are fully responsible for their destiny) directs every single policy and decision. The regime has instituted fear and irrationality, and people are forced to do the most insensible things: in anticipation of the 7th Congress of the Workers' Party, the government enforced a 70-day campaign of increased productivity and extra working hours for all North Koreans. This means that bureaucrats have to stay a few hours longer every day, that industries have to multiply output, and that people in the countryside need to show, by working for the community, commitment to their leader and the country. As a result, I saw hundreds of people lining up along the roads fixing patches, picking weeds, planting trees in the middle of nowhere, or simply sweeping the road, all of these activities being undertaken with their bare hands and rudimentary tools.

After three generations of iron-fisted control, the North Korean people have grown massively ignorant and indoctrinated. Kim Il-sung (the "Great Leader") is adored as a god; his son and successor Kim Jong-il (the "General") is considered a visionary and a genius. The examples of irrational devotion to their leaders were sometimes so absurd that they made me crack up with laughter: during my visit to the Songnam Caverns, the guide started by saying that her explanations should be listened to very attentively because the General said so during his visit 30 years earlier. Pictures and statues of both the Leader and the General are everywhere, always smiling—however, they are the only ones who smile in the DPRK.

There is not a large display of Kim Jong Un's "visionary" ideas yet, but of course he has only been in power for a short time and there is still plenty of time for him to become a "legendary" figure. So far, his appearances on local TV are usually associated with the country's nuclear weapons arsenal and his ability to "wipe out" both the Blue House (South Korea's government headquarters) and the White House. He is referred to as "the Marshall," due to his "Songun" policy, which prioritizes the military over anything else.

It has been frustrating to see that North Koreans know much less about North Korea than we as outsiders know. Neither my guide nor any of the locals I talked to knew that Kim Jong Un had attended a Swiss boarding school, that his father was born in the Soviet Union (interestingly, one of the touristic attractions in the northern part of the country is Kim Jong-il's mythical birthplace), or that he has a five-year-old son. It goes without saying that they also had no idea what either Google or a "selfie" is. North Koreans think that the DPRK won the Korean War in 1953 (they call it the "Fatherland Liberation"

War). They have evolved believing that the regime is the result of Kim Il-sung's divine intervention and not affiliated in any way with the USSR, which is not mentioned in any history books. The United States is their eternal imperialistic enemy. North Koreans pride themselves on inflicting violence, suffering, and humiliation on Americans, which was on display in the Fatherland Liberation War Museum with 20 depictions of dead American soldiers. North Koreans ignore the mysterious circumstances surrounding the deaths of Kim Jong Un's uncle Jang Song-thaek and Kim Jong-il's first mistress, Song Hye-rim. The willingness of the party to rewrite history explains why the country is air-tight to foreigners, and why we are seen as a dangerous threat to the country's cult-like mindset. My movement was strictly limited. I had a guide everywhere I went including during my jogging sessions in Pyongyang, when my annoyed escort was doing his best to keep up in his official uniform. I think that only with the distance of time will I be able to make sense of the irrational fear, the nonsense, the lack of freedom that I experienced (although at a level that probably pales in comparison to what North Koreans go through), and the locals' blind belief that their country is paradise.

The problem with political failures is that they are sometimes very difficult to resolve. My impression is that the current regime is going to last for a long time, even in the absence of its current, tyrannical dictator. The North Korean population is not only prepared to go to war now, but they are also willing and prepared to suffer continued hardship and starvation. As my guide said, "We are not afraid of war; if provoked, we will go to war." The consequences of the famine in the 1990s have been corruption and a certain tolerance toward black markets by authorities, but indeed the lesson that North Koreans have learned is that they can survive (most of them) if the situation were to repeat itself. Besides, they are absolutely behind their political leaders, whose propaganda is extremely effective. Changing the mindset of the population won't happen from one day to the next, especially using outside force.

Therefore, the current embargo is insufficient and economic sanctions will only make people suffer while not weakening the political system. Perhaps closing the borders to stop foreign products and equipment, especially oil, from entering would make the average North Korean more inclined to revolt against their leaders, but that would be impossible, not to mention cruel and inhumane.[16]

Does it matter? Competitiveness and stock markets

It is when I joined the IMD 14 years ago that I heard for the first time the acronym "BRICS." These countries—Brazil, Russia, India, China, South Africa—are the future of the world economy, I was told, and any company that wants to succeed in the next decades needs to operate in these countries. They have large economies and domestic markets, growing populations, natural resources, and uncovered potential. The term is attributed to then Goldman Sachs' Chief Economist Jim O'Neill, who would later become chairman of Goldman Sachs' asset management division.

As O'Neill would comment later, "I got two out of four countries right" (South Africa would be added to the BRIC countries later),[17] in reference to China and India, the two countries that, in his opinion, delivered to expectations. Alas, Table 2.3 shows that, in terms of overall competitiveness, China has definitely improved, but India has not. The privilege of being the most improved BRICS nation goes to Russia; despite being among the 20 least competitive countries in the IMD rankings, it improved four positions between 2011 and 2018.

Table 2.3 BRICS Position in the IMD World Competitiveness Rankings

	2011	2012	2013	2014	2015	2016	2017	2018	2019	Performance 2011–2019
Brazil	44	46	51	54	56	57	61	60	59	Down 15 positions
China Mainland	19	23	21	23	22	25	18	13	14	Up 5 positions
India	32	35	40	44	44	41	45	44	43	Down 11 positions
Russia	49	48	42	38	45	44	46	45	45	Up 4 positions
South Africa	52	50	53	52	53	52	53	53	56	Down 4 position

© IMD WORLD COMPETITIVENESS ONLINE 1995–2019.

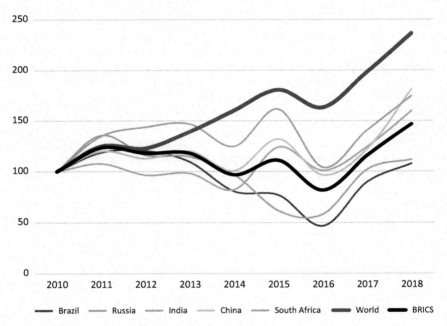

Figure 2.3 The Performance of BRICS in Stock Markets

Source: Datastream.

In reality, even the Goldman Sachs' chief economist got it wrong. If what he wanted to predict was the "countries of the future" as of 2011, Figure 2.3 shows that USD 100 invested in an equally weighted portfolio (a portfolio with 20 percent of the money invested in each of the five countries) would have generated USD 146 by the end of 2018, or equivalently 4.9 percent per year. By contrast, the world portfolio has generated an average return of 11.35 percent. Not even the best-performing countries (China, South Africa, and India) did better than the world portfolio, despite what we may have suspected, given that China has been considered the most successful economy of the last decades.

If we claim that competitiveness is the right tool to measure the success of a country, then competitiveness should be correlated with stock market returns, at least as long as stock returns track the performance of the overall economy. The problem with stock markets is that returns are primarily commensurate with risk; therefore riskier markets (countries) should also yield higher stock returns. Let us try to assess both, using the 2000 IMD World Competitiveness Rankings. I have classified countries into three groups: most competitive (ranking 1–16), average (ranking 17–33), and least competitive (ranking 34–47).[18] For each country, and using the Datastream country index (which tracks the stock price performance of the largest publicly traded companies in the country), I have computed annual returns and volatilities, where the volatility is measured as the annual volatility of monthly stock returns of the country index.

Can we predict stock market returns and risk (volatility) using competitiveness rankings? The answer is in Figure 2.4. Countries are classified on the horizontal scale by their competitive ranking. The vertical scales measure, respectively, annual returns and annual volatilities for the groups of countries. Surprisingly, the more competitive a country is ranked, the lower the stock market returns. For the most competitive economies in 2000, annual market returns were 5.4 percent on average over the period 2001–2018; for the least competitive, this figure is 12.3 percent. So what is going on?! Obviously, less competitive economies are also riskier. While the most competitive economies display an annual volatility of 1.6 percent (meaning that returns are confidently within a band of 3.8–7 percent, that is 5.4 ±1.6 percent), volatility is 1.9 percent (with returns that vary between 10.4 and 13.2 percent). Volatility differences are not dramatic at the index level, but they are much greater at the individual stock level.

Overall, the best risk-return trade-off is provided by the countries in the middle, those that author Parag Khanna has called *The Second World*.[19] Intuitively, investing in competitive economies is a safe bet: they are *"value"* economies ready to generate returns, but because the market already incorporates that information, they are highly priced and also low risk. Indeed, less competitive economies are *"growth"* economies with

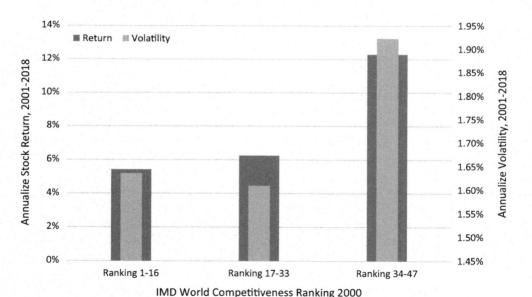

Figure 2.4 Competitiveness and Stock Returns

Source: Datastream and IMD World Competitiveness Center.

development potential, but also with high risk. Surprisingly, the BRICS countries are neither of these. Over the period, they have displayed low(er) returns with high volatilities, possibly because they were declared so publicly as the "successful countries of the future."

Summary

In summary—productivity is the result of endowments, good institutions, and reliable infrastructure. But despite the fact that productivity is the main anchor of competitiveness, its presence within a particular country is not a guarantee of success. Sometimes, productive economies fail to generate prosperity because of government malfunctioning. In democracies, very often the political cycle is an obstacle for long-term policies—an issue that we will discuss extensively in the next chapter—because politicians favor short-term and easily acceptable reforms that guarantee re-election, at the expense of necessary and painful reforms that only pay off in the long term. In dictatorships, the North Korea example above demonstrates that people depend to a great extent on luck when it comes to being ruled by the right dictator. In both democracies and dictatorships, corruption, bureaucracy, suboptimal decentralization, and the excessive influence of exclusive institutions (like the military) in politics result in economies that are not competitive.

Fiscal rules need to prioritize people's quality of life and job creation. Sometimes, tax rules are implemented in order to attract capital and investment, but they subsequently give advantage to a few. In other cases, the economic structure of the country is such that, despite being productive, tax revenues have to be diverted to government spending that is not necessarily value-creating. An example of the former is the UAE, not only with no income taxes and yet an amazing ability to attract foreign business, but also with non-existing public education and healthcare systems. An example of the latter is Japan, where public finances are held captive thanks to a demographic structure dominated by an aging population that needs to be supported by the government pension system.

In order for productivity improvements to result in more competitiveness, it is also paramount that salaries guarantee a decent standard of living for workers. As we will discuss in the next chapter, in some industrialized countries there is an increasing wedge between productivity and salaries, with a detrimental impact on prosperity, as well as lower tax revenues. Meanwhile, salaries for the public sector are usually pretty low in such countries. Ultimately, health and education systems, infrastructure, and the quality of human capital typically deteriorate in such societies, and competitiveness suffers as a result.

Finally, external conditions do matter a lot as well. These can be geopolitical conflicts (Ukraine, Israel), the hostility of neighbors (Russia, Israel, Taiwan), or the global economic context, when the country is extremely open to foreign trade (Mexico). In those cases, even a productive economy will fail to deliver prosperity to its citizens, and competitiveness will also be conspicuous by its absence.

Why is competitiveness our choice? Why is it the best measure of a country's success? In the next section, we look back to history, and analyze how economists and policymakers assessed the performance of countries, and the metrics that were used.

30. LOOKING BACK TO HISTORY

Early economists believed that economic development was mainly dependent on a nation's natural resources and extracted wealth. Wealth used to be expressed in two main forms—capital and labor. The most populated nations had more human capital than less populated ones, and nations waged wars to obtain additional human capital in the form of slaves and war prisoners. Hence, this doctrine stipulated capital and labor as being the main source of wealth for nations.

But if natural and human resources determine wealth, a corollary follows that, in order to develop, countries need to generate and increase the supply of both. Therefore, early economic growth theories were focused on the extraction of natural resources. As an economy grows, it depletes the availability of minerals, fisheries, and forests. And, at the same time, it increases the quality of human capital, gains access to unexplored sources of materials, and drives innovation to create new ones. This conflicting and contrasting process is described by what economists refer to as "endogenous growth models." However, the main limitation of economic growth theories is that they are limited by the amount of natural resources and the environmental issues caused by intensive manufacturing, and the sustainability of resources extraction.

Commenting on this process, Robert Solow—currently Emeritus Institute Professor of Economics at the Massachusetts Institute of Technology, and the 1987 winner of the Nobel Prize in Economics—formulated in the 1970s an exogenous-growth framework (the so-called *Solow Growth Model*), in which a sustainable economy is possible as long as non-renewable natural resources can be substituted with another factor of production such as physical capital, consequentially balancing the economic growth path.

The availability of natural resources partly explains why the United States, Canada, and Australia report higher than average levels of income per capita. However, this phenomenon fails to explain why India, Venezuela, and the Democratic Republic of Congo are underdeveloped. India has the fourth largest coal reserves on earth and significant reserves of limestone, petroleum, diamonds, natural gas, chromite, titanium ore, and bauxite. Over 12 percent of the world's thorium production and over 60 percent of global mica production come from India, which is also the leading producer of manganese ore.[20] At the end of 2017, Venezuela possessed 24.9 percent of the world's reserves of crude oil,[21] more than those of the United States, Canada, and Mexico combined. It is also the leading exporter of bauxite, coal, gold, and iron ore.[22] The Democratic Republic of Congo has the world's largest reserves of cobalt and significant quantities of the world's diamonds, gold, and copper. This makes it potentially one of the richest countries in the world.[23] Yet, despite this apparent wealth of natural resources, poverty ratios in these three countries are particularly high, suggesting that rich endowments do not guarantee economic development. Economic development models in these cases fail to acknowledge the impact of openness and globalization on domestic access to these resources.

Of course, some countries are lucky enough to sit on top of a massive source of wealth, and rightfully exploit it. From the 16th century up to the 1930s, Dubai and Abu Dhabi were the leading ports and pearling centers of the Middle East.[24] In fact, pearls provided the foundation for the region's growing prosperity during that period. Most of these pearl exports were directed to the West, but India and Turkey were also frequent recipients. The demise of the pearl industry was caused by World War I, the Great Depression, and primarily the Japanese invention of the cultivated pearl, and the slump in prices that this caused. In any case, the attractiveness of the pearl sector for a society that had been mostly rural and poor for centuries was disrupted by the discovery of oil in 1958, after a 30-year search that had started in 1936, when the first British geologists arrived in Abu Dhabi. From this point, until the creation of the United Arab Emirates in 1971, the wealth of the region increased massively. By 1980, the country's GDP per capita was USD 113,000 (constant 2010 USD), compared to USD 28,700 for the United States and USD 54,800 for Switzerland in the same year.[25] Alas, between 1980 and 2017, the UAE's GDP per capita fell 61 percent. Natural resources do not last forever, but even with the fall in oil prices, Abu Dhabi's GDP per capita was USD 71,600 in 2017,[26] while Dubai's was USD 40,700. Such a difference exists because, while Abu Dhabi produces oil, Dubai does not.

But the UAE, and Dubai in particular, also tell a different story on how to succeed through trade, independently or at least in parallel to abundant natural resources. In 2006, Sheikh Mohammed bin Rashid Al Maktoum took over as leader of Dubai. Through a parallel strategy designed to attract talent and capital, Sheikh Mohammed successfully turned Dubai into the global business hub of the Middle East. He did so by eliminating corporate and income taxes to begin with. Dubai is funded primarily with the profits of state-owned enterprises and consumption taxes, and its economy relies primarily on logistics and services—depending heavily on foreign trade.

Originally, those economists who defended trade as the key to economic development were called mercantilists—and their doctrine mercantilism. The mercantilists viewed trade as the main source of wealth generation, and eventually economic development. David Ricardo (1772–1823) developed an international trade theory based on comparative advantage and specialization. The theory was first introduced in his book *On the Principles of Political Economy and Taxation* in 1817. The main argument proposed by Ricardo is summarized as follows—countries should specialize in the production of goods in which they have not only an absolute advantage, but also a relative advantage over other countries, in order to gain the benefit of international trade. Since China is specialized in labor-intensive products, and the United States is specialized in capital-intensive products, China should export wheat to the United States, and the United States should export cars to China.

Mercantilism was dictated by the economic environment of that age, at a time when the primary factors of production (capital and labor) did not interact through technology. Trading nations are no longer necessarily the wealthiest countries. In fact, free trade has hardly ever been the factor behind the success of the great powers of the past. Joe Studwell puts it bluntly in *How Asia Works*:

> The shocking truth, however, is that every economically successful society has been guilty, in its formative stages, of protectionism. Outside the anomalous offshore port financial havens such as Hong Kong and Singapore, there are no economies in the world that have developed to the first rank through policies of free trade.[27]

The intensive trade doctrine was eclipsed by the Industrial Revolution, allied with the rising importance of technology. Early in the 20th century, nations raced in technological advancement and qualitative economic development. Modern theories of economic development are no longer dependent only on the accumulation of capital, either physical or human. Academics now argue that there is a third form of capital that is equally important to the performance of production—a favorable institutional environment.

The importance of institutional quality rose in popularity with Daron Acemoglu and James Robinson's (from MIT and the University of Chicago, respectively) 2012 book *Why Nations Fail: The Origins of Power, Prosperity, and Poverty*. The authors form their main hypothesis around the fact that economic institutions are the key determinants of a country's success; hence, economic growth and development. In this framework, wealth creation can only be achieved through political freedom. The political environment of a country formulates economic institutions, and the quality of those institutions is the key element that determines the success or failure of nations. Their work is extensive and extremely relevant, as they test the hypothesis that institutional development determines success, at the expense of two other alternatives. These two alternatives are that the geographical position of the country is of primary importance, so that rough climate areas and exposure to diseases hinder economic development, or that cultural aspects, such as the business orientation of a nation, its creativity, and hard work, determine success. In the end, they conclude, the quality of a nation's ruling elite, and whether they form and apply relevant policies, are the keys to fighting poverty and securing economic development.

Institutional quality explains why Singapore and Argentina differ so much in their degrees of prosperity, being ranked 59th and 3rd, respectively. Obviously, Argentina is quite a rich country with significant natural deposits, extensive territory, and a population of around 44 million. In contrast, Singapore is a small island-country with limited natural resources, land, and population. Argentina was a highly developed nation at the turn of the 20th century, but has since experienced a raft of major crises, announcing defaults eight times over the following 100 years. We have touched upon some of Argentina's more recent problems elsewhere in this book. Upon gaining independence from Malaysia in 1965, Singapore was already viewed as the "Monaco of the East,"[28] securing steady economic growth and development. The main driving force of Singapore's economic progress has been the policies of Singapore's first prime minister, Lee Kuan Yew, particularly since the 1970s.

First, Singapore curtailed corruption and established equal business rights, attracting foreign investments by offering a competitive tax policy, and securing investors by instigating property protection regulations. These astute development policies led businesses to grow, prompting an increase in foreign direct investment's portfolio, which eventually resulted in capital stock rising by 33 times (note: does this mean it rose on 33 occasions, or rose 33-fold? It's not entirely clear—CM) by 1992. Ultimately, this helped the nation in constructing a world-class airport and establishing modern business districts, which have also boosted both its physical and intangible infrastructures.

Thus, natural endowments, trade openness, and institutional quality combine in different ways to drive a nation's success. But none of them can be considered either entirely necessary or sufficient. Institutions (see Chapter 3) require economic foundations, since stock markets, trade unions, political parties, and business associations are the result of, not the reason for, a productive economy. Trade openness is partly the cause for the emergence of new powers in the last decades (China and the European Union, for instance), but protectionism has helped most big countries in the early stages of development. Natural resources are usually a distraction from effective policies, and in most cases those countries with massive access to natural resources have failed to develop welfare-enhancing economic and social institutions. Prosperity is therefore the combination of different approaches and policies, the interaction of the public and private sector, and the ultimate choice of a country's rulers, taking into account each nation's unique historical and social background.

A detailed look at productivity data

World data

We live in amazing times. At the end of 2017, the difference between the richest country in the world (Luxembourg: 107,000 in constant 2010 USD per person) and the poorest (Burundi: 212 USD per person) is more than 500 times. That is way more than in 1960, when the difference between the richest and the poorest was 176 times (Bermuda: USD 27,800; Myanmar: USD 158). Countries are more disparate, but both the richest and the poorest countries are today richer than they were 58 years ago. Indeed, Myanmar's per capita GDP multiplied nine times between 1960 and 2017, and Luxembourg's grew four-fold. For the average country in the world, the increase is 2.87 times.

Angus Maddison from the University of Groningen has calculated the performance of the world economy in a colossal book.[29] When measured in 1990 international USD, the average output of a world citizen has grown from USD 450 in the year 1990 to USD 6,516 in 2003, or 14 times. However, most of the prosperity that we enjoy today has been generated over the last decades: world GDP per capita has grown after 1950 at the same rate as it did between 1000 and 1913.[30]

In the period 1500–1820, the world's per capita output grew 0.14 percent per year on average, but it grew 3.92 percent per year in 1950–1973, 1.77 percent in 1973–2003, and 1.5 percent between 2003 and 2017. Today, we grow in 10 years as much as we did in a century before 1900. Low-income countries enjoy the same living standards today as Norwegians in 1820.[31]

As a result of our economic development, and above all the consequences of the Industrial Revolution, more people work, and therefore output is higher. In the United States alone, Maddison reports that while only one-third of the population was employed in 1820, almost 50 percent was working by 2003. And because output has grown much more than employment, the world population is also significantly more productive.

The best source of information for productivity figures is the Total Productivity Database provided by the Conference Board. Productivity is measured as output (in 2017 USD) divided by employed persons and adjusted based on a 2011 price index. To gain a feel for the performance of this indicator at the world level, Figure 2.5 illustrates the average growth in labor productivity across countries in the world in the period 1990–2018.

Overall, the average of the world's labor productivity is expanding, but its changes (in percentage terms) are fluctuating. Specifically, labor productivity has decreased since the period 2003–2009, and has then increased in an upward curve.

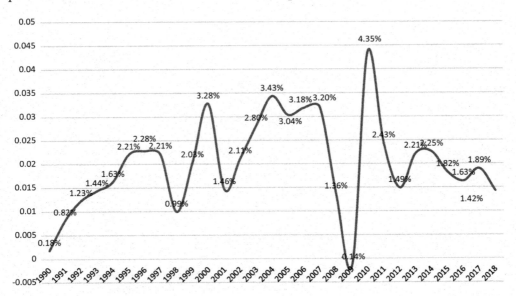

Figure 2.5 World Change in Productivity

Source: The Conference Board.

However, the positive trend of productivity does not necessarily reflect the progressiveness of its growth. The annual percentage change of the world's labor productivity seems to have increased since 1990, but, in fact, turns out to have been weakening since 2000. Similarly, the growth of productivity plummeted in the early 1990s—which was primarily due to the US recession—and again in 2008 due to the global financial crisis. At those two points, labor productivity fell by 3.17 and 2.05 percent, respectively, relative to the previous year.

The average measure of labor productivity at the world level can provide us with valuable insight regarding global productivity. Unfortunately, there are also some concerns about these conclusions. First, the average index is calculated using equal weights, which therefore implies that more productive countries can shift their production to less productive nations, which is not logical. Second, every country is treated equally, which should not be the case. Third, the "average" also implies that the impact of economic shocks in one country can spread to all other nations, while this is not always true. Thus, in the following section, we would like to narrow our observation of labor productivity to smaller country samples. We will present the countries in two groups, namely the G8 nations and other developing countries.

G8 countries

Established in 1975, the group of eight (G8 countries) refers to the group of eight most industrialized countries. They are the United States, France, Germany, Canada, Japan, the Russian Federation, Italy, and the United Kingdom. According to World Bank data, the total GDP of the eight countries in 2017 accounted for 47.48 percent of the world's total GDP. Figure 2.6 illustrates the movement of labor productivity in the eight countries in the nominal value (USD) during the period 1950–2018.

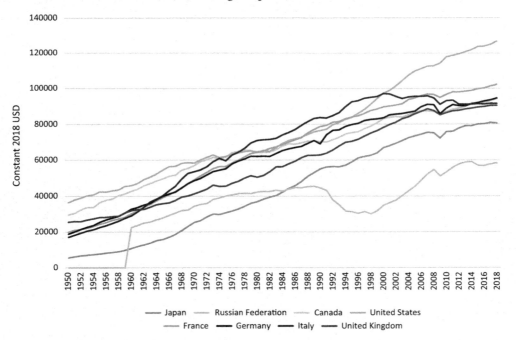

Figure 2.6 Labor Productivity in G8 countries

Source: Conference Board.

Overall, except for Italy, the path of labor productivity in the G8 countries is one of continuous increase. In 2018, the United States led the rest of the countries regarding labor productivity level, while the Russian Federation had the least labor productivity in the group. Russia experienced the lowest labor productivity in 1998, when the financial crisis occurred, causing the country to default on its debt. The Asian financial crisis, and the decline in metal and crude oil demand, were two external shocks triggering the Russian financial crisis at that time, which then subsequently turned into a political mess. However, Russian productivity gradually rebounded to its initial path as the country's financial institutions started to diversify their assets.

In what is a significantly different case than Russia, Italy is currently under prolonged distress, and still unable to wake up from its weakening productivity. Fiscal management was the greatest challenge for Italy in 1998, which was also the start of a persistent slump in labor productivity. Subsequently, its high ratio of public debt to GDP makes Italy one of the most vulnerable countries in Europe to any form of external shock.

Let us look at the data in a different fashion. We will now measure the percentage growth in labor productivity every decade since 1950. Figure 2.7 illustrates the productivity growth for the eight countries in the group. Surprisingly, unlike the positive movement on its nominal value, the productivity growth across the countries in the group is decreasing.

Every decade, labor productivity growth is showing a downturn, with the smallest growth experienced in the period 2011–2018. Even for Italy, productivity growth fell below zero percent in the period 2011–2018. How can the increasing welfare gained by industrialized countries correspond to the fall in productivity growth? This phenomenon is known as the "productivity puzzle," associated with a number of possible causes. We will get more deeply into this issue in the next section.

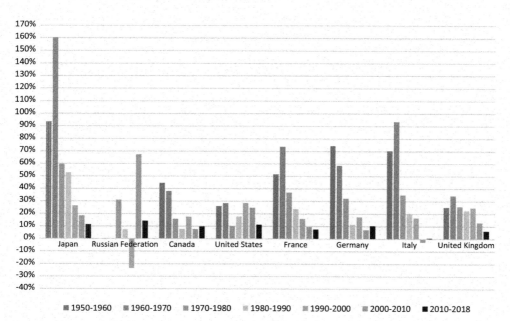

Figure 2.7 Changes in Labor Productivity for G8 countries
Source: The Conference Board.

Other countries

To have a better understanding of labor productivity across the globe, let us make a similar analysis as we did in the G8 countries to the other countries. To have a fair comparison, a similar analysis will be implemented in some leading developing countries, namely China, India, Brazil, South Korea, Switzerland, and Saudi Arabia. According to World Bank data, in 2017 the GDP of these six countries made up 24.52 percent of total GDP in the world. China, in particular, was the world's second largest economy after the United States, constituting 15.16 percent of the world's GDP.

Figure 2.8 illustrates labor productivity in nominal level (USD) for the six countries. In comparison to Figure 2.7, we can see that the level of labor productivity in developing countries is below that of industrialized countries, except for Saudi Arabia and Switzerland. Recall that labor productivity is measured as output per employed person. Thus, in the case of China, although its economy is rapidly growing, its labor productivity is still below the United States, as more population is employed as labor than in the United States. Some economic issues, such as excess inventory, an asset bubble, or a trade war with the United States, also potentially pressures Chinese productivity in the upcoming years.

Labor productivity in Saudi Arabia, in particular, behaves quite differently from others. With oil resources and a smaller number of employed persons, Saudi Arabia reached its peak labor productivity up to USD 250,000 per employed persons in the 1970s, which is superior to any country. However, productivity plummeted in the mid-1980s as the oil price crisis hit the economy. Currently, the labor productivity in this country is hovering at USD 150,000 per employed person, which is still way above the average of the world's labor productivity. Furthermore, Switzerland reaches a similar level of productivity as its peers, i.e., France, Germany, the United Kingdom, and Italy. Finally, Brazil and India are

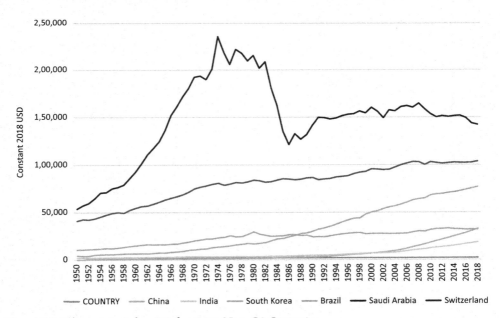

Figure 2.8 Changes in Labor Productivity, Non-G8 Countries
Source: The Conference Board.

currently reaching a similar level of labor productivity, except more economic turbulence in Brazil has decreased its labor productivity since the 2010s.

Interestingly, the phenomenon of the productivity puzzle is also happening in some developing countries, particularly the one with a high productivity slope. Figure 2.9 illustrates the percentage change of the labor productivity index, the so-called productivity growth, which is measured every 10 years.

As shown above, the weakening productivity growth is obviously seen in South Korea, Switzerland, Saudi Arabia, and Brazil, where the first three countries place at the top three in Figure 2.9. In China and India, there is an upturn trend in labor productivity. However, even when China and India are considered, the labor productivity growth in all countries during 2011–2018 is found to plummet compared to the previous decades.

Overall, as we read thus far, several results stand out. First, diving into the productivity issue in individual countries can give us a better insight regarding a nation's competitiveness, in addition to only relying on aggregate measures, such as the IMD World Competitiveness Ranking or the world's average ratio. Using the labor productivity index, defined as output per employed person, can give us more information regarding the level of productivity, its speed, and how it grows over time. Second, the level and growth of productivity in industrialized countries still outperform those in some leading developing countries. Third, although the level and growth of productivity between industrialized and developing countries are different, the phenomenon of the productivity puzzle remains in both groups. This gives us a signal that the slowdown in productivity growth might be caused by a systematic pattern or similar economic factors across countries, regardless of the various economic issues that every country is facing. In the following section, we are going to look more deeply into the productivity puzzle: what it is, and what factors are actually affecting the phenomenon.

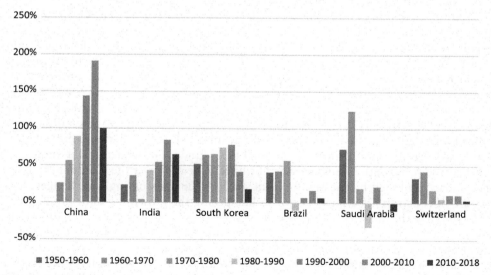

Figure 2.9 Change in Labor Productivity

Source: The Conference Board.

The productivity puzzle

In March 2016, the Bank of International Settlements (BIS), based in Basel (Switzerland), proclaimed the productivity puzzle as one of the biggest risks in the world economy.[32] This is a well-known phenomenon: the puzzle because the productivity growth of a country tends to decline while technology is developing rapidly. Figures 2.8 and 2.9 give us a clearer view regarding the downturn trend in productivity growth in the G8 and other developing countries; except for China and India, the labor productivity growth declines during 1950–2018. Between 2008 and 2018, labor productivity in Germany, Switzerland, the United States, the United Kingdom, and most other developed economies stagnated.

The irony is that while in the last decade the world has enjoyed the fastest technological revolution ever seen, our economies have not become more efficient. This seems like a paradox; automated production and services should be able to produce more with fewer people. If we took this to its natural conclusion, full automation implies infinite productivity. While we're obviously not at this level, major progress has been made. For example, car manufacturing in Germany has achieved levels of automation whereby 80 percent of the jobs can be made redundant. Intuitively, this should imply that the industry has become extraordinarily productive, because very few hands produce many cars, with the help of machines. But such a phenomenon has not happened.

Why is it that, in the most technologically advanced decade of our history (between 2000 and 2010), in the years when we saw the explosion of Google and Apple, robotics, the industrial internet, automation, and big data, the world economy had not been able to improve the productivity of labor? Labor productivity is a simple equation—output is the numerator, number of employees is the denominator. If technology allows us to produce more with fewer people, why is it instead that countries like Germany, Switzerland, and the United States are as productive today as they were in 2010? Answering this question is extremely important because we are effectively saying that the world economy (with the exception of a handful of countries) is less competitive today than it was 10 years ago.

Let me venture some potential explanations:

Credit crunch: One of the popular ideas regarding the reason behind this puzzle is the impact of the economic crisis. For instance, economists Carmen Reinhart and Ken Rogoff from Harvard University have taught us[33] that financial crises affecting economies can create a permanent scar on productivity. This logic is similar to an incident in which a footballer breaks his or her leg; he or she may not be able to perform at the same level afterwards. During its lifecycle, the global economy has experienced economic turbulence of various kinds, such as oil price shocks, financial crises, and geopolitical turmoils. One similarity across the crises mentioned is the constraint on credit activity, which is due to the excessive risk aversion of the financial sector. This fear affects the way that banks are able, and choose, to channel their funds. Consequently, the more constrained and prudent the credit provided by banks, the narrower the room for economic agents to expand their businesses. A recent study by the Bank of England[34] suggests that this credit constraint is a major factor in hampering the growth of labor productivity. Unfortunately, the financial channel does not fully explain why, even when credit activity has been stabilized and countries have implemented exit policies from their crises, that the productivity puzzle continues unanswered.

Misallocation of capital and labor across sectors: This is a very interesting avenue, since it suggests that in most countries, skills and resources are not matched to jobs, so both the public and the private sector invest inefficiently in sectors that do not necessarily create added value. A research piece written by Gita Gopinath, currently chief economist at the International Monetary Fund, and various co-authors has shown[35] in the context of the recent European crisis that the decline in real interest rates in the period 1999–2012 led to a significant decline in sectoral total factor productivity. This was due to the fact that capital inflows were misallocated to firms that had higher net worth, but that were not necessarily more productive. The UK National Institute of Economic and Social Research and the Bank of England have also provided evidence showing that resource misallocation between capital and labor during the crisis was the factor that weakened productivity in the United Kingdom.[36]

Data is wrong: One can obviously argue that output, measured by GDP, does not take into account all productive activities of an economy (more below), nor the quality of its output. The first mobile phone ever launched, the Motorola StarTAC,[37] cost about USD 1,000 in 1996, which is, in real terms, much more than consumers pay today for the market-leading iPhone X. However, of course, the features of the latter are stellar compared to the former. While this is true, the fact that productivity is no higher today than it used to be, and consequently salaries have not increased, remains. Therefore, today we are less able to enjoy our technology than before, because our productivity, and hence our salaries and purchasing power, are lower.

Even though we produce higher-quality products, what we produce is cheaper: This argument unfortunately does not stand up to scrutiny, because the data in the previous graphs and tables is in inflation-adjusted dollars.

The McKinsey Global Institute released a study in 2018 assessing the role of demand on the productivity puzzle.[38] They suggested that the momentum of the productivity boom during the 1990s has faded. If you were employed during the 1990s, you might still remember how tremendous the impact of the use of PCs, software, and information technology was on the way people worked at that time. Unfortunately, that type of euphoria has faded. This thinking explains why the high productivity boom in the past occurred, as the way that people worked changed dramatically, from manual to automation, which resulted in high productivity growth. But today, technology has become widespread in every type of work, in all companies, of all sizes. So, we cannot expect similar productivity jumps as occurred in the past.

It takes time for technology to impact productivity: That is, today's innovations need a lag effect to materialize and impact on labor productivity. Regarding innovation, the study from McKinsey releases similar statements to those of Gordon (2012) and Cowen (2011), who asserted that the type of technological progress in the past may not continue as progressively in the future. However, Gordon (2012) claimed that current innovation may not be as substantial as in the past, which is understood, as ongoing innovation is more focused on internet technology rather than the physical machine. Decker et al. (2016) even argued that current innovation is sufficiently mature that marginal productivity emanating from future innovation may not be as high as it was in the past. However, this latter point is quite debatable.

Technology does not make us more productive: Some economists contend that current innovation disentangles labor further from productivity. For instance, the invention of Twitter and Facebook is found to make people less productive. Furthermore, some also argue that the development of technology today is based more on market orientation rather than pushing users to be more productive. Nevertheless, McKinsey (2018) believes that it is only a matter of time before modern innovation has a significant impact on labor productivity.

Lack of investment: Without investment, job creation deteriorates and productivity suffers. In the post-crisis period, and especially in Western economies, there has been a lack of investment in tangible capital, less research and development, less capital replacement by companies, and consequently a smaller stock of capital.[39] The recognition of intangible assets such as patent and research and development (R&D) should be measured in the same way as physical capital in GDP, yet they are not. This thinking leads many to believe that the lack of recognition for this type of asset hinders the growth of innovation even more, which eventually decreases labor productivity.

The slow diffusion of innovation to firms has also been blamed for the slowdown in productivity, although not the slower rate of innovation itself.[40] However, this slow diffusion can also be triggered by other factors. For instance, less-skilled workers in a company can ensure that any innovation is effectively useless. Or, less innovative company leaders' unwillingness to innovate can also ensure that innovation stalls. Finally, besides the slow diffusion process, some studies also blame governments that help to ensure that productivity is seriously slowed. The blame for this is based on the argument that government policy stabilization, such as fiscal policy or monetary policy, is executed inappropriately, which subsequently destroys productivity itself. For instance, a tight fiscal policy can impose a tax rate that is too high, and this then disincentivizes business to grow, labor to work, or even individuals to save their money. Furthermore, an over-tightened monetary policy to prevent economic overheating is also believed to have a persistent impact on weakening credit activity, which subsequently restrains credit offered to firms, and causes labor productivity to fall.

There are two final explanations that are worth considering. Our productivity data is reported as output per capita, not output per hour. It could well be that, if we work fewer and fewer hours as our economies develop, we would end up living in a more efficient world (higher productivity per hour) but with less productive employees as they work less. Unfortunately, when one looks at productivity per hour, the results are the same as those reported here.

Besides, the explanation could simply be that we work in less productive jobs. If this is the case, then the productivity puzzle is almost a red herring. But this is at odds with the observation that, during recent decades, the world economy has moved from farming to manufacturing, and then to services. And services are more productive than manufacturing, which is, in turn, more productive than farming—irrespective of technology.

In conclusion, as argued above, many factors impact on the productivity puzzle, ranging from crisis-related causes to technology, human capital, diffusion dynamics, and many others. However, although the theories mentioned earlier are sufficiently logical, no single answer can actually explain the puzzle. The best guess among all alternatives is that the productivity puzzle is a dynamic phenomenon, which has an equilibrium that is prone to various shocks. By the same logic, if this is a dynamic phenomenon, then a cure to accelerate productivity in an upward curve should also be identifiable. More importantly, when economic shocks—such as crises, technology, lack of human capital—infiltrate the economy and dislocate productivity from its equilibrium, government policies are of critical importance. For instance, from the fiscal policy side, more budget can be allocated to support education and training, so that human capital can be strengthened. Equally, the government can also assign more budget to prioritize investment in productive sectors, according to the country's endowments and profile, in order to advance its dynamic comparative advantage. Beyond that, other supporting factors of productivity must also be promoted, such as employees' incentives, innovations, and other aspects that can result in a better quality of life.

Productivity and wages

Productivity matters because, in an economic equilibrium, individuals should be paid according to how productive they are.[41] If I generate USD 20 per hour of work because I am a lumberjack, while my neighbor is a soccer star who sells USD 1,000 official club T-shirts in an hour, he should be paid 50 times more than me. Besides, if technology makes me more productive, or I simply work harder, so that next year I generate USD 30 per hour in output, my wage should increase by 50 percent. Certainly, I am not entitled to all the proceeds from my job, because production costs are incurred, and my company will need to invest in technology and advertising. But it should be the case that, over a long period of time, productivity increases should be *approximately* equal to salary increases.

In Figure 2.10, I show the dynamics of labor productivity and average compensation in the United States in the period 1948–2016. The data is collected by economists Anna Stansbury and Larry Summers[42] from Harvard University. Between 1948 and the 1973 oil crisis, productivity and wages grew in parallel, and in 25 years there was an impressive doubling in the average prosperity of American workers. However, the wedge between productivity and pay began in 1973, and grew systematically until today. In their analysis of the most recent period, Stansbury and Summers show that, while productivity grows 1.16, 2.33, and 1.15 percent in the periods 1973–1996, 1996–2003, and 2003–2014, the wage share of such increases is −0.26, 0.32, and −0.34 percent, respectively. In other words, we can even see that in the last decade, productivity increases are accompanied by reductions in real wages.[43] There is also a big difference between what the US Bureau of Labor Statistics calls "production/nonsupervisory compensation," which essentially corresponds to blue-collar workers, and the average worker, who represents industry and services employees. For the former, the wedge between productivity and salaries has widened even more.

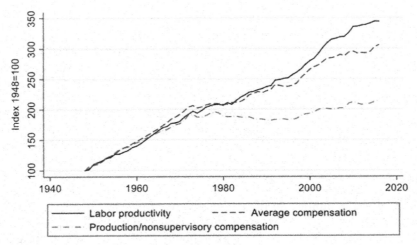

Figure 2.10 The Gap between Productivity and Salaries

Source: Stansbury and Summers (2018).

What has happened? The good news is that while there is an increasing gap between productivity and *average* pay, there is still a substantial linkage between productivity and *median* compensation in the 1973–2016 period. To understand what this means, note that as income inequality increases because the top 5 percent becomes richer and richer, average compensation increases, but median compensation does not. In a hypothetical country with 100 workers who earn USD 30,000 per year, both the average and the median salaries are USD 30,000. If, instead, 5 out of 100 workers get a pay raise to USD 300,000, the median salary remains at USD 30,000, but the average salary has now increased to USD 43,500.

Interestingly then, what Stansbury and Summers find is that

> even as productivity growth has been acting to push workers' pay up, other factors not associated with productivity growth have acted to push workers' pay down. So while it may appear on first glance that productivity growth has not benefited typical workers much, [their] findings imply that if productivity growth had been lower, typical workers would have likely done substantially worse.[44]

All in all, these results suggest two important features of our economies in the recent years: productivity increases have been enjoyed by only a few, and labor has lost in favor of capital (i.e., machines). Few reasonable people would doubt this conclusion, so it is important to discuss the reasons behind it. Non-technological explanations would attribute the gulf to the increasing lack of skills of employees faced with technological innovation, immigration, and globalization, and a decline in the power of unions.[45] As for technology, obviously automation and digitalization have reduced the relevance of manual labor, and human skills now require investments in new technologies that are typically implemented at the expense of labor income. These issues will be discussed in the next section.

Governments have a lot of say over most of these issues, and it is the responsibility of public policy to curtail the resulting income inequality by attacking the root causes of the pay–productivity gap. For what it is worth, let me add to the explanations above, one that has not been discussed enough, namely, the growing power of shareholders in publicly traded firms.

Governance rules after the 2008 crises have prioritized the interests of shareholders over other stakeholders, very often against the original intent of protecting customers, employees, and wider society from the excesses that led to the financial crisis itself. Originally, corporate governance rules were enacted to protect the interest of shareholders against self-dealing executives, because of the very essence of a corporation in which ownership and control are separated. Consequently, the focus of governance rules was to encourage fair representation of shareholders on the board of directors, adequate internal controls to monitor executives, and appropriate compensation rules, disclosure requirements, and accounting policies. The conflict today is between large and small shareholders, or more precisely between owner-managers and minority shareholders. In March 2017, Snap Inc., the popular social media company, went public through an initial public offering (IPO) underwritten by Morgan Stanley, and sold 200 million shares at USD 17 per share, thus raising USD 3.4 billion. However, all the shares issued carried no votes, stripping shareholders of any decision-making power in the newly listed company. The trick involved was that the company has three classes of shares—A, B, and C. In the IPO, Snap issued only Class A shares. Class B shares carry

1 vote, and Class C shares carry 10 votes. Snap's IPO prospectus explicitly declares that the holders of all outstanding Class C shares are "a founder, an executive officer, and a director of the company."[46] Why would anyone invest in Snap Inc. then? If you do, you will consider that, even though you do not have any decision-making power over the company's future, you are at least entitled to a share of the company's profits. Wrong. With respect to dividends, Snap Inc. states before the IPO, "We intend to retain all available funds and future earnings, if any, to fund the development and expansion of our business, and we do not anticipate paying any cash dividends in the foreseeable future."[47] Once you have lost all your rights, your only reason to invest in the company is the expectation that the stock price will increase due to the performance of its leaders. Wrong again. As of January 2019 (almost two years after the IPO), Snap's stock price is close to USD 7 per share. *The New York Times'* "DealBook" columnist Steven Davidoff Solomon called Snap Inc's deal "the most shareholder-unfriendly governance in an initial public offering, ever."[48]

Unfortunately, the Snap approach to corporate governance is not unique. There are dual-class shares in 222 out of the 3,000 companies[49] in the US Russell 3000 Index, including Alphabet (the parent company of Google), Facebook, and Zynga. Among the recent arrivals to the stock market, Alibaba and Spotify give minority shareholders restrictive voting power. Additionally, 84 companies in the S&P 500 do not pay, nor intend to pay, any dividends to their shareholders. These companies indeed account for a large share of the total market capitalization of the index, and include Facebook, Alphabet, TripAdvisor, and Paypal Holdings, among others.

Lighter corporate governance standards imply more power for controlling shareholders, and subsequently less employee rights. In his seminal book *Capital in the Twenty-First Century*, Thomas Piketty sees capital accumulation as the reason for the increasing levels of income inequality in the world and proposes a universal wealth tax as the solution. An analysis of the recent stock market trends also shows that government policies could curtail inequality without resorting to taxes; instead, they just need to guarantee the empowerment of minority shareholders.

Technology and competitiveness

A pertinent question is: to what extent technology, and particularly technology in the productive system, makes countries more productive, and consequently more competitive? We praise technology for the improvements in productivity and quality of life that the world has enjoyed in the last 70 years. However, in previous sections, we have discussed the puzzling observation that, in the last decade, when our technological development has exploded and we have implemented the most disruptive transformations, world productivity has stagnated.

The optimistic view of technology posits that robots make humans more productive, and therefore contribute to economic growth. The only systematic study of the impact of robots on the economy has been conducted by Georg Graetz and Guy Michaels from the London School of Economics.[50] They studied the implementation of robots in 17 European countries between 1993 and 2007 and found that robots accounted for 10 percent growth in GDP over the period. One channel through which robots contribute to growth is the acceleration of production that reduces production costs and prices, and subsequently increases aggregate demand. A survey[51] conducted by the OECD in 2017 uncovered very similar impacts in the period 1993–2016.[52]

Technology can have other positive *spillover* effects. Automation can encourage a country to move its supporting supply chain closer to its homeland, rather than having this outsourced to other countries. A study by the International Federation of Robotics[53] shows that 70 percent of respondents in a survey conducted by Citigroup trust that automation would encourage companies to move their manufacturing closer to home. Indeed, Whirlpool, Caterpillar, and Ford Motor Company in the United States, and Adidas in Germany, have already done so.

The anti-robot school of thought posits that they overtake human jobs and increase unemployment. To the extent that the competitiveness of a country relies on its ability to generate jobs, if robots only make us more productive but push people out of the job market, they should not be encouraged. It is undeniable that the implementation of robots in industries is widespread, and it has even become a necessity for enterprises to survive in the hugely competitive globalized marketplace. In its 2017 report,[54] the McKinsey Global Institute predicts that up to half of the total productivity growth required to ensure a 2.8 percent growth in GDP over the next 50 years will be driven by automation. However, McKinsey surprisingly states that "our productivity estimates assume that people displaced by automation will find other employment,"[55] without further pursuing the question of what jobs will be created. If I adopt David Graeber's terminology, I suspect that most of these will be *bullshit* jobs,[56] tasks that do not create value for society beyond self-fulfillment and that they will almost inevitably be low-paid jobs with poor long-term outlooks.

Technology has two other detrimental effects on economic development, well-documented by *Financial Times* associate editor David Pilling in his book *The Growth Delusion*.[57] When digitalization removes activities from the formal economy, and instead moves them into the informal or black economy, GDP reduces automatically. For example, we use email instead of the postal service, listen to music through our unlimited subscription to Spotify instead of buying a record, and use a car-sharing internet platform to move across the city instead of taking a taxi. Second, technology makes stuff cheaper, thereby reducing the nominal and, more importantly, the real GDP. This is the case because technology actually substitutes products and services; it does not merely make the same product cheaper. Thirty years ago, we had to buy a flashlight, a camera, an agenda, a voice recorder, a watch, an alarm clock, a telephone, and even a heart sensor in order to perform several tasks that can be done today with just a smartphone.

Overall, competitiveness policies related to robotization should be analyzed through the employment lens, and more broadly by considering whether technology improves the quality of life for all citizens, including those displaced from the labor market.

Value drivers and key performance indicators

In the same way that companies distinguish between value drivers and performance indicators, government officials also have to be careful not to pull the wrong levers when managing an economy. We are frequently confronted with this distinction in our executive classes. When company strategy specifies that the goal is to be the market leader, for example, two important decisions must be made. First, determining which key performance indicators (KPI) the company is going to use in order to measure market leadership: market share (which market? share in revenues or in profits?), sales volume, the number of countries in which the company is number one in its product market, etc. In some cases, choosing a KPI is straightforward. If my objective is to generate double-digit growth, I will look at revenue growth. If my objective is to be highly profitable, I will set a benchmark based on a minimum operating profit margin. As Peter Drucker used to say: "If you can't measure it, you can't manage it." The second decision is both more important and more difficult to tackle. This is because KPIs are not directly affected by a company's decisions, but are indirectly impacted by managing a corresponding *value driver*. To manage profitability, value drivers are pricing, marketing strategy, product mix, quality control, failure tolerance, cost discipline, and cost of capital. To manage growth, value drivers are acquisition strategy, market entry approach, innovation, financing costs, and service quality.

Competitiveness, or a competitiveness ranking, is, at the end of the day, nothing but a country's KPIs. As a performance indicator, it encompasses several other ingredients that we have discussed earlier, namely productivity, prosperity, quality of life, attraction of foreign capital, job creation, the image of the country abroad, and the talent capital of the nation. These are all KPIs that allow countries to translate competitiveness into measurable macroeconomic figures. But they should not be considered managerial tools. For instance, productivity cannot be managed directly, and surprisingly the strategies of many countries fail because they do not tackle the factors that determine productivity, instead mistakenly choosing to tackle productivity itself. I once spoke to a high-level government official from a government that shall remain nameless who told me that the country had put emphasis on improving their ranking in the World Bank's Ease of Doing Business ranking. The country did indeed manage to improve its ranking in a relatively short period of time (they have a good dictator), but to the chagrin of the government, "the country did not see any increase in the number of businesses being created."

Thus, productivity is the key to achieving competitiveness, particularly in the long run. More productive countries correspond to their higher levels of competitiveness, which in turn are expected to increase the country's social welfare. However, productivity alone cannot guarantee the realization of strong competitiveness. It must be supported by the soundness of other pillars, such as institutions, infrastructure, macroeconomic environment, health and primary education, higher education and training, goods market efficiency, labor market efficiency, financial market development, technological readiness, market size, business sophistication, and innovation.

Managing wages is one way to manage labor productivity. Theoretically, higher wages can incentivize workers to be more productive. However, this may also deter companies from hiring employees. Therefore, considering whether minimum wages, for instance, increase competitiveness boils down to carefully considering these two sets of effects.

31. SETTING THE COMPETITIVENESS PATH

In this section, we will discuss the importance of the starting conditions in order to be competitive. Countries rich in natural resources, with a privileged geographical position, and with long-standing entrepreneurial values and a law-abiding culture, find it easier to be competitive. But as important as the initial conditions, it is the path that countries follow, and that it is normally shaped by good/bad decisions, luck, and external events. Let me illustrate this point with the example of Slovenia and Belarus, two Slavic countries, located in Europe, both with a moderate amount of population, not a big territory compared to their neighbors; both countries young after they gained their independence from the USSR in the early 1990s. And yet so different in terms of diplomatic reputation, political freedom, economic prosperity and life expectancy, and competitiveness today.[58] How did that happen?

The Slav people spread through Europe from the 6th century and, as their area of influence extended, they also started to separate into smaller groups. Belarusians and Slovenians have existed as such since the 10th century, when the Slavs divided into three groups—south, east, and west, where Slovenian territories belonged to the south and Belarusian to the east. As time went by, those three groups splintered into smaller groups, which became proto-nations of the modern ones.

Both countries were constantly affected by some of their numerous influential neighbors. That influence continued for such a long time that there were no official names for those states until the 20th century. Speaking of Slovenia, over history it had several names: *Slavic tribes* under Venetian ruling, *Carinthia* in the Holy Roman Empire, *Inner Austrian Provinces* when led by the Habsburgs, *Illyrian* provinces, *Carniola* as part of the Austro-Hungarian Empire. The first time the Slovenes declared themselves not just a minor ethnicity was in the 19th century during the Spring of Nations. At that time, the Slovenes had spent roughly a thousand years under German/Austrian feudal domination and their territories were heavily Germanized.

Still, the Slovenes managed to preserve their culture and places of origin. As the Slovenians talk about their history they say: "We were not Germanized, rather Europeanized." That is, they took the best ideas they could, learned from the Europeans, who were the pioneers of various technologies back then, and decided to go their own way.

Actually, from the beginning of the 11th century, their territories were slowly assimilated into the Roman Empire, and only natural borders, such as mountain ranges and rivers, protected Slovenians from the Germanic influence and helped them preserve their own culture. That changed in the beginning of the 17th century when the preacher Jurij Dalmatin printed the Bible in the Slovene language. The Bible spread across the national lands and gave the Slovene language and thus its culture a second life.

As for Belarus, its name first appeared on the map during World War I, when local citizens proclaimed the Belarusian People's Republic under the reign of German Kaiser Wilhelm II. The republic was never recognized; however, the Belarusians made it clear they were a nation. And soon after the war, the Byelorussian Soviet Socialist Republic was created within the boundaries of the Soviet Union.

Of course, the Belarusians appeared as a nation much earlier. The eastern group of Slavs initially consolidated their lands into Kievan Rus', and then the group divided into more autonomous principalities. The proto-principality for Belarusians was the Polotsk Duchy which was conquered by the Principality of Lithuania, which later created the Commonwealth with Poland and was subsequently partitioned by the Russian Empire. That is three centuries under moderate Lithuanian influence, three centuries under more intense Polish influence, and 200 years under the Russians. Each of the historical periods shaped the future nation. And from the establishment of the Lithuanian Duchy, the Belarusians began to emerge as a new culture aside from the Ruthenians. The Ruthenian lands were the southern lands of the former Kievan Rus'. They differed from the northern Muscovite and Novgorodian lands in culture and dialect and had such names as Red, White, and Black Ruthenia, which would later become Ukraine, Belarus, and the Baltic states, respectively.

After the dissolution of Austria-Hungary, Slovenia joined the newly born Kingdom of Serbs, Croats, and Slovenes. Slovenian territories suffered significant destruction from its involvement in World War I battles. Instead of being divided among several powers, the Slovenes agreed to become a part of a new state.[59] However, the Slovenian capital—Ljubljana—had been untouched by the war and the country could enjoy a stronger economy than Serbia and Croatia in the period between the two world wars. Even though the region of Koroška in the north voted to join Austria in a referendum and Primorska on the west went to Italy under the Treaty of Rapallo, the Slovene economy and culture developed significantly during the 1920s—the main city saw the foundation of the University of Ljubljana, the National Gallery, and the Academy of Sciences and Arts.[60]

It all came to an end during the Axis invasion of Yugoslavia. Germany considered the Slovene territories as part of Styria, a former part of Austria and Italy that had claims over territories all over the Adriatic. After the invasion, Slovenia was partitioned among these three countries. World War II had taken a heavy toll on Slovenia—during the war many Slovenes fought a guerilla war against the Nazis under the leadership of the Communist resistance leader, Marshal Tito. The Slovenians lost 5 percent of the population.[61]

Slovenia made great progress under Yugoslavia's market-oriented "self-management" form of socialism. Slovenes made up less than 10 percent of Yugoslavia's population, produced 20 percent of the country's wealth, and generated 30 percent of its exports. By the 1980s, the Yugoslav economic system was in debt and stagnation, and resentment over the Belgrade central government's policy of distributing subsidies from the more prosperous northern republics to the less-affluent and often corrupt southern republics led to Yugoslavia's breakup.

Slovenia, deprived of a secure market and confronted with economic dislocation that forced Slovenes to compete for business in a broader market, started to show the weaknesses of its *socially owned* enterprises: featherbedding, limited professional skills, poor competitiveness, undercapitalization, outmoded production methods, and resistance to innovation. On the other hand, its modern infrastructure and its traditionally strong social discipline became countervailing factors.

In the early 21st century, the Slovene economy is based primarily on services and trade. The shift to a market economy has improved the standard of living in rural localities despite only modest changes in the traditional smallholding pattern of landownership. It has also produced a small group of newly wealthy individuals—*tajkuni* or tycoons. Most of the economy is now privatized, and a significant source of income comes from the manufacture of automotive parts, pharmaceuticals, and electrical appliances.

While some aspects of the former socialist rule have been maintained, the Slovene government has adopted several democratic measures, including a parliamentary form of government. The president is the head of state and supreme commander of the armed forces and cannot be elected for more than two five-year terms. Executive power is held by the prime minister and a 15-member cabinet. There are seven political parties in Slovenia that support ideologies ranging from the far right to the center-left. The majority of Slovenes, approximately 71 percent, identify themselves as Roman Catholic; Roman Catholicism has undoubtedly influenced Slovene culture more than any other religion.

Among the numerous commercial activities in Slovenia, tourism is of great importance. Slovenia's proximity to the Alps and the Mediterranean, along with its climate, makes it a popular tourist destination. The business derived from tourist hotels, ski resorts, golf courses, and horseback-riding centers provides employment for a growing number of Slovenes.[62]

Belarus went through the same circumstances and events—World War I, World War II, a nation inside a socialist state, independence. There were some crucial differences, though.[63] When World War I ended, another war erupted immediately between Russia and Poland, with Belarus and Ukraine caught in the middle. The Russians were ultimately defeated and forced to cede Western Ukraine and Western Belarus to Poland. Russia kept part of the remaining Eastern side, so "Belarus" was restricted to a small strip which included the capital city Minsk.[64] Over the 1920s, the Eastern territories were gradually returned to Belarus. However, some of the traditional Belarusian territories, such as the Smolensk and Bryansk regions, remain under Russian domination.[65]

Western Belarus was returned in 1939 right before the start of World War II and had to be integrated into the rest of the country. Only two years passed before the Eastern Front of World War II opened on the borders of Belarus. The war was catastrophic for the country—20–25 percent of the people died. The destroyed state was to be reconstructed from the ashes. It took 26 years to reach the pre-war level of population. Belarus became part of the USSR after 1945.

The economy recovered much faster—instrument-making, radio engineering, and radio-electronic industries were developed. The enterprises of these industries supplied electronic computers, optical, electrical, control devices, cinema equipment, TVs, watches, and more. Belarus became an assembly workshop of the Soviet Union. The chemical and petrochemical industry specialized in the production of mineral fertilizers, tires, plastics, and synthetic materials, mainly chemical fibers. The country hosted the largest production of potash fertilizers in the USSR.

In 1986, the nuclear accident at the Chernobyl power plant, which is only 150 kilometers from the Belarusian border with Ukraine, had a devastating effect on the Belarusian agricultural industry. As a result of the radiation, the agriculture sector in a large part of the country was destroyed, and many villages were abandoned. Since gaining its independence from the Soviet Union, Belarus has moved relatively slowly on privatization and other market reforms, emphasizing instead its close economic relations with Russia. About 80 percent of all industry remains in state hands, and foreign investment has been hindered by a political climate not always friendly toward business. The Russian financial crisis that began in autumn 1998 severely affected Belarus's Soviet-style planned economy. Belarus is almost completely dependent on Russia, which buys 70 percent of its exports.[66]

The movement toward a market economy in Belarus was slower than that of other former Soviet republics, with only a small percentage of state-run industry and agriculture privatized in the years following independence. Largely in response to this economic upheaval, Belarus sought closer economic ties with Russia. In the early 21st century, Russia remained a major trading partner, although relations between the countries had become tense as a result of disputes over the price of imported gas and oil.[67] And the last but not least fact—about half of Belarusians consider themselves non-religious or atheist. Roughly two-fifths of the population adheres to Eastern Orthodoxy, which, while not the official religion, maintains a privileged status in Belarus. Roman Catholics constitute the largest religious minority.

As we can see, Slovenia and Belarus have a lot in common and still Belarus is stagnating in life standards. Both countries were quite well-developed as part of a system of a larger federation and both had an issue, trying to diversify their economies to a broad market. Slovenia succeeded and Belarus slowed down. So, the reason is not in their development but in their history, geographical position, and the people themselves.

The main difference between those states since olden days is religion. Although Catholicism and Orthodoxy are branches of Christianity, Catholicism proved to be more flexible to changes while the main value of the second branch was conservatism. Those two values are great; however, if we speak about economics and technology, flexibility is more profitable. Conservatism still affects the Belarusians to some extent.

The second difference is geography. Slovenia enjoyed being a traffic hub in Europe, located close to the technologically and scientifically superior Western countries. It played the role of a bridge between eastern and western Europe. The country has always been strongly identified with central Europe, maintaining a balance between its Slavic culture and language and Western influences.

Belarus, which is situated much further to the east, lacking access to the sea hindered the speed of receiving any sort of useful goods and information from abroad. After the dissolution of the Soviet Union, several countries from the former Union and the Warsaw Pact would become a trade node between Russia and Europe. Poland achieved this goal first despite being in as bad an economic condition as Belarus.[68]

Slovenia chose to be more of a Western country and preserved its connections with the east and former Yugoslavian states. In fact, some of the most developed countries are main partners of Slovenia and have greatly helped to develop the country.[69]

Belarus, however, managed to exact some profit by being in the middle of the roads, connecting the European Union and Eastern countries with Russia. Actually, the first steps of the new country were to turn to the West, encouraging nationality, changing the coat of arms and flag to the historical ones, and introducing a new economic model—capitalism. The state didn't know exactly what to do with new possibilities and freedom. That was because the previous Belarusian model of economics was entirely based on a social economy and was a part of the system. The difference between Slovenia and Belarus at that stage was that Slovenia got stuck into another economic model, based on Titoism—the social model of Yugoslavia.

Yugoslavia was the first socialist country to attempt far-reaching economic reforms. Because of its early start and frequency of systemic changes, it was considered the most reformed socialist economy. For over 40 years, Yugoslavia tried to develop its own model of socialism based on workers' self-management, ample decentralization, social ownership, and increasing reliance on the market mechanism. Continuous experiments with economic reforms produced an economic system with specific characteristics based on a combination of socialist, self-managed, and market features, facilitated by the country's international relations. Another distinctive feature of Yugoslavia was that the socialist model emerged from a grassroots revolution led by Tito's partisans during World War II.[70]

This way, Slovenia was more ready than Belarus to change its politics and economy. Belarus went through the same first complicated years as an independent country. The state was being westernized, when an economic crisis occurred in the 1990s. Belarus stood between a longer path to further development and a quicker way—reconnection with Russia. What was supposed to be a temporary arrangement led to a prolonged union between Russia and Belarus until now.[71] While Russia supported the Belarusians, its influence became greater than was expected.

So the reasons for such a difference are as follows:

- History and religion, which had a huge impact on both countries.
- Geography, where Slovenia is a transit between the countries, comparable in size and force, and Belarus is a transit between the EU and huge Russia, with many ambitions on the Belarusians.
- The 20th-century historical developments outside of the two countries, which led Slovenia to end up with a social-capitalist economy and Belarus purely socialist.

- Belarusian culture, which sent it first into the EU's arms for quicker stabilization of its economy and later into the Russians' arms. Yes, it was the president's decision, but few people stopped him back then.
- Sitting between the EU and Russia, Belarus had still not decided which side to pick and consequently chose a social-capitalistic economy, whose disadvantages were already proved by Yugoslavia.
- The main one—Belarus intends to join the EU but closer ties with Russia and their influence only allow Belarus to withstand an unlikely accession.

The Belarusian opposition is not on the list, because they have already shown their inability to bring Belarusians together, nor to affect Belarusian culture. There may be a window, however. Any change of politics depends purely on the people, their culture. The situation with Crimea made many Belarusian elders turn to the EU instead of Russia, while the youth has always mainly supported integration into the EU. If not the opposition, the new generation of Belarusians will definitely strive toward Europe.

32. HAPPINESS: AND THE SEARCH FOR THE MODERN-DAY SHANGRI-LA

I argue that competitiveness is the right metric of a country's success, and that GDP is not. There is, however, a long list of alternatives to either one that we can use with more or less accuracy to measure prosperity. My main concern with these indicators is that in many cases those key performance indicators of a country are not easy to manage. For example, *The Economist*'s Quality of Life Index, or a country's stock market return. Some others only take into account a particular aspect of an economy, ignoring the other foundations of prosperity and economic success—for instance, the Ecological Footprint and the Environmental Sustainability Index. Some countries have made efforts to find the right metric that can be managed as well. However, in their attempt they leave economic development playing a secondary role, thereby jeopardizing the sustainability of the country's success. I am specifically referring here to Bhutan's Gross Happiness Index.

Bhutan: the happy country

The one-hour flight between Nepal's capital Kathmandu and the city of Paro in Bhutan is interesting for many reasons. The plane flies through the Himalayans so the view of Mount Everest is one of the most stunning that one can imagine. Besides, to go from one country to the other you have to adjust your watch by 15 minutes, the weirdest time difference due to the choice of standards made by Nepal. Furthermore, Paro has the reputation of being one of the most dangerous airports in the world, and only eight pilots are currently licensed to land there. The 2.5 kilometer runway is short by international standards and the pilot can only see the runway when the plane is about to touch the ground.

Nepal and Bhutan are also interesting countries to compare. Both have been monarchies for centuries, although Nepal only until 2001. Both are landlocked and surrounded by big neighbors such as India and China. Both have strong ties to the British Empire, even though they managed to remain independent for their whole history as nations. Both are natural beauties with tourism and the environment as prime industries. It is true that Nepal's population of 30 million exceeds by far the less than 1 million people in Bhutan; that Nepal is prominently Hinduist while Bhutan's official religion is Buddhism; and that their recent histories are massively different.

Nepal's last two decades have been marked by two disasters—one political and one natural. On June 2001, 10 members of the royal family, including King Birendra and Queen Aishawarya, were killed in a mass shooting during a family gathering allegedly committed by Crown Prince Dipendra. He also shot himself in the head and was severely wounded,[72] passing away three days later. His uncle Gyanendra (brother of King Birendra) was proclaimed king after the massacre.[73] Over the next years, his popularity fell as he deposed and appointed new governments at his will. Ultimately, in 2007, and after several rebellions, seven political parties (including the Maoist rebels themselves) declared Nepal a federal republic. In the first elections after Gyanendra was deposed, the Maoist won by a simple majority. Subsequently, different governments alternated and in February 2014 the country chose a prime minister from the Nepali Congress Party, which started working on a new constitution that was proclaimed in 2015.[74] During this period, corruption and bureaucracy became rampant. As one of my Nepali friends says: "with the Kings, we knew that they were stealing us, but they were only a few. Now there is a whole political class that is stealing and the coffer has not become bigger. We miss the King."

The second disaster occurred in April 2015, when a terrible earthquake with an epicenter 80 kilometers north of Kathmandu killed 9,000 and destroyed a big part of the country's already poor infrastructure. The reconstruction process is still going on, and it has required a significant amount of international investment. A voracious and corrupted public sector is not helping, and the life of the average Nepali citizen is becoming harder. For example, cars in a developing economy like Nepal are subject to a 150% tax, something that only people in countries such as Singapore can afford.

Not surprisingly, between 2000 and 2017, the average GDP per capita in constant international 2011 USD went to 2,456 from 1,539 (an average annual growth of 2.8%).

In the meantime, Bhutan grew from USD 3,538 to USD 8,536 (or 5.3% per year). It has not been as unlucky as Nepal, but it has followed a completely different path.

How did Bhutan do it?

Bhutan brands itself as the real Shangri-La

Shangri-La was a legendary, remote sanctuary where everyday life was steeped in spirituality and shared happiness, and where encircling, impenetrable mountains prevented the troubles of the world from entering. Such paradise was made popular in the West by the author James Hilton in his 1933 novel *Lost Horizon*. Hilton described Shangri-La as a mystical, harmonious valley enclosed in the rugged western end of the Kunlun Mountains, ruled with great benevolence by wise men who made their home in an opulent monastery. In the novel, the people who live in Shangri-La are almost immortal, living hundreds of years beyond the normal lifespan and only very slowly aging in appearance. If they leave Shangri-La, they rapidly grow old and die.

Shangri-La has become synonymous with any earthly paradise, particularly a mythical Himalayan utopia—a permanently happy but disciplined land, ringed by towering mountains, isolated from the world. Like many fictional creations, the story has deep roots in ancient myths; many scholars believe that the Shangri-La story can be traced back to Shambhala, a mythical kingdom in Tibetan Buddhist tradition.

Wouldn't it be amazing if there were a real country that was a peaceful, happy paradise, ringed by spectacular mountains, filled with people who were content, and ruled by a benevolent monarch?

It is unknown if this was his intent, but in 1972, during an interview with a British journalist for the *Financial Times* at Bombay airport, the then-king of Bhutan, Jigme Singye Wangchuck, said, "Gross national happiness is more important than gross national product."[75]

This was the beginning of the positioning of the Kingdom of Bhutan as the Land of Happiness. The foresightedness of the Happy King, as well as his subsequent heirs, has marked the history of Bhutan since.

At the time, Bhutan was a sleepy backwater kingdom sandwiched between the eastern arm of India to the south, Nepal to the west, Tibet to the north, and Arunachal Pradesh, a state of India, to the east. With only 38,394 square kilometers of landlocked, mountainous terrain, and a population of less than 800,000 (in neighboring China, there are 180 cities—*cities!*—with larger populations than all of Bhutan), Bhutan was never going to be an economic powerhouse. Today, it is classified by the United Nations as a "least developed country" (LDC). Such nations exhibit the lowest indicators of socioeconomic development, with the lowest Human Development Index ratings of all countries in the world. A country is classified among the least developed if it meets three criteria:

- Poverty—adjustable criterion based on gross national income (GNI) per capita averaged over three years. As of 2018, a country must have a GNI per capita less than USD 1,025 to be included on the list, and over USD 1,230 to graduate from it.
- Human resource weakness (based on indicators of nutrition, health, education, and adult literacy).
- Economic vulnerability (based on instability of agricultural production, instability of exports of goods and services, economic importance of non-traditional activities, merchandise export concentration, handicap of economic smallness, and the percentage of population displaced by natural disasters).[76]

Bhutan was added to the inaugural LDC list in 1971, a year before the king's announcement. As of December 2018, it was still there. Other nations on the list are all too familiar to people who watch the news: Afghanistan, Haiti, Mali, Myanmar, Somalia, Yemen.[77]

Bhutan's economy is based on agriculture, forestry, tourism, and the sale of hydroelectric power to India. Over half of the population depends on agriculture for their main livelihood. (By way of comparison, the last time that 50 percent of citizens in the United States were involved in agriculture was in 1880.)[78]

Agrarian practices consist largely of subsistence farming and animal husbandry. Handicrafts, particularly weaving and the manufacture of religious art for home altars, are a small cottage industry. Being landlocked, and with a topography mostly of steep and high mountains crisscrossed by a network of swift rivers forming deep valleys before draining into the Indian plains, the building of roads and other infrastructure is difficult and expensive.

There are no trains and not a single kilometer of railroad track. In contrast, the densely populated and highly developed island nation of Taiwan is slightly smaller than Bhutan in land area, and yet boasts 1,691 kilometers of rail that carry an average of 2.99 million passengers per day.[79]

Timber is important, as about 60 percent of the total land area is covered in forest. A permit is required before any tree can be chopped down, making Bhutan the most ecologically pure land in Asia and possibly the world.[80]

You could look at endless statistics about a nation, but the one statistic that matters above all others is the bottom line: How long do its citizens expect to live? Between birth and death, how many years do they get?

In terms of life expectancy, despite their relative poverty, the people of Bhutan are in the middle of the list. On the 2010–2015 UN list, the average citizen of Bhutan could expect to live 68.88 years, which put the mountain kingdom at #136 out of 201.[81] In 2018, the overall life expectancy had risen to 70.6 years—better than both India and Pakistan.[82]

The slow evolution toward a democratic constitutional monarchy

The development of Bhutanese democracy has been marked by the active encouragement and participation of reigning Bhutanese monarchs since the 1950s. The process of modernization and democratization was initiated by the Third King of Bhutan, Jigme Dorji Wangchuck (reigning from October 27, 1952 to July 21, 1972). Three years prior to his ascension to the throne, India and Bhutan had signed the Treaty of Peace and Friendship, which provided that India would not interfere in Bhutan's internal affairs as long as Bhutan accepted guidance from India in its foreign policy. This was the first international agreement that unambiguously recognized Bhutan's independence and sovereignty.

Early movement toward democratization began in 1952, when King Jigme Dorji Wangchuck established the 130-member National Assembly. Slavery was officially abolished, and the king endeavored to build foreign ties and for Bhutan to develop its own infrastructure with a series of five-year plans.

The Fourth King of Bhutan, Jigme Singye Wangchuck (reigning from July 24, 1972 to December 14, 2006), instituted political and legal reforms that have shaped the constitutional monarchy and democracy in Bhutan. But his reign also saw the enactment of restrictive citizenship laws and the expulsion and flight of thousands of Lhotshampa (ethnic Nepalese) refugees from Bhutan in the 1990s.

He also promulgated an increased emphasis on cultural assimilatory *driglam namzha* laws. The Driglam Namzha is the official behavior and dress code of Bhutan. It governs how citizens should dress in public and how they should behave in formal settings. It also regulates a number of cultural assets such as art and architecture. In English, *driglam* means "order, discipline, custom, rules, regimen," and *namzha* means "system." The term may be read as, "The Rules for Disciplined Behavior."

In 1989, the government elevated the status of the dress code from recommended to mandatory. All citizens were then required to observe the dress code in public during business hours (see Image 2.3).

Born February 21, 1980, Jigme Khesar Namgyel Wangchuck is the current reigning Druk Gyalpo or "Dragon King" of the Kingdom of Bhutan. After his father, Jigme Singye Wangchuck, abdicated the throne in his favor, he became king on December 9, 2006.

In July 2013, the country held its second general election, in which the former opposition People's Democratic Party gained a majority of the seats in the National Assembly, resulting in the country's first democratic transfer of power to the opposition. International election observers reported the elections were generally free and fair.

The most significant human rights issues include continued incarceration of Nepali-speaking political prisoners; restrictions on freedom of assembly and association; and the government's refusal to readmit certain refugees who asserted claims to Bhutanese citizenship.[83]

Image 2.3 The author with HE Lyonpo Loknath Sharma, Minister of Economic Affairs, Bhutan. Photo taken by the author

On the Cato Institute's Human Freedom Index 2018, Bhutan scored an overall 6.81 out of 10. The median of 162 countries in 2016 was 6.89. The index uses 79 distinct indicators of personal and economic freedom in areas including rule of law, safety, religion, freedom of assembly, and property rights.

Given its consistently middling economic and social welfare performance, out of all the nations on earth, why should Bhutan be focused on the happiness of its citizens?

It is because the government has made the promotion, cultivation, and measurement of citizen happiness a *national priority*.

Gross National Happiness (GNH)

In the 1970s, the young King Jigme Singye Wangchucthe began to promote the idea of gross national happiness as an alternative to the accepted idea that gross domestic product was the only way for a country to judge its success. This was part of a set of larger political reforms; he also believed in the legitimacy of public deliberation and discussion, and as a result, in 2008 the Kingdom of Bhutan became a constitutional monarchy and held its first vote for parliament.

The king's decision to focus on the happiness of his subjects was not simply invented; it was deeply rooted in Bhutanese tradition. Bhutan's legal code of 1729 stated that, "If the government cannot create happiness for its people, then there is no purpose for government to exist." The code stressed that Bhutanese laws must promote happiness for all sentient beings, and as a predominantly Buddhist nation, it was clear to the king that the cultivation of compassion stemmed from this ancient wisdom—that the focus needed to be on not only the economic progress of Bhutan, but also a "flourishing human society living in harmony with nature."

GNH aims to measure the quality of human life in a more holistic way and believes that the beneficial development of human society takes place when material and spiritual development occurs side by side.[84]

There were many other reasons why the king promoted the idea of gross national happiness. He wanted to ensure the traditional culture of Bhutan did not become a victim of mass modernization; that corruption in Bhutan was eradicated; and there was increased transparency between the government and the citizens of the country. The king stated that corruption had only started appearing when development in Bhutan started picking up; too many people, down to local government level, were corrupt, and he sought to end it and bring a new age of transparency to Bhutan.[85]

During the 1980s and 1990s, the king further elaborated the concept of GNH. He proclaimed that the development in Bhutan should be defined as a harmonious psychological, social, and economic environment that could lead to the blossoming of happiness.[86] Happiness itself should not only be related to individual fulfillment, but should also be a collective behavior that is touchable through the implementation of public policies.

When Bhutan embraced democracy in 2008, the Constitution of Bhutan, Article 9 further ensured the inclusion and continuity of GNH values by defining duties such as: "The State shall strive to promote those conditions that will enable the pursuit of Gross National Happiness." Therefore, Bhutan ensures enabling conditions for happiness to be the sole purpose of its development. Over the years, GNH has evolved from a noble aspiration into a more quantifiable tool, partly in response to the unexpected global attention it has garnered.[87]

A nation's happiness can be measured

Of course, "happiness" is a very broad term whose meaning and definition depend on culture, language, and society. Most definitions simply use synonyms to describe happiness, such as Webster's: "a state of well-being and contentment: joy; a pleasurable or satisfying experience."[88]

Aristotle said, "Happiness is a state of activity."[89]

Mahatma Gandhi said, "Happiness is when what you think, what you say, and what you do are in harmony."[90]

Jeremy Bentham, an 18th-century English philosopher, social reformer, and jurist, defined it as "the sum of pleasures and pains."[91]

Since the dawning of the Industrial Revolution, Western societies have assumed that having a high income is the key to personal happiness, because with more money you can buy more security, luxuries, and healthcare. Therefore, one way to measure the success of a nation is with its GDP. A high GDP indicates a wealthy country with high standards of living, income levels, and rate of employment, and therefore happier and more satisfied people.

According to the World Bank, in 2017 the nation with the highest GDP was the United States, followed by China, Japan, and Germany. Near the bottom of the list is Bhutan. But

Table 2.4 Bhutan Compared to Similar Economies

Nation	Population 2018	GDP 2018 (USD billion)
Bhutan	817,054	2.52
Macao SAR, China	632,418	50.36
Luxembourg	590,321	62.40
Guyana	789,508	3.62
Solomon Islands	635,254	1.30

Source: World Bank Development Indicators.

to be fair, its GDP should be compared not to giants like China and the United States but to nations with a similar population. Table 2.4 displays how Bhutan ranked with some nations of similar population.

As can be seen from Figure 2.6, the individual productivity of nations within a group can vary wildly, from very high to very low. But are people in Macao and Luxembourg 20 times *happier* than people in Bhutan and Guyana? Do high income and high GDP invariably lead to high happiness? Can a people be happy with a low GDP?

The Government of Bhutan says "yes," with a qualification:

Any discussion of the GNH in Bhutan must begin from the understanding that it is distinct from the Western literature on 'happiness' in two ways. First it is multi-dimensional—not focused only on subjective well-being to the exclusion of other dimensions—and second, it internalizes other regarding motivations.[92]

And as the first elected prime minister of Bhutan under the new Constitution of Bhutan, adopted in 2008, said,

We have now clearly distinguished the "happiness" … in GNH from the fleeting, pleasurable "feel good" moods so often associated with that term. We know that true abiding happiness cannot exist while others suffer, and comes only from serving others, living in harmony with nature, and realizing our innate wisdom and the true and brilliant nature of our own minds.[93]

How the GNH Index works

In creating the Gross National Happiness Index, Bhutan sought to create a measurement tool that would be useful for policymaking and create policy incentives for the government, NGOs, and businesses of Bhutan to increase GNH.

The GNH Index includes both traditional areas of socioeconomic concern such as living standards, health, and education, and less traditional aspects of culture and psychological well-being. It is a holistic reflection of the general well-being of the Bhutanese population rather than a subjective psychological ranking of "happiness" alone.[94]

Based on the Alkire–Foster methodology of multidimensional measurement, the GNH Index identifies four groups of people: unhappy, narrowly happy, extensively happy, and deeply happy. The analysis explores the happiness that people enjoy already, then focuses on how policies can increase happiness and sufficiency among the unhappy and narrowly happy people.

The GNH Index is implemented by the Gross National Happiness Commission, which is composed of the secretaries of each of the ministries of the government, the prime minister, and the secretary of the GNH Commission. The GNH Commission's tasks include conceiving and implementing the nation's five-year plan and promulgating policies.

The GHN Index is created from data collected in a massive national survey of citizens of Bhutan. The first GNH survey was conducted in 2008. It was followed by a second one in 2010, and a third in 2015. The GNH survey covers all 20 districts (*Dzonkhag*) and results are reported for varying demographic factors such as gender, age, abode, and occupation. The first GNH surveys consisted of long questionnaires that polled the citizens about living conditions and religious behavior, including questions about the times a person prayed in a day and other Karma indicators. It took several hours to complete one questionnaire. Later rounds of the GNH Index were shortened, but the survey retained the religious behavioral indicators.[95]

Here are a few excerpts from the 2015 Questionnaire.[96]

Question 15 relates to psychological well-being:
> *Q15. Please think deeply and tell me, what are the most important things (sources) that will make you lead a truly happy life?*

Question 22 asks:
> *Q22. How many people are very close to you that you can count on them if you …*
> - *Are sick*
> - *Have financial problems*
> - *Have emotional problems*
> - *Have to attend to important personal events (childbirth, funeral, wedding, etc.)*

Question 58 asks about barriers to healthcare:
> *Q58. On the last occasion you or your family visited a healthcare center within the past 12 months, how long did you have to wait before receiving the healthcare service?*

Question 80 is in the Good Governance section. A *zomdue* is a public meeting held periodically, at the village level, to discuss local issues. It asks:
> *Q80. In the past 12 months, have you attended a zomdue?*

Question 124 relates to ecological diversity and resilience:
> *Q124. Did an earthquake significantly affect you or your family or property in the past 12 months?*

Question 134 relates to financial security:
> *Q134. With your current total household income, how difficult or easy is it for you to manage your daily necessary expenses such as for food, shelter and clothing?*

The four pillars of GNH

As a public policy, Gross National Happiness is based on four pillars.

1. **Good governance.** Good governance is considered a pillar for happiness because it determines the conditions in which Bhutanese thrive. While policies and programs that are developed in Bhutan are generally in line with the values of GNH, there are also a number of tools and processes employed to ensure that the values are indeed embedded in social policy.

2. **Sustainable socioeconomic development.** A thriving GNH economy must value the social and economic contributions of households and families, free time, and leisure, given the roles of these factors in happiness.
3. **Preservation and promotion of culture.** Happiness is believed to be contributed to by preserving the Bhutanese culture. Developing cultural resilience, which can be understood as the culture's capacity to maintain and develop cultural identity, knowledge, and practices, and able to overcome challenges and difficulties from other norms and ideals.
4. **Environmental conservation.** Environmental conservation is considered a key contribution to GNH because in addition to providing critical services such as water and energy, the environment is believed to contribute to aesthetic and other stimuli that can be directly healing to people who enjoy vivid colors and light, an untainted breeze, and silence in nature's sound.[97]

The nine domains

The four pillars are further elaborated into nine domains, which articulate the different elements of GNH in detail and form the basis of GNH measurement, indices, and screening tools.

1. Living standards
2. Education
3. Health
4. Environment
5. Community vitality
6. Time-use
7. Psychological well-being
8. Good governance
9. Cultural resilience and promotion

These nine domains clearly demonstrate that from the perspective of GNH, many interrelated factors are important in creating the conditions for happiness. [98]

The nine domains are further supported by 33 indicators. The survey makes the analysis of the nation's well-being with each person's achievements in each indicator. In addition to analyzing the happiness and well-being of the people, it also guides how policies may be designed to further create enabling conditions for the weaker scoring results of the survey.

Criticism of Bhutan's GNH index

GNH has been described by critics as a propaganda tool used by the Bhutanese government to distract from the ethnic cleansing and human rights abuses it has committed. As writer Saurav Jung Thapa noted, "Between 1987 and 1992, the absolute monarchy and northern Drukpa elite carried out a systematic and sustained campaign of ethnic cleansing against its Lhotsampa minority who live mostly in the south."[99]

By 1992, an estimated 80,000 Bhutanese of Nepali ancestry had been pushed across the Bhutanese border into Indian territory.[100]

According to Human Rights Watch, "Over 100,000 people of Nepalese origin and Hindu faith, or 1/6 of the population of Bhutan, were expelled from the country because they would not integrate with Bhutan's Buddhist culture."[101]

The Government of Bhutan is clear about the rules under which its citizens must live. "Bhutan is a friendly and engaging place," wrote *The Economist* in 2004,

> but there is an Orwellian tinge to its government. Last month it became the first country to ban tobacco. Citizens must return to their village each year to obtain their identity card. Those who travel abroad surrender their passports on return and can reclaim them only by going to the capital, Thimphu.[102]

It is strictly forbidden to kill any animal (including fishing); however, the country imports tons of meat annually from India. Between religious freedom (Buddhism does not ban meat consumption) and environmental values, the country has chosen the latter.

Honestly, I have mixed feelings on whether measuring and managing happiness is conducive to real prosperity. Bhutan has made amazing achievements in terms of quality of life, but it is a small, closed economy whose future prospects are not economically glorious and where its major risks are a massive dependence on India and its physical proximity to China. As Minister Sharma told me, "we chose a middle path between capitalism and socialism. Our focus is not on industrialization, but on sustainable development." Essentially, public policy promotes happiness by reducing people's choices: they cannot smoke, travel easily, have same-sex relationships, dress any way they want. By not focusing on material wealth, they are also restricting the needs of the population, as one cannot aspire to what one cannot access. Whether the happy country remains economically sustainable is still an open question to me.

The concept of GNH spreads beyond Bhutan

No matter what you think of the Bhutanese version of happiness, there is no doubt that the concept of Gross National Happiness, first promulgated by King Jigme Singye Wangchuck, has been picked up by other nations, states, and even cities.

They include Victoria, British Columbia, where a shortened version of Bhutan's GNH survey was used by the local government. In Seattle, Washington, a version of the GNH Index was used by Seattle City Council and Sustainable Seattle; Eau Claire, Wisconsin; Creston, British Columbia; and the US state of Vermont, also used a version of the GNH Index.

In 2016, Thailand launched its own GNH Center. In the Philippines, bills have been filed in the Philippine Senate and House of Representatives in support of Gross National Happiness in the Philippines.

Many other cities and governments have undertaken efforts to measure happiness and well-being, including the national governments of the United Kingdom's Office of National Statistics and the United Arab Emirates; and cities including Somerville, Massachusetts, and Bristol, United Kingdom.[103]

The United Nations world happiness report

Compiled and edited by John F. Helliwell, Richard Layard, and Jeffrey D. Sachs, and published by the United Nations Sustainable Development Solutions Network, the annual *World Happiness Report* seeks to measure and quantify the degree of happiness in 156 nations of the world. The results are obtained by surveying 1,000 people in each nation per year. This is done in association with the Gallup World Poll.[104]

It all began in July 2011, when the United Nations General Assembly adopted resolution 65/309, "Happiness: Towards a Holistic Definition of Development," inviting member countries to measure the happiness of their people and to use the data to help guide public policy.

The first World Happiness Report was released on April 1, 2012, as a foundational text for the UN high-level meeting: Well-Being and Happiness: Defining a New Economic Paradigm.

The Gallup World Poll questionnaire measures 14 areas within its core questions: (1) business & economic, (2) citizen engagement, (3) communications & technology, (4) diversity (social issues), (5) education & families, (6) emotions (well-being), (7) environment & energy, (8) food & shelter, (9) government and politics, (10) law & order (safety), (11) health, (12) religion and ethics, (13) transportation, and (14) work.

As of March 2018, Finland was ranked the happiest country in the world, followed by Norway, Denmark, Iceland, and Switzerland. Bhutan came in at #97 out of 156, above Nepal (101), Bangladesh (115), Myanmar (130), and India (133).

Regardless of how objectively happy the Bhutanese people are—perhaps seeing how *unhappy* their immediate neighbors are makes them feel better—it is undeniable that the idea of striving for national happiness, and trying to measure it, has captured the interest of the world. Today, the UN has declared a World Happiness Day. Experts and dignitaries attend World Happiness summits. Students enroll in happiness courses. Yale University offers a course in how to live a happy life. Citing Bhutan, the Delhi school system has added happiness to its curriculum.

There's even a Gross National Happiness Institute, a non-profit civil society organization (CSO) established with the purpose of promoting the science and education of happiness policies around the world. As they say on their website:

> The happiness movement begins with you, your family, friends, neighbors, colleagues and community. You take responsibility for your own happiness and for the happiness of the people you care about. The movement is about communication, education, and cooperation on promoting scientific-based policy decisions that contribute to our well-being and happiness.[105]

33. CONCLUSION: WE MANAGE WHAT WE CAN MEASURE

The last chapters have discussed the concept of competitiveness and I have argued that it is the best measure of the performance of a country that we can use today. First of all, we understand very well what the inputs of a competitive model are and can therefore compare—and thus benchmark—countries. Second, we have discussed that the black box that converts inputs into outputs is complex but in essence consists of two technologies. The first one is a productive and efficient economic system. Without performing productive activities, there is no way a society can create value. Even if valuable natural resources are endlessly available, a nation will need investments to extract them, access to international markets to monetize them, governmental institutions to distribute the gains, and leadership and governance in order to secure that all these resources are not wasted against the interests of future generations. That is why the second technology that converts inputs into prosperity is the set of institutions, values, and regulations that promote job creation and individual quality of life. In that context, competitiveness refers to the ability of a nation to generate value for its citizens. It boils down to national policy to define what value is: for some economies (China) it will be job creation and economic growth; or happiness (Bhutan); for some others (Norway, Sweden) it will be social welfare and sustainability; for a few (Maduro's Venezuela, Lula's Brazil) it will be about providing minimum resources for the majority of the population in order to guarantee the survival of a non-inclusive elite. In all cases, the common denominator in all these approaches to competitiveness is inclusive prosperity: fairness, quality of life for people, promotion of talent, preservation of physical health, provision of high-quality infrastructure, absence of extracting minorities (corruption), and provision of financial resources for companies and citizens.

These are all the ingredients of a country strategy. That is why, in the next part, I characterize what a good country strategy is.

NOTES

1 IMD, World Economic Outlook, May 2000—Chapter V: The World Economy in the Twentieth Century 1/32.
2 China, indeed, displays positive GDP per capita growth in all but two years between 1968 and 2017. The question is to what extent one can trust Chinese statistics.
3 World Bank Group, "The Human Capital Project," 2018.
4 Mankiw (2010).
5 Kuznets (1934).
6 Siggel (2006).
7 Porter (1990).
8 Nadal-Belda, Alberto (2005), "La Competitividad de la Economía Española," *Revista del Instituto de Comercio Exterior*, 438–452.
9 Martín, César (2014), "¿Qué es la Competitividad de un País?" *Revista Índice*, 6–8.
10 Porter et al. (2008).
11 Global Competitiveness Report, www3.weforum.org/docs/GCR2017-2018/05FullReport/Th eGlobalCompetitivenessReport2017%E2%80%932018.pdf, last accessed January 7, 2019.
12 Porter (1990).
13 Paul Krugman (1994).
14 OECD (1992).
15 CIA Factbook.
16 However bleak North Korea's future looks, one thing that's for sure is that China will play a key role in determining it. If and only if China decides that the DPRK is not sustainable, it will not be. Reform, domestically driven change, or a social revolution, all currently seem unthinkable. The experience in Europe with West and East Germany, and the dissolution of the USSR, are not applicable to the two Koreas. The two countries have evolved too far apart, and their political systems are incompatible. North Koreans live like South Koreans did 50 years ago while South Korea has become one of the world's most developed nations. North Korea has stagnated into nothingness.

Consequently, only through a gradual and cautious re-establishment of the relationships between the two Koreas will we see an improvement in the quality of life of North Koreans. A glimmer of hope has been sparked by the two sides' expressed wishes to form a type of confederation. In the foreseeable future, we could see the border between the countries being reopened for people and goods. And the dream in two or three generations is that, as China Mainland and Hong Kong did, we end up with "one country, two systems."
17 www.cnbc.com/2016/05/18/i-got-2-out-of-4-countries-right-mr-bric-jim-oneill-says.html.
18 In 2010, there were only 58 economies in our ranking, and we obtained stock prices from Datastream for only 47 of these.
19 Khanna (2008).
20 World Atlas, www.worldatlas.com/articles/countries-with-the-most-natural-resources.html, last consulted on December 10, 2018.
21 OPEC, www.opec.org/opec_web/en/data_graphs/330.htm, last consulted on December 10, 2018.

22 World Atlas, www.worldatlas.com/articles/countries-with-the-most-natural-resources.html, last consulted on December 10, 2018.
23 Swali Arica, http://blog.swaliafrica.com/dr-congo-richest-in-resources-yet-poorest-country -in-the-world/, last consulted on December 10, 2018.
24 Morton (2016).
25 Source: World Bank Development Indicators.
26 *Arabian Business*, July 23, 2017.
27 Studwell (2013), 63.
28 www.bbc.com/news/business-32028693.
29 Maddison (2017).
30 Ibid.
31 Ibid and World Bank Development Indicators.
32 https://positivemoney.org/2016/03/bis-warns-of-a-global-debt-crisis-and-a-lack-of-policy-r esponse-options-time-to-update-the-boes-policy-toolkit/.
33 Reinhart and Rogoff (2009a, b).
34 Bank of England (2014).
35 Gopinath et al. (2017).
36 Riley et al. (2015); Barnett et al. (2014a, 2014b).
37 www.technology.org/2017/09/18/cell-phone-cost-comparison-timeline/.
38 McKinsey Global Institute (2018).
39 Bank of England (2014).
40 Comin and Hobijn (2010).
41 The relationship between wages and productivity has been part of economic theory for a long time. In his book *The Wealth of Nations* (1776), the Scottish philosopher Adam Smith thought that wages were determined naturally by two forces, of supply and demand. In practice, this simple definition implies that wages are a legal agreement between workers and employers. Thus, wages also reflect the level of payment representing workers' willingness to give up their leisure for work instead. As economic research is developing, wage is defined as the marginal productivity of labor. In the ideal world of an economy with no government intervention, no frictions, and no external shocks, the level of wage should equal the marginal productivity of labor.
42 Stansbury, Anna, and Lawrence H. Summers (2018). "Productivity and Pay: Is the Link Broken?," Peterson Institute for International Economics working paper 18-5.
43 Other academic work has documented the same phenomenon for other countries. Sharpe et al. (2008) from the Centre for the Study of Living Standard find the same pattern in Canada. They argue that in the period 1980–2005, real wages of Canadian workers were stagnant while labor productivity increased by 37 percent. See Schwellnus et al. (2017); Vaisburd et al. (2016); Tamasauskiene and Stankaityte (2013) for the UK and OECD countries. Other interesting studies are Bosworth and Perry (1994); Fisher and Hostland (2002); Blanchard and Giavazzi (2003); and Passimeni (2008).
44 Stansbury and Summers (2018).
45 See references in Stansbury and Summers (2018).
46 Snap Inc.'s preliminary prospectus, available at www.sec.gov/Archives/edgar/data/1564408/ 000119312517029199/d270216ds1.htm#rom270216_6.
47 Ibid.
48 *The New York Times*, February 3, 2017.
49 Source: Council of Institutional Investors.
50 Graetz and Michales (2018).
51 OECD (2017).
52 There are other studies that also provide some evidence regarding the positive impact of automation on labor employment. For example, the study from Zierahn et al. (2016) reveals that automation created over 10 million jobs in European countries during 1999–2010.
53 International Federation of Robotics (2017). "Key Messages: The Impact of Robots on Productivity, Employment, and Jobs," available at https://ifr.org/img/office/Robots_and_Jo bs_Key_Messages.pdf.
54 McKinsey Global Institute (2017).
55 Ibid.

56 Graeber (2018).

57 Pilling (2018).

58 Slovenia ranked #48 in the 2018 IMD World Competitiveness Rankings. Belarus is not included in either the IMD or the WEF rankings because of the low quality of their statistical data.

59 www.slovenia.si/slovenia/history/the-state-of-slovenes-croats-and-serbs/,   last   accessed January 2, 2019.

60 www.ljubljana.si/en/about-ljubljana/history-of-ljubljana/restless-20th-century/, last accessed January 2, 2019.

61 www.elitepropertyslovenia.com/a-history-of-slovenia, last accessed January 2, 2019.

62 www.britannica.com/place/Slovenia.

63 A fantastic tool to explore the history of Belarus is http://map.letapis.by/en/#1295.

64 www.economist.com/europe/2005/06/16/bordering-on-madness.

65 http://map.letapis.by/en/#19210318.

66 www.everyculture.com/A-Bo/Belarus.html.

67 www.britannica.com/place/Belarus.

68 https://mfa.gov.pl/en/p/msz_en/foreign_policy/europe/european_union/poland_ineu/centr e_of_europe/?channel=www.

69 www.themeditelegraph.com/en/markets/finance-and-politics/2018/04/21/germany-and-austria-pull-slovenian-economy-itZvllXMJpA8i4VUTgqvkN/index.html.

70 https://doc-research.org/2018/03/rise-fall-market-socialism-yugoslavia/.

71 http://mfa.gov.by/en/courtiers/russia/.

72 Interestingly, the investigation that ensued reported that Prince Dipendra had two bullet wounds, which makes it difficult to believe he inflicted them himself.

73 BBC News, June 2, 2001.

74 Source: https://en.wikipedia.org/wiki/History_of_Nepal, last accessed April 6, 2019.

75 Dorji, Tashi (15 June 2012), "The story of a king, a poor country, and a rich idea," *Business Bhutan.*

76 UN Economic Analysis & Policy Division, "Criteria for Identification of LDCs," www.un.org /development/desa/dpad/least-developed-country-category/ldc-criteria.html.

77 United Nations, "List of Least Developed Countries (as of December 2018)," www.un.org/ development/desa/dpad/wp-content/uploads/sites/45/publication/ldc_list.pdf.

78 Ezra Klein (2014), "40 maps that explain food in America." Vox.com., www.vox.com/a/ explain-food-america.

79 Wikipedia. https://en.wikipedia.org/wiki/Rail_transport_in_Taiwan.

80 BBC News (1998), "Country profile—Bhutan: A land frozen in time," http://news.bbc.co.uk/2 /hi/country_profile/54627.stm.

81 United Nations Department of Economic and Social Affairs (2015), "United Nations World Population Prospects: 2015 Revision."

82 Indexmundi.com, "Bhutan Demographics Profile 2018." www.indexmundi.com/bhutan/ demographics_profile.html.

83 US Department of State. "Bhutan 2017 Human Rights Report," www.state.gov/documents/o rganization/277523.pdf.

84 GNH Centre Bhutan, "History of GNH," www.gnhcentrebhutan.org/what-is-gnh/history-of -gnh/.

85 G. Dorji (2015), "The origins of GNH," www.kuenselonline.com/the-origins-of-gnh/.

86 Allison (2012).

87 GNH Centre Bhutan, "History of GNH."

88 Merriam-Webster, www.merriam-webster.com/dictionary/happiness.

89 Goodreads quotes, www.goodreads.com/quotes/31240-happiness-is-a-state-of-activity.

90 Ibid.

91 Munich Personal RePEc Archive (2017), "Measures of Gross National Happiness," https://mp ra.ub.uni-muenchen.de/11280/1/MPRA_paper_11280.pdf.

92 The Centre for Bhutan Studies, (2012), "A Short Guide to Gross National Happiness Index," www.grossnationalhappiness.com/wp-content/uploads/2012/04/Short-GNH-Index-edited .pdf.

93 Opening Address of 'Educating for Gross National Happiness' Conference: Lyonchhen Jigmi Y. Thinley, Thimphu, Bhutan (2009).

94 Oxford Poverty & Human Development Initiative, "Bhutan's Gross National Happiness Index," https://ophi.org.uk/policy/national-policy/gross-national-happiness-index/.
95 The Centre for Bhutan Studies, (2012), "A Short Guide to Gross National Happiness Index," www.grossnationalhappiness.com/wp-content/uploads/2012/04/Short-GNH-Index-edited .pdf.
96 Centre for Bhutan Studies and GNH Research (2014), "The Third Gross National Happiness Survey Questionnaire."
97 GNH Centre Bhutan, www.gnhcentrebhutan.org/what-is-gnh/the-4-pillars-of-gnh/.
98 Ibid.
99 Saurav Jung Thapa (2011), "Bhutan's Hoax: Of Gross National Happiness," https://web.arc hive.org/web/20110713000732/http://wavemag.com.np/issue/article3775.html.
100 Kai Bird, "The Enigma of Bhutan," *The Nation*, www.thenation.com/article/enigma-bhutan/.
101 Bill Frelick (2008), "Bhutan's ethnic cleansing," *New Statesman*, www.hrw.org/news/2008 /02/01/bhutans-ethnic-cleansing.
102 *The Economist* (2004), "The pursuit of happiness," www.economist.com/christmas-specials /2004/12/16/the-pursuit-of-happiness.
103 Wikipedia, https://en.wikipedia.org/wiki/Gross_National_Happiness#cite_note-60.
104 2018 World Happiness Report, https://s3.amazonaws.com/happiness-report/2018/WHR _web.pdf.
105 GNH Institute. "About the Gross National Happiness Institute," http://gnh.institute/about-gro ss-national-happiness-gnh-institute-happiness-movement.htm, accessed February 9, 2019.

REFERENCES

Allison, Elizabeth (2012), *Gross National Happiness* (Great Barrington, MA: Berkshire Publishing Group).
Atkinson, Robert D. (2013), ¨Competitiveness, Innovation and Productivity: Clearing up the Confusion, *Information Technology and Innovation Foundation)*
Bank of England (2014), "The Productivity Puzzle," *Investment News: Monthly News Bulletin*.
Barnett, Alina et al. (2014a), "Impaired Capital Reallocation and Productivity," *National Institute Economic Review* 228(1): 35–48.
Barnett, Alina, Sandra Batten, Adrian Chiu, Jeremy Franklin, and Maria Sebastiá-Barriel (2014b), "The UK productivity puzzle," *Bank of England Quarterly Bulletin* 54 (2): 114–128.
Blanchard, Olivier, and Francesco Giavazzi (2003), "Macroeconomic Effects of Regulation and Deregulation in Goods and Labor Markets," *Quarterly Journal of Economics* 118(3): 879–909.
Bosworth, Barry, and George L. Perry (1994), "Productivity and Real Wages: Is There a Puzzle?," *Brookings Papers on Economic Activity* 25(1): 317–343.
Comin, Diego, and Bart Hobijn (2010), "An Exploration of Technology Diffusion," *American Economic Review* 100: 2031–2059.
Competitiveness Advisory Group-Ciampi Group (1995), "Enhancing European Competitiveness," *First report to the President of the Commission, the Prime Ministers and the Heads of State*.
Cowen, Tyler (2011), *The Great Stagnation: How America Ate All the Low-Hanging Fruit of Modern History, Got Sick, and Will (Eventually) Feel Better* (New York: Penguin Group).
Decker, Ryan A., John Halriwanger, Ron S. Jarmin, and Javier Miranda (2016), "Where Has All the Skewness Gone? The Decline in High-Growth (Young) Firms in the U.S.," *European Economic Review* 86: 4–23.
Fisher, Tony, and Doug Hostland (2002), "The Long View: Labor Productivity, Labor Income and Living Standards in Canada," in Sharpe, Andrew et al. (eds.), *The Review of Economic Performance and Social Progress 2002: Towards a Social Understanding of Productivity* (Montreal: Institute for Research on Public Policy).
Gopinath, Gita, Şebnem Kalemli-Özcan, Loukas Karabarbounis, and Carolina Villegas-Sanchez (2017), "Capital Allocation and Productivity in South Europe," *Quarterly Journal of Economics* 132(4): 1915–1967.

Gordon, Robert J. (2012), Is U.S. Economic Growth Over? Faltering Innovation Confronts the Six Headwinds (No. 18315). NBER Working Paper, August.

Graeber, David (2018), *Bullshit Jobs: A Theory* (New York: Simon & Schuster).

Graetz, Georg, and Guy Michaels (2018), *Robots at Work* (No. 1335). Centre for Economic Performance, London School of Economics, CEP Discussion Paper.

Khanna, Parag (2008), *The Second World: How Emerging Powers Are Redefining Global Competition in the Twenty-first Century* (New York: Random House).

Krugman, Paul (1994), "Competitiveness: A Dangerous Obsession," *Foreign Affairs* 73(2): 28–44.

Kuznets, Simon (1934), "National Income 1929–1932. A report to the U.S. Senate,' in 73rd Congress, Second Session (Washington, DC: U.S. Government Printing Office).

Mankiw, N. Gregory. (2010), *Macroeconomics*, 7th Edition (New York: Worth Publishers).

McKinsey Global Institute (2017), *A Future that Works: Automation, Employment and Productivity*.

McKinsey Global Institute (2018), *Solving the Productivity Puzzle: The Role of Demand and the Promise of Digitation*.

Organisation for Economic Co-operation and Development (OECD) (1992), *Technology and the Economy: The Key Relationships*. (Paris, France: OECD).

OECD (2017), *The Risk of Automation for Jobs in OECD Countries: A Comparative Analysis* (Paris, France: OECD).

Pilling, David (2018), *The Growth Delusion: Wealth, Poverty, and the Well-Being of Nations* (New York: Tim Duggan Books).

Porter, Michael E. (1990), *The Competitive Advantage of Nations* (New York: Free Press).

Porter, Michael E. et al. (2008), "Moving to a New Global Competitiveness Index," in Porter, Michael E., and Klaus Schwab (eds.), *Global Competitiveness Report 2008–2009*, World Economic Forum, 43–63.

Reinhart, Carmen M., and Kenneth S. Rogoff (2009), "The Aftermath of Financial Crises," *American Economic Review* 99(2): 466–72.

Reinhart, Carmen M., and Kenneth S. Rogoff (2009), *This Time is Different: Eight Centuries of Financial Folly* (Princeton, NJ: Princeton University Press).

Riley, Rebecca, and Chiara Rosazza-Bondibene (2015), *The UK Productivity Puzzle 2008–2013: Evidence From British Businesses*, NIESR Discussion Paper.

Schwellnus, Cyrille, Andreas Kappeler, and Pierre-Alain Pionnier (2017), *Decoupling of Wages from Productivity: Macro-Level Facts* (No. 1373). Economics Department Working Papers, OECD.

Sharpe, A., J.F. Arsenault, and P. Harrison (2008), *The Relationship Between Labor Productivity and real Wage Growth in Canada and OECD Countries*, Research Report. Centre for the Study of Living Standards (CSLS).

Siggel, Eckhard (2006), "International Competitiveness and Comparative Advantage: A Survey and a Proposal for Measurement," *Journal of Industry, Competition and Trade* 6: 137–159.

Tamasauskiene, Zita, and Aiste Stankaityte (2013), "Evaluating of the Relationship between Wages and Labour Productivity in Lithuania: Territorial and Sectoral Approaches" working paper, Faculty of Social Sciences, Siauliai University.

Vaisburd, Victor A. et al. (2016), "Productivity of Labour and Salaries in Russia: Problems and Solutions," *International Journal of Economics and Financial Issues* 6(S5): 157–165.

Part 3
What it takes to have a national strategy

34. INTRODUCTION

That I require a country strategy should not be interpreted as a defense of planned economies as a recipe for success. A strategy can consist of an industrial policy completely led by the private sector, or a list of a country's unique and differentiating assets that all politicians preserve and promote over time. On the contrary, there is no country that becomes competitive by chance—inclusive prosperity is the result of stable, long-lasting, agreed-upon, and based-on-a-vision choices and policies.

Therefore, the first prerequisite of competitiveness is a country strategy. In the next chapters, I describe the ingredients of a good strategy. I do not deviate from the concept of strategy that corporate executives and business consultants use and promote. First of all, a strategy cannot be just aspirational—it must be winnable and henceforth realistic given a country's starting conditions. A country strategy must be based on the uniqueness of the country itself, whether it is its natural resources, intangible infrastructure, historical legacy, or political constraints. As I claim in earlier chapters, many governments try to replicate what others have already done successfully. This is not enough. Today, politicians are learning from each other, and this is desirable as long as it pertains to some aspect of economic policy. For instance, Estonia has become the role model of e-government, attracting numerous government delegations to visit each year (so that Estonia has opened a showroom to display its achievements). Israel is today a model of innovation and fintech, and Tel Aviv is the ecosystem that everybody wants to copy. When it comes to the promotion of tourism, Thailand is the country of reference, and Singapore is the world reference for education, artificial intelligence, smart city policies, and the structure of government departments. But as a systematic, comprehensive choice of vision and choices in all dimensions, there is no perfect example that fits all economic conditions, endowments, and cultures.

The requirements of a country strategy are surprisingly obvious. However, very often, governments—especially in democratic regimes—ignore strategy and focus on tactics. Short-term approaches to economic growth and prosperity are useless, particularly when they are based on partisan ideology. A first and essential ingredient of a country strategy is national consensus—the shared understanding of what the country needs. When implementing policies, politicians will often ignore that building consensus comes first. We will discuss extensively the challenges of building a national consensus with several examples—Lithuania, in particular, but also Mexico, South Africa, France, Finland, Portugal, and India. I will clearly distinguish between dictatorships and democracies— in dictatorships, building consensus is very easy because politicians are not exposed to social accountability and opposing views. The future challenge of democracies is how to preserve consensus over time, or what I will call *policy stability*—which is not the same as *political stability*. Switzerland, the Netherlands, the United States, and Norway are all examples that come to mind of countries with fundamental political choices that are independent of the volatility of an electoral process.

Because strategies are long term by definition, there are two requirements to make them long-lasting. One is political leadership. By that I refer to the selflessness, vision, generosity, and commitment of individuals who make a difference in their countries. I will share examples of not only historical figures such as Winston Churchill and Franklin Roosevelt, but also the more recent examples of Lee-Kuan Yew (founder of Singapore) and other benevolent dictators, as well as Maksim Liksutov (head of the Transport Department of the city of Moscow).

The second ingredient is having a long-term view. This is obviously complementary to the previous one, but most often the lack of a long-term vision is a consequence of the political system. If I am exposed to re-election every four years (or worse, if I cannot be re-elected), my incentives to implement long-term policies are non-existent. That is why discussing the case of Mayor Marty Walsh of Boston is extremely interesting in my opinion. Despite the constraints of a demanding political process for re-election, he has committed to a strategy for Boston to be completed by 2030.

There are two other important aspects to consider. One is the importance of execution—at the end of the day, policies have to be implemented. The second issue is the recent phenomenon of business consultants involved in designing country policies and strategies. To me, this is one of the most pervasive behaviors of politicians because it denotes a lack of vision, commitment, personal leadership, long-term view, and inability to build a consensus. The involvement of consultants in public policy is very seldom described, so I go into details about it, especially in some countries.

To start, let us describe a poster child of a good strategy—Abenomics.

35. A GOOD STRATEGY

Every time we receive a government delegation in our center, I always ask the same question: "What is your country strategy?" Sometimes, answers are too vague, like, "We want to be the Switzerland of Latin America" or "We aim to attract capital to our nation." Other times, politicians take too long to answer and provide a one-hour presentation about the country's present and future achievements, but lack a clear vision, objectives, key performance indicators (KPIs), and relevant policy decisions. A few times, the country completely lacks a strategy.

In these situations, I follow the *Strategy-In-One-Slide rule*: if our visitor is able to produce a single page describing the country strategy—and such that we can understand it—then the country passes the first test in our competitive assessment and we can move on to analyzing detailed policies. This is no different than what we do with our corporate clients, but in the case of a government, it should be much easier to formulate because planning departments are humongous in some countries and hundreds of people are full-time devoted to deciding, planning, and executing.

For an example of a non-strategy document, check the 1,000-page document that McKinsey produced for the Government of Lebanon (more about it later).[1] Abenomics, being more comprehensive, can be summarized in one page.

The strategy-in-one-slide rule: Japan as a poster child

The Japanese economy

In terms of the size of gross domestic product (GDP), Japan is the third largest economy in the world, after the United States and China. Together with Germany and South Korea, this country was once recorded as one of the fastest growing in the world's history. Japanese growth during 1960–1980 gave the country the consideration of a "growth miracle." The Japanese economy relies heavily on some industries. The core industries are banking, insurance, real estate, retail, transportation, telecommunication, and construction. Japan also operates highly technological industries such as automotive, electronic, steel, machineries, chemical, textile, and foods. Japan is also a substantial player in various research and robotics industries. As an advanced economy, around 75 percent of the country's GDP is generated through the service sector.

As the second most advanced economy after the United States, Japan is the only Asian country included in the G8. Japan is also a member of some international organizations such as the United Nations, the Organization for Economic and Cultural Development (OECD), the Asia-Pacific Economic Cooperation (APEC), and the Association of Southeast Asian Nations (ASEAN) plus 3. In international trading, Japan is the fourth biggest exporter as well as the sixth biggest importer in the world. Many analysts predict that Japan, South Korea, India, and China will outperform the supremacy of Western countries in dominating the global economy.

In 2018, Japan was ranked the 25th most competitive economy (out of 63 countries) in the world. The country also placed 39th in ease of doing business index (out of 190 countries), based on a World Bank report. Hence, despite its stagnant economic performance judged by many economists and policymakers nowadays, it is undeniable that the growth miracle has laid a strong foundation for Japanese competitiveness at the level that other nations are still dreaming today. Thus, understanding how this country's economic strategy works, how to measure it, and how to implement the strategy is considered beneficial to present in this book.

The Japanese economic miracle

After World War II, Japanese economic growth rapidly accelerated, up to 10 percent on average over four decades before it diminished following the 1990s' economic crisis that hit the country.

The story of the Japanese growth miracle started after the country's defeat in World War II. At that time, the country experienced great suffering as all resources were spent on financing the military Japan suffered tremendously at the time, both economically and socially. Starvation, malfunctioning production activity, soaring inflation, and a high unemployment rate left the country behind in the development of Western civilization. During the suffering, the allied American forces stepped in and occupied the country. However, the occupation of the country was not followed by the replacement of the Japanese government, meaning that the Japanese government was submissive to American directions. The American occupation was a turning point of further reforms taking place in the country. At least four major reforms were implemented during the American occupation in an effort to revive the country's economy.

First, the United States implemented demilitarization reform in Japan, to stop Japan from continuing to expand its military expenditure, produce domestic military equipment, and force people to war. Through demilitarization, Japan could temporarily concentrate on not involving itself in further war, while gaining protection from American occupation.

The second reform was to promote market liberalization. The market in the Japanese economy at the time was not competitive at all. Some family companies monopolized the economy as a giant cartel known as Zaibatsu, governing such aspects as manufacturing companies, financial services, and production sectors. Zaibatsu was also served well by the government through lower taxes, creating large social inequality. Although its role in making the market inefficient was not preferred, Zaibatsu played an eminent role in supporting military expenditure during World War II. One major reform to liberalize the

Japanese market was to break up Zaibatsu holdings by selling its stocks to the public. In this way, the power of the cartel was significantly minimized, and the entry barrier was loosened, reviving competition among companies and making the price of goods more competitive.

The third reform was to prevent landlords from charging rental prices to farmers. This reform also promoted the redistribution of land to be held by farmers who were able to cultivate it very well. This way, the return from capital could be enhanced in a more effective way. Also, this reform encouraged the production of agricultural goods, which could then support the Japanese economy suffering from food problems.

The final reform that the Unites States initiated was labor reform through the formation of the labor union and consolidating its relationship with the internal management of companies. Before World War II, the style of management in most companies was very closed, as they were mostly working under family management. The breakup of Zaibatsu, followed by the increasing ownership of public shares, motivated labor to join the labor union and increased its competitiveness collectively. This way, labor could bargain its real wage more competitively and boost employment. Also, a stronger bond between labor and management made companies work better together.

These four reforms performed as the baseline for Japanese economic recovery after the war, having a positive effect on the Japanese economy. With a more competitive market, companies could increase their production, gain more profit, and enjoy higher salaries, which eventually boosted consumption and GDP. Furthermore, one important outcome of the implementation of the four reforms was the significant improvement in human capital performance. In addition to the four reforms, in 1948 the Unites States implemented the Dodge plan in Japan. Three sub-plans were introduced as part of the Dodge plan, namely, fiscal consolidation, suspension of loans, and abolition of subsidies. The three sub-plans were intended to dampen inflationary pressure on the Japanese economy and ensure that the national budget was powerful enough to support economic recovery.

However, although the four reforms worked well during the recovery, the significant gain happened when the Korean War broke out in 1950. During that period, given its stabilizing manufacturing companies, Japan received an abundant order of military tools to support the United States and other countries in the Korean War. Hence, Japan's production experienced an increase of up to 70 percent and provided the country with abundant income to further strengthen its economic recovery. In addition to the large stream of income, human capital in Japan also played an important role. The Japanese were very talented in replicating the technology they observed from imported products. Later, they implemented their understanding and improved similar technology into their own system. This intelligent strategy was able to refocus Japan to develop its technology and multiply its total factory productivity. Finally, with higher productivity, Japan multiplied its level of production and with even better quality, opened the door to more intense international trade and more income from export activity.

Finally, the political environment also supported the Japanese economy in reaching its growth miracle. Under the Hayato Ikeda administration, Japan experienced a heavy industrialization era by focusing on giving incentives to the production of manufacturing, electric power, coal, and steel. The government encouraged the role of the Ministry of International Trade and Industry to support the rapid expansion of Japanese industrial growth. Accordingly, the central bank of Japan also implemented an aggressive monetary policy by giving direct credit to banks, which then directed the funds to corresponding companies in those production sectors. The government also eradicated the rise of

Keiretsu, a monopoly power similar to Zaibatsu, in order to maintain market competitiveness in the economy. Overall, these series of reforms delivered Japan as the only Asian country equally competitive in comparison to Western civilization.

Japan's economic challenges

There is no perfect country on this planet, including Japan. The growth miracle that made Japan the leader among Asian countries faced its biggest challenge during the 1990s, when the asset price bubble crisis hit its economy. Since then, the Japanese economy has been gradually sluggish, posting downward economic growth and even worse, times when its economic growth has turned negative. Figure 3.1 illustrates the four biggest challenges that Japan is currently facing.

The first biggest challenge for the Japanese economy is its shrinking population. As shown in Figure 3.1, population growth in Japan is diminishing, even up to today. Improving life expectancy and falling birth rates mean smaller numbers in the next generations. This is surely a problem for the government, as population growth is the key to supplying more labor, expanding the tax base, increasing government income, and eventually accelerating GDP.

Furthermore, having continuous generation growth is also important to maintain the chain of innovation in the country, and more importantly, to maintain competitiveness in the long run with other countries. These potential benefits are starting to fade for the Japanese economy. As the old age dependency ratio (the number of those aged 65 years and above as a share of the total population) is expected to exceed 50 percent by 2030, Japan is threatened with high pressure on some expenditures in the future, such as pension funds, healthcare, social benefits programs, and so forth. Without a sufficient income stream from the working generation, these expenditures pose a serious problem. National competitiveness is also believed to be affected by this issue. For instance, according to the World Bank report, Japan's ease of doing business ranking has been worsening, from 13th in 2008 to 39th in 2018.

The economic impact of a shrinking population is also seen in Japan's GDP growth. Since 1990, when the crisis hit the economy, Japan's GDP growth has experienced a structural break, which is a permanent change on the path to its economic growth. Simply put, its GDP growth keeps weakening and reached its lowest level in 2008, which was when the US subprime crisis hit the global economy. At that time, Japan's economic growth had contracted by almost 6 percent. The persistent falling economic growth is primarily reinforced by another issue, namely, the deflationary expectation. As shown in Figure 3.1, inflation in the Japanese economy has been very low and even fell below zero after the recession of 1990. Numerous expansionary policy measures were activated, ranging from a very low official interest rate and tax incentives, to abundant credit injection, but they all ended up having an insignificant impact on the country's inflation rate.

Accelerating inflation is important because it is ideally reflecting increasing economic activity. As long as inflation is not overheating, having positive inflation is always preferred by any country. Therefore, the deflationary expectation in the Japanese economy implies that economic agents in the country strongly expect that the economy will continue to weaken in the future. Theoretically, this pessimistic perception also reflects how the Japanese do not easily believe in government promises. Or, it can also imply a problem with the central bank's credibility.

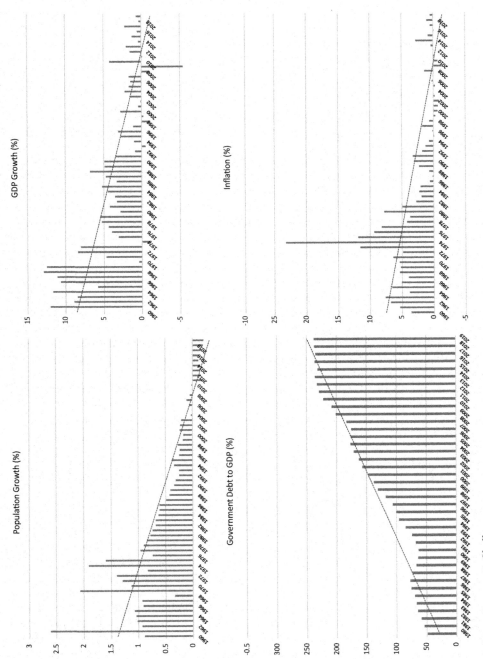

Figure 3.1 Japan Economic Challenges

Source: Datastream.

Higher expenditure on an elderly population amid a decreasing labor supply from younger generations forces Japan to rely on technology in maintaining its productivity. Unfortunately, that's not enough to fill the government budget deficit. Japan must also rely on public debt to maintain its sustainability, which makes the government debt to GDP ratio soar. Public debt is the amount of money that a country owes to lenders, including individuals, businesses, and even other governments. Higher public debt occurs because expenditure is higher than tax revenue. Hence, when a country experiences a consistently increasing public debt, this means that every year the government suffers from absorbing tax and must support the expenditures by borrowing from the public.

Actually, in the short run, public debt is a good way for a country to gain extra funds to support the economy. However, when debt is constantly rolled over, this can lead investors to question the country's repayment capacity. At that rate, investors can demand higher interest rates to compensate for the credit risk. Consequently, with higher interest rates, the ability to repay is reduced and the need for further indebtedness increases. In cases when the country is no longer able to sustain the debt pressure, that country can fall into a debt crisis. Since 1991, the ratio of debt to GDP in Japan has been increasing at a very high pace, which will eventually make the country the most indebted in the world, with total public debt accounting for 237 percent of its GDP in 2019.

Fortunately, up to this point, Japan's creditworthiness remains high in the eyes of investors, both local and foreign. In 2018, Standard & Poor's credit rating for Japan stood at A+, with a positive outlook. Similarly, Moody's credit rating also granted Japan an A1, with a stable outlook, while Fitch's credit rating gives Japan an A score, with a stable outlook. These strong credit ratings reflect how the country's fundamental confidence is resilient and that Japan remains as one of the safe havens for global investors.

There are some reasons why the most indebted country in the world can still stand with confidence among global economic players. First, although Japan's public debt is enormous, almost all of that debt is held domestically. In other words, Japan does not rely on foreign debt to finance its public sector. Over decades, around 60–70 percent of national debt is held by the Bank of Japan, while the rest is owned by trust and investment funds. Second, Japan consistently posts a surplus current account, which remains valuable to attract foreign direct investment. Japan's current account stayed positive at 1.82 trillion yen in 2018, with net foreign direct investment at 12.53 billion yen in the same year. Third, the government has made tremendous efforts to create sound macroeconomic policies—such as low interest rates, credit injection, and fiscal consolidation—to stimulate the Japanese economy. Investors consider that as a strong commitment to prevent the country's situation from worsening.[2]

The Japanese economy remains stable because people just believe so. However, that kind of bonding is not a permanent factor to guarantee that such trust will be long lasting. Thus, the public debt still needs a change of trajectory to further ensure investors that the economy is well managed. A study from the European Central Bank[3] states that risks from debt can have a negative impact on a country when its level has reached 70–80 percent of GDP, which Japan has long surpassed. One of the efforts that the Government of Japan is striving for is to increase inflation. By inducing inflationary pressure, the real value of debt can be depressed. Furthermore, the Japanese government is also struggling to boost its domestic economy with aggressive fiscal stimuli. These aggressive actions are well known as Abenomics, which is explained in detail below.[4]

Abenomics

As described previously, despite its economic glory in the past, Japan is now a normal country facing many challenges in maintaining its long-term competitiveness. Deflation, high government debt, and shrinking labor supply due to an aging population are the major hardships that the country's economy is dealing with nowadays. In tackling such economic issues, Japan's former prime minister, Shinzo Abe, endorsed a fundamentally new concept that he believes would put an end to the crisis—a strategy popularly known as Abenomics.

By the time he was elected and took office in November 2012, the prime minister decided to promote an intensive cooperation between the government and the Bank of Japan (BOJ), without losing independence from each other. Abenomics is known as the package of economic policies that focuses on the simultaneous implementation of three economic pillars, called "Arrows," to revive Japanese economic activity. The names of the three pillars are: aggressive monetary policy, flexible fiscal policy, and structural growth reform.

Since Abenomics was implemented in 2012, the Government of Japan claims that the country has achieved remarkable progress. For example, the nominal GDP grew positively from 496 trillion yen in 2012 to 432 trillion yen in 2015. The economy also experienced a declining unemployment rate, from 4.3 percent in 2012 to 3.1 percent in 2016. More importantly, the deflationary mindset is starting to diminish, which is shown by the improvement in the consumer price index (CPI) growth at 3 percent between 2012 and 2016. Furthermore, Japan's annual corporate ordinary profits also increased by 20 trillion yen from 2012 to 2015. Finally, the pace of government debt to GDP ratio has been stabilized since the strategy was implemented in 2012, increasing by only 12.4 percent between 2012 and 2016, compared to 46.2 percent in the period from 2008 to 2012.[5]

However, Abenomics is not a one-time implemented strategy. Rather, this is a strategy that needs continuous execution to ensure that its positive impact can be permanently embedded in the domestic economy. Therefore, before we jump into the recent result of what Abenomics has been achieving, it is important to understand how this strategy works.

The three arrows in Abenomics are depicted in Figure 3.2. The first arrow is aggressive monetary policy, which functions to dampen the deflationary mindset in the Japanese economy. The second arrow is the flexible fiscal discipline, which aims to boost domestic economic growth. Finally, the third arrow is structural growth reform, which aims to enhance labor productivity and improve societal norms to promote openness for investment. These three arrows are planned to work simultaneously and actively interact with each other. Let us dive deeper to explore each in greater detail.

Arrow 1: aggressive monetary policy

The first arrow is related to monetary policy, which surely goes to the responsibility of the BOJ. Before Abenomics began in 2012, the BOJ implemented a zero-policy rate to ensure that banks can lend and borrow money with low interest rates to each other. Additionally, the BOJ also pushed conventional quantitative easing by providing a credit stimulus to the financial sector with the hope to accelerate credit activity and raise inflation expectations in the future. Unfortunately, these two samples of policy formulations ended unsuccessfully. That is, deflation and low GDP growth still haunt the country's economy. Hence, the main objective of the first arrow is to get rid of the mindset of deflationary pressure from Japan's economy.[6]

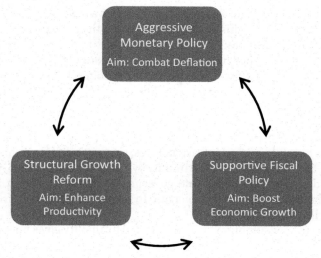

Figure 3.2 Japan's Abenomics.

Given the failure of conventional monetary policy, Abenomics acknowledges the need for a more aggressive one. This includes a series of policy interventions from the BOJ aiming to reach the long-term inflation target of 2 percent within two years. In realizing this, the first program that the BOJ executed was a significant asset purchase, in addition to a zero-policy rate. This program resulted in a massive increase in the monetary base, which went from 29 to 87 percent of GDP in the period 2012–2017. The rationale is that a higher monetary base increases inflation expectations, which subsequently expands government's tax base and revives economic growth.

If the base remains high in the long run, the BOJ needs to discourage investors from purchasing low-risk government bonds by expanding the average maturity of the assets held. Hence, the BOJ altered its asset maturity from three years to seven years on average and implemented the yield curve control (YCC) policy to keep 10-year government bonds' yield at zero. These policies were expected to encourage investors to invest in more short-term risky assets, such as stocks, thus creating inflationary expectations. Finally, the BOJ also consolidated all assets purchased under the previous BOJ governor into a single program to enhance the transparency of its policy.

In other words, to keep it simple, the mechanism in the first arrow is to flood the domestic economy with a surge of fresh money while forcing investors to take more risks in the short term. Therefore, with abundant money, inflation increases, the interest rate is pressured down, domestic currency can be weakened, exports rise, and the debt ratio of the government decreases.

Arrow 2: flexible fiscal policy

However, to ensure that Abenomics works, the other arrows must ensure that monetary policy has a significant impact on the real economy. The second arrow—expansionary fiscal policy—plays a major role in reconditioning the tax system and boosting domestic economic growth.

The aim of fiscal policy under Abenomics is to achieve "flexibility" between fiscal consolidation and fiscal stimulus. This flexibility means that the government budget plan must be adjustable enough to accommodate any emergency stimulus in the future. Practically, Abenomics' flexible fiscal policy intends to achieve a record 600 trillion yen of GDP and a primary surplus by 2020.[7] The fiscal policy also targets to reach 3 percent growth of nominal GDP and steady real economic growth by 2 percent. In realizing this, fiscal policy must design various fiscal stimuli and facilitate several government spending projects.[8]

The first fiscal stimulus was started in 2013 by spending 20.2 trillion yen on many government projects focusing on protecting citizens' lives and revitalizing citizens' environment, such as building critical infrastructures, bridges, buildings, etc. Following this, the government further increased its stimulus by injecting a separate 5.5 trillion yen in April 2014. Besides injecting money into government projects, another significant step in reducing the budget deficit was the increase in the consumption tax from 5 percent to 8 percent in April 2014.

The increase in the consumption tax was intended to amplify government revenue, but it ended up having an adverse impact on the country's economy and pushed Abe to reschedule the tax increase to April 2017 instead of the originally planned date of October 2015.[9]

Arrow 3: structural growth reform

The third arrow in Abenomics is known as structural growth reform. That is, this arrow focuses on reforming working values and structural regulation that hinder the Japanese from being more productive and attracting foreign investment (see Figure 3.3). We might

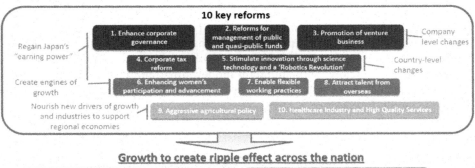

Figure 3.3 Abenomics: The Third Arrow in One Slide

Source: Prime Minister's Office of Japan.

question how one of the richest countries in the world still needs such reforms. As we will see if we take a closer look, Japanese working values are still facing many obstacles, indeed.

Historically, a rigid bureaucratic system plays a significant part in Japanese corporate values. This bureaucratic system causes most regular workers to work based on quantity rather than quality. According to a government survey in 2017, around 25 percent of Japanese companies require their employees to work more than 80 hours per month, with 12 percent working more than 100 hours overtime, which made Japan one of the countries with the longest working hours in the world.[10] Even worse, deaths due to overwork, known as "karoshi," are frequent, with workers suffering heart attacks and strokes and committing suicide.

In addition to bureaucracy, a seniority-based system is also very entrenched in Japanese corporate values. Managers are mostly unreceptive to change, and employees spend most of their lifetime in the same company. This situation is destructive for labor productivity. In comparison to OECD countries, labor productivity in Japan is a quarter below the top half of countries. More ironically, despite its longest working hours, Japan is the least productive country in the G7. In addition to efficiency problems, Japan also suffers from other working cultural problems such as gender inequality, low entrepreneurial spirit, and a wide salary gap between permanent and temporary workers.

It is therefore no wonder that this third arrow of Abenomics is considered the most important of the three. It was put into practice through a plan called the Emergency Economic Measures for the Revitalization of the Japanese Economy, which was released by the cabinet in 2013. The government planned to execute the growth strategy under three main points. First, the government aims to develop the system for implementing bold regulatory and institutional reform in the areas that have the potential for high growth. This step includes significant corporate governance reform, which hopefully covers the issues of a seniority-based system and overtime working policy. Abenomics also emphasizes the importance of women in working life and intends to increase women's participation at the senior management level.

Second, the government also aims to encourage business investment and innovation. This step includes the strategy to expand Japanese business to overseas markets, enhancing Japanese human capital, and improving small- and medium-sized enterprises (SMEs), which includes real success measures for the agriculture, forestry, and fishery sectors. Third, the government also aims to be more open to foreign investment by promoting Japan as "the most business-friendly country in the world" (to understand how to brand a country, see Chapter 51). In realizing this objective, the government decided to create more incentive for investment, such as tax reforms and labor flexibility, encouraging foreign workers to participate in the Japanese labor market.

The three arrows of Abenomics are designed to operate simultaneously with the objective of enhancing economic growth. Such an objective is formalized in two important key performance indicators: an inflation target of 2 percent and a nominal GDP growth rate of 3 percent. Given that no real KPIs are set for the third arrow, the first two arrows are more observed and measurable than the third. However, the existence of the third arrow is a foundation for the other two and can be seen from the realization of social policies in the country. In order to assess the progress of Abenomics thus far, the next section will provide an updated report of its performance.

Japan's economic strategy today

It has been seven years since Abenomics was introduced, which is a considerable time for anyone to observe whether or not the framework has worked well. Before moving into the facts of Abenomics' achievements so far, it is fair to say that Abenomics is a set of structural reforms which will pay off in the very long run. This understanding is sometimes absent in discussions between supporters and critics of Shinzo Abe, not only in Japan but also around the world.

Figure 3.4 illustrates the grand design Japan is trying to achieve through the implementation of Abenomics. The ultimate goal of the Japanese government is to reach 600 trillion yen of GDP, which needs to be bolstered by achievements in six important pillars: rising consumption, creation of new demand, increasing capital investment, improving corporate performance, higher employment, and higher income. Furthermore, three primary engines are utilized to achieve the objective in the six pillars: (1) to boost productivity, (2) to drive innovation and trade, and (3) to energize corporate strategies. Let us go deeper to understand how these three pillars support the ultimate objective of the Japanese government.

Engine 1: boosting productivity

The first engine is boosting productivity by the change in work style and labor diversification, which suits the third arrow of Abenomics. This engine is eventually expected to increase wages, encourage higher labor demand, create higher income, and eventually increase consumption.

Under the first step, the Government of Japan has made many efforts to reform the work style issue in Japanese corporate culture. For instance, in March 2017, the Council for the Realization of Work Style formed a promising plan to realize a society where everyone can choose various and flexible work styles. The government is also planning to

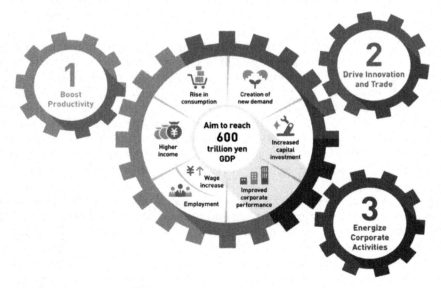

Figure 3.4 Abenomics in One Slide
Source: Government of Japan.

issue rules and guidelines for a pay-for-performance system, a regulatory limit on overtime work with penalty, and a new system to encourage children to attend higher education regardless of their economic conditions. The government also encourages women to achieve more promotions by lessening the burden for working parents, such as providing additional childcare services to 500,000 families by 2017, increasing childcare leave benefits from 50 to 67 percent, and providing female candidates with executive leadership training programs.[11]

These kinds of policies have turned in remarkable results. For instance, the number of women joining the workforce increased by about 1.5 million during 2012–2016,[12] and women taking roles in management positions in the private sector increased by 10 percent.[13] Finally, in filling the labor shortage, the government also encourages foreign professionals to arrive for employment by expediting permanent residency through the program of the Japanese Green Card for Highly Skilled Foreign Professionals, which increased the number of highly skilled professionals by 97 percent during 2015–2016.[14]

Engine 2: driving innovation and trade

The second engine is driving innovation and trade, which is implemented through structural reforms such as deregulation in the agricultural sector and other areas with growth potential. This strategy is implemented to promote international trade. Through this engine, it is expected that Japan will receive more capital investment and attract more foreign demand. In the agricultural sector, the government aimed to double the integrated market value from 5.1 trillion to 10 trillion yen by 2020. Agriculture, forestry, fishery, and food exports reached 750.2 billion yen in 2016, which was the highest of the previous four years. In enhancing food distribution abroad, the government also introduced eight agricultural policy reform bills and strengthened export promotion through the Japan Food Product Overseas Promotion Center (JFOODO).

Besides agriculture, the government also promotes development in the healthcare and energy sectors through a series of investment and incentive programs. The government also provides assistance to SMEs so they can expand their business abroad and modernize their processes to meet international standards. In the service industry, the government aims to double labor productivity growth to 2 percent in an industry that covers 70 percent of the country's GDP. In realizing this, the government has decided to customize plans for legal restructuring, tax reduction, and financial support in hospitality, transportation, nursing, and child care, wholesale and retail. In the tourism industry, the government aims to reinforce tourism as the centerpiece of regional revitalization. In December 2016, the government enacted the Integrated Resorts Promotion bills. The government also improved tourist experience with additional free Wi-Fi spots and 3,000 new ATM machines for international transactions. Thus far, the government has deregulated private room rentals for lodging in Tokyo, Osaka, and Kitakyushu City. Furthermore, in March 2017, an additional 222 rooms were authorized in the Tokyo and Kansai areas to support tourism.[15]

Engine 3: energizing corporate activities

The last engine to support the ultimate objective of the Japanese economy is energizing corporate activities. This engine is implemented with the aim to create a business-friendly environment and promote incoming foreign investment through strong corporate governance and tax incentive. One of the incentives that the government gives to investors is a corporate tax reduction. In practical terms, the government reduced the corporate tax from 40.69 percent before the Abenomics era to 30.86 percent in 2018.

Furthermore, besides stimulating growth through friendly taxation, the government also attracts inward foreign investment by increasing corporate transparency. In 2014, the government issued a code of conduct for investors, which is known as Japan's Stewardship Code. Japan's Stewardship Code is aimed at ensuring that investors will fulfill their fiduciary responsibilities; for example, by assuring the corporation that their behavior will always benefit the host companies. This is because for many years, institutional investors in Japan were criticized for not acting in the best interests of minority shareholders. The introduction of Japan's Stewardship Code attracted huge enthusiasm from companies. Since December 2016, Japan's Stewardship Code has been accepted by 214 institutional investors. Moreover, the Stewardship Code was further improved in 2017, including new guidance related to the role of asset owners issuing mandates and monitoring their asset managers.[16]

On the other side, besides imposing responsibilities on investors, the government must also ensure investor protection. The Stewardship Code has been complemented with new regulated corporate principles, known as Japan's Corporate Governance Code. One significant requirement of the code is the obligation to include independent directors on boards. Before Abenomics in 2013, roughly 600 of the 1,400 largest listed Japanese companies worked without independent directors. By June 2015, 100 percent of Japanese publicly listed companies had at least one independent director.[17]

In conclusion, the economy of Japan was facing hardships following the economic crisis of 1990. Abenomics was the solution that the government offered. Implementation of the major reforms is still in progress and there are already some indications of success.

36. THE IMPORTANCE OF NATIONAL CONSENSUS

In mid-December 2008, and only a few weeks after having been elected as prime minister of Lithuania, Andrius Kubilius announced the most draconian set of policy measures that the country had seen since World War II—the package was nicknamed "Night Tax Reform" to symbolize the urgency and speed of the changes. Faced with rising deficits that threatened to bankrupt the country, the Seimas (Lithuanian parliament) had approved a cut in public spending by 30 percent and a reduction in public sector wages by 20–30 percent, and slashed pensions by as much as 11 percent. In total, more than 60 new laws and amendments were implemented.[18] To ease the pain to his citizens and to show solidarity and a willingness to walk the talk, Andrius Kubilius himself took a pay cut of 45 percent.

Figure 3.5 shows the damage. The reduction in salaries was accompanied by tax increases on a wide variety of goods, such as pharmaceutical products and alcohol. Corporate taxes rose to 20 percent, from 15 percent.[19] The value-added tax rose to 21 percent, from 18 percent. It was estimated that the impact of these measures on the country's economy would be equal to 9 percent of GDP, the second-largest fiscal adjustment in a developed economy, after Latvia's, in the post-2008 crisis.[20] And Kubilius' plan had been announced only three months after Lehman Brothers had filed for bankruptcy.

It was not easy for the Lithuanian population to take the pill. From the beginning, the prime minister stated his commitment to defend the living standards of the lower classes:

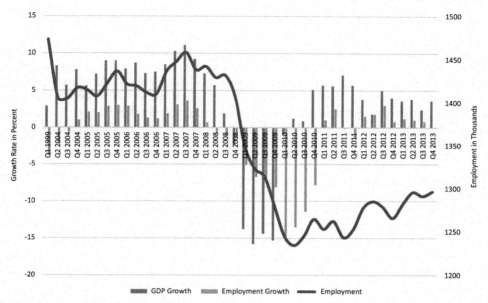

Figure 3.5 The Lithuanian Crisis

Source: Datastream.

> We have to show that the state knows how to take care of the weakest ones in difficult times, that it does not leave its citizens to suffer without any hope or prospect. Therefore, we will do everything [so] that the crisis combat plan would affect the people with lowest income as least as possible.[21]

However, in the subsequent months, the country lost one-third of its population (who fled to other European countries), and entered into a massive recession that destroyed 15 percent of all jobs in the country in less than two years (see Figure 3.5). In the same period, foreign net savings, that is net capital inflow, swung from 11.9 percent of GDP in 2008 to a net capital outflow of 3.8 percent of GDP, meaning that aggregate demand fell by 15.7 percent of GDP.[22] By mid-January 2009, demonstrations in the country had spread, and 7,000 people gathered outside the parliament where violence ensued.[23] People's perception was summarized by one of them: "They are taking away our last money and providing nothing. I am fed up with the lies, corruption and those grinning, fat faces behind the windows of Parliament."

In their seminal book *The Set-Up-to-Fail Syndrome: Overcoming the Undertow of Expectations*, my colleagues Profs. Jean-Francois Manzoni and Jean-Louis Barsoux from IMD analyzed the ability of executives to lead organizations through painful changes. Their premise is that "turkeys do not vote for Thanksgiving." That is, employees will not accept changes unless leaders share the pain and the gain with them, and they recommend leaders stick to the following principles:

People's views have to be heard
Decisions are applied with consistency
Decisions receive timely feedback
Decisions are based on sound facts and reasoning
Communication is sincere/genuine

When building national consensus, political leaders usually ignore these recommendations. In fact, leading change is today one of the most typical reasons why reform agendas have failed: as in France, Italy, Mexico, Argentina, and the Philippines. The case of Andrius Kubilius is a good example of a good change process, not only a good change program. Reflecting on his experience as prime minister, he would later recall the key lessons from this period: "Our recipe how to become slimmer – first of all, you need to have a good crisis, and then you need to understand that a deficit of political will is more dangerous than fiscal deficit." He also summarized his approach through three key achievements:

Political will to implement effective austerity measures through an internal devaluation. It was made without delay from the very beginning.

National consensus. Besides political will to implement austerity measures and internal devaluation, the ability to keep national consensus was of greatest importance. "You have to have a dialogue with your social partners, and you have to do the most difficult cuts as quickly as possible," Kubilius told *The New York Times*. "I told them this is history. You need to decide now how you want to be described in our history books."[24]

Support for business by reducing red tape. A time of crisis is the best time to implement major reforms such as slimming down the public sector. Lithuania cut the public sector by 10 percent, and it implemented major reforms to university education, its healthcare system, and other areas, creating a competitive environment in larger areas of the public sector.

Achieving national consensus, that is, "making the Turkeys walk into the oven," was the trickiest part, and it was done by asking social stakeholders to sign a *national agreement* on such austerity measures. Major labor unions, business associations, and an association of pensioners signed it, which partially limited social unrest. *People were heard.*

When presenting the Annual Government Report to the Seimas on April 15, 2010, Kubilius argued that 2009 had been a huge success, and that disaster had been averted in Lithuania. He stated:

The 15th Government can argue with confidence that the most severe crisis in Lithuania's history has been handled – public finances, which were on the verge of disaster, have been stabilised and we can take a more optimistic view of the future.

He even claimed that 2009

will be discussed in textbooks and scientific theses on how to survive a 15 percent recession, reduce GDP deficit by 9 percent (i.e., almost LTL 9 billion), avoid a collapse and preserve public, political, and social stability, stable currency, and regular payments of retirement pensions and salaries.[25]

The economy recovered very rapidly, as Figure 3.5 shows. If, in 2009, the national GDP dropped by 15 percent, it was growing again in 2012 by 3.5 percent. "Such a development allowed us to come back to international financial markets in the second half of 2009, with the borrowing cost rapidly going below the level which we had before the crisis," says Kubilius.[26]

However, it did not end well politically for Kubilius. During his mandate, the Social Democrat opposition party was proactively increasing the tension in the country. They blamed Kubilius and the Night Tax Reform for being the cause, not the solution, to the economic crisis. During the 2012–2016 election campaign, the Social Democrats were promising the nation to correct the mistakes made by the reforms, to end austerity, increase the minimum wage, and increase public spending. Kubilius lost the election[27] and his opponent, Social Democrat Algirdas Butkevičius, became the new prime minister.

Achieving national consensus in any political system can be complex. When politics is considered, it is usually in the context of blistering arguments, profound disagreements, and endless debate and counter-debate. Yet, what we often view as a rambunctious process is, in fact, increasingly steered toward crafting a consensus within certain political parameters, which can be at least palatable to all those concerned.

There is a precedent for this in the work of the 18th- and early 19th-century German philosopher Georg Wilhelm Friedrich Hegel, and his Hegelian dialectic. In philosophy, dialectics can be seen as a discourse between two parties that hold differing views, with the intention of establishing objective truth through reasoned arguments. While there is always a fair helping of vested interest involved in the political process, the dialectical method still offers a reasonable representation of political debate.

Hegel's insight deemed discourse and debate to be subject to three stages of development. First, there is a thesis (for the sake of argument, we can imagine that this thesis is initially offered by a government); at this stage, there is a reaction to the thesis, which gives rise to an antithesis, contradicting or negating the thesis. And from this point of conflict, the tension of the two points is resolved by means of a synthesis.

This thesis → antithesis → synthesis process is at the heart of modern political discourses, with all "sides" understanding that a practical political consensus must be crafted, no matter the scale and scope of disagreements that may underpin it. Lithuania in 2008 is a clear example of this. Kubilius was the candidate of the Homeland Union-Lithuanian Christian Democrat Party. He had defeated the Social Democrats in the election, who had been in a coalition government until then. The Social Democrats opposed the December 2008 plan, even though the previous finance minister had denied any upcoming crisis in the country.

So, what we will see as this chapter unfolds is that consensus in politics can occur in a wide variety of different theaters, across national borders, and on a supranational basis, as well as within individual countries. But we're going to begin this examination by looking at how political consensus between governments and populations can be achieved within individual countries.

Building consensus in democracies

Democracy is a political concept that has existed for over 2,500 years, owing its origin to the ancient Greeks. Athenian democracy developed around the 5th century BC in the Greek city-state of Athens, comprising Athens itself and the surrounding territory of Attica. Derived from the Greek words dêmos, meaning people, and kratia, meaning power or rule, the principle of democracy is that it enshrines self-ruling powers in the everyday lives of the general population.

And the notion of political consensus remains highly important today, particularly in a world in which everyone has an opinion, and the internet, and social media in particular, has provided an instantly accessible platform to announce it. One could quite reasonably argue that achieving political consensus today is harder than at any other time in human history.

Political consensus can reasonably be described as when all interested parties within a particular political region can broadly concur on certain policies, or on a general political direction. It is important to note that consensus does not mean blanket political agreement, but rather that the vast majority of views can be catered for within the parameters of debate that result from a particular approach. It is also important to note that sociocultural influences have a massive impact on what consensus is reached. While we live in an increasingly globalized culture—which we will discuss shortly—regional and national differences are still of paramount importance.

For example, in Britain there is a general consensus on the importance of the National Health Service (NHS), and the welfare state in general. Admittedly, the consensus on the NHS is less strong than in the immediate post-World War II period. Nonetheless, culturally, Britons believe very strongly in the concept of healthcare that is comprehensive, universal, and free at the point of delivery. Conversely, in the United States there is considerable opposition to the notion of "socialized" healthcare. Many in the United States view the NHS as an abomination, and as literally antithetical to their way of living.

It is hard to believe that the NHS could be so cherished in the UK, and so demonized in another English-speaking country, but this can, first, be attributed to the social climate in Britain immediately following World War II, which devastated Britain physically, economically, and psychologically. There was an intrinsic mood of empathy for the downtrodden at this time, which played a major role in the creation of the NHS and other aspects of British life and political culture that endure to this day.

Conversely, the United States has long been a market-driven society and culture, in which anything that impedes individual freedom and choice is seen as being highly suspect. This has advantages and disadvantages, but it means that the political culture and general public is forcefully opposed to the idea of the NHS, believing it to be an imposition on personal freedom. Which of these perspectives is correct is debatable, but any political leader wishing to create a consensus around openly privatizing the NHS in the UK would be faced with an almost impossible task.

We will discuss particular case studies later, but let me spend some lines on one of them. One country that has been through a particularly turbulent period in its history is Argentina. The South American nation was forced to endure a particularly intense financial crisis, the roots of which can be traced back to 2001.

Following a raft of factors, including International Monetary Fund (IMF) intervention in the country, millions of Argentinian bank accounts were frozen in January 2002, and the people were told that they would not be allowed to access their accounts until June 2003.[28] During the height of the crisis, in a country that was previously used to enjoying a reasonable standard of living, in October 2002, over 57 percent of the Argentinian population were living below the government-defined poverty line.[29]

In 2004, the then president of Argentina, Néstor Kirchner, blamed the IMF for impoverishing 15 million people. An obituary for Kirchner in *The Guardian* was subtitled "his bold defiance of the IMF paved the way for South America's progress." *The Guardian* article also acknowledged that in September 2003, Kirchner refused to go along with the

IMF's conditions, and defaulted on Argentina's commitments to them. The IMF backed down and rolled over the loans.

This was a bold move at the time as it went against the international community and conventional wisdom. But Kirchner sought a broad coalition of political and public support for the direction that he envisaged for Argentina. Thanks to the horrifying conditions that had been imposed on the public, the late president was able to achieve this, and Argentina asserted its independence, in what was an extraordinary situation.

As a result of Kirchner's economic policies, Argentina went on to grow at an average of more than 8 percent annually through 2008, pulling more than 11 million people, in a country of 40 million, out of poverty. The policies of the Kirchner government, including the central bank targeting of a stable and competitive real exchange rate, and taking a hard line against the defaulted creditors, were not popular in Washington or among the business media. But they worked.

Kirchner's successful face-off with the IMF came at a time when the fund was rapidly losing influence in the world, after its failures in the Asian economic crisis that preceded Argentina's collapse. It showed the world that a country could defy the IMF and live to tell about it, and contributed to the ensuing loss of the IMF's influence in Latin America and middle-income countries generally.

However, this certainly wasn't the end of the story, with Argentina recently plunged into a major currency crisis. This has even necessitated the existing government returning

Image 3.1 The Author with Andrés Ibarra, Former Minister of Modernization of Argentina

to the IMF for assistance. Such conditions arise due to a complex international picture of commingled factors and are not necessarily indicative of the wrong direction of Argentina's economic policy.

Indeed, the original scenario in the Latin country stemmed from what is often referred to as the "Washington Consensus," which included macroeconomic stabilization, trade liberalization, privatization, deregulation, and related market-oriented policies.[30] This direction was largely accepted by the Argentinian public at the time, but once the country was plunged into a state of crisis, it was obvious that it couldn't maintain this direction indefinitely. The future of Argentina will be dependent on delivering a new political consensus that reflects the shifting situation in the country and convinces an increasingly revolutionary population. What is clear is that consensus politics can only work in a situation of stability, and the ability of consensus decision-making to indeed contribute to this stability must be one of its primary characteristics.

Another example of consensus decision-making comes from the Southeast Asian country of Myanmar (formerly Burma). Noted for the military dictatorship that emerged under the Burma Socialist Program Party, Myanmar has had an extremely unstable recent history, and although it cannot be considered a full democracy, it is worth considering here.

Following a general election in the country in November 2010, a new civilian government was forged, which led to a wholly new political architecture. Union and regional parliamentary sessions, a new president and cabinet, chief ministers, parliamentary committees, open political dialogue with various stakeholders, including Daw Aung San Suu Kyi (leader of the National League for Democracy),[31] new civil society groups, national-level workshops, held in Nay Pyi Taw, the capital city of Myanmar—all of these important instruments of a civil and democratic society became enshrined in Myanmarese culture.

Out of this new structure emerged a new political culture, focused on achieving policy decisions through consensus. Experts of Myanmar's politics and history note that this was a radical change from the previous society, which was always fixated on placing power in the hands of a few aristocratic individuals.

Of course, there will be many challenges ahead for Myanmar, in a country that has been ravaged by internal conflict, and in which no such democratic culture has previously prevailed. It remains to be seen whether the government will enact this political consensus going forward, and the military remains both influential and potentially brutal. But there is at least hope in this poor country that a more reasoned and consensual political dialogue will emerge. If militarism wins out over discourse, then it will be hard for any such consensus to remain credible in the eyes of the public.

In conclusion, what we can observe from these examples is that political consensus requires the acceptance of the population in order to work. Hard and unyielding policies such as internal devaluations, responses to financial crises, or abandoning a currency peg are contentious by their very nature, and ultimately populations are less likely to accept them, particularly if they result in what are perceived to be undesirable consequences.

The likelihood of such policies then being overturned in the next political cycle becomes quite high. Stability and consensus go hand in hand, and both are required if a meaningful political direction is to be followed for a significant period of time. Successful countries are those where policies can be formulated and implemented in the context of a general popular consensus, even if populations can sometimes be resistant to them to some extent. If a government can find broad-based backing for a certain policy or political direction then it can be maintained for a period of time, even in the midst of public opposition.

This idea of consensus is also important for business and the corporate sector, as it tends to be associated with coherence and stability. Obviously, these are qualities that the business community values, and it is only when they are tangible within a certain nation that big corporations will get involved on a significant scale.

How consensus is built

Let us look at some examples of political administrations that successfully built consensus, and thrived as a result. We begin by examining some case studies in which consensus was not established adequately, and problems resulted as a consequence.

Mexico

When he was elected president of Mexico in December 2012, Enrique Peña Nieto was viewed very much as a modernist and reformist. The relatively young, handsome, and charismatic Nieto pledged to deliver 608 *compromisos* (promises) as part of his election campaign. Having received 7 percent more of the vote than his closest rival, Nieto was comfortably elected, and began the process of delivering his ambitious program of reform.

Nieto's policies particularly focused on rapid economic change within Mexico. In particular, Nieto was responsible for attempting an expansive breakup of monopolies, liberalizing Mexico's energy sector, reforming public education, and modernizing the country's financial regulation. The BBC also reported on Nieto's extensive reform of education in the early months of his presidency.

None of these policies should be seen as unreasonable or necessarily bad for Mexico or its people, but often the success of a legislative program is based on consensus. Nieto singularly failed to achieve this consensus for his program of reform, and made numerous other errors of judgment.

Central to the problems with the Nieto administration was his inability to seek political alliances, and to gain popular support for his overall vision. This led to a hierarchical form of leadership that sowed the seeds of his own unpopularity, and indeed his downfall, at a later date.

Political gridlock was to defeat most of Nieto's plans for Mexico, and even forced the president to instate the multilateral Pact for Mexico, which was intended to address political infighting. However, it should be said in mitigation that the rapid descent in global oil prices, largely brought about by new sources of oil being tapped into via fracking, was also a massive economic blow to Mexico, and would have been problematic for any leader.

It should also be acknowledged that Mexico does have significant demographic, economic, and logistical problems that will pose challenges for any political ideology or regime. But, for example, there is little evidence that Nieto's education policies have been successful. Research from the non-profit organization WorldFund indicates that Mexico still spends less per capita on education than other comparable Organization for Economic Co-operation and Development countries, while students in Mexico score 81 points below the OECD average on math.[32]

Furthermore, only 35 percent of Mexicans graduate from high school. The International Community Foundation charity attributes this lack of success in reforming education to continuing poverty, inequality impacting on indigenous communities, growing gender equality, and, most damningly, shrinking education budgets. This latter issue can be squarely aimed at the Nieto regime, and indeed, *The Guardian* reported on the failure of Nieto's much vaunted education reform, noting in May 2018 that Mexico still ranks last in education among the 35 OECD countries.[33]

Other reforms were similarly unsuccessful, with many believing that Nieto's failure to seek broad political consensus from within the Mexican system ended the effective implementation of his vision. And within a relatively short period of time, even more serious allegations were being leveled at the Mexican leader.

Nieto has been widely accused of using propaganda techniques in order to deprive the Mexican population of important information. This included so-called *peñabots*, automated accounts on social media which attempted to spread pro-government propaganda and marginalize dissenting opinions. Most with an informed view of Mexican politics would agree that Nieto's presidency certainly contributed to the so-called "fake news" phenomenon.

Furthermore, testimony in an ongoing drugs-related trial in Mexico suggested that Nieto was guilty of taking bribes. Alex Cifuentes Villa testified that Nieto took a bribe worth USD 100 million from Joaquín Guzmán Loera—the infamous crime lord known as El Chapo.[34] This extremely serious allegation has yet to be proven, but the former president's handling of several contentious issues was criticized as being dictatorial, controversial, and ill-judged.

Nieto vacated his position in November 2018, by this time considered to be one of the least popular and successful presidents in Mexico's history. And this precipitated an almost inevitable lurch to the left in Mexican politics. The incumbent president, Andrés Manuel López Obrador, has promised to bring about what he describes as "the fourth transformation of Mexico," by breaking the "neoliberal consensus" that has plagued Latin America.[35]

Whether this is successful remains to be seen. But in order to achieve this, Obrador will need a far less top-down approach than was the case with Nieto, a willingness to negotiate with allies and opposition alike, and the ability to craft a political consensus that can follow through on this vision for the future. Otherwise, Mexico will remain the somewhat chaotic and impoverished nation that it has been for some time.

South Africa

The election of Jacob Zuma in South Africa was indicative of a healthy shift in South African politics, continuing in an encouraging direction away from the hideous apartheid era. The fact that Zuma was sworn in as president of South Africa is a significant triumph in and of itself, and critiques of his time in office must be seen in this context, as well as the inherent issues in South African society caused by its previous political malaise.

Zuma's time as president between 2009 and 2018 wasn't entirely without its successes. The former president was praised for his youth initiatives, which helped many young South Africans back into work, while the increasing stability of South African society that occurred under his tutelage was cited as a major factor in an increase in tourism. Zuma also oversaw the completion of a 700 kilometer pipeline from Durban to Gauteng, which has been economically important for South Africa.[36]

However, many believe that Zuma's failures far outweigh his successes. Zuma was strongly criticized for yo-yoing on the appointment of former president Thabo Mbeki. His proposals to redistribute land were never delivered. Zuma failed in the country's fight against the HIV/AIDS epidemic. Crime increased under his premiership. The economy stagnated, with the sovereign credit rating of South Africa being downgraded. And there is a massive energy crisis in the nation.[37]

But it was Zuma's political positioning and machinations that perhaps most obviously illustrate his failed regime, and entire approach to the presidency. The former president ducked key questions in parliament, undermining the political process and constitution. Zuma was also criticized for avoiding accountability on the Public Protector's report on Nkandla—a private home of Zuma, over which he is accused of using public money to fund.[38]

And the former president has done little or nothing to clamp down on the billions of dollars of corruption that is almost endemic in South African society, nor to break the chain of vested interest between business and state. Critics of Zuma also denigrate his leadership for increasingly politicizing the communications machinery associated with the state. African media has accused the president of turning the South African Broadcasting Corporation into a virtual propaganda mill. It is indeed hard to imagine anything less democratic, unconstitutional, or libertarian than this, yet similar accusations have been made regarding the politicization of supposedly independent institutions within the criminal justice system.

Zuma also failed to unite South Africa, a deeply divided country. This was essential in order for his presidency to be viewed as a success, and in order for his policies to stick. He was seen as the ideal figure to achieve a political consensus across the tripartite alliance—an alliance among the African National Congress (ANC), the Congress of South African Trade Unions (COSATU), and the South African Communist Party (SACP)—that defines South African politics.

Unfortunately, by the time he left the presidency in February 2018, most observers concurred that relations within the alliance were at an all-time low. By his final months in office, Zuma didn't even consult COSATU and SACP on matters of government. The president was also roundly booed at the COSATU Worker's Day rally, held in Bloemfontein in May 2017.[39]

Zuma also failed to end fractionalization within the ANC. Despite promising to unify the party, by 2017 the ANC entered its 54th National Conference in a state of disarray and division. Media stories were focused on a possible split, with many in the party apoplectic over Zuma's conduct and what they saw as his corruption and misappropriation of public money. By the end of his tenure, most considered Zuma an unhelpful, and even destructive, presence, while even his own party had become hugely divided. Zuma had done everything other than achieving a political consensus.

His was not a quiet exit, though, as Zuma initially refused to step down, defying the orders of the ANC to resign. Thus, the Council on Foreign Relations wrote of the "painful exit" of Zuma. National Public Radio concluded that Zuma "never escaped the taint of corruption," while the BBC described him as "the most colorful and controversial president South Africa has had since white-minority rule ended in 1994."

What we can say with some certainty is that Zuma emphatically failed to achieve the consensus that was so dearly needed in South Africa, and the consequences were both obvious and sobering.

France

One final example of a political leader failing to achieve consensus relates to the proudly independent and rebellious nation of France. Emmanuel Macron assumed office as the president of France on May 14, 2017. In this sense, it is perhaps a little early to assess his presidency. However, there are already clear patterns and themes emerging, a political soufflé from which Macron will struggle to extricate himself.

As is so often the case with political figures, Macron entered office promising an ambitious reform agenda. And many French political commentators felt that he had begun to implement this during 2017. In particular, Macron had promised to negotiate with the powerful unions, which wield such influence in France, and, with Muriel Pénicaud, his employment minister, had conducted 300 hours of closed-door talks with union bosses by December 2017.[40]

While many initially applauded this, Macron had already hit problems within a matter of months. Economic problems were afoot, with unemployment growing, hardly something likely to find favor with the unions. Furthermore, the perception of Macron is of an increasingly right-wing figure, something that grates with the French public that is traditionally, and emphatically, left-wing. Macron's plans to jettison 120,000 public-sector jobs in the coming years have been highly unpopular, and he has already been strongly criticized by Jean-Luc Mélenchon—an experienced and popular socialist figure.

In a speech at the end of 2018, Macron went on the attack, defending his legacy. He noted that France "can't work less, earn more, cut taxes and increase spending."[41] But his popularity and approval rating have already slid to all-time lows within France,[42] and his political isolation is such that pushing through his reform agenda appears hugely problematic.

Macron's current position underlines the importance of skillfully aligning one's political position and image with the prevailing values of a country. Failing to do this will see you isolated and marginalized, no matter how significant your position within the political hierarchy may be. Macron now faces a massive challenge to resurrect his image, win another term in office, and gain support for policies that go against the grain of what France has stood for socially, politically, economically, and culturally.[43]

So, failing to achieve political consensus can definitely have a massively negative impact on outcomes. But let's now examine a few case studies where achieving consensus has reaped rewards.

Finland

The Nordic country of Finland may not be one of the biggest, most powerful, or even well known on the planet. But it does have one particular claim to fame: its education system is frequently ranked as the very best in the world. To some degree, this can be traced back to Finland's Lutheran past, with education being a huge part of this branch of Western Christianity.

The successes of Finnish education can be largely attributed to the 1968 School System Act. After this historical piece of legislation, the organization of education in Finland was "focused on the primary school curriculum, and offered a compelling vision of a more humanistic, child-centred school," as had been worked out by three successive reform commissions, intended to ensure that all Finnish people have equal educational opportunity.[44] This belief in equality is reflected in other areas of Finnish society as well; Finland has the lowest wage inequality of any country in the EU.[45]

Finland has also placed a huge emphasis on the importance of teachers within the system, getting these key professionals on side with the ideas of the government. The selection of teaching candidates is stringent, yet once teachers are selected they are given far more autonomy within the system than in many comparable nations. The judgment of teachers is trusted in assessing students, and the same pressures of performance and exam results are not placed on young people in Finland.[46] Indeed, there is no standardized testing.[47]

Another key aspect of Finland's education system is that its schools are publicly funded. This is symptomatic of the cooperative nature of schooling in Finland. There are no league tables of schools, no lists of top-performing teachers. Education in Finland is focused on preparing young people for the real world, and in being an instrument to address social inequality.

Smaller class sizes, fewer years spent in formal schooling, less homework and outside working foisted on children—these principles are the backbone of an education system that is the envy of the rest of the world. It is all about making people feel included, about giving everyone the same opportunities, about building trust in teachers, about achieving an educational consensus within a nation.

Portugal

Another European country that faced massive economic difficulties in the wake of Europe's sovereign debt crisis was Portugal. Although a Western European nation, Portugal is not as wealthy as some of its more prominent neighbors. Consequently, when the country was forced to go cap-in-hand to the IMF, seeking a EUR 78 billion bailout, it was considered a depressing and debilitating day for the nation.[48]

Nonetheless, the authorities struck a note of cautious optimism at the time. "This programme's success will require a truly national effort," the EU and IMF commented in a joint statement back in 2011. The plan at the time was to reduce the national deficit, stimulate long-term growth, and restabilize Portugal's banking and finance sector.

Crucially, the president of the European Central Bank at the time, Jean-Claude Trichet, indicated that the Government of Portugal would have to work diligently in order to make the bailout work. "The program contains the necessary elements to bring about a sustainable stabilization of the Portuguese economy. We are confident. Of course, it calls for the present government … and future governments to do the job," Trichet commented in Helsinki.[49]

Certainly, Portugal experienced some difficult years following this unsavory time in its history. But the Portuguese government, led by Aníbal Cavaco Silva, put in place the necessary measures to cut the Portuguese deficit, and slowly but surely the economy began to recover.

By the end of 2016, there were tangible signs of improvement. The Portuguese government achieved a 2.1 percent budget deficit in 2016—which was the lowest since democracy had been restored to the nation in 1974,[50] following the Carnation Revolution—while the economy grew by 2.7 percent,[51] the best economic result since the turn of the century, and, overall, probably the best economic performance in Portugal's history.

Portugal's maneuvering in the bond market at that time would arguably not have been possible without a broad political consensus, which then helped achieve the relative acquiescence of the people for what was unquestionably an austere culture for some years.

Yet, key economic data for 2016 outlines what a remarkable recovery has been achieved in Portugal. Even the unemployment rate in the country had been shaved considerably, to 9.5 percent.[52] Although this was still slightly higher than the country's 43-year post-democratic average, it represented a massive reduction from the peak level of 17.5 percent just a few years earlier.

Another contributing factor to Portugal's recovery has been the country's tax regime, which has encouraged people to participate in society economically and uphold the plans of the government to achieve recovery.[53] The effective low tax burden that is standardized across society has been praised by many economic commentators, while Portugal also has a special tax regime for non-habitual tax residents, enabling the country to attract wealthy people, who have then contributed to the Portuguese economy.

The flat 20 percent tax rate for both employment and self-employment has enabled the Portuguese government to bring people together in Portugal, and reward ambition and success, without penalizing the poor and needy. It is this spirit of togetherness and consensus which means the country can look forward to the future with some optimism.

India

Finally, it is also worthwhile briefly mentioning the example of Manmohan Singh. The Indian economist and politician served as the prime minister of India from 2004 to 2014. It was arguably his decision-making as Minister of Finance in the early 1990s that demonstrated the value Singh placed on political consensus.

Singh's budget in 1991 had a massive impact on the course of India's history.[54] India had been considered a primitive nation up until that point, enduring a rather hand-to-mouth existence as an impoverished nation. Singh helped set the wheels in motion for a new India, which has become one of the most successful and modern economies on the planet.

The former prime minister has specifically spoken of how he sought a broad-based consensus for his economic plans from day one. Singh was able to breach the divide between political parties and set India on a course from which millions of the world's poorest people have hugely benefited.

...

As we have seen in this chapter, national consensus often results in a more coherent policy framework that also produces enviable results in domestic politics. National consensus is also a desired feature by the business community. Achieving national consensus can often be a tricky proposition considering the level of debate, discourse, and disagreement that inevitably occurs in the political systems of diverse nations. But those political figures that have negotiated these choppy waters have been far more likely to be rewarded, whereas those that have set out unilaterally, in a lone dinghy, have all too frequently capsized.

37. POLITICAL LEADERSHIP

Political leadership is undoubtedly an important aspect in any stable and successful country. The direction of a nation can be profoundly impacted by its leader, both positively and negatively. Yet, many political supremos fail to understand what is required in order to succeed in a particular territory. This does vary significantly from one country to another, yet we can identify common tropes and characteristics among successful leaders from hugely differing countries.

How a single man changed an entire city

You may be surprised to know that the car-sharing capital of the world is Moscow, not San Francisco or London. Car sharing is a rather new trend. It has been actively developing for the last decade. This is how the system works: you use a smart application that tells you which cars are available around you. Once you find the car you like, you get in it and drive for as long as you want (typically for short distances), and when you are done you park anywhere in the city, pay with your app on a per-minute basis, and move on. You are responsible for the costs of parking and traffic violations, if any. Car sharing is much more popular in Europe than in the United States, where due to lesser restrictions on services such as Uber and Lyft, ride hailing—sharing a ride with another passenger and a private driver—is the dominant trend.

In Moscow, just in January 2019, there were 2.7 million rides like that, a massive increase relative to the previous year—in January 2018, there were 700,000 rides. The mayor of Moscow, Sergey Sobyanin, declared recently that

> car sharing is gaining popularity in Moscow. Twenty-three million rides were made with its help last year. In 2019, the service companies intend to purchase another 5 thousand new cars. Thus, the Moscow car sharing fleet will increase up to 21,500 cars.[55]
>
> The popularity of the service is growing due to the increase in the number of cars, flexible tariffs, and new services for customers. Today, citizens have access to almost 17 thousand cars for car sharing.[56]

The impact on Moscow's traffic congestion has been impressive.

What is the reason for such popularity of car sharing particularly in Moscow? Moscow is a 12 million-people megalopolis. Approximately one in every seven Russians lives in greater Moscow, the most populated urban area in Europe, with 20 million people. Its historical development was not meant for such a human flow. Although Moscow was rebuilt after World War II and the architects kept in mind the potential future expansion of the city, they could not anticipate it would grow so big. Moscow suffocates in traffic jams; the roads cannot handle the amount of transport moving inside the city, transferring through it, from the outskirts and from nearby towns such as Khimki and Zelenograd, which are closely interconnected with the capital. Congestion is such that government officials use special lanes call "ZiL lanes" (also sometimes called "Chaika lanes") which run along the main arteries of the city and can be only used by vehicles carrying senior government officials. Even though they were introduced in the 1960s during Leonid Brezhnev's presidency, they are still widely used by Kremlin officials.

Any traditional methods such as building additional roads or underground lines are very expensive so the government turned to the "limit traffic, not widen the roads" way. Reducing the number of personal vehicles in the city center thus became a policy priority.

The man responsible for such a transformation is Maksim Liksutov, head of the Transport Department of Moscow.

Maksim Liksutov

In 2011, at the age of 35, Estonian-born Maxim Liksutov, a member of the *Forbes* ranking of the richest people in Russia (USD $500 million, 189th place), became a transport advisor to Moscow's Mayor Sergey Sobyanin. Simultaneously, he was appointed as head of the Transport Department of the Moscow government. His professional career had started, however, exactly 20 years before.

With the dissolution of the Soviet Union in 1991, Estonia lost the Soviet coal that once made a significant share of the transshipment of the port of Tallinn. Sergey Glinka—not only a future partner of Liksutov, but also a former sailor and port worker—solved the problem. He managed to have all coal mined in Kuzbass, a Russian mining region close to the Mongolian border, transported to and exported from the port of Tallinn to the European market. The business had huge potential, but there were problems with product quality—the Kuzbass mines had never independently accessed the export market outside the former Soviet Union, and the coal was loaded into wagons without cleaning the dust and sludge. Glinka barely had time to organize the supply, so he offered his housemate and friend Liksutov control over cleaning and handling the coal import. Liksutov immediately proved himself to be able to negotiate with people in the port who were not used to getting up from their chair over the previous 20 years. He found the equipment and set up all the processes for cleaning and transshipment.

During the 2000s, and as a result of the privatization of Russian assets, Iskander Makhmudov and Andrei Bokarev became the new owners of Kuzbass. They did not change the established distribution channels but created the joint business transport company "TransGroup AS" with Liksutov and Glinka. TransGroup was no longer just a freight forwarder back then, but a freight railway operator with its own fleet. In 2002, the company owned several dozen cars, but even this number gave it an advantage over competitors—almost none of the forwarders had their own wagons. After 10 years, a small forwarding company became a giant transport forwarder with revenues of USD 900 million.

Which roles did the partners share in the TransGroup? Makhmudov and Glinka proposed the strategy of business development, and Liksutov was a successful performer. He was responsible for operational management. TransGroup competitors admitted that Liksutov was not the main figure but was best suited for the role of a public person.

As political changes were unraveling in Estonia, by 2005 Sheremetyevo still remained the only Moscow airport without a railway connection to Moscow. After an agreement at the end of that year, the Sheremetyevo Corporation created a subsidiary limited liability company called Aeroexpress. Since the company needed huge investments for the purchase of new trains and the construction of a railway terminal in Sheremetyevo-2, Sheremetyevo sold 74 percent of Aeroexpress to Delta-Trans-Invest, a private company owned by Liksutov and Glinka. Liksutov, who had connections with Russian Railways back in the 1990s when he was engaged in the transportation of coal from Russia to Estonia, became chairman of the board of directors of Aeroexpress.

Practically speaking, most of Liksutov's business interests were by now in Russia. In April 2007, the Estonian authorities dismantled the monument to Soviet soldiers in the center of Tallinn and moved it to a military cemetery. Mass protests and riots broke out in the city. Liksutov then decided to move his company's head office from Estonia to Russia. Only an idle terminal and a small restaurant in Tallinn were left in Estonia. A new phase of Liksutov's life had begun.[57]

Liksutov's idea was to bring the company out of the state regulation over ticket prices, which applies to suburban transportation, and focus on wealthy passengers. "Our passengers are businessmen, foreigners, tourists, as well as staff working at airports. They differ from ordinary commuters and are willing to pay for comfort"—was the official statement of Aeroexpress.

Aeroexpress invested approximately 12 billion rubles in the purchase of trains, the construction of the terminal in Sheremetyevo, and the additional required equipment. Funds were obtained from loans by VTB Bank and TransCreditBank, as well as personal money from Makhmudov and Bokarev.

For almost one year, trains to Sheremetyevo airport had barely any passengers, and they became popularly known as пустовозы (*pustovozy* or *empty-wagon trains*). Neither Russian Railways nor Liksutov felt troubled by the absence of passengers: the traffic jams in Moscow were such a problem that people would come sooner or later, irrespective of the frequency of the trains. Even expensive business-class wagons were пустовозы. Gradually, by 2010, the number of commuters increased to reasonable levels. By 2013, Aeroexpress[58] was successfully fighting with its main competitor—Moscow taxi drivers. Confidence grew and Aeroexpress carried out a large-scale advertising campaign with the slogan: "Honest taxi drivers recommend Aeroexpress." Liksutov did not skimp on the campaign financing that cost 3 percent of Aeroexpress' total revenue that year.

The turning point in Liksutov's career was the ride by Aeroexpress with Prime Minister Vladimir Putin on March 28, 2011. The ride was quick and took only half an hour, while Liksutov was expressing the advantages of this transport and the future benefits to the premier. In short, the successful Estonian-Russian businessman became the advisor and then the deputy mayor. We already know the ability of Liksutov to present his business with gloss but it is no less important to know what happened in the Transport Department of Moscow before his appointment. Putin's support would prove key to Liksutov's career.

The previous head of the Transport Department was Nikolai Lyamov—another experienced official, who was appointed shortly after Sobyanin as a member of a new team of officials in 2010. One of the main tasks of the city—the fight against traffic jams and the development of public transport—was assigned to him. It was his duty to create separate road lines for public transport in Moscow. This initiative was later called one of his main mistakes: the lines were created, but the smooth operation of public transport was not implemented as quickly as possible.[59]

Under Lyamov's watch, the city began to develop an intelligent transport system and he organized the work of a legal taxi service. But the official did not have the courage to take decisive measures. The scientific head of the Research Institute of Transport and Road economy, Mikhail Blinkin, said: "Moscow needs some revolutions, and one of them is the organization of our parking space." Lyamov was unable to move this project from a standstill point.

One year later, Liksutov was appointed head of the Transport Department. With Liksutov's arrival, the transport strategy of Moscow had acquired real shape. Not afraid of tough measures, he reduced the parking space in the center and introduced paid parking; additionally, he restricted freight transport entry into the city.

As Blinkin concluded:

Age contributes to determination. This is a young generation which has international experience; they see the world not only as tourists, but also as locals. They have traveled by car through London and Paris. They have ridden high-speed trains in Tokyo as well.[60]

At that point, Liksutov saw the potential of the new emerging transportation method— car sharing. He then granted car-sharing companies free parking in Moscow concurrently increasing the parking price for all other vehicles. Confronted with the anger of taxi drivers and residents, he completely ignored their protests. As of today, Liksutov has been implementing such a policy for a relatively long time and he is still in charge despite all the irritation he has caused among both drivers and some influential officials.

Maksim Liksutov is certainly not the standard case of a political leader: moving into public service after (or during) a successful career as a businessman, he managed to implement changes in people's lives despite massive opposition and hardships. With no personal interest vested in reducing traffic congestions in Moscow, he was able to stick to an initial strategy without losing his superiors' support. How did he do it? The first time I heard about his story, I felt that his case summarizes very well the key successful factors that we tend to observe more generally among "good" political leaders. We will explore these next through other examples, but let me state them here. Successful political leaders:

> Tend to be doers more than mobilizers, and they gain their experience typically in the private sector before they start their political careers.
> Have nothing to lose, and they are not scared of losing the next election. Liksutov was already rich, having built a fortune in the private sector. He did not come into the job to make money.
> Typically have full support from a close entourage of supporters, either above or below them. Liksutov has always enjoyed the full support of the country's prime minister (and then president) Vladimir Putin, as well as the mayor of Moscow.
> Are very often amazing communicators. In his case, Liksutov's presence has always been an asset.
> Are always lucky to be in the right place at the right time—I guess this is clear in this example.
> Are able to use their opponents' weak spots to their advantage. Lyamov's lack of drive became Liksutov's political advantage.
> Act decisively—in the case of Liksutov, again with respect to his predecessor.
> Always take their superiors' intentions into consideration.

In the next section, I provide additional insights. However, it is very important to distinguish the role of political leaders in democracies vs. dictatorships. A dictator can easily share and implement a vision without challenges to his or her authority, and therefore leadership is exercised much more easily. The difficult task comes when you need to satisfy voters or a superior authority.

Leaders must be willing to sacrifice: weapons in Australia

On April 28, 1996, 29-year-old Martin Bryant stepped into the Port Arthur historical prison tourist spot in Southern Tasmania armed with two AR-15 semi-automatic rifles. What followed was the deadliest mass shooting in Australian history, claiming 35 lives. At the time, Australia had generally very lax gun laws that varied by state. Bryant's assault rifle was purchased through a Tasmanian newspaper ad. In the aftermath of Port Arthur, Australia rewrote its gun laws to prevent future massacres. However, the reason the Australian case is interesting is that gun reform was led by Prime Minister John Howard, a member of the conservative Liberal Party (LP), whose base was largely farmers, hunters, and other sections of society that would have otherwise opposed any gun control legislation. Howard governed with a coalition made up of his own Liberal Party and the center-right National Party (NP), which had a similar base. The Australian gun reform episode showcases the costliness of unpopular but necessary political decisions in a democracy. After the 1996 reforms, many high-ranking members of the National–Liberal government coalition were voted out of office, most notably Robert Borbidge (NP), the premier of Queensland, one of Australia's most conservative states. The country also saw the rise of the One Nation party, which flanked the government coalition from the right, taking large parts of its base.[61]

According to Howard, his decision to implement gun reform was a direct result of the Port Arthur shooting. Howard and his government immediately began discussing the possibility of implementing a total ban on automatic and semi-automatic weapons. The main obstacle to gun reform was that the federal government had in effect very little power over policy in this respect, since gun ownership rights were determined entirely at the state level. The federal government would therefore have to negotiate with the states to convince them to pass new gun laws independently. The one thing the government could do was to ban the import of semi-automatic weapons, which Howard's government did immediately.

Despite the institutional barriers, the gun reform initiative would prove to be more politically costly than politically difficult. Reform was widely popular, particularly in cities. According to Howard, if the states had refused to play ball with the new gun reform proposals, he would have called for a national referendum on the issue that he claims would have undoubtedly carried. The numbers seem to back this up. According to polls on Howard's government's performance a year into its term (it took office six weeks before Port Arthur), its actions on gun reform were ranked as favorable by 63 percent of Australians. This was one of the only two issues ranked favorably by more than 50 percent; the other was interest rates. On other issues, Howard polled at 27.5 percent on average. Two months after Port Arthur, a national poll showed that 80 percent of Australians agreed with "Howard's gun control laws."

The problem was that where there was opposition to reform, it came from the National and Liberal parties' own bases. The image of John Howard delivering a speech to a crowd of angry Liberal voters, screaming and booing at him, while Howard exclaims "There's no other way! There's no other way!" speaks for itself. Gun registration laws already existed in some Australian states and the types of weapons citizens could own also varied regionally. The states of Queensland and Tasmania had no registration laws, and the norms that did exist were lax at best. In other states, laws varied, with some only permitting registered handguns and not automatic or semi-automatic weapons. As a result, it was quite easy to buy an unregistered gun in one of these states and take it back to places like Victoria, which had tighter regulations. Tasmanian laws are what allowed Bryant to purchase his semi-automatic through the newspaper ad in the first place. Gun reform, therefore, had to be universal and include Queensland and Tasmania, which would prove to be tough battlegrounds. As of the 1996 election, the National–Liberal coalition was extremely strong and had not only crushed the Labor opposition in parliament, but also dethroned it after over a decade in power. The Liberal Party alone held 75 of 148 seats in parliament and governed with the 18 seats the NP had plus one independent.

The 1996 gun reforms were based on the following points:

- Ban on the importation, sale, and ownership of all automatic and semi-automatic weapons as well as pump-action shotguns and self-loading center-fire rifles.
- Mandatory registration of all firearms.

- All gun owners must first apply for a gun permit that cites a *"valid reason"* for owning a gun. These include farming and hunting but *not* personal protection.
- Gun owners must also apply for a license for each individual gun they own as well as undergo a mandatory 28-day background check. Gun owners must also follow storage regulations for their weapons and incur heavy penalties for breaking any of the rules.
- Individuals with a criminal record or mental health problems may not possess firearms.

Finally, the most important of all the policies was the national gun buyback scheme. According to John Howard, this policy was instrumental in getting the states to comply with the government's proposal, since it was government funded. The Australian government issued a temporary amnesty on the possession of unregistered weapons and allowed citizens to sell their unregistered guns to the state at market price. They also bought all registered weapons that were made illegal from the public at market price (this was mandatory), as well as any other guns that Australians did not want, possibly because they did not want to deal with the new regulations. All in all, the Australian government bought 661,000 weapons from the public at a cost of USD 500 million in federal money.

As a result of the reforms, many NP and LP politicians never held office again after the next election. The most notable of these was Rob Borbidge the Queensland premier. Borbidge held a strange position because in the Queensland government, unlike other state governments or the federal parliament, it was his National Party that held most of the seats and not the Liberals with which they were in coalition. Howard later recognized that Borbidge agreed to go along with the gun reforms knowing it would be "extremely difficult"[62] for him politically. Indeed, in interviews, Borbidge said on gun control that "[he] took the stand, [and he] was prepared to face the political consequences."[63] In Borbidge, the political cost of gun control is clear because not only did he lose the next election, but his entire party was booted from power in Queensland. After 1996, a new political party called One Nation emerged as a more right-wing alternative to the Nationals and Liberals. They secured only a minority in federal parliament, but did take Borbidge's old position and control of the Queensland government. The NP and LP themselves had been a right-wing alternative to what had been viewed as a stagnant Labor government, but many rural voters who had enthusiastically voted for the new coalition felt betrayed by their gun control policy pivot and deserted to One Nation at the next election in 1998. Howard believes that gun control was an "important reason"[64] that One Nation rose in the late 1990s.

The reforms had some silver linings, notably that John Howard himself did not lose his next election as a result of his gun policies and proceeded to serve four terms as prime minister until 2007, which is a testament to taking politically costly actions that are political suicide and having the public realize that this is the case. In interviews, his supporters have stated that although their initial reaction to the reforms was outrage, they eventually came around and accepted that the reforms were reasonable. All in all, the case of Australian gun control is an interesting example of political actions that are socially beneficial but extremely politically difficult. Gun violence has never been as high in Australia as it was before 1996 and suicide rates have plummeted. Suicide is, after all, the most common form of violence, accounting for over two-thirds of it. This is also usually why gun violence is seen as less pressing than it is: most people who shoot a gun at someone shoot them at themselves.

Effective leadership

Unfortunately, not every leader is successful in inspiring their particular nation and achieving their political goals. Let us examine some case studies of heads of state that have achieved the delicate balancing act involved in being perceived positively as a political leader, and discuss what these notable individuals have in common.

Winston Churchill

Winston Churchill is perhaps the most noteworthy political leader of all-time, and one of the most successful. Presiding over the British campaign during World War II, there have certainly been few heads of state placed in more pressurized circumstances. Yet, Churchill took this almighty challenge in his stride and proved himself to be the ideal wartime leader for the United Kingdom.

Churchill was known for his powerful oration and mastery of the English language. During some of the darkest days in the history of Britain, Churchill delivered speeches that are considered among the most powerful ever spoken. His speeches were defiant, heroic, yet always human, and were sprinkled with dashes of humor as well. As President John F. Kennedy said of Churchill: "He took the English language and sent it into battle."[65]

The level of popularity achieved by Churchill is almost inconceivable today. Indeed, between July 1940 and May 1945, there were never less than 78 percent of people polled who approved of Churchill as the British prime minister. This popularity was partly derived from Churchill's incredible work ethic, with the prime minister regularly working 18-hour days during the war effort. But the nature of his speeches was also highly populist, using simple but precise language to inspire the largest swath of people possible. This enabled the general population to identify with Churchill and trust his vision that the almighty war effort required.

However, before discussing the reasons for Churchill's political success, it is also worth noting that he was deposed from his position as prime minister shortly after the end of World War II. The population sought the reformation and reconstruction of Britain, and Labor, under Clement Attlee, was deemed more suitable to govern Britain in the immediate post-war world. This indicates that just because a political leader is ideal for a particular time period, it does not necessarily follow that he or she will succeed in all circumstances. Context is all-important.

Yet, there are many leadership skills that others can learn from Churchill, aside from his highly regarded ability with communication. Churchill went out of his way to connect with the average man and woman on the street, at a time when the morale of the United Kingdom was understandably fragile. This involved visiting factories and bombed houses, and regularly speaking with everyday people. Undoubtedly, this had a positive impact on his image as a political leader, and even on the war effort in Britain.

Churchill also spoke with passion about the spirit of the British people, which only served to steel the resolve of the population. For example, one quote attributed to Churchill is as follows:

It was the nation and the race dwelling all round the globe that had the lion's heart. I had the luck to be called upon to give the roar. I also hope that I sometimes suggested to the lion the right place to use his claws.

Churchill was also highly passionate about his position, and an avowed patriot. He was dedicated to the betterment of the United Kingdom and had devoted his entire life to this exalted goal. He previously worked as a war correspondent, a soldier, and a writer before becoming a statesman. This meant that Britons could relate to their leader and really get behind him, at probably the most testing time in the entire history of the United Kingdom.

It was also important for Churchill to be a visionary, as he needed a wider spectrum of analysis of the war situation in order to be successful. He was then able to put this vision into practice with both courage and decisive action, which was critical in order to bring the British people along with him during World War II. This spirit and togetherness are perhaps exemplified best by what is possibly Churchill's most famous speech, in the House of Commons on June 4, 1940:

> We shall not flag or fail. We shall go on to the end, we shall fight in France, we shall fight on the seas and oceans, we shall fight with growing confidence and growing strength in the air, we shall defend our Island, whatever the cost may be. We shall fight on the beaches, we shall fight on the landing grounds, we shall fight in the fields and in the streets. We shall fight in the hills. We shall never surrender![66]

Churchill perfectly captured the mood of Britain at a time when this was absolutely essential to his premiership. He also intimately understood the character of the British people, and was able to tap into this national character and engender a collective spirit. However, when the climate of Britain changed, and the public perception was that a more thoughtful and considered approach was required in order to rebuild after the demoralizing and destructive war effort, Churchill was no longer seen as the right man for the job and was quickly voted out of office.

This underlines the fact that the conditions of a particular country are critical to the success of a political leader. Not only is it important to understand and respect the culture of a nation, but it is also critical to comprehend that this is a shifting entity. If a political leader becomes too associated with one mode of behavior or rule, he or she can be quickly deposed when this is no longer deemed appropriate.

Franklin Roosevelt

There are many great leaders in the history of the United States, but Franklin Delano Roosevelt, who served as the 32nd president of the United States from 1933 until his death in 1945, can perhaps be considered the most successful modern president. Not only did Roosevelt win a record four presidential elections—before this became impossible due to a change in the Constitution—but he was also an absolutely central figure in world events during a critical time in human history.

Roosevelt was responsible for directing the federal government during the majority of the Great Depression, and oversaw the United States' intervention in World War II. Thus, Roosevelt dealt with the greatest economic downturn in the history of the United States, and the longest period of sustained global conflict. Yet, he came out of this tumultuous period with an unblemished reputation and is often regarded by academics and scholars as one of the three greatest American presidents of all-time, alongside George Washington and Abraham Lincoln.

While Roosevelt was responsible for implementing a vast legislative program, probably the policy that is most associated with his period of presidency is the New Deal. This was a series of programs, public work projects, financial reforms, and regulations enacted in the United States between 1933 and 1936, effectively creating support for the poor and a genuine welfare state in America, as the country attempted to recover from the crippling depression that had occurred in the early years of the decade.

To give a flavor of this policy, major federal programs introduced during the New Deal included the Civilian Conservation Corps, the Civil Works Administration, the Farm Security Administration, the National Industrial Recovery Act of 1933, and the Social Security Administration. Help was offered to farmers, unemployed people, youth, and the elderly and retired. Safeguards and restraints on the banking industry were also put in place, which were deemed essential after the financial sector was primarily responsible for the market collapse which preceded the Great Depression.

This was a highly debated course of action, but one that history has judged extremely favorably. The United States was able to rise out of the Great Depression, and once again establish itself as the predominant economic power of the 20th century. Nonetheless, a huge amount of political wrangling was associated with the New Deal, as it was particularly opposed by certain Republican factions.

Thus, in order to cement his legacy as a hugely successful president, and push through this program of reformation, Roosevelt needed several leadership skills that particularly meshed with the American character and society. It is often noted that Roosevelt was a particularly curious person, always keen to learn more about a wide variety of subjects. This meant that he was generally held in high esteem by the American public, and this aspect of his character could be easily contrasted with such recent presidents as George W. Bush and Donald Trump.

Roosevelt's presentation skills were also exemplary. Despite dealing with paralysis from the waist down due to polio, he nonetheless cut an imposing figure with his brimming confidence and booming voice. He also used radio to good effect, becoming a master of the brand-new technology, and is generally regarded as one of the best orators of the 20th century. It is notable that Roosevelt received a huge number of letters of appreciation during his time as president, something that was unheard of prior to his tenure.

Another aspect of Roosevelt's presidency was its extreme decisiveness, driven by his self-confidence and belief in his own opinions and decisions. However, this had to be measured with a desire to listen, in what was an extremely delicate political situation for the United States. Nonetheless, Roosevelt was always ready to ignore his closest advisors on major issues, most notably when he threw his weight behind the Allied forces in what many people consider a defining moment that swung the balance of power away from the Axis nations.

Roosevelt also showed a doggedness and ability to overcome significant personal adversity that particularly appealed to the American people and culture. Roosevelt had contracted polio in 1921, which left him paralyzed from the waist down. Yet, he refused to be seen publicly in a wheelchair, instead relying on a combination of canes and mechanical braces in order to stand upright, and even walk short distances. This determination appealed to the American people, while it helped with his public image and statesmanlike qualities.

Jimmy Carter

It is interesting to contrast these successes of Roosevelt with the failings of another Democratic president. There are many similarities between the period over which Jimmy

Carter presided, in the late 1970s, and the times of Roosevelt. When Carter became president, the country was experiencing a turbulent period, during which the economy was suffering from stagflation. This was characterized by low output and high inflation and unemployment, which meant that Carter had to seek radical solutions, particularly as economists in the White House considered it to be an unexplained phenomenon.

With this in mind, Carter put in place an energy conservation program, which introduced higher oil taxes in order to discourage consumption. Carter would instead rely on oil importation in order to keep US cars on the road, but this turned out to be a spectacular misreading of the American public.

The US population was not prepared to drastically change its consumption patterns overnight, or wear sweaters in order to offset heating, as Carter himself claimed (rather implausibly) that he did. Instead, the American public still remembered the golden years of the 1950s and 1960s, and considered the state of the nation to be something of a comedown. Carter also underestimated the importance of the motor car in American culture, and thus his energy policy is widely considered to be unsuccessful.

Carter also demonstrated a lack of flexibility, and this is perhaps best underlined by the fact that he still considers his energy policy to be successful to this day, even though it is cited as a primary reason why he was not able to secure a second term in office.

In terms of foreign policy, Carter also displayed a lack of prudence, despite the fact that he had advocated strong adherence to human rights principles. This can be praised in principle, but in practice, examining his approach to dealing with foreign leaders does not reflect favorably on his presidency.

Most of the leaders with whom Carter built relationships were ironically dictators, frequently violating human rights legislation. Yet, Carter tended to establish controversial, friendly relations with such people, which undermined the ethos of his presidency. Carter not only lacked experience in the field of international politics, but he was also unable to learn from his mistakes, being reticent to implement prudence and ingenuity, which ultimately caused massive problems when the Soviet Union invaded Afghanistan and the Iranian Revolution took place.

Carter can be viewed as an idealist who failed to understand that the implementation of his ideology was more important than the vision itself. Although the definition and intentions of his foreign and domestic policies were often morally appreciated, the enforcement of them proved to be problematic. Carter showed himself to be a soft negotiator who was unable to establish the level of authority and respect that is required for any American president. He also failed to act decisively over certain foreign policy issues, and thus his presidency is usually judged to have been a failure.

Above all else, Carter fails to understand the political culture of the United States, and what Americans actually require from their president. Rather than relying on values-based arguments, Carter underestimated the importance of appearing strong and charismatic, and speaking to everyday working people on their level. It is therefore perhaps not surprising that the dominant political figure in the United States in the 1980s, Ronald Reagan, was able to do precisely these things with aplomb, and secured two well-received terms in office as a result.

Political dictatorship

However, although liberal democracy has come to dominate the Western world, it is not the form of government that operates in every region of the planet. Democracies are not always in place, and sometimes political leaders are *de facto* dictators, in whom a vast amount of power and influence is invested.

While this may run contrary to our Western values, the reality is that not every country is ready to implement a system of democracy. The people living in these nations still wish to have as enjoyable and valuable an existence as possible, and this means that strong and effective political leadership is required in these countries.

Of course, there are many examples of despotic and corrupt dictators, but amid the chaff there is also some wheat to be found. And one of the most benevolent and effective political leaders in this context is Lee-Kuan Yew, the first prime minister of Singapore.

Lee-Kuan Yew

Yew was in office for seven years, between 2004 and 2011, but was also a central figure in Singapore achieving its independence from British colonial rule in 1963. Yew always characterized Singapore as a "Chinese society," and thus advocated strong leadership in accordance with traditional Chinese society, culture, and government. An illustration of this is one of his most famous quotations:

Anybody who decides to take me on needs to put on knuckle-dusters. If you think you can hurt me more than I can hurt you, try. There is no other way you can govern a Chinese society.

In accordance with this, Yew abandoned any pretension of being popular in favor of what he deemed to be long-term socioeconomic planning. As a leader, though, Yew was always in favor of meritocracy and multiculturalism as governing principles, even ensuring that English was the common language in the nation, in order to integrate immigrant society and facilitate trade with wealthy countries.

But Yew also mandated bilingualism in schools in order to preserve the mother tongue of students and protect their ethnic identity. In a sense, Yew was willing to make a practical decision in order to preserve both the cultural and economic aspects of Singapore.

While Yew's leadership was strongly criticized for the curtailment of civil liberties, particularly with regard to media control and public protests, there were underlying reasons for these decisions. By Western standards, Yew's decision to bring libel suits against political opponents was particularly mendacious, but here he strongly argued that such disciplinary measures were necessary for political stability in an embryonic nation. Certainly, Singapore faced massive economic challenges in becoming an independent country, yet it has established itself as particularly stable in the early decades of self-rule.

Yew did encourage the open and free exchange of ideas but understood that strong political leadership was essential for Singapore at that time. In arguing that open dialogue was important, the statesman drew a comparison with America. "China will inevitably catch up to the U.S. in absolute GDP. But its creativity may never match America's, because its culture does not permit a free exchange and contest of ideas," Yew had commented.

He convincingly argued that a country which has never been a democracy will struggle to successfully implement a democratic system. Yew argued:

I do not believe you can impose on other countries standards which are alien and totally disconnected with their past. So, to ask China to become a democracy, when in its five thousand years of recorded history it never counted heads … All rulers ruled by right of being the emperor, and if you disagree, you chop off heads, not count heads.

Yew also understood the importance of technology in transforming the country, and in changing how government would operate. He particularly noted the often-quoted statistics that around 70 percent of the population would be urban based by the year 2030. Yew understood that this would require a change in government in years to come, and that the population would become increasingly well-informed, even in a traditionally dictatorial society such as Singapore.

As a leader, Yew encouraged the Singaporean population not only to be outward looking, but also to understand that balancing the books in a nation the size of Singapore would be of critical importance. Yew was vocally critical of the economic management of several Western nations, particularly in relation to the persistent government budget deficits and high public debt that have been commonplace in recent years.

Yew understood Singapore on every level: socially, culturally, and economically. He saw that raising the standard of living for the general population would be deemed more important than lofty ideals of installing democracy. Indeed, he always paid close heed to the history of Singapore, and emphasized how important it was to know history, and then build that into your medium- and long-term planning.

Above all else, Yew promoted a modern notion of economic competition, and the idea that this was central to the human psyche. Yew commented:

> Human beings are not born equal. They are highly competitive. Systems like Soviet and Chinese communism have failed because they tried to equalize benefits. Then nobody works hard enough, but everyone wants to get as much as, if not more than, the other person.

In summary, Yew knew how to appear credible in the eyes of the population, and the best way to deliver an inspiring and strong system of government that would appeal to the general public. Strong leadership, economic modernization, a steady shift toward a more open society, and protection of traditional aspects of culture were all part of his recipe for a prosperous Singapore. And this political stew that he created was well-received by the people, successful on the political stage, and ultimately resulted in Yew becoming a highly regarded leader.

Again, context is critically important, and it should be emphasized that what worked in Singapore would have been reviled elsewhere.

In the Western world, dictatorships are typically branded as unstable, untrustworthy, and undemocratic. Certainly, it is impossible to argue against the last of these claims, as a dictatorial government is undemocratic by its very nature. But contrary to the impression that most Westerners have, dictatorships can actually be successful, and deliver optimum conditions for the general population. That may grate with our collective values, but examining the political system of two prominent dictatorships can begin to reveal that the situation is more nuanced than we might imagine.

The political system of Singapore

Since the country declared independence in 1959, Singapore has transformed from a relatively underdeveloped and impoverished agrarian society into one of Asia's wealthiest nations. Today, Singapore is a sophisticated center of international banking, business, and shipping. And it has achieved this without ever becoming a true democracy.

Nonetheless, Singapore is not some shotgun nation, lacking basic freedom, rights, and opportunities, just because it hasn't embraced liberal democracy. First, constitutional supremacy in Singapore is the highest law, which means that the constitution is the foundation of all laws in the country. This means that all other laws must be formulated in conjunction and have no contradictions with the constitution. In this regard, parallels can be drawn immediately with the United States, which is, of course, a constitutional republic.

What operates in Singapore is a system in which there are checks and balances, but the government is not accountable to the people in the direct way that we would associate with a Western nation (although many believe that even in current democratic systems, governments have become far too powerful and unaccountable).

The government in Singapore is classified into three powers, namely, the executive, legislative, and judiciary. Essentially, the executive is the executor of government policies, consisting of the president and the cabinet. The legislature consists of people's representatives in parliament. And the judiciary consists of a supreme court and its subordinates, which has the power to examine the actions of the legislative and executive through judicial review. The judiciary must ensure that every law passed through the legislature does not violate the constitution. Likewise, the judiciary must also check that administration actions carried out by executives are constitutional. On the other hand, the legislature also has the legal right to check the executive through questions and answers in parliamentary sessions.

In Singapore, the president is elected by all citizens, and then has the right to choose one member of parliament as his prime minister and choose other members of parliament as ministers, based on the advice of the prime minister. Therefore, the prime minister and ministers of the cabinet are also the members of parliament. So, each power is a watchdog over the other. In this regard, the government owns a self-internal control system rather than solely relying on public supervision. This means that although Singapore cannot be accurately described as a democracy, it does function in a coherent fashion, rather than investing too much power and control in one person, or a small group of people. Nonetheless, Lee-Kuan Yew is widely recognized as having been a benevolent dictator in the nation for decades. But we'll return to that concept later.

While the president is the head of state of Singapore, she or he must always adhere to advice from the prime minister, and any minister acting under the cabinet. Thus, the actual work of governing the country is mostly executed by the prime minister and ministers in the cabinet; hence, the prime minister is usually considered to be the most important person in Singapore. Nonetheless, reformation has taken place in Singapore, in order to expand the role of the president. But what is crucial to note is that the key political players in Singapore are never elected by vote, and never directly accountable to the electorate. The president, and other checks and balances, are intended to ensure that the system functions adequately, but the people have no direct say in this, other than electing the president, who then takes a back-seat role.

Presidential elections are held in Singapore, consisting of the issuance of a writ of election, application for president eligibility, political donation, nomination, campaigning, and the day of election. The part of the president eligibility and political donation are the two processes that make elections in Singapore notably different from liberal democracies.

In the first step, the prime minister issues a writ of presidential election to the returning officer. The writ of election contains information regarding the exact day and place of nomination. One of the documents that the presidential candidate needs to obtain is a valid certificate of eligibility, along with a community certificate. This community certificate functions as proof of the candidate's objectivity with regard to all majority and minority groups in Singapore. The candidate is required to submit a community declaration, in the event of him or her deeming himself or herself to be part of a member minority group such as Chinese, Malay, Indian, etc. Alternatively, candidates can also state that they are not a member of any such community.

The next step after obtaining the certificate of eligibility and the community certificate is political donation. This is intended to prove that every candidate only receives political donations from permissible donors. The total amount of donations received must be at least USD 10,000. Furthermore, if the candidate is eligible for nomination, then she or he must submit a nomination paper to the returning officer, together with a statutory declaration that he or she has passed the qualification and is no longer a member of a political party.

Once the nomination is official, candidates are allowed to run campaigns. Presidential candidates are permitted to campaign through all forms of modern media, as long as there is no excessive expenditure, or provable links with big business involved. Finally, before the day of the election arrives, the cooling off period occurs, when candidates are not allowed to campaign.

This may seem quite a quaint system to the uninitiated, but it has proved to be highly supportive for socioeconomic progress in Singapore. The country has indeed flourished since becoming an independent nation in 1965. Prime Minister Lee-Kuan Yew took firm control of the country at this time, but, thankfully, committed himself to building a coherent and prosperous society.

The results were staggering. Over the next 20 years, Singapore's economy grew by over 800 percent. Average income per capita rose more than fourfold. The percentage of families living in poverty dropped to 0.3 percent (in the United States, this figure is deemed to be over 20 percent). The population of the country has stabilized, and unemployment is extremely low. By every reasonable measure, Singapore is a stable, modernized, successful society, and it is one that has achieved this without the direct political accountability that is deemed essential in the West.

38. A LONG-TERM VIEW

Political leadership and national consensus come together in practice through the implementation of long-term policies. The success of such policies requires a sustainable commitment by leaders and society to implement them. In their formulation, it is paramount that politicians put the interest of people ahead of their electoral interests. This is so difficult to achieve in democracies that it is hard to find examples in our recent history of successful long-term plans that are preserved through time, political cycles, and politicians. As I will show next, it is necessary that the design of the political process, or the characteristics of the electorate, is such that the chances of remaining in power after the next election are already guaranteed. It is as simple as this. Long-term policies have proven impossible in Mexico, where by the constitution a president cannot be re-elected for a second term. In contrast, as I discuss below, through its recent history, Boston has only seen Democratic mayors. As, on top of this, the electoral system is non-partisan (that is, candidates do not run under the official umbrella of the party), and a candidate can be re-elected as many times as possible, it is easy to enact long-term policies (such as Imagine Boston 2030).

Boston's colorful political history

First settled by European immigrants in 1630, and named by its Puritan inhabitants after the port town of Boston in Lincolnshire, England, for over a century the city of Boston, Massachusetts, was the largest town in British America. The city's location on the coast of the Atlantic Ocean made it a lively port, and during the colonial era its merchants engaged in shipping as well as fishing.

In the 19th century, Boston's population grew rapidly, and the city's ethnic composition changed dramatically with successive waves of immigrants. Irish immigrants dominated the first wave of newcomers during this period, especially following the Irish Potato Famine, which lasted from 1845 to 1849. By 1850, the Irish were the largest ethnic group in Boston.

Then came Italians, Germans, Lebanese, Syrians, French Canadians, and Russian and Polish Jews. By the end of the century, Boston's core neighborhoods had become enclaves of ethnically distinct immigrants, with the Irish dominating South Boston and Charlestown, Italians in the North End, and Russian Jews in the West End.

More Italians arrived following World War I, and again after World War II. Most settled initially in the North End. Despite the fact that the vast majority of both groups were Catholic and politically aligned with the Democratic Party, the Irish often clashed with the Italians. Thousands of Irish immigrants had settled in the North End in the 19th century, displacing the established English ("Yankee") residents. Then, in the early 20th century, the Irish were crowded out by newly arriving Italians. The two groups competed for jobs as well as housing, and there were cultural differences, including different styles of Catholic worship.

In the 20th century, Boston's African-American community slowly grew, thanks to an influx of immigrants from the West Indies and Cape Verde as well as blacks from the American South and West. In the 1920s, the community began expanding from the South End into the Roxbury district of the city, eventually becoming one-quarter of the city's population.

Mayor James Michael Curley

For much of the 20th century, the political life of Boston was characterized by intense ethnic rivalries, flamboyant characters, anti-Semitic violence, and corruption. In that regard, it was no different than any other big American city.

Perhaps no Boston political figure was more colorful than James Michael Curley. Between 1914 and 1950—a span of 36 years—he served four terms as mayor of Boston, including part of one term while incarcerated in prison. In addition to serving a term in the US House of Representatives, he also served a single term as governor of Massachusetts, a period characterized by one biographer as "a disaster mitigated only by moments of farce." [67]

Curley was born in Boston's Roxbury neighborhood in 1874. His father, Michael Curley, had landed in Boston from Oughterard, County Galway, Ireland, at the age of 14. His mother, Sarah Clancy, was also from County Galway. As Curley came of age, Boston's politics reflected the growing power of the Irish Catholic immigrants, a trend that was opposed by existing Yankee Protestant powers. He was a flamboyant figure and a populist who, because of his well-publicized efforts at helping those who were disadvantaged, became known, unofficially, as "the mayor of the poor." His motto—"Work harder than anyone else, preserve your self-respect, and keep your word"—earned him the loyalty of working-class voters.[68]

His first public notoriety came in 1904 when, while in prison on a fraud conviction, he was elected to Boston's board of aldermen. The prison sentence came after he and a colleague tried to help two men get jobs with the post office. To do this, Curley and the other man took the civil service exam under the names of the office seekers. Though the incident gave Curley a bad reputation among the city's gentrified Yankees, among the Irish poor it cemented his image as a man who would do whatever it took to help his constituents.

In 1946, newly elected to his fourth and final term as mayor of Boston, Curley was convicted of mail fraud. As *The New York Times* reported on January 19 of that year, Curley and two codefendants had been charged with misrepresenting their ability to obtain government contracts for their clients and had bilked these clients out of a total of USD 60,000. The *Times* noted,

> The mail fraud indictment against Mr. Curley, who enjoys great popularity in Boston, cast not the slightest shadow over his candidacy in the Boston Mayoralty election in November. Representative Curley was elected by the largest plurality ever given a Mayoral candidate there. His 115,000 votes almost equaled the combined total of his five rivals.[69]

When he reported to prison, he refused to relinquish the mayor's office, although it is unclear how much day-to-day influence he exerted over the city during his incarceration. Curley served just five months before President Harry Truman pardoned him; the president was responding in large part to a petition listing the names of over 100,000 Boston residents.[70]

The death of James Michael Curley in 1958 marked the end of an era. Many people loved "The Rascal King" (so named by his biographer, Jack Beatty), and many—primarily the wealthy Protestant Yankees whom he loved to skewer—hated him. But even a longtime opponent had to admit, "The city would be a shabby place today without having had him."[71]

With the passing of Curley, the nature of Boston politics evolved, ethnic differences eased, and the old neighborhood strongholds of power slowly gave way to more professionalized candidates controlled not by local bosses but by campaign consultants.

Boston's non-partisan city government

Boston, with its city proper population of 685,000, making it roughly equal to Sarajevo, Bosnia and Herzegovina or Sheffield, UK, has a mayor-council system of government. Specifically, it is a *strong mayor* system. Under this system, the mayor is the chief executive and is elected by voters, while a unicameral council serves as the legislative branch. The popularly elected mayor is given almost total administrative authority and a clear, wide range of political independence, with the power to appoint and dismiss department heads without council approval and little or no public input.

The Boston City Council is made up of 13 members: 9 district representatives and 4 at-large members. Councilors are elected to two-year terms and there is no limit on the number of terms an individual can serve. The council is responsible for approving the city budget, which is prepared by the mayor; monitoring, creating, and abolishing city agencies; making land use decisions; and approving, amending, or rejecting other legislative proposals.

It is important to know that all municipal elections in Boston, including elections for mayor and city council, are non-partisan. This means that like any citizen, candidates for office are entitled to have a personal party affiliation, but this party affiliation does not appear on the ballot. Candidates are not chosen by a political party's primary elections. Under US federal law, "non-partisan election" has a legal definition. According to 5 CFR 151.101 [Title 5. Administrative Personnel; Chapter I. Office of Personnel Management; Subchapter B. Civil Service Regulations; Part 151. Political Activity of State or Local Officers or Employees General Provisions], the term means "an election at which none of the candidates is to be nominated or elected as representing a political party any of whose candidates for Presidential elector receives votes in the last preceding election at which Presidential electors were selected."[72]

Proponents of non-partisan elections say that when it comes to providing services, political parties are irrelevant. The famous saying for this situation is, "There is no Democratic or Republican way to pick up the garbage." They also suggest that cooperation between officials belonging to different parties is more likely. Politicians in non-partisan offices are likely to be focused more on getting their job done than making the other party look bad, as is often seen at the national level.

In addition, because candidates must seek votes from across the political spectrum, non-partisan elections are more likely to encourage and reward moderate candidates. This also leads to elections that are more competitive.

Of the 30 most populous American cities, 22 have non-partisan elections. Cities that have partisan elections—where parties (generally Republican vs. Democratic) openly compete—include New York City, Houston, Texas, Philadelphia, Pennsylvania, and Indianapolis, Indiana.[73]

In Boston, mayors are elected to terms of four years. There are no term limits—a mayor could be re-elected over and over again.

While Boston's city government is non-partisan, like the Commonwealth of Massachusetts it tends to be overwhelmingly composed of people who are affiliated with the Democratic Party. The last Republican mayor of Boston was Malcolm Nicholls, who served one term from 1926 to 1930. For better or worse, this *de facto* one-party rule—even though the parties themselves cannot take an active role in elections—provides great stability and continuity from one mayoral or city council term to the next. It ensures that unless the voters specifically mandate sweeping changes—which in Boston they haven't done in decades—a current mayor can act with substantial assurance that his successor is not going to dismantle everything he did. If a project is started under one mayor, it is very likely to be continued under the next.

Contrast this with the highly partisan nature of national politics in the United States. In Washington, DC, the Republicans and Democrats seem to be caught in an endless high-stakes competition in which whoever controls a particular branch of government—executive, the Senate, the House of Representatives, and increasingly even the Supreme Court—seeks to ram through their party agenda while opposing initiatives made by the other side. On the presidential level, in the modern era it had been accepted that the incoming president, while pursuing his own agenda, would respect the laws passed by his predecessor. Changes would be made gradually, and international agreements and treaties were not touched. This tradition allowed presidents to act with considerable assurance that their successor wouldn't reverse everything they did.

When Donald J. Trump, a Republican, assumed the office of president of the United States in 2017, he immediately abandoned this decades-long tradition. His goal—openly stated—was to destroy every agreement and accomplishment of his predecessor, Barack Obama. For example, on May 8, 2018, Trump announced the United States was leaving the 2015 Iran Nuclear Agreement reached by seven countries after more than two years of grueling negotiations. Trump said the United States would reimpose the stringent sanctions it had imposed on Iran before the deal and was considering new penalties. In response, Iran said it would remain in the deal. So did France, Germany, Britain, China, and Russia, who joined Iran in accusing the United States of sabotaging the accord.[74]

In the case of Donald Trump, his intense focus on reversing the accomplishments of his Democratic Party predecessor has gone well beyond the typical desire of one party to realign the nation along its vision and policies. His animus was—and is—deeply personal. He simply *hates* Barack Obama. Whatever Obama did as president, Trump wants to do the opposite. Many analysts speculate his hatred has its roots in the infamous 2011 White House Correspondents dinner, where Trump—who had for months been demanding that then-President Obama produce his birth certificate—was mercilessly skewered by both the president and the emcee, comedian Seth Meyers.[75]

While the full consequences of Trump's "wrecking ball" approach to federal policies remain to be seen, political observers agree that his abandoning of traditions dating back to the end of World War II has ushered in a new era of instability. This extends beyond politics and into the nation's industrial production. As part of their everyday jobs, business leaders try to plan years in advance and anticipate market conditions. Trump's impulsive actions, seemingly fueled only by his desire to dismantle everything Obama did, make long-range planning much more difficult, particularly for companies engaged in foreign trade and who use foreign suppliers. They do not know if tariffs will suddenly be imposed, or if Trump will make a regulation favoring one industry over another. On January 2, 2019, Apple's chief executive officer (CEO) Tim Cook announced that the tech giant had lowered fiscal first-quarter sales expectations, and he cited as a primary culprit China's faltering economy amid Trump's escalating trade war with that nation. "We believe the economic environment in China has been further impacted by rising trade tensions with the United States," Cook told CNBC. Apple's shares plunged on the news, adding to steep losses for the Dow Jones Industrial Average.[76]

As for Trump, he had made his attitude clear. A tweet from December 4, 2018, was typical:

I am a Tariff Man. When people or countries come in to raid the great wealth of our Nation, I want them to pay for the privilege of doing so. It will always be the best way to max out our economic power. We are right now taking in $billions in Tariffs. MAKE AMERICA RICH AGAIN.

Mayor Thomas M. Menino

As mayor of Boston, James Michael Curley was succeeded in 1950 by John Bernard Hynes, another son of Irish immigrants. Hynes, who served as acting mayor during Curley's imprisonment in 1947, and subsequently defeated Curley three times at the ballot box, was very different from his predecessor. Hynes was a modern big-city mayor, and during his 10 years in office he began to transform Boston from a rowdy collection of fractious neighborhoods into a cohesive metropolis. It was Hynes and his successors, John Collins and Kevin White, who were most responsible for the modernization of the city of Boston.

It is a testament to the effectiveness of Boston's city government that during the late 1960s—and even beyond—when violent race riots erupted each summer in most major American cities, Boston was largely spared. The black residents of Boston, while not immune to the effects of the entrenched racism that was a hallmark of American society for centuries, didn't feel the deep and corrosive sense of alienation that urban blacks felt in other big cities.

Kevin White served as mayor for 16 years—when Boston voters like their mayor, they re-elect him over and over again—and when he left office in 1984, he was succeeded by another son of Irish immigrants, Raymond Flynn. A devout Catholic, Flynn served as mayor for three terms—nearly 10 years—until President Bill Clinton appointed him US Ambassador to the Holy See, where he served until 1997.

The person in the line of succession to fill the remainder of Flynn's term was the president of the Boston City Council, Thomas Michael Menino. On July 12, 1993, Menino became acting mayor of Boston until the upcoming November 1993 election.

He won that election, and as the 53rd mayor of Boston, Menino would be re-elected four times, eventually serving until January 6, 2014—a span of over 20 years. Instead of running for a sixth term, which he could have won easily, due to ill health he chose to retire.

It was Tom Menino who established the modern-day template for the successful and popular mayor of Boston, and it can be argued that the reason Marty Walsh cruised to an easy victory in the mayoral election of November 5, 2013, is that voters saw him as a continuation of the style and substance of Tom Menino—not just in his politics but in the very way that he spoke.

Menino was the city's first mayor of Italian descent. The son of Susan and Carl Menino, Thomas Menino was born on December 27, 1942, in Boston's Hyde Park neighborhood. His father was a factory foreman at Westinghouse Electric. His paternal grandfather had emigrated from Grottaminarda, a town and commune in the province of Avellino (Campania), situated 80 kilometers (50 miles) northeast of Naples, in the southwest of Italy. His paternal grandmother was from Roccagorga, a commune in the province of Latina.[77] They lived on the first floor of the family's Hyde Park home.

After graduating from St Thomas Aquinas High School in Jamaica Plain in 1960, Menino didn't want to go to college. "Truman didn't go to college," Tom told his father. President Harry S. Truman was Menino's favorite president and a personal hero.[78]

Menino worked as a housing relocation specialist for the Boston Redevelopment Authority, was a research assistant for the state legislative committee on housing and urban development and served as an aide to state senator Joseph F. Timilty. In November 1983, Menino was elected as a Boston City councilor, where he served until being made acting mayor in 1993.

As mayor, Menino promoted an agenda of social liberalism, fiscal responsibility, and economic growth. In 2001, *Governing* magazine named Mayor Menino "Public Official of the Year" for effective neighborhood development in Boston. He also spearheaded many development projects designed to bring jobs into the city and help reverse the "white flight" to the suburbs that Boston, like many American cities, had experienced during the decades following World War II.

Perhaps most of all, it was for two reasons that residents of Boston loved Tom Menino.

He was a tireless worker and hands-on mayor who always *showed up*. When there was a shooting, a fire, or any significant public event, regardless of the time of day, Mayor Menino would be there. People in the high-crime neighborhoods of Mattapan and Roxbury knew that while the mayor couldn't solve all their problems, he was aware of their pain and did his best to comfort them.

His attentiveness to detail and to delivering services to his constituents—right down to fixing potholes in the streets—earned him the nickname "The Pothole Mayor." At the same time, he had the respect of the city's big money interests—the downtown financial firms and high-tech companies that were the engines of Boston's economy.

The other reason people loved Tom Menino was his distinctive way of speaking. To put it simply, he spoke as if he had a mouth full of marbles. When you heard him give a speech, it was likely that at some point you'd turn to your neighbor and ask, "Can you tell me what he just said? I couldn't understand a word of it." His thick Boston accent was combined with *malapropisms*—the actual garbling and mixing-up of words. As a result, some commentators took to referring to the mayor as "Mumbles Menino."

As Britt Peterson wrote for *The Boston Globe*, "As Boston's 'Mayor for Life' Thomas M. Menino prepares to step down in January, he leaves many legacies, from filled-in potholes to new skyscrapers downtown. But the mayor's most personal legacy may be his impact on the English language."

> Over his twenty years in office, 'Mumbles' Menino's colorful slips of the tongue, delivered in his shambling Boston accent, have provided endless humor and fascination for journalists and the public. When he wasn't (allegedly) calling Boston's lack of parking spaces 'an Alcatraz around my neck,' he was mixing up player names on just about every local team; just this October, he expressed his hope that the Boston Red Sox would win 'the World Series Cup.' How could a man who couldn't get through a sentence without ten 'ums' and several false starts be mayor of the Athens of America?[79]

His fascinating speech pattern told Boston voters two things: First, because his way of speaking would never play outside of Boston, there was no danger he would see being mayor as a mere stepping stone to national office. In contrast, Mayor Kevin White had aspirations for national office, as did Mayor Ray Flynn, who left the job of mayor to be ambassador to the Vatican, before running for Congress. Mayor Menino never set his sights beyond the city limits of Boston.

Second, he was *authentic*. He was truly a man of the people. As Menino himself said in his 1993 victory speech, "I'm not a fancy talker, but I get the job done."[80]

Did Tom Menino have a long-term vision for the city of Boston? Curiously, he denied it. Sensitive to those who said that the "urban mechanic" lacked a big vision, he derided visionaries as people who can't get anything done.[81] In his two decades as mayor of Boston, he never communicated a comprehensive vision of the city's future. Nor did he seem to want to. He focused squarely on the day-to-day problems of Boston's present, none of them too small to occupy his interest.[82]

In reality, he had a vision—he just did not talk about it. He knew that successful mayors deliver the everyday services their constituents expect: good schools, low crime, clean streets, prompt trash removal, potholes that get filled in. The "big picture" decisions he made quietly, without fanfare. In 2010, he successfully spearheaded the Innovation District, an urban environment fostering innovation, collaboration, and entrepreneurship on 1,000 acres of the largely empty South Boston waterfront. The barren area is destined to be one of the biggest mixed-use developments in the entire country when it is done.[83]

That same year saw the establishment of a new city department: New Urban Mechanics. Many people thought Menino gave the department that name as a wry commentary on his reputation as an "urban mechanic" who lacked vision. But New Urban Mechanics was conceived as a bold innovation laboratory dedicated to solving real-life problems using technology and new ideas. Formed as the mayor's civic research and development team, the department tackles research and design projects over a wide range of topics. The mission is to "work across departments and communities to explore, experiment, and evaluate new approaches to government and civic life."[84] This includes everything from civic engagement to city infrastructure to education.

Many of the projects promoted by New Urban Mechanics seek to leverage technology to make city government more responsive to citizens. BOS:311 (originally called Citizens Connect) is a mobile smartphone app that helps residents report quality of life issues, such as graffiti, directly to the right person at City Hall to take action. As of January 2019, the app had logged 1.4 million 311 service requests.[85]

Street Bump is an app that allows Bostonians to transmit information on potholes and other road problems directly to City Hall. The One Card is a school ID, a library card, and a community center membership card, as well as a transit pass. The website Discover BPS (Boston Public Schools) provides information for families about possible schools for their children. The site Where's My School Bus lets parents learn if their child's ride to and from school is on schedule.

In late 2011, Menino announced an ambitious plan to jump-start nearly USD 600 million in development along the East Boston waterfront. He championed the idea of a Downtown Boston Business Improvement District. In low-income Dudley Square, the rehab of the old Ferdinand Building into a modern office complex for the city schools' headquarters transformed the blighted neighborhood.

With Tom Menino, Bostonians had a mayor who wasn't a fancy talker and who got the job done while quietly spearheading visionary projects. His first loyalty was to the neighborhoods of his city. In his private life, he was the same, living modestly with his wife, the former Angela Faletra, who kept her job as an accountant at John Hancock Financial Services. "Work gives me my own identity," she told Boston.com News. "It is a little private piece of me." Her husband agreed: "Angie is the real thing. She does not have to work. She could have a driver, and somebody to clean the house. But she will never give it up. She's stubborn that way."[86]

Mayor Marty Walsh

In Martin Joseph Walsh, Boston voters found a mayor who would continue the policies and the down-to-earth image of Tom Menino. They chose continuity over change.

With two exceptions.

One difference was that with Walsh, Boston voters returned to the traditional archetype of the Irish-American mayor. Walsh was raised in the Savin Hill neighborhood of Boston by parents who were first-generation Irish—his father, John Walsh, had immigrated from Callowfeenish, a townland near Carna, County Galway, while his mother, Mary (born O'Malley), hailed from Rosmuc, County Galway. The couple came to the United States in the 1950s, and Marty was born on April 10, 1967.

Diagnosed with Burkitt lymphoma at age seven, years of chemotherapy disrupted his schooling; but at age 11 a scan revealed no traces of the cancer. He went to high school at The Newman School and received a bachelor's degree from the Woods College of Advancing Studies at Boston College.

His working-class credentials could not be more authentic. At age 21, he joined the Laborers Local 223 union, and rose to become the union's president, where he served until elected mayor of Boston. He also served as secretary-treasurer and general agent of the Boston Metropolitan District Building Trades Council, a union umbrella group, and as head of the Boston Building Trades.

In 1997, Walsh was elected to the Massachusetts House of Representatives, where he served until elected mayor of Boston. In April 2013, he announced he would run in the 2013 mayoral election. He resigned the Trades Council position. On September 24, 2013, among 12 candidates in the mayoral preliminary election, Walsh received a plurality of the vote, and advanced to the general election, facing the second-place candidate, Boston City Councilor John R. Connolly. On November 5, 2013, Walsh defeated Connolly in the general election.

The second major difference between Marty Walsh and Tom Menino is that Walsh was unafraid—and even eager—to publicly champion a long-range plan for the city.

Imagine Boston 2030

On May 6, 2015, during the Innovative Design Alternatives Summit (IDeAS) at Boston's historic Faneuil Hall, Walsh announced the launch of Boston's first citywide planning process in 50 years. Imagine Boston 2030 was a two-year public engagement process to create a "roadmap for success" leading up to Boston's 400th birthday. The mayor encouraged residents to get involved in the conversation by visiting a new website: Imagine .Boston.gov.

"It has been fifty years since we had a comprehensive plan for Boston," Mayor Walsh said in a video message that played before his remarks.

> In 1965 people were looking for the confidence to believe that the city's decline had ended. Today we're a thriving, healthy, and innovative city. Now is our chance to set the course for the next generation. I'm inviting you to join us in imagining the Boston of 2030. From economic development to open space, from education to equality, your voice is the key to our success.[87]

Through Imagine Boston and the power of the internet, the city hoped to take a more dynamic approach to community engagement than had been done with planning efforts in the past. As a first step to inform the process, Mayor Walsh asked community members to share their preferences for how they wanted to be engaged by completing a short online survey on the website. People could also participate on Twitter or reach out to their neighborhood coordinators to give feedback.

At the time of the mayor's announcement, a wide array of planning was already underway, including work on transportation, housing, climate action, arts and culture, aging, open space, and education. Imagine Boston sought to weave those initiatives together with other key themes to guide Boston into the next decades.

Imagine Boston aimed to address at least eight key themes, including:

- Housing: Building housing that keeps Boston accessible to all.
- Mobility: Creating an efficient, equitable, sustainable transportation system.
- Environment and adaptation: Using natural resources wisely while preparing for the impacts of a changing climate.
- Parks and open space: Providing world-class spaces for recreation and public life.
- Prosperity and equity: Creating jobs and supporting education and workforce development infrastructure to broaden economic opportunity.
- Arts, culture, and creativity: Enriching Boston and harnessing our creative potential in all endeavors.
- Design and placemaking: Building on a rich tradition of creating vibrant urban places and neighborhoods.
- Health: Improving and sustaining the health of Boston's population.[88]

So that citizens can get an idea of how the program is faring, its website at Imagine .Boston.gov offers voter-accessible metrics. The metrics dashboard features 14 metrics that are evaluated on a yearly basis to measure and track the city's overall progress toward achieving the plan's goals. As the website says,

> The metrics reflect Boston's data-driven approach to guiding long-term growth to boost quality of life, equity, and resilience in every neighborhood across Boston. The dashboard allows users to interact with data available on historic trends, current benchmarks, and how we will achieve the goals laid out in the plan.[89]

For example, one goal of Imagine Boston 2030 is to "encourage affordability, reduce displacement, and improve quality of life."

Under this heading are four metrics:

- Reduce housing cost burden for Bostonians. Metric: Decrease the portion of low- and middle-income households that are severely housing-cost burdened.
- Improve health outcomes for all Bostonians. Metric: Reduce disparities in premature mortality by neighborhood.
- Improve the walkability of each neighborhood. Metric: Increase Walk Score® ranking of neighborhoods.
- Keep Boston a safe city. Metric: Lower or maintain Boston's crime rate to be below the crime rates of peer cities.

If you click on goal number 2, "Improve health outcomes for all Bostonians," you're presented with the current metrics for "Reducing disparities in premature mortality (death before age 65) by neighborhood." As of January 2019, they include:

- Approximately 1,000 Bostonians die before age 65 each year. (The goal is to lower this number.)
- The city has experienced a 26 percent reduction in the premature mortality rate since 2000.
- In the low-income Roxbury section, there has been a 35 percent reduction in the premature mortality rate since 2002. You can click on any of the city's 15 neighborhoods to see the statistics for that neighborhood.

Anyone can go to https://imagine.boston.gov/ and peruse the data.

It is remarkable that Mayor Walsh would advocate the public display of metrics that reflect the performance—for better or worse—of his administration. This transparency is possible because the city has embraced digital technology as a tool of both results measurement and constituent communication; because the city's government is non-political and focused only on results; and because Boston voters tend to favor candidates who are down to earth and deeply involved with the city's diverse neighborhoods. The next mayoral election is in November 2021. Given the current performance by Marty Walsh, it is hard to imagine any candidate campaigning against him who would advocate abandoning Imagine Boston 2030.[90]

39. THE IMPORTANCE OF EXECUTION: DELIVERY UNITS

From the saying to the doing there is a long distance. This is particularly true in national and local politics. Most national strategies fail at the execution stage, and that is why I now analyze the current trend toward efficiency in political execution as a pillar of national success. Because *delivery units* are becoming the role model and are rapidly extending worldwide, I am devoting this section to their detailed analysis.

Prime Minister's delivery unit in the United Kingdom

As many other countries, the United Kingdom has adopted several public services reforms over the past decades. One of these reforms was the Prime Minister's Delivery Unit (PMDU), which was praised by several politicians, experts, officials, and institutions in the United Kingdom as well as abroad. The PMDU is one of the efforts by governments in many countries to address universal challenges in how to improve the management of public services and the quality of the provided services.[91] The introduction of PMDUs is primarily associated with the advocacy of Tony Blair, the prime minister of the United Kingdom at the time, and Professor Michael Barber, his chief adviser on delivery at the time.[92]

The PMDU was first introduced in the United Kingdom in 2001 during Tony Blair's second-term government. It was a center of government institution to assist and direct the prime minister and his administration on ways to improve public services, such as health education, transport, and crime. A *center of government* (CoG) institution(s) differs from ministers and other government institutions as it is an establishment formed to provide direct assistance or support to the prime minister or similar chief executives, and does not deliver direct services to the people but focuses instead on broad policy areas. Professor Michael Barber was the first head of the delivery unit, followed by Ian Watmore, the chief information officer in 2005, and finally by Ray Shostak in mid-2007. The delivery unit was brought to an end in the United Kingdom in October 2010 by the coalition government led by David Cameron.[93]

The delivery unit worked closely with, and was later integrated into, Her Majesty's Treasury, as well as other departments and agencies of the government and relevant stakeholders. The Treasury is the government department responsible for developing and implementing the government's public finance and economic policies. The PMDU worked closely with other government departments to evaluate delivery outcomes and provide performance management for the main areas in the delivery system. Together with the Treasury, the PMDU shared the responsibility to "improve public services by working with departments to help them meet their PSA targets consistently with fiscal rules."[94]

The forming of the PMDU was a by-product of the introduction of the public service agreements (PSAs) by Chancellor Gordon Brown and his then economic adviser Ed Balls in the early years of Blair's first government in 1998. The PSAs had direct and simple goals: "to define clear, long-term, outcome-focused goals; to provide ambition and a sense of direction; and to represent a contract between the public and government, adding a degree of accountability and transparency rarely seen before."[95] The PSAs were part of a comprehensive spending review which addressed nearly 35 policy areas of government through pointing to around 600 measurable targets. These targets were then reduced to 160, covering 18 areas in the spending review of 2000.[96] The PSAs were proposed by the special adviser to the Chancellor only a few days before the approval of the spending review of 1998. The PSAs were seen as a political announcement by the Labour Party that it would be aiming at tough measurements for the government's departments to improve the performance of the public services and deliver measurable improvements. However, the early execution of the PSAs was not promising and was characterized by weak political leadership, with practically no functioning model.[97] The short-term targets of the PSAs and the general political cycle made it difficult to expand these agreements into longer-term policies that would need 10–15 years to be realized. Moreover,

> it was unclear who was responsible for delivering PSAs and whether officials would even be held to account for failure. The accountability 'wasn't observable in any way.' More critically, PSAs were not tied to any levers, since spending allocations had already been agreed prior to their announcement.[98]

The PSAs were only firmly put into action in 2001, when Tony Blair gave his instructions to Michael Barber to "deliver" these agreements and to achieve 17 "priority" PSA targets.

As public services became controlled by market mechanisms, there was increasing public pressure to develop efficient monitoring mechanisms and transparent measurements on the performance of various local governments and agencies to enable public choice and establish a means of accountability. Prior to the PSAs, previous attempts were made by the UK government to improve the performance of local governments and agencies. The Financial Management Initiative (FMI) and Next Steps were earlier initiatives in this way. Moreover, the Citizen's Charter was adopted in 1991 to involve the public directly in the assessment of public and local services, and in 1992, the Local Government Act was introduced to allow the Audit Commission to implement statutory performance indicators for local government.[99]

PSAs established a clear framework for setting long-term targets and efficient methods to mobilize sufficient organizational resources to implement these targets. Prior to the adoption of the PSAs, it was clear that there was public dissatisfaction with health and education services, as well as the crime rates and poor-quality transportation. At the time of the introduction of the PSAs, there was increasing concerns regarding the long waiting times for patients to access health services provided by the National Health Service, and the quality of schools. Regardless of the type of government in charge, there was a widespread public view that the government's departments were unable to focus enough attention and resources toward improving these services.[100]

The initial work of the PMDU faced some resistance from government officials; however, Blair's support and Barber's credibility had succeeded in influencing government departments in accepting and collaborating with the PMDU. Barber managed to gain the support of the Treasury, and focused prioritized targets allowed him to create a well-functioning delivery model.[101] The reliable and resilient operating model relied on a diverse team that was well-resourced and had a collaborative system of working.[102] In 2007, the PMDU was officially incorporated as part of the Treasury and mobilized sufficient funds for its mission. Furthermore, the goals of the PSAs became more ambitious by setting cross-cutting targets that addressed several ministers and government departments at one time. However, the federal nature of the civil services fractionalized the impact of these PSAs, especially as the third Labour government was coming to an end. The coalition government led by David Cameron axed the PSAs and the PMDU as they were both considered symbols of the influence and control of Tony Blair in the government.[103] But the recent Implementation Unit is seen as the re-emergence in disguise of many of the methods and mechanisms of the PMDU.[104]

Professor Michael Barber, the first head of the PMDU, described the main approach of the unit's work through identifying three main components in addition to an overarching fourth component: first, creating a small team concentrating on performance; second, collecting data on performance to identify reliable targets and trajectories; third, requiring clear procedures to lead and safeguard the concentration on performance. And throughout all these components runs a significant component, which is creating and maintaining strong relationships within the unit and with all levels of relevant government departments that are responsible for delivery and implementation.[105]

Similarly, the national archives of the United Kingdom's Cabinet Office[106] describe the purpose of the Prime Minister's Delivery Unit as "to help Government to deliver better and more efficient public services." It aimed to do so through:

- monitoring the delivery of key policies and reform priorities and directly reporting to the prime minister,
- identifying the main problems and challenges to achieve the aimed improvements and recommending the needed action to strengthen delivery,
- strengthening the capacity of the involved government's departments to deliver, through reviewing their capabilities and facilitating the share of knowledge about best practices in delivery, and
- assisting in identifying and developing the targets of the PSAs to efficiently accelerate improvements in the quality of public services.

The main structures of the PMDU's work as stated in the cabinet's archives are:

- close collaboration and partnership with relevant government departments to make sure of the presence of a common shared understanding of current and foreseen challenges and a shared commitment to take the required actions,
- close engagement with officials involved in the delivery system at all levels to ensure a shared realization of the influence of the adopted policies and the benefits and risks of the planned required actions,
- objective, external challenge to departments to ensure the delivery and implementation of the proposed actions, and
- gathering of high-quality data that enable efficient monitoring of the progress against predefined trajectories and identify the effects of the main implemented policies.

The head of the delivery unit was appointed by the prime minister, and the unit had around 50 staff members. The staff of the PMDU came from within the civil service, the public sector, and major consultancy firms, in addition to relying on the knowledge and experience of a broader group of associates who were experts in successful delivery systems in the public, private, and voluntary sectors. The structure of the unit was as follows:

- eight delivery teams where each team was headed by a senior civil servant;
- one analytic function department;
- one support team;
- one commissioned projects and delivery knowledge team; and
- one capability reviews team.

In the public services areas targeted by the PMDU there is a strong legacy of efficient delivery by government departments and several success stories.

A good example of success in execution is the national education policies.[107] The PMDU, in collaboration with the Department for Education (DfE), had targeted 60 schools in five boroughs in London where their performance was below the national performance by approximately 17.5 percentage points. Tim Brighouse, who was the chief education officer of Birmingham at the time, worked closely with the boroughs and the targeted schools and with the assistance of expert practitioners whom were mostly head teachers. They coordinated on the ground with these schools and developed a tailored package based on existing best practices to assist the schools in improving the quality of their performances. Accordingly, the gap between the performance of these schools and the national performance decreased to only 8 percentage points by 2005, although the overall national performance was continually increasing.

Another success story is healthcare service,[108] involving reducing the waiting time of patients treated or admitted to four hours. In doing so, the PMDU worked closely in collaboration with the Department of Health and Social Care, and the National Health Service introduced weekly monitoring of hospitals. The new indicator was included in the star rating. Moreover, they encouraged the "see and treat" best practice method in all hospitals, in order to immediately treat minor injuries rather than using triage, which is the method of prioritizing the treatment of patients based on the urgency and severity of their condition. They also sought to adjust or overcome programs that had not delivered satisfactory results, such as the emergency care collaborative. They assessed, identified, shared, and increasingly adopted best practices on bed management in all hospitals. Moreover, the PMDU was helped in reducing the rate of unfounded asylum applications by 78 percent.

Although the success of any reform should be viewed in the long-term changes it institutes in the civil service and not in the instant moment, the PMDU had fundamentally changed the accountability of the government and civil servants.[109] A report[110] published in 2014 reported interviews with a number of permanent secretaries (the highest senior civil servant in a ministry in the government of the United Kingdom) and other senior civil servants to explore the impact and legacy of different reforms that took place in the British government in the last decades. Here, I present some of the respondents' opinions on the PMDU and PSAs' impact on the civil service.

One permanent secretary stated that the PMDU had

> changed the entire game [...] on accountability and responsibility. It fundamentally
> said: 'You as ministers, and you as civil servants, are responsible for delivery. It is
> not enough anymore to just launch the policy and think that's the job done.' And
> that, in a sense, sounds so obvious, but you remember back, that just wasn't people's
> mentality, so I think you cannot underestimate that.

Similarly, another permanent secretary mentioned that "Every perm sec knows that
delivery is a massive chunk of what their job is about now. And that just wasn't the case
fifteen years ago." The United Kingdom was quite successful in adopting an outcomes-
focused "comprehensive performance and evaluation system that embraces everything
from central government ministries down to frontline services."[111] These reforms had
significantly enhanced the performance of health and education services as well as criminal justice. The key difference that PSAs made was the clarity of objectives and targets
that government departments can follow and achieve as well as their affiliated agencies
and local departments, instead of the understanding and vision gap that always existed
between politicians and civil servants.[112]

Another permanent servant indicated that the PSAs and the PMDU were

> a great step forward in clarifying what departments were for and beginning to
> measure that in some systematic way. It allowed me in managing the department
> to assess a sort of balanced scorecard and so on and so forth against some clear
> objectives.[113]

Delivery units around the globe

Dissatisfaction with the capability of the government to deliver quality services is a
global phenomenon and has become a constant driver for distrust and doubt in national
states. Governments are used to overselling their promises and achievements to their
citizens, while undermining the increasing complexities and challenges faced to deliver
quality public services. Restructuring the government aims to restore trust in its ability
to provide quality public services and narrow the gap between government's promises,
citizens' expectations and demands, and the realized delivered services. That requires
governments to rethink how they work in terms of planning and budgeting, monitoring
and evaluation, identifying the responsibilities and accountability of each ministry and
government agency, and how implementations are executed. For governments to achieve
good governance, they need legitimacy, being responsive and accountable to their own
citizens, and independent from partisan and political interference. That is why there is
growing interest in improving a government's capacity to deliver, its effectiveness, and
the establishment of democratic accountability.[114]

In order to improve the delivery of public services, many countries and local governments as well as international organizations have opted to adopt the United Kingdom's
approach, dubbed *Deliverology*.[115] This approach is based on three main components:
"establishing a small team focused on performance [the delivery unit], gathering performance data to set targets and trajectories, and having routines to drive and ensure a focus
on performance."[116] There is no one-size-fits-all model for improving governments' effectiveness and delivery, but delivery units can be an extremely effective tool for enhancing

governments' delivery and implementation. However, delivery units need to be carefully designed to fit the existing institutional framework of each government or organization in order to have a successful impact on transforming delivery performance. The OECD has highlighted the key factors that contribute to the success of delivery units.[117] First, they differ in terms of their scope, especially with regard to the type of priorities addressed and outcomes expected; for instance, whether these are few or many priorities. Second, the scope and focus of delivery units should be clearly identified, ideally being narrow. Finally, good collaboration and coordination between the center of government and ministries and other stakeholders is the most crucial factor to identify the responsibilities and expectations of each involved agency. Currently, more than 15 countries have created delivery units in their national governments in addition to other delivery units established at state level, as in Maryland in the United States and Pernambuco in Brazil or at a local level such as the Borough of Haringey in London, as well as The World Bank, which created a President's Delivery Unit in 2014.

In Chile, President Sebastián Piñera established the President's Delivery Unit in the same year he took office, in 2010. Again, the President's Delivery Unit is a center of government agency created to achieve key priorities which the new administration identified. These seven programmatic priorities covered healthcare; education; employment; economic growth; civil security; poverty; and perfecting democracy.[118] The President's Delivery Unit had four key functions: "(i) strategically manage the planning for government actions, (ii) coordinate policy, mainly exercised through the DCI, (iii) monitor and improve performance, and (iv) accountability."[119] At the establishment of the unit, the president stated that its mission was "[to establish] a permanent evaluation and results monitoring system that regularly reports to the President of the Republic on the state of progress."[120] The President's Delivery Unit was responsible for monitoring and evaluating the achieved results and directly reported to the president. In order to achieve the programmatic priorities, the unit was also responsible for developing key milestones and results for each priority, clarifying how these results could be practically translated into formal decisions, and developing clear protocols to coordinate between responsible committees. It also participated in drafting the president's speech at the State of the Union in March 2010 on the public budget, and was seen as a key instrument in imposing discipline on ministries and other government agencies.[121]

Because of the huge power and authority given to the President's Delivery Unit over government ministries and agencies, it was important to be perceived as an invisible partner and collaborator and not as a competitor. This was very important to gain confidence and reliability from the government and ease collaboration with it. The PDU's contribution had less influence on creating the substance and content of the actions to be unrolled, but focused instead on securing coherence and integration.[122]

In Brazil, Eduardo Campos took office in 2007 as the governor of the state of Pernambuco, which has a population of around nine million and is located in one of the poorest regions in Brazil. Campos founded a center of government delivery unit to directly report to him, instead of the 66 agencies that were directly reporting to him at the time. He sought to build a delivery unit that could facilitate his mission and adopt a data-driven management approach. The new unit took responsibility of management, planning, budgeting, and monitoring the delivery of key results and implementations of his administration, in order to ensure efficient integration of several functions performed by the departments of the government. Campos headed a weekly meeting with the delivery unit to foresee implantation progress of his 12 strategic objectives identified in his initial strategic plan. The 12 strategic objectives covered 750 priority goals and were said to be developed through citizens' participation through 12 regional seminars that involved around 13,500 participants, led by the governor himself. The delivery unit had a significant impact on improving civil services and achieving tangible and measurable results.[123] For instance, one of the priorities of Campos' administration was to control crime rates and violence, so that homicides decreased by 30 percent in Pernambuco between 2007 and 2012, at a time when the national homicide rate in Brazil had increased. The delivery unit aims not only to achieve immediate results but also to improve the overall delivery of civil services and the institutional context of implementations. "Engaging employees from all levels of the civil service, from managers to a range of frontline staff, has begun to change the organizational culture of Pernambuco's public administration."[124]

In Rwanda, the Government Action Coordination Unit (GACU) was established in 2008.[125] The GACU is a small technical unit established within the Ministry of Cabinet Affairs and has around 10 analysts and a coordinator. The GACU is responsible for policy analysis, monitoring the implementations, and preparing cabinet meetings and quarterly and annual reports. In addition, the role of the unit includes preparing the National Leadership Retreat, National Dialogue Council meetings, and Imihigo planning and evaluation (Republic of Rwanda 2019). Dissatisfied by the failures in civil services delivery, public sector inefficiency, and duplication of duties across ministries, President Paul Kagame established two units to improve coordination among high levels of the government: a strategy and policy unit under the president's office and an action coordination unit within the prime minister's office. The two units were headed by the Minister of Cabinet Affairs and aimed at redefining the responsibilities and roles at the center of government, and improving planning and monitoring efforts, as well as coordination and accountability at all government levels.[126]

The President's Delivery Unit in Senegal was created in 2014.[127] The Senegalese delivery unit emerged with the "Emerging Senegal Plan" presidential initiative by President Macky Sall which aims to implement 27 projects and 17 key reforms covering a broad range of development areas from the investment environment to energy and land management to be achieved by 2035. The President's Delivery Unit is responsible for ensuring the delivery of five of these projects and three reforms, closely monitoring the progress on these projects and reforms, and providing a weekly report to the president.[128] The unit is also responsible for developing proposals for consideration by the president. Key responsibilities are

> reporting to the president about the level of progress of each project or reform;
> assessing the performance of delivery;
> identifying any additional financial or technical needs to support the implementation of the targeted projects and reforms;
> identifying major challenges faced during implementation and propose practical solutions as well as strategic decisions that require immediate action by the government.

To achieve its mission, the delivery unit works closely in collaboration with all ministries, local departments, and stakeholders, especially those directing the projects, in order to ensure effective coordination and that implementation is realized in line with the initial plans within the sectoral ministry of supervision.

Similarly, the office of President Uhuru Kenyatta in Kenya established the President's Delivery Unit in 2015 with a primary aim to improve the coordination within the programs of the national government, as well as monitoring, evaluating, and reporting directly to the president on the timely implementations of key development priorities. The delivery unit is a center of government agency based in the office of the president and works and coordinates with relevant ministers as well as key offices and departments within the office of the president. The delivery unit works within Kenyatta's Big Four agenda to improve civil service delivery and have the public achieve higher developmental goals that can uplift his nation and the standard of living of Kenyans. The Big Four initiative aims to enhance manufacturing, food security and nutrition, universal health coverage, and affordable housing. It is divided into flagship programs covering: information and communication technology; healthcare; land management; infrastructure; social inclusion; education; food security; energy; youth and women; security; ease of doing business; and ease of access to government services (Huduma Centers). Besides the head of the President's Delivery Unit and his secretary, the delivery unit has four sector delivery directors and around 45 staff.[129]

Following the recommendations of the second National Development Plan, Uganda established the Prime Minister's Delivery Unit in 2016 to improve the delivery of services provided to its citizens. The website of the office of the prime minister gives a detailed description of the history, aim, and working mechanism of the delivery unit. The unit aims to foster the delivery of public services, and to assist and facilitate the implementation of national development priorities. The Ugandan government seeks to achieve fast visibility of results and develop a culture of civil service performance based on speed and consistency in the public sector, and to transform the overall approach of service delivery in the government and how the public sector operates. For that, the unit's purpose is to enable the delivery of these national priorities through a methodical approach of planning and execution. The delivery unit established a rigorous system of monitoring and reporting on key national priorities and works on identifying challenges that appear during implementations to promptly address them. Moreover, similar to delivery units established elsewhere, the Ugandan Prime Minister's Delivery Unit bases its work on close collaboration with ministers and local authorities as well as other stakeholders to ensure that key priorities are met by the public as well as private sector and other developmental agencies. Again, collaboration and coordination play a vital role not only for implementation but also to clearly identify the responsibilities and expectations of each stakeholder. The creation of the delivery unit within the office of the prime minister was motivated by the lack of periodically short-term monitoring and evaluation mechanisms, and the government's willingness to achieve rapid progress on key selected development areas identified by the National Development Plan.[130]

The government identifies three main goals for the delivery unit. First, making results achieved on key national priorities clearly visible. Second, developing and anchoring a culture of speed and rigorous performance within the public services. And finally, to introduce flexible initiatives that identify and respond to the challenges of effective service delivery. The key services priorities that the delivery unit is responsible for are education, healthcare, employment, and household incomes.[131]

Other countries had established delivery units under different names. Within the department of the prime minister and cabinet in Australia, the Cabinet Implementation Unit was established in 2003 with a relatively small staff of around 10 experts. The unit works with government departments and agencies to guarantee the timely implementation of government decisions and plans, and to see that results are achieved in accordance with the set budget and expectations. The unit drafts policy proposals for consideration by the prime minister to ensure that the cabinet has clear and achievable goals that can be periodically assessed. The unit works in collaboration with other departments and agencies to develop implementation plans and to evaluate and manage any challenges and implementation risks. The unit is also responsible for monitoring the progress achieved to meet key government decisions and directly reports to the prime minister and the cabinet on the progress of these implementations.

Similarly, in Canada, the Privy Council Office was established within the government in 2016 as a delivery and results unit. The unit works on monitoring and reporting on the status of the implementation of the 364 commitments identified by Prime Minister Justin Trudeau in his mandate letters to ministers, in various areas including gender equity, employment, budgeting, and refugees. The commitments cover 12 key priorities identified by the government and documented through the prime minister's mandate letters sent to each cabinet minister.[132]

The experience of Malaysia's PEMANDU

In 2009, Malaysia established the Performance Management and Delivery Unit (PEMANDU) headed by Idris Jala as its chief executive. Jala was appointed within the office of the prime minister in line with the government's vision to move the country from middle-income status into a high-income country by 2020, and for that Jala was responsible to lead the Government Transformation Program (GTP) and the Economic Transformation Program (ETP).[133] Since then, the PEMANDU has become one of the largest and most successful delivery units in the world, and many governments seek to study and learn from its experience.[134] In the World Bank report on Malaysia's experience with the PEMANDU, it states that at the time of his appointment as head of the PEMANDU, Jala "was given the assurance by the prime minister in 2009 that the government is altogether committed in the pursuit of sustainable and inclusive socio-economic transformation."[135] The main aim for the creation of the PEMANDU was to assist in designing the National Transformation Program (NTP) and ensure that the NTP is being realized and implemented by the responsible ministries, departments, and agencies (MDAs), while the PEMANDU is responsible for planning, monitoring, and reporting on the progress of implementations and addressing the challenges faced.

The success and legacy of the PEMANDU must be placed within the broader context of Malaysia's public sector performance culture and development progress. Malaysia has always had a strong public sector which created the desired environment for the establishment and success of the PEMANDU. Since its independence from the British Empire in 1957, the country has built an effective public sector that focuses on improving the economy through diversified growth, reducing poverty rates, and building the country's infrastructure. Even before the PEMANDU, the Malaysian government had always attempted to focus on results more than on strategies. "This performance orientation created elements of a performance culture."[136]

The eight steps of transformation

The PEMANDU plays several well-defined and successive roles. The PEMANDU follows its own "Eight Steps of Transformation" methodology that ensures the unit is involved with key tasks at every stage of implementation. The transformation steps start with strategic workshops that include the unit with high members of the cabinet to identify the strategic direction of the government. The PEMANDU is responsible for assisting in identifying the key priorities of the cabinet as well as breaking down these key priorities in order to be translated into concrete interventions in line with the National Transformation Program and to identify the owners of these interventions. Following that, the PEMANDU provides technical support to ministries, departments, agencies, and other stakeholders involved in the National Transformation Program. This technical support includes setting key performance indicators and methods to monitor them. The PEMANDU also works to promptly identify obstacles faced during implementation and reporting them to higher levels of decision-making to quickly resolve them. By the end of the cycle, a third independent party audits and verifies the reported KPIs and disseminates its results to all stakeholders as well as the public in the annual report.[137]

Transformation is a continuous process that every institution must endorse in its daily culture, yet the transformation process might be unclear and difficult to embed and codify, and for that the PEMANDU adopts a "decoding transformation" approach. From the PEMANDU's website, the "Eight Steps of Transformation" methodology is explained. "The Eight Steps of Transformation is a radical and structured approach incorporating clear diagnosis, planning, implementation, execution, and feedback, in a sequence which ensures transparency and accountability during your transformation."[138] The Eight Steps of Transformation are as follows.

Step 1: Strategic workshop

Sometimes politicians have a clear vision about the future, but such vision does not come with clear and measurable outputs. This is especially the case when responsibilities spread across many agencies and resources are spread across many tasks. In these cases it is crucial to make sure that well-thought objectives are reachable and resilient to bottlenecks. Strategic workshops bring together senior decision-makers and key staff in the ministries, departments, and agencies to collectively identify the desired goals to be achieved and to ensure that decisions are clear, achievable, and quantifiable. The higher desired goals are called "True North."

Step 2: Develop your implementation plan with our lab approach

The PEMANDU's main work is done through labs that bring together all public sector agencies involved in the delivery of a specific priority together with other private sector actors to work on a specific policy area. These labs are organized in order to make the desired goals as concretely detailed as possible with clear identification of responsibilities, timelines, step-by-step actions, financial resources, and measurable targets. The lab is also important to ensure that all stakeholders share the same understanding of their roles and the desired goal.

Step 3: Secure feedback with the hosting of an open day

Open Days are regular meetings between the delivery unit and the ministries, departments, agencies, and other stakeholders to collect feedback from shareholders and keep the prime minister or responsible ministers informed of implementation progress and any challenges faced. Stakeholder feedback is a crucial element to ensure optimum understanding and cooperation of the general agenda.

STEP 4: Ensuring accountability and commitment through a roadmap

Roadmaps help in ensuring transparency which is realized into commitment. Roadmaps include details about project owners, actions, activities, timelines, milestones, and targets to be achieved. Roadmaps are crucial to identify points of reference for implementing the transformation program to all ministries, departments, agencies, and other stakeholders.

Step 5: Setting key performance indicators

"People do not do what you expect, but what you inspect." KPIs are first set in the labs (Step 2) and are measured on an annual basis. The head of ministries, departments, and agencies and other implementation leaders are responsible for ensuring that implementation is progressing according to a given scorecard that includes multiple KPIs to be measured, in order to achieve the desired goals or the "True North."

Step 6: Rigorous implementation to ensure delivery

Monitoring cycles take place on a weekly and monthly basis in order to closely oversee implementation progress, identify any obstacles and challenges faced, and promptly work on resolving them at the operational level. The unit works to ensure that the prime minister's office or responsible ministers provide support and high visibility.

Step 7: Credibility via independent validation and verification

Successful implementation and transformation cannot be attained without reliable data. Reliable data that accurately reflects outcomes and results will facilitate the close monitoring and measuring of implementation progress toward achieving the desired goals or the True North. For that, the PEMANDU relies on external and independent auditing to provide data on implementation progress to ensure the accuracy of the data provided about delivery.

Step 8: Annual report to inform the public of progress

The annual report shows how close the ministries, departments, agencies, and all stakeholders are to achieving the desired goal or the True North. The annual report provides needed information for all stakeholders on the progress and achievements attained in the transformation program, as well as obstacles faced throughout the implementation process.

The PEMANDU's mission and responsibilities are clearly identified in order to have optimum focused results and ensure accountability. The important element for the success of the PEMANDU is its focus on a specific number of clear priorities. These high-level priorities are well defined in the National Transformation Program, which includes 8 national key results areas (NKRAs), 6 strategic reform initiatives (SRIs), and 12 national key areas (NEKAs). The priorities are further detailed and broken down into staged projects with defined KPIs and timelines that the PEMANDU works on to ensure that they are achieved. Whereas ministries, departments, and agencies are responsible for the budgeting and implementation of the projects highlighted in the NTP, the PEMANDU, guided with the NTP, works on designing, adjusting, monitoring, and facilitating collaboration and communication, as well as de-bottlenecking. The labs (Step 2 in the Eight Steps of Transformation) play a crucial role in identifying and anchoring ownership of the projects among the involved stakeholders.

Key lessons learned from PEMANDU

The key factors that enabled the PEMANDU to effectively support the Malaysian public sector and successfully attain the desired goals of the NTP can guide other countries that are considering the establishment of delivery units. One of the key elements for the success of the PEMANDU is the existence of a strong support system from the high levels of the cabinet. The PEMANDU's success relies heavily on the direct support of the prime minister and his involvement in its operations. As the PEMANDU works on monitoring the implementation process and tries to identify and resolve challenges and bottlenecks faced by ministries, departments, and agencies, the regular support and involvement of the prime minister facilitates the de-bottlenecking through problem-solving meetings and performance reviews.[139]

The PEMANDU works through a focused and concrete results platform that is connected to the central national framework. The PEMANDU works within the NTP's results platform that helps the unit to maintain its focus on narrow, well-defined strategic priorities and avoid wasted or unfocused efforts. Moreover, the PEMANDU's approach combines "top-down control with bottom-up voice."[140] Through the strategic workshops, policy decision-makers set the desired goals and policies, thereby ensuring a command-and-control system; the labs organized by the PEMANDU allow for ministries, departments, agencies, and other implementing stakeholders to express their opinions and voice in order to operationalize the government's strategic priorities.[141]

In addition, the PEMANDU's institutional structure and mandate allow for recruiting external talent from the private sector. This arrangement adds value to the public sector through introducing a private sector corporate culture. Under the prime minister's "special-purpose vehicle," the PEMANDU is authorized to seek experience and recruit staff from outside the public sector. The PEMANDU is able to attract private sector staff through its pay structure, which does not fall under the civil service pay scale, allowing the PEMANDU to attract experts and highly skilled staff from both the public and private sectors. Such a mechanism allows for the existence of diversified and progressive ideas that meet best practices and improve designing and implementation processes.[142] Finally, the PEMANDU's collaboration and work with various stakeholders within the government as well as outside the government are a crucial factor to facilitate the implementation and problem-solving process. The implementation and delivery of the NTP is supported by key institutional arrangements, such as delivery management offices (DMOs) that are established within the ministries, and which allow the PEMANDU to collaborate with the ministries to implement the NTP.[143]

Limitations and challenges of PEMANDU

The PEMANDU's main limitations arise from its strength elements. The same factors that work in favor of the PEMANDU's effectiveness can be significant obstacles if they were wrongly managed or if the conditions changed. For instance, the presence of a strong institutional environment that focuses on a quality public sector performance is an effective factor until it becomes very complex. The PEMANDU depends on the existing sophisticated public sector of planning, monitoring and evaluation, and reporting; however, the involvement of several institutions at the center of government as well as ministries, departments, and agencies at the implementation level can create overlap, coordination problems, and unclear ownership and accountability. Besides the PEMANDU's responsibility to monitor the KPIs of implementations in accordance with the NTP, involved ministries have similar performance-tracking responsibilities. This may create excess reporting tasks on implementing agencies, as they have to report for different institutions that may have dissimilar KPIs which may be complex or even conflicting.

While the incorporation of experts from the private sector helps infuse a successful corporate culture into the public sector management and use of top talent, it can also discourage public sector staff from collaborating and they may perceive the staff of the PEMANDU as outsiders with no or limited public sector experience. The strain might be unavoidable, and it has occurred in other delivery units in other governments that have adopted a similar model. In addition, the salary gap between civil servants and the staff of the PEMANDU will create potential tension and uncollaborative behavior. For that, the staff of the PEMANDU aims to emphasize their added-value responsibilities such as close monitoring, timely problem-solving, and de-bottlenecking through prompt assistance from higher levels in the cabinet. Generally, the PEMANDU is perceived in some ministries, departments, and agencies as a valuable institution that adds to the overall implementation process, while other ministries are more skeptical toward the unit.[144]

Labs are important to design the transformation program in accordance with the NTP; however, designing projects through the lab may not allow it to connect the achieved results to the NTP or to coexisting efforts. The NTP does not include all government efforts and public services but rather specific priorities to be achieved under the five-year plan; thus "the questions of attribution of the outcomes are often raised." For instance, it would not be clear to link improving literacy rates in Malaysia due to the NTP interventions or other education programs that are implemented outside the many other non-NTP initiatives. "Rather, the question is whether the overall impact was a result of a narrow strategic intervention in the NTP or of a multitude of other programs that are ongoing in parallel."[145]

40. AVOID CONSULTANTS!!!

In nations where citizens have a voice in choosing their leaders—and even in those where the dictator or ruling family seem benevolent—people expect their leaders to possess experience, knowledge, insights, and other qualifications that enable them to effectively perform their jobs. These attributes may be acquired from public service, higher education, military service, or perhaps just life experience. Such qualifications both validate the leaders' positions of authority and reassure citizens that their leaders are making wise decisions that, while likely informed by one political viewpoint or another, are good faith efforts to do what's best for the average citizen, and in keeping with the cherished traditions of the nation.

At the same time, no human being can be an expert in everything. Politicians, especially, are required to consider and then offer judgment on a dizzying array of issues.

Agriculture, taxes, business subsidies, voting rights, national defense, healthcare, immigration—politicians are tasked with making decisions on a wide range of important policy areas. While a leader may be well-versed in one area, it is likely that he or she will be less familiar, and less confident, in another. For this reason, to gain more information about a topic before rendering a decision or casting a vote, the wise leader will seek counsel from specialists.

Since the dawn of humanity, kings have had their courts and their advisors. There's always an official body of advisors—from King Arthur and his Knights of the Round Table to the modern-day cabinets of presidents and prime ministers. But in many cases, close advisors have been people lurking in the background, out of the public eye. Indeed, history is replete with examples of "the power behind the throne." The medieval Merovingian kings, relatively weak in power, depended upon their "mayors of the palace." Tsar Nicholas II had Rasputin. Presidents and prime ministers have their unofficial circles of advisors, such as the "kitchen cabinet" of President John F. Kennedy, which included his brother, attorney general Robert Kennedy; his appointment secretary, Kenneth O'Donnell; his special assistant, Lawrence O'Brien; and others.

Today, US President Donald Trump has surrounded himself with a similar "kitchen cabinet" of people who appear to have no other roles than to advise him on matters great and small. They include his daughter Ivanka Trump, his son-in-law Jared Kushner, senior adviser Stephen Miller, and counselor to the president Kellyanne Conway.

What all of these advisers have in common is that they are, at least nominally, a part of the government. They have some connection to the history and heritage of the office they are serving. While their advice can be self-serving (there are many who believe that US Vice President Dick Cheney urged his boss, President George W. Bush, to invade Iraq so that Halliburton, the company where Dick Cheney was chief executive from 1995 until he left in 2000 to run for vice president, could reap lucrative construction contracts), it is a generally accepted tenet that presidents have the right to choose their advisors, regardless of how flawed they may be, and to bring them into their administrations.

Paid outside consultants are more like mercenaries. You hire them, they perform a specialized function, and then the relationship ends. Unlike most political advisers, they do not care about the client's political affiliation or agenda. They will work for any leader who can write the check. While paid outside consultants have long been used in political campaigns and are deemed necessary both for their technical expertise and their cool objectivity, their use has traditionally been limited to the period of the campaign itself: Get the candidate elected, get paid, and then go away until the next election.

Meanwhile, in the world of business, the role of the paid outside consultant has become ubiquitous. Few big-company CEOs or boards would venture to make a key decision without first commissioning a report from a consulting company. For example, if a business wants to enter a new market, the leader will hire a consultant to analyze the proposed venture, make a list of the pros and cons of the idea, and provide a recommendation of action.

Doing so gives the business leader two important benefits:

1. Employing a consultant on a project is intended to provide the leader with information that is valuable and impartial and has been obtained and presented by someone with no stake in the outcome. Ordinarily, this should be a good thing.
2. The consultant provides political cover for the leader. By hiring an outside expert who is free from bias, the leader inoculates himself or herself against criticism

should the project fail. "Do not blame me," the leader will say. "I hired the finest experts and followed their advice. I am not to blame for the disaster." In fact, it is even better than that, because if the project turns out to be a success, the role of the consultant can be minimized. "Yes, we had some outside advisors," the leader will say. "But at the end of the day it was my call to make. I alone made the correct decision. The consultants had nothing to do with it."

This is why, for many business leaders, using an outside consultant is always a win-win proposition.

The big business of consulting

Business management consulting is the practice of helping organizations to improve their performance by analyzing existing organizational problems and developing plans for improvement. Organizations may draw upon the services of management consultants for a number of reasons, including gaining access to the consultants' specialized expertise and acquiring external (and presumably objective) advice. And, as was noted above, it is often wise to hire a management consultant to provide political cover for a leader who needs to make a tough decision.

While business consultants had long practiced in London, in the United States the first management consultancy was started by Frederick Winslow Taylor, who in 1893 opened an independent consulting practice in Philadelphia. His business card read "Consulting Engineer—Systematizing Shop Management and Manufacturing Costs a Specialty." With his system of scientific management, Taylor promoted the first method of organizing industrial work. Then, in the 1930s, the federal Glass–Steagall Banking Act ushered in a new era of government regulation and accelerated the demand for professional advice on finance, strategy, and organization.

Today, management consulting is a USD 250 billion industry. Whether the focus is strategy, taxes, finance, human resources, operations, or information technology, business consultants are a staple of corporate life. Today, in every corner of the world, over 700,000 consulting firms provide services across every aspect of business. From defining strategic direction to simply serving as an additional pair of hands for outsourced work, consultants have become inextricably linked to the success of most large organizations.[146]

The biggest consulting firms in the world include:

Deloitte. Founded in 1845 by William Welch Deloitte, and headquartered in London. Revenue: USD 38.8 billion (2017). Employees: 263,900 (2017).

PricewaterhouseCoopers. Formed in 1998 with the merger of Price Waterhouse and Coopers & Lybrand, each dating to the mid-19th century. Headquartered in London. Revenue: USD 37.7 billion (2017). Employees: 236,000 (2017).

Accenture. Founded in 1989 (from Andersen Consulting) and headquartered in Dublin, Ireland. Revenue: USD 34.85 billion (2017). Employees: 435,000 (2018), including 130,000 in India.

EY. Founded in 1989 from the original component company established in 1849 and headquartered in London. Revenue: USD 31.3 billion. Employees: 250,000 (2017).

KPMG. Founded in 1987 with the merger of Klynveld Goerdeler and Peat Marwick, and headquartered in Amstelveen, the Netherlands. Revenue: USD 26.4 billion (2017). Employees: 188,982 (2016).

McKinsey. Founded in 1926, headquartered in New York. Revenue: Over USD 10 billion (2018). Employees: 27,000 (2018).

Boston Consulting Group (BCG). Founded in 1963 in Boston, USA. Revenue: USD 5.6 billion (2016). Employees: 14,000, including 6,200 consultants worldwide.

Bain & Company. Founded in 1973 and headquartered in Boston, USA. Along with McKinsey and BCG, it is one of the Big Three management consultancies. Revenue: USD 4.5 billion (2017). Employees: 8,000 (2018).[147]

The Big Three

Many of these global consulting companies offer accounting, auditing, and other services that are not considered management consulting. The Big Three, or MBB, refers to the name colloquially given to the world's three largest strategy consulting firms by revenue. They are McKinsey, Boston Consulting Group, and Bain & Company.

A visit to the McKinsey website reveals the breathtaking scope of the industries they serve, from agriculture to semiconductors.[148] Tucked into the long list is the category of "Public Sector." A tour of the public sector services page reveals another list, entitled "How We Help Clients." (This means clients that are governments.) This list includes:

- Customer Experience
- Defense & Security
- Economic Development
- Education
- Healthcare
- Information Technology
- Operations
- Organization
- Public Finance
- Public Safety & Criminal Justice
- Strategy[149]

One featured service is "government transitions." McKinsey tells the visitor, "Our expertise extends across the full range of public-sector capabilities … . From advising on government transitions across the world, we've developed an approach to help you prepare to serve your constituents from day one."[150]

There are lots of punchy little text boxes describing the services offered by McKinsey in the category of government transitions. For example, one reads:

"Build risk-management capabilities. Support development of an appropriate risk strategy for the state and help build its internal capabilities, processes, and culture to identify, prevent, and mitigate risks."[151]

McKinsey also provides consulting services in the category of defense and security. The website informs the visitor:

Our work in defense and security covers a wide range of topics. For instance, we help clients develop and execute strategic plans, analyze organizational behavior, explore new methods to improve operational efficiency, and redesign and implement

IT infrastructure and systems. In the past 5 years, we have supported defense ministries, military forces, police forces, and justice ministries in 15 countries on more than 180 defense and security projects.[152]

On their website, Boston Consulting Group offers a nearly identical list of industries they serve, including the public sector. On their "Defense, Justice, and Border Protection" page, the company writes,

> Faced with decreasing budgets and changing or resurging threats, governments must reform and modernize defense forces while preserving their military readiness. At the same time, leaders must bolster homeland security by improving the organizational effectiveness and efficiency of supporting functions like justice, immigration, border protection, and intelligence—which themselves are facing new challenges and budgetary restraints.[153]

Likewise for Bain & Company. They serve the same industries as the other two, including the public sector. The website does not mention providing consulting services for defense and security, but plenty of advice on other topics of concern. For example, under the "Public Sector & Government" heading, there are links to various articles written by Bain executives. One typical article lives on an associated website, livemint.com. Entitled "Liberalization's lasting impact," the article discusses the Government of India and its efforts to manage and grow the economy. The authors—Sri Rajan, chairman of Bain & Co., India; Nikhil Prasad Ojha, a partner with Bain & Co. in Mumbai; and Shyam Unnikrishnan, a Bain principal and a member of the strategy and consumer products and retail practices in India—write,

> To show it means business, the government should continue on its path of disintermediation, retreat from being a direct service provider in major sectors, and let the private sector fill up that space. We have seen the intent, but reality needs to catch up.[154]

Presumably, this is the advice they're offering the government in New Delhi—to please let the private sector take care of business while the government sticks to governing.

Isn't this a good thing?

At first glance, it would seem to be a good thing that a national government, especially one in a developing country, would be willing to seek the advice of coolly detached professionals, who would come in, do their objective analysis, provide unbiased advice, and if necessary help the government implement that advice. This is what McKinsey says on its website:

> We study markets, trends, and emerging best practices, in every industry and region, locally and globally. Our investment in knowledge also helps advance the practice of management. We publish our findings extensively, and we engage with leading thinkers on the most pressing issues facing our clients and society.[155]

And this is the mission statement of the Boston Consulting Group:

> Our mission is clear. We go deep to unlock insight and have the courage to act. We bring the right people together to challenge established thinking and drive transformation. We work with our clients to build the capabilities that enable organizations to achieve sustainable advantage. We are shaping the future. Together.[156]

And Bain:

> Bain & Company helps transform the world's most important businesses into vigorous, agile organizations that anticipate the unpredictable, adapt rapidly to disruption, and outcompete their opposition.[157]

Who could argue with that? If the world were full of businesses and national governments that were rational, ethical, and interested only in doing what was best for their people, then this "expertise for cash" business model would be a good thing. Most of us would agree that if we could help our neighbors by providing our expertise to help them solve a problem, we would. Business consultants like to see themselves as non-partisan service providers, like plumbers or electricians. If your house has a leaky pipe, the plumber comes and fixes it, or perhaps even installs a better, newer pipe. If your wiring is bad, the electrician will install wiring that's up to code.

What could be wrong with that?

Big consultants grab business where they find it

Given the arguments on both sides of the fence—that doing business with authoritarian regimes is a good thing because it helps liberalize them, versus the idea that doing business with authoritarian regimes serves only to strengthen them and their hold on their own people—it is not surprising that the leading management consulting firms, and in particular McKinsey, have chosen the former stance. Indeed, the use of American and European consulting firms by the leaders of emerging and authoritarian nations has been growing.

Here are just a few examples.

McKinsey in Oman

Oman, a nation on the Arabian Peninsula, was until January 2020 ruled by Sultan Qaboos, who has absolute power and issues laws by decree. He has been the hereditary leader of the country since 1970. According to the US Department of State, Omani law prohibits criticism of the Sultan in any form or medium and does not provide citizens with the right to change their government. The Sultan retains ultimate authority on all foreign and domestic issues, and public officials are not subject to financial disclosure laws. The practice of torture is widespread in Oman's state penal institutions and has become the state's typical reaction to independent political expression.[158]

On the EIU Democracy Index 2018, Oman, considered an authoritarian regime, received a score of 140, only slightly above Cuba and Russia.[159] But with a tiny population of barely three million people and reasonable amounts of oil, Oman is a fairly prosperous place, with money to spend on professional consultants.

As Consultancy-me.com reported in 2018, McKinsey & Company has been working with Oman on plans to integrate the sultanate's refining and petrochemical sectors into a single entity.

The Oman blueprint for economic diversification sits alongside many other national transformation programs released across the Gulf Cooperation Council (GCC) in response to the drop in global oil prices. This includes the Saudi Vision 2030, which many assume was devised by McKinsey, with a focus on breaking the local reliance on oil resources which, according to Deloitte figures, in 2016 accounted for approximately 90 percent of Omani government revenues and more than 50 percent of the national GDP.[160]

McKinsey in Lebanon

In July 2018, Consultancy-me.com reported that following McKinsey's enlistment to help boost Lebanon's troubled economy, McKinsey had delivered to the government a 1,000-page report containing its recommendations.

The five-year economic plan sought to shrink Lebanon's massive debt, currently at 150 percent of economic output and projected by the International Monetary Fund to reach 180 percent in 2023, which prompted action from certain sections of the international community following the Council for Economic Development and Reconstruction (CEDRE) investment conference in Paris in April 2018.

Despite constant political turmoil and the lack of a domestic budget for the 12 years up to 2017, Lebanon's fragile economy had sustained itself through remittances from the two-thirds or more of its population living abroad, along with record foreign reserves of around USD 43 billion. In a situation not unlike the ongoing crisis in Jordan, with unemployment hovering above 20 percent, since 2011 the influx of some 1.5 million refugees had placed the Lebanese economy under increasing pressure.

In an effort to correct the soaring debt to GDP ratio, which places Lebanon alongside Greece as one of the three most indebted countries on earth, and a trade deficit approaching USD 12 billion in the fourth quarter of 2017, in 2018 the Government of Lebanon[161] hired McKinsey, the presumed or acknowledged architect behind the portfolio of radical national transformation programs currently underway across the GCC.[162]

But the opposing political interests in Lebanon may make the effort nothing more than an expensive boondoggle. As Bloomberg reported,

> 'The divisions could reduce the McKinsey report to a theoretical exercise,' said Sami Nader, head of the Levant Institute for Strategic Studies in Beirut. 'The effort is laudable … . But anything that touches the economy will need political consensus in Lebanon because we do not have a functioning democracy.'[163]

Bain in Moscow and Beijing

In the 1990s, Bain joined the wave of American consulting companies hired by emerging post-Communist nations to teach them about Western management structure and strategy. The company's involvement came at a critical point when government leaders in both Moscow and Beijing sought Western intervention to absorb the fundamentals of capitalism.[164]

"The Chinese got a lot of advice from a wide array of U.S. consulting shops and it had a significant impact on China's ability to develop a more efficient market-oriented economy," said Kenneth G. Lieberthal, a China expert at the Brookings Institution. "The consultants were all trying to get in on the ground floor and build relationships with the government."[165]

In 1993, under the oversight of then-CEO Mitt Romney, Bain went to Beijing, where the firm's consultants held a series of management seminars for Chinese government trade officials. At the same time, Bain consultants were advising Russian officials and conducting seminars to aid the post-Soviet business privatization campaign.

In his book, *No Apology: The Case for American Greatness*, Mitt Romney—then a politician running for the office of president of the United States—described China's economic success as "free enterprise on steroids." But during the campaign, he followed the Republican Party line by castigating the Chinese for "cheating" on trade and accusing Beijing of cyberspying and intellectual property piracy.[166]

Boston Consulting Group in Dubai

Following continuous project work in the region since 2005, BCG in Dubai opened its office in 2007. As the company's website states:

> Having earned a reputation as one of the world's premier boomtowns, Dubai is a hot spot not only for the real estate sector but also for tourism, trade, transportation, and financial services. Large Dubai businesses are increasingly rolling out their business models abroad and becoming global competitors.[167]

What do these consultants actually *do* in these hyper-wealthy nations with their ancient traditions? As former BCG executive Keith Yost wrote about his experience working in Dubai, sometimes it seems like it is all for show:

Early on, before I began case work, one manager I befriended gave me some advice. To survive, he told me, I needed to remember The Ratio. Fifty percent of the job is nodding your head at whatever is being said. Twenty percent is honest work and intelligent thinking. The remaining thirty percent is having the courage to speak up, but the wisdom to shut up when you are saying something that your manager does not want to hear. [...]

I spoke up once. And when it became clear that I would be committing career suicide to press on, I shut up.[168]

Consultants in Saudi Arabia

Saudi Arabia is a booming center of business consultancies. According to Consultingcase101.com, there are 31 business consulting firms with offices in Riyadh. All of the big players are there, including Boston Consulting Group (BCG), Deloitte, KPMG, McKinsey, and PricewaterhouseCoopers (PwC).[169]

Since 2008, Boston Consulting Group has been in Saudi Arabia, working with key stakeholders on topics of the highest national importance. The BCG Riyadh office opened in June 2015. The company says,

> BCG provides specialized consulting services to Saudi-based clients in all sectors ....
> In addition to working with clients in Saudi Arabia, BCG realizes the importance

of making a difference within local communities. We participate in social-impact programs—including one that fosters youth entrepreneurship—in order to help the Kingdom thrive socially and economically.[170]

Deloitte says,

> We have expanded our specialized professional services in the Middle East, leveraging our local and global talent in areas such as Financial Advisory Services, Enterprise Risk Services, and International Tax Services. We have also continued to play a pivotal role in serving the region's high-growth industry sectors such as tourism, hospitality and leisure, construction, telecoms and financial services, as well as major sectors such as oil and gas, the public sector, and the Gulf region's sovereign wealth funds.[171]

Bain's two largest client bases in the region include large corporations and family-owned businesses, particularly in Saudi Arabia. When it comes to financial services, Saudi Arabia is a growing market for Bain. Jean-Marie Pean, managing director of Bain & Company Middle East, told Tamara Walid from *Arabian Business*,

> We help them restructure their business because a family-run business or a traditional corporate entity is absolutely unable to take the company to the next level without recommendation. If they want to become regional they have to change their organization, and that's what we help them do.[172]

McKinsey has a significant presence in Saudi Arabia. The company says, "Our Saudi Arabia Practice helps Saudi leaders realize the Kingdom's full potential: a vibrant middle class with the right standard of living based on a more competitive private sector and modern public sector."[173] The global managing partner of McKinsey & Company, Kevin Sneader, told *Financial Review* that McKinsey was a "force for good" in Saudi Arabia, and that he was "quite proud" of the firm's work on the country's economic, education, and healthcare development.[174]

Over the past several decades, global consulting companies and government agencies—both national and local—have developed a deeply symbiotic relationship. The consultants need the hefty paychecks, as well as the prestige of serving national governments. The governments need one of two things: either actual managerial expertise so that public services can be outsourced to the consultant, or the political cover of having hired an expert firm to give them advice that may or may not be useful. The former—privatization of public services—can be dangerous because of a loss of accountability. The latter can be dangerous because consulting firms can, knowingly or unknowingly, help support repressive authoritarian regimes.

Tangled webs and dark alliances

I have already provided an overview of the management consulting industry, introduced its biggest players, and gave a few examples of their global involvement with the public sector, with particular attention paid to the volume of business done by the Big Three—McKinsey, Boston Consulting Group, and Bain & Company—with governments that rank very low on the Democracy Index.

There are many who believe that the interaction of American and European consulting companies with repressive or troubled governments is a good thing because it exposes these governments to liberal political, social, and economic ideas that they ordinarily could avoid. Much is made, for example, by companies like McKinsey of their employment of women in Saudi Arabia, as if this would show the king—an absolute ruler—the virtues of social progressiveness.

There are many others who are troubled by the mercenary attitude of these companies, who seem to follow the paycheck no matter into what dark hole it leads. These companies send their people to serve repressive regimes, provide assistance to those regimes in strengthening their hold on power, cash the check, and then look the other way as their work is used to oppress.

In addition, many analysts see politicians, in their eagerness to dodge responsibility, massively delegate their legislative and administrative responsibilities to external agents who are self-interested, unaccountable, and biased. As we always say in management, "strategy cannot be delegated," and there is no reason to believe that a company like McKinsey will have a better understanding of a nation's economy than any well-educated local person. As we glimpsed in the story of Boston Consulting Group executive Keith Yost and his work in Dubai, it seems that many high-priced consultants are expected to serve in a wide range of roles, from being pointless window dressing to a real influence on a government that has abrogated its responsibilities. For these companies, either extreme is fine as long as the check is in the mail.

We often see evidence of an unholy alliance between a consulting company and its government client in the sense that each one has an objective that may not have much to do with improving the lives of ordinary citizens. Too often, consulting mandates produce reports that:

Promote growth and innovation while ignoring that a country's objective should be competitiveness and widespread prosperity.

Make vague and general recommendations, very often off the shelf, so they end up advising the same thing to all client countries.

Then, when it comes to execution, they move aside; and when their recommendations fail, they can always blame the government and its lack of execution ability.

Surprisingly, we also see evidence of outside consulting firms being involved in not just program direction or problem fixing, but also in devising entire national strategies. It is hard to see how this could be done effectively by a group of outsiders, even if they were bolstered by local recruits.

McKinsey: bad optics in China

In what seems like a decision designed to give McKinsey's critics a reason to accuse the company of being oblivious to serious human rights issues in authoritarian states, in December 2018 the company held a lavish retreat in the desert in Kashgar, the ancient Silk Road city in China's far-west region of Xinjiang. As *The New York Times* reported:

Hundreds of the company's consultants frolicked in the desert, riding camels over sand dunes and mingling in tents linked by red carpets. Meetings took place in a cavernous banquet hall that resembled a sultan's ornate court, with a sign overhead to capture the mood.[175]

While on the retreat, McKinsey consultants chronicled on Instagram their many activities, including camel rides, while during the business portion they spent their time discussing their work with state-owned Chinese firms.

The problem? Just four miles away—close enough to see the warm glow in the sky from the festive McKinsey bonfire—thousands of ethnic Uighurs languished in a sprawling internment camp, just one of a vast archipelago of similar facilities.

As Reuters has reported, the UN Committee on the Elimination of Racial Discrimination cited estimates that up to one million Uighurs may be confined in detention camps in Xinjiang Province. Its findings were issued after a 2018 review of China's record, the first since 2009.

Reports indicate that China has created a massive police state in Xinjiang dedicated to the surveillance, imprisonment, and forced re-education of Chinese Muslims. China's foreign ministry insists Xinjiang faces a serious threat from Islamist militants and separatists who plot attacks and stir up tension between the mostly Muslim Uighur minority and the ethnic Han Chinese majority.[176]

McKinsey has a long history in China. As the McKinsey website says, in 1995 McKinsey opened offices in Shanghai and Beijing, "cultivating Chinese clients and committing to the development of the country." An early client was a bottled-water company founded by four farmers; within a few years, according to McKinsey, it was valued at USD 200 million. Over the following decade, McKinsey's presence in China expanded from just a handful of people to hundreds of consultants.[177]

Today, the company says it has more than 450 consultants and over 70 partners located across five locations in Greater China: Beijing, Shanghai, Hong Kong, Taipei, and Shenzhen. They are supported by more than 100 research professionals and over 250 professional support staff. The company notes that "over 90 percent of our more than 350 consultants are of Chinese descent and speak fluent Mandarin as well as one or more dialects of Chinese. More than 80 percent of our seventy partners are of Chinese descent."[178]

The company works directly with Chinese government entities. In the past decade, McKinsey has served over 20 different central, provincial, and municipal government agencies on a wide range of economic planning, urban redevelopment, and social sector issues. The company has

> advised several central government ministries on a range of high-impact issues, from designing healthcare reform policies, to providing talent and leadership development programs for the next generation of government leaders, to crafting policies and specific measures aimed at spurring more domestic consumption.[179]

As Michael Posner noted in *Forbes*, McKinsey and other consultants working for the Chinese government may have to do some soul-searching. "As the Chinese government continues its crackdown on dissent and engages in the mass incarceration in internment camps of as many as one million ethnic Uighurs in Xinjiang Province," Posner wrote in December 2018,

> the test for McKinsey will be its willingness to address these actions with Chinese government clients in a meaningful way. Although some of this is perhaps

happening behind closed doors, there is little evidence that the firm has adjusted its engagement with the Chinese government in response to the rapid deterioration of rights. It now must do so.[180]

McKinsey and Viktor Yanukovych

Since it declared independence in 1991, Ukraine has been traveling a bumpy road toward a market economy. In February 2010, a formerly disgraced politician named Viktor Yanukovych—he had two prior criminal convictions—won the Ukrainian presidential election and became the fourth president of Ukraine. During the election campaign, Yanukovych had stressed the necessity to reform the country. But despite his campaign promise of "improvement of life starting today," the new president quickly applied his efforts to concentrating his personal wealth and power. Yanukovych rejected a pending European Union Association agreement, choosing instead to pursue a Russian loan bailout and closer ties with Russia. The opposition from pro-EU Ukrainians was intense, and on February 22, 2014, the Ukrainian parliament voted to remove Yanukovych from the post of president of Ukraine on the grounds that he was unable to fulfill his duties. He fled the country, and citizens who entered his lavish compound were astounded at the amount of wealth he had somehow accumulated on his modest salary.

The reason why Viktor Yanukovych had been able to win the presidency in 2010 was because his public image had been polished by McKinsey and Rinat Akhmetov, the country's richest oligarch. As reported by *The New York Times*, Akhmetov had rescued Yanukovych by hiring two consulting groups: Paul Manafort, whose Russian-linked team had worked for dictators with little regard for human rights, and McKinsey.

This was at a time when Yanukovych was currying favor with the Russians and engaging in massive corruption. According to diplomatic cables released by WikiLeaks, Akhmetov assured the Americans that his candidate was "a strong McKinsey supporter," while Yanukovych emphasized that he had instructed his aides "to work directly with McKinsey experts."

Manafort burnished Yanukovych's personal reputation and strengthened his pro-Russia Party of Regions. McKinsey provided an economic plan that Yanukovych could use to portray himself as a market-based reformer who was in alignment with the European Union.[181]

In reality, Yanukovych was none of those things.

Offended by *The Times* article, the very next day McKinsey issued a rebuttal. Among other points, McKinsey said,

> The Times' suggestion that we undertook this work to polish the image of Mr. Yanukovych is deeply misleading. The local Partners who led this work were committed to the cause of reform; yet when it became clear that the country's President would not follow through on his stated reform agenda, we made the tough decision to walk away and end our service. And let us be clear: the innuendo linking our work to Paul Manafort's reported public affairs and lobbying activities is plain wrong.[182]

The Australian government's growing dependence on consultants

The increasing number of professional consulting firms hired by the federal government in Australia came to the attention of Stephen Easton, a writer from TheMandarin.com.au. In his article of September 19, 2017, he questioned the outsized influence of the global firms that provide these services in public life. "They seem able to turn out a thick report full of impressive figures and charts to justify almost any argument," he wrote, "and also donate plenty to the major political parties."

He noted that a controversy over the use of consultants to supplement public service capability had emerged in New South Wales. Budgetary documents tabled in parliament revealed that government agencies were increasing their spending on outside expertise. The Department of Premier and Cabinet had earmarked USD 10.8 million, roughly triple its consultant spending the previous financial year. The Department of Planning and Environment had set aside USD 11.1 million, 10 times the amount it had previously spent. The Technical and Further Education (TAFE) commission intended to pay out more than four times its previous annual consulting budget.

Earlier in 2017, it was reported that since coming to power in 2013, the federal government had spent nearly USD 1 billion on consultants, despite a platform calling for the reduction of public sector spending through job cuts and a strict approach to enterprise bargaining with its agencies.

David Schmidtchen, a human resources expert from the consulting firm of E&Y, said that in theory, consultants should not be acting as decision-makers. But in practice, he sometimes privately questioned the way agencies used his expertise. "Increasingly I go in," he told a seminar audience,

> and I become the coach, the mentor to the senior executive, the mentor to the middle management, and I often ask myself why. It is leadership, management, capability, how do you organize a task, all that sort of stuff. There is something missing in that capability; I should not be filling that gap. And yet, routinely, that's what we do. And that, for me, should already exist.

Schmidtchen said he told his clients they should never "abrogate the responsibility of knowledge" to consultants.[183]

Many believe government should be run like a business. Really?

Among many policymakers—and voters—a common belief is that private enterprise (that is, business) is inherently more efficient than government. Because private industry must make a profit, while government seeks to spend as much taxpayer cash as it can, government should therefore strive to be more like business.

As Bessma Momani wrote in "Management Consultants and the United States' Public Sector," public sector agencies are increasingly being told to operate "like a business," which means that "it should be cost-efficient, as small as possible in relation to its tasks, competitive, entrepreneurial, and dedicated to 'pleasing the customer.'" This mantra has spurred accounting and consulting firms to open public sector divisions, while opening the door for management consultants to give advice on public sector reform. As consulting firm Capgemini put it, "funding constraints require governments to adopt more business-like approaches when addressing the pressing challenges facing our federal government. And, taxpayer expectations are intensifying. More and more—success comes from being ready to respond to complex and unpredictable challenges."[184]

Management consultants promote the idea that they are providers of innovative solutions stemming from their unique and independent expertise. In the organizational behavior literature, they are discussed as change agents coming to the rescue of the archaic public sector.

Almost without exception, management consulting companies advocate for the increased privatization of government programs and services. This is not surprising because any government entity that hires an outside consulting firm has already engaged in privatization. Therefore, it is logical that the consulting firm would urge even more privatization.

As Lee Cokorinos wrote for the Center on Policy Initiatives, acceptance of the business model of government is becoming increasingly widespread, and the public sector practice divisions of big consulting firms including Accenture, BearingPoint, Boston Consulting, Carlyle, Capgemini, Deloitte, Goldman Sachs, Grant Thornton, McKinsey, and PricewaterhouseCoopers are exerting pressure for the privatization of government assets, procurement practices, and services.

The language of privatization has also evolved, with the friendly sounding concept of "public private partnerships" (PPPs or P3s) coming into common use. These are contracts between government agencies and private sector entities that promote private sector involvement in services (information technology and social services delivery) and infrastructure projects (roads, water delivery, waste disposal).

"The large consulting and project financing firms, and a raft of smaller companies in the privatization and contracting industry, have moved in to take over public assets and services on an unprecedented scale," wrote Cokorinos. "Through their management consulting practices, they have also changed the face of decision-making within the federal, state, and local governments, enabling them increasingly to drive the agenda of public services."

Due to the high rate of turnover among public sector personnel, consultants often have better access and deeper institutional knowledge than the people who are hiring them. "They know our business better than us," one Pennsylvania state worker, who requested anonymity for job security reasons, told the *Harrisburg Patriot-News*.[185]

Increasingly, municipalities and local governments in the United States are outsourcing many of their basic services to private sector managers. Cokorinos noted the example of four newly incorporated towns in the state of Georgia: Chattahoochee Hill Country, Johns Creek, Milton, and Sandy Springs. In 2006, these towns signed contracts with consulting company CH2M HILL OMI to manage all of the municipal facilities except fire and police. In Sandy Springs, where the company manages all staff, CH2M HILL employees, wearing Sandy Hill uniforms and driving trucks with Sandy Hill emblems, are tasked with enforcing municipal ordinances and grass-cutting and parking regulations.

With USD 5.24 billion in 2016 sales and 20,000 employees, CH2M HILL Companies, Ltd., based in Englewood, Colorado, is one of the leading engineering and infrastructure firms providing services to federal, state, and local governments. Working in over 50 countries, its public sector practice includes government facilities design and construction, redevelopment, base operating support, and base closing management for the military.[186]

Determining if a consultant is worth the investment

If you hire a consultant for your business and you say, "We want you to help us increase our market share by 10 percent," it is pretty easy to evaluate the results. At the end of the contract, the company has either increased its market share by 10 percent or it hasn't.

But governments are not businesses. Their goals are not to increase market share or stockholder return. Their goals are more difficult to pin down: alleviate poverty, attract new industry, improve the delivery of services to the population.

In its 2010 report titled "Management Consultants and Public Sector Transformation," the Association of Chartered Certified Accountants (ACCA) addressed this challenge. "It can be hard to identify useful measures that are suitable for all types of projects, and attributing cause and effect is not always easy, even where performance has improved," wrote the ACCA. "This has not stopped a plethora of toolkits developing to help managers make the best use of management consultants and assess their value, whether through peer review or post-contract evaluations."[187]

And on what basis do management consultants sell their services to client governments? How can a problem faced by China be related to a problem faced by Brazil? According to the ACCA, much of the critical research in this area has focused on whether management consultancy sells itself as a profession. For example, a coach can demonstrate the value of his or her services by emphasizing his or her knowledge of behavioral sciences to solve an organizational problem. This approach suggests to the client a level of professional status. But in other cases, performance claims may be vague and difficult to prove, leading management consultants to strive to convince the client that they have a unique specialization or knowledge base. To succeed and obtain the contract, they will resort to references to results of previous work or claims to having core or unique products.

The ACCA pointed out some examples of consultant engagements that are unproductive or even wasteful.

- A consultant may be commissioned to undertake a project to deliver messages that the public sector clients do not want to deliver themselves. As *The Guardian* wrote,

  If a management wants to slash its workforce, then it is obviously better that the bad news be delivered by outsiders who can be blamed later. This evasion of responsibility may well be worth a great deal to the managers concerned, if not to the other stakeholders of the enterprise.[188]

- The public sector has too many initiatives to project manage them all effectively. Consequently, evaluation teams and peer-review teams are often composed of other management consultants, leading to conflicts between competing consultants.

- Because a minority of senior managers are involved in decision-making, junior-level bureaucrats can hire consultants for quixotic projects. For example, a small consultancy project requiring five London boroughs to agree to performance targets for the 2012 London Olympic Legacy over a three-day period was never going to be achievable or value for money.

- Consultants fail to understand that government is not business. As the ACCA wrote:

  In the case of healthcare it was recently reported in *The Guardian* that there has been a 'proliferation of management consultants within the NHS and it is not clear whether they have a true appreciation of the complexities of healthcare delivery—healthcare is not the same as selling clothes off a rack in a shop.'

- As *The Guardian* pointed out in a 2017 editorial, there can be an element of "The King Has No Clothes," whereby consultants are assumed to have superior knowledge for no other reason other than they're consultants, and no one will dispute it. *The Guardian* wrote, "Someone who comes along with an air of confident command will always find followers even if they know nothing about their subject, providing the followers are more painfully confident of their own ignorance."

McKinsey's vision 2030 for Saudi Arabia

On April 26, 2016, the government of Saudi Arabia announced the Council of Ministers had, during its session under the chairmanship of the Custodian of the Two Holy Mosques, endorsed King Salman Saudi Arabia's Vision 2030.

The cabinet session was devoted to a discussion of the vision, which the *Saudi Gazette* said was drafted by the Council of Economic and Development Affairs upon the instructions of the Custodian of the Two Holy Mosques.[189]

The real story behind Saudi 2030 was revealed by Hilal Khashan in the *Middle East Quarterly* (Winter 2017). The reason for the development of the strategic plan was the dramatic drop in oil prices, which had depleted Saudi Arabia's cash reserves by a whopping USD 150 billion. This drove the ruling family to "contrive hastily a financial rescue plan."

Based on a December 2015 report by the McKinsey Global Institute (MGI) entitled "Saudi Arabia Beyond Oil: The Investment and Productivity Transformation," the Vision 2030 plan sought to reinvigorate a Saudi economy that had yielded an annual gross domestic product growth of only 0.8 percent between 2003 and 2013, less than most emerging economies. The plan advocated the reduction of the role of the public sector and bureaucracy while simultaneously empowering the private sector to become the main employer and vehicle for economic growth. It called for the creation of a huge sovereign wealth fund to be funded by an unprecedented initial public offering (IPO) of a 5 percent stake in Aramco.[190]

The US Chamber of Commerce effusively praised Vision 2030, writing in March 2018:

> Since the Saudi Crown Prince, His Royal Highness Mohammed Bin Salman (or known by his nickname "MBS") unveiled Vision 2030 in 2016, significant economic and social reforms have swept across the country at a breakneck speed. This ambitious initiative focuses on diversifying Saudi Arabia's economy beyond oil and gas, promoting private sector and small-to-medium size enterprise engagement, and creating jobs for its large youth population, where nearly 70 percent of its citizens are under the age of thirty.[191]

Adel Abdel Ghafar from the Brookings Institution pointed out that the Saudi leadership has been effusive in its praise of McKinsey. In a wide-ranging interview with *The Economist* in January 2016, Prince Mohammed himself said, "McKinsey participates with us in many studies." According to the *Financial Times*, Saudi businessmen have sarcastically dubbed the Ministry of Planning as the "McKinsey Ministry."[192]

Despite the widespread enthusiasm for the plan, Ghafar highlighted a glaring oversight. The report did not adequately address the *human* element (oh, those pesky constituents!). A major hurdle to the success of Vision 2030 will be changing the mindset of everyday Saudi Arabian citizens, who have long been accustomed to state largesse that included fuel subsidies, loans, free land, and public sector jobs. "How will everyday citizens react to the reforms?" wrote Ghafar.

> The Saudi government will be asking more of its citizens—will the citizens in turn ask for more accountability and representation? Since January [2016], the prices of gasoline, electricity, and water have gone up. There was a public outcry against higher utility prices, which led King Salman to fire the water minister to absorb the public's anger.[193]

Another critical assessment by John Edwards, a member of the board of the Reserve Bank of Australia, warned that, in order for the plan to be successful, it must "profoundly change Saudi society and politics."[194]

Riyadh's cultural values do not support the objectives of Vision 2030, noted Hilal Khashan. Saudi society is closed, status oriented, and tribally structured. Saudis treat expatriates, especially laborers from poor countries, as non-entities unworthy of human dignity. Under the guise of promoting religious moderation, the Saudi government is suppressing the freedom of expression, which was dismal to begin with. The modern Saudi state rests on the three pillars of religion, tribalism, and oil, which will be extremely difficult to change.[195]

The question is, why did McKinsey ignore these obvious realities? You do not need to be an expert in Saudi society to see what Khashan and others see. Couldn't McKinsey address these serious foundational issues in its supposedly objective reports and recommendations?

The answer is no—not if it wanted to keep cashing Saudi government checks.

Saudi Arabia is a state with an absolute ruler whose authority is maintained and exercised by an extended family of ministers. They hire a company like McKinsey not to challenge them but to parrot back to them what they already believe. Indeed, Khashan noted that each Saudi development plan resembles the previous one.

> Vision 2030 looks pretty much like a continuation of the ninth development plan (2010-15), with its emphasis on promoting sustainable development and raising the competence of the Saudi workforce while creating a knowledge economy in an environment of progressive structural development.[196]

In October 2018, McKinsey's deep involvement with the Government of Saudi Arabia was called into question following the disappearance and presumed murder of Jamal Khashoggi, a critic of the Saudi government who was a contributing writer for *The Washington Post*. The firm said it was "horrified" that a report it prepared to measure public perception of Saudi Arabia's policies may have been used by the kingdom to silence dissidents. But, as *The New York Times* reported in November 2018:

> While Mr. Khashoggi's death prompted investors from around the globe to distance themselves from the Saudi government, Booz Allen and its competitors McKinsey & Company and Boston Consulting Group have stayed close after playing critical roles in Prince Mohammed's drive to consolidate power.[197]

The people at McKinsey—and many of the other big global consulting firms—know not to push their authoritarian clients too far. Challenging them means risking being fired. And so they tell their clients what they want to hear, even if it is unrealistic and will change nothing, or even if it presents a moral dilemma. Authoritarians expect to remain in power, and they're not looking for a plan that will weaken their hold over their people. But neither do they want to go broke, so what consultants including McKinsey deliver are plans that have appealing ideas for transformations in industry but nothing about the deeper social reforms that will make those changes possible and lasting.

The one-size-fits-all syndrome

Consulting companies are in the business of efficiency. Therefore, it is logical that consulting companies will seek to "package" their solutions to sell to more than one client.

After all, if a program works for Nation A, why wouldn't it work for Nation B and even Nation C?

In "The Pain of Withdrawal: The Saudi 2030 Vision," Peter Ward noted that Western management consultants appear to have inordinate influence over Saudi Arabia and the Gulf States. Saudi Arabia's Vision 2030 was unveiled in 2016. Bahrain (in 2008) and the UAE (in 2008) had their own Economic Vision 2030, and Oman had its "Vision 2020." All these reports shared the concepts of fiscal tightening, reform of energy and water subsidies, privatization, and anticipation of foreign investment. All bore the hallmarks of a McKinsey-inspired plan.[198]

As Keith Yost, working in Dubai for Boston Consulting Group, wrote,

> I got the feeling that our clients were simply trying to mimic successful businesses, and that as consultants, our earnings came from having the luck of being included in an elaborate cargo-cult ritual. In any case it fell to us to decide for ourselves what question we had been hired to answer, and as a matter of convenience, we elected to answer questions that we had already answered in the course of previous cases—no sense in doing new work when old work will do.

He even makes this startling confession: "It did not bother me therefore when I was handed consulting reports that had been stolen from our competitors."[199]

He describes writing a report that showed his client's present course of action would result in a loss of a billion dollars. His manager, upon reading the report, told him that the client did not want to hear anything about losing a billion dollars. The client had given a clear indication of what he wanted to hear in the report, and it wasn't that he was going to lose a billion dollars. So Yost changed the report to please the client.

While management consultants do good work, they also know how to play the game: Speak with authority; give the client some interesting ideas; and never, ever challenge the client or their fundamental belief system. If you think your client is morally bankrupt, just keep your mouth shut, do the work, and cash the check. If you go too far, you will get fired, and the client will hire someone else who will tell them what they want to know.

NOTES

1 www.consultancy-me.com/news/1118/mckinsey-delivers-1000-page-report-to-government-of-lebanon.
2 Source: World Economic Forum, www.weforum.org/agenda/2016/09/explained-why-the-japanese-economy-is-stuck.
3 European Central Bank (2010)
4 www.thebalance.com/japan-s-economy-recession-effect-on-u-s-and-world-3306007.
5 Source: Government of Japan.
6 Reuters, September 13, 2018.
7 Source: Government of Japan, www.japan.go.jp/abenomics/_userdata/abenomics/pdf/170313_abenomics.pdf.
8 Source: OECD Economic Surveys, Japan, April 2015.
9 *Japan Times*, October 15, 2018.
10 CNBC, June 1, 2018.
11 Source: Government of Japan.
12 Source: Ministry of Internal Affairs and Communications: "Labor Force Survey."
13 Source: Ministry of Health, Labor and Welfare: "Basic Survey on Wage Structure."
14 Source: Ministry of Justice: "Number of Recognitions of Highly Skilled Professionals."
15 Source: Government of Japan.

16 Source: Investopedia, March 29, 2018, www.investopedia.com/articles/investing/062515/jap ans-stewardship-code.asp.

17 Tokyo Stock Exchange: "Appointment of Independent Directors by TSE-listed Companies."

18 Interestingly, in summer 2008 the Social-Democrat government had been proposing an increase in pensions. They claimed that there would be no crisis in Lithuania.

19 In 2010, the corporate tax rate was restored to 15 percent, which remains to this day. It is important to note that personal income tax was reduced from 24 to 21 percent.

20 *The New York Times*, April 1, 2010.

21 www.baltic-course.com/eng/analytics/?doc=7419.

22 https://euobserver.com/opinion/114419.

23 www.express.co.uk/news/world/80362/Protests-over-Lithuania-government.

24 *The New York Times*, April 1, 2010.

25 www.lrs.lt/sip/portal.show?p_r=7694&p_k=2&p_t=96498.

26 Andrius Kubilius (2016), "The Story How To Become Slimmer," at www.munich-economic-summit.com/wp-content/uploads/2016/04/Andrius_Kubilius_MES2013.pdf.

27 Homeland Union, Kubilius' party, won 33 seats in parliament, out of 140. Social Democrats (38 seats) and the Labour Party (29 seats) built the winning coalition.

28 *The Daily Telegraph*, January 12, 2012.

29 The World Bank (2019), "Urban poverty headcount ratio at national poverty lines (percent of urban population)."

30 Tedesco (1999), *Democracy in Argentina: Hope and Disillusion*, 83.

31 BBC (2010), "Burma releases pro-democracy leader Aung San Suu Kyi."

32 WorldFund (2019).

33 *The Guardian*, May 15, 2018.

34 https://wgno.com/2019/01/18/el-chapo-guzman-associate-claims-kingpin-paid-100m-b ribe-to-former-mexican-president/.

35 *The Washington Post*, July 5, 2018.

36 Mafu (2017), "Hey, Here Are 5 GOOD Things President Jacob Zuma Has Done."

37 www.jbaynews.com/president-zuma-has-failed-south-africa/.

38   www.npr.org/sections/parallels/2018/02/14/584631829/s-africas-zuma-leaves-office-as-he -entered-accused-of-corruption?t=1549631762441.

39 www.news24.com/SouthAfrica/News/cosatu-cancels-main-workers-day-rally-as-zuma-is -heckled-20170501.

40 Lafitte (2017), "Macron fulfilling his reform agenda," Official Monetary and Financial Institutions Forum.

41 Frost and Rose (2018), "France's Macron pledges more reform medicine in 'decisive' 2019," Reuters.

42 Schaart (2018), "Macron's popularity drops to new low as French fuel tax revolt rages," *Politico*.

43 www.politico.eu/article/emmanuel-macron-popularity-drops-to-new-low-as-french-fuel-ta x-revolt-rages/.

44 Centre for Public Impact (2016), "Finnish educational reforms following the 1968 School System Act," at www.centreforpublicimpact.org/case-study/education-policy-in-finland/.

45 www.helsinkitimes.fi/finland/finland-news/domestic/10727-finland-has-lowest-income-in equality-in-eu.html.

46 www.theguardian.com/teacher-network/2017/aug/09/worlds-best-school-system-trust-teachers-education-finland.

47 Hancock (2011), "Why Are Finland's Schools Successful?" *Smithsonian* magazine.

48 BBC, May 24, 2011.

49 www.reuters.com/article/us-eurozone/portugal-faces-tough-road-under-78-billion-euro-b ailout-idUSTRE7443EA20110505.

50 *Financial Times*, May 24, 2017.

51 https://qz.com/1207039/portugals-economy-is-growing-at-its-fastest-rate-for-17-years/.

52 https://econews.pt/2017/06/30/unemployment-rate-in-portugal-falls-to-9-5-in-april/.

53 PricewaterhouseCoopers and Associados (2014), "Europe's best kept secret: Why Portugal should be your top tax choice."

54 *Hindustan Times*, July 23, 2016.

55 https://carsharik.ru/21-5-tysjach-avtomobilej-v-moskovskom-karsheringe/.
56 https://carsharik.ru/moskovskij-karshering-2-7-mln-poezdok-za-janvar/.
57 www.forbes.ru/sobytiya/lyudi/80116-pochemu-dlya-borby-s-probkami-sobyanin-pozval-biznesmena-s-zheleznoi-dorogi.
58 Aeroexpress engaged in regional projects—transportation in Olympic Sochi, Vladivostok, the city of the APEC summit, and the capital of the Universiade 2013, Kazan. In three cities, Russian Railways built railways, tunnels, bridges, and terminals required for the delivery of passengers to airports, totaling 28.4 billion rubles. Aeroexpress was not able to repeat its Moscow success in the regions and transportation in these cities remains unprofitable.
59 Two important events disrupted Liksutov's comfortable life in 2012: in February, the Estonian government had to consider Liksutov's application for deprivation of his citizenship. Later that year, a scandal broke out: he was blamed for his involvement in private sector businesses while in public office. The problem was solved in the traditional way: the Moscow official transferred his assets to his wife and soon after divorced her. Suddenly, Liksutov's wife Tatiana Liksutova became one of the richest persons in Estonia.
60 www.kommersant.ru/doc/2464246.
61 This section is partly based on a radio interview with Prime Minister John Howard in Richard Fidler (2016), "John Howard: guns, politics and power," ABC (ABC Australia).
62 Simon Chapman (1997), "Over Our Dead Bodies: Gun Law Reform after Port Arthur," *Pluto Press*, Australia.
63 John Oliver (2013), "Gun Control & Political Suicide," *The Daily Show*.
64 Simon Chapman, "Over Our Dead Bodies: Gun Law Reform after Port Arthur."
65 www.nysun.com/new-york/how-churchill-mobilized-the-english-language/87862/, last accessed July 28, 2020.
66 https://winstonchurchill.org/resources/speeches/1940-the-finest-hour/we-shall-fight-on-the-beaches/, last accessed July 28, 2020.
67 MassMoments.org (2019).
68 MassMoments.org (2019).
69 *The New York Times*, January 19, 1946.
70 Brendan Koerner (2004).
71 MassMoments (2019).
72 USLegal.com (2019).
73 National League of Cities (2019).
74 Mark Landler (2018).
75 Maya Oppenheim (2017).
76 Kevin Breuninger and Jeff Daniels (2019).
77 Simons (2014).
78 Andrew Ryan (2013).
79 Britt Peterson (2013).
80 Alex Kingsbury (2013).
81 David Boeri (2014).
82 Alan Ehrenhalt (2014).
83 Tom Acitelli (2014).
84 New Urban Mechanics (2019).
85 Ibid.
86 Louisa Kasdon Sidell (2004).
87 Imagine.Boston.gov (2015).
88 Ibid.
89 Imagine. Boston.gov (2019).
90 For a detailed description of the Smart City Boston policies, see Bris et al. (2019).
91 Gold (2014).
92 Etheridge and Thomas (2015).
93 Panchamia and Thomas (2014).
94 Source: Cabinet Office (2006).
95 Etheridge and Thomas (2015).
96 Gay (2005).
97 Etheridge and Thomas (2015).

 98 Panchamia and Thomas (2014).
 99 Ibid.
100 Panchamia and Thomas (2014), Etheridge and Thomas (2015).
101 Etheridge and Thomas (2015).
102 Panchamia and Thomas (2014).
103 Etheridge and Thomas (2015).
104 Harris and Rutter (2014).
105 Etheridge and Thomas (2015).
106 United Kingdom's Cabinet Office (2006)
107 Etheridge and Thomas (2015)
108 Ibid.
109 Panchamia and Thomas (2014); Etheridge and Thomas (2015).
110 Panchamia and Thomas (2014).
111 Talbot (2010).
112 Panchamia and Thomas (2014).
113 Ibid.
114 Santiso (2015).
115 OECD (2018).
116 Barber et al. (2011).
117 OECD (2018); Gold (2017).
118 Alessandro et al. (2014).
119 Ibid.
120 Ibid.
121 Kamensky (2015).
122 Alessandro et al. (2014).
123 Ibid.
124 Ibid.
125 Gold (2017).
126 Iyer (2012).
127 Gold (2017).
128 Carnemark (2014).
129 Source: Kenya's President's Delivery Unit (2018).
130 Government of Uganda (2019).
131 Ibid.
132 OECD (2018).
133 Chin (2015).
134 The World Bank (2017).
135 Ibid.
136 Ibid.
137 Ibid.
138 PEMANDU (2019).
139 The World Bank (2017).
140 Ibid.
141 Ibid.
142 Ibid.
143 Ibid.
144 Ibid.
145 Ibid.
146 Soren Kaplan (2017).
147 Sameer Kamat (2018).
148 McKinsey & Company (2019).
149 McKinsey & Company, "How We Help Clients" (2019).
150 McKinsey, "Public Sector" (2019).
151 McKinsey, "Our Capabilities" (2019).
152 McKinsey, "Defense & Security" (2019).
153 Boston Consulting Group, "Defense, Justice, and Border Protection" (2019).

154 Mint (2016), "Liberalization's lasting impact: rules-based regime, disintermediation", available at https://www.livemint.com/Politics/DuMcxbGyLGsfDJcUvmkqfL/Liberalizations-lasting-impact-rulesbased-regime-disinte.html
155 McKinsey, "About Us" (2019).
156 BCG, "Mission" (2019).
157 Bain & Co. (2019).
158 The Gulf Centre for Human Rights (GCHR) (2014).
159 *The Economist* Intelligence Unit (2018).
160 Consultancy-me.com (2018).
161 www.consultancy-me.com/news/339/lebanon-calls-in-consulting-firm-mckinsey-to-revamp-its-economy.
162 Consultancy-me.com (2018).
163 Donna Abu-Nasr (2018).
164 As reported by Stephen Braun in Onlineathens.com.
165 https://greatriversofhope.wordpress.com/tag/bain-capital/.
166 Stephen Braun (2012).
167 BCG.com (2019).
168 Keith Yost (2010).
169 Consultingcase101 (2019).
170 Boston Consulting Group (2019).
171 Deloitte (2019).
172 Tamara Walid (2008).
173 McKinsey "Middle East" (2019).
174 Edmund Tadros (2018).
175 Walt Bogdanich and Michael Forsythe (2018).
176 Stephanie Nebehay (2018).
177 McKinsey.com, "History of Our Firm" (2019).
178 McKinseychina.com, "An Introduction to McKinsey Greater China" (2019).
179 McKinseychina.com, "Public sector & non-profit institutions" (2019).
180 Michael Posner (2018).
181 Walt Bogdanich and Michael Forsythe (2018).
182 McKinsey.com, "Statement on *The New York Times* Article" (2018).
183 Stephen Easton (2017).
184 Besma Momani (2013).
185 Lee Cokorinos (2009).
186 ch2m.com (2019).
187 The Association of Chartered Certified Accountants (2010).
188 *The Guardian*, February 27, 2017.
189 *Saudi Gazette*, "Vision 2030" (2016).
190 Hilal Khashan (2017).
191 Carrie Rising (2018).
192 Adel Abdel Ghafar (2016).
193 Ibid.
194 John Edwards (2016).
195 Hilal Khashan (2017).
196 Ibid.
197 Michael Forsythe et al. (2018).
198 Peter Ward (2017).
199 Keith Yost (2010).

REFERENCES

Abu-Nasr, Donna (2018), "Banking to Cannabis: McKinsey Has a Plan for Lebanon's Economy," *Bloomberg News*, https://www.bloomberg.com/news/articles/2018-07-06/banking-to-cannabis-mckinsey-has-a-plan-for-lebanon-s-economy (Accessed January 23, 2019).

Acitelli, Tom (2014), "Mapping Mayor Tom Menino's Real Estate Legacy," *Boston.curbed.com*, https://boston.curbed.com/maps/mapping-mayor-tom-meninos-real-estate-legacy (Accessed January 2, 2019).

Alessandro, Martin, Mariano Lafuente, and Carlos Santiso (2014), "Governing to Deliver: Reinventing the Center of Government in Latin America and the Caribbean," *.Inter-American Development Bank*)

The Association of Chartered Certified Accountants (2010), "Management Consultants and Public Sector Transformation," https://www.accaglobal.com/content/dam/acca/global/PDF-technical/public-sector/tech-afb-mcps.pdf.

Bain & Company (n.d.), "About Bain," https://www.bain.com/about/ (Accessed 22 January 22, 2019).

Barber, Michael, Paul Kihn, and Andy Moffit (2011), "Deliverology: From Idea to Implementation," McKinsey & Company.)

Boeri, David (2014), "'Urban Mechanic' Menino Never Wanted to Be Anything More Than Mayor," *WBUR.org*. https://www.wbur.org/news/2014/10/30/menino-remembrance-boeri (Accessed 2 January 2019).

Bogdanich, Walt and Michael Forsythe (2018), "How McKinsey Has Helped Raise the Stature of Authoritarian Governments," *New York Times*, https://www.nytimes.com/2018/12/15/world/asia/mckinsey-china-russia.html (Accessed January 24, 2019).

Boston Consulting Group (n.d.a), "Defense, Justice, and Border Protection," https://www.bcg.com/industries/public-sector/defense-justice-border-protection.aspx (Accessed 21 January 2019).

Boston Consulting Group (n.d.b), "Mission," https://www.bcg.com/about/mission/default.aspx (Accessed January 21, 2019).

Boston Consulting Group (n.d.c), "Working in Dubai," https://www.bcg.com/offices/dubai/working-in.aspx (Accessed January 23, 2019).

Boston Consulting Group (n.d.d), "Working in Riyadh." https://www.bcg.com/en-us/offices/riyadh/working-in.aspx (Accessed January 23, 2019).

Boston.gov (2019), "New Urban Mechanics," https://www.boston.gov/departments/new-urban-mechanics#join-us (Accessed January 2, 2019).

Braun, Stephen (2012), "Romney's Bain advisers aided China, Russia growth," *Onlineathens.com*, https://www.onlineathens.com/national-news/2012-10-10/romneys-bain-advisers-aided-china-russia-growth (Accessed January 23, 2019).

Breuninger, Kevin, and Jeff Daniels (2019), "Apple's Shocking Revenue Warning about China Is Yet Another Example of Trump's Impact on the Tech Industry" *CNBC.com*. https://www.cnbc.com/2019/01/03/apples-china-warning-is-another-example-of-trump-impact-on-tech.html (Accessed January 3, 2019).

Bris, Arturo, Christos Cabolis, and Bruno Lanvin (2019), *Sixteen Shades of Smart* (Lausanne, Switzerland: IMD World Competitiveness Centre).

Bureau Opérationnel de Suivi du Plan Sénégal Émergent (n.d.), http://www.senegal-emergent.com/fr/dispositif.

The Cabinet Office (2006), "Prime Minister's Delivery Unit (PMDU)," *National Archives*, https://webarchive.nationalarchives.gov.uk/20060715135947/, http://www.http://cabinetoffice.gov.uk/pmdu/.

Carnemark, Curt (2014), "Ministers Share Experience on Leadership for Delivery," *World Bank*, http://www.worldbank.org/en/news/feature/2014/06/06/ministers-share-experience-on-leadership-for-delivery.

Chapman, Simon, and Rebecca Peters (1997), *Over Our Dead Bodies: Gun Law Reform after Port Arthur* (Annandale, Australia: Pluto Press Australia Pty Ltd).

Chin, Vincent (2015), "Malaysia on the March," *Centre for Public Impact*, https://www.centreforpublicimpact.org/malaysia-on-the-march/.

Cokorinos, Lee (2009), "The Government Consulting Industry: A Landscape Map," *Center on Policy Initiatives*.

Consultancy-me.com (2018a), "McKinsey Delivers 1,000-page Report to Government of Lebanon," https://www.consultancy-me.com/news/1118/mckinsey-delivers-1000-page-report-to-government-of-lebanon (Accessed January 21, 2019).

Consultancy-me.com (2018b), "Oman Calls in McKinsey on Refining and Petrochemical Industry Integration," https://www.consultancy-me.com/news/789/oman-calls-in-mckinsey-on-refining-and-petrochemical-industry-integration (Accessed January 22, 2019).

Consultingcase101.com (n.d.), "List of Consulting Firms in Riyadh, Saudi Arabia," https://www.consultingcase101.com/list-of-consulting-firms-in-riyadh-saudi-arabia/ (Accessed January 23, 2019).

Deloitte.com. "More about Deloitte in Saudi Arabia," https://www2.deloitte.com/sa/en/pages/about-deloitte/articles/about-deloitte-saudi-arabia.html (Accessed January 23, 2019).

Dower, John W. (2003), *Embracing Defeat: Japan in the Wake of World War II* (New York: W.W. Norton & Co.).

Easton, Stephen (2017), "Why Do Government Agencies Need So Many Consultants?" https://www.themandarin.com.au/83789-what-is-the-point-of-public-service-consultants/ (Accessed January 24, 2019).

The Economist Intelligence Unit, Democracy Index (2018), http://www.eiu.com/topic/democracy-index (Accessed January 21, 2019).

Edwards, John (2016), "Vision 2030 (part 1): Saudi Arabia's bold reinvention plan," The Lowy Institute, https://www.lowyinstitute.org/the-interpreter/vision-2030-part-1-saudi-arabias-bold-reinvention-plan (Accessed January 25, 2019).

Etheridge, Zina, and Peter Thomas (2015), "Adapting the PMDU Model: The Creation of a Delivery Unit by Haringey Council, London: A Case Study," Institute for Government.

Forsythe, Michael et al. (2018), "Consulting Firms Keep Lucrative Saudi Alliance, Shaping Crown Prince's Vision," *New York Times*, https://www.nytimes.com/2018/11/04/world/middleeast/mckinsey-bcg-booz-allen-saudi-khashoggi.html (Accessed January 25, 2019).

Gay, Oonagh (2005), "Public service agreements: Parliament and Constitution Centre," *UK Parliament*, available at https://researchbriefings.files.parliament.uk/documents/SN03826/SN03826.pdf

Ghafar, Adel Abdel (2016), "Saudi Arabia's McKinsey Reshuffle," *Brookings Institution*, https://www.brookings.edu/blog/markaz/2016/05/11/saudi-arabias-mckinsey-reshuffle/ (Accessed January 25, 2019).

Gold, Jen (2017), "Tracking Delivery: Global Trends and Warning Signs in Delivery Units", Institute for Government.

Gold, Jennifer (2014), "International Delivery: Centres of Government and the Drive for Better Policy Implementation," Institute for Government and Mowat Centre.

Government of Japan (2013), "Emergency Economic Measures for The Revitalization of the Japanese Economy," available at https://www5.cao.go.jp/keizai1/2013/130111_emergency_economic_measures.pdf

Government of Japan (2017), "Abenomics."

Government of Uganda, Office of the Prime Minister (2019), "The Prime Ministers Delivery Unit (PMDU)," https://opm.go.ug/the-prime-ministers-delivery-unit-pmdu/

The Guardian (2017), "The Guardian View on Management Consultants: The Trick Is Confidence: Editorial," https://www.theguardian.com/commentisfree/2017/feb/27/the-guardian-view-on-management-consultants-the-trick-is-confidence (Accessed January 24, 2019).

The Gulf Centre for Human Rights (2014), "Torture in Oman," https://www.gc4hr.org/report/view/20 (Accessed January 21, 2019).

Harris, Josh, and Jill Rutter (2014), "Centre Forward: Effective Support for the Prime Minister at the Centre of Government," Institute for Government.

Hayashi, Fumio, and Edward C. Prescott (2002), "The 1990s in Japan: A Lost Decade," *Review of Economic Dynamics* 5(1): 206–35.

Ihori, Toshiro et al. (2005), "Public Debt and Economic Growth in an Aging Japan," IDEAS.

Ito, Takatoshi (1996), "Japan and the Asian Economies: A 'Miracle' in Transition," Brookings Institution.

Iyer, Deepa (2012), "Improving Coordination and Prioritization: Streamlining Rwanda's National Leadership Retreat, 2008–2011," *Innovations for Successful Societies, Princeton University*, https://successfulsocieties.princeton.edu/publications/improving-coordination-and-prioritization-streamlining-rwandas-national-leadership.

Johnson, Chalmers A (1982), *MITI and the Japanese Miracle: The Growth of Industrial Policy, 1925–1975* (Stanford: Stanford University Press).

JPX Tokyo Stock Exchange (2018), "Japan's Corporate Governance Code: Seeking Sustainable Corporate Growth and Increased Corporate Value over the Mid- to Long-Term," available at https://www.jpx.co.jp/english/news/1020/b5b4pj000000jvxr-att/20180602_en.pdf.

Kameer, Samat (2018), "Top Consulting Firms in the World," *MBACrystalBall.com*, https://www.mbacrystalball.com/blog/2018/07/06/top-consulting-firms-world/ (Accessed January 21, 2019).

Kamensky, John (2015), "Delivery Units Around the World," *GovLoop.com*, https://www.govloop.com/community/blog/delivery-units-around-world/.

Kaplan, Soren (2017), "The Business Consulting Industry Is Booming, and It's About to Be Disrupted," *Inc.com*, https://www.inc.com/soren-kaplan/the-business-consulting-industry-is-booming-and-it.html (Accessed January 21, 2019).

Kawagoe, Toshihiko (1999), *Agricultural Land Reform in Postwar Japan: Experiences and Issues* (Washington, DC: World Bank).

Ke, D.S. (2012), "Overwork, Stroke, and Karoshi-death from Overwork". *Review Article Acta Neurol Taiwan* 21.

Khashan, Hilal (2017), "Saudi Arabia's Flawed 'Vision 2030.'" *Middle East Quarterly*. https://www.meforum.org/6397/saudi-arabia-flawed-vision-2030 (Accessed January 25, 2019).

Kingsbury, Alex (2013), "Menino Took Small Steps, Made Major Changes," *WBUR.org*, https://www.wbur.org/news/2013/12/30/menino-small-steps-major-changes-boston (Accessed January 1, 2019).

Koerner, Brendan (2004), "How to Govern from the Clink," *Slate*, https://slate.com/news-and-politics/2004/12/how-to-govern-from-jail.html (Accessed December 2, 2004).

Landler, Mark (2018), "Trump Abandons Iran Nuclear Deal He Long Scorned," *New York Times*, https://www.nytimes.com/2018/05/08/world/middleeast/trump-iran-nuclear-deal.html (Accessed January 3, 2019).

Lechevalier, Sebastien, and Brieuc Monfort (2016), *Abenomics: Has It Worked? Will It Fail?* (IDEAS).

MassMoments.org, (November 3, 1929), "Mayor Curley Jeopardizes Election." https://www.massmoments.org/moment-details/mayor-curley-jeopardizes-election.html (Accessed January 1, 2019).

McKinsey.com, (n.d.a), "Creating Change That Matters," https://www.mckinsey.com/about-us/overview (Accessed January 21, 2019).

McKinsey.com (n.d.b), "Defense & Security," https://www.mckinsey.com/industries/public-sector/how-we-help-clients/defense-and-security (Accessed January 21, 2019).

McKinsey.com (n.d.c), "History of Our Firm," https://www.mckinsey.com/about-us/overview/history-of-our-firm (Accessed January 24, 2019)

McKinsey.com (n.d.d), "Middle East: Riyadh," https://www.mckinsey.com/middle-east/riyadh (Accessed January 23, 2019).

McKinsey.com (n.d.d), "Our Capabilities," https://www.mckinsey.com/industries/public-sector/how-we-help-clients/government-transitions/our-capabilities (Accessed January 21, 2019).

McKinsey.com (n.d.e), "Public Sector," https://www.mckinsey.com/industries/public-sector/how-we-help-clients/government-transitions/our-capabilities (Accessed January 21, 2019).

McKinsey.com (n.d.f), "Public Sector," https://www.mckinsey.com/industries/public-sector/how-we-help-clients/overview (Accessed January 21, 2019).

McKinsey.com (2018), "Statement on New York Times Article on McKinsey Work in Southeast Asia, China, Eastern Europe and the Middle East," https://www.mckinsey.com/about-us/media-center/statement-on-new-york-times-article (Accessed January 24, 2019).

McKinsey.com (2019), "China," http://mckinseychina.com/about-us/ (Accessed January 24, 2019).

Ministry of Health, Labour and Welfare of Japan (n.d.), "White Paper on Measures to Prevent *Karoshi*, etc.," http://fpcj.jp/wp/wp-content/uploads/2017/11/8f513ff4e9662ac515de9e646f63d8b5.pdf.

Momani, Bessma (2013), "Management Consultants and the United States' Public Sector," *Business and Politics* 15(3): 381–399.

Nakamura, Takafusa (1981), *The Postwar Japanese Economy: Its Development and Structure* (Tokyo: University of Tokyo Press), 56.

National League of Cities (n.d.), "Partisan vs. Non-Partisan Elections," https://www.nlc.org/partisan-vs-nonpartisan-elections (Accessed January 3, 2019).

Nebehay, Stephanie (2018), "U.N. calls on China to free Uighurs from Alleged Re-education Camps," *Reuters*, https://www.reuters.com/article/us-china-rights-un/u-n-calls-on-china-to-free-uighurs-from-re-education-camps-idUSKCN1LF1D6 (Accessed January 24, 2019).

The New York Times (1946), "Curley Convicted for Mail Frauds with Two Others," https://timesmachine.nytimes.com/timesmachine/1946/01/19/93013357.html?action=click&contentCollection=Archives&module=ArticleEndCTA&region=ArchiveBody&pgtype=article&pageNumber=1.

Ohno, Kenichi (2006), *The Economic Development of Japan: The Path Travelled by Japan as a Developing Country* (Tokyo: GRIPS Development Forum).

Ono, Hiroshi (2018), "Why Do the Japanese Work Long Hours? Sociological Perspectives on Long Working Hours in Japan," *Japan Labor Issues* 2(5): 35–49.

Oppenheim, Maya (2017), "Remembering Donald Trump's Traumatic Experience at the 2011 White House Correspondents Dinner," *Independent*, https://www.independent.co.uk/news/world/americas/donald-trump-white-house-correspondents-dinner-dropped-out-twitter-2011-roasting-barack-obama-seth-a7600156.html (Accessed January 3, 2019).

Organisation for Economic Co-operation and Development (OECD) (2018), *OECD Public Governance Reviews: Paraguay: Pursuing National Development through Integrated Public Governance* (Paris: OECD), http://dx.doi.org/10.1787/9789264301856-en.

Panchamia, Nehal, and Peter Thomas (2014), "Civil Service Reform in the Real World: Patterns of Success in UK Civil Service Reform," Institute for Government, available at https://www.instituteforgovernment.org.uk/sites/default/files/publications/260314%20CSRW%20-%20final.pdf.

PEMANDU (2019), "Decoding transformation," https://www.pemandu.org/8-steps-of-transformation/.

Peterson, Britt (2013), "A defense of Menino's language gaffes," *The Boston Globe* (Accessed January 1, 2019).

Posner, Michael (2018), *"How McKinsey & Co. Fails as a Global Leader,"* Forbes, https://www.forbes.com/sites/michaelposner/2018/12/18/how-mckinsey-co-fails-as-a-global-leader/#6818e0a376d1 (Accessed January 25, 2019).

President's Delivery Unit (2018), "The Journey of Transformation," *Office of the President, Government of Kenya*, https://www.delivery.go.ke/.

Ragusa, Frank, and Nathaniel Barzideh (2014), *Abenomics and Japanese Monetary Policy: A Path to Economic and Ethical Recovery* (Wharton Research Scholars, University of Pennsylvania).

Rajan, Sri et al. (n.d.), "Liberalization's Lasting Impact: Rules-based Regime, Disintermediation," *Livemint.com*, https://www.livemint.com/Politics/DuMcxbGyLGsfDJcUvmkqfL/Liberalizations-lasting-impact-rulesbased-regime-disinte.html (Accessed January 21, 2019).

Republic of Rwanda (2019), "The Ministry of Cabinet Affairs," *Office of the Prime Minister*, https://www.primature.gov.rw/index.php?id=12.

Rising, Carin (2018), "The Pivotal Role Women Will Play in Saudi Arabia's Economic Future," *U.S. Chamber of Commerce*, https://www.uschamber.com/series/above-the-fold/the-pivotal-role-women-will-play-saudi-arabia-s-economic-future.

Ryan, Andrew (2013),"Harvard to Give Menino Honorary Degree," *The Boston Globe*, https://www.bostonglobe.com/metro/2013/05/29/from-hyde-park-harvard-yard-menino-receive-honorary-degree-from-prestigious-college/QomTJxX6vTyzSsHotV1zPP/story.html (Accessed January 1, 2019).

SAMPAN.org (2015), "Mayor Walsh Announces 'Imagine Boston 2030' at Design and Architecture Summit," https://sampan.org/2015/05/mayor-walsh-announces-imagine-boston-2030-at-design-and-architecture-summit/ (Accessed January 2, 2019).

Santiso, Carlos (2015), "Governing to Deliver: Three Keys for Reinventing Government in Latin America and the Caribbean," *Governance* 28(2): 123–126.

Saudi Gazette, Riyadh (2016), "Vision 2030," http://english.alarabiya.net/en/perspective/features/2016/04/26/Full-text-of-Saudi-Arabia-s-Vision-2030.html (Accessed January 25, 2019).

Sidell, Louisa Kasdon (2004), "Boston's Reluctant First Lady," *The Boston Globe*, http://archive.boston.com/news/globe/magazine/articles/2004/11/14/bostons_reluctant_first_lady/ (Accessed January 1, 2019).

Simons, D. Brenton (2014), "Thomas M. Menino 1942–2014," *Vita Brevis*, https://vitabrevis.americanancestors.org/2014/10/thomas-m-menino/ (Accessed January 1, 2019).

Suzuki, Toru (2009), "The Latest Development in Population of Japan," *Japanese Journal of Population* 7(1): 87–90.

Szekeres, Valéria, and Aleksandra Szczepańska (2015), *Abenomics: A Way to Accelerate the Japanese Economic Growth* (Hungary: Obuda University, Keleti Faculty of Business and Management).

Tadros, Edmund (2018), "McKinsey 'Quite Proud' of Saudi Arabia Work, Says Global Head," *Financial Review*, https://www.afr.com/business/accounting/mckinsey-quite-proud-of-saudi-arabia-work-says-global-head-20181217-h196xm (Accessed January 23, 2019).

Takada, Masahiro (1999), *"Japan's Economic Miracle: Underlying Factors and Strategies for the Growth,"* Lehigh University working paper.

Talbot, Colin (2010), *Performance in Government: The Evolving System of Performance and Evaluation Measurement, Monitoring and Management in the United Kingdom* (No. 24). ECD Working Paper Series, World Bank.

USLegal.com (n.d.), "Nonpartisan Election Law and Legal Definition," https://definitions.uslegal.com/n/nonpartisan-election/ (Accessed January 3, 2019).

Walid, Tamara (2008), "Bain Looks East," *Arabian Business*, https://www.arabianbusiness.com/bain-looks-east-49942.html (Accessed January 23, 2019).

Ward, Peter (2017), "The Pain of Withdrawal: The Saudi 2030 Vision," *The Asan Institute for Policy Studies*, http://en.asaninst.org/contents/the-pain-of-withdrawal-the-saudi-2030-vision/ (Accessed January 25, 2019).

The World Bank (2017), *Driving performance from the center: Malaysia's experience with PEMANDU* (Washington, DC: The World Bank)

WorldFund (2019), *Education Gap in Latin America* (New York: WorldFund)

Yoshino, Naoyuki, and Farhad Taghizadeh-Hesary (2014), "Three Arrows of 'Abenomics' and the Structural Reform of Japan: Inflation Targeting Policy of the Central Bank, Fiscal Consolidation, and Growth Strategy," Asian Development Bank Institute.

Yost, Keith (2010), "The Story BCG Offered Me $16,000 Not to Tell," *TherapieTech.com*, https://thetech.com/2010/04/09/dubai-v130-n18 (Accessed January 23, 2019).

Zhu, Huaiqing, and Changfeng Pan (2011), "Condition Constraints and Player Behavior in China's Stock Market," in Xu, Lilai (ed.), *China's Economy in the Post-WTO Environment: Stock Markets, FDI and Challenges of Sustainability* (Cheltenham, UK: Edward Elgar Publishing), 29.

Part 4
The path to competitiveness

41. INTRODUCTION

Without doubt, Switzerland is one of the most successful economies of the last decades. It sits on top of most international rankings in terms of productivity, innovation capacity, life satisfaction, and competitiveness. Some of its companies are the leaders in their industries; it has contributed to the world with some of the most value-enhancing innovations, from Velcro to the Red Cross. Switzerland also possesses one of the most efficient financial systems in the world.

These achievements add to the attractiveness of the country for foreign multinationals (MNCs) which, in the last years, have chosen this small country in the middle of Europe as a center of manufacturing, marketing and sales, and supply chain operations. In parallel, many other foreign MNCs' headquarters have moved to Switzerland, with particular emphasis on international operations.

This has happened despite the country's inherent conditions which make it unnatural as a focal point of attention for foreign MNCs. Its geographical position is usually praised as one of the advantages of Switzerland; yet, Switzerland does not have direct access to the sea, and we know that most of the current and future trade routes are maritime. Moreover, the United Nations estimates that about 40 percent of the world's population currently lives by the sea. Not only that—Switzerland's largest city (Zurich) hosts circa 400,000 people. This is in contrast to a world where close to 20 percent of the population lives in urban areas of 10 million people or more, with this number expected to double in the next two decades.

Switzerland is also one of the most expensive countries in the world. It ranks second to last in the Institute for Management Development (IMD) World Competitiveness Rankings in terms of cost of living (only better than Hong Kong), its currency has appreciated massively throughout 2015–2018, and the Big Mac index released by *The Economist* puts prices in Switzerland in January 2019, 13 percent more expensive than the second most expensive country (Norway), and 20 percent overvalued with respect to the US dollar (USD).[1] As a result, remuneration of employees, executives, and professionals is the highest in the world, which makes relocation very costly for foreign MNCs.

The Swiss National Bank reports that 11,500 subsidiaries of foreign companies are located in Switzerland,[2] employing almost 500,000 people, or about 10 percent of the employment in the country.[3] Why do MNCs such as Philip Morris and ABB have Switzerland as a base for their operations? Why, after the merger between Lafarge from France and Holcim from Switzerland, the latter was chosen as home of the new entity? Simply put, because Switzerland is a competitive country. Hopefully the discussion in Part 4 clarifies that this is equivalent to the nation being able to generate sustainable, inclusive prosperity for its people through a productive economic system, job creation, and appropriate institutions.

In this part, I highlight the ingredients of a national strategy—what makes a nation competitive. First and foremost, I emphasize the two necessary conditions: education and infrastructure. This is important because both a good education and a reliable infrastructure cannot develop in a short period, especially when a country starts from scratch. Because building a solid education system and investing in infrastructure is a long process, these two should also be the priorities of any government that aims to become competitive. With both education and infrastructure there is no magic: both require massive levels of public investments. In the next chapters, I shed some light on successes (Finland) and failures (Brazil), not ignoring that in some countries (Singapore, and especially the United Arab Emirates [UAE]) the attraction of foreign talent is a complement to investing in the domestic talent pool.

Coming back to Switzerland, the country is a European democracy with a sound and reliable legal system. For corporations this is not enough, yet Switzerland offers policy stability within a system where the rule of law is upheld which has no rival in the world. Here, the importance is not on the preservation of democratic values (more in Chapter 61) but on respect for the law as the only way to organize a society. I disagree with the view that acceptance of the law is a cultural trait. In Chapter 45, I show how insider trading regulation (to prevent the leak of private information ahead of corporate news in financial markets) was useless at curtailing fraud, and it was only when courts effectively did their job that prosecutions started. Rule of law is preserved through courts and good judges, and it can be achieved in Singapore as well as in India.

On the other side of the coin of the rule-of-law principle is corruption. When I arrived in Switzerland 14 years ago, one of my friends told me the story of his 12-year-old son's school assignment. He had been asked to write a report along the following guidelines:

"you are walking down the street and you see a car parked on a pedestrian crossing. Write a letter to the police reporting the misbehavior." The next week, his son came home with a new assignment with similar instructions: "you are waiting the bus and you see a car passing and the driver is using her cellphone. Write a letter to the police reporting the misbehavior." Ultimately—my friend says—"it was impossible to get in the car without my son advising me to wear the seatbelt." A country like Switzerland ranks so low in corruption levels not only because its laws are appropriately enforced, but also because the population is well educated to make the right choices. Most admired is the case of Hong Kong which I describe extensively in Chapter 46 because it is the poster child of success against corruption in a short period of time.

Because the starting conditions matter, I cannot ignore that any general recipe is useless. In Switzerland, the country's manufacturing excellence is outstanding; thus the "Swiss made" label is a reliable guarantee of quality. In parallel, Switzerland has developed a culture of innovation which finds its roots in the Swiss education system, a spirit of entrepreneurship, and a constant search for new ideas in a country that lacks natural resources other than the human brain. The situation is completely different in Ecuador, Indonesia, Jordan, etc. Finding a unique path to competitiveness is therefore important, because every country is a special case. Uniqueness is also emphasized through country branding, and it is interesting to compare the cases of Thailand, South Africa, and the small new state of Timor-Leste in their efforts to market their economies to the external world. Our research has shown that one of the best predictors of the level of foreign investment in a country is the image of the country abroad. Chapter 51 makes this visible.

A country cannot survive, however, without access to financing, especially for small and medium enterprises (SMEs). The economic development of Switzerland has happened as the financial sector has grown. Today, Switzerland is the country where executives consider that access to finance is among the easiest in the world. When asked about the availability of credit in the country, respondents to the IMD World Competitiveness survey ranked Switzerland #1 in the world, with Sweden, Hong Kong, and Denmark right below.

Additionally, regulation is business friendly and policy is regularly oriented to favor entrepreneurship and the creation of firms. Within a Europe that is slowly moving to a more flexible labor market, Swiss labor regulations provide a different landscape for employment protection and labor costs, resulting not only in low unemployment, but also very low costs of hiring a very qualified labor force. Labor market rules allow not only large MNCs, but also small and medium enterprises to create jobs. In Switzerland, SMEs account for 99 percent of the companies and generate two-thirds of the jobs.[4] It is interesting to analyze in detail the case of South Korea, as I do in Chapter 50, where large enterprises (chaebols) not only operate together with small enterprises, but also compete with them for talent and financial resources.

One aspect of the Swiss competitiveness model is the generation of prosperity through internal regional competition, be it in taxes, academic institutions, or business locations. The level of decentralization of policy allows fiscal rules to be different across cantons. And while the design of curricula in education is the responsibility of the confederal government, cantons are responsible for funding, teachers' salaries, and school quality.

Last, it is important to note that, for any economy to excel, it needs to rely on private initiatives—not the public sector—to create jobs. In our rankings, public subsidies are an impediment to prosperity because they eliminate people's incentives to educate themselves, invest, and innovate. While it may look as if helping the poor through subsidies contributes to well-being, it is only when such subsidies are part of a larger ecosystem that they are efficient. I formalize these ideas in two chapters. Chapter 48 details the subsidized economies of Tunisia and Oman. Some of the facts about these two countries may be surprising for the Western reader, more used to paying high taxes and high prices for food and gas. The result of subsidized economies is not only lack of incentives, but also poor public finances, because most of the government budget goes down the drain through current expenses, without generating economic growth. In Chapter 49, I compare plain subsidies with the more sophisticated ecosystems in China and Saudi Arabia, where the public sector does not directly subsidize individuals, but does so through the private sector. Companies, in exchange for providing basic products and cheap services, are granted a license to operate (through monopoly power or access to financial resources) which compensates them for the subsidy itself. At the root of these ecosystems is a new way of understanding capitalism in which the public sector is not a passive actor in the economy.

42. EDUCATION

When advising governments on the best policies to increase prosperity, I often say that it is best to start with the reforms that take the longest to implement. This is obviously difficult when politicians do not stay in power forever and they focus on too-short-term agendas. In fact, recent examples of successful countries (Singapore, Switzerland, Estonia) show that once the long-term issues are resolved, it is easy to promote economic growth, innovation, the financial health of the country, and attract foreign investments.

The most important of such long-term reforms is education. In the same way that money is the currency of transactions, talent is the currency of a country's prosperity. Education is the ultimate driver of entrepreneurship, the ability to innovate, efficiency and productivity, life satisfaction, and economic growth.

Innovation ecosystems are mushrooming everywhere in the world today: Silicon Valley of course, but also Cryptovalley in Switzerland, the various innovation parks in Singapore, Hong Kong, Thailand, South Korea, the Skolkovo Innovation Center in Russia—to cite a few. The model is always the same and quite simple: to innovate, we need capital and regulation. Additionally, the most important factor is talent and ideas. These are always the result of good education policies that foster creativity, out-of-the-box thinking, and, overall, technical training. Innovation ecosystems are discussed in Chapter 54.

The productivity of a country, and therefore its wage levels, depends to a great extent on the quality of human capital and the talent of the labor force. As the world has moved massively into a services society (something that, in China and India, is happening too rapidly), the value of human skills and education has also increased. A hundred years ago, the importance of brains was less compared to the power of a machine, the availability of sources of energy, and the heads of cattle possessed. Nowadays, there is a direct relationship between productivity and talent. This is so because the human brain has become more important than human legs and hands. The approximately 80,000 employees of Tata Motors generate an annual revenue of USD 520 per capita. Similarly, the 22,000 employees of DBS in Singapore produce USD 509. In contrast, Tencent's 38,000 employees have a productivity of USD 924 per head. This is not because China is more competitive than Singapore or more efficient than India, quite the opposite. The reason is that Tencent's is less capital and more labor intensive. As we evolve into a digital society this will be more and more prevalent.

Talent and education should be promoted not only for economic reasons. A recent survey in the UK has shown that graduates display a higher degree of life satisfaction than non-graduates. Bhutan incorporates the quality of the education system as a major driver of its happiness index. And as life satisfaction increases, people are more productive, spend more, improve the image of their country, attract foreign visitors and investment, and pay more taxes.

All in all, talent and education are the major drivers of long-term economic growth. At the IMD World Competitiveness Center, we have collected evidence for the last 30 years showing that countries that succeed in the long run (Singapore, Malaysia, Taiwan) also display relatively higher-quality education systems. Similarly, countries that have ranked lower for long periods (Philippines, Indonesia) report disproportionally lower levels of public investment in education.

South East Asia has made amazing progress in the last years. The Philippines, which invested only 2.47 percent of its gross domestic product (GDP) in education in 2015 (compared to a world average of 4.5 percent), now invests 3.07 percent. South Korea invests 5.07 percent. These are good signs, but not enough: Estonia, a country with a stellar performance in all international comparisons, invested 6.07 percent of its GDP in education in 2017 (compared with 5.63 percent in 2015). So, there is much more to be done: India, Singapore, Taiwan, and Thailand have reduced their levels of investment in the last years.

In the meantime, countries in the region have primarily relied on attracting foreign talent by offering life quality, high salaries, and a safe environment. This is the case with Singapore, replicated as well by Hong Kong and Taiwan. Others such as Thailand, Indonesia, and the Philippines still struggle to prevent a talent drain. However, attracting talent is not a long-term solution. Because by opening borders to talent competition, countries can end up in a segmented labor market between expats and locals. Unless the government promotes policies to incorporate local talent (as happens in the UAE and Saudi Arabia), local employees will be displaced to low productivity/low salary jobs. Global talent is desirable in order to incentivize the local labor force to improve their skill level to be able to compete, but this is never possible if the national education systems are not ready. This is, today, the problem of South East Asia (with remarkable exceptions). Not surprisingly, and with the exception of Canada, all the countries in the top 10 of the 2018 IMD World Talent Ranking are European.

Governments should focus more on the reforms that drive long-term competitiveness. Education is the most important.

Better education yields more productive individuals

Explaining differences in educational achievement, whether at the individual level or between groups, has become an increasingly prominent research topic in the fields of sociology and labor economics. The observed heterogeneity in the return to education has often been attributed to a large variety of factors ranging from socioeconomic variables such as race or household income to more structural components like the quality of the learning environment and teaching style. The role of more behavioral factors such as trust and parental involvement in education has recently been integrated into this analysis, as well as other preconditions necessary for successful personal development, namely good mental and physical health dispositions. Taking these factors into consideration, it is fair to assume that national governments play a pivotal role in shaping the effectiveness and extent of the return to education through their respective policy choices.

Two important questions about education systems are relevant to address. The first one is the importance of education in determining economic outcomes such as salaries, employment opportunities, and job satisfaction. These are private returns on education that have an effect on society as a whole, and have been widely studied and analyzed.[5] While important, this is not the question I am interested in.

The second question is which type of policies determine the quality of the education system, and of course what it means to have a "good" education system. The latter will be addressed more extensively in Chapter 59, and I will assume in the next paragraphs that the systems of Finland, Singapore, and Switzerland are the best in the world. This chapter therefore explains how countries achieve excellence in education, and specifically the type of financial investments required.

Systemic inefficiencies? Toward explaining the observed mismatch

In a very interesting foreword to a study conducted by McKinsey on the world's best-performing school systems, Andreas Schleicher, former Directorate for Education at the Organization for Economic Cooperation and Development (OECD), affirms that there is still significant scope for improving education efficiency across the OECD; to such an extent that taxpayers could expect up to 22 percent more output for their levels of investment in schooling. He further stresses that measuring performance does not necessarily lead to pertinent insights into what policies can do to help students learn better, teachers teach better, and schools become more effective in delivering productive knowledge. In his eyes, the root of the problem behind the observed mismatch in education investment and achievement lies within adaptability. Countries whose education systems work best are those that are "swift to adapt, slow to complain and open to change."

In fact, high-performing schools around the globe are those that do not complacently hold onto ideals of tradition and past reputation, but rather seek to innovate and provide solutions to address future labor market challenges. This, however, is not necessarily analogous to exorbitant costs. Countries such as Singapore, for example, continue to demonstrate that it is possible to achieve extremely high education outcomes with reasonable levels of investment. The study conducted by McKinsey on the world's 10 most effective education systems sheds light on some of the factors that may translate into an efficient transmission of knowledge:

1. getting the right people into teaching jobs,
2. developing these individuals as effective instructors, and
3. ensuring that the education system provides the best possible learning outcomes for every child, regardless of social background or inherent ability.

These best practice measures demonstrate that the implementation process required to substantially improve the learning outcomes of pupils is achievable not only in a short time frame, but also at reduced costs.

An aspect of education and productivity that is often overlooked in our modern societies is the crucial role of fostering creativity. This is especially true in the day and age of artificial intelligence (AI) and computerized production processes, where the contribution of human capital to output increasingly involves our ability to think critically and creatively about real-time solutions. The concept of fostering creativity in education goes back as far as the age of Plato[6]; however, the idea regained policy interest in the late 1950s when US and European engineers' perceived failure to outperform Soviet engineers was deemed a direct consequence of their lack of creativity. This eventually led to the US National Defense Education Act, which declared creativity as important for the prosperity and survival of society.[7] Since then, many Western economies in the developed world have made policy efforts to combine knowledge and creativity in a way that places this quality at the center of "curriculum and pedagogy."[8]

In this respect, it may go some way to providing an explanation as to why East Asian and European economies have been faring considerably better in education achievement compared to some of their developing counterparts. For many developing economies, creativity remains a neglected aspect of education as policy objectives have primarily focused on obtaining a workforce that is well-tailored to the demands of export-led growth, whereas in more developed economies, policies have been able to integrate creativity as a means to achieve future growth and student self-actualization. According to Oral (2006), developing economies' integration of creative thinking skills in education is a crucial and necessary step in shaping their future political orientation and economic reform.

Key success factors

Investment in education

Overall, this is a crucial driving force behind the development of an education system. Most of the countries that have succeeded in establishing competitive education systems in the world have focused their resources toward their education system from the elementary levels to the higher and advanced education levels.[9]

Taking a closer look at data made available by the Program for International Student Assessment (PISA) educational assessment survey along with the United Nations Educational, Scientific, and Cultural Organization (UNESCO), EUROSTAT, and other national sources, it is striking to note that some of the world's best-performing 15-year-old students in science and maths stem from countries who spend relatively less on education. For instance, within the scope of IMD's World Competitiveness country rankings, the top 10 most performing economies with regard to overall PISA scores include six Asian economies, of which none appear in the top 10 for public expenditure on education. Conversely, economies such as Brazil (6.2 percent), Israel (6.8 percent) and Iceland (7.2 percent)—which all figure in the top 10 spenders on education as a percentage of GDP—fare extremely poorly in educational achievement with PISA scores of 389, 468, and 481, respectively.[10] On first inspection, these statistics illustrate a potential mismatch between the cost and effectiveness of education in different countries; however, the figures need some further context and exploration as the numbers employed do not take into account factors such as demographics or purchasing power parity.

Note that investment in education as a percentage of GDP is the standard metric of government funding of education. The OECD uses such a metric to measure "Public Spending on Education."[11] Consequently, countries such as Singapore, Hong Kong, and Japan—that spend a relatively smaller proportion of their GDP on education than

Brazil for instance—appear less prolific in their efficient use of resources on education. Although the ratio is a good indicator of the priority of education that a country adopts, it is not a reliable metric, especially when comparing countries with different GDP sizes and economic capacities as well as different population sizes.[12]

Figure 4.1 reports a more meaningful measure that takes into account the country's demographics by reporting public investment per student, not as a percentage of GDP. The figure only includes OECD countries, which on average spent USD 9,722 per capita in 2015 (compared to USD 9,722 for Japan and USD 17,737 for Singapore). Within the OECD, the United States is the second most spending country (USD 15,776 per student), yet it remains in the middle of the PISA rankings in science (496 vs an OECD average of 493), reading (497 vs an OECD average of 493), and math (40 vs an OECD average of 490).

Therefore, investment is important, but it does not tell the full story.[13] Why do some economically advanced countries such as the United States obtain less efficient outcomes in educational achievement than some countries that spend proportionally less per student?

Teachers' salaries

Teachers' salaries are important because they directly affect motivation and morale and indirectly the quality of the education system.[14] Additionally, competitive salaries mean that the teaching profession will attract some of the best talent, which enhances

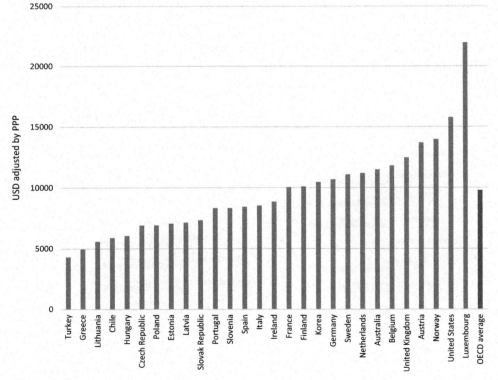

Figure 4.1 Total Expenditure on Education Per Full-Time Student, 2015
Source: OECD.

the quality of the education that students receive, and the overall quality of the education system. Figure 4.2 illustrates countries offering the best salaries to teachers. Data is obtained from research done by Oscar Williams-Grut from the Business Insider.

Out of the best paying countries, Canada, Japan, Germany, Korea, and Switzerland also make an appearance in the top 10 PISA scores performance in the world.[15] This indicates a strong correlation between teacher salaries and the performance of the education system. However, this correlation does not mean that offering the best salaries directly translates into a good education system. At the same time, it does not mean that offering the lowest salaries means the education system is directly poor. For example, New Zealand ranks consistently as one of the ten worst paying countries in the world for elementary (USD 43,000) and high school (USD 46,000) teachers.[16] The statistics here reveal a consistent correlation between the salaries provided to teachers and performance. Therefore, performance is a function of teacher salaries for most countries as illustrated in Figure 4.3, based on research from Peter Dolton from the University of Sussex and Oscar Marcenaro Gutierrez from the University of Málaga.

The size of the class (number of students per class) also has a direct impact on the quality of education delivered, because it influences the effectiveness of the teacher. Firstly, a small class reduces the teacher workload. This allows the teacher the energy and time to improve his or her performance as a teacher and focus on improving students.

Secondly, a small class size makes the classroom less chaotic. A big class with students displaying different types of temperament and intelligence and occupying the same space poses a significant challenge in their management. For teachers facing a huge class, management is difficult to achieve consistently on a daily basis and still provide the best education and learning experience.[17] A small class offers privacy for the students while engaged in in-group work with less disruption of their work, which leads to higher levels of student focus and translates to improved performance.

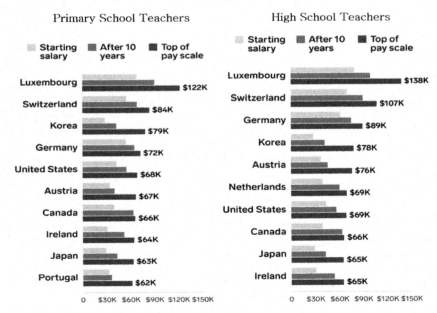

Figure 4.2 The 10 best-paying countries

Source: Willams-Grut (2016).

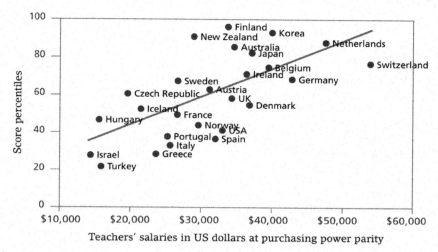

Figure 4.3 Educational Performance and Teachers' Salaries

Source: Dolton and Marcenaro-Gutierrez (2011).

Thirdly, a small class size enhances teacher–student engagement. It allows the teacher to give more attention to each student, thereby individualizing the learning experience. This enables the identification and understanding of the student's weaknesses and strengths, which allows the teacher to design the learning process in a bespoke manner. This benefits the learning ability of the students.[18] Figure 4.4 highlights the number of students for every teacher (staff) averages across the world.

From the numbers shown in Figure 4.4, the best-performing countries such as Finland, Germany, and Japan (appearing in the top 10 PISA score ranking) also have, on average, small classes. Finland's primary school class size is at 14, below the OECD average of 15. Germany's is 15, while Japan's is 16. In secondary schools, Finland's class size is 14, equal to the OECD average.[19] The graph also shows that Italy's class size is smallest in the subsample of countries—and it ranks worst in PISA scores.

Reducing class sizes only works if the country has the ability to bring in equal or even better teachers to meet the extra need. Countries such as Finland, Germany, and Japan have demonstrated the capacity to add more teachers to make the difference as they reduce class sizes. On the other hand, reducing class sizes without hiring teachers of equal quality to make the difference might end up making things worse.

Class size affects the behavior of the children individually and as a group. It also affects the effectiveness of the teacher—in providing individualized and targeted education. Therefore, countries that balance class size with quality teachers end up performing better than nations with class sizes within the OECD standard but are not matched with the quality of teachers.

Education philosophy

The overarching education philosophy adopted by the education system in Singapore, Switzerland, and Hong Kong focuses on providing education to all students, but differentially according to what individual students can afford intellectually.[20] This means

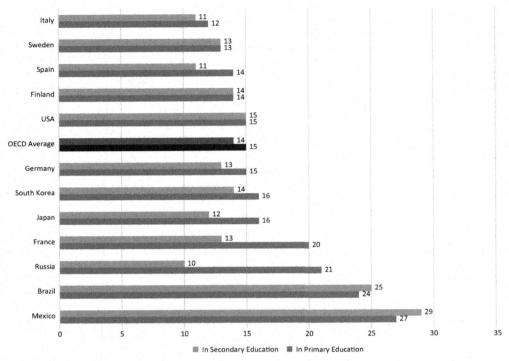

Figure 4.4 Average Number of Students per Teacher in 2017

Source: OECD.

that the philosophy has planned around the fact that some students are more gifted than others. Therefore, students that do not excel in classwork are not condemned to a life without education.

Instead, the education system provides them with alternative high-quality education options to further their talents and abilities. Additionally, students who do not qualify for higher education courses do not get any less professional opportunities after they have completed second-level education.

For example, in Switzerland, the apprenticeship system that provides vocational training has established an education system that not only produces all-round graduates, but also expands the opportunities for many of the students, especially those who do not make it into the country's higher education colleges or internationally.[21] The dual-tracked approach—where students get apprenticeship training for three to four days gaining hands-on experience and receive classroom instruction for the remainder of the school days—not only allows for diverse training but also provides more choice to students when it comes to professional decisions. I describe the Swiss system in detail below.

The vocational training program's importance is underscored by the fact that two out of three students in Switzerland choose to pursue training in a vocational program. Moreover, these programs are closely correlated with the labor market.[22] This enhances the success of the education system in offering students with the skills and preparation to be absorbed into the labor market once they graduate. It also means that students do not necessarily need a college degree to have the skills and wherewithal to be employable.

The education philosophy in Singapore, Finland, Switzerland, and Hong Kong adopts a personalized level of education that is more than is typically seen in countries such as the UK and the EU. On many metrics such as teacher salaries, investment in education per GDP, investment in education per student, and class size, the United States and the UK are competitive with Singapore, Switzerland, and Hong Kong.[23] However, when it comes to performance on the PISA scores and other metrics, the United States and the UK lag behind countries that are performing very well.[24] This highlights that the overall philosophy behind the education system plays a crucial role in its success.

An education philosophy affects the way teachers and students interact, the instructional design (ID), the focus of the curriculum, and the choice students have regarding their professional development. Singapore, Switzerland, and Hong Kong offer significantly more choices to students when it comes to paths towards professional development compared to fellow OECD countries such as the United States and the UK.[25] This is characterized by the focus on vocational training, which gives professional meaning and purpose even with the lowest levels of education certification.

Why nations fail in education

Lack of attention to education policies

The failure to establish an ideological and intellectual foundation behind an education system means that the overall system does not get the best from the students, and does not offer the students much in the way of skills or preparedness for the world generally and the labor market specifically.

For example, fundamental challenges face the education system in Brazil. Firstly, teachers are not well paid, are demotivated, and mostly disinterested. They do not take seriously the role of being the agents who shape the future. Secondly, the Brazilian public is not largely inclined to seek education.[26] The value of education in Brazilian society and within the larger Brazilian culture is not emphasized compared to successful countries such as Singapore, Hong Kong, Switzerland, and Finland. Thirdly, investment in education per GDP and per student is significantly below the OECD and global averages. This means that teachers and students do not have access to the requisite tools and facilities (classrooms) to meet the core demand (number of students) in the country.[27]

In South Africa, the basic intellectual investment in education, especially the quality of education that students receive, is significantly below par. This is underscored by the fact that a significant number of students are leaving school without the ability to read, write, and use arithmetic.[28] This results from the fact that most South African teachers lack the basis pedagogic and content expertise and competencies to impart knowledge to the learners.[29] Other challenges include inefficient utilization of resources, corruption, inadequate organizational support of teachers, and constant curricular shifts.[30]

Primary school not mandatory

The best example is Brazil where primary education is not mandatory. This has exacerbated the situation where more and more members of society do not value education, and where a significant number of young boys and girls do not go to school to gain basic literacy. Additionally, this also means that the cost of primary school education in the country is beyond the means of many, especially those living in rural areas and the unemployed or poor of the country.

Lack of social consensus

There is a significant connection between the education system and its ethos and the overall societal dispensation. This is because the education philosophy is a reflection of the collective aspirations of a country or a society. As a result, a lack of consensus on the philosophical and structural aspects of the education system affects the overall quality of the education offered. This issue is observed in Spain, where there are constant changes to the education structure depending on the political party in power. This back and forth means that intellectual investment, structural development, and philosophical advantages are lost because of the constant changes. Most of the best-performing education systems such as Hong Kong, Singapore, Switzerland, and Finland have stable structural, philosophical, and ideological approaches to education. Political changes do not necessarily mean a significant upending of the system in place. This has allowed the professionals and stakeholders in the education sector to cement some of the gains, to work on limiting or eliminating the weaknesses, and to work overall toward making the education system better year on year.

Education for all in Switzerland

Switzerland's education system is born by two distinct figures with opposing opinions influencing the Swiss education space. The first opinion advocates for the unification of the education system at the federal level and the harmonization of the educational institutions of each canton. The other opinion considers that the federal state is not authorized to intervene in school decisions and that the cantons must retain their sovereignty in terms of education.

The first unifying ideas came from Philippe-Albert Stapfer, an influential figure in Berne where he held high office in teaching. Inspired by a number of public education projects, Stapfer brought together well-known Swiss pedagogical figures such as Fr Grégoire Girard, Johann Heinrich Pestalozzi, and Daniel Johannes Heinrich Zschokke, to design an education plan that would contribute to the forging of this one and indivisible Republic. The main aim of Stapfer was to spread education through a country that was distinguished by its cultural, religious, linguistic, and traditional diversity.[31] He also insisted on the development of an education plan that aimed to establish a federal organization of the public education system. In this plan he wanted to:

- Unify the school structure at the federal level in order to harmonize the system and the pedagogical content in particular to the primary school.
- Establish a national teacher training school which would ensure unified training and the quality of all teachers throughout the country.
- Unite all students in a single university so as to concentrate the most intelligent scholars and to make science and the arts shine.

Knowing clearly that the Swiss population struggles to have a unified opinion, Stapfer proposed a solution, which could be considered as the premises of the famous "Swiss compromise": this centralization would be compensated by the establishment of councils of education within each canton. Approved by the Directory, Stapfer's Education Plan of 1798 would then have a destiny similar to that of most educational projects. It was the subject of endless debates and commissions arousing controversies, amendments, and compromise. In the end, the plan was abandoned as Stapfer left office. But what is crucial is that the public education councils he set up in each canton remained. Following the adoption of the constitution of 1848 and the unification of the cantons, the debates re-emerged; however, it was resolved that the cantons would retain their sovereignty. Debates in the Federal Chambers discussed establishing normal schools at the expense of the Confederation and a federal university. This idea remained controversial:

> the French-speaking cantons fear the Germanic intellectual hegemony, the Catholic cantons the Protestant hegemony, the conservative cantons the hegemony of the liberals. On the other hand, the cantons that already have a university fear the reduction of its audience. In other words, the latent conflicts between cantons always have repercussions on school issues and retain initiatives to delegate real responsibilities to the Confederation.[32]

Two main events marked the turning point toward the unification of the education system. The first event was in 1875, when Switzerland adopted one of the first systems of centralized evaluation of school performance. The school results were made public to encourage comparison between cantons. As a result of this competition, the cantons rivaled to conceal their weaknesses and improve their results. These examinations were abolished just before the Great War and were reintroduced at the end of World War II.

The second event took place during the second half of the 19th century. Economic crises and tensions in the labor market had intensified migration flows within the country. Parents and teachers demanded greater coherence of school structures and curricula between cantons. From the 1860s, teachers' associations demanded this harmonization and wanted their diploma to be recognized throughout the national territory. In response to these interpellations, and in order to prevent the increasingly organized and influential teaching associations from taking over too much power, the cantonal ministers formed an alliance. This was followed by a conference, which brought together all the directors of the Public Instruction of Switzerland (CDIP) in 1897. In this context, the directors would laboriously but gradually multiply the concordats allowing for the first harmonization of the Swiss school. Following numerous efforts by the CDIP, such as the introduction of federal statistics on school attendance, number of pupils per class, proportion of graduates in the population, among others, the harmonization of school structures, programs and calendars, a concordat was signed in 1970 which updated the constitution.

The latest addition to the harmonization of the Swiss education system was legalized on May 21, 2006 (HarmoS concordat) following a half decade of negotiations by the CDIP. The HarmoS project's aims were

- To define the age at which school begins (four years of age as of July 31).
- The duration of compulsory school (11 years, including 2 years of kindergarten) and the length of each school year.[33]

Today, after two centuries of talks, the Confederation is given the right and the duty to control Swiss education.

Funding

In 2018, public expenditure on education represents 5.1 percent of GDP. Compulsory schooling represents the largest share of expenditure in this field. The Confederation finances 17.0 percent of education, the cantons 51.7 percent, and the communes 31.3 percent. However, financing of education is not always done directly, but also in the form of contributions to other levels of government; 55 percent of the confederation's funds are spent directly and the rest is paid to the cantons.[34] Switzerland's expenditure on tertiary education and research is high in international comparison. This is partly due to the fact that research plays a central role in Switzerland's universities which is confirmed by the high proportion of doctoral graduates. Initially, each canton financed their own university, the confederation responsible for the federal institutes of technology. But the federation later began to contribute funding for the promotion of research and development. Moreover, the state started granting subsidies and covering needs that the cantons could not afford.

In terms of apprenticeships, Switzerland spends more than 1 percent of its GDP on its vocational education and training (VET) system. In contrast to the overall education system which is funded by public funds, the VET system relies on a strong public to private relationship. In fact more than 60 percent of the VET system is funded by private companies.[35] However, due to the productivity of apprentices, the private sector gets a return on its investment. This return enables private companies (even small ones) to accept many apprentices who will, if they choose to stay after their training, increase the firm's profit.

Curriculum and structure

The Swiss education system is known for its high permeability between its different sectors "no degree without further education possibilities."[36] This feature contributes to the high popularity of apprenticeships. Furthermore, thanks to its prestigious universities, many foreign professors are attracted to Switzerland. This leads to a larger concentration of highly qualified researchers and teachers which, in turn, contributes to higher education levels among students, resulting in a more competitive workforce.

Nowadays, the Swiss school system is divided into three parts: primary grades, secondary grades I and II, and the tertiary education system. The cantons are still partly sovereign in terms of education, which is why there are 26 ministries of education, one for each canton. Since the HarmoS concordat has yet to be implemented in all cantons, where it has been implemented kindergarten begins at age 4, and school is compulsory until the age of 15. It consists of eight primary years (Grades 1–8) and three secondary I grades (Grades 9–11).

After finishing compulsory school, several options are available. Either continue on with secondary II (i.e., the gymnasium) or start an apprenticeship. After gymnasium (or, under certain conditions, also with an apprenticeship), there is the possibility to attend 1 of the 12 Swiss universities without taking entrance exams and for a lower price than in other OECD countries.

Although Swiss pupils reached very high scores in the PISA, Switzerland still struggles with pupils coming from modest socioeconomic backgrounds. In fact, the difference between native and first-generation immigrant children is among the highest in OECD countries. Integrating children with an immigration background into school is particularly important as well as particularly challenging, as they make up a large share of pupils: 22 percent of 15pyear-old children have an immigration background.[37] This education gap translates into lower upper secondary degree attainment. One explanation of this is the fact that fundamental cognitive and non-cognitive abilities are produced in the early years of childhood, long before children are five years old. Children from disadvantaged families receive much less cognitive and emotional stimulation than other children, hindering development. For these children, attending childcare and pre-school education facilities is effective in avoiding learning difficulties later on. Substantial evidence shows that schooling at a very young age raises educational opportunities at later stages, especially for those with fairly poorly educated parents. It also raises the share of pupils who are able to pursue education at the tertiary level.[38]

The tendency to prefer having a university degree has increased over the past years. This might be perceived as positive but what makes Switzerland so innovative is the "jack of all trades" type of education, which is achieved by accumulating a certain set of practical skills in addition to a large theoretical baggage. In fact, companies prefer an apprentice who has continued his or her studies than a freshly graduated university student who has not done any practical work. In other words, university and apprenticeships should be viewed as being complementary and not mutually exclusive.[39]

Continuing education also plays an important role especially in an era of rapid changes. Switzerland does not spend as much as other top OECD countries on continuing formation. It is largely left to private companies that have no obligation partake in such programs. This lack of federal funding leads to a less up-to-date workforce that gets too comfortable with the everyday workload and does not see the necessity to innovate. Moreover, because the profitability of continuing training increases with the level of education, companies tend to invest more on their educated workers than on their less educated ones. This disparity tends to widen the gap between qualified and non-qualified people. In addition, there is also a difference between the two genders. Companies are far less likely to financially support women than men. This is why there is a much higher proportion of women financing their own continuing education.[40]

Teachers first in Finland

For decades, Finland has constantly been top ranked by PISA. Since its first publication in 2001, Finland has been seen as an international leader in education. What makes Finland special is that this country not only delivers great performance in respect of their students' intellectual ability, but also their education system is uniquely centered at the students' happiness. Although some other countries might sit on the big 10 of the PISA's chart, no other country can compete with Finland in their homogeneous quality across all schools. Specifically, the quality difference between the best and the worst school in Finland is miniscule, which simply means that they are all equally good.

As mentioned earlier, no pain no gain. The achievement that Finland is enjoying today is not far from what they sacrificed in the past. Some people may hardly believe that this education system experienced a turmoil of social problems and economic collapse in the past. Therefore, understanding the evolution of how this country transformed its hardships into successfully delivering the most attractive education system would be beneficial for us, especially for countries that are still struggling to elevate their human quality.

Political history behind Finland's success

The development of the Finnish education system has been a slow process that started at the end of World War II and continued until the 1980s. Finland is a small country that gained independence from the Soviet Union in 1917. The first post-war election in 1945 created a parliament where the seats were composed of three political parties: the Social Democrats, the Agrarian Centre Party, and the Communists. As a newly independent country, the three political parties reached a consensus on a few major reforms. One such area was education. Before the reform took place, the education system in Finland was conventional, with Germanic influence and based on memorization. Understandably, the system intended to fulfill the needs of an agricultural society rather than a modern industrial society. In that period, 60 percent of Finland was rural with income per capita levels less than half of the United Kingdom or the United States.[41]

By 1950, only a quarter of young people in Finland were able to access middle school. The reason is that schools were not evenly distributed throughout the country. Hence, only those who lived in towns could attend. Also, not all middle schools were public, some were private. Hence, wealthy children had greater access to middle schools.[42]

Those social imbalances raised the awareness of political leaders to create a more inclusive education system. Additionally, as the Finnish economy was recovering from the war, public awareness of greater access to education was also rising. In response to social demands, the parliament created three successive reform commissions which were responsible for producing recommendations to reform the education system. The first reform was implemented in 1945 by focusing on the primary school curriculum. This reform was intended to transform the primary school curriculum to be more humanistic and child centered. The second reform was released one year later by introducing a common school which covered Grades 1–8. However, this idea failed to be implemented due to strong rejections from universities and grammar teachers.[43]

Finally, the third reform was implemented in 1955 and created the system of *comprehensive schools*. Under this reform, parliament expanded the basic education from six to nine years under a municipally run comprehensive school. That is, parliament recommended that all comprehensive schools be managed directly by local governments. Such a policy created an education system where middle schools were more evenly distributed geographically. Finally, in 1968, the Finnish parliament legislated to design an education system around comprehensive schools.[44] The legislation obligated all young Finnish to gain nine years basic education in a comprehensive school under a municipality's management. Therefore, all schools were public schools. Although debate regarding the reform was rising, the legislation gained a majority vote, as the country was very ambitious to enhance its future competitiveness. Besides, the authority considered that prioritizing education reform was crucial as it would establish a foundation for all reforms that would take place in the country.[45]

Subsequently, the Finnish governments embarked on a long process to formulate a national curriculum. Its design took five years from 1965 to 1970 before it was implemented in 1972. The basic principle underpinning the school curriculum was equality, that is, the idea that schools could not differentiate depending on students' interests or skills. Teachers were not allowed to treat children differently in order to eradicate socioeconomic barriers.[46]

To ensure that the new comprehensive school treated all students equally, another challenge that the government faced was the quality of teachers. In order to raise their level, the government implemented a new rule which required all teachers to hold at least a master's degree. In addition to that policy, the Finnish government also provided intensive and comprehensive training programs for all teachers across municipalities. This intensive training was implemented during the period 1972–1977, in parallel with the implementation of the new education system to schools throughout municipalities. The transition to this new system was implemented slowly and carefully. The first implementation of the new system was in 1972 covering municipalities in northern Finland, while it gradually spread to municipalities in the southern regions in 1977.[47]

In 1985, the government took a significant step in reforming the traditional structure of academics in upper secondary school. Precisely, the government brought up the concept of trust between the government and schools by giving schools more independence to develop their internal curriculum with a more flexible and modular structure. Surprisingly, the trust given to schools and teachers was able to deliver exceptional results. As teachers were given more autonomy, their commitment to high-quality education increased. At the same time, with more trust came more transparency between the national school inspectorate, municipalities, and schools.[48]

Eventually, the series of continuous, steady, and careful reforms by the different Finnish governments paid back with a solid education performance since 1970. For example, in 1970 only 30 percent of adults had completed middle school education; today, it is 90 percent.[49]

Brazil and the irrelevance of education

Brazil is the fifth largest country in the world in terms of both size and population. The lack of a proper education system and teachers has been pulling the South American country behind. Although the state has made remarkable progress in the recent past, including allocating more funds to the sector, a lot still needs to be done.

The biggest problem facing Brazil is poor public education. A whopping 18 percent of the population is functionally illiterate. They cannot perform basic arithmetic or communicate effectively orally and in writing. A more worrying fact is that 38 percent of Brazilian undergraduates are functionally illiterate. The public education system is almost a failed one, there are no teachers, classes are overcrowded, and there is poor infrastructure and inadequate security at schools.

Teachers in these schools are not qualified, and the few who are qualified are underpaid. Teachers' salaries start at USD 350 a month, and because their jobs are secure, most of the times they are absent from work.

43. OPENNESS/TALENT ATTRACTION

Without doubt, the fast changes in technologies that we are currently enjoying are going to contribute to economic growth. However, together with technology, some observers indicate that the best predictor of future growth is access to human capital. In this context, the need for technological knowledge has shifted the demand for workers toward those with exceptional skills, competencies, and training. Technology thus makes it essential for the competitiveness of enterprises, and economies in general, to be able to continuously tap into the global highly skilled talent market. What do countries do to attract talent? What motivates highly skilled talent flows?

In principle, in a world where borders are blurring and globalization has spread, it should be easier to attract movable human capital. English is becoming the world's lingua franca; it has become much easier and faster to travel across countries, and culturally we are more alike thanks to social networks, communications, and technology. Today, workers—especially those highly educated—have a choice.

The traditional approach to attracting talent is that highly skilled labor gravitates toward those economies with higher income per-capita levels. If, additionally, the tax system in the country favors high incomes, a higher return on skills can increase the attractiveness of a host economy. In addition, the availability of opportunities to access high positions and the possibilities of professional development can increase the appeal of a country. Highly skilled talent moves, for example, to countries that offer opportunities to further their skills which could, in turn, lead to better jobs and higher wages. Increasing evidence, however, suggests that there are several attractiveness factors beyond economic incentives.

For example, the institutional quality of a destination country is one of these factors. An effective legal system that protects the rights of individuals contributes greatly to attracting and retaining talent. In addition, the level of immigration restrictions plays a significant role. More restrictive immigration policies can, for instance, discourage highly skilled individuals from pursuing a job opportunity in a particular country. Conversely, policies that establish highly skilled labor as a policy target—that is, selective admittance based on skills—and consequently ease the migrating process for individuals, increase the attractiveness of countries. Selective admittance policies can determine whether or not spouses can gain access to a country's labor market.

Additionally, my own work with Shlomo Ben-Hur, José Caballero, and Marco Pistis from the IMD World Competitiveness Center[50] suggests that skilled workers tend to move to countries that use the same language as their own, or at least to countries where their own language is spoken extensively even if it is not the native language of the destination country. We have also found that the level of openness toward foreigners in destination countries and the quality of life they offer can be more significant than the existing economic conditions. For instance, despite the high earning potential and attractive fiscal regimes in a particular economy, highly skilled talent may gravitate more toward other countries that offer a diversity of lifestyles that can result in individuals' greater well-being and life satisfaction.

Also fundamental are policies that facilitate entrepreneurship. Highly skilled talent, in other words, is drawn toward countries that promote innovation and risk-taking. Evidence also suggests that the level of technological innovation in a destination country is key to attracting highly skilled talent. Countries that develop and implement policies that entice and favor technological innovation tend to attract more talent. Importantly, entrepreneurial activity can ultimately have a significant impact on a country's innovative trends. Therefore, the interaction between entrepreneurship and technological innovation can lead to a virtuous cycle. If highly skilled talent is attracted to countries that encourage entrepreneurial activities and technological innovation, then the increasing flows of highly skilled talent can foster greater entrepreneurship and generate further technological innovation. This, in turn, can lead to greater talent attraction, and so on.

In the future, governments that develop policies to attract talent will enjoy economic competitive advantages coming from more innovation and higher economic growth. In addition, attracting well-prepared talent creates positive spillovers on the domestic labor force, because they are obliged to compete and step up their own skills and education. How can countries foster such policies? First and foremost, by creating new job opportunities by investing in industries that are at the forefront of technology. Second, by facilitating the integration of migrant workers into the local culture and institutions. Finally, by providing tax incentives, access to services, and civil rights to foreigners.

Abed Shaheen and InfoFort

Bowling Green is a small community in Wood County in Ohio, its closest largest city being Toledo, with 250,000 inhabitants. It is also a one-hour drive from Lake Erie, and it is famous for hosting the National Tractor Pulling Championship[51] since 1967. It was here, at Bowling Green State University (BGSU), and specifically in the School of Business, where Abed Shaheen was finalizing his MBA in 2003. Born in 1978 in Beirut, Lebanon, Abed received a full scholarship to go to the United States after finishing his degree in computer science at the Lebanese-American University in Beirut. "Technology changed my life," says Abed, because even during his two years in business school he had always considered that programing and computing would be at the center of his professional life, even though he knew that he wanted to become a businessman.

Job prospects were gloomy at the end of 2003, especially in the technology sector after the internet bubble had burst. Abed received a couple of job offers from regional companies in information technology (IT)-related jobs, but he was at the same time targeting the Middle East market. Ultimately, it meant a lot to him to be close to his family back in Lebanon, and he did not have a working visa to stay in the United States, so he would need not only a company that wanted to recruit him in the United States, but also a company that would sponsor his H-1 visa. Besides, any position he would take would not be comparable in terms of quality of life to living in say Dubai. Instead of a 12-day annual vacation in the United States and relatively high taxes, he could live very comfortably in Dubai with a high salary, no income tax, and close to home.

Abed applied online for a job in Aramex, the logistics company founded by Fadi Ghandour who was also the chief executive (CEO) at that time. With no hesitation, and upon graduating from BGSU, he accepted an offer in the supply chain solutions team and moved to the United Arab Emirates. Aramex is located in the Jebel Ali Free Zone (Jafza), set up by Sheik Mohammed in 1985. It started with only 19 businesses, but today, Jafza hosts 7,000 companies.[52] At the time of Abed joining Aramex, the company was mainly focused on logistics and transportation within the Middle East and North Africa (MENA) region, with Dubai one of its major hubs.

On 2009, Fadi Ghandour asked Abed to join InfoFort. The company had been established in 1997 by two partners and it was the leader in information management solutions in the Middle East. InfoFort was a B2B company that collected documents from banks, schools, insurance companies, and public sector organizations, and stored them in secure warehouses for compliance, recording, or security reasons. Typically, a bank would accumulate cashed checks and, at some point, would need to store them safely, in case a potential legal claim arose in the future. InfoFort's service consisted of collecting, recording, and storing these documents, and delivering them on request. Because Aramex was primarily a courier operator in the UAE, massive synergies justified a majority stake being acquired from the two company founders. The storage business was very much driven by governance and regulation, so it had to be managed separately.

Six years after arriving in the UAE, and when he was only 31 years old, Abed became the CEO of InfoFort. Within the next eight years, the company changed from a storage facility into the leading digital transformation solutions provider in the Middle East, Africa, and South East Asia, with services in the UAE (Abu Dhabi, Dubai), Saudi Arabia (Riyadh, Jeddah, Dammam), Egypt (Cairo, Alexandria), Qatar, Oman, Bahrain, Kuwait, Jordan, Algeria, Bangladesh, Turkey, Kenya, Ghana, and Uganda. InfoFort not only stores documents, but it first scans them and creates a digital record that it shares with the client, charging a managing fee for this procedure. Additionally, it has moved into the software business to capture more value, by designing search tools that allow the client to search for any specific key or field in a series of thousands of documents; in advance, the client would buy very expensive software from third-party vendors to process the data. Today, InfoFort provides the entire array of services, including a new blockchain solution to secure and verify documents in order to prevent the forging and duplication of records. InfoFort's clientele includes global and local companies, ranging from small- and medium-sized organizations to multinationals and Fortune 500 enterprises that span a broad range of industries such as financial services, legal, healthcare, engineering, government, public services, energy, oil and gas, information technology, and media.[53]

Abed's personal life also changed and he went from living in a small apartment next to the Free Zone, to renting a bigger, newly constructed apartment with magnificent views over the Persian Gulf, in The Palm, a gigantic real estate project sponsored by the Dubai government in 2001. In 2016, he got married in Santorini (Greece); he is a member of the Young Presidents Organization (YPO) and drives a Tesla Model S.

Dubai as a talent attractor

The UAE ranks second in the world in the indicator "Foreign highly skilled personnel are attracted to your country's business environment." This is part of the annual IMD World Competitiveness Executive Survey, completed by thousands of executives across the world. The top country is Switzerland. The first graph in Figure 4.5 displays the question score (from 1 to 10) for a subsample of countries. Figure 4.6 compares the evolution of the UAE with Brazil and Taiwan, which rank 51 and 54, respectively, in 2018 in the first indicator, and 47 and 44, respectively, in the second indicator.4.5

Where does the UAE's talent attractiveness come from? As Abed's example shows, not only do low taxes and high salaries play an important role, but also its infrastructure and quality of life. "Here anybody can become a CEO at age 30," says Abed. In most countries, the private sector drives innovation. In Dubai, the public sector drives innovation and the private sector tries to catch up. This means that the process of the digital transformation of the corporate sector is led by the government through proper IT infrastructure and quality of services. The principle is that if you build the infrastructure, visitors and foreign talent will come. And in the region, the UAE is unique because no other country focuses on people as its major asset. In Dubai, foreign individuals are the product and feed the tax revenues of the Emirate by spending and investing. The government therefore wants to improve the quality of life, and does so by providing a stable environment for businesses and individuals.

The availability of jobs and the bright career prospects of executives in Dubai incentivize competition, which in turn benefits companies and improves the pool of talent available. Companies need to provide good incentives for talented staff to stay because

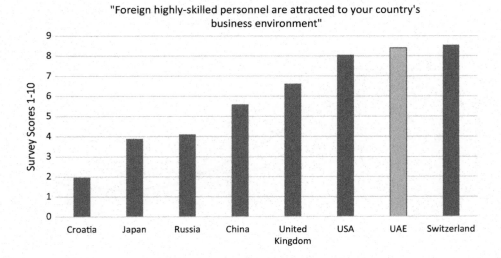

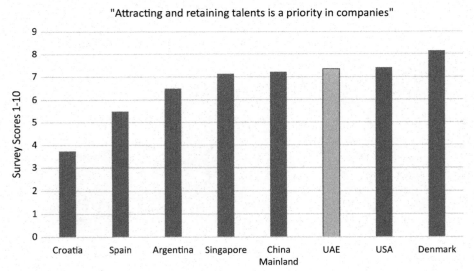

Figure 4.5 Talent Attractiveness of Countries

Source: IMD World Competitiveness Center.

mobility across companies is high in Dubai. Foreign talent makes local talent better off as well, although in the UAE the Emiratization Program, which guarantees a job for Emirati, is also removing incentives to train and improve performance.4.6

Still, the UAE is not paradise since Abed is under a three-year, renewable visa. Only recently has the Emirate introduced a longer-term, 10-year visa for foreigners. And there is no social safety net in Dubai, which means that your visa is canceled if you lose your job. Additionally, there is no public education or health system to speak of in the UAE, and lack of democracy means that policies tend to be unpredictable. That is why, overall, the UAE ranks 18th out of 63 countries in the "Attracting and Retaining Talent is a priority for companies" indicator, below the United States, Japan, and Israel, for example. It is highly unlikely that Abed will ever become Emirati, and even less so a permanent resident.

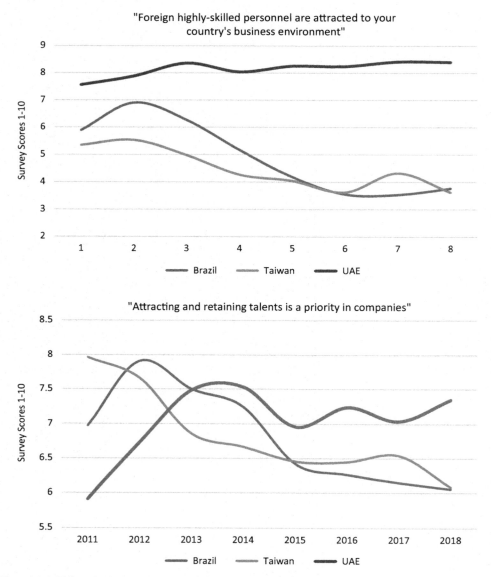

Figure 4.6 Talent Attractiveness over Time

Source: IMD World Competitiveness Center.

Which countries attract talent?

Attracting talent is a combination of factors. First and foremost is the quality of life in the country, which depends on the weather, language difficulty, cultural openness, and social norms and habits. Finland is a developed, technologically advanced, and stable country; however, it fails to attract talent (our survey shows that it ranks 39 out of 63 countries in the availability of foreign workers). Second, it is a function of taxes, especially those who affect foreigners. Portugal has made amazing progress moving from 55th to 33rd position in Talent Attractiveness through a policy of fiscal incentives to foreign corporates[54] and individuals. New residents from the European Union and some other countries are eligible for the non-habitual residence regime (NHR) for the first 10 years they are in Portugal, which taxes income at a 20 percent flat rate.[55] After that, they are subject to Portuguese rates of taxes, with a maximum of 48 percent which is still lower than in some European countries.

Fiscal incentives can target a specific type of talent. Since August 2016, individuals who work in Romania in the research and development (R&D) and IT fields benefit from a complete exemption from income taxes (which are already at a low 16 percent rate for the overall population).[56] Not surprisingly, Romania is today one of the most important IT hubs in Europe. Andrei Pitis, a Romanian tech entrepreneur, launched Vector Watch in 2015. Vector Watch was a pioneer in the new wave of wearables so, and was bought by Fitbit (from San Francisco, CA) in January 2017, together with its team and technology. Two other companies founded by Romanians and that ended in North-American hands are LiveRail (acquired by Facebook in 2014 for more than USD 400 million) and UberVu, acquired in 2014 by Hootsuite.[57]

The third factor that drives talent inflows is compensation levels. The average CEO salary (including base salary and bonuses) for the top 10 countries in talent attractiveness in the IMD World Competitiveness Rankings (Ireland, Japan, Denmark, Switzerland, Austria, Netherlands, Belgium, Luxembourg, Estonia, and Sweden) is USD 434,000. In contrast, the CEO salary in the bottom 10 countries (Slovak Republic, Argentina, Russia, Italy, Colombia, Spain, Ukraine, Peru, Greece, and Croatia) is USD

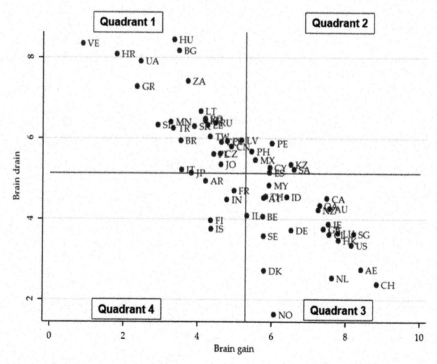

Figure 4.7a Global Talent Distribution in 2017

Source: Ben-Hur et al. (2020).

250,000 on average.[58] This is also self-fulfilling but counterintuitive, for if a country wants to attract foreign talent, it must open itself by paying higher salaries. At the same time, if facing a larger pool of potential candidates, it would seem logical that executive salaries drop, not increase. This is, however, not observed, because international talent also have access to a larger set of opportunities, and therefore are unwilling to accept below-average salaries.

Finally, talent attractiveness relies on stability and the rule of law. Amid the instability created by a potentially illegal independence referendum in Catalonia (Spain) in 2017, more than 3,000 companies changed their headquarters to Madrid and other regions. Companies that moved out included the Spanish headquarters of IKEA, and Caixabank, the second-largest Spanish bank by assets.[59] In more extreme situations such as armed conflicts, academics have found a strong correlation between capital (and talent flight) and violence. Economists Adriana Camacho and Catherine Rodríguez from Universidad de los Andes in Colombia have estimated that a one standard deviation in the number of guerrilla and paramilitary attacks in a Colombian municipality increases the probability of plant exit by 5.2 percent.[60]

Retaining talent and avoiding brain drain are usually about preventing local, well-educated workers from leaving the country in search of better opportunities. This is not undesirable at the personal level, as Abed Shaheen will never regret leaving his country of birth. But it is a waste of resources because the education and labor system has developed talent that is then enjoyed by companies in another country. The same success factors that favor talent attraction are at play here. However, it is not always the case that countries that attract the most talent, lose the least. My recent study cited earlier[61] classifies countries into four quadrants depending on whether they rank weak/strong in talent attraction/retention. Naturally, countries such as the United States and Switzerland are attractors of foreign talent, and do not suffer from brain drain. Conversely, Venezuela and Italy are net exporters of talent (they lose a lot, they attract a little). But in other parts of the world, talent flows are more interesting. Finland, India, and France neither attract nor export talent, for the reasons we have mentioned above. Spain and the Philippines not only suffer above-average brain drain, but they are also significant attractors of foreign workers. The cases of Japan and Sweden are interesting: Japan used to be a country with little brain drain and also very low brain gain, and it has become a country that is currently exporting skilled workers to other countries. Sweden has succeeded in attracting foreign talent between 2005 and 2018, so in the 2018 rankings it is second (only after Denmark) in attracting foreigners.

Finally, let me stress that opening a country to foreign talent should not just be a response to the needs of the labor market, in case local talent is not available—as it would be in the cases of Singapore and the UAE. There is a beneficial effect of foreign talent on domestic talent through the incentives provided to compete and develop. My country Spain is the 12th largest economy in the world, but ranks 33 out of 63 countries in the quality of its senior managers, below Germany, Italy, and Portugal. The reason is quite simple: among the top 35 companies in the Spanish stock market (the so-called Ibex-35 index), only in two of them (Santander and BBVA) is the CEO a non-Spaniard (Greek, in the case of Santander, and Turkish, in the case of BBVA, both appointed in 2018). This contrasts with neighboring countries, such as Italy and France, where the CEOs of large international and global companies, such as AXA, LafargeHolcim, Airbus, PSA Peugeot

Percentage of foreign board members

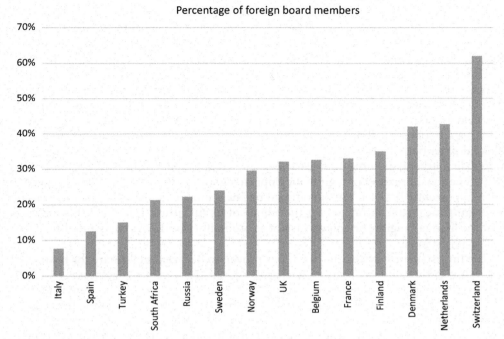

Figure 4.7b Percentage of Board Members in Publicly Traded Companies, 2015
Source: Spencer Stuart.

Citroen, Generali, Unicredit, Telecom Italia, and Alitalia are foreigners. Companies that do not internationalize their headquarters can never be global, since globalism results from global talent.

At the root of the lack of global talent at the top is usually corporate governance. In Spain, only 12.5 percent of board members in the largest companies[62] are foreigners, compared to 62 percent in Switzerland (see Figure 4.7). Implementing policies to make boards more international (as for example Japan has done) is paramount to attracting foreign talent.

44. INFRASTRUCTURE

IKEA, the Swedish-founded multinational firm that designs and sells ready-to-assemble furniture, has embraced the internationalization model, and tapped into the global market.[63] The biggest appeal to the company is the surge of the middle class in many of the emerging economies. The middle class, as a result of economic growth and diversification, makes these nations prime markets for multinational businesses such as IKEA. Primarily, IKEA has positioned itself as a low-priced, mass-market brand. However, while expanding into the emerging markets, IKEA has designed its brand to target customers who desire to live an international lifestyle and thus consume international products.

IKEA's interest in the emerging markets can be underscored by its heavy presence in China with 18 stores and in Russia with 14 stores. The firm seeks to expand further in China, with a plan to open three new stores in Suzhou, Guangzhou, and Chengdu. In Russia, IKEA's presence in the market fueled its revenue by 11 percent in 2015.

However, out of the BRICS countries (Brazil, Russia, India, China, and South Africa), only South Africa and Brazil do not have a presence of IKEA in their markets. This is despite the fact that both countries bear a similar profile when it comes to their consumer markets, middle-class surge, and a reliance on imported goods. In the case of Brazil, a cursory look shows it as a typical emerging market that could provide a viable and potentially lucrative market for IKEA products. However, its absence from the Brazilian market is an indication of a subtle but significant difference with the rest of the BRICS nations. Brazil's tax regime for imported goods is significantly high—pegged at over 75 percent. However, the operational business model adopted by IKEA focuses on leveraging local subcontractors for the supply of its furniture. Therefore, this indicates that the high tax regime on imports is not as prohibitory of IKEA's entry into Brazil as it seems at first look.

The infrastructure system in Brazil has proven to be a real nightmare for businesses operating in the country. The supply chain and logistics aspect of businesses is significantly reliant on a well-developed and a strongly interconnected business environment. In Brazil, logistics is a massive challenge because of its slow ports, and the limited and expensive nature of its internal transportation network. Inadequate infrastructure makes the cost of production skyrocket significantly. It also affects the delivery time to consumers, increases the inefficiencies of supply chain and logistics, and thus affects the lead time in the production process. This aspect reveals Brazil to have a largely underdeveloped infrastructure, which puts it at a disadvantage against, for instance, China. Although India also has infrastructure challenges, it is significantly better developed than Brazil. As a result, foreign direct investments (FDIs) prefer countries such as China, India, and Russia over Brazil.

The relationship between infrastructure and business, and by extension the reason why IKEA is not operational in Brazil, highlights the failures of the Brazilian strategic growth aspect. In this case, infrastructure refers to basic physical systems that are crucial to running a business (big or small); these include communication, transportation, electricity (energy), water, and sewage. Typically, these are high-cost systems that are often developed by the government to create a business-friendly environment. A lack of, or inadequate, infrastructure significantly increases the cost of doing business, making a country ominously unattractive to foreign investments.

Infrastructure in Brazil

Brazilian infrastructure in the IMD world competitiveness rankings

The infrastructure ranking here refers to the position that Brazil occupies relative to its direct competitors among the emerging markets, the rest of the developing world, as well as the developed world. It reveals the competitive capability of the country when it comes to attracting foreign investment. Concurrently, it is indicative of the country's environment as not only a business destination, but also its ability to support small- and medium-sized local businesses that are crucial in the economic growth of the country.

Within the IMD World Competitiveness Rankings, we will focus on basic infrastructure (Table 4.1) and technological infrastructure (Table 4.2). These two areas establish the environment's capacity to support a dynamic modern business as well as the availability of the resources needed in building an innovative business model to adapt to the constantly changing global economy driven by emergent technologies such as machine learning, blockchain, and artificial intelligence.

Basic infrastructure

Basic infrastructure is fundamental to the operations within a country. In this case, basic infrastructure refers to the road network, railroad system, air transport, and energy production and distribution (electricity/power), and the maintenance systems for all these systems. As illustrated in Table 4.1, Brazil is competitive in water resources (ranking 9th) because of the Amazon region; air transport (ranking 10th) because of its advanced aircraft manufacturing sector; and indigenous energy production (ranking 19th) primarily because of the Amazon region's indigenous tribes and the massive wealth of resources, including oil. However, the Brazilian basic infrastructural performance is abysmal by international standards. Figure 4.8 illustrates the comparison between Brazil and other global powers in terms of paved roads and vehicle density.

Roads

The road network is one of the most basic and important aspects of infrastructure. It enhances the mobility of goods, services, and human resources over short and long distances. Therefore, an effective road network is crucial in enhancing productivity, reducing cost, speeding up lead time, and allowing for the proper and high-quality management of organizations within a market economy. Having an effective road

Table 4.1 Basic Infrastructure in Brazil

Basic Infrastructure	Rank	Year
Water Resources	9	2014
Management of Cities	60	2018
Roads	33	2014
Railroads	52	2014
Air Transportation	10	2016
Quality of Air Transportation	55	2018
Distribution of Infrastructure	62	2018
Water Transportation	61	2018
Maintenance and Development of Infrastructure	61	2018
Energy Infrastructure	59	2018
Indigenous Energy Production	19	2015
Electricity Costs for Industrial Clients	37	2017

Source: IMD World Competitiveness Center.

network, in itself, does not translate into an improved business environment. In many cases, there is a need to balance it out with vehicle density. Therefore, the road network coverage-to-vehicle density is crucial in determining the speed and efficiency of road transport.[64] When vehicle density increases too much, the economy is bound to experience massive traffic jams, slowing down transport and increasing inefficiencies in the operations of businesses.

In 2014, Brazil was ranked 33rd in terms of road network, as illustrated in Table 4.2. However, a World Bank analysis indicates that Brazil's ratio of paved roads-to-vehicle density is significantly poor compared to regional powers such as Mexico and Argentina, as well as its BRICS competitors such as China and India, as illustrated in Figure 4.8.

The underdevelopment of the road transport system in Brazil is exacerbated by the country's reliance on this means of transport for most of its core industry operations. For example, as illustrated in Figure 4.9, Brazil relies heavily on its highways:

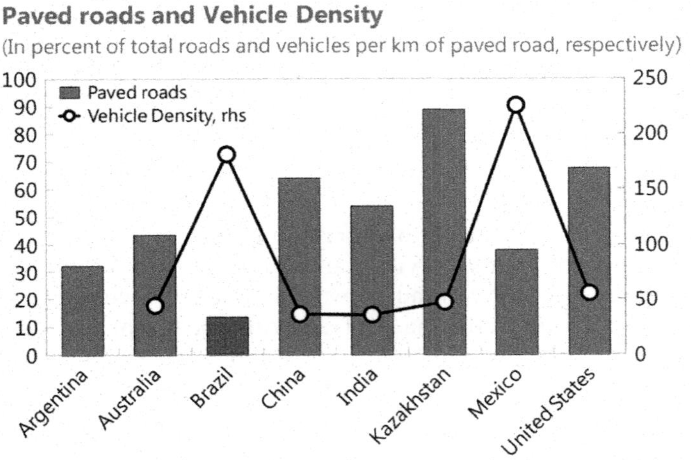

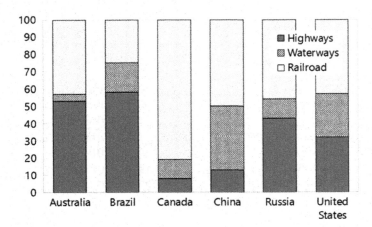

Figure 4.8 Paved Road and Vehicle Density

Source: World Bank, Brazil: Selected Issues Paper, May 2015.

Figure 4.9 Share of Goods Transport

Source: Karpowicz et al. (2018).

60 percent of Brazil's agricultural commodities are transported by road while most of the country's iron ore is transported via rail. Therefore, this transportation mix is one of the biggest sources of the country's lagging performance in exports and competitiveness against some of its primary competitors such as China, Russia, and the United States.[65] The reliance of the agricultural sector on an unreliable and underdeveloped road network, coupled with the fact that most of the agricultural products are perishable, combines to increase the losses to farmers and business operators. Additionally, it has discouraged any meaningful investment in agriculture because the margins simply do not exist.

Aside from the export industry, the inefficiency of road transport is taking a massive toll on local and intra-Brazil businesses in agribusiness and other core operations-heavy firms. Increasing the cost of production makes it hard for small- and medium-sized enterprises to be profitable. As a result, this is discouraging small businesses from either starting or smothering the existing ones that have not established an expansive resource pool to absorb the inefficiencies resulting from the inadequate and unsupportive infrastructure.[66]

If you have ever driven in Brazil, you will agree with statistics that put Brazil as the 7th worst country in terms of traffic across the world, with an average of 36 hours in congestion.[67] The epicenter of Brazil's traffic problem is in Sao Paulo, the country's most populated city. I still remember that, the very first time I traveled to Sao Paulo, my first impression of the country on leaving the airport and traveling toward the city center was a human corpse on the side of the road, by itself. On average, peak traffic consumes around 86 hours of a driver's time. According to BBC's Paula Cabral, in an article appearing on bb.com entitled "Sao Paulo: A City with 180 km Traffic Jams," tailbacks in and out of Sao Paulo extend a total of 180 kilometers on a Friday evening's commute.[68] Paula Cabral argues that traffic jams cause challenges in many places around the world; however, in Sao Paulo, they have become increasingly more than just a nuisance. They are described as part of the culture and life in the city that has more than 11 million inhabitants. Quoted in the Cabral article is Crespo, a Sao Paulo resident and commuter, who says that "we have become slaves of traffic and we have to plan our lives around it."

To explain how big the problem of the traffic in Sao Paulo is, Paula Cabral's article provides Crespo's tale of how she met her future husband. They were stuck in traffic, driving slowly beside each other. The initial flirting gave way to intermittent conversations. In the end, he convinced her to give him her number. He later called and the result has been their happy marriage. It is ironic yes, but it also underscores the challenge that commuters in the city have to endure on a daily basis. Individual's conducting businesses, delivering goods, and depending on the efficiency of transport to keep time and enhance the supply chain, will be terribly disappointed with the speed of things in the city. This is a massive challenge, because with 11 million people, Sao Paulo also offers a massive consumer market for a broad range of businesses.

This has become a nightmare especially for modern technology-based businesses, particularly the retail sector, that are heavily reliant on delivery as part of their customer service package. That is the case for fast-moving goods, the fashion industry, and even the telecommunications sector that depend on delivery to their doorstep. As global trends indicate that the retail sector is evolving toward consumer-centric approaches, it is increasingly difficult for the retail sector in Sao Paulo to adapt to these approaches. This is because it will be extremely difficult to keep deliveries on time.

Additionally, it might not make business sense, since deliveries are only possible for a reduced number of customers within a day's traffic, which will squeeze the margins even more.

According to *The Rio Times*, a study conducted by Dutch transport technology Company TomTom reveals that Rio de Janeiro ranks the third worst in the world in terms of traffic.[69] The TomTom study utilized data collected from GPS from approximately 146 cities across the world, and subsequently ranked them according to their traffic congestion over the entire day. On average, commuters on Rio de Janeiro roads lose around 100 hours annually stuck in traffic. The only cities worse than Rio are Istanbul and Mexico City. According to *The Telegraph*, recent investments in infrastructure in Rio seem not to have had any effect on the city's traffic challenges.[70] *The Telegraph* further indicates that 47 percent of Rio de Janeiro is considered congested, which means that, on average, a driver loses around 43 minutes on the road every day.

The challenges facing Rio de Janeiro and Sao Paulo are emblematic of the challenges facing the road transport network in Brazil. They reveal how the underdevelopment of roads, and infrastructure as a whole, has led to massive adverse effects on the entire business supply chain—starting from production, logistics (transport), delivery, and even sales. This underdevelopment has been one of the biggest aspects cited by businesses that either leave the Brazilian market or decline to enter the market at all.

Airports

The airports in Brazil are significantly developed. As illustrated in Table 4.1, Brazil ranks 10th in the number of passengers carried by the major air travel companies operating in the country. However, when it comes to the quality of air transport (which is the capacity of the air travel sector to support business development), Brazil is ranked 55th in the world. These two rankings demonstrate both the country's strengths and weaknesses in the air transportation sector. Brazil is one of the leading manufacturers and exporters of aircraft to the global market.[71] Both air travel technology and expertise exist in Brazil, which is demonstrated by the global 10th ranking of the number of people carried by its major air travel companies.

Brazil's airports face a steady surge in demand for air travel. As one of the emerging economic powers in the world, a burgeoning middle class and a decline in the cost of air travel (ticket prices) have combined to make air travel a significantly attractive prospect as well as accessible to a broader population of the country. Major companies in Brazil such as Gol and Azul have adopted low-cost models, aimed at "democratizing" air travel—which means making it more accessible to more people in the Brazilian market.[72] When, in 2010, these firms introduced the low-cost model, they saw a 27.6 percent surge in passenger transit.

However, Brazil has not developed the air travel sector extensively enough to meet all the travel demands of the country. As a result, air travel is faced with massive bottlenecks, such as insufficient airport terminals, which often leads to flight delays. In and around the airports, there is insufficient parking and the feeder roads to the airport are not sufficiently expansive to handle the traffic. Brazil's National Civil Aviation Agency [ANAC], in charge of air travel security) has always sought to limit the number of operations in the country's major airports. However, the demand is growing significantly.[73] Therefore, limiting air travel is denying many of the businesses in the sector a massive pool of revenue flow. Broadly, the limitation hampers the transfer of intellectual property and business operations and management, while squeezing the hotel and hospitality and tourism sectors as well.

Across the world, the United States ranks first in the world in terms of number of airports, with 14,712 airports. Brazil comes in second with 4,093 airports, followed by Mexico and Canada with 1,714 and 1,467 airports, respectively.[74] The distance between first and second is massive; however, the United States is a fully developed country. Brazil scores an impressive second on the list, a significant distance from its BRIC competitors such as China (with 200 airports as of 2015) and India with 134 airports. Despite the large number of airports, the infrastructural foundation and capacity in Brazil is significantly lagging other major countries on the global stage. For example, access to the airports is extremely difficult, and the subways are massively underdeveloped. Additionally, Brazil's airport capacity is significantly small compared to first-world nations such as the United States.

Ports

Typically, especially in most of the developed world and emerging nations such as China, water transport is crucial for the movement of goods. Ports are a crucial cog in expanding markets and growing economies. They allow the movement of goods and services to and from a country, which increases the trading capacity of a trading nation.

As the Brazilian economy has expanded and its markets have grown, its ports have faced operational challenges that the country must address to create a suitable environment for further growth, especially for the import and export sectors. However, this growth has been met with slow and overworked Brazilian ports. Additionally, most of the operations at these ports are massively underdeveloped and unsupported by technology, modern approaches, and standard procedures. Consequently, they are unable to accommodate the surge in the quantity of large ships and other advanced systems they continually face.

The Brazilian government is responsible for the operations and administration of ports in the country under the Law of Ports—*Lei dos Portos 8.630/93*. However, the involvement of the government means that the running of these ports lacks the flexibility and innovation of a privately run port which focuses on efficiencies and value for money. The public sector does not operate on competition; therefore, competition among the ports has ground to a halt, and the status of these ports is on a downward trajectory or stagnating.[75] Additionally, the rigidity of the public sector means that the changes that these ports need to modernize and improve their activities are not forthcoming.

Furthermore, the specific operations of these ports are filled with bureaucracies that slow down the clearance of goods, make it expensive to import, and thus lead to a surge in the prices of imports once they get into the country. The inefficiencies also have a significant impact on the lead time and effectiveness of businesses in the country. Some emerging SMEs that focus on the importation of goods face massive wait times caused by bureaucracy and the resulting inefficiencies have a significant cost in business terms.[76]

The Brazilian government has made attempts to transition the ports from their reliance on paper to paperless approaches. However, these small changes do not meet the core aspects that these Brazilian ports need to undertake to be competitive against some of the most expansive and modernized ports seen in the United States and their BRIC competitor—China. China and the United States are the world's first- and second-largest economies, as well as the biggest traders with each other. Such large-scale trade is conducted because of world-class ports and effective water transport with efficiency, security, and a massive clearance rate.

In trade and business, the speed of delivery can make a huge difference. Therefore, there is a need for the Brazilian government to undertake significant and holistic reviews and changes to the core approaches to the operation of its ports. Additionally, it is crucial to encourage individual ports to seek benefits through instituting competitive advantages for businesses. This will establish a foundation for the growth and modernization of the ports in Brazil, and bolster their competitive edge. As a result, this will enhance the country's ranking when it comes to ports, its capacity to handle the massive movement of goods, thereby developing its capabilities for growth in international trade.[77]

Technological infrastructure

The role of technology as a core infrastructure has an expansive role to play in modern economic development, growth, human resource development, and competitive advantage in the local, regional, and international markets. Some of the most advanced economies in the world such as the United States, the EU, and Japan are also leading in technological development and innovation, and harnessing such technology to create value. The core area heavily influenced by technology is communication. For an economy to expand, grow, and be dynamic and diversify, communication not only has to be enabled, but it also has to be efficient, effective, and on par with global standards.[78] This means having access to the internet, computers, and smartphones, developing digital and technological skills, and having the ability to turn these skills into value in the market.

Among the emerging economies, the biggest example when it comes to technological development is China. In a few years, the country has moved from being a seller of trinkets to a leading competitive force in the world of innovation. In 2017, China was

Table 4.2 Technological Infrastructure in Brazil

Technological Infrastructure	Rank	Year
Mobile Broadband Subscribers	29	2016
Mobile Telephone Costs	8	2016
Communication Technology	60	2018
Computers in Use	7	2017
Computers per Capita	48	2017
Internet Users	46	2017
Internet Bandwidth Speed	53	2017
Digital/Technological Skills	62	2018
Qualified Engineers	49	2018
ICT Service Exports	5	2016
Cyber Security	54	2018

Source: IMD World Competitiveness Center.

ranked, for the first time, number one in the number of patents accepted in the United States, behind the United States itself, Japan, South Korea, and Germany. This indicates that China has taken a leap to become one of the leading countries in the development of technology and innovation. This allows the country to create value from such technologies and thus engineer the development and use of such technologies in the economic and social realms as well.

In the field of science and technology, the biggest challenge facing Brazil is that it lacks a long-term policy to facilitate the scientific and technological development to reach the nation's population with the aim of improving quality of life.[79] As opposed to India and China, Brazil's technological development in the areas of innovation is lagging. This puts it at a disadvantage in the information age, where more and more businesses are embracing big data, machine learning, and artificial intelligence, as not only the current boosters of their business models, but also the future of enterprise.

However, in the access and utilization of the available technology, Brazil performs impressively. For example, Brazil ranks 8th in the cost of mobile phones, 7th in computer use, and 5th in information and communication technology (ICT) services exports. This indicates that access to technologies such as broadband and computers is significantly competitive around the world. It also means that there is an extensive presence of personnel in the market with technology skills, forming a crucial foundation for businesses entering the Brazilian market seeking qualified personnel in the areas of technology and science.

Why infrastructure investment has been lacking in Brazil

In recent years, Brazil has made efforts at revitalizing its infrastructure. Under the leftist Workers' Party (PT) that was in power between 2003 until President Dilma Rousseff was impeached in 2016, the country sought to invest in a series of projects and proposals aimed at enhancing the country's infrastructure. Proposals ranged from developing a bullet train connecting Rio de Janeiro and So Paulo, to a mass housing project for the poor. This program, as proposed by the government, was designed to be funded by the government's development bank, the BNDES. The bank was to provide subsidized long-term financing for these projects. However, this project did not take off and thus failed to meet the projected targets of infrastructural revitalization and modernization to meet the emerging needs as the country gains the status of an emerging economy.[80]

Much of the program's funds were wasted in the spending that surrounded the 2015 World Cup, as well as corruption-riddled developments in the oil-refining sector. An article by Joe Leahy in the *Financial Times* in 2017 revealed corruption to be a massive challenge to the process of modernizing Brazil's infrastructure. Much of the resources assigned to the development of infrastructure have been siphoned off through bribes and mismanagement. This has caused, historically, a massive delay in the development of infrastructure. It means that the current structures and networks have faced decades of under-investment, which has led to the current underdeveloped infrastructure ranging from ports, to airports, to railroads, to roads.[81]

Lack of strategic planning has also been a massive challenge in the development of infrastructure. The best approach to establishing an infrastructure that meets the demands of a market economy is to do it strategically not only taking into consideration the current needs of the nation, but also instituting the expected changes in the demands of the market in the near and far-future.[82] Brazil's lack of such strategic approaches has seen a massive growth in the economic capacity of the country and an increased demand for transportation (people and goods), without a corresponding expansion of the infrastructural capacity of the country.

The other challenge in developing the Brazilian infrastructure is funding. So far, the Brazilian government has been the chief source of funding for developing infrastructure across the country. It is challenging when the government does not have money. It has been difficult for the country to get alternative sources of funding. Not many developers and companies, local or foreign, have been willing to take on infrastructure development in Brazil. This has meant that the country does not have reliable partners in consistently developing its infrastructure to meet the overall demand in the market economy.[83] This is especially the case as Brazil emerges from recession and embarks on a growth trajectory.

For example, Danish AP Moller-Maersk, the largest shipping company in the world, has invested over USD 2.7 billion in infrastructure in Brazil since 2010. This includes USD 400 million the company has plowed into the Santos container terminal. The firm has invested over USD 2.2 billion in 16 Sammax vessels that are designed to sail between Brazil, Europe, and Asia. However, despite this heavy investment in the country, the company still faces challenges with supporting infrastructure. For example, there is only a single highway overpass leading to this port. As a result, truck drivers face massive delays at the railway crossings. Additionally, the port authorities' failure to dredge the access canal has led to massive silting, which has lowered the draft and prevented ships from loading to full capacity.

The Maersk example points to a massive lack of coordination in infrastructure policy. In this regard, the investment in the port without the expansion of the supporting infrastructure is useless. There is a need for a strategic approach to infrastructural development, where the aim of developing is to free up the flow of goods, improve speed and safety, thereby cutting the lead time within the Brazilian business environment.

A final note: the Olympic games

The Rio 2016 Olympic Games were seen as a massive opportunity for Brazil to showcase itself to the rest of the world. It was a massive infomercial for the country to steal a march on its competing rivals such as China, India, and Russia, to establish itself as one of the most attractive business and investment destinations, thereby creating an Olympics boom in business that would have a positive ripple effect on the country as it recovered from recession. Massive promises were also made around the issue of infrastructure. In this regard, the development of stadia in Rio and the upgrading of travel infrastructure including modernizing roads and air travel in Brazil could have had a positive impact on the whole economy. Alas, USD 12 billion later, Brazil is facing massive cash problems, with the "Olympics legacy in ruins."[84]

Brazil is facing a massive economic crisis as characterized by its inability to pay its workers, the majestic arenas showcased in the Olympics are crumbling in disrepair, and there is a surge in public anger toward the government's choices and the level of spending on the Olympics, coming hot on the heels of the spending on the 2014 World Cup also hosted in Brazil.[85] Unemployment in Rio de Janeiro has doubled since the end of the Games. An analysis also shows that GDP has fallen by 8.4 percentage points. Public employees have faced a cut to their pensions and wages by up to 30 percent.

An evaluation of the period during and in the immediate aftermath of the Olympic Games shows that the city of Rio experienced a boom. Businesses were booming, the hotel and hospitality industry experienced a massive surge in customers and revenue, and the ripple effect on the city's economy was significantly impressive. However, in the medium to long term, the legacy of the Games has not been sustained. Many argue that the decline has coincided with the economic recession in the country. However, the efforts by the local and national Brazilian authorities to harness the buzz created by the Games to establish a more lasting socioeconomic legacy on Rio and Brazil as a whole have not been effective.

Additionally, the projects surrounding infrastructure did not extend beyond the Games. There was a need for the Brazilian government to establish a coalition of investors during and after the Games with the aim of expanding investment into the development and modernization of various infrastructural systems in the country.[86] The failure to have such a coalition meant that many of the resources spent on the Games with a real, tangible, and long-term impact on the socioeconomic landscape of the city and the country, in hindsight, were a massive waste. The country, and especially its people and workers, are paying the ultimate price, as the government reaches for their wages, and squeezes their pensions.

45. RULE OF LAW

Broadly speaking, the rule of law can be defined as society's acceptance and adherence to the supremacy of the law above all other forms of power in a country. It is a political principle that encompasses all members of a population by considering them as equally subject to well-defined and established legal codes and processes, fundamentally restricting the arbitrary exercise of power. It is a very powerful tool against authoritarianism and corruption, often acting as a control mechanism against many forms of instability. A strong and respected rule of law can therefore be considered as one of the most efficient checks and balances on modern politics. Under its influence, public and private actors are made accountable for their actions and justice is provided through transparent processes.

These aspects matter greatly for the economic and political stability of countries, and the rule of law is therefore not void of competitiveness considerations. For instance, given that they are respected, laws play a decisive role in allowing governments to promote and implement new policies. They provide the legitimacy and assurance that policies will be implemented in ways that can be effectively monitored and enforced. Similarly, through channels such as strong enforcement regulations, secured property rights, and effective dispute settlement mechanisms, the rule of law further reinforces the perceived level of business security within an economy. This, in turn, sends positive signals to domestic and foreign investors who feel much more inclined to invest. Additionally, an effective rule of law assigns accountability, reduces levels of corruption, and improves the living conditions of a country's citizens, all of which contributes to a more competitive environment.

Further benefits of having a "good" rule of law are explored in the literature and include the provision of quality public goods and the more efficient tackling of collective action problems (like environmental degradation). Indeed, the efficiency and quality of public infrastructure such as road networks, bridges and even buildings are highly dependent on having strong safety and regulatory enforcement mechanisms which guarantee the security of the physical infrastructure and minimize the waste of scarce resources. Likewise, adherence to the rule of law is essential to holding governments, businesses, civil society, and communities accountable for protecting public health and the environment from illicit practices that degrade the status quo.

The World Justice Project (WJP) Rule of Law Index

The WJP Index attributes a value between 0 (weak) and 1 (strong) to 126 countries around the globe, reflecting their degree of adherence to the rule of law. The scores and rankings are based on eight factors and are derived from the opinions collected from more than 120,000 household and 3,800 expert surveys. As a result, the index is a unique and very useful primary data source that captures a country's *perceived* adherence to the rule of law according to the average person in that locality. Despite its many advantages, such as identifying a country's strengths and weaknesses and tracking changes over time, the index is also victim to a few inherent flaws. For example, the interpretation of the rule of law may not be homogeneous across the sample, creating skewed data. However, it remains a strong analytical tool and it is interesting to explore some of the common trends that arise between the WJP's Rule of Law Index and the IMD's World Competitiveness data. This section attempts to shed light on some of these trends and explain both how and why they are relevant.

Geopolitical considerations

Some trends instantly catch the eye when glancing over the WJP's top 20 indexed countries in Figure 4.10. Firstly, the geographical distribution of the top 10 performers appears noteworthy, nine of which are located on the European continent. More specifically, the top four countries in which the population perceives the rule of law as being most strongly implemented are all Nordic. The reasons behind this are certainly very diverse and heterogeneous; however, one may put forward a few credible hypotheses to explain this phenomenon: for instance, the long history binding these countries with the practices of law or the populations' profound trust in their welfare-oriented governments. Perhaps more surprising to some might be the United States' 20th position. However, I would argue that this observation can also be traced back to issues of governance. Indeed, the perceived importance of the rule of law might be hampered by pervasive national dynamics such as racial and socioeconomic inequalities, both of which currently play a predominant role in US politics.

Similarly, the bottom 20 countries from the WJP's Rule of Law Index demonstrate a blatant bias toward political instability and a general mistrust of their governing bodies. Venezuela, for example, also ranked bottom in the IMD's World Competitiveness Ranking, is currently experiencing a crisis with implications that now reach far beyond economic or political considerations: the country is often described as a failed state. Civilian society has slowly resorted to an anarchic form of resistance against the daily military coercion experienced. Under such conditions, it is difficult to imagine how any

Country/Jurisdiction	Overall Score*	Global Rank	Country/Jurisdiction	Overall Score*	Global Rank
Denmark	0.90	1	Madagascar	0.43	107
Norway	0.89	2	Mozambique	0.43	108
Finland	0.87	3	Turkey	0.42	109
Sweden	0.85	4	Myanmar	0.42	110
Netherlands	0.84	5	Angola	0.41	111
Germany	0.84	6	Bangladesh	0.41	112
Austria	0.82	7	Uganda	0.40	113
New Zealand	0.82	8	Nicaragua	0.40	114
Canada	0.81	9	Honduras	0.40	115
Estonia	0.81	10	Zimbabwe	0.40	116
Australia	0.80	11	Pakistan	0.39	117
United Kingdom	0.80	12	Ethiopia	0.39	118
Singapore	0.80	13	Bolivia	0.38	119
Belgium	0.79	14	Cameroon	0.37	120
Japan	0.78	15	Egypt	0.36	121
Hong Kong SAR, China	0.77	16	Mauritania	0.35	122
France	0.73	17	Afghanistan	0.35	123
Republic of Korea	0.73	18	Congo, Dem. Rep.	0.33	124
Czech Republic	0.73	19	Cambodia	0.32	125
United States	0.71	20	Venezuela	0.28	126

Figure 4.10 Rule of Law Around the World: Top and Bottom 20
Source: World Justice Project, Rule of Law Index 2019.

country could set up the necessary preconditions for the population to adhere to the rule of law (given the lack of trust in state institutions). In countries like Egypt, Congo, Afghanistan, and even Cambodia, the devastating consequences of political and armed conflict go a long way to explain the population's general distrust of the law and its rejection as the supreme form of power. In Latin America, cases such as those of Nicaragua or Honduras might be explained by the historical dominance of political instability and the perceived lack of effective law to protect basic human rights. Indeed, in countries where the informal sector is sometimes more affluent than the formal economy, this leads to unwanted outcomes where formal institutions are undermined by corruption, thus reducing its efficacy and trustworthiness.

Attractiveness considerations

Another interesting trend is the strong positive correlation between a country's adherence to the rule of law and its ability to retain talent. Derived from the IMD's 2018 Talent Report, the correlation illustrated in Figure 4.11 has interesting implications for competitiveness as it underlines a dynamic where young professionals make

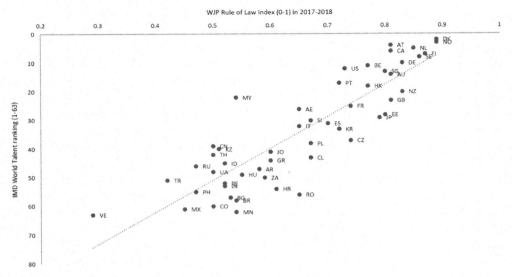

Figure 4.11 Talent Competitiveness and Institutions

Source: IMD World Competitiveness Center.

the conscious decision to relocate to countries that offer a strong legal environment and framework. Similar to foreign investors' need to be reassured of an economy's business health and legal security before committing to personal investments, talent also needs to be reassured that the legal framework of a country is effective and reliable before moving there. Poorly enforced labor rights, ineffective dispute mechanisms, and ill-defined contract rights may all act as a red light in discouraging the economic migration of foreign talent or the loss of domestic talent (also known as the brain drain). From the graph, we can see that some countries deviate quite considerably from the general pattern observed. Romania, for example, appears to have a proportionally better respect for the rule of law than its ability to attract talent would suggest. This might be explained by the diffusion of legal norms imposed by the European Union on its member states and the relatively sparse employment opportunities in the country. On the contrary, despite Malaysia's strong ability to attract talent, the country boasts a relatively weak respect for the rule of law.

Exploring the rule of law's four pillars: Thailand and Switzerland

According to the World Justice Project, the rule of law is a framework of laws and institutions that embodies four universal principles: accountability, just laws, open government, and the accessibility and impartiality of dispute resolutions. The following section aims to explore the definition of these four pillars and provide some first-hand anecdotes underlying everyday instances where these pillars are visibly in action (or conversely, not at all!).

Accountability

This pillar ensures that all actors within an economy are held accountable under the law, meaning that public and private actors such as government officials, firms, and citizens abide by the rules. Factors used to measure accountability include constraints on government power, sanctioning against misconduct, and, most importantly, the existence of mechanisms that punish corruption. A very important aspect of this pillar is therefore ensuring that government officials active in all branches (executive, judicial, and military) do not use public office for private gain. However, in a country like Thailand where public sector' salaries are relatively low, it is not uncommon to see discrete instances of corruption for quick self-gain. For example, policemen on Khaosan Road, Bangkok, do not hesitate when they spot foreign backpackers engaged in minor illicit activities such as public urination or smoking marijuana. Swift arrests followed by convincing blackmail (Thai drug enforcement laws are extremely tough) often lead to cash inflows that can represent as much as a month's salary.

Just laws

This pillar is self-explanatory and seeks to measure if laws are clear, publicized, stable, and just. Their aim and application should enhance the protection of fundamental rights, including the security of persons, core human rights, as well as contract and property rights. This is currently sparking huge debate in Switzerland, with politicians and workers' unions asserting that the proposed bilateral "accord cadre" between Bern and Brussels goes against such equity concerns. Many fear that accepting the conditions imposed by the EU will substantially increase the number of foreign workers who would benefit from salary dumping by undercutting Swiss salaries (who are notably among the highest paid in the world) while not imposing any social security costs on contractors because such new labor would be domiciled abroad. In the case of Thailand, the enforcement of such rights is also quite precarious due to the political situation with some of the country's neighbors. For instance, many construction workers who actively contribute to the infrastructural boom of the Thai capital Bangkok are illegal Burmese migrants whose rights are not guaranteed.

Open government

Here, the World Justice Project aims to measure government transparency. It attempts to analyze the processes by which laws are enacted, administered, and enforced, to see if these are accessible, fair, and efficient. Over the last few years, many countries have seen significant improvements in these factors due to continuous positive developments in the provision of public data and the right to information. Another important aspect of open government is civic participation mechanisms and the ability to freely express opinions. Although Thailand and Switzerland have relatively free media outlets, both are strongly exposed to political biases that are circulated through the affiliation of their respective media owners.

Accessible and impartial dispute resolution

This pillar is concerned with the impartiality of police forces and criminal judges who enforce the law. It also explores whether the criminal justice system discriminates in practice based on socioeconomic status, gender, ethnicity, religion, or sexual orientation and identity. Some measures include the accessibility and affordability of civil courts, including whether people are aware of available legal options; can access and afford legal advice and representation; and can access the court system without incurring unreasonable fees, encountering unreasonable procedural hurdles, or experiencing physical or linguistic barriers. Generally speaking, countries that experience lower scores in this pillar tend to be countries where there is greater inequality between the rich and the poor. In an ideal world, the rule of law is best represented and respected when justice is delivered by competent and ethical legal representatives who have adequate resources and reflect the makeup of the community they serve. This can sometimes be challenging as inequalities in opportunity hinder the ability of the criminal system to proportionally represent minorities (such as the southern Muslim population in Thailand for instance).

Insider trading regulation

> When some favorable piece of news occurs, such as the discovery of a rich mineral deposit, it is alleged that the insiders are the first to know and they act, buying the stock and causing its price to rise. The insiders then tell their friends, who act next. Then the professionals find out the news and the big institutions put blocks of the shares in their portfolios. Finally, the poor slobs like you and me get the information and buy, pushing the price still higher.
>
> Burton G. Malkiel, *A Random Walk Down Wall Street*[87]

Burton G. Malkiel's take on how stock market movements occur may not always hold true, but it is safe to say that the random walk which equity prices are said to follow is more random for some traders than others. Indeed, as this chapter will show, the stock markets of some countries barely take a random walk at all, suggesting significant levels of insider trading.

For a long time, insider trading wasn't even considered a significant misdeed by most stock market regulators. The first account of any regulation dealing with insider trading appeared in 1909, when the United States Supreme Court established the so-called Insider Rule. The case, sometimes referred to as *Strong v Repide*, ruled that directors of companies had to either disclose their insider information or abstain from trading altogether.[88] Although a full ban on insider trading followed in 1934, the first prosecution for breaches of the regulation only occurred in 1961.

Elsewhere, in Great Britain, there were no insider trading regulations until as late as 1980. In fact, it really wasn't until the 1990s that insider trading laws became a globally recognized issue. During that decade, the number of stock markets with insider trading regulation more than doubled from 34 of 79 to 87 of 103. In most instances across these markets, the pattern established by the United States was followed; the regulation was enacted, but no little or no enforcement followed.

We can speculate that the lack of enforcement is at least in part because publicly traded companies are effectively the clients of these markets and upsetting them wouldn't be good business. Furthermore, the largest companies often have several listings on different indices at once. In extreme cases, this could even lead to these companies engaging in regulatory arbitrage—focusing efforts on exchange with loose insider trading laws at the expense of another.

Advocates of loose regulation around insider trading generally say that less stringent regulation means that stock market prices reflect all available information faster, making them more efficient. They also argue—with some justification—that insider trading is nearly impossible to prove; when we see the price of a stock rising in the days before major news about the stock emerges, it is not as though the stock was being purchased by the CEO. Insider traders are usually discreet enough to ensure that the timing of their trades can be passed off as circumstantial evidence.

On the other side of the fence, there is a body of individuals—and if the enforcement of regulation is anything to judge by, it is a growing one—who support the enforcement of regulation against insider trading. They typically cite a number of motives to advance their case, most of which revolve around the integrity of markets: by allowing insider trading, the average trader or investor faces near impossible odds of beating the market return when faced with highly asymmetric information. Or more simply, the markets are called "public" for a reason.

Discouraging the average trader or investor from participating on the stock market may not initially seem like much to worry about, but their participation brings much needed liquidity to the market. Liquidity is the lifeblood of any stock market—it is the reason that companies are listed there in the first place. As authors Utpal Bhattacharya and Hazem Daouk point out in their 2002 paper, "The World Price of Insider Trading,"[89] less liquidity ultimately means higher equity cost, the consequence of which is likely to be less investment on the stock market as a whole—or an invisible cost of something in excess of USD 4 trillion.

In that light, the decision of many stock market regulators to cut back on the practice is more understandable. In the past decade, both the Securities Exchange Commission (SEC)[90] and the Department of Justice[91] in the United States have openly stated that prosecuting illegal insider trading is a priority. This is reflected in the increased number of "enforcement actions" taken against the crime by the SEC over the past number of years (see Figure 4.12).

The fervor to bring down those trading on privileged information is not limited to the United States. In the past decade, it has spread as far as emerging markets, such as Brazil and Russia. Perhaps speaking for the motives of many emerging market indices, Maria Helena Santana, the head of Brazil's securities regulator, said in 2011: "after having

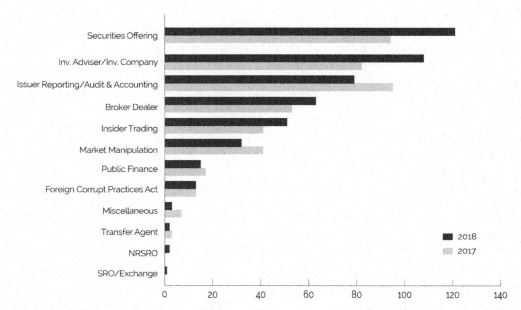

Figure 4.12 Standalone Enforcement Actions 2017, 2018

Source: SEC Division of Enforcement Annual Report.

investors consider our legislation and regulatory environment not safe enough or strong enough," it had to "gain credibility."[92]

The word credibility is fundamental here. The Brazilian securities regulator, the CVM, initiated regulation outlawing insider sales as far back as 1976 (making insider trading regulation older than democracy in the country); however, only in 2011[93], a full 35 years later, was the decision taken to make it a priority. In its defense, Brazil is not alone in being lenient on insider trading despite having regulations in place. It appears that the general tendency that existed across most markets was to have laws in place as a signaling function more than any real intention to prosecute.

Rule of law and insider trading in Mexico

The case of Mexico is indicative. The OECD's 2017 Corporate Governance Handbook looks at the corporate governance standards of all member countries Of Mexico, it says: "Listed companies are characterized by a high degree of concentration. Company groups are the common feature in the market, and many of them are owned by family groups."[94] In other words, with its small close-knit circles being privy to privileged information, Mexico's stock market, the *Bolsa Mexicana de Valores* (BMV), is prime territory for insider trading.

Indeed, there appears to be plenty of evidence to suggest that this was the case. A 2002 paper[95] by Utpal Bhattacharya, from Indiana University, and Hazem Daouk, from Cornell University, looked at the returns of Mexico's stock market, the *Bolsa Mexicana de Valores*, over the three-year period between 1994 and 1997 and found that news announcements that one would reasonably expect to cause movement in stock prices (earnings announcements, dividend announcements, merger announcements, etc.) had little or no effect. As Utpal and Hazem point out, this is compelling evidence that insider trading across the BMV was rampant at the time.

Viewed from a distance, it may have appeared that everything was in working order. After all, Mexico's regulator, the CNBV, introduced insider trading legislation on January 2, 1975, as part of *la Ley del Mercado de Valores*[96] ("Security Markets Law" or "SML") with the intention of bringing the BMV up to modern standards. In 1983, the SML was updated. The rules on insider trading were relatively stringent—particularly so, given how few countries had any laws at all—including making insider trading a civil offense. However, fines on offenders were limited to twice the amount of gains obtained.[97]

In theory then, the country had regulations. But this mostly amounted to nothing more than window-dressing. Looking back, a memorandum of understanding signed between the SEC and the CNBV in 1990 was effectively a rubber-stamp exercise.[98] It changed almost nothing in practical terms. Until relatively recently, for example, brokerage houses in Mexico shared common control with the corporations themselves. Given this set of circumstances, if someone with access to privileged information hadn't been trading on it, you might be forgiven for thinking that they were missing a wonderful arbitrage opportunity.

By the end of the 20th century, the CNBV had never prosecuted anyone for insider trading, despite having explicit laws in place for 25 years. However, soon things began to change. In the first years of the new century, there was a flurry of prosecutions against insider trading on the BMV. It is difficult to say exactly what stimulated the sudden CNBV response from its 25-year passivity. In my view, a combination of different factors—both Mexican and non-Mexican—came together that led to a crackdown, not just inside Mexico but everywhere.

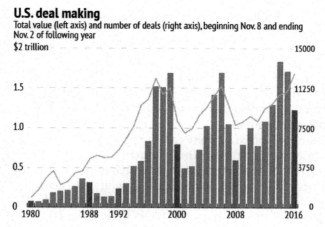

U.S. deal making
Total value (left axis) and number of deals (right axis), beginning Nov. 8 and ending Nov. 2 of following year

Figure 4.13 US Deal Making, Total Value (Left Axis) and Number of Deals (Right Axis)
Source: Thomson Reuters.

On a global level, markets were witnessing one of the world's largest ever merger waves (see Figure 4.13), driven by a combination of deregulation, globalization, and companies taking part in the landgrab for nascent internet technology. Mergers and acquisitions (M&A) is prime territory for insider trading given that target firms are typically offered premiums well in excess of their market price by the buyer. Utpal Bhattacharya[99] notes that the cases of SEC investigations into insider trading—measured as cases per 1,000 companies—more than doubled between 1998 and 1999. It continued to rise into the next decade, never again returning to the relatively low rate that it had been in the 1990s.

Second, the internet revolution mentioned in the last paragraph also opened up trading on markets to the masses as never before. A spokesperson for the SEC told CNN in 1999: "Insider trading is now on the Main Street level rather than the Wall Street level. We're bringing more cases about individuals who know about the companies rather than people involved in the deals." He went on to give the case of a spouse of a director trying to profit from obtaining privileged information in the household and an increase in younger people trading on the internet.[100]

Third, we can speculate that a high-profile case brought against a large group of Mexicans insider trading in the United States in 1999 raised the heckles of the SEC. These included the CEO of Grupo Mexicano de DeSarrollo, a large Mexican construction company and his nephew, Juan Pablo Ballesteros Gutierrez, who is vice chairman of GMD and the former director of Illinois-based Nalco Chemical Co. Ballesteros along with several other Mexicans were alleged to have traded in Nalco's stock on non-public information.[101]

Finally, and perhaps most significantly of all, the CNBV probably came to realize that its lax attitude to insider trading was doing it more harm than good—or as one Mexican expert said at the time: "There is a herd effect, where you do not want to get left behind as a market."[102] This can be seen in June 1999, when the CNBV established a new Corporate Governance Code for Mexico, whose express purpose was "to encourage more transparent management practices in order to enhance the confidence of local and foreign investors and thus attract more investment to benefit the Mexican economy."[103] Reading between the lines, it is not difficult to see how clamping down on insider trading could fall under that remit.

A high-profile example of the CNBV's stricter approach came in 2007, when it fined two board members of Telmex, the publicly listed Mexican telecoms operator, 402,469 pesos (approximately USD 39,000).[104] The sanctions which were issued against Telmex weren't alone; advisors and executives at several other large Mexican corporations were fined at the time for the same misdemeanor. These included an advisor for Grupo Modelo and a board member at Finamex.

The miniscule fines involved in these cases tell their own story. A USD 39,000 fine—the biggest ever in Mexico until that time—must have raised some sniggers in boardrooms across the country. Insider trading was treated more as an administrative offense than a criminal one. This largely continued for about a decade, until 2017, when the CNBV dished out fines totaling 25 million pesos (approximately USD 1.3 million) to 15 different people.[105] Of these, Ignacio del Valle Ruiz, a director of Mexichem, had to pay USD 220,000—the highest fine ever handed down for insider trading in Mexico.[106]

The fines probably only made a ripple. A *Bloomberg Businessweek* article[107]cited numerous instances of suspicious stock market activity which the CNBV could investigate. These included a 10 percent drop in Desarrollada Homex SAB's share price two days before an accounting scandal at the firm was announced; a 5.2 percent rise in the stock of construction company OHL Mexico SAB hours before it announced to the market that it had received a take-private offer; and a decline of 14 percent in the shares of Alfa SAB in the days before it announced that it was calling off an initial public offering (IPO) for one of its units. Even the most trusting of analysts would have suspicions.

The most commonly given reason for the CNBV's inaction is their lack of technology to deal with the issue of insider trading. The last sizable investment made by the exchange was in 1990, when it purchased a Vancouver-based securities exchange. However, telling everyone that your technology is inadequate to deal with the issue might as well be an invitation to those possessing privileged information to trade on it for their own benefit. And with insider trading, the more you think it is happening, the more you're likely to be right; as part of my own research, I was able to show a 90 percent correlation between cases where insider trading was highly likely to exist and cases where a prosecution for the crime was made.[108]

The case of Mexican regulation of insider trading is a lesson in behavioral economics all on its own. Despite being highly proactive in introducing insider trading laws, the CNBV has been extremely passive in issuing prosecutions. Research by myself and others, including Bhattacharya and Daouk (2002), has shown that the passing of laws in the area of insider trading has no discernible effect on the cost of equity in a stock market – instead, it is the ongoing enforcement of that regulation. Thus, as with Mexico and others, including Norway and Russia, it is worse to have a law that fails to prosecute those that violate it than to have no law at all.

46. CORRUPTION

If a citizen living in Hong Kong in the 1960s were to suddenly be transported, via time machine, to the Hong Kong of today, he or she would be deeply shocked. Not by the gleaming skyscrapers or the teeming activity of Hong Kong's world-class banks and corporations—those things they would have expected. Not by the outgoing, friendly, and industrious people—Hong Kongers have always been that way.

The shocking change would be the amazing lack of corruption.

The person arriving from the 1960s into present-day Hong Kong would likely step onto the streets with a pocket full of cash, ready to participate in the rampant culture of graft that typified life in Hong Kong for as long as anyone could remember.

When the British acquired Hong Kong in 1841, corruption was already a way of life, and graft thrived at all levels of government, with the police being the most corrupt of any agency. Over the years, in an effort to dampen bribery and theft, the British authorities passed various anti-corruption laws, including the Misdemeanors Punishment Ordinance of 1898, the Prevention of Corruption Ordinance (POCO) in 1948, and the Prevention of Bribery Ordinance (POBO) in 1971.

The laws didn't make much difference, nor did the Anti-Corruption Office (ACO), established in 1971 under the jurisdiction of the very agency it was designed to oversee: the Royal Hong Kong Police Force (RHKP). During Hong Kong's post-war economic growth, salaries of government employees remained low, and the culture of corruption among public officials blossomed. Perhaps out of a sense of deprivation, officials at all levels of government began to supplement their wages with demands for "tea money," "lucky money," or substantially larger sums.

For example, when firemen arrived at a burning house, they'd greet the owner by saying, *"Mo chin mo sui"*—"No money, no water!" Having been paid to extinguish the fire, they'd then ask for money to turn *off* the water, preventing water damage to the already damaged house.[109]

Ambulance crews would demand tea money before picking up a sick person. Even hospital amahs asked for "tips" before giving patients a bedpan or a glass of water. Offering bribes to the right officials was also necessary when applying for public housing, schooling, and other public services. Officials in Lands and Public Works departments demanded cash for consultation and approvals before they'd allow developments and projects to proceed. Civil servants often had to pay for promotions. The Royal Hong Kong Police organized entire stations to profit from hawkers and licenses, and were enriched through many other illicit schemes.

Many detective superintendents amassed enormous wealth from their corrupt dealings with corporations and triads—the Chinese organized crime families, of which Hong Kong had several branches. There were nine main triads operating in Hong Kong, dividing territory by ethnic group and geographic location, with each triad in charge of a region. From the 1950s to the 1970s, the Kowloon Walled City in Hong Kong was controlled by local triads.

The names of triad gangsters have been seared into the memories of the older generations, and their stories adapted into popular movies such as *To Be Number One*. This 1991 Hong Kong film was based on the rise and fall of gangster Ng Sek-ho, whose empire ended with the establishment of the Independent Commission Against Corruption (ICAC).

The RHKP was so saturated with corruption that post-war colonial governments avoided confronting the problem, fearing that an aggressive cleanup would lead to the total breakdown of law and order. In the 1960s, so powerful were corrupt policemen that they succeeded in getting a committee of inquiry to lay the blame for a series of riots on the territory's few prominent anti-police corruption campaigners.[110]

The RHKP was sarcastically referred to as "the very best that money could buy."

It wasn't just public officials and the police who expected payments from civilians for services rendered. When China's mercantile compradors—agents for foreign organizations engaged in investment, trade, or economic or political exploitation—were in the ascendancy, transactions were made based on commission. In essence, it was a glorified system of tipping. The procurement, delivery, and shipment of goods being traded, the engagement (and dismissal) of staff, guarantees of their conduct and reliability—everything that took place on or passed through the premises was subject to tips, of which the comprador took his cut.[111]

It is worth noting that street-level officials had to deal with an immigrant Chinese population distant from a government over which it had no electoral influence. As Alan Smart wrote in his paper "The Unbearable Discretion of Street-Level Bureaucrats: Corruption and Collusion in Hong Kong," many refugees brought from Republican China the ingrained belief that dealing with the government was best avoided and, if necessary, required bribes. Since many had to break laws to survive, opportunities abounded for squeezing squatters, hawkers, and unlicensed factory operators. The problem emerged in part because the colonial legal rules concerning corruption collided with Chinese "folk norms," and what the law regarded as corrupt, ordinary Chinese people often saw as a normal part of life.

Any aspect of civil life that is regulated creates opportunities for profits by those with discretion over control of the activity. Domains where the government tolerated informal practices, such as squatting, were particularly prone to corruption. Unlicensed street vendors were exceptionally vulnerable to shakedowns. The police had ready opportunities for corruption because they were responsible for issuing licenses to massage parlours, dancing schools, public dance halls, billiard rooms, and money changers."[112]

The case of Peter Godber

Many people believe the tipping point came in 1973 when Chief Superintendent Peter Godber, a senior officer stationed at Wan Chai Police Station and later at Kai Tak Airport Police Station, was caught up in a massive scandal.

Godber's career of graft began to unravel in 1971, when an internal police unit happened to discover an unusual remittance from Hong Kong to Canada: 12,000 Canadian dollars had been transferred to a Canadian bank account under the name "P. F. Gedber." Police launched an internal investigation, code-named "Havana." But with limited powers, the anti-corruption unit made little progress. Then, another tip came in, and police began contacting international banks.[113]

They discovered that in the years before his expected retirement in July 1973, Godber had opened bank accounts in Canada, Australia, Singapore, the United States, England, and Hong Kong, where he had stashed away at least HK$ 4.3 million (approximately USD 600,000).

When his wealth was exposed, Godber immediately arranged for his wife to leave the colony. He then used his police airport pass to bypass immigration and passport checks and board a plane for London. Godber's flight from justice spurred a public outcry over the integrity and quality of the police's efforts at self-investigation and a new call for reforms in the government's anti-corruption efforts.

Students spearheaded a mass rally in Victoria Park, protesting and condemning the government for failing to tackle the corruption problem. Demanding prompt government action, protesters with slogans including "Fight Corruption, Arrest Godber" insisted that Godber be brought back to stand trial.

The government responded to the scandal by appointing a commission of inquiry to investigate how Godber could have committed his crimes and to determine the effectiveness of the Prevention of Bribery Ordinance. Under the direction of Sir Alastair Blair-Kerr, the commission concluded that for "political and psychological reasons," Hong Kong needed to establish a new anti-corruption agency that was fully independent of the RHKP.[114]

The independent commission against corruption

In a speech delivered to the Legislative Council in October 1973, Hong Kong Governor Sir Murray MacLehose said

> I think the situation calls for an organisation, led by men of high rank and status, which can devote its whole time to the eradication of this evil … . A further and conclusive argument is that public confidence is very much involved. Clearly the public would have more confidence in a unit that is entirely independent, and separated from any department of the Government, including the Police.[115]

On February 15, 1974, Sir Murray founded the Independent Commission Against Corruption. Unlike the old police anti-corruption branch, the ICAC was answerable only to the governor. The ICAC was empowered to fight corruption using a three-pronged approach of law enforcement, prevention, and education.

The independence of the organization was assured by three human pillars—the commissioner, the head of operations, and the Operations Review Committee (ORC).

The Operations Department was accountable not to the commissioner but to the ORC, largely comprising members of the public appointed by the chief executive.

The founding commissioner was Sir Jack Cater, a former Royal Air Force fighter pilot who arrived in Hong Kong to work with the British military jurisdiction after the Japanese surrender in 1945. The commissioner is the public face of the ICAC, and is mainly responsible for policy, public image, and international relations. Although generally considered the top official in the organization, the commissioner often has little knowledge of the organization's core business of investigation until the very last minute of a case because the ICAC is guided by a "need-to-know" principle which acts as a *de facto* separation of functions.

The ICAC has three divisions: operations, community relations, and corruption prevention.

The Operations Department is the largest and is responsible for all high-profile arrests. The person in charge of the Operations Department is appointed not by the ICAC commissioner but by the chief executive. By custom and practice, the head of operations is usually bestowed the title of deputy commissioner. This department considers itself all-powerful, and reportedly tends to resist all attempts to interfere with its investigations.

The first important task of the ICAC was to bring Peter Godber to justice. In early 1975, Godber was extradited from England to stand trial. The charges consisted of one conspiracy offense and one of accepting bribes. Godber was found guilty on both counts and sentenced to four years' imprisonment.

From its inception, the ICAC had teeth, and corrupt officials soon felt its bite. The investigations and arrests of many police officers created a furore among the police, who protested against the ICAC and on one occasion even tried to overrun the headquarters.

In 1977, the governor, realizing that too much change too quickly could be dangerous, issued a blanket pardon against petty cases committed before that year. But the pardon did not extend to higher-level detective superintendents, and many high-level Chinese officers, notorious for their unexplained wealth, left for exile to Taiwan, which had no extradition treaty with Hong Kong.

The following year, as a result of its investigations, the ICAC oversaw a mass purge in which 119 officers, including one customs official, were asked to leave under the provisions of Colonial Regulation 55 to fast track the decisions in the public interest; a further 24 officers were held on conspiracy charges, and 36 officers and a customs official were given amnesties.

In his 2004 book, *A Modern History of Hong Kong*, Steve Tsang, a Chinese studies professor at the University of Nottingham, described the ICAC as "one of the best parting gifts from the colonial government," which "made the right psychological impact on the general public."[116]

Hong Kong in the rankings

Over the years, the ICAC has transformed Hong Kong from a swamp of corruption to one of the most transparent and corruption-free territories on earth. (Officially, the territory is the Hong Kong Special Administrative Region [SAR] of the People's Republic of China. It is governed under the principle of "one country, two systems," under which China has agreed to give the region a high degree of autonomy and to preserve its economic and social systems for 50 years from the date of the handover in 1997.)

The following are four ranking reports from global organizations that pay attention to corruption within nations. In every case, Hong Kong ranks near the top.

Transparency international ranking

In its Corruption Perceptions Index of 2017, Transparency International, a non-profit organization based in Berlin, Germany, ranked Hong Kong #13 out of 180 countries surveyed. The Corruption Perceptions Index ranks countries and territories by their perceived levels of public sector corruption according to experts and businesspeople. It uses a scale of 0–100, where 0 is highly corrupt and 100 is very clean. In 2017, the index found that more than two-thirds of countries scored below 50, with an average score of 43.

For example, the nation with the lowest perceived level of corruption was New Zealand, which received a score of 89 and a ranking of #1. A Nordic trio: Denmark, Finland, and Norway, followed. Rank #13 was actually a three-way tie between Australia, Iceland, and Hong Kong, with each receiving a score of 77.

The United States came in at #16. At the very bottom of the list were the dismal places you'd expect to see there: Syria, South Sudan, Somalia.[117]

As Krista Lee-Jones wrote in her 2018 report for Transparency International titled "Best Practices in Addressing Police-Related Corruption," Hong Kong's ICAC is noted for its three-pronged approach to fighting corruption through enforcement, education, and prevention. She noted,

> Public education is a crucial element of its three-pronged strategy to reduce corruption. Early efforts of the ICAC saw community liaison officers place special emphasis on publicising the arrest and successful prosecution of prominent police members. This helped establish the commission's strong reputation for a determined crack-down on large scale corruption. Large scale public education campaigns also

enhance the legitimacy of the ICAC, promote the knowledge of anti-corruption laws, and mobilise the public to report corruption.[118]

The World Bank Group's Worldwide Governance Indicators

The Worldwide Governance Indicators (WGIs) are a research data set summarizing the views on the quality of governance provided by a large number of enterprise, citizen, and expert survey respondents in industrial and developing countries. The reports aggregate individual governance indicators for over 200 countries and territories over the period 1996–2017, for six dimensions of governance:

- Voice and accountability
- Political stability and absence of violence
- Government effectiveness
- Regulatory quality
- Rule of law
- Control of corruption

Under the dimension of control of corruption, in the past five years Hong Kong has consistently been placed within the top 20. In the 2018 indicators, Hong Kong is ranked #17 out of the 209 economies surveyed, the second highest in Asia.[119]

Rule of Law Index 2017–2018, World Justice Project

The Rule of Law Index described in Chapter 45 assesses the extent to which countries/ territories adhere to the rule of law in practice by examining eight factors, namely constraints on government powers, absence of corruption, open government, fundamental rights, order and security, regulatory enforcement, civil justice, and criminal justice.

In the 2017–2018 index, Hong Kong is ranked 16th out of 113 countries and jurisdictions for its overall rule of law performance and #10 under the factor of "absence of corruption." Hong Kong also ranks high in political stability, government effectiveness, regulatory quality, and rule of law.[120]

Political and Economic Risk Consultancy, Ltd. Reports

A consulting firm specializing in strategic business information and analysis for companies doing business in the countries in East and South East Asia, Political and Economic Risk Consultancy, Ltd. (PERC) produces a range of risk reports on the countries of Asia, paying special attention to critical socio-political variables such as corruption, intellectual property rights risks, labor quality, and other systemic strengths and weakness of individual Asian countries.

In their report "Perceptions of Corruption in Asia, the US and Australia in 2018," out of 16 nations PERC ranked Hong Kong at #4, after Singapore, Australia, and Japan. The survey was based on 1,802 responses—at least 100 from each of the countries surveyed, except for Cambodia, from which they had 97 responses. Almost all respondents were business managers or professionals. Some were nationals of the countries surveyed; others were expatriates working for companies or organizations in these countries.[121]

ICAC mission and regulations

The mission of the ICAC is very simple: "With the community, the ICAC is committed to fighting corruption through effective law enforcement, education and prevention to help keep Hong Kong fair, just, stable and prosperous."

Those three words—enforcement, education, and prevention—represent the three-pronged strategy pursued by the ICAC as it strives to root out corruption in Hong Kong wherever it exists. A fair question to ask is, what constitutes corruption?

There are legal definitions. In general, according to the ICAC,

> corruption occurs when an individual abuses his authority for personal gain at the expense of other people. Corruption erodes fairness and the rule of law, and in some cases, puts lives and property at risk. The spirit of the Prevention of Bribery Ordinance (POBO) enforced by the ICAC is to maintain a fair and just society.

The full text of POBO is available online, but the ICAC provides this summary:

> Public servants (for definition of "public servant," please refer to the Text of the Law) include prescribed officers and employees of public bodies. POBO does not apply only to government employees, such as police officers or politicians. Parts of it also apply to employees of "public bodies"—those corporations that exist to serve the general public. Prescribed officers are subject to Sections 3, 4, 5, and 10 of POBO while employees of public bodies (e.g., power company, bus company, hospital, etc.) are subject to Sections 4 and 5.

In the Ordinance:

> "Advantage" includes money, gifts, loans, commissions, offices, contracts, services, favors, and the discharge of liability in whole or in part, but does not include entertainment.
>
> "Entertainment" means the provision of food or drink for consumption on the occasion when it is provided, and of any other entertainment provided at the same time, for example singing and dancing. Although the acceptance of entertainment does not breach the POBO, individual departments will still stipulate the conditions for staff's acceptance of entertainment.

The following are a few recent examples of accusations of fraud made by the ICAC. All of them are collected from their own reports.

- **Operator of consultancy firm charged with HK$ 680,000 bribery over HKJC membership application.** An operator of a membership consultancy firm has been charged by the ICAC today with conspiracy for members of the exclusive private Hong Kong Jockey Club (HKJC) to accept a share of a HK$ 680,000 bribe for assisting a person in applying for its racing membership.
- **Ex-welder of engineering company charged with accepting HK$ 48,000 illegal "referral fees."** A former welder of an engineering company has been charged by the ICAC with accepting illegal "referral fees" totaling over HK$ 48,000 for referring two men to serve as construction workers for the company.

- **Company director brought to court for bribing bank staff.** A director of a trading company was brought to the Kwun Tong Magistracy after being charged by the ICAC with offering a bribe to an employee of a bank for unfreezing an account for his company. [122]

A survey of offenses charged shows that most are made against employees of public bodies, not politicians, judges, or police officers. In fact, in the 1970s, 8 out of 10 graft complaints were against public officers. Over the years, this trend has reversed. Complaints against police officers have declined, and nowadays, only 3 out of 10 complaints relate to public servants. Meanwhile, private sector cases have been on the rise.

Has the ICAC ever been compelled to prosecute one of its own? The answer is yes. The most recent internal problem was in 2013, and involved the commissioner himself. Timothy Tong, who had served as commissioner from July 2007 until June 2012, was found to have overspent on entertaining and gifts for Mainland and other overseas officials. Tong was criticized by the Legislative Council Public Accounts Committee for his dozens of work trips costing taxpayers almost HK$ 4 million (USD 513,000) and lavish gifts to both Mainland and overseas officials. The committee expressed its concern as to "whether Mr Tong had thoroughly considered that unduly close contacts between him and mainland officials in Hong Kong during his tenure might have shaken public confidence in the impartiality of the ICA."

As of this writing, the case continues. Tong denies that his behavior is a problem. "I believe this investigation will not affect the international reputation of the ICAC," he said in June 2018.

His remarks were rejected by former ICAC investigator Lam Cheuk-ting, who said, "It is ridiculous. What he has done has seriously damaged the ICAC's reputation."[123]

The case of Donald Tsang

Just as the ICAC will pursue ordinary bureaucrats and corporate managers who cross the ethics line, it will also pursue offenders at the highest levels of government.

In 2005, Donald Tsang became Hong Kong's chief executive (the position was created to replace the governor of Hong Kong, the representative of the monarch of the United Kingdom during British rule), and was re-appointed to the position in 2007. In February 2010, Tsang began negotiating with Bill Wong Cho-bau, a major shareholder of Wave Media, over a penthouse flat in Shenzhen, where Tsang planned to retire. At that time, the invitation was issued for digital audio broadcasting license applications, to which Wave Media, Phoenix U Radio, and Metro Broadcasting Corporation responded.

On July 16, 2010, Tsang's wife Selina Tsang Pou Siu-mei deposited HK$ 350,000 in cash into her Bank of East Asia account. As ICAC investigators discovered, this was only 35 minutes after Wave Media shareholder David Li Kwok-po withdrew HK$ 350,000 in cash from the same branch. The prosecution said Li gave the money to Tsang to help pay for the Shenzhen penthouse.

On November 5, 2010, the Executive Council approved Wave Media's digital broadcasting license.

Twelve days later, a payment of 800,000 yuan (HK$ 943,000) was made from Tsang's wife's account to East Pacific Holdings, a company owned by Wong. The prosecution suggested that the payment could have been Tsang buying the property for less than the market rate, while the defense said it was a rent payment. There were also allegations of an unethical deal with an interior decorator. To investigators, it seemed clear that Wave Media—soon to be renamed Digital Broadcasting Corporation (DBC)—was giving Tsang and his wife a sweetheart deal on the penthouse in exchange for approval of the broadcasting license.

On February 29, 2012, the ICAC launched an investigation into Tsang's actions. In June, Tsang completed his term in office as chief executive of Hong Kong. On October 5, 2015, Tsang was charged with two counts of misconduct in public office, becoming the most senior public official in Hong Kong to be arrested.[124]

Since that time, there has been a series of trials. On February 17, 2017, a jury found Tsang guilty on one charge of misconduct in public office over the penthouse rental and not guilty on the misconduct charge for the penthouse decoration, but failed to reach a verdict on the count of accepting an advantage from an agent. On February 22, 2017, he was sentenced to 20 months in prison. As of this writing, he's out on bail. The prosecution has not yet applied for a third trial.

The three pillars of an anti-corruption policy

To put Hong Kong—long and rightfully regarded as a swamp of corruption—on the path to transparency and fairness in the business and political dealings of its citizens, the government chartered the Independent Commission Against Corruption to not only enforce the laws against corruption but also to go one step further and take proactive measures to reduce corruption in the future.

To fulfill its tripartite mission, the ICAC is organized into three divisions.

Enforcement: the operations department

As the investigative and enforcement arm of the ICAC, the mission of the Operations Department is to:

- Receive and consider allegations of corrupt practices.
- Investigate any alleged or suspected offenses under the ICAC Ordinance, the Prevention of Bribery Ordinance (POBO), and the Elections (Corrupt and Illegal Conduct) Ordinance.
- Investigate any alleged offenses of blackmail committed by a prescribed officer through misuse of office.
- Investigate any conduct of a prescribed officer, which is connected with or conducive to corrupt practices, and report thereon to the chief executive.

As the largest department of the ICAC, the Operations Department is divided into two divisions—one for investigating corruption and related offenses in the public sector, and one in the private sector. Because corruption is a secretive crime and difficult to detect, the department cannot be passive; instead, it takes a proactive approach to investigate and uncover graft through several means.

To exchange information and facilitate cooperation, the agents and employees of the ICAC maintain extensive contacts in the public and private sectors. Essential in fighting corruption is close cooperation with other law enforcement agencies in Hong Kong, the Mainland, Macau, and overseas. Liaison channels have been established with many of these agencies either directly or through their consulates in Hong Kong. The ICAC also participates in international anti-corruption initiatives, conferences, symposia, and work groups.

When fighting corruption, human resources are important, and so is technology. The Operations Department leverages advanced equipment, information technology, and specialized skills including computer forensic skills to preserve, seize, examine, and analyze electronic data and present it as admissible evidence in court. Advanced financial investigation skills allow ICAC agents to trace the paper trails left by criminal acts and corrupt payments. To ensure smooth prosecutions, suspects' interviews are always video recorded. The recorded interview process has become an established and accepted practice with full support from the courts and lawyers.

As we saw in the case of Peter Godber and many others, one key to uncovering graft is the ability to trace illegal payments across time and borders. Established in 2011, the Forensic Accounting (FA) Group provides support to frontline investigators in dealing with cases involving increasingly sophisticated *modus operandi* from a financial perspective. Dedicated officers with professional qualifications and extensive forensic accounting experience provide expert opinions on financial and accounting matters and assistance in search operations. To bolster their skills and knowledge in financial investigations, frontline investigators receive training sessions by FA Group officers.

To enhance the capability of the commission to deprive criminals of their corrupt and illicit crime proceeds, in 2010 the ICAC established the Proceeds of Crime section. It deals with the restraint, disclosure, and confiscation of assets under the Organised and Serious Crimes Ordinance (Cap 455).

In addition to its own investigative assets, the ICAC relies on citizen informants to provide tips about suspected corruption. The ICAC must walk a fine line between accepting and pursuing all legitimate tips without trampling on the rights of the accused—who may, after all, be innocent. The Hong Kong Bill of Rights Ordinance Article 11(1) recognizes the principle of the presumption of innocence: "Everyone charged with a criminal offence shall have the right to be presumed innocent until proved guilty according to law."

Furthermore, the Hong Kong Bill of Rights Ordinance Article 11(2)(g) ensures the right against self-incrimination and the right to silence: a suspect may not "be compelled to testify against himself or to confess guilt." Suspects in Hong Kong also enjoy the right to request a writ of *habeas corpus* and the right to trial within a reasonable time or release.

The ICAC encourages citizens to report possible crimes in person rather than electronically or anonymously. Reports made in person can be more detailed and convey more information crucial to effective follow-up and investigation. On its website ICAC .org.hk, the ICAC states that in recent years more than 70 percent of reports have been made in person, leading to more successful investigations. In general, they say, only about 10 percent of anonymous reports can be followed up by the ICAC.[125]

Tips lead to prosecutions of both petty offenders and high-profile criminals.

In December 2018, as the result of a tip, a 21-year-old man admitted that on two consecutive occasions he had obtained employment with property agencies by using false representations and academic proof, thereby inducing the property agencies to pay him salaries totaling over HK$ 30,000. When applying for the positions, he had presented forged graduation certificates from a Hong Kong secondary school. The magistrate adjourned the case to the next year for sentence, pending a community service order report. The defendant was granted bail.

Although far less common than in the past, police officers occasionally succumb to the temptation of graft. In October 2018, a superintendent of police (SP) and two operators of two private clubs were found guilty of accepting and offering bribes of HK$ 570,000 in total in relation to the operation of the private clubs in Wan Chai. Apparently, the officer disclosed to the club owners confidential information relating to police investigations of the clubs, and rendered advice or assistance to the owners so that they could evade inspections and investigations by the police. All three were sent to prison.

The Corruption Prevention Department

The Government of Hong Kong and the ICAC recognize that from both a practical and a moral perspective, if a society can work to *prevent* corruption, then fewer people will commit acts of corruption and life will be better for everyone.

The Corruption Prevention Department believes that opportunities for corruption can be removed through transparent and accountable procedures, effective leadership and supervisory control, and improved system controls and safeguards.

The mission of the department is twofold:

- Examine the practices and procedures of government departments and public bodies and secure revision of any that may be conducive to corruption.
- Advise upon request from private organizations or individuals on how to prevent corruption.

In discharging these duties, the department does not merely make announcements or issue directives; it works closely with the management of organizations and acts as their consultants.

To effectively plug "corruption loopholes" in a wide spectrum of public and private functions, the department employs a team of professional staff experienced in a wide range of fields including accounting, auditing and financial analysis, engineering, information technology, law, and surveying. These experts work closely with client organizations to identify functions and systems vulnerable to corrupt practices. To provide timely advice to government bureaux, departments, and public bodies to ensure anti-corruption measures are built in from the start, the department closely monitors developments in public policies, law, and government initiatives.

Assisting private companies

While it may seem obvious that the ICAC should be charged with supervising and investigating the activities of people in the public sector—politicians, judges, police officers, bureaucrats—an equally important part of its mission is to assist (and if necessary prosecute) private companies, which, after all, were deeply entrenched in the old "tip economy" under which nothing got done without money changing hands. In fact, under Section 12(e) of the Independent Commission Against Corruption Ordinance, Cap. 204, the ICAC has the *statutory duty* to instruct, advise, and assist any person, on the latter's request, on ways in which corrupt practices may be eliminated by such person.

Professional corruption prevention advice and services to private companies, organizations, and individuals are provided by the Corruption Prevention Advisory Service (CPAS), a specialized unit in the Corruption Prevention Department of the Hong Kong ICAC. CPAS believes that the prevention of corruption is a vital element of good governance of any enterprise, essential for its long-term success, development, and health. A company that fails to effectively manage the risks of corruption, fraud, and malpractice will see its profits decline and its reputation tarnished.

The services of CPAS are free, confidential, and available to any organization. For example, operators of Hong Kong's elite private kindergartens can learn how to avoid becoming the target of bribes ("advantages") offered by desperate parents. As the Sample Code of Conduct for Managers and Staff of Kindergartens admonishes,

Advantages offered in connection with the following activities must not be accepted:

(a) Admission or promotion of students (registration fees approved by EDB are not regarded as advantages);
(b) Recommendation of students for admission to primary schools;
(c) Discount, commissions, or gifts by a supplier or contractor to an individual rather than to the Kindergarten;
(d) Vacation packages for Managers or staff offered by suppliers, contractors or any persons having business dealings with the Kindergarten;

And so on.[126]

With such attention to detail, it is no wonder that Hong Kong has earned the reputation as a place of high ethics and honest public officials.

To business owners, CPAS offers guidance in the interaction of private companies with public officials who may either overtly ask for a bribe or offer suggestive hints. In one of many case studies published by CPAS, a law enforcement officer visited a restaurant shortly after its opening. The officer informed the restaurant's owners that he could visit the restaurant regularly, but that his visits required the payment of monthly "travelling expenses." Believing that the officer would protect the restaurant from triads— organized crime groups that would demand protection money—the owners agreed to pay. CPAS noted that both the official and the restaurant owners were guilty of violating Section 4 of POBO, which prohibits both the offering of any advantage to a public servant as an inducement or reward, and the solicitation by a public servant of an inducement or reward.

CPAS urges, "Any payment to a public servant which does not follow clear and proper procedures must be avoided. Business operators should decline any demand for bribe and report to the ICAC immediately."[127]

It is not always the public servant who is looking for a bribe. Sometimes, as this story provided by CPAS illustrates, a business owner will offer a bribe to an official, who turns it down and then—to add to the misery of the business owner—contacts the ICAC:

A mah-jong school operator submitted an application to a government department for a licence to establish a new mah-jong school. The operator was informed that his application would likely be turned down as his proposed premises was close to a school and a church, and there were objections from local community. Upon the operator's request, the subject officers met with the operator to discuss his licence application. At the meeting, the operator offered an envelope of winning lottery tickets to the officers, and solicited the latter's assistance in his licence application. The officers refused to accept the advantages and referred the incident to the ICAC.

It seems as if the mah-jong school operator wasn't very smart. Mah-jong is an immensely popular tile-based game originally developed in China, and it is often used for gambling—hence its prohibition near schools and churches. Did the mah-jong school operator believe that no one in the community would notice his mah-jong school nestled up against the school and the church?

Listed companies

Hong Kong is a leading international financial center with one of the biggest stock markets in the world. Publicly held corporations are particularly vulnerable to schemes involving the manipulation of share prices. Because of the increasingly common practice of paying top executives with stock options, as well as judging the performances of top executives largely on the short-term price of a company's stock, during the past few decades this problem has become more acute.

CPAS provides a case study of a director of a financial corporation who oversaw a merger project of two companies. In order to facilitate his work, the director and his team were given access to inside information on the details of the merger plan. The team members were fully aware that if this inside information regarding the merger were made public, such knowledge would materially affect the share prices of both companies. However, the unscrupulous director disclosed the information to a past client, who in return gave the director a luxury car. Armed with this confidential inside information, his past client then bought shares in these companies. A week later, when the announcement of the merger was made public, the share prices of the stocks rose. The past client then sold the stocks and took a profit.

The director's action in abusing the information violated not only Section 9(1) of POBO but also insider dealing provisions of the Securities and Futures Ordinance.[128]

The Convoy case: ICAC and the SFC join forces

While the ICAC routinely handles many cases of simple bribery, it also has the capability—and the determination—to investigate highly complex financial frauds, often with the close collaboration of other government agencies.

One of the biggest cases of alleged corporate fraud involves Convoy Global Holdings Limited, a limited liability company incorporated in the Cayman Islands,[129] and a member of the Convoy Financial Group. Reports indicate that the company's ultimate owner may be a shadowy entity known as Perfect Team Group Limited, based in Tortola, British Virgin Islands.[130]

As early as March 2017, Convoy Group Holdings was among 50 Hong Kong companies named by shareholder activist David Webb in his blog post titled "Enigma Network: 50 Stocks Not to Own." The problem was a murky shareholder network: Convoy was intertwined with at least ten other companies, including Town Health International Medical Group, Lerado Financial Group Company, Jun Yang Financial Holdings, and China Wah Yan Healthcare. Because their cross-shareholdings were below the disclosure threshold, the true identities of shareholders with significant voting power were impossible to determine—even if they were to act in concert to achieve a corrupt goal.[131]

Sources tipped off the ICAC that some employees were suspected of using the company to solicit an advantage of about HK$ 47 million between March and June 2015. On December 7, 2017, the Securities and Futures Commission (SFC) and the ICAC, following a joint investigation, raided Convoy Global's office, charging alleged corruption of the company's share trading and lending activities. The deputy chairwoman and executive director of financial advisers, Rosetta Fong Sut-Sam and executive director, Christie Chan Lai-yee were arrested.

The next day, chairman Quincy Wong Lee-man was arrested by the ICAC. Also implicated is Cho Kwai-chee, an executive director of Convoy and a well-known local investor nicknamed "Doctor Cho" because he is a medical doctor.

As of this writing, the exact charges have not been made public. Analysts know that Town Health International Medical Group, of which Cho is executive deputy chairman, was ordered by the SFC to suspend trading in its shares on November 27, 2017, after the regulator said it found the company's earnings report for the first half of 2016 and its annual report for 2016 included "materially false, incomplete or misleading information."[132]

In addition, Cho's flagship company Town Health, which has been steadily gaining control of Convoy since 2013, has been communicating via emails and diaries to arrange for the appointment of Mark Mak Kwong-yu and Christie Chan Lai-yee as executive directors of Convoy.

According to reports, Cho is the mastermind behind the circular financial arrangements that siphoned off HK$ 4.04 billion of Convoy's funds to companies associated with him, according to Convoy's lawsuit. Meanwhile, Convoy Global Holdings has filed three lawsuits against Cho and scores of other defendants, in a claim amounting to HK$ 715 million (USD 91.41 million).

To escape prosecution, Cho may have fled Hong Kong.[133]

Education: The Community Relations Department (CRD)

The statutory duties of the Community Relations Department are to educate the public against the evils of corruption, and to enlist public support in combating corruption.

It operates through two divisions:

Division 1 publicizes anti-corruption messages through the mass and new media, and plans strategies on business ethics and youth integrity promotion.
Division 2 provides face-to-face preventive education to the public, and reaches out to different levels of the local communities to enlist support for the ICAC's work.

The department's strategy consists of four initiatives:

1. Adopt an "ethics for all" approach to tailor preventive education programs to different target groups.
2. Leverage a partnership approach involving strategic partners in planning, implementing, and evaluating the programs.

3. Increase use of the new media.
4. Enhance the integration of media publicity and face-to-face contact.

The department has apportioned its efforts among various demographic groups including the general public, the business sector, young people, building management, district organizations, and new arrivals and ethnic minorities.

The general public

Anti-corruption messages are disseminated through TV and radio advertisements, posters, and the internet. The TV drama *ICAC Investigators* (in Chinese only) has become a popular series.

The ICAC website provides the public with the latest news of the commission, information on corruption prevention, and access to the ICAC's audio-visual products and other publications, including iTeenCamp.icac.hk, a special website for teenagers. Here, the ICAC offers information, online games, animation, and comics.

To promote anti-corruption messages, two online video platforms feature episodes of the ICAC TV drama series as well as training videos. On Facebook, the "All for Integrity" fanpage leverages ICAC initiatives to enlist public support and foster a probity culture in Hong Kong. On Instagram, ICAC's icon is Greedy_kin, a lazy and greedy sloth that, from its bad examples, encourages young people to reflect on their behaviors, engage in self-examination, and build positive values.

And, of course, there's an ICAC smartphone app that offers educational and informational features, allowing users to access the latest news and activities of the ICAC, as well as a convenient channel for watching integrity videos.

The business sector

To fortify the business sector's resistance to corruption, the Community Relations Department of the ICAC established the Hong Kong Business Ethics Development Center (HKBEDC).

The Hong Kong Business Ethics Development Center offers a full range of consultancy services on ethical management, including:

- Business and professional ethics training programs to enhance the ethical standards of the workforce.
- Codes of conduct training to help ICAC-assisted business organizations formulate and review a code of conduct—the statement of the standard of behavior expected by a company of its management and employees.
- System control offers practical advice to plug common corruption loopholes in various functional areas and to introduce effective mechanisms to prevent malpractice, fraud, and corruption.
- Publications and resources on the handling of ethical issues in the day-to-day operation of various trades and professions.

The resource center offers an in-depth collection of books and publications on local and overseas anti-corruption laws and researches as well as training packages and practical guides for different trades and professions.

Publications and resources include a variety of practical guides and training packages, videos, feature articles, e-learning packages, and case studies addressing the ethical issues faced by practitioners; and a database of case studies that may be used as reference for enhancing the ethical management and staff integrity of business organizations.

There are lots of case studies used as training tools.

For example, "Defrauding by giving false information" relates the tale of the chief engineer of a hotel who oversaw the repair of the air-conditioning system. The engineer conspired with a spare parts supplier to defraud the hotel by falsifying orders for a batch of extra and unnecessary spare parts for the project. After submitting false invoices to the hotel and getting paid, the supplier gave the chief engineer HK$ 60,000 in kickbacks.

The chief engineer, eventually being brought to book, was found guilty of conspiracy to defraud and was sentenced to prison for 12 months. The supplier was fined HK$ 10,000.

In case the reader misses the point, the case study includes an informative case analysis, explaining

> the chief engineer abused the trust of his employer and misused his authority to defraud in the process of procuring goods for his company, failing to fulfill his duty of loyalty to his employer. Using false documents to deceive and mislead his employer for personal gain, he finally could not escape from legal sanctions.[134]

Hong Kong ethics laws are strict. For example, the case study "Hidden agenda in sponsorship" relates the story of Dr E., a consultant ophthalmologist in a public hospital who was often party to the procurement of high-value medical equipment for his department. During the procurement of equipment for oculoplastics, Billy, the sales director of a potential supplier, asked Dr E. to comment favorably on the equipment produced by his company. To sweeten the request, Billy offered to pay for Dr E.s' passage and accommodation to visit the company's laboratory in New York while also attending an important medical conference there. Sure enough, after the trip, Dr E. recommended that the hospital offer the contract to Billy's company.

In some nations, this behavior would hardly be noticed. But in Hong Kong, Dr E. was in violation of Section 4 of the Prevention of Bribery Ordinance, and Billy also committed the offense of corruption for offering the bribe to Dr E.

In addition, Dr E. might have breached Section 16.1 of the Professional Code and Conduct issued by the Medical Council of Hong Kong (November 2000), which specifies that doctors should avoid accepting pecuniary inducement from commercial firms that might compromise the independent exercise of their professional judgment.

Moral education for youth

ICAC believes that by educating children and young people about the evils of corruption, they will be less inclined to succumb to temptation when they get older.

And, showing a keen understanding of how to get and keep the attention of children, the ICAC offers a wide range of educational materials in formats already familiar to kids, including videos and colorful activity packages.

A popular activity package is "Gee-Dor-Dor," produced by the Community Relations Department of the ICAC. The package seeks to support teachers as they develop kindergarten and primary students' positive values such as fairness, honesty, and care. In developing "Gee-Dor-Dor," the CRD invited kindergarten and primary schools to conduct demo teaching for the package. The launching seminar of the package was held in June 2015.

In "Gee-Dor-Dor's Space Adventure" cartoon movie, three friends are beamed up to a spaceship hovering overhead. Once inside the spaceship—named Gee-Dor-Dor—they are informed by the friendly commander of the spaceship that levels of positive energies on Earth—specifically fairness, honesty, and love—have fallen to dangerously low levels. But there is a solution: an energy source exists in space that can reverse this dire trend, but they have to find it.

Gee-Dor-Dor flies to a distant planet, where one of the friends competes in a battle contest, with the prize being a crystal ball of super positive energy. Further adventures ensue, and eventually the three friends return to Gee-Dor-Dor, where the positive energies of fairness, honesty, and love are fully restored and the people on Earth can live in peace and harmony.[135]

The ICAC YouTube channel features dozens of videos, including 36 Gee-Dor-Dor adventures. With 392,900 views, the most popular video is 康署潮文動畫系列】邊一個發明了衰工(3)自己「工自己救, which Google translates as "ICAC tidal animation series] one invented the dying work (3) to save their own work."

Image 4.1 Gee Dor Dor in ICAC Museum. Photo Taken by the Author

The ICAC offers an interactive moral education e-book, which includes a variety of stories showcasing various ethical dilemmas faced by young people. In *Outstanding Security Guard Election*, written by Poon Kam-ying and Pearl Poon, an election has been scheduled to choose the best security guard in an apartment block. One of the guards, Gina, is unscrupulous and attempts to win votes by bribing kids with candy and flattering the adults. The other security guard, Richard, makes no attempt to campaign, but simply goes about his daily job and is very helpful to all the residents.

A young resident named Joyce is asked by her father to assess the candidates. As the story goes,

> That evening, Joyce reported to Dad what she had observed. Dad shook his head and sighed, "Gina is lazy at work and always shirks responsibilities. In order to get votes, she even resorted to lies, brags and candy treats for kids. It's really bad!"

Then, her mom Mom took out the form for the security guard election and said, "Now let's cast our votes in the fairest way to safeguard our home!" The book does not reveal for whom Joyce and her family voted—that's left for the readers to decide.[136]

Enforcement, prevention, and education—these are the three pillars of the ICAC leading Hong Kong into a bright future of fairness, honesty, and love.

47. FINANCIAL SYSTEM AND STOCK MARKETS

By the end of 2016, almost 50,000 companies listed their stock in exchanges all over the world. The combined market capitalization of these companies was approximately USD 70 trillion,[137] roughly similar to the world's GDP. Publicly listed firms include not only Apple and Alibaba, but also small companies who find in this way easy access to finance. In fact, the World Federation of Exchange (WFE) states that the size of publicly listed firms is as small as USD 10 million in market capitalization.[138] All in all, these firms, small and large, are also significant employers: WFE estimates suggest that the 24,000 companies across a set of 26 of the 55 WFE's equity market exchanges employ over 127 million people.[139]

A country's financial system is more than its stock exchange of course, and it includes the monetary system, the banking system, and all markets where investors trade financial instruments. The role of the financial system in the economy is to allocate capital efficiently. By collecting, processing, and providing information, financial intermediaries reduce the transaction costs of obtaining capital by firms, and allow individual and institutional investors to place their savings in assets that provide the best combination of risk and return.

Very often, we tend to associate developed financial markets with competitive economies. Not surprising, the economies of the United States, Hong Kong, and the Netherlands rely heavily on their financial systems. And certainly, as countries become more and more prosperous, a natural consequence is the need to create markets and systems that allocate capital. And since the financial system needs to be regulated, financial development comes together with the passing of corporate governance, accounting, tax, and transparency laws. There is a view then that the financial sector does not matter very much, and that any relationship between financial development and growth is due to growth leading financial development. In 1988, Robert Lucas, who won the 1995 Noel Prize in Economics, wrote in a famous paper that

I will [...] be abstracting from all monetary matters, treating all exchange as though it involved goods-for-goods. In general, I believe that the importance of financial matters is very badly over-stressed in popular and even much more professional discussion and so am not inclined to be apologetic for going to the other extreme.[140]

Less-developed economies can at first function with a relatively unsophisticated financial system as long as they have decent banks.[141] In many African countries for instance, bank debt may be the only source of funding because they lack the legal framework and accounting practices necessary to develop a stock market. As the economy develops, the financial system contributes to economic growth and leads the development process—not results from it. In need of financial resources, corporations organize informal financial markets that become regulated once they grow. These financial institutions improve the way companies operate through the need to provide transparent information and maintain clear records of operations. The pressure from external investors is, in this way, a driving force of economic development. Moreover, through the provision of credit, the monetary and banking systems allow individuals to invest and increase their quality of life, with better access to education and infrastructure. Finally, financial markets also make it easier for foreign capital to flow into the country, contributing to the positive dynamics created by financial regulation.

Therefore, this chapter shows that well-functioning financial systems are not only the consequence, but also the reason for the competitiveness of countries. Over a long period of time, the interaction between Wall Street and Main Street—or between the financial system and the real economy—reinforces each other, and we gradually observe the positive impact that a good financial system has on economic growth and quality of life. Conversely—and I want to use here the example of India—those countries that forget the financial sector are not able to develop a competitive economy despite their apparent strengths in innovation and talent.

Figure 4.14 plots the typical measure of financial development in a country—the size of financial markets to GDP—in relation to the country's GDP per capita and for

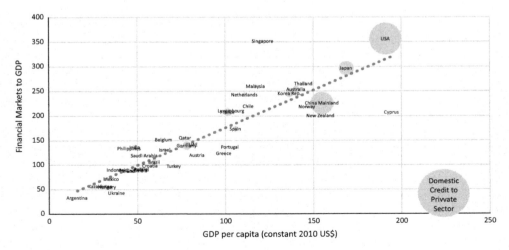

Figure 4.14 Importance of Financial Markets

Source: World Bank Development Indicators.

a sample of countries. Data is for 2017. The size of financial markets is computed as the sum of the market capitalization of domestic companies, relative to GDP, and the private credit in the country, also relative to GDP. Private credit is represented in absolute values by the size of the circle to indicate the size of credit markets irrespective of stock markets. The line of fit suggests a positive relation between financial development and economic development. Those countries whose position is above the line are *over-financed* in the sense that their financial system is larger given the degree of economic development. This group of countries includes Singapore and the Netherlands. Among the countries in the graph, the United States is the country with the largest capital markets relative to GDP, and although it seems that bank credit to the economy is small in absolute terms, financing from credit amounts to about 191 percent of GDP, with another 164 percent corresponding to stock market capitalization. Developing economies below the line, such as Brazil, Mexico, and Argentina, are also financially underdeveloped. And as GDP per capita grows, other countries such as Portugal, Greece, and Turkey display a relatively weaker financial system.

Figure 4.15 plots the relationship between the size of capital markets and IMD's competitiveness ranking. Again, there is a significant relationship between both, and competitiveness increases as financial development grows (and vice versa).

The benefits of finance are important and have been very well documented by academics and international organizations. In 2000, in a paper published in the *Journal of Financial Economics*, Professor Jeffrey Wurgler (then at the Yale School of Management

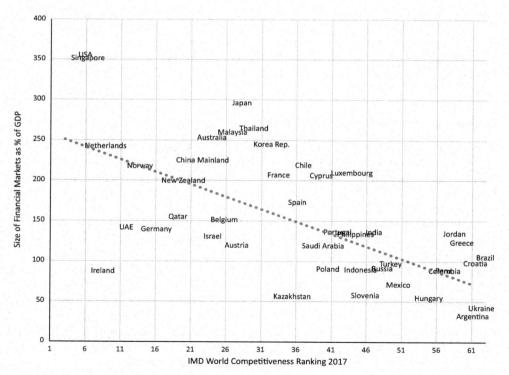

Figure 4.15 Competitiveness and Financial Development

and currently at NYU) showed that more financially developed countries allocate capital more efficiently across industries.[142] Specifically, Jeff found that "developed" financial markets (measured by the size of the domestic stock and credit markets relative to GDP) such as the United States and the United Kingdom increase investment more in growing industries, and decrease investment in their declining industries. This means that financial development is associated not necessarily with more investment in domestic companies, but a better distribution of funds. Consequently, financial development is positively related to economic growth, and the link between one and the other happens because financial systems:

- Produce information *ex ante* about possible investments and allocate capital.
- Monitor investments and exert corporate governance after providing finance.
- Facilitate the trading, diversification, and management of risk.
- Mobilize and pool savings.
- Ease the exchange of goods and services.[143]

By performing these functions, financial markets help to improve the economy. Let me share two important studies that confirm such causality. The work of R.E. Wright has provided plenty of examples of how the success of the US economy is partly due to the role of financiers. He recounts how in the 18th century, US corporations increasingly forced managers to hold large quantities of stock in the corporation to align their personal financial interest with those of the firm.[144] Once interests were aligned, companies would perform better. Similarly, and at a local level, Italian economists Luigi Guiso, Paola Sapienza, and Luigi Zingales analyzed data from regions in Italy and found that differences in local financial development explain the probability that an individual starts a business, as well as the growth of firms.[145]

In summary, and as Prime Minister William Gladstone of the UK said in 1958: "Finance is, as it were, the stomach of the country, from which all the other organs take their tone."[146]

Financial sector development in China

Let me now describe two case studies in detail. First, a description of how the failure to develop a banking system is behind India's lack of competitiveness in recent years. The process that India followed is exactly the opposite of what happened in China. From 1949 through the 1970s, the banking industry in China operated as a part of the centrally planned economy.[147] The People's Bank of China (PBOC) was China's Central Bank; at the same time, it was also a commercial bank offering deposit, credit, and settlement businesses. From the late 1970s, as part of China's reform and opening-up agenda, the banking industry transformed significantly. The four major specialized banks, known as the "Big Four," namely Agricultural Bank of China (ABC), Bank of China (BOC), Construction Bank of China (CCB), and Industrial and Commercial Bank of China (ICBC), were either spun off from the "monolithic" Central Bank or were newly incorporated. The Big Four were designated to specialize, respectively, in agricultural finance, foreign exchange and trade financing, construction and infrastructure financing, and urban commercial financing. In 1983, after spinning off its commercial banking businesses, the PBOC began to focus primarily on central banking activities. In December

1993, the central government restructured the Big Four into state-owned commercial banks, after which they began to operate independently, managing their own risks and operations, and taking full responsibility for their profits and losses.

In 2003, state-owned commercial banks were restructured under the joint-stock system (*gufenzhi*), during which reform measures including capital injection by the government, financial restructuring, internal reform, and strict oversight were introduced. Such efforts set the stage for their local and offshore listing.

Through years of development, small- and medium-sized commercial banks such as CITIC Industrial Bank, Shenzhen Development Bank, and Guangdong Development Bank have grown rapidly. At the end of 2015, China was home to 12 joint-stock commercial banks, 133 city commercial banks, 5 private banks, 859 rural commercial banks, 71 rural cooperative banks, and 1,373 rural credit cooperatives.[148] The rapid rise of small- and medium-sized banks has broken the monopoly of large state-owned banks under the planned economy. In its place is a new financial landscape featuring multiple layers of banking and different types of banking institutions. Cooperation, functional complementarity, and fair competition among financial institutions are conducive to the development of the financial service system, and that serves the goal of building a socialist market economy. I will pay more attention to the Chinese banking ecosystem in Chapter 47.

Instead of moving from a system of state-owned banks to privatizing them, India went from a system of many, dispersed, and unsophisticated banks, to nationalizing them starting in 1955. This is the time when the economy needed an efficient payment and credit system. However, and lacking monopoly power as in China, the state-owned banks grew bureaucratic and inefficient. The process of privatization and liberalization was thus very difficult and is still going on. If I need to point to a significant difference between the competitiveness paths of India and China, it is their completely different banking systems.

India and the effects of financial underdevelopment

Over the past five decades, India has made significant progress, securing dynamic economic growth and maintaining long-term economic reforms aimed at increasing India's stability and competitiveness. Despite India's strong economic performance, the banking sector is often viewed as the weakest sector of the economy, even though it has been developed and has grown rapidly in the past decade. Although the banking sector in India was heavily influenced by government and subsequently nationalized, it has achieved significant development as a result of its liberalization over the last decades.[149]

Historically, India's banking sector has undergone major regulatory and structural changes that have resulted in institutional development. Such changes happened through three major phases:[150] before nationalization, the period of nationalization, and the period after nationalization. The periods of transformation were the result of institutional and regulatory reforms by the Indian government.

The first phase includes the colonial period and the early years of India's independence (1947). The phase is observed with the establishment of the first commercial banks in India and lasted till the late 1950s and early 1960s—the phase of the nationalization of India's banking sector. The first bank in India was established in 1786—the Bank of India, followed by the Bank of Hindustan. The first banks were established with foreign capital, and the East India Company played an essential part. Many of the early established banks were re-established as the Imperial Bank of India as a private shareholders bank. The first Indian-owned bank was Punjab National Bank. The period was observed with a large number of small-sized banks; however, the banking sector did not experience significant growth or development due to lack of confidence in commercial banks, which was consequently reflected in the low levels of deposits. On the institutional level, India implemented banking regulatory action in the early years of its independence. The Government of India introduced the Banking Companies Act in 1949. The act of 1965 granted the Reserve Bank of India (RBI; established in 1935) a supervisory role over banking activities, eventually reorganizing the Reserve Bank of India as the Central Bank. This phase of the establishment of the early banking sector was turbulent and unstable; however, the phase came to an end in the early 1960s with governmental reforms, and was followed by the phase of structural and institutional changes that shaped the development of India's banking sector for the next decades.

The next phase of the Indian banking sector's evolution came with a contradictory reform policy—the banking sector's nationalization. The phase began with the Government of India embarking on major banking sector reforms in the early period after independence. The early years of the banks' nationalization were noted with the first nationalized bank; in 1955, the Imperial Bank of India was nationalized. The bank had large banking facilities and specialized in rural and suburban areas of financing. Additionally, India's government established the State Bank of India as an actor for the Reserve Bank of India. Later, in 1959, seven subsidiary banks of the State Bank of India were nationalized. Nevertheless, this phase of nationalization peaked in 1969, when the prime minister of India, Mrs Indira Gandhi, increased the efforts of nationalization, consequently nationalizing 14 major commercial banks. The second wave of India's banking sector nationalization reforms was enforced in 1980 when six more banks were nationalized. The second banking nationalization reforms almost nationalized the entire banking sector in India, with 80 percent of the banking sector under the government's control and ownership.

Initially, the banking sector's nationalization reforms were successful. The banking sector rose significantly, increasing the number of branches in the public sector–owned banks eight-fold. The nationalization reforms boosted confidence in India's banking sector, with the institutional reforms stimulating an immense rise in deposits and consequently the development of the Indian banking sector. Nevertheless, by 1990, India faced stagnation in its banking sector. The public sector–owned banking system was unable to provide competitive and modern services to customers, bringing up mismanagement issues of the government-owned banking sector. Even though the nationalization of the banking sector was, to some extent, a success, India's government faced development challenges in the banking sector. The developing private sector required a progressive and modern banking sector. Additionally, with the liberalization of the economy and the banking sector, India required new reforms.

In the early 1990s, the banking sector required modernization, and bank's profitability and innovativeness became a priority for upcoming banking reforms. In 1991, M. Narishimham established working groups dedicated to the liberalization of banking activities. The phase of liberalization that began in 1991 aimed to increase financial stability and develop a competitive banking sector in India. In light of banking liberalization reforms, the process of the banking sector's nationalization was halted; moreover, the government took action in the development of the private sector's banking by granting licenses to ten commercial private banks.[151]

Private and foreign banks have become major players in India's banking sector. Free of government's management, these banks focus their efforts on providing satisfactory services to customers. The banking sector has developed innovative technologies to access their customers, including online and mobile banking, and increased the number of ATMs.

The modern banking sector in India is a rapidly developing industry. It is relatively stable, due to a flexible exchange rate regime and a large number of external reserves. However, the process of liberalization and the rapid growth of the banking sector has brought new challenges. Nowadays, India's banking sector is a dynamic and growing sector with 151 commercial banks operating in the market. The Indian banking market is the 4th largest among emerging economies, grossing up to USD 281 billion in 2017. The banking sector in India consists of 27 state-owned and nationalized banks, 27 old and new private sector banks, and 49 foreign banks. While the biggest banks in terms of total assets and banking network are the public sector banks, the foreign-owned banking sector is the largest in number of banks. The number of foreign banks has grown rapidly over the past two decades due to the growth in the banking market and the economic development dynamics in India.

The biggest bank in India is the State Bank of India with USD 430 billion in total assets and 14,000 branches. Among other national and state-owned banks are the Bank of Baroda and Punjab National Bank. ICICI Bank is the largest private-owned bank in India, with over USD 100 billion in assets and a large banking network. The Bank of India is one of the leading Indian banks. It underwent the process of nationalization and was established as a private bank; however, it was nationalized in 1960 and is now a public sector bank. India's banking sector liberalization reforms have opened up the market to foreign banks. Nowadays, there are 45 foreign banks in India with around 300 branches. The biggest foreign banks in India, in terms of branches, are Standard Charter, HSBC, and Citibank, of which Citibank is the most profitable foreign-owned bank. The foreign-owned banks are an essential part of the Indian banking sector development. Despite a relatively minor role in terms of market share, foreign banks increased the efficiency and competitiveness of the banking market, launching modern financial products and financial technologies.[152]

Despite the rapid growth of India's banking sector, this sector is one of the weakest aspects of the country's economy vis-à-vis its counterpart countries. The Indian banking sector showed great resilience in the financial crisis of 2008; however, nowadays, it is facing major challenges and issues. The main issue for India's banking sector is the rising amount of non-performing assets (NPA). The NPA ratio in India accounts for 9.85 percent, a ratio that is far ahead of developed countries such as the United States, the UK, and Japan. A high NPA ratio is typical in countries with unstable financial systems and crises states—Ireland, Greece.[153]

The NPA crisis in India is the result of unsupervised and unwise borrowings and is reflected in mismanagement, poor accounting standards, and a large amount of banking fraud. Arguably, the state-owned banks are not doing that well, as 70 percent of India's bank market is composed of the public sector. In this regard, foreign-owned banks show lower NPA ratios and better profit performance.[154] These issues in the public and private banking sector underline the importance of banking regulations in India, where further control and reforms have been implemented both by the government and the RBI.

48. IT IS THE PRIVATE SECTOR THAT CREATES JOBS

Recalling Chapter 29, competitiveness countries manage their natural resources, geographical position, regulation, infrastructure, etc., in an optimal way so as to generate jobs, attract investment, improve people's quality of life, and generate overall prosperity in an inclusive way. In other words, inputs are optimally transformed into outputs. What is key to understand is the engine—or the black box—which connects inputs and outputs in the economic system, and by that I mean the productive system that employs people so the country generates products and services that, once sold in either the domestic or foreign markets, allow the government to raise taxes and invest in people.

In these dynamics, it is the responsibility of the private sector to create jobs. The government must ensure that the economic environment is efficient, that the physical and digital infrastructure is sufficient, that there is provision of domestic or foreign talent, and that regulation is transparent, inclusive, and conducive to business. But it is not the role of the state either to directly create jobs (unless they are necessary to maintain the government machine), or to waste the national budget ignoring economic—that is, value-creating—considerations.

Aren't subsidies provided by the state a way to improve life conditions? I am often asked this question because our rankings do penalize governments who provide subsidies, that is, who spend instead of investing. And I want to explain why.

Subsidies can serve two alternative purposes. A "subsidy" may be a tax deduction when a company builds a new plant, or when it hires people in a particular geographical area. In 2007, and 30 years after being acquired by Nestlé, American company Alcon, a world leader in eye care products, decided to move its headquarters to Switzerland. As a way to attract the company, the tax authorities of Canton de Fribourg, where the company is currently located, gave Alcon a "ten-year investment tax incentive" which drastically reduced the company's tax bill. The conditions were that Alcon would employ a certain minimum number of employees in the region, and that it would stay there until 2017.[155] Such tax subsidies are investment incentives, and here the key word is "incentives": they help companies create jobs, and therefore they improve the competitiveness of the country.

But there are other subsides that are dangerous. This is the case when people receive money from the state to have a better life, but in doing so they are *disincentivized* to seek better opportunities, innovate, work hard, and be part of the economic system. In February 2019, Finland announced that it had stopped its basic income experiment as the results were disappointing (more about minimum guaranteed incomes in Chapter 60). The experiment was conducted in 2017 and 2018. During this period, 2,000 randomly selected unemployed individuals received a basic income of EUR 560 per month that was not conditional on whether these people would get a job or not. The participants were selected among persons between 25 and 58 years of age who had in 2016 received basic unemployment allowance or labor market support from Kela, the social insurance institution of Finland.[156,157]

Such subsidies are detrimental to competitiveness for two reasons. First, they do not help the competitiveness machine because subsidies can make people idle. I am not saying that this is not sometimes necessary: unemployment subsidies are socially desirable, but only to the point where a jobless person is better off not working than working. Second, subsidies naturally detract resources from the national budget that could otherwise be used in productive investments—their opportunity cost is huge for the economy.

It is interesting to explore a couple of cases where subsidies are detrimental to the competitiveness of a country. I have chosen Oman and Tunisia because, as the Middle East and North Africa countries, they represent very well the spirit of social policies in that region—in order to maintain people's satisfaction with the government, the government subsidizes them. Tunisia is also interesting because, as a result of the Arab Spring, the country has managed to move from a subsidized economy to a much more market-oriented country. In contrast, Oman has followed the opposite path, and only in the context of falling oil prices and the need to diversify the economy, has it been forced to lower subsidies on basic products, with the subsequent social discontent.

Tunisia and Oman

The countries of Tunisia and Oman in the economic region of the Middle East and North Africa exhibit middling economies relative to their peers. On the 2019 Index of Economic Freedom by The Heritage Foundation (2019),[158] Tunisia declined in competitiveness to the rank of 125th place, earning it a Mostly Unfree categorization, while Oman rose five spots to 88th place, earning it the Moderately Free moniker. While a myriad of issues, from the size of government to the inconsistent application of the rule of law, plague these countries, one of the most egregious marks against their global competitiveness is their complex system of subsidies that distorts their economies and prevents market-based reallocation of investment in the pursuit of economic growth.

The subsidies given out in these nations, most extremely in the form of energy subsidies, have racked up debt for both countries, and have led them to run perpetual deficits. Efforts to improve the subsidy environment often achieve mixed results as numerous concessions are made and reversals are common. To understand the impact that subsidies have had on the culture and economic situation of these nations, their unique paths to modernization must first be explored. Following a historical understanding of their development, the current economic situation in these two countries must be contrasted with other, less subsidized economies. Finally, an exploration of their public finances, and the impact subsidies have on their governmental performance, will further clarify the causes for their meager economic competitiveness.

Tunisia

History and political context

Modern Tunisia traces its lineage to the ancient Carthaginian civilization, whose capital was located near Tunisia's modern capital Tunis. Following successive occupations, first by the Romans, then by various Islamic Caliphates through to the Ottoman Empire, and finally as a French colony, Tunisia gained its independence on March 20, 1956. Established initially as a constitutional monarchy under King Lamine Bey, its first prime minister, Habib Bourguiba, abolished the monarchy on July 25, 1957, establishing the Republic of Tunisia, and becoming its first president. Ruling until 1987, Bourguiba was greatly inspired by the rationalism and secularism of revolutionary France and the Napoleonic era. The government advanced women's rights and suppressed Islamic fundamentalism, but in economic matters it was heavily state directed, focused on nation-building and not free enterprise.[159]

In January 1961, socialist organizer Ahmed Ben Salah was appointed Minister of Planning and Minister of Finance, instituting economic plans to transition Tunisia into a fully socialist economy. The government became more directly involved with the economy throughout the decade through large public works programs, transforming agriculture into worker-owned cooperatives, and attempting to nationalize much of Tunisia's industry. A regime that valued investment in public services and popular support, finances were in poor order, and foreign investors fled. In 1969, The World Bank threatened to revoke financial aid to the country unless it opened its market.[160] Bourguiba responded to this pressure declaring "the end of the socialist experience" on September 22, 1969. Ben Salah was fired and the cabinet was moved to support economic liberalization.[161]

Despite attempts to introduce more market-friendly reforms through the privatization of industry and opening trade, Bourguiba's strong state vision prevented full economic liberalization. Industries were heavily state directed even if they were privately owned. A national vision based on food self-sufficiency led to heavy subsidies for agricultural development, at the cost of national competitiveness. Economic growth went in fits and starts, and it was only in 1987, when a coup ousted Bourguiba and replaced him with Zine El Abidine Ben Ali, did Tunisia accelerate its pace of market-based reforms.[162]

While the country experienced steady economic growth throughout the 1970s, as tourism and foreign investment increased, increasing the nation's productivity, and the discovery of oil improving the financial situation, problems continued. The lack of decent urban jobs led to a drain of skilled workers from the nation, and the agriculture sector continued to be plagued by inefficiency, relying on government subsidies to ensure affordable food. The IMF, seeing problems with public financial management, imposed subsidy restrictions in 1983, which led to a rise in the price of bread, and major riots.[163] Over 100 protesters were killed in the ensuing chaos. The government, plagued by popular backlash, increased its repressive practices to maintain power, leading to a rise in terrorist activity.

This attempt at subsidy reform accelerated Bourguiba's decline as the military, given a more prominent role in public life, was increasingly fed up with the government's policies. A peaceful coup took place, replacing Bourguiba with Ben Ali on November 7, 1987, while the former leader was in ill-health.[164] The economic state of the country was in ruin at this time, debt stood at 46 percent of the GDP of the young nation and annual inflation hovered around 10 percent.[165] Under Ben Ali's leadership, Tunisia's economy began to be seen as one of the best performing in all of Africa. Trade with the European Union steadily increased, and agricultural reforms alleviated some of the inefficiencies that plagued the country. State involvement in industry, however, continued, and government bureaucracy remained problematic. Nonetheless, Tunisia's GDP growth between 1987 and 2010 averaged 5 percent per year, and the country was listed as one of the eight African Lions, which accounted for 70 percent of the African continent's GDP.[166]

Despite the economic performance of the Ben Ali regime, it began to grow deeply unpopular among the Tunisian public. In political matters, the government backtracked on liberalizing reforms, restricting a free press, cracking down on political rivals, and jailing dissidents. The economic liberalization of the country corresponded with extensive political repression. As youth unemployment increased in the 2000s, many saw that the regime's authoritarian corruption was siphoning off prosperity for the connected elite at the expense of the majority. In December 2010, mass protests began, leading to a state of emergency being declared the following month. On January 14, 2011, Ben Ali fled the country and Prime Minister Mohammed Ghannouchi assumed power.[167] Promising new political and economic reforms, Ghannouchi announced his new cabinet on January 17, which was met with protests over the inclusion of members from the Ben Ali regime. Protests continued even after a second cabinet was announced, criticizing Ghannouchi's presence in political transition. Finally, on February 27, 2011, he resigned from the government.[168] Mohamed Beji Caid Essebsi, who served as Minister of Foreign Affairs in the latter years of Bourguiba's government, became prime minister and began enacting reforms, including elections to a Constituent Assembly tasked with rewriting the constitution, and the dissolution of the secret police.

The transition years after the Tunisian revolution proved to be economically disastrous.[169] Political gridlock resulted in few of the promised reforms being enacted for years, with instability and conflict further reducing Tunisia's appeal to investors. After parliamentary elections on December 24, 2011, and until the elections on October 26, 2014, following the ratification of the new Tunisian constitution, a ruling "Troika" government presided over economic decline, rising unemployment, and mass refugee migration from neighboring Libya. The rising influence of Islamists in Tunisia, who aimed to co-opt the constitution to build an Islamic State was routinely criticized.

Following ratification of the new Tunisian constitution and the establishment of the Second Republic, Caid Essebsi returned to power, sworn in as president on December 31, 2014.[170] His secular party, Nidaa Tounes, also garnered a plurality of seats in parliament. Since 2014, the economy has stabilized as governance has once again normalized, though economic growth has not returned. Concessions made to various protesting parties have kept an intricate bureaucracy alive, while public finances remain in disarray, unemployment remains high, and foreign investment and tourism are down following both the chaos of the revolution and the 2015 terrorist attacks.

The subsidized economy

Tunisia has had significant subsidies in place in most of its crucial industries since the 1970s, and any attempts at reform have been met with stiff resistance. According to The World Bank, subsidies are core to Tunisia's development model.[171] The population of Tunisia is highly sensitive to price changes on essentials, especially bread, as evidenced by the bread riots, which led to the fall of the Bourguiba regime. This has made reforming the subsidy system difficult. The existing model of subsidies "relies on untargeted food and energy subsidies, which have been proven to be unequitable and increasingly expensive."[172] Despite this, the subsidy system prevents an estimated 700,000 Tunisians from falling into poverty, making reform of such an entrenched institution difficult.[173]

The largest subsidies are reserved for energy, to ensure that the price of petrol and electricity remains affordable, followed by food products. Based on 2013 World Bank data, it was estimated that these subsidies accounted for 94 percent of the government's spending on social programs.[174] The government also invests highly in agricultural production, education, and tourism, but these are not classified as explicit subsidies on Tunisia's balance sheet.

Energy

The energy subsidy system, built during the 1970s after Tunisia's move away from socialist governing models, has had a central place in Tunisia's budget for decades, as reform was almost never on the table. During the Ben Ali regime, subsidies remained stable and constant. For an authoritarian regime that lacked legitimacy in the eyes of many Tunisians, harming their standard of living, even if in the short term, through subsidy reform was unjustifiable.[175] The regime governed on tacit consent, in which it made concessions to appease the public in order to remain in power. The generous subsidy system was seen as one of these sacrosanct concessions.

Energy subsidies in Tunisia do not primarily benefit the poorest. The blanket nature of the subsidies, which are both unlimited and untargeted by need, has meant that high energy consumers receive the greatest share of the returns. Poorer households consume considerably less electricity than urban, middle-class ones, and thus capture far less of the subsidy. In 2014, The World Bank estimated that the bottom four income deciles captured only 29 percent of the total energy subsidy.[176] The post-revolution interim government acknowledged this skew toward the middle class in its efforts to reform the subsidy system. Its hand had been forced to make a change as a result of the currency shock brought about by the revolution.

The interim government desired a managed transition that would allow Tunisia's domestic energy market to reflect global prices. This transition, only partially completed, ballooned the cost of energy subsidies on the balance sheet. Prices for energy, gasoline, and diesel rose by 7 percent in both September 2012 and March 2013, though this did little to improve public expenditure.[177] In addition,

> Energy subsidies to cement companies were halved in January 2014 and fully removed in June 2014. Electricity tariffs on low- and medium-voltage consumers were increased in a two-step process, by 10% in January 2014 and another 10% in May 2014. The government introduced a lifeline electricity tariff for households consuming less than 100 kWh per month in 2014.[178]

These changes were combined with new social programs, such as social housing and tax deductions for the poor, which were aimed at offsetting the costs of energy on its poorest citizens.

Despite the interim government's caution in reforming energy subsidies extensively, the IMF in 2014 applauded their efforts, arguing that the comprehensiveness of their plans justified the gradualness of the change. Proposals by the interim government to change electricity subsidies touched the entire breadth of the complex subsidy system in place.

After elections in 2014, the new government worked with the IMF to increasingly reform its fuel subsidies, but left electricity more or less unchanged since the initial enthusiasm for reform. Fuel price reform became more politically tangible as the price of crude oil dropped dramatically at the end of 2014. In January 2016, a change to the structure of fuel prices was enacted which levied greater excises on gasoline, kerosene, and other fuel products, while dropping the price of diesel by 20 percent.[179] In July 2016, a symmetric fuel price mechanism was adopted, which was to ensure that the cost of outputs better reflected changes in the price of inputs.

As of January 2019, the cost of 1 liter of petrol in Tunis sits at 1.985 dinars (USD 0.67), following four consecutive price increases in 2018, which began the year at 1.75 dinars

(USD 0.59 USD).[180] In the global context, this is incredibly low, with the world average being USD 1.09 per liter as of January 2019.[181] Tunisia's gas prices are lower than almost every other North African nation, aside from Sudan and Ethiopia, and are comparable to more oil-rich Middle Eastern nations. The price rises in 2018 were met with fierce resistance, but were concessions made to the IMF after extensive debt negotiations.

While a comprehensive medium-term plan has been developed to combine subsidy elimination, a gradual price change to reflect global prices, and targeted interventions to alleviate poverty, little has been enacted regarding electricity.[182] Unlike the price of fuel, which was raised in 2018, the price of electricity was left unchanged, much to the chagrin of the IMF. Electricity prices sat at 0.21 dinars (USD 0.07) per kWh as of June 2018, compared to a global average of USD 0.14 per kWh. Tunisia is more in line with the rest of the MENA region with these low prices, as almost all of its neighbors heavily subsidize electricity. According to crowd-sourced data from Tunis, the average basic monthly utility bill for a single person living in an 85 square meter apartment is 105.61 dinars (USD 35.55), less than a quarter of the average cost across the OECD.[183]

Basic products

While energy subsidies have taken an increasing share of overall subsidies since the Arab Spring, subsidies for basic products such as food have been an untouchable staple of the Tunisian government's social policy. Bourguiba's vision of a self-sufficient agricultural sector made support for the domestic agricultural industry and generous subsidies for food distribution primary aspects of the government's program after the transition away from socialism. Even more so than energy subsidies, subsidies to food have created intense price sensitivities among the public, prompting mass backlash if touched.

Especially important to the Tunisian public is the price of bread, a core staple of the North African diet. This importance placed on bread can make or break a regime. Bread riots, as a result of subsidy restrictions in 1983, which doubled the price of cereal-based products including bread and couscous, played a pivotal role in weakening the Bourguiba regime and the rise of his successor Ben Ali. The riots were initiated in poverty-stricken regions far from Tunisia's urban districts, mostly by young men who had suffered from unemployment or the instability of seasonal work. Solidarity between students, the rioters, and Islamist opponents of the regime compounded its nationwide impact and prompted a violent response by the government. The lingering aftermath of the bread riots influenced the Ben Ali's regime to leave subsidies more or less intact.

A worsening fiscal situation, and general knowledge that most subsidies favored the wealthy, led to a gradual and careful reform of food subsidies between 1991 and 1993.[184] The government maintained subsidies for lower-quality bread products, but lifted any support for luxury wheat products, coupling this effort with strengthened social protection programs designed to aid the poor. The careful political weight that the government placed on awareness among rural citizens and the poor indicates the lasting impact of the bread riots on Tunisian political psychology.

Subsidies as a whole increased their primacy in the final years of the Ben Ali regime, and food subsidies were no exception. A report found that the government's support for food was detrimental to Tunisia as a whole.[185] Tunisia's priority for food independence has meant that an unproductive agricultural sector produces food to be sold at below market cost to Tunisians, when they could import food from neighboring countries for less. This has kept the facade of low prices a heavy burden on taxpayers. The consumer subsidies for food cannot be disentangled from this concern for Tunisia's agricultural sector, which compounds the inefficiencies of the system.

Post-revolution, Tunisia's government has left nominal food subsidies largely untouched, meaning that they are highly variable in cost as a result of currency fluctuations. The cost of food has nonetheless increased through an increase in the nation's valued-added tax (VAT). In early 2018, this prompted protests due to the costs borne by poor Tunisians, some of them violent.[186] The rise in VAT on both basic and luxury goods, such as cars, phones, and internet connectivity, was a shock to many Tunisians, leading to widespread vandalism and the petrol bombing of police stations. The government reacted with concessions, pledging 170 million dinars (USD 57.2 million) to aid the poor.

This largely tumultuous experience has kept food prices more or less stable, and far below global costs. Tunisia has the lowest cost of bread in the world as of January 2019 at 0.36 dinars (USD 0.11). The average across all cities in Europe in the same period is USD 1.27, more than 1,100 percent higher. Bovine products, extremely unproductive aspects of the country's agricultural sector, are nonetheless quite affordable. In Tunis, a liter of milk costs 1.23 dinars (USD 0.41), while a kilogram of beef costs 22.42 dinars (USD 7.55).[187]

Much criticism has been targeted at the government for continuing with general subsidies on foods, which has allowed exploitation by non-Tunisians who purchase cheap food within the nation's borders and then transport the food to sell at higher prices elsewhere at the cost of the taxpayer. The current situation, however, makes it quite difficult to expect significant reform anytime soon.

Cost to public finances

Before the Tunisian revolution, subsidies stood at approximately 2 percent of GDP, hitting 2.5 percent just before the revolution in 2011. In the wake of the revolution, these subsidies ballooned, reaching 7 percent of GDP in 2013.[188] As global oil prices increased around 2011, the Central Bank lifted Tunisia's fixed exchange rate policies to remain competitive, but the devaluation contributed to a greater subsidy bill.[189] Annual budget deficits before the revolution hovered around 3 percent of GDP, but spiked to 6.8 percent of GDP following the revolution in 2012, and standing at 5.3 percent of GDP as of 2017, with its 2017 debt to GDP ratio sitting at 69.2 percent.[190]

While the continued instability following the revolution has increased the instability of the country's public finances, it is this same pressure that has increased the vulnerability of Tunisia's population. An exchange rate of 1.4 dinar to USD in 2011 before the revolution, it has since been devalued to a rate of 3.32 dinar to USD as of February 2019.[191] Inflation has also increased as a result of economic instability, though drastic measures taken by the Central Bank have prevented it from reaching double digits.[192]

Extrapolating from these findings, it is clear that the economy of Tunisia following the revolution has been driven almost exclusively by consumption[193] The fallout of the 2015 terrorist attacks harmed the tourism industry and accelerated investor flight, and despite the interventions of the Central Bank, exports have not picked up. The subsidization of the economy has helped Tunisians continue to spend domestically, while all indicators remain poor, and market processes are unable to improve productivity or the attractiveness of the country for foreign investment. As a result of meager productivity and investment, Tunisia has lost its catch up growth. Tunisia's GDP per capita is below 29 percent of the OECD average, being above 30 percent before the revolution.[194]

The failure of the country to implement reforms at the pace encouraged by the IMF has created longer-term strains on economic recovery. Tunisia was urged to implement drastic and urgent reforms in 2018 as unemployment remained very high, and the government expanded public sector jobs to appease its citizens.[195]

As subsidies continue to eat into large portions of the government's finances, strategic investments in improving Tunisia's attractiveness remain unlikely. Its otherwise skilled workforce is unable to be utilized and the incentives to modernize its economy remain non-existent. The longer this burden remains on Tunisia's economy, the more entrenched these fiscal problems will become, making reform down the line more unlikely.

Oman

History and political context

Oman is a sight of pre-historic human activity, and its geographic desirability at the mouth of the Persian Gulf, where the Arabian Sea forms its coast to the southeast, and the Gulf of Oman to its northeast, has resulted in numerous conquests and invasions over the centuries. From 1892 to 1971, the Sultanate of Muscat and Oman, which encompassed modern-day Oman, and parts of the United Arab Emirates and Pakistan, was a British Protectorate and an absolute monarchy governed by the Al Said dynasty.[196]

The Sultanate featured internal tensions between the more secular coastal parts of Muscat, and the conservative, orthodox Muslim parts of inland Oman. This conflict was exacerbated by the discovery of oil in the Persian Gulf and the growing economic value it had to Middle Eastern economies following World War II. In 1954, an insurgency led by Ghalib Bin Ali, the last Imam of Oman, was launched to limit the power of the Muscat Sultanate who granted oil drilling rights to the Iraq Petroleum Company, and would have profited from oil in the inland territory.[197] After being suppressed for a few years, the insurgency was again launched in 1957 with support from Saudi Arabia and Egypt, though British relations with the Sultan led to them supporting him in the conflict. The insurgency was put down in 1959.

Only three years later, however, the Dhofar Rebellion began, a long conflict between the Sultanate and Communist rebels who had initially collected weapons from the failed insurgencies, but went on to receive the support of China and the Soviet Union.[198] The British grew increasingly frustrated with Sultan Said bin Taimur's ability to control rebellions and reflect national unity. In 1968, the British formally announced their withdrawal from the Gulf region by 1971, though relations with Oman were stronger and longer lasting than with other Gulf countries.[199] Immediately before its withdrawal, the British supported a palace coup, replacing Said bin Taimur with his Western-educated son, Qaboos bin Said al Said. One of his first acts on ascension was to rename the Sultanate of Muscat and Oman as the Sultanate of Oman in a show of national unity, though Muscat remained the capital city. The country remains an absolute monarchy and Qaboos bin Said al Said has remained its leader, making him the longest-serving current leader in the Middle East.

With British support, a renewed counterinsurgency campaign began after the coup, and a program of modernization was undertaken to support Oman's harmony and prosperity. The Dhofar Rebellion was later put down in 1976.[200] Oman rapidly advanced women's rights, as well as increasing investments in health, education, and welfare. Oman experienced massive economic growth during the 1970s and into the 1990s, with moderate sustainable growth throughout the 1980s.[201] The government complied with trade liberalization requirements throughout the 1990s to accede to the World Trade Organization, where it received member status in 2000.[202] Investments in technology have been a high priority of the government, especially given the difficulty of oil drilling in a country with as complex a geography as Oman. Oman's growing prosperity allowed the government to expand its provision of services to its population, a common practice in oil-rich Middle Eastern nations. From energy to healthcare to basic needs like food, public subsidies insulated Oman's residents from global market and price fluctuations.

In recent years, the government has faced financial hardship as a result of this generosity, mostly due to the declining oil prices since the end of 2014. Initiatives to relieve Oman's dependence on oil and an expansive foreign labor force through investments in economic diversification, job creation, and training programs have taken shape. While Oman seeks to be a global player, complying extensively with international law, maintaining strong diplomatic relationships with others, and boasting strong economic growth, it has nonetheless had a strongly nationalized economy.

During the Arab Spring, riots in Oman were not as intense or violent as those in Tunisia and other neighboring states, but focused instead on the lack of good jobs for Omani citizens. In response, the government engaged in a large job creation program led by the private sector, and has increasingly supported initiatives to privatize its energy holdings. In 2017, it is estimated that 53 percent of Oman's GDP was from the services sector, resembling many modern, advanced economies.[203]

The subsidized economy

Historically, Oman had one of the lowest rates of subsidies in the Gulf Coast, relying on high oil revenues and an expansive foreign workforce, but this changed as a result of a process referred to as *Omanization*.[204] This was a practice in which the Omani government would invest in domestic citizens to diversify the economy and make more good jobs accessible to locals, not only by investing in education and healthcare, but also through subsidizing basic necessities such as food and water. As oil prices rose toward the end of the 2000s and into the early 2010s, the percentage of the public budget dedicated to subsidies ballooned. In 2011, when expenses from transfers were highest, nearly 26 percent of the budget was dedicated to subsidies and other transfers.[205] The recent slump in global oil prices has, however, forced a rethink of Oman's public finances and generosity to its citizens. The government has since gradually phased out certain subsidies and undertaken a broader reform mechanism.

While not as oil rich as some of its neighboring nations, Oman has nonetheless managed to leverage its oil production to undertake significant modernization projects over the last 30 years, leading to a high standard of living, despite an untrained workforce. Among the public expenses of Oman, the highest shares are taken by education, health, housing, and welfare spending, while electricity subsidies continue to rise. The 2019 budget, which has still failed to balance the national budget, has nonetheless come a long way from the chaotic state of the public finances in 2015 following the oil price crash.

Energy

In 2012, prior to the oil price shock, electricity was provided to all citizens and workers in Oman at 26 percent of the market price, while gasoline was sold at 48 percent of the market price, leading to substantial dependence on government assistance.[206] As oil prices began to slump, the government was very anxious about reforming prices for fear of protests similar to those of neighboring countries during the Arab Spring. In 2015, one of the first actions taken was to double natural gas prices.[207]

In 2016, after the government realized that the oil slump would continue and result in sustained deficits, the Omani government launched a major initiative to balance its budget. In 2015, subsidies to oil products stood at 479.8 million riyals, falling to 17.1 million riyals in 2016, while electricity subsidies were cut by nearly 108 million riyals, dropping from 386.4 million to 278.8 million.[208] The government believed that the negative effects from the cuts to residents would be short-lived, and personal fiscal responsibility would return as a result of the transition.

In 2017, the government was faced with the growing problem of youth unemployment, which sat at 49 percent.[209] Many of these young people were adversely affected by subsidy reforms, as higher fuel costs were seen as jeopardizing their access to work. Public expenditure rose in 2017 by 800 million riyals, with electricity subsidy rising to 500 million riyals.[210]

A new fuel subsidy scheme was enacted in 2018 to ensure support for the vulnerable, while also maintaining fiscal responsibility through more discretionary targeting. The new National Subsidy System (NSS) allows Omanis over 18 years of age who own a vehicle of any type and have a total monthly income under 600 riyals to receive a subsidy card.[211] When first released, the card enabled holders to purchase up to 200 liters of Mogas 91, the national regular-grade fuel, for a guaranteed rate of 0.18 riyals per liter. In August 2018, however, the maximum salary was raised to 950 riyals a month, making 69 percent of working Omanis eligible for the NSS. As of January 2019, nearly 328,000 people are on the NSS system, receiving subsidized fuel.[212] While the overall costs of this system are lower than previous fuel subsidies, as it has removed expatriate workers who continue to make up most of Oman's labor force, it nonetheless remains costly for the government.

While reforms to electricity subsidies along the lines of fuel reform were on the table in 2018, talks have stalled. In 2018, the total cost of electricity subsidies ballooned to 550 million riyals.[213] Electricity demand has been growing in Oman, especially in urban areas, with the general favorability of electricity subsidies doing little to curb consumption. The 2019 budget included a 3 percent increase in the expected cost of electricity subsidies for the year.[214]

Oman has among the lowest fuel prices in the world even when exempted from fuel subsidies. At 0.21 riyals per liter it has the 18th cheapest fuel prices in the world according to global petrol prices, though most Omanis face nearly 15 percent lower prices.[215] Oman's willingness for fuel reform has been tempered by how accustomed its population has grown to generous government handouts.

Residential tariffs for electricity in Oman are 0.01 riyals per kWh for the first 3,000 kWhs, which then rises to 0.015 riyals for the next 2,000 kWhs, followed by 0.02 riyals for the following 2,000 kWhs, 0.025 riyals for the following 3,000 kWhs, and 0.03 riyals for everything over 10,000 kWhs[216]. In Muscat, the cost of basic utilities for a month sits at 21.84 riyals.[217]

Basic products

One of the most persistent subsidies in place in Oman has been support for water.[218] Middle Eastern nations are afflicted by constant water shortages, and one of the flagship aims of the government during development was to provide low-cost potable water to its citizens. The mandated low cost of water has, however, plagued the water infrastructure in Oman with a lack of self-sufficiency and development. Combined with subsidies to Oman's agricultural sector, it has been increasingly difficult for Oman to meet its demand for water given the subsidies, but reform is difficult due to the popular need for low-cost water.[219]

Water demand skyrocketed in Oman as a result of the low costs, and stands far above the international average. Oman's Public Authority for Electricity and Water reported that the nation "is expecting demand for residential water in Oman to reach 630mn m³ by 2025 against 215mn m³ in 2011, an increase of threefold."[220] This is 321 percent of the average per capita water consumption per day.[221] Water in Oman in 2013 cost 0.44 riyals (USD 1.14) per 1,000 liters for the first 5 million liters, a price far lower than any OECD nation.[222]

As demand continues to rise despite falling oil prices, the burden of the water subsidy on the government has increased. In 2016, the water subsidy rose by 3 percent as reforms were refused.[223] As opposed to subsidy reform, strategic investment in upgrading its desalination facilities has been undertaken to manage the country's water, an uncertain and costly procedure.

Water subsidies have been more or less untouchable, despite recommendations by analysts to raise the cost of water to curtail demand.[224] The nation has been less attached to its food subsidies, which came into effect more recently than the government's subsidization of water. Similar to rising water demand, food demand began to rise as the country became wealthier. The country only produced 2 percent of its cereal demands for staple foods in 2012.[225] Oman has struggled to improve its food security as its water demand has skyrocketed, leaving little for extra agricultural capacity. The reliance on food imports, rather than domestically subsidized production, has in contrast to water, however, enabled greater subsidy reform. In the first quarter of 2015, a 173 million riyal (USD 443 million) cut to subsidies was made, mainly targeting foods such as rice, flour, and sugar.[226] Cuts to food were expanded in 2016.[227]

Food prices today in Oman are much more in line with global costs. A loaf of white bread in Muscat costs 0.41 riyals, while 1 liter of milk costs 0.59 riyals, and 1 kilogram of beef round costs 3.20 riyals. The new prices stand in stark contrast to the pre-oil collapse costs.[228]

Cost to public finances

Despite failing to resolve much of its fiscal tensions, the Government of Oman has come a long way in handling the financial burden caused by declining oil prices. Budget deficits surpassed 15 percent of GDP in 2015, reaching 20.8 percent of GDP in 2016, but have since declined, with expectations of a 2019 deficit just above 10 percent of GDP, mostly achieved by reduced expenditures.[229] Stopgap financing through oil reserves had been utilized in 2015 to help assuage the deficit, though debt has risen as a result of foreign borrowing. The debt to GDP ratio in 2014 was 5 percent, while it is projected to hit 50 percent of GDP by 2020.[230]

While Oman has struggled with its public finances as a result of a decline in oil prices, this has not triggered a crisis on the scale of some of its neighbors. The Omani riyal's value has stayed more or less constant, and the country's sovereign wealth fund has been leveraged in diversification initiatives.[231] Subsidy reforms have focused on targeting Omani citizens, which while saving money and preventing a rise in poverty, have failed to produce the degree of productivity increase the nation requires. The IMF has warned that Oman's plan for managing its budget deficit still relies too much on oil prices picking up in the near future.[232]

For Oman to fully realize its ambitions of a diversified and "Omanized" economy, its continued subsidization of its citizens has prevented economic reallocation and more productive investments in industry. Half of all Omanis work in the state sector, which provides higher-paying jobs than the private sector, though a hiring freeze triggered by low oil prices jeopardizes this continued reliance on Omani welfare.[233] Unless significant reforms to subsidies are made, the correct incentives to improve Oman's economy will not be in place.

Conclusion

An analysis of Tunisia and Oman reveals the degree to which entrenched subsidies create dependence on state aid, which in turn limits a country's ability to respond to economic shocks. Despite attempts by the governments of both nations to respond to changing global economic situations, the political economy of subsidies raises thorny issues. Rapid adjustment in a state that is so heavily involved in its economy proves to be impossible.

Global competitiveness is often harmed by insufficient incentives for domestic citizens to respond to global market fluctuations, which makes productivity growth hard to achieve in times of downturn, further doubling down on negative economic situations. Given that subsidies in MENA nations often affect essentials, such as electricity, fuel, food, and water, the ability for vital inputs to be reallocated to more productive uses is harmed by high residential consumption and political unwillingness to reform.

49. PUBLIC-PRIVATE PARTNERSHIPS

The analogy described in the Introduction assimilates the competitiveness race to a cyclist riding his or her bicycle through a paved road. The cyclist is the private sector, the bike is the government, and the road includes both the physical and intangible infrastructures of the economy. I hope the comparison helps the reader understand that, unless the public and the private sectors collaborate and work together, neither one of them is able to make a country successful.

Public–private partnerships can take several forms. In Chapter 57, I discuss how the Sustainable Development Goals are implemented through partnerships and I describe some recent experiences. More generally speaking, I want to stress in this chapter that the future of the capitalist system goes by redefining the role of the state, from a mere agent preserving the institutional and legal environment. There are no pure capitalist systems any more, where the invisible hand of the market operates freely subject to the constraints set by the legal environment. This is even more true in the West, compared to China for example. In April 2012, Harvard historian Niall Fergusson stated that "China is leading a shift away from the state, but the developed world is moving in the wrong direction."[234] I think it is worth stopping for a second to reflect about what model (or models) of capitalism are thriving in the 21st century, particularly in relation to the traditional, hands-off capitalism where the government only monitors, but does not interfere in the productive economy too much.

Let us remember that the basic pillar of the capitalist system as we have got to know it during the 20th century is based on three pillars:

- Perfect competition, where monopolies are undesirable unless forced by the conditions of a particular market.
- Passive governments vis-à-vis businesses, and where regulation only provides guidelines and rules of behavior.

- Shareholder-value maximization as the objective value of a firm, and with social objectives as a means and not as goals.

This chapter shows examples of how nations are redefining such concepts and, in parallel, redefining the role of the private sector. From China to Saudi Arabia and many others, it is worth noting that more and more, governments are intervening in businesses, creating social pressure on corporations to incorporate "shared value" objectives, resulting in an expansion of the boundaries of firms.

The Chinese ecosystem: the role of the state

Shaanxi, Northwest China: a discovery

The largest city of the Shaanxi Province in northwest China—Shaanxi is not to be confused with its neighbor Shanxi[235]—as well as the region's main educational and industrial hub, is called Xi'an. The city of Xi'an, however, is mostly known as the oldest of the Chinese four great ancient capitals.[236] Through history, Xi'an was the starting point of the Silk Road over which merchants used to travel to bring goods between China and Europe.

As I listen to the guide's inspired voice, images overflow my mind. Xi'an is the birthplace of the ancient Chinese civilization, home to age-old attractions like the City Wall and the Terracotta Warriors, and a place deeply steeped in the traditional culture. But we are not going to visit these fascinating historical sites today. We're en route to a village called Lining, famous for apple orchards, in order to meet some of the local farmers.

Our car ride shouldn't take long—Lining is about 65 kilometers northwest of Xi'an. As we leave the cityscape behind, the guide tells me more about the region we're driving through. His English is near-perfect, with a barely notable accent; he paints a colorful picture of the area and its inhabitants, and I find myself captivated by his tales.

Shaanxi is inhabited by approximately 39 million people who live in an area of about 205,000 square kilometers—slightly more populous than Canada; the province is similar in size to Kyrgyzstan and Senegal. Looking at a map of China, Shaanxi is 880 kilometers long with a width that varies between 160 and 490 kilometers; the province is particularly narrow in its less populated northern half. From south to north, Shaanxi is naturally divided into three parts by the North Mountains and the Qin Mountains. The northern area is called Shanbei and the southern Shannan. Xi'an is located in the central part of Shaanxi, called Guanzhong.

In addition to being an important part of the country's cultural history, Shaanxi is also the province that borders most other provinces in China.[237] Two of the longest rivers in Asia, the Yangtze River and the Yellow River, run through Shaanxi; the yellow loess from the silt of the Yellow River covers large areas. Due to widespread soil erosion, only about one-third of the province is under cultivation and, over the last decades, the government has tried various measures to reverse its effects.[238]

Despite the terrain challenges and a great variety of climates—from temperate continental to temperate monsoon and subtropical—Shaanxi is one of China's major agricultural bases. It is famous for producing grain, vegetables, cured tobacco, and Chinese chestnuts, as well as being a major production and processing center for fruits. In fact, the specific physiographic features and climate conditions in the northern and central parts make Shaanxi one of the world's most suitable regions for fruit, particularly apples.

Apple farming and its impact on the farmers' lives

Together with two other provinces, Shandong and Henan, Shaanxi grows a staggering quarter of the world's apple production. It has been at the forefront of China's fruit production since 2011; by 2018, it had reached 60 percent of the 1.2 million hectares devoted to apple plantation nationwide.

Consequently, apple production is the local farmers' main source of income in Shaanxi. The per-capita net income, however, is still behind the national average, which is reflective of China as a whole. Although about 35 percent of the population works in agriculture, rural incomes are much smaller compared to those in urban areas.

Investigating this disparity as well as learning more about the farmers' lives is the reason for my trip to Lining. The journey is the starting point for research about rural development, the financial help the government provides to the most vulnerable part of its population, and the modern Chinese economy.

As we approach our destination, apple orchards line the horizon as far as the eye can see. My guide introduces me to a farmer called Zhou Yan. He is a petite, slender-framed man of indiscernible age. He seems to be well over 60, yet I can't tell for sure—his weathered face might be a reflection of having worked the land alongside his parents since he was a boy.

I learn that Zhou Yan's orchard is small: about 0.8 hectares, or 12 mu.[239] Technically speaking, the orchard is not really his. The current land laws are a holdover from the commune era and stipulate that all land belongs to the state; farmers are only able to lease it from their local governments. The 2008 reform[240] introduced some improvements to this law. While selling and mortgaging land is still prohibited, farmers are now allowed to lease contractual rights to other farmers or to agricultural companies. These rights are derived from the local government or the collective landowner for 30 years and can be further leased to others.

In practice, China's farmers still do not control "their" land's fate, even if it has been worked by their family for generations.

I ask Zhou Yan what apple farming means to him and his family. He shares that they used to grow corn and wheat but, like many others in the area, they changed crops when they learned that the local weather and soil conditions were optimal for apple growing. In spite of the challenges they face with their crop—from natural disasters to fluctuations in apple prices due to oversupply—their average yearly income has since increased tenfold, resulting in a significant improvement in their living conditions. Before developing their orchard, Zhou Yan's family struggled to cover their monthly expenses as most of what they made went on land taxes and lease fees; he himself never got a higher education since his parents couldn't afford it. Nowadays, the family lives in a bigger house with electricity, they own more possessions, and Zhou Yan's two children are studying at a university in Xi'an.

Farmers in this part of Shaanxi started growing apples after China opened its agriculture to the broader export market in the 1980s; since then, large areas of arable land have been gradually converted into orchards. This transformation changed many farmers' lives due to the fact that apples produce higher economic returns. These days, China as a whole produces about half of the world's supply of apples and the government is encouraging farmers to further optimize apple production. The state's efforts to support modernization include updated rural policies as well as improved financing and agricultural bank loan opportunities.

Zhou Yan is open to modernization—he'd like to redesign his orchard in order to boost productivity—and is in need of financial help to move forward. While some farmers prefer to get loans from private lenders such as friends and relatives, he has decided to resort to a bank. He wants to apply for a working capital loan from one of China's so-called Big Four,[241] the Agricultural Bank of China.

Agricultural loans in China: ABC bank example

The Agricultural Bank of China is the third-largest bank in the world and a pioneer in inclusive finance in China. The bank was established in 1951, and when it went public in 2010, it was the world's biggest initial public offering.

As a major state-controlled publicly listed bank, ABC positions itself as "the Bank of the Party, the nation, the people and the market."[242] While ABC provides urban commercial banking services both within China and overseas, its core mission—and political responsibility—is to provide financial services for rural development. In that respect, the bank focuses on three areas: basic financial services in rural areas, financial poverty alleviation, and loans to rural households.

The commitment to inclusive financial services that benefit farmers, in turn, enhances ABC's brand reputation and social image; in fact, ABC is the only bank among the Big Four that serves *Sannong* development. *Sannong* issues are those relating to agriculture, rural areas, and farmers; they are considered vital to China's economic prosperity and social stability.

Between the 1950s and the 1970s, China's agricultural system was egalitarian: farmers were compensated based on a complex point system linked to their performance. Monitoring agricultural production, however, was difficult, and farmers' income became stagnant because there were no incentives as motivation to work hard. At the end of the 1970s, the Communist Party introduced an incentivized production system and gave farmers the autonomy to grow the types of crops based on market demand. The government then summed up the issues relating to agriculture, rural areas, and farmers in the phrase "*Sannong* issues" (San 三 means "three," and all three words begin with the Chinese character Nong 农).

In China, like in most developing countries, there is a polarity between urban and rural areas. One of the major setbacks for socioeconomic rural development is a lack of basic financial services and difficulty accessing loans. Therefore, ABC's financial services, adherent to the *Sannong* policies, aim to close that gap. In addition to financing agricultural operations, the bank also supports housing, education, and healthcare initiatives—those that improve the rural infrastructure and farmers' lives.

ABC aims to serve a huge and widely dispersed rural population,[243] which makes setting up traditional physical bank outlets highly challenging. As a consequence, large parts of China have either very rudimentary credit services or no credit services at all. This is not a problem for Zhou Yan and the other farmers in the village, given Lining's proximity to Xi'an. However, even areas where credit is in supply could be further aided with credit access and delivery. In order to address this issue, ABC has deployed self-service banks in rural townships and developed mobile financial services.

Compared to other loan products, farmer loans require more staff to process: it typically takes two credit officers to review one loan application. Additionally, while the costs and risks of agriculture financing are somewhat made up for by the lower interest rate on deposits and the higher interest rate on loans, agriculture financing is, ultimately, less profitable than urban retail and corporate banking.

For ABC, nonetheless, the road to becoming a world-class commercial bank leads through ventures that improve rural conditions and through creating a climate that enables both *Sannong* and sustainable development.

The modern Chinese business ecosystem

To better understand the social role of ABC bank, one needs to examine the particularities of the modern Chinese business ecosystem. At times called "capitalism with Chinese characteristics," this continually evolving system is, in fact, very different from capitalism in the West.

The phrase "invisible hand," originally introduced by Adam Smith,[244] represents the essence of Western capitalism: it is the invisible hand of the market that operates without government's involvement. Adam Smith believed in a free market where everyone works in his or her own interest. His is the so-called "perfect model," one that maximizes the profit and cash flow, social surplus, and shareholder value, and in which the market regulates itself by means of competition, supply and demand, and self-interest.

Such capitalism model rests on three pillars: "perfect competition" in which monopolies are viewed as bad; passive governments whose regulation provides only guidelines; and shareholder value maximization where social objectives are not a goal but simply a means.

This is not the case with the ecosystem in China. Rather than allowing businesses to freely operate within the parameters of its regulations, the Chinese government, instead, grants monopoly power to companies within an industry. That way, the government dominates a number of industries—for example, banking and technology—through state-owned enterprises.

In this particular economic model, there is a triangle between the state, the companies, and the public. The state provides businesses with monopoly power, license to operate, financial resources, and subsidies; the businesses provide services to customers; and the customers, finally, support the state. The strength of the connection between the government and the businesses is, therefore, very strong in China, although the share of state-owned enterprises in industrial output has been dropping as the country steadily moves toward free-market capitalism.

In the case of ABC bank, not only does the Chinese state own most of ABC's shares but it also protects the bank's competitive position. Moreover, the state caps ABC's interest rates and subsidizes the non-performing loans. Strategically, ABC's urban banking operations buffer the lower profit and higher risks of *Sannong* banking operations. Lending to agricultural enterprises not only reduces ABC's credit risks but also provides a sustainable and long-term solution to alleviate poverty and improve the livelihood of farmers. Providing small amount loans to farmers alone cannot continue to grow the business or achieve business sustainability.

All these measures exemplify that it is, in fact, in the government's best interest to have farmers like Zhou Yan bank with ABC.

State-directed capitalism is closely related to a quasi-monopoly market structure that focuses on social monopolies and that some advanced Western economies have been moving toward. In such a model, governments assume a greater economic role by allowing themselves to intervene in business. This involvement creates social pressure on corporations and, as a consequence, the public, the corporations, and the government develop "shared value" objectives. As a result, companies expand their boundaries—thus maximizing business sustainability and social welfare—and maintain their competitive position.

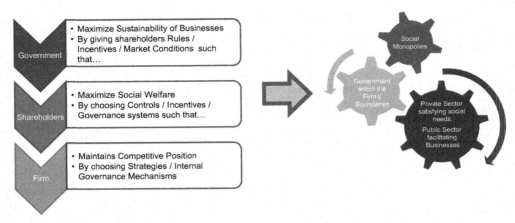

Figure 4.16 The Chinese Business Ecosystem

This process enables the creation of social monopolies, among which there is no objective competition. Figure 4.16 illustrates this process.

When a market is based on social monopolies, incentives are in equilibrium as the public and the private sectors work together to create a win-win economic situation. The role of government becomes preserving positions of market dominance in exchange for social investments; the companies further contribute to society in exchange for government incentives. Finally, this process teaches shareholders that maximizing social welfare leads to their value maximization as well.

The role of the state in granting a license to operate: Saudi Arabia

Hamad Al Otaibi works as a taxi driver in Jeddah, a major city in the Kingdom of Saudi Arabia (KSA). His dream had always been to become financially independent and to own his own vehicle, even if this meant joining the other 35,000 taxi drivers[245] populating the roads of Jeddah, one of the most dangerous cities in the world to drive a car.[246]

In 2003, taxi companies were ordered by Royal Decree to increase the number of Saudis employed in the sector. This would have given Hamad a clear advantage over Indian or Pakistani drivers who had dominated the market until then.[247] But Hamad, like many of his friends, was not interested in working for a taxi company. Not because the decree had created an excess of job openings for nationals, which meant he could choose a much better-paying job, but because it would be easier for Hamad to purchase his own car if he was not working for someone else.

Hamad's life started to change the moment he saw an advertisement that read: Job Opportunities for Young Saudi Males through the Taxi Ownership Program at Bab Rizq Jameel.[248]

The "Taxi Ownership Program" was started by Bab Rizq Jameel (part of the Abdul Latif Jameel Community Services that focused on job creation) in 2002. The program participants could own their vehicle after paying for it by easy monthly installments.[249] The only requirements to benefit from the program were to be a Saudi national and to make a down payment of SR 3,000 (Saudi riyals) (about USD 730). For Hamad, this was great, because over time he could own more than one car, provided he had paid off the installments on his first vehicle.

At 27 years old, Hamad was happily driving his Toyota Camry as he had been doing for the last two years, and he was bringing home about SR 5,000 per month (about USD 1,300), which was enough to support his mother, younger sister, and brother.

Abdul Atif Jameel

Founded in 1945 by the late Sheikh Abdul Latif Jameel, Abdul Latif Jameel (ALJ) started with a single Toyota dealership in Jeddah. The group became the sole distributor of Toyota Motor Company (TMC) vehicles in 1955. This monopoly was not granted by Toyota but by His Majesty Saud bin Abdul-Aziz Al Saud. The exclusivity included service and spare parts. With the discovery of massive oil reserves in the country in 1938, the Kingdom had already started a growth trend that would be unstoppable in the years to come. Moreover, the lack of public transportation in a country that spanned 2.15 million square kilometers (4 times Spain, 50 times Switzerland) meant that a monopoly on automobile distribution was certainly a valuable concession.

In 1972, ALJ expanded into customer finance, shipping, and general trading services. The car financing arm of the group, United Installment Sales (UIS), was started in 1979 to only serve Toyota customers. ALJ Co Ltd, the parent company, was formed in 1980. Since then, it has grown into an internationally diversified group, with operations in the United Kingdom, Monaco, Morocco, Algeria, Egypt, Sudan, Syria, China, and Japan. It further expanded into healthcare, hotels, consumer electronics, real estate, media communications, and even air-conditioning. Every company in the group was typically headed by one of the Abdul Latif Jameel family members.

Sheikh Abdul Latif Jameel passed away in 1993 and since then his son Sheikh Muhammed Abdul Latif Jameel has been running the group. The automobile division is obviously the largest and the most profitable. In 2007, ALJ was ranked Toyota's 7th largest distributor worldwide. It has a strong presence in the Kingdom, as well as in Syria, Morocco, Algeria, and Turkey. It also owns dealerships in China, Monte Carlo, Germany, and the UK. In addition, ALJ is the exclusive distributor for all Lexus vehicles in the KSA, and since November 2004 it has been the sole distributor of Daihatsu vehicles and parts in the KSA, Syria, Morocco, Algeria, Sudan, Egypt, and Turkey.[250] Since 2003, ALJ has had a technical agreement with TMC to produce (and distribute) all accessories for Toyota cars as well. ALJ became the sole distributor of Toyota in Turkey in 2009.

By the beginning of 2012, ALJ was the largest private company in the KSA and the largest Toyota distributor in the Middle East. Other ALJ businesses are also leaders in their corresponding markets. UIS is currently the market leader in installment sales and leasing services to the Saudi market. It operates with a strong network of over 200 branches in the KSA. The company is not publicly listed.

Strong company values

This statement by the company's president is strongly incorporated into ALJ's culture. ALJ is recognized in the Kingdom as equivalent to "socially responsible," employees are referred to as "associates," and customers are known as "guests." The company's mission is to "Empower our associates to provide delightful guest experiences, drive sustainable growth & make a difference to everyday life."[251] Not surprisingly, ALJ's values are "respect, improve, pioneer, empower." However, neither ALJ's guests nor its associates include women. ALJ does not employ women, and women do not usually buy cars, at least not directly, because they are not allowed to drive in Saudi Arabia.[252] Even though the KSA does not have a written ban on women driving, Saudi law requires citizens to use a locally issued license while in the country. But such licenses are not issued to women, which effectively makes it illegal for women to drive. Consequently, women are forced to hire personal drivers (usually immigrants from South Asia) as full-time employees. Ironically for a company that does not employ women, ALJ has endowed a Poverty Chair at the Massachusetts Institute of Technology (MIT), currently held by a female professor.

The KSA is the Middle East's largest importer of motor vehicles[253] and auto parts and the largest car market in the region. Saudi Arabia is expected to enjoy a GDP compound annual growth rate (CAGR) of 4 percent in that period, with a slightly growing population (from 26 million at the end of 2009 to about 33 million in 2017).

At the end of 2016, Japanese brands accounted for 38 percent of sales, South Korean brands for 31 percent, with the rest corresponding to auto makers from the United States, Germany, France, and Malaysia. TMC (and consequently ALJ) dominates the market with a share of around 31 percent.[254]

TMC's Australian unit, Toyota Motor Corporation Australia (TMCA), exported its 500,000th vehicle to Saudi Arabia on October 21, 2010, achieving an export milestone. The subsidiary shipped the Toyota Camry from Melbourne as part of a shipment of about 1,500 Australian-produced Camry and Aurion vehicles destined for Saudi Arabian dealerships.

ALJ Group has three major competitors. Al-Jazirah, Ford's importer-dealer in the KSA, is currently the exclusive distributor of Ford and Lincoln in the country. Al-Jazirah's market share is almost 5 percent, still far below ALJ's. Aljomaih Automotive Company (AAC) is the largest GM dealer in the Middle East, with a 12 percent market share in the KSA. Finally, Al-Hamrani United Company (AUC) is a (non-exclusive) distributor of Nissan vehicles and holds an estimated 8 percent market share. Although relatively small, AUC is strong in the central province (which includes the capital Riyadh), with over 30 percent of the province's market share.

In 2003, ALJ established Community Initiatives (ALJCI) to centralize its community investments and support the many initiatives with which the group had to deal. Fundamentally, ALJCI's objective was to create new opportunities for young entrepreneurs. These included:

- Assisting young Saudis (male and female) to obtain job opportunities.
- Providing training programs supported with interest-free loans.
- Cooperating with the government and the private sector to alleviate poverty and reduce the level of unemployment.
- Supporting small businesses and assisting the owners to achieve and develop their projects.[255]

Thus, ALJ's view of corporate social responsibility (CSR) was different to how it was viewed in the West, even in concepts that were predicated as "new." Michael Porter's influential article is an example of the current view on CSR:

Companies must take the lead in bringing business and society back together. [...] The solution lies in the principle of shared value, which involves creating economic value in a way that also creates value for society by addressing its needs and challenges. Businesses must reconnect company success with social progress. Shared value is not social responsibility, philanthropy, or even sustainability, but a new way to achieve success.[...] Shared value, then, is not about personal values.[256]

Sheikh Mohammed Abdul Latif Jameel, president of ALJCI, summarized his thinking as follows:

> My father taught me an important lesson in running a business: Never to forget that life is not just about you—it is about what you can do for others. Our company should always look for ways to help societies help themselves, in a business-like – and therefore sustainable – way. We hear much talk about «Corporate Social Responsibility». I do not like this expression. It makes responsibility sound like an obligation. It is not. It is a privilege and makes it sound like an issue for the business. For me, and for everyone who works with me, it is more than that—it is personal. Which is as it should be.[257]

ALJ's approach was neither philanthropic nor profit-seeking. Rather than providing local charities with donations in the form of money or food, ALJ's initiatives were focused on allowing individuals to grow into active members of society and eventually benefit the community.[258] The company's 2011 goal was to create 50,000 jobs by investing in several initiatives:

- Bab Rizq Jameel, seeking to create job opportunities for the youth. Its goal is to create 500,000 job opportunities by the year 2015 through several programs: training and employment, taxi ownership (the program that Hamad Al Otaibi benefitted from), truck ownership, small business,[259] productive household program for women (to start their own micro project), and franchising support.
- Education and training, mostly consisting of scholarship programs at secondary, higher secondary, and university level.
- Health and social programs, for example by financing hospitals and health centers. ALJCI also pioneered the "Family Day Initiative for Prisoners," which allows family members of prison inmates to maintain relationships.[260] ALJCI built 44 living units in the Briman Prison in Jeddah for that purpose.

ALJCI prides itself on the creation of the first social business in the Arab world, the Grameen-Jameel. Established in 2003, it helps alleviate poverty by providing technical and financial assistance to microfinance institutions. It operates in nine countries in the MENA region. It was incorporated in 2007 as a joint venture between the Grameen Foundation and ALJ. In 2011, Grameen-Jameel facilitated local currency financing worth USD 53 million to nearly 520,000 microfinance clients.[261]

ALJ has contributed to the arts, with the financing of the Jameel Gallery of Islamic Art at the Victoria and Albert Museum in London. In addition, ALJCI endowed the Jameel Prize for contemporary art and design.

Similarly, the company invests heavily on poverty alleviation, specifically with the Abdul Latif Jameel Poverty Action Lab at MIT,[262] a network of 66 affiliated professors from around the world whose mission is to "reduce poverty by ensuring that policy is based on scientific evidence."[263]

Monopoly power in exchange for social investment

The auto distribution industry in Saudi Arabia is a value ecosystem where dealerships are monopolies by royal decree. Such market dominance obviously preserves their long-term profitability at the expense of customers who have to pay a price for their car that is higher than what it would otherwise be if competition were allowed. In exchange for receiving monopoly powers, and as an implicit contract with the government, those firms invest heavily in social programs (and they call it "corporate social responsibility") which, in turn, reduces the pressure on the government to invest in poverty-alleviation programs, build infrastructure, develop human capital, etc. In this case, higher prices compensate consumers for higher taxes that they would have to pay if companies did not exploit their monopoly power to the benefit of society.

The Agricultural Bank of China (as well as the other state-owned banks in China) receives a *de facto* monopoly power in their market with the mandate to bear social responsibilities: financing farmers, providing subsidized loans, operating in non-bankable areas, and relaxing credit conditions to favor the poor. By financing the farming sector, the economic development in Chinese agricultural regions is fostered by the (quasi) private sector, thereby substituting the state.

The public–private capitalist system that the ALJ and ABC represent is effective, but also easily implementable because both countries are dictatorships. How can they be possible in Western democracies? I will discuss this issue in the last part of the book. Let me say by now that we have not come up with good models that work in democracies. However, the future of solutions such as minimum guaranteed income schemes and social monopolies, and the implementation of innovation ecosystems will require governments to find mechanisms so companies optimally choose social objectives without penalties (taxes) or incentives (financial subsidies).

50. NATIONAL CHAMPIONS, BUT ALSO SMES

Capitalism is defined as an economic system in which private citizens control the various means of production. The government takes no direct role in allocating production or setting prices; these are determined by the free market, where value is the result of supply and demand or the relationship between private producers and private consumers.

Traditionally, the opposite of capitalism has been socialism, where the government controls the various means of production and makes decisions about production and price.

Today, the era of Soviet-style socialism seems to be over, and capitalism exists in some form nearly everywhere in the world. We live in an increasingly globalized economy, which is based on an international free market with no single government having the authority to control the means of production or the value of commodities globally. The international economy is basically capitalist, but not all nations practice capitalism on the domestic scale. And nowhere is there "pure" unfettered capitalism of the sort that flourished in the United States and England in the late 19th century; every government exerts varying degrees of regulation on private businesses. Capitalism comes in various shapes and sizes, and every country has its own model.

Monopolies

In capitalism, a monopoly is an entity that is the sole supplier of a particular commodity. It is, by definition, the largest supplier that can exist within a given market. Industrialized nations tolerate certain monopolies, such as water utilities or mass transit systems, because to allow competing companies would result in highly inefficient congestion. As a condition of their existence, these "natural monopolies" are regulated by government, and must, for example, receive government permission to raise prices.

In the United States, the last true industrial monopoly was Standard Oil. Established in 1870 by John D. Rockefeller, Standard Oil grew to control nearly all of the nation's oil production. The company also controlled the refineries, most of the wells, and the transportation of the oil. At its peak, Standard Oil controlled up to 90 percent of the petroleum industry in the United States, and was expanding globally. In 1911, the United States Supreme Court ruled that Standard Oil was an illegal monopoly and ordered it broken up into 34 independent units.[264]

More recently, in April 2012, the US Justice Department filed an antitrust lawsuit against Apple and a group of book publishers, asserting that they colluded to fix e-book prices. The scheme was created to thwart Amazon, which was selling e-books at below cost and gaining monopolistic control of the market. Several of the publishers agreed to settle the case.[265]

Oligopolies

While monopolies are uncommon in democracies, the next level down on the corporate food chain is very common. An oligopoly—from the Ancient Greek olígos ("few") + poleîn ("to sell")—is a market form wherein a market or industry is dominated by a small number of large sellers (oligopolists). While you might assume that a market dominated by a handful of "national champions" would be characterized by fierce competition between them, this is not always the case. In some situations, oligopolies may employ restrictive trade practices such as collusion or market sharing in order to inflate prices and restrict production in much the same way as a monopoly. Whenever there is a formal agreement for such collusion between companies that should be competing against one another, this practice is known as a cartel. A prime example of such a cartel is the Organization of the Petroleum Exporting Countries (OPEC), which has a significant influence on the international price of oil.

Examples of oligopolies in Western industrialized nations include Boeing and Airbus, which together control the large passenger aircraft market. In their case, because there are two of them, they make a duopoly. The massive, long-term investment of time and money involved in developing new passenger aircraft models leaves emerging companies with little chance of competing against the two behemoths, which can far more easily afford the outlays. Even as players from Brazil, Canada, Russia, and China are making serious attempts to challenge the dominance of Airbus and Boeing, the odds are stacked against them. As a result, analysts say, the Airbus–Boeing duopoly is likely to persist and even strengthen in the foreseeable future.[266]

One might assume that with just a handful of big players in a market (which is then called a concentrated market), these companies would enjoy the freedom that you'd expect comes with economic power. In fact, the opposite is often true. Oligopolies often exist in a tense state of interdependence, where they cannot act independently of each other. A firm operating in a market with just a few competitors must take the potential reaction of its closest rivals into account when making its own decisions. Because firms cannot act independently, they must anticipate the likely response of a rival to any given change in their pricing or other activity. Decisions may include whether to compete with rivals, or collude with them.[267]

An example of alleged collusion came to the surface in the German auto industry, which is dominated by five companies: Volkswagen, Daimler, BMW, Porsche, and Audi. (Actually, you might say there are three; the Volkswagen Group owns Audi, Bentley, Bugatti, Lamborghini, Porsche, and Volkswagen.) In 2017, the five were accused of forming "working groups" that would decide, for example, how fast a convertible top should be raised and lowered. "The conclusion," wrote Frank Dohmen and Dietmar Hawranek,

> is that Daimler, BMW, Audi, Porsche, and Volkswagen often no longer compete with one another. Instead, they secretly cooperate, very closely, in fact, in the same way one would normally expect of the subsidiaries of a single company to work together, as something like a "German Cars Inc."—or a cartel.[268]

The labor market relationship between large caps and SMEs

Like fish that swim in the ocean, the relationships between large "national champions" and the smaller SMEs that share the same waters are complicated—especially in regard to the labor market and employment.

On the one hand, big companies often eat smaller ones, swallow the bits they want, and spit out the rest. Typically, when a big company acquires a smaller one, the big company will use its scale of efficiency to cut redundant roles, resulting in a net job loss. While most acquisitions of smaller companies don't make the headlines, big mergers do. In December 2018, for example, entertainment giant The Walt Disney Company announced an agreement to acquire 21st Century Fox for USD 52.4 billion in an all-stock deal. The deal between Disney (the second-largest media and entertainment conglomerate in the United States after Comcast) and Fox is an attempt by Disney to strengthen its TV and film businesses against new competitors and technologies in the content arena. As reported by *International Business Times*, employees at 21st Century Fox are bracing for the day in June 2019 when anywhere from 4,000 to 10,000 employees will lose their jobs once the merger with The Walt Disney Company takes effect. Fox has a total workforce of 22,400 employees worldwide.[269]

On the other hand, like whales followed by pilot fish, big enterprises often provide jobs and revenues to the SMEs that surround them. For example, Volkswagen AG is Europe's largest auto manufacturer with worldwide revenues approaching USD 110 billion and manufacturing facilities on every continent. To manufacture its roughly 11 million vehicles per year, the company relies on a vast network of SME supplier companies—and managing it is a challenge. As IBM noted in a white paper, "Given the sheer scale of Volkswagen's procurement activities—global purchasing volume approaches \$80 billion annually—the company is constantly buffeted by external events. Forecasts change. Commodity prices rise and fall. Suppliers go out of business."[270]

Volkswagen AG employs about 302,000 people directly, but when you add its thousands of SME contract suppliers, the number of people who depend on VW for their livelihood is incalculable.

The number of SMEs that informally cater to the employees of a big company like Volkswagen is also huge. These are the hotels, garages, restaurants, trucking companies, builders, taxi drivers, and schools that provide services to employees in a "company town." To appreciate the importance of these jobs, you need only read a news report about what can happen to a town when a factory closes.

Swindon is a large town in Wiltshire, South West England. At the 2011 census, it had a population of 182,441. And since 1989, it has been the site of a Honda factory that produces bestsellers such as the Honda Accord and the Honda Civic. In February 2019, Honda announced it was closing the plant in 2021, putting 3,500 jobs directly at risk. But thousands more could be affected. Next to the Honda plant stands a smaller one making Mini sedans for BMW. Both rely on the same supply chains, and some locals think the Mini plant will be the next to go.

"It is devastating for Swindon. I think Swindon's finished without Honda, that's my opinion," said Sue Davis, a 49-year-old financial worker whose husband works at the plant.[271]

As Robert Buckland, MP for South Swindon, told Euronews, he reacted with "concern and surprise" upon hearing the news. "Honda is a major employer here in Swindon. The closure of the factory will also affect many of the company's local supply chains in and around the town."[272]

With the anticipated closure of the Swindon plant, component makers operating across the UK have suddenly found themselves without a key customer. Yokohama, Japan-based Unipres employs about 100 people at a Birmingham plant where car frames are assembled for Honda. But with the automaker planning to exit the country, "We will start considering our options, including shutting down," a Unipres representative told *Nikkei Asian Review*.[273]

How national champions coexist with smaller competitors

In Germany, the Big Five automakers aren't the only vehicle manufacturers. There are others, including:

- Ford-Werke Gmbh, headquartered in Niehl, Cologne, North Rhine-Westphalia. It is a subsidiary of Ford of Europe, which in turn is a subsidiary of Ford Motor Company. The company employs 28,800 people.
- Opel. Once a part of GM, it's been a subsidiary of French automaker Groupe PSA since August 2017. Opel employs 37,000 people.[274] Groupe PSA is the second biggest in Europe, after Volkswagen. Both Ford and Opel are not really "smaller" competitors because they are parts of much larger automakers.
- Weineck Engineering, the manufacturer of Weineck Cobra Limited Edition.
- Borgward Group, an international automobile brand established in May 2008. The company is headquartered in Stuttgart, Germany, and carries the identity of former German brand Borgward. Borgward currently employs nearly 5,500 people globally and has more than 2,300 engineers.

There are an additional 17 small manufacturers, ranging from Apal, a small-scale automobile company originally from Belgium, to YES!, a brand of high-performance sports cars manufactured by YES! Beteiligungs-undbesitzgesellschaft mbH. Many of these small manufacturers produce customized variants using the components of Big Five vehicles. For example, Lotec is a German sports car powered by a Mercedes-Benz V-12 engine.

Why don't the big companies just swallow up these little guys? Because the little guys pose no threat, it's just not worth it, and the little guys buy parts from the big guys, like the Mercedes-Benz engines that Lotec buys from Daimler.

Sometimes upstarts can be seen as a threat, or at least a force to be reckoned with. Electric car maker Tesla, founded in 2003 and, as of 2018, employs 45,000 people, is going head to head with big companies including General Motors. In response, analysts say that GM is going to reposition its venerable Cadillac marque as a luxury electric vehicle brand. Just in time, too—in 2018, Tesla sold 191,627 cars in the United States with just three models, while Cadillac sold only 154,702 with a full portfolio of vehicles. The Cadillac electric car will reportedly arrive in 2021, just as GM rolls out 20 new electric cars through 2023 globally. Reports say most of the 20 planned electric cars would be Cadillacs.[275]

The relationships between big national champions and the universe of SMEs that serve them, compete with them, and occasionally supplant them are complex and symbiotic, not unlike the vast array of creatures large and small that live in the world's oceans.

South Korea—The land of chaebol

At first glance, South Korea—especially Seoul—appears to be an advanced, overwhelmingly metropolitan area teeming with technology. Everyone has the latest smartphone, most of them from Samsung or LG, though Apple's iPhone does have a strong following as well. In South Korea, as in many other developed markets, there are apps for everything from getting a taxi or car-share service, to ordering food.

But one of the biggest things I can't help but notice is the overabundance of brand names—nearly all of them large, family-owned companies. You cannot go anywhere in Seoul without seeing Samsung, LG, Lotte, SK, and many others.

South Korea is a country long dominated by these large companies even though a majority of its workers are employed at small- and medium-sized enterprises. However, even among these industry behemoths, SMEs have found ways to carve out their own little niches.

CEO Sophie Kim admits that it was selfish motivation that led her to starting Market Kurly—an SME and online shopping platform that provides fresh, organic produce. She had a passion for food that led her to spend her weekends at various food markets and organic farms. However, these wholesalers did not offer products in small quantities, which meant many of the food items she bought went bad before she could eat them.

From this conundrum, Market Kurly was born and after three years, it has 500,000 subscribers and makes more than 9 billion won (USD 8.37 million) a month in revenue with famous conglomerate Shinsegae rumored to be interested in buying out the platform.[276]

Market Kurly is just one of a few examples of a small- and medium-sized enterprise in South Korea that has found a niche market and has been able to thrive in a business environment long dominated by large family-owned corporations—known locally as "chaebol." Just how was this small company able to do so and why is it so difficult for others to follow its lead?

In order to understand that, first, one must understand the history of the chaebol and the role they played in South Korea's meteoric economic growth.

The history

Chaebol literally means "wealthy clique" in Korean and is essentially just that. It is a group of large family-owned companies—many established during the Japanese occupation before the end of World War II—that led the country's stunning economic growth following the Korean War. Today, many of these companies have gone global and employ hundreds of thousands of people both in Korea and abroad.

After the Korean War, aid from the United States and other countries around the world flooded into South Korea and the government provided hundreds of millions of dollars in special loans and other financial support to rebuild the country, with special attention paid to companies in the construction, chemicals, oil, and steel sectors.[277]

Furthering this movement, after taking power through a coup in 1963, late President Park Chung-hee launched a modernization drive through which the government selected companies to undertake major projects that were often financed by government-backed loans. This, in turn, created a close relationship between the government and chaebol, with many politicians over the last several decades—and some still today—needing financial support from the companies to fund their political campaigns.[278]

Part of Park's strategy was to prioritize preferential loans to export businesses and insulate domestic industries from external competition. As a result, exports grew from 4 percent in 1961 to 40 percent by 2016, leading to what is now called "The Miracle on the Han."

However, many economists have noted that this led to an imbalance—money meant for the common people ended up in the hands of the wealthy. Even current President Moon Jae-in has referenced this imbalance today, vowing to set it right. This along with government crackdowns on the labor movement created resentment of the chaebol among the general population.

The Asian financial crisis of the late 1990s stirred up concerns about the chaebol and their effect on the country's overall economy. As the large companies drove so much of South Korea's economic growth and made up such a large portion of its GDP, the fear surfaced that close ties between the companies could lead to a major economic disaster should one fail. What is more, as the economy matured over the years, more consumers began to worry about the political power and corruption within the chaebol. An increasing number of South Koreans began to consider white-collar crime a major issue.[279]

In exchange for a bailout from the IMF, the South Korean government agreed to reforms that would weaken the chaebol structure, which led to many being broken up into smaller portions.[280]

Chaebol today

Today, there are a total of 45 companies in Korea that are defined as chaebol, according to the South Korean Fair Trade Commission, with the top 10 companies owning more than 27 percent of all business assets in the country.[281] The top five companies represent roughly half of the South Korean stock market's value and the chaebol drive the country's investment in research and development.[282]

The companies have expanded beyond their original business areas and now have many affiliates in a broad range of fields including electronics, food, chemicals, construction, household appliances, life insurance, and more.[283] As of 2018, they employ around 12 percent of South Korea's workforce, but hold 77 percent of the country's market capitalization (see Figure 4.17).

Many chaebol have maintained their cozy ties with the government, becoming nearly inseparable as many politicians look to these companies to fund their election campaigns. And while South Korea's economic growth has dropped from near double digits to around 3 percent, the chaebol have continued to grow and have moved many jobs overseas.[284]

In recent years, however, the South Korean government has pushed for reform measures such as simplifying complex cross-shareholdings which have allowed owner families to control a wide range of businesses despite having small direct shareholdings. It also pressured the chaebol to discontinue intra-group deals and allow more opportunities for SMEs. This pressure prompted some conglomerates, such as the LG Group, to move to a holding company structure, though due to the large amount of cross-shareholding, this is not seen as something completely feasible for the largest of the chaebol.[285]

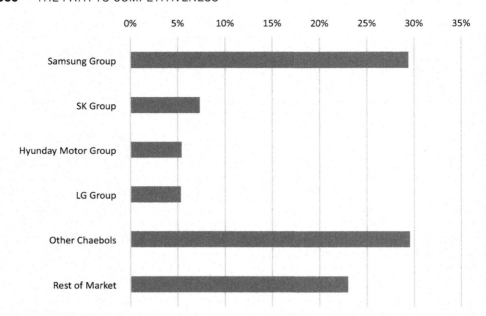

Figure 4.17 Market Capitalization of South Korean Chaebols. Several Sources: www.businesskor ea.co.kr/news/articleView.html?idxno=19558 and www.koreaherald.com/view.php?ud=20170709 000153.

Corruption scandals

Over the past few decades, a growing number of chaebol leaders and executives have been convicted of corruption, embezzlement, and various other white-collar crimes. Despite these convictions, rarely did these businessmen see the inside of a jail, or if they did, they were quickly released and pardoned. Some of the most recent cases include Samsung Chairman Lee Kun-hee who has been pardoned twice, the last time so he could help in South Korea's bid for the 2018 Winter Olympics. Chey Tae-won, chairman of SK Group, was indicted on charges including embezzlement in 2012, though after receiving a four-year prison term, he was released and pardoned in 2015. Chung Mong-koo from Hyundai Motor was indicted on charges including breach of trust in 2006 and given three years in prison, though suspended for five years. He was then pardoned in 2008. Lee Jae-hyun of CJ was given two and a half years for various charges including embezzlement in 2013, though he was granted a special pardon in 2016.

Public ire hit fever pitch in 2017 when a corruption scandal surrounding then-President Park Geun-hye erupted. The daughter of former dictator Park Chung-hee was implicated in an influence-peddling scandal that eventually led to her ouster in December 2017. She was later sentenced to 24 years in prison and fined around USD 17 million in the spring of 2018.

As part of this scandal, Jay Y. Lee, *de facto* head of Samsung Group, was arrested and later convicted of bribery. He was sentenced to five years in prison.[286] It was found that Lee had been paying bribes to a close confidante of the deposed president. However, he was later released when an appeals court shortened and suspended his sentence and then allowed him to retake control of the company.[287]

The same year that Lee was convicted, the chairman of Lotte's retail group was convicted in a different corruption trial related to former President Park and sentenced to 30 months in jail. Later, an appeals court suspended his sentence, freeing him.

Top five chaebols

Although there are still many that fall under the category of chaebol, it is generally agreed that these are the top five in the country.

Samsung

Now the largest chaebol in South Korea with businesses encompassing electronics, insurance, ships, luxury hotels, hospitals, an amusement park, and even an affiliated university, Samsung got its start in 1938 as a small company that exported fruit, dried fish, and noodles. It was started by Lee Byung-chull in the small city of Daegu with only 40 employees before later moving to Seoul in 1947 and then leaving the country during the Korean War. After the war, the company opened up a sugar refinery in Busan—Cheil Jedang—and then expanded into textiles. Today, it is led by second- and third-generation members of Lee's family—Jay Y. Lee is considered the *de facto* head, though his official title is vice president of Samsung Electronics. It makes up one-fifth of South Korea's exports and for the past decade has accounted for more than 14 percent of the GDP.[288]

Hyundai

Now known mostly for its car-making company, Hyundai started as a construction business in 1947. Over the following years, it rapidly expanded into areas such as shipbuilding, finance, electronics, and department stores. In 2003, the government forced the company to split up and downsize to write off some of its debts in the aftermath of the 1997 financial crisis—namely Hyundai Automotive Group, Hyundai Department Store Group, and Hyundai Heavy Industries. Hyundai Motor has since become the third-largest carmaker in the world, with Hyundai Heavy Industries now the world's largest shipbuilding company. Hyundai Group itself focuses on elevators and container services. It is also known for its arm that built a resort on Mount Kumgang in North Korea, though the North Korean government has since seized control.[289]

SK group

Also known as SK Holdings, SK Group got its start in 1953 when the Chey family acquired Sunkyong Textiles. They then rebuilt all the factories and facilities of the company and began work in the textile industry. Today, the company has approximately 80 subsidiaries operating in such industries as energy, chemicals, finance, shipping, insurance, and construction. In 2014, more than half of its sales came from energy and chemicals, and it made a collective USD156.6 billion in revenue. One of its best known companies is SK Telecom, the largest wireless carrier in Korea and one of only three major telecoms. It is also known for its semiconductor company SK Hynix, which is the world's second-largest memory chip maker.[290]

LG

Established in 1947, LG Corporation first focused on the chemicals and plastics industries, though today it is best known for LG Electronics, which is considered one of its core companies. After its start in 1958, LG Electronics was the first producer of radios, TVs, and appliances in the country, though it is currently ranked second behind Samsung Electronics. In the 1960s, the company adjusted its focus to consumer electronics, telecommunications networks, and power generation. Its chemical business also expanded into cosmetics and household goods and within the group is one of South Korea's three telecommunications companies—LG U+. Other affiliates include LG Display and LG Innotek, which produce liquid crystal display panels and electronic parts.[291]

Lotte

Lotte Group was started in Tokyo in 1948 by Shin Kyuk-ho, and later brought to Seoul in 1967. The group mainly focuses on food products, discount and department stores, hotels, theme parks, and entertainment, though it also includes companies in the finance, construction, energy, and electronics sectors. Lotte Confectionery is the third-largest gum maker in the world. In recent years, Lotte Group made headlines for the massive infighting among founder Shin Kyuk-ho's children over who would take control, namely between his two sons—Dong-ju and Dong-bin.[292]

Small- and medium-sized companies in South Korea today

It is easy to understand why smaller companies in South Korea may struggle to gain market share when you understand the sheer size of chaebol and the extent of their power. Among the flashy advertisements that are ubiquitous throughout the cities of South Korea, I have often been hard-pressed to find any for companies that are not chaebol.

However, I have found that the popularity of online and mobile shopping in South Korea—which boasts the world's fasted internet—has led to an opening for many SMEs and startups, including Market Kurly.

What is it that makes Market Kurly different from other shopping experiences in South Korea? CEO Sophie Kim says in an interview with Joongang Ilbo that part of it is their approach to quality control, going as far as to say it is the real key to the business.

She continues that she uses strict quality and safety control to enlighten customers and elevate their standards. From its start in groceries, the company has since expanded into products that many consumers in South Korea worry about in terms of safety, namely diapers, sanitary pads, and some household products—all items that have made headlines in recent years for lax safety control from some of the country's biggest conglomerates.

Outside of that, Market Kurly's structure is fairly straightforward. Customers can browse the website and order whatever products they wish. The orders are then delivered directly to their homes in Seoul and Gyeonggi Province by 7 a.m. the next day as long as the order is placed before 11 p.m. the previous night. Many products are also offered in small quantities—an attractive feature for the country's growing number of single-person households.

Kim says that the company has a team devoted to finding products, admitting that most of the people on the team are foodies who stay on top of changing food trends and are eager to try new things. Ultimately, however, every product must gain her approval before it is added to the website. She keeps the company's ties to other small companies by sourcing from multiple small wholesalers, continuing to help other SMEs. She can also rotate wholesalers if demand is high.

However, at times Kim admits that government regulations can get in the way of doing business. She has had to drop a few partner companies because of laws that require a food company or restaurant to go through a separate hygiene approval process applied to food manufacturing companies before they are allowed to sell products through a different retail platform. This process includes such requirements as having a separate ingredient storage room, baking room, and packaging room, which is costly and difficult for small companies to comply with.

But it is through these struggles that Market Kurly has found ways to help SMEs band together to continue staying in business—namely a collaboration with startup OTD to establish a facility with manufacturing equipment that small eateries can share. It is impossible for these small companies to afford a building and to staff it on their own, so they are making such a facility accessible to them in order to get around the hygiene regulation. Market Kurly also lends its logistics system to other small businesses.[293]

But outside Market Kurly, what is the situation in South Korea like for other SMEs?

Facts about SMEs

According to South Korea's Ministry of SMEs and Startups, 87.9 percent of all Korean employees work in SMEs, with that breaking down into 25 percent in medium-sized companies, 25 percent in small companies, and 38 percent in micro-enterprises. SMEs make up 99.9 percent of all enterprises in the country and account for 37.5 percent of exports. See the graphic depiction in Figure 4.18.

The largest industries for SMEs include wholesale and retail (1 million businesses, 2.9 million employees), accommodation and restaurants (708,387 businesses/2 million employees), manufacturing (408,459 businesses/3.1 million employees), transportation (375,490 businesses/965,255 employees), and construction (133,373 businesses/1.1 million employees). The average pay for employees of SMEs is only 63 percent of those at chaebols.

The government has worked over the years to support SMEs in the face of chaebol dominance across many industries, though some experts feel this may have led to more negative effects, the largest being the emergence of the Peter Pan Syndrome—where SMEs hesitate to grow into larger companies due to the requirements for government aid.[294]

From 2015, in order to obtain support, firms have to keep employees below 300 and capital below USD 8 million and once those numbers are surpassed, the company is no longer eligible for 160 SME support programs. Not to mention, once a company's assets are more than USD 5 billion, it then faces various investment restrictions. While South

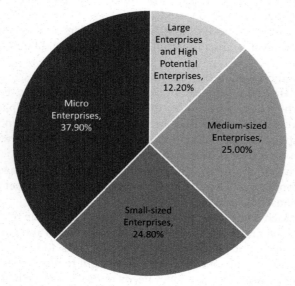

Figure 4.18 Employment in South Korea by Business Size
Source: South Korean Government.

Korea has been regarded as a good model for small business support programs—ranging from credit guarantees, subsidized loans, and tax deductions, to partial exemptions for hiring people with disabilities—clearly the system should change. From 2002 to 2012, only 629 SMEs out of several million companies grew beyond 300 employees.

Relationship between SMEs and chaebol

Expounding this is the complicated relationship between South Korea's chaebol and SMEs, with many claiming that the large corporations often use their power and clout to squeeze smaller companies.

The government's previous policies favoring large family-owned companies helped the country grow into an exports powerhouse, though many now question whether that is enough to support continued growth. The country's SMEs remain far behind chaebol. I think that South Korea should focus on building more vibrant SMEs and further developing the inefficient service sector in order to create more jobs. In a report in 2013, McKinsey and Consultants said that it is becoming increasingly apparent that the export-oriented growth formula that helped large companies drive economic development is losing steam.[295]

Not to mention, the spread of large corporations into many unrelated domestic markets is said to have encroached into business areas traditionally reserved for SMEs. Many accuse them of choking smaller companies by forcing them to cut prices or by buying them out to strip them of assets and repress competition.

One such example is that of the conglomerate Shinsegae, which runs the country's largest supermarket chain e-mart. Since 2016, when e-mart was separated from Shinsegae, the unit has spread quickly, selling its own private brand products in its own stores alongside those purchased from small and medium manufacturers. As of 2017, there were 145 e-marts in the country, though the company also launched its own ready-to-eat food brands Peacock and No Brand. There are currently around 30 No Brand outlets in the country and it has even started its own warehouse-style outlet called e-mart Traders, which is competing with foreign-run Costco—in just eight years, there are now 14 e-mart Traders outlets compared to 13 Costco's.

All this has led to e-mart becoming #1 among retailers with about 12 million won (USD 11.3 billion) in revenue. In addition, there are now over 1,000 products under the Peacock brand.

Competition has increased in the ready-to-eat market for mid-size food manufacturers despite the fact that many still retain a pool of loyal customers. For local packaged kimchi Daesang, which has been running the kimchi brand Jonggajip for 30 years, while sales have increased, its market share has been gradually decreasing and more challenges have emerged. Despite this, the company remains positive that they will maintain their customer base with their quality and unique packaging process.

In order to stay afloat, many small and medium companies will need to differentiate research and development in areas such as packaging as well as target the newly emerging single-person household market.

Shinsegae's approach could seem menacing to some, though the retail unit says that it displays its products separately from others produced by SMEs and vows that it does not intentionally place more of its items on the shelves. Experts add that it is impossible for the government to step in and control a consumer's right to buy.

In these circumstances, the government needs to find a more efficient way to control retail giants from monopolizing the market without hurting the natural market order. Professor Choi Bae-gun from the economics department at Konkuk University, has said that it is interesting that the domestic retail market is dominated by large corporations that only make up 1 percent of the market—the remaining 99 percent are SMEs. But yet, many of these smaller companies are suppliers, manufacturing and selling their products through the retail giants. Because of this, government policies to try and stem large corporations' growth could inadvertently end up hurting smaller companies.[296]

A more specific example is found in the government's policy that all large super stores close two days a month in order to even out competition with small grocery stores and traditional markets in South Korea—it was shown that for every large store like e-mart that opens up in a neighborhood, around 22 smaller stores shut down. However, over the years, this policy has proven to be mostly ineffective with small stores and markets still shutting down at the same rates, and many consumers—especially those in the restaurant business—complaining of inconvenience. Rather than protecting small businesses, it has ended up hurting them as many rely on these large retailers in order to stay open.[297]

Government policy

With a new president and administration after the candlelight protests of 2016, a new policy direction was ushered in, attempting to undo the damage many felt an over-reliance on chaebol inflicted. President Moon Jae-in called for equal opportunities, fair processes, and just results at the beginning of his presidency in early 2017, initially taking a hard stance against the unfettered market dominance of chaebol.

While previous administrations had rained favors on large companies through policy and special treatment, the Moon administration took a sharp turn in the opposite direction, vowing to help promote SMEs and startups, while punishing chaebol found involved in corruption and attempting to scale back the companies' dominance in the Korean market.

However, since then, many of Moon's previous supporters have turned into critics, accusing the administration of abandoning its policy goals of helping small- and medium-sized companies in the wake of the stalling economy, and more importantly in their eyes, harshly downscaling its drive to punish the chaebol and their executives who were complicit in the corruption scandal that cost former President Park Geun-hye her job.

Between the protesters and the government are the many still-struggling SMEs, who say the new laws meant to help them have only added to their strife.

The promises and policies

The Moon administration promised to create a level playing field for SMEs as well as setting the goal of creating 160,000 jobs by fostering innovative entrepreneurs during his five-year term. As part of this, the administration also hoped to tackle the growing youth unemployment rate, which hit a high of 10 percent in 2016.

Among these promises were five especially geared toward fostering new startups and SMEs. The government aimed to issue 2.5 trillion won (USD 2.2 billion) annually to support startups and SMEs with a new specialized fund especially for young entrepreneurs. The government also vowed to lower the investment barrier from 5 billion won (USD 4.5 million) paid-in capital so that early entrepreneurs could more easily establish a venture. Other startup regulations would be eased in order to allow them access to special tax reductions and exemptions for SMEs.

Plans also included education for entrepreneurs geared toward teaching them to start again after failure. As 6 in 10 startups tend to fail within the first three years, a deep-seated fear of failure emerged in the business world—a fear that experts attribute to South

Korea's highly competitive environment that starts for many in school—but Moon hoped further education as well as a special fund to help failed entrepreneurs start over would encourage more to keep trying. The earliest start to this was a fund created in 2017 to help startups with a technological edge to start over after a failed business.

The Moon administration also vowed to encourage large businesses to help out small companies, jumping onto a trend that some conglomerates had already been using to foster new tech. It set a goal to boost 3,000 tech ventures by supporting startup subsidies and R&D for in-house incubators at medium and large companies and establishing a special tax exemption for in-house startup R&D.[298]

The year 2018 was a whirlwind of new regulations and policy changes. In January, the government raised the minimum wage 16.4 percent to 7,530 won (USD 6.71) per hour. Following that, in May, USD 3.5 billion was added to a special budget geared toward helping create jobs for youth and support hard-hit industrial regions. Three new policies were passed in July—the government introduced a cap on working hours with the new maximum set at 52 hours per week for companies with more than 300 employees, down from 68, then it raised the minimum wage by another 10.9 percent for 2019 to 8,350 won per hour. At the end of the month, it presented tax benefits and other support measures for small business owners and the self-employed. In the following two months, the government proposed its largest budget increase in 10 years for 2019 to create jobs and increase welfare spending, and then rolled out the first installment of a USD 9 billion investment fund to foster startups.[299]

Moon also launched the Ministry of SMEs and Startups in 2017 to better meet the needs of such ventures and to help set policy direction for the future. During his campaign, Moon promised to reform chaebol and began a campaign to eradicate corruption, which led to the arrest and conviction of several political figures for corruption, the biggest being former President Park Geun-hye and then former President Lee Myung-bak, who received 15 years in prison for bribery, embezzlement, and abuse of power.[300]

Supporters turned critics

Just two years into his term, more and more of President Moon's followers have begun to step up and call for more, claiming the polices his administration have enacted haven't been helping. What is more, they claim the government hasn't been doing enough to actually eradicate corruption among large family-owned conglomerates. In November 2018—just over two years after the candlelight protests started in October 2016, many took to the streets, protesting the lack of improvement made by Moon and the government.

While the government-led crackdown on corruption did result in several arrests and convictions, high-profile chaebol executives—most notably Jay Y. Lee from Samsung and Shin Dong-bin from Lotte Group—were handed suspended sentences and allowed to return to work at their companies, continuing the long-held tradition of the judiciary treating such leaders with kid gloves.

Recent studies have shown that a leader of a top chaebol convicted of bribery has a more than 70 percent chance of receiving a suspended sentence, while in such cases for non-chaebol leaders, the chance drops to 40 percent. For those convicted of so-called "street crimes" such as theft, the chance is even lower—20 percent.

There was some success in the beginning, though. Moon appointed Kim Sang-jo, considered a long-time crusader on reining in chaebol excesses, to head the Fair Trade Commission, which resulted in several large companies simplifying their corporate structures after pressure to clear out cross-shareholdings and step away from unfair intra-group deals. But many detractors say that when the economy began slowing, the government began losing a lot of its fight in going after chaebol.

They even began to criticize some of the president's recent decisions, such as who he chose to take with him on a business delegation to North Korea—which was largely made up of executives and representatives from the top family-owned conglomerates. This was viewed as being no different than the deposed Park administration, which was often criticized for its cozy relationship with chaebol, even before the corruption scandal broke out.

Park Sang-in, a professor at Seoul National University, went so far as to comment that the government has done nothing to lay the foundation for fair competition between smaller players and decreasing chaebol's dominance.

Despite this, Moon has continued his call for a fair economy. He was quoted in media reports in November 2018 as saying, "In the past our people worked day and night under the goal of building a well-off nation and became an economic powerhouse in just half a century, but fairness was lost along the way."[301]

But even before the protests, a group of Korean intellectuals—The Intellectuals' Declaration Network—that had previously supported Moon issued a joint statement in July calling for the Moon administration to be more aggressive in implementing various social and economic reforms. It was the first time since the president took office that a group of progressive intellectuals released a collective opinion on the current government's course. A total of 323 such people signed the declaration.

Among the recommendations, they demanded bold policy in income-driven growth, innovation growth, and a fair economy. Specifically, they pushed for stronger chaebol reform, including the eradication of "deep-rooted vices" in the system. The group accused the administration of taking steps back from its previous promises, namely the revisions to the real estate tax system and the half-hearted approach to true chaebol reform.

They also criticized the government's apparent move away from establishing a "three-wheel economy"—income-driven growth, innovation growth, and a fair economy. The group said that Moon had the perfect opportunity to get the approach on track with his original tough stance on chaebol reform, but dropped the ball and opened the window for the new minimum wage hike to be blamed for the declining performance of SMEs and the reduction in jobs.

While the group expressed their hope for Moon's ultimate success and stated that this was not them parting ways with support for the president, they felt without making necessary corrections to the current trajectory, he would eventually fail.[302]

Ministry of SMEs and startups

Despite growing concerns over the short-term future of SMEs, the government is determined to push forward with support, and none is more eager than the new Ministry of SMEs and Startups (MSS).

The ministry announced three main goals for its policy direction in 2019—resolve a respectable ecosystem for venture firms and business startups; build a firm corporate growth ladder; and spread a creative economy to the middle-class economy and enhance policy efficiency. One of its biggest pushes through these goals is to help the globalization of SMEs, which it sees as crucial for the sustained growth of these companies.

To help in this endeavor, the ministry offers a plethora of programs and support specially geared toward SMEs and startups. Domestically, it runs a public procurement system through which the government and public sector companies purchase products made by SMEs, and has established shopping areas exclusively made up of SMEs in high traffic areas. The ministry also helps to promote SME products to large, domestic home shopping channels. In addition to this, the MSS also promotes the fostering of small and medium companies owned by women.

The ministry has also started supporting specialized vocational high schools, Meister high schools, technological academies, and a customized industry-academic technology manpower cultivation program in order to help resolve the shortage of manpower seen in small- and medium-sized companies. It hopes to better connect the companies with talent seeking jobs, as well as creating much needed conditions at the companies to attract more talent. It has also introduced a fund that will compensate achievements made by SME employees and award designations to companies that foster competent employees.

The globalization of SMEs is seen as a key goal for the ministry and crucial to creating more jobs for South Koreans. To further this, the ministry has launched 14 export support centers at regional offices throughout the country where these companies can not only seek help with policy, but also link up with other organizations that seek to help further their growth.[303]

The actual effects of government policy

With the South Korean economy stalling over the last year, many SMEs are struggling to make ends meet, in part due to some of the new laws that were put in place to help them, but also due to growing competition from overseas firms as well as the long dominance held by large conglomerates within the country.

Jinyong Packaging, an SME that makes packaging for some of the biggest companies in the country and at one time generated millions of dollars in revenue, dropped its employment from 15 to 4 over the course of five years after orders decreased 80 percent. The CEO, Oh Yoon-min, said that he also cannot afford to pay the increased minimum wage and may be forced to further cut his workforce. Nokstop Chem, another SME, reported that days can pass without work as orders and prices keep dropping.

Even though SMEs contribute a small portion of South Korea's GDP, any trouble they experience still has a large impact on the job market and consumption.

In 2018, SMEs showed the largest drop in output since the 2009 global financial crisis. Additionally, nearly 45 percent of the more than 3.5 million SMEs in Korea were classified as zombie companies, meaning they have been unable to pay capital costs with operating profits for three consecutive years. The rate of corporate bankruptcy was also growing, with a 9 percent annual increase in the number of defaulting companies, as well as the number of SMEs up for sale, which grew by 44 percent.

With more clients turning to other countries such as India and China for cheaper products, this has left many SMEs in the lurch—many rely on large Korean conglomerates for orders but they are moving manufacturing overseas.

On top of that, the recent minimum wage hikes (Figure 4.19) and cuts to the maximum working hours have left many smaller companies with their hands tied. In 2019, the minimum hourly wage was KRW 8,350 (about USD 7). They cannot afford the wage increases and end up cutting the number of workers. With the wage gap between SMEs and conglomerates also increasing, workers in smaller companies look to overtime to make more money but are now facing hurdles as they can no longer work more than

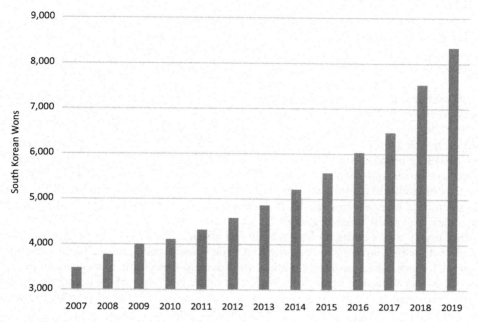

Figure 4.19 Minimum Hourly Wage in South Korea

Source: Minimum Wage Commission of South Korea.

52 hours a week. Many have been forced to pick up non-regular work at other companies, though reportedly even these jobs are dwindling due to the minimum wage hike.

Some companies report that chaebols are still sticking to the practice of squeezing SME subcontractors on price or blocking them from making contracts with other conglomerates. [304]

The complaints about the new laws and regulations have Moon's administration stuck on where to go next, likely worsening the situation for SMEs down the road. Former Finance Minister Kim Dong-yeon suggested adapting future government measures in August 2018, while at the same time chief of staff for policy Jang Ha-sung was reported as saying that the weakening job market was due to structural problems, calling for the administration to stay the course.[305]

Both officials were later replaced by Moon in November 2018, potentially paving the way for new ideas on how to fix the economy, though the administration has yet to make any significant change in its policies. President Moon has reiterated his commitment to creating a fair economy, though many experts have called them empty words, asking what the point of replacing officials is if the government is not going to shift its approach or policy.[306]

51. BRANDING THE COUNTRY

The nation branding of Timor-Leste

If you go just about anywhere in the Americas, Europe, or Africa, stop a random person on the street, and ask them their opinion of Timor-Leste, you would probably receive a reply that was something like this:

"Timor-Leste? Never heard of him."

"Is not that a boy band?"

"I have heard it is a type of fruit sold at organic food stores."

"Is not that one of the galaxies discovered by the Hubble telescope?"

But if you happened to encounter someone who was well-versed in the geography of East Asia, the answer might be very different:

"The Democratic Republic of Timor-Leste? Ah, it is a beautiful little island nation! Nestled in the Timor Sea between Indonesia and Australia, its high rugged mountains and sparkling beaches are surrounded by crystal-clear waters and vivid coral reefs. Its people are warm and friendly, with a multi-layered cultural history that is a rich combination of traditional Timorese, Portuguese, Chinese, and Indonesian influences. This vibrant mix is revealed in their local architecture, cuisine, clothing styles, and artistic endeavors. You really must go there!"[307]

That pretty much sums up how people feel about Timor-Leste: Either they've never heard of it, or they love it. For me, the first time I heard about such a small nation was from my former colleague, now coauthor and friend Willem Smit, a professor of marketing at the Asia School of Business in Kuala Lumpur. Willem's wife is Portuguese which I guess provided the initial bond between a Dutch academic then living in Singapore and the former Portuguese colony. It is he who has taught me everything I know about Timor-Leste, and in fact this section is primarily based on the case study about country branding that Willem has written with Manuel Soares.[308]

The basic facts

A constitutional republic, the nation of Timor-Leste, or East Timor, comprises the eastern half of the island of Timor and a few surrounding islands. The western half of the island is part of the nation of Indonesia. To the south, across the Timor Sea, Australia is the country's largest neighbor. In land area, Timor-Leste is a small nation—about the same size as Montenegro or the Bahamas—with a population of 1.3 million, which is equal to Estonia or Trinidad and Tobago.

The island has been inhabited by humans for over 40,000 years. Timorese origin myths tell of ancestors that sailed around the eastern end of Timor arriving on land in the south, or Timorese ancestors journeying from the Malay Peninsula or the Minangkabau highlands of Sumatra. By the 14th century, the island was exporting aromatic sandalwood, slaves, honey, and wax. It was the abundance of sandalwood in Timor that attracted European explorers to the island in the early 16th century. Currently one of the most expensive woods in the world, both the sandalwood itself and its oil exude a distinctive fragrance that has been highly valued for centuries.

These European explorers reported that the island was governed by a number of small chiefdoms or princedoms. Long-term European occupation began in 1769, when the city of Dili was founded on the northern coast and the colony of Portuguese Timor declared. In 1914, the border between the Dutch-colonized western half of the island and the Portuguese-colonized eastern half of the island was established by the Permanent Court of Arbitration.

During World War II, the Japanese occupied the island. At the end of the war, the Portuguese returned. In the wake of the 1974 Portuguese revolution, Portugal effectively abandoned its colony on Timor, opening the door for a hostile takeover by Indonesia.

Decades of Indonesian occupation left the country in tatters, with much of the infrastructure in the city of Dili destroyed and poverty rampant throughout rural areas. Following years of bloody conflict, on August 30, 2001, with the help of the United Nations, the East Timorese voted in their first election to elect members of the Constituent Assembly. On May 20, 2002, the Constitution of the Democratic Republic of East Timor came into force and the UN recognized East Timor as an independent nation. The city of Dili became the new capital.

As specified in the constitution, the head of state of East Timor is the president of the Republic. He or she is elected by popular vote for a five-year term. Following elections, the president appoints the leader of the majority party or coalition as prime minister, and then, on the proposal of the latter, the cabinet. The unicameral East Timorese parliament is the national parliament, whose members are each elected by popular vote to five-year terms.

Unfortunately, the independence of Timor-Leste in 2002 did not usher in a period of internal peace and stability. The build-up to the May 2007 presidential elections saw renewed outbreaks of political violence. In February 2008, the elected president, José Ramos-Horta, was critically injured in an attempted assassination. Separately, Prime Minister Xanana Gusmão also faced gunfire, but escaped unharmed. The United Nations intervened with security forces. In March 2011, after the tension had eased, the UN handed over operational control of the police force to the East Timor authorities, and on December 31, 2012, fully ended its peacekeeping mission.[309]

What this meant is that for nearly a decade after independence, if you happened to read about Timor-Leste in the news, or saw a report on television, you were likely to get the impression that the island was nothing more than an impoverished, third-rate banana republic, and not a safe place to visit.

The branding of Timor-Leste

In 2007, presidential elections were held in which incumbent Prime Minister José Ramos-Horta emerged as the victor.

The newly elected government started laying the foundation of reforming the image of the island nation. This was driven by practical economic reasons as well as ethical ones. The Timorese economy has long been highly dependent on two exports, oil and coffee. Dependence upon commodity exports is not the basis of a resilient economy for any nation, especially a poor one. In fact, as Gobie Rajalingam wrote for the Asia Foundation, "with warnings that if it does not diversify its economy beyond oil extraction, the country's petroleum wealth fund may be exhausted by 2030."[310]

Meanwhile, South East Asia is one of the world's most tourist-rich regions, but with a reputation for violence and instability, Timor-Leste was not going to get its share of tourist spending. "With Timor-Leste's natural beauty, rich history, and cultural heritage," wrote Rajalingam, "there is significant untapped potential to develop tourism as a diverse and inclusive industry to drive economic development."[311]

For the island to further develop its tourism sector, the public perception of the island had to improve, thereby attracting not only tourists but also foreign investment. A key part of this effort included increasing the number of hotel rooms, improving the island's infrastructure to boost accessibility, and increasing opportunities for sightseeing and organizing events.

The government's key priorities included increased transparency in the Department of State Budgeting and Spending, with new openness about how much money government agencies received and spent, as well as how decisions were made. As a part of this effort, in August 2011, Timor-Leste hosted the Extractive Industries Transparency Initiative (EITI) regional conference.

The Extractive Industries Transparency Initiative is the global standard to promote the open and accountable management of oil, gas, and mineral resources. In each of the 51 implementing countries, the EITI is supported by a coalition of government, companies, and civil society. "Guided by the belief that a country's natural resources belong to its citizens," says the EITI, the organization

> has established a global standard to promote the open and accountable management of oil, gas, and mineral resources. The EITI Standard requires the disclosure of information along the extractive industry value chain from the point of extraction, to how revenues make their way through the government, and how they benefit the public.[312]

The goals are to promote understanding of natural resource management, strengthen public and corporate governance, and provide the data to inform reforms for greater transparency and accountability in the extractives sector.

President José Ramos-Horta referred to EITI as "a cornerstone of our institutional framework to ensure transparency."[313] He also asserted that the nation's Transparency Portal would enhance transparency and improve public service delivery.

Many of the attendees at the two-day conference in Dili expressed support of the efforts of the Timorese government to achieve greater financial transparency. "For me," said then-World Bank director and former Indonesia minister of finance, Sri Mulyani,

> there is no better illustration of what is meant by the EITI than East Timor, a country that just a decade after independence, has developed a worldwide system of revenue management and achieved the criteria of the EITI compliance. Timor-Leste is the first country in Asia Pacific, and third worldwide, which meets these criteria.[314]

The five pillars of transparency

A key part of the initiative is the Transparency Model that Timor-Leste developed for itself, consisting of five pillars:[315]

1. The Transparency Portal, which since 2002 has made available online information about Timor-Leste's government accounts. One of the features of this tool is a daily information update. For example, as soon as money is withdrawn or received, this information is published in the website. This website is available in Tétum, Portuguese, and English languages.
2. Compliance with the EITI rules. The initiative and the rigor demonstrated by the government gave Timor-Leste the distinction of being the first Asian Pacific country, and third in the world, to comply with the EITI rules, which guarantees transparency and responsibility in those nations rich in natural extractive resources, such as oil.
3. The Petroleum Fund. Created in September 2005, the fund's purpose is to contribute to the responsible management of petroleum resources and for a solid fiscal policy. It is managed by the Banking and Payments Authority of Timor-Leste (BPA).

4. Direct televised broadcasting of the complete discussion of the state budget, which, since the swearing in of the constitutional government, takes place during an average of 13 days. It broadcasts not only the final vote but also the debate carried out in the national parliament.

5. The Council of Ministers press releases in the government website and also in their dissemination through mailing lists of citizens and/or institutions to whom the decisions and issues analyzed by the government may be of interest. This information is also available in Tetum, Portuguese, and English.

The transparency portal

On the occasion of its launch on March 17, 2011, Prime Minister Kay Rala Xanana Gusmão remarked,

> This Portal represents much more than the development of a mechanism for promoting transparency, accountability, and control in regard to the public accounts of the State. This Portal represents the true transformation of our State, particularly in Public Administration, which "step by step" has been adopting new efficiencies, innovation and accountability standards.[316]

The first pillar of the Transparency Model, the Transparency Portal is divided into four sub-portals:

1. Budget Transparency

The Budget Transparency Portal lets the user interactively:

- Get complete financial information on how the national budget is being spent.
- Access historical and recent data.
- Monitor the progress of the Timor-Leste government's budget execution.

The portal is updated every day so information is current, and it is accessible to any member of the public, groups, and development partners. You do not need a user name or password to access it.

2. Aid Transparency

Like many small, developing nations, Timor-Leste accepts foreign aid from its wealthier neighbors. For example, as Arie Kusuma Paksi wrote in 2013,

> from 1999 to 2009 the international community channelled USD5.207 billion to support post-conflict recovery in Timor-Leste .... Foreign aid has come in the form of grants, projects, or operations of foreign institutions involving the UN and bilateral and multilateral actors and donors.[317]

Openly tracking the receipt and expenditure of aid is an important task. Initiated under the Development Partnership Management Unit (DPMU), the Ministry of Finance of the Government of Timor-Leste, the Aid Transparency Portal (ATP) is an official development assistance (ODA) database. The objective of the ATP project is to strengthen the capacity of the DPMU to manage, track, and report on aid flows, and to ensure that aid is being properly recorded, allocated, and utilized to benefit the citizens of Timor-Leste.

The ATP tracks donor commitments and disbursements to Timor-Leste on a quarterly basis. This is accomplished through the implementation of an internet-based Aid Information Management System (AIMS).

The goal is to support the implementation of the Timor-Leste Strategic Development Plan, reduce administrative costs and time, facilitate more informed decision-making, and improve the efficiency, effectiveness, and coordination with and among government agencies and development partners.

3. eProcurement

The Government of Timor-Leste uses the Timor-Leste eProcurement Portal to purchase and acquire goods and services. All types of procurement processes, including tenders and requests for quotes, are published to the Timor-Leste eProcurement Portal. The goal is to provide more transparency in government procurement, and to allow all citizens and vendors to download tenders, providing equal opportunity. It also allows government procurement to be used as an instrument to promote private sector development and helps to protect against monopoly.

The Timor-Leste eProcurement Portal is a website which lets the user:

- View all open tenders, grouped by the type of business, and
- access and review all awarded tenders.[318]

4. Government Results

Based on the Timor-Leste Strategic Development Plan, the Timor-Leste Government Results Portal shows outcomes information for the most important government targets, projects, and programs. The Timor-Leste Results Portal enables government agencies to set the targets for each goal, to track progress, and make adjustments to the programed targets. It also has the ability to control performance goals in order to determine the progress for a specific fiscal year and fiscal periods.

The portal allows the public to obtain information about goals progress, descriptive information of government programs and projects, and budgetary information. This information can be converted into measurable results in order to quantify public financial resources.[319]

Much progress ... and a long way to go

While the island culture is ancient, as a self-governing nation Timor-Leste is still very young. The Indonesian occupation was brutal, and as it moves forward the country needs to patiently build its regulatory framework and infrastructure.

As the United States Agency for International Development (USAID) reported, Timor-Leste has faced daunting challenges to establishing a viable state and a representative democracy. The country still lacks the fundamental governance systems essential to adequately respond to persistently high rates of poverty, unemployment, growing socioeconomic inequality, and unresolved conflict.[320]

Timor-Leste is striving to rebalance the country's economy away from such a heavy reliance on its oil industry and to grow private sector business. The government has identified tourism as an industry that could help boost the economy. Neighboring New Zealand is working with the government to create an environment for high-quality tourism, where the money goes into the communities. As New Zealand tourist writer Laura Walters commented, in 2018, the New Zealand government was slated to give USD 16.7 million in aid and development, with one-third of it going toward improving economic diversification. That meant focusing on developing industries including coffee, cocoa, aquaculture, and now tourism.

With continued progress, in the near future you will be able to ask anybody about Timor-Leste, and they might reply, "I have heard so many good things about it—I really must plan a visit!"

South Africa: Turmoil, new hope, and a positive national brand

For most people who do not live in South Africa, the history of that nation is clearly divided into two eras by the date of April 27, 1994. This was the day of a historic national election. Before that time, South Africa was a deeply fractured nation that had once been colonized by the British and whose most notable feature was its brutal system of apartheid. Under this system, the white minority held political and economic power, while the people of the indigenous African majority were used as a low-wage workforce.

After decades of violent struggle and painful transformation, with the election of April 27, 1994, the African National Congress (ANC) took the reins of government. Nelson Mandela, who had been imprisoned for opposing apartheid, assumed the office of president of South Africa. The Government of National Unity was established, and the government embarked on the Reconstruction and Development Program (RDP), designed to address the socioeconomic consequences of apartheid. Its goals included alleviating poverty and addressing the massive shortfalls in social services across the country.

In 1995, South Africa adopted a new constitution, and the government also established the Truth and Reconciliation Commission (TRC), designed both to expose the crimes of the apartheid era and to offer opportunities for mutual forgiveness.

In the post-apartheid world, South Africa has become an economic leader on the continent, where the size of its economy is second only to that of Nigeria. As one of the most industrialized countries in Africa, The World Bank classifies South Africa as an upper-middle-income economy; alongside Botswana, Gabon, and Mauritius, it is one of only four such countries in Africa. Once crippled by international sanctions designed to force an end to apartheid, by 2011 South Africa's gross domestic product had nearly tripled to USD 400 billion, but has since declined to roughly USD 295 billion in both 2016 and 2017.

There are many bright spots in the economy. For example, South Africa carries the perception of having some of the world's most secure banks. It ranks high for the healthy balance sheets of its banking sector, and for the extent that companies raise money by issuing shares or bonds on the capital market. In its list of the top 10 Most Valuable Brands and Most Strongest Brands, Brand Finance, a business valuation and strategy consultancy company, has cited ABSA, Capitec, FNB, Nedbank, and Standard Bank among the top 10 strongest South African brands.[321]

South Africa is not without its problems, however, and the IMD World Competitiveness Report 2018 put the country in 53rd position and revealed the areas which remain a hindrance to businesses competing in the country.[322] Significant problems are the high levels of structural unemployment, lack of access to quality education, plus poverty and inequality.

According to the 2016 *BusinessTech.co.za* article "Sixteen Things Businesses Hate about South Africa," business leaders believed the top five challenges to doing business in the country were inefficient government bureaucracy, restrictive labor regulations, a shortage of skilled workers, political instability, and corruption.[323]

These problems continue to be a challenge. As Martin Kingston, the vice president of Business Unity South Africa wrote, confidence in transparency, accountability, and fairness in the country has declined, in large part because of ongoing and widespread "state capture."[324] This is a type of systemic political corruption in which private interests significantly influence a state's decision-making processes to their own advantage. For example, in 2016 there were allegations of an overly close and potentially corrupt relationship between the wealthy Gupta family and the South African president Jacob Zuma, his family, and leading members of the African National Congress.

South African business leaders rank corruption as the most problematic factor for doing business. Trust in both public institutions and the ethical conduct of business is low. According to Kingston, 83 percent of South Africans have seen corruption getting worse over the last few years—the highest of any country in Africa.[325]

The importance of public perception: brand South Africa

Every nation has its problems, and every nation should have the opportunity to solve those problems while at the same time attracting foreign investment and developing the international business connections that are the lifeblood of any economy.

Based in Johannesburg, Brand South Africa was established in August 2002 to help create a positive and compelling national brand image. It is an office of the federal Department of Communications (DOC), which itself is tasked with

> creating an enabling environment for the provision of inclusive communication services to all South Africans in a manner that promotes socio-economic development and investment through broadcasting, new media, print media and other new technologies, and to brand the country locally and internationally.[326]

Brand SA grew out of the International Marketing Council of South Africa (IMC), which had been established in 2000 by the administration of then-President Thabo Mbeki to "create a positive, unified image of South Africa; one that builds pride, promotes investment and tourism, and helps new enterprises and job creation." It was later rebranded as Brand South Africa.[327]

Currently, Brand South Africa is headed by Dr Kingsley Makhubela. He formerly served as the director-general of the Department of Tourism, and prior to that, held, among others, the position of chief of state protocol at the Department of International Relations and Co-operation.

Brand South Africa was launched with the intention to attract tourism and investment. This required a consolidated and consistent brand image.[328] In pursuit of its mission, Brand South Africa provides a wide range of services while promoting a positive message about South Africa to the nation and the world. This involves work both domestically and internationally.

Play Your Part

Domestically, the main branding tool is called "Play Your Part." Play Your Part is a program designed to inspire, empower, and celebrate active citizenship in South Africa. It targets a broad cross-section of the population, from businesses to individuals, non-governmental organizations (NGOs) to government, churches to schools, and those of all ages. It aims to encourage South Africans to use some of their time, money, skills, or goods to contribute to a better future for all.

The 16 Days of Activism for No Violence against Women and Children campaign took place from November 25 to December 10, 2018. Over that period, the government convened a series of dialogues on violence against women and children to raise awareness of the problem, explore the causes, and seek appropriate solutions. Through the dialogue sessions, government representatives hoped to interact with community members who had experienced violence and abuse.[329] The campaigned was launched on November 25 in Melmoth, KwaZulu-Natal, under the theme of #HearMeToo: End Violence against Women and Children!

Direct government action included the Women Empowerment and Gender Equality Bill, passed in 2014, which provided government with the legislative authority to promote the empowerment of women and addressed issues of enforcement and compliance toward the attainment of the national target of 50/50 gender parity. Other measures included the Prevention and Combating of Trafficking in Persons Act (Act No 7 of 2013), which penalized the trafficking of young girls and women; and also the practice of *ukuthwala*, a form of abduction that involves kidnapping a girl or a young woman by a man and his friends or peers with the intention of compelling the girl or young woman's family to agree to marriage.[330]

Global South Africans

Abroad, South Africa exercises what we can call "rugby diplomacy." Global South Africans (GSA) is a project led by Brand South Africa to enlist the talent, experience, and credibility of South Africans living abroad, permanently or temporarily, with the goal of capitalizing on the "Miracle of 1994" (the coming to power of the African National Congress) and reaffirmed with the nation's unexpected victory in the rugby World Cup the following year, which did much to bring the splintered nation together.

The World Cup did much to break down stereotypes about South Africa and to demonstrate that, in spite of a number of very real challenges, the newly unified nation deserved a place in the upper echelons of emerging market economies. Brand South Africa sought to build on the reputational momentum the World Cup had given them and on what it had done to bring the nation together.[331]

Not to be outdone by the men, in December 2018, South Africa's women's football team, Banyana Banyana, made history in Ghana. After a nail-biting tournament, Banyana Banyana (which means "The Girls") reached the finals of the Africa Women's Cup of Nations, and for the first time ever, earned a spot in the all-important FIFA Women's World Cup taking place on June 7, 2019, in France.[332]

Brand South Africa launched the Global South African program in the conviction that South African citizens of every color could be a priceless resource for the nation as it strived to compete in the global economy. The term "brand ambassador" has lately become popular among consumer products companies, and Brand South Africa adopted it by encouraging visitors to the website—and indeed all citizens of South Africa—to become part of the GSA network and act as brand ambassadors for the country. As they said, "You believe in South Africa, love the place, and want to help us reach our full potential for the benefit of all our people and the continent of which we are part."[333]

"Amazing Thailand"

While the Kingdom of Thailand is an ancient country, the nation we know today can be said to have begun in the 1960s with the American war in Vietnam. The Thai government—which contributed troops to the war effort—allowed the US Air Force to use Thai air and naval bases. At the height of the war, almost 50,000 American military personnel were stationed in Thailand, mainly airmen. Thai entrepreneurs, many with connections to the government, constructed new hotels, restaurants, and bars to serve the battalions of cash-laden American GIs visiting on R&R. The GIs added USD 111 million to the Thai economy.[334]

The American presence and the exposure to Western culture hastened the westernization and modernization of Thai society. Before the war, the impact of Western culture was limited to a highly educated elite in society; but with US dollars pumped into the economy, the service, transportation, and construction industries grew phenomenally. The negative effects of drug abuse and prostitution also grew, and the traditional rural family unit was broken down as more and more rural Thais moved to the cities to find employment.

In 1965, the population of Thailand was 30 million people, and by the end of the 20th century this number had doubled. Bangkok's population had grown 10-fold since 1945 and has tripled since 1970.

With modernization and a growing middle class came political instability. After the student-led revolution of October 14, 1973, the following decades were characterized by a tenuous democracy, with military rule being reimposed after a bloody coup in 1976. For most of the 1980s, Thailand was ruled by Prime Minister Prem Tinsulanonda, a strongman who restored parliamentary politics. Apart from a brief period of military rule from 1991 to 1992, the country remained a constitutional monarchy, whereby the prime minister was the head of government and a hereditary monarch was head of state. The judiciary was independent of the executive and the legislative branches.

This period ended with the coup d'état May 22, 2014. The 2007 constitution was revoked, and since that time Thailand has been under the rule of a military organization called the National Council for Peace and Order (NCPO). In practical terms, negotiations between politicians, bureaucrats, influence peddlers, corporate leaders, and army officers create a sense of political stability. In 2016, the Economist Intelligence Unit rated Thailand as a "hybrid regime."[335] This is defined as a nation "where consequential irregularities exist in elections, regularly preventing them from being fair and free." Such a nation has a government that applies "pressure on political opponents and non-independent judiciaries," and has "widespread corruption, harassment, and pressure placed on the media, anemic rule of law, and more pronounced faults than flawed democracies."[336]

For centuries, a symbol of stability has been the Thai royal family. Although the current Chakri dynasty was created in 1782, the existence of the institution of monarchy in Thailand is traditionally considered to have its roots in the founding of the Sukhothai Kingdom in 1238. In 1946, Prince Bhumibol Adulyadej (Rama IX), then aged 19 years old, ascended the throne. He died on October 13, 2016, at the age of 88; at the time of his death, King Bhumibol was the world's longest reigning monarch. The Thai military leadership has traditionally backed the monarchy; in 2015 alone, it spent USD 540 million—more than the entire budget of the Ministry of Foreign Affairs—on a promotional campaign called "Worship, protect and uphold the monarchy."[337]

Despite its volatile political history, Thailand has long been a popular tourist destination, renowned for its vibrant cultural heritage and natural beauty. Traditional Thai culture features a number of performing arts including drama and Thai dance. Medical tourism is a large and growing sector. Food is a big attraction—in 2016, gastronomy was Thailand's fourth-largest portion of tourism income. Elephant trekking has been an attraction for tourists for decades, and ever since logging in Thailand was banned in 1989, elephants have been brought into camps to perform for tourists and to give them rides.

Buddhist temples are a very popular attraction. As of December 31, 2004, there are a total of 40,717 Buddhist temples (*Wat* in Thai language) in Thailand, of which 33,902 are in current use, according to the Office of National Buddhism. One of the most spectacular is Bangkok's Temple of the Reclining Buddha, which hosts the largest collection of Buddhas in Thailand, including a reclining Buddha that is 45 meters (150 feet) long. Built on an island close to the Grand Palace, the temple complex is considered the best of the best royal temples. The oldest temple in Thailand is Phra Pathom chedi, which means "Holy chedi of the beginning" (*chedi* is a part of *Wat*), which dates to the third century BCE, when Buddhism was introduced to Thailand.

A recent addition to Thailand's temples is Wat Rong Kun, better known to foreigners as the White Temple, in Chiang Rai Province. Opening to visitors in 1997, it is a contemporary, unconventional, privately owned art exhibit in the style of a Buddhist temple. It is owned by Chalermchai Kositpipat, who designed and constructed it. And yes, it is all white. A work in progress, Kositpipat considers the temple to be an offering to Lord Buddha, and believes the project will give him immortal life. The temple is not expected to be completed until 2070.[338]

Muay Thai, or Thai kick boxing, is the national sport of Thailand, and a trip to a stadium to witness the "science of the two limbs" is top on the agenda of many tourists.

Sex tourism has been an unfortunate reality in Thailand; of the 26.74 million visitors recorded by the Tourism Authority of Thailand (TAT) in 2013, 11.23 million were men suspected by NGOs to have come to Thailand explicitly to engage in prostitution.[339] The government regularly expresses its displeasure; on February 21, 2017, Prime Minister Gen Prayut Chan-o-cha announced that he would order the police to dismantle the booming sex industry in the coastal city of Pattaya. "I do not support prostitution," said Prayut.[340]

If you think anything has changed, just Google "Pattaya sex" and you will see what's possible.

The tourism authority of Thailand

In 1924, a government office called Tourism of Thailand was founded by Prince Purachara Jayakara, the Prince of Kamphaengphet. When he was sitting as a train commander, he would send stories about Thailand to get published in the United States. He set up an advertising department for the State Railway of Thailand to help tourists who visited Thailand and promote Thailand among foreigners. The office was originally at the State

Railway of Thailand but was later moved to Hua Lamphong Railway Station. After Prince Purachara Jayakara went to work for the Ministry of Commerce and Transport, the office also moved there, but it was still working closely with the State Railway of Thailand.[341]

For the next half century, responsibility for attracting tourists to Thailand shuttled between the State Railway of Thailand, the Ministry of Commerce, the Ministry of Commerce and Transport, and the Office of the Prime Minister. On May 4, 1979, the Tourism Authority of Thailand (TAT) was formally established as an arm of the Ministry of Tourism and Sports. Its mandate is to promote Thailand's tourism industry.

The "Amazing Thailand" campaign was launched in 1998 to mark the 72nd birthday of His Majesty King Bhumibhol Adulyadej. It also marked the end of the last millennium and the start of a new one. In addition, it presented the chance for Thailand to highlight the importance of tourism as part of recovery efforts from the 1997 Asian crisis.

The TAT partnered with public and private organizations to launch the campaign, which featured sales and unique Thai tourism products including accommodation, entertainment, souvenirs, and new destinations. This resulted in a 7.53 percent growth in visitor arrivals to 7.76 million in 1998, and a further 10 percent increase to 8.58 million in 1999.[342]

Various other campaigns have followed, including "Unseen Thailand" (2003), Thailand Grand Invitation (2006), Thailand Talk to the World (2007), Amazing Thailand It Begins with the People (2013–2014), and most recently, Discover Thainess Campaign (2015). As an example of the "spirit of Thainess," TAT informs us that

> Thai boxing incorporates the Thai way of life in the *wai kru* dance as a way of paying respect to the trainer; the Thai fun in the enjoyment of the crowd; the Thai wisdom in the techniques and training handed down over centuries; and the Thai wellness in the many techniques used to treat wounds or bruises.[343]

In 2018, tourism revenue was expected to climb to 3 trillion baht, with gastronomy accounting for 750 billion. "The TAT will heavily promote gastronomy tourism as well as street food, especially in Bangkok," said Yutthasak Supasorn, governor of the Tourism Authority of Thailand. "Local food will be one of our core tourism products in the coming year. The TAT aims to push the country to become a destination for gastronomy in Asia."[344]

One initiative included an effort to create a Michelin Guide for Thailand. In 2017, the government approved a 144 million baht budget (USD 4.5 million) to fund the Michelin Guide in a five-year (2017–2021) contract to create Michelin Guides for Thailand. Bangkok was the first city Michelin explored to find the best restaurants. *The Michelin Guide to Bangkok* was released on December 6, 2017. There were just 17 starred restaurants in Bangkok, including 14 locations with one star and three with two stars. No Bangkok restaurant was awarded three stars. The list was small, especially for a city with a population of more than 8 million people.[345]

Reflecting the impressive diversity of street food in Bangkok, which is one of the most attractive spots for visitors from around the world, the Michelin Guide selected a total of 28 street food stalls. The project is expected to expand to other Thai cities.

Today, tourism is a major economic contributor to Thailand. Estimates of tourism receipts directly contributing to the Thai GDP of 12 trillion baht (USD 378 billion) range from 9 percent (1 trillion baht) (2013) to 17.7 percent (2.53 trillion baht) in 2016. When indirect travel and tourism receipts are included, the 2014 total is estimated to have accounted for 19.3 percent (2.3 trillion baht) of Thailand's GDP.[346]

Thailand consistently receives high reviews and rankings as a tourist destination. In 2013, Thailand was the #10 "top tourist destination" in world tourism rankings compiled by the United Nations World Tourism Organization, with 26.5 million international arrivals.[347]

In the MasterCard 2014 and 2015 Global Destination Cities Index, Bangkok ranked #2 in the world's top 20 most visited cities, trailing only London. The US News' 2017 Best Countries report ranked Thailand at #4 globally for adventure value and seventh for cultural heritage.[348]

In 2018, Thailand again appeared in the MasterCard top 10 list of global cities for dining and shopping. In the MasterCard Global Destination Cities Index, Bangkok was ranked third on the list of the Top Global Cities for Dining and sixth on the list of the Top Global Cities for Shopping.

The GDCI Indulgences survey is a part of the MasterCard Global Destination Cities Index (GDCI). It ranks cities that tourists had visited in the previous year. In 2018, the result indicated that Bangkok was the #1 global destination for the third consecutive year, with Phuket and Pattaya ranked 12th and 18th, respectively. This has resulted in Thailand being the only country to have three cities in the top 20 list. "Dining and shopping are the key expenditure items that connect visitors to local culture, traditions, and history," said Donald Ong, director of MasterCard Thailand and Myanmar:

> MasterCard has created an amazing city experience for tourists through the Priceless Cities program, including Bangkok. Whether it is a vacation in a boutique hotel or tasting famous food in Thailand, MasterCard believes that opening up new experiences will create impressive memories for tourists from all over the world.[349]

52. CONCLUSION

Competitiveness is best understood as a country's ability to generate prosperity by using all the resources and competencies of its economy. There is no single way for a country to top the competitiveness rankings, and that is fine. The problem is that country competitiveness itself is frequently misinterpreted.

Country competitiveness is not a zero-sum game. Countries do not compete in the same way that companies and industries do. Firms compete to gain market share, enjoy economies of scale, or exploit first-mover advantages in new products and markets. Traditionally, competition at the company level is a zero-sum game: you win, I lose. By contrast, making countries more competitive involves cooperation as well as competition. In particular, trade and markets enable economies to collaborate to increase prosperity for all. World Bank data shows that, between 1994 and 2019, there is no single country among the 63 included in the IMD World Competitiveness Yearbook where GDP per capita has declined over the period. Therefore, if economic growth is an indicator of long-term competitiveness then, in the competitiveness race, everybody wins.

Country competitiveness is not just about exporting more. It is true that the ability to export is a fundamental driver of competitiveness. A closer look at the data shows a positive correlation (of 0.41) between a country's IMD World Competitiveness score and the criterion that measures its contribution to world exports (in percentage terms, and based on 2018 data).

However, some of the most competitive economies in our 2018 rankings are net importers, including the United States in first position. Developing a strong domestic market of consumers and companies that buy foreign goods and services can be desirable if a country lacks a significant comparative advantage in certain industries.

Achieving export excellence should be a governmental priority only to the extent that it creates jobs and prosperity in the country. Exporting construction or banking services, for instance, does not necessarily generate jobs at home. Exporting tourism and travel-related services, manufactured goods, and agricultural products does. A country can hinder its competitiveness if it promotes sectors that create jobs mostly abroad.

Country competitiveness does not require democratic institutions. Of the top 10 countries in the IMD World Competitiveness Ranking for 2018, 4 are among the world's 20 least democratic countries according to the Economist Intelligence Unit. History shows that democracy leads to lower levels of corruption, more transparency, and better respect for property rights—all drivers of competitiveness. However, democracy seems to be a sufficient rather than a necessary condition for greater competitiveness. (It is an interesting empirical question whether democracy leads to more competitiveness, or whether competitiveness ultimately results in a demand for democracy.) Countries such as Singapore and the United Arab Emirates rank very highly without having developed democratic institutions.

For countries in the early stages of building competitiveness, the question is which model to follow. Contrary to what international organizations such as the IMF or The World Bank would have advised 20 years ago, a dispassionate and objective economist cannot suggest that democracy is clearly the starting point to achieve prosperity.

Country competitiveness does not mean greater happiness. The IMD World Competitiveness Rankings do not indicate where people are happier or live better, unless quality of life is identified with the availability of economic resources and financial means. The most competitive countries are the most prosperous, yet not necessarily the happiest. Happiness is a relative concept, usually measured by asking people how they feel with respect to a reference group. Happiness cannot be an objective of economic policy and is therefore not a key performance indicator in the competitiveness race. There is no consistent relationship between happiness and competitiveness.

Country competitiveness is not just economic growth. Growth is only a long-term byproduct of competitiveness. There is a growing consensus now that the so-called MINT countries (Mexico, Indonesia, Nigeria, and Turkey) are some of the most promising economies for the next few decades.[350] But it would be a mistake to focus on macroeconomic figures as the only indicators of their success.

As IMD's World Competitiveness research during the last 30 years has shown, competitiveness results from the combination of economic performance, perceptions, values, resources, and competencies. Only by excluding incorrect interpretations of competitiveness will countries be able to respond to the challenges of global markets.

NOTES

1 *The Economist*, January 10, 2019, in www.economist.com/news/2019/01/10/the-big-mac-index, last checked March 12, 2019.
2 www.swissinfo.ch/eng/business/big-business_switzerland-s-love-affair-with-multinationals/44342642, last accessed March 12, 2019.
3 https://data.snb.ch/de/topics/aube#!/cube/opanmumkpbs, last accessed March 12, 2019.

4 Source: Swiss Confederation data: www.kmu.admin.ch/kmu/fr/home/politique-pme/po
   litique-pme-faits-et-chiffres/chiffres-sur-les-pme/entreprises-et-emplois.html, last checked
   March 12, 2019.
5 For example, Angrist and Krueger (1991) and Aakvik et al. (2010) attempt to determine the
   causal impact of education on earnings. Psacharopoulos and Patrinos (2004) create a model
   for the relationship between education and earnings. Studies by Trostel et al. (2002) and
   Harmon et al. (2003) analyze the impact of the parents' education level as a determinant of
   the education level of the children, and their relationship with income.
6 Cropley (2004).
7 Esquivel (1995).
8 Wilson (2005).
9 Paananen et al. (2015).
10 PISA scores are scaled so that the OECD average in each domain (mathematics, reading, and
   science) is 500 and the standard deviation is 100.
11 See https://data.oecd.org/eduresource/public-spending-on-education.htm, last accessed
   March 12, 2019.
12 Hanushek and Woessmann (2015).
13 Popkova et al. (2015).
14 Gal (2019).
15 Investopedia (2019).
16 Data.worldbank.org. (2019).
17 Marsh (2014).
18 Rushe (2018).
19 Walker (2014).
20 Willams-Grut (2016).
21 Duchesne and McMaugh (2018).
22 Biesta (2017).
23 Biesta (2015).
24 Pratt et al. (2017).
25 Ibid.
26 Schwartzman et al. (2015).
27 O'Cadiz (2018).
28 Clark and Worger (2016).
29 Schwartzman et al. (2015).
30 Shay (2017).
31 This part is based primarily on Hofstetter (2012).
32 Hofstetter (2012).
33 Accord intercantonal sur l'harmonisation de la scolarié obigatoire (concordat HarmoS)
   (2007).
34 Federal Statistical Office (2016).
35 Marti (2017).
36 Ibid.
37 Fuentes (2011).
38 Ibid.
39 Bauer (2013).
40 CSRE (2015).
41 Sahlberg (2009).
42 Risku (2014) and Routti and Ylä-Anttila (2006).
43 Antikainen and Luukkainen (2008).
44 Aho et al. (2006).
45 Risku (2014).
46 Antikainen and Luukkainen (2008).
47 Ibid.
48 World Bank (2006).
49 OECD (2010).
50 Ben-Hur et al. (2020).

51 Source: www.bgfalconmedia.com/city/bowling-green-hosts-th-annual-national-tractor-p ulling-championships/article_7deba90a-68f1-11e6-b892-87c73a1bd841.html, last consulted December 12, 2018.

52 Jafza brochure, last consulted December 12, 2018.

53 See www.infofort.com/about-infofort/.

54 http://taxsummaries.pwc.com/ID/Portugal-Corporate-Tax-credits-and-incentives, last consulted December 12, 2018.

55 https://algarvedailynews.com/news/11080-tax-benefits-attracted-10-000-foreigners-to-p ortugal-in-2016, last consulted December 12, 2018.

56 Ernst & Young, "HR and Tax Alert," July 2016.

57 *Financial Times*, September 19, 2017.

58 Source: IMD World Competitiveness Rankings 2017–2018.

59 *Business Insider*, December 22, 2017.

60 Camacho, A., and C. Rodríguez (2011), "Firm Exit and Armed Conflict in Colombia", Universidad De Los Andes working paper.

61 Ben-Hur et al. (2020).

62 Cinco Días, https://cincodias.elpais.com/cincodias/2018/08/24/fortunas/1535129090_76737 2.html, last consulted on December 18, 2018.

63 Emerging Markets Today (2016), "Why Brazil still is a no-go for IKEA," https://emergin gmarkets.today/2016/02/03/why-brazil-still-is-a-no-go-for-ikea/, accessed January 20, 2019.

64 Moraes and Ferrer (2010).

65 Karpowicz et al. (2018).

66 Amann, E., Baer, W., Trebat, T., and Lora, J.V. (2016), Infrastructure and Its Role in Brazil's Development Process. *The Quarterly Review of Economics and Finance*, 62, 66–73.

67 CbSnews.com. (2019), Cities with the worst traffic in the world. [online] www.cbsnews.com/ pictures/worst-traffic-cities-in-the-world/23/, accessed January 20, 2019.

68 BBC News (2019), The city with 180km traffic jams. [online] www.bbc.com/news/magazine -19660765, accessed January 20, 2019.

69 *The Rio Times* (2015), Rio Has Third Worst Traffic of 146 Cities in the World | *The Rio Times*. [online] https://riotimesonline.com/brazil-news/rio-real-estate/rio-has-third-worst-traffic -of-146-cities-in-the-world/, accessed January 20, 2019.

70 *The Telegraph* (2019), The world's worst cities for traffic. [online] www.telegraph.co.uk/travel /galleries/The-worlds-worst-cities-for-traffic/traffic-rio/, accessed January 20, 2019.

71 Raiser, M., Clarke, R., Procee, P., Briceno-Garmendia, C., Kikoni, E., Kizito, J., and Viñuela, L. (2017), Back to Planning: How to Close Brazil's Infrastructure Gap in Times of Austerity.

72 Ibid.

73 Fearnside, P.M. (2002), Avanca Brasil: Environmental and Social Consequences of Brazil's Planned Infrastructure in Amazonia. *Environmental Management*, 30 (6), 0735–0747.

74 Ibid.

75 BBC News (2019), The importance of infrastructure investment. [online] www.bbc.com/ news/business-11642433, accessed January 20, 2019.

76 *The Rio Times* (2015), Rio Has Third Worst Traffic of 146 Cities in the World | *The Rio Times*. [online] https://riotimesonline.com/brazil-news/rio-real-estate/rio-has-third-worst-traffic -of-146-cities-in-the-world/, accessed January 20, 2019.

77 Transport for Development (2017), Are roads and highways the Achilles Heel of Brazil? [online] http://blogs.worldbank.org/transport/are-roads-and-highways-achilles-heel-brazil, accessed January 20, 2019.

78 Smartcitiesdive.com (2019), Study: Rio de Janeiro and São Paulo Lost USD 43 Billion from Traffic Congestion in 2013 | Smart Cities Dive. [online] www.smartcitiesdive.com/ex/sus tainablecitiescollective/study-rio-de-janeiro-and-s-o-paulo-lost-usd-43-billion-traffic-co ngestion-2013/307346/, accessed January 20, 2019.

79 Global Sherpa (2012), Infrastructure Fuels Growth in BRIC Countries—Global Sherpa. [online] http://globalsherpa.org/infrastructure-development-china-india-brazil/, accessed January 20, 2019.

80 Revista.drclas.harvard.edu (2019), Why is Brazil "Underdeveloped" and What Can Be Done About It? [online] https://revista.drclas.harvard.edu/book/why-brazil-underdeveloped-and-what-can-be-done-about-it, accessed January 20, 2019.

81 *Financial Times*, September 19, 2017.

82 *The Economist* (2019), The road to hell. [online] www.economist.com/special-report/2013/09 /28/the-road-to-hell, accessed January 20, 2019.

83 Latin America & Caribbean: Opportunities for All (2017), To close the infrastructure gap, Brazil needs to spend better – not necessarily more. [online] http://blogs.worldbank.org /latinamerica/close-infrastructure-gap-brazil-needs-spend-better-not-necessarily-more, accessed January 20, 2019.

84 *Mail Online* (2017), Brazil's $12 billion Olympic legacy lies in ruins. [online] www.dailym ail.co.uk/news/article-4241412/Brazil-s-12-billion-Olympic-legacy-lies-ruins.html, accessed January 20, 2019.

85 Ibid.

86 Ft.com (2019), The long haul to recovery for Brazil's infrastructure | *Financial Times*. [online] www.ft.com/content/9c0595a2-7eb4-11e7-ab01-a13271d1ee9c, accessed January 20, 2019.

87 Malkiel, B. (1973), "*A Random Walk Down Wall Street*," W.W. Norton and Company, New York. ISBN: 978-0-393-35224-5.

88 *New York Times* (2016), "Timeline: A History of Insider Trading."

89 Bhattacharya, A. and Daouk, H. (2002), "The World Price of Insider Trading," *The Journal of Finance* 57 (1), pp. 75–108.

90 SEC (2015), "SEC Enforcement Actions: Insider Trading Cases."

91 US Department of Justice (2018), "Securities fraud charges announced today against former junior analyst for major investment bank and current NFL player," August 29, 2018.

92 *The Economist* (2011), "Tipping the Scales."

93 Bris, A. (2005), "Do Insider Trading Laws Work?" *European Financial Management* 11 (3), 267–312.

94 OECD (2017), "OECD Corporate Governance Handbook, 2017."

95 U. Bhattacharya, U., Daouk, H., Jorgenson, B. and Kehr, C., "When an Event is Not an Event: The Curious Case of an Emerging Market." *Journal of Financial Economics* 55.

96 Phillip, W.F. (1993), "La actuación de «insiders» en México."

97 Pitt, H.L. and Hardison, D.B. (1992), "Games without Frontiers: Trends in the International Response to Insider Trading." *Law and Contemporary Problems* 55 (4).

98 See www.sec.gov/about/offices/oia/oia_bilateral/mexico-mou.pdf.

99 Battacharya, U. (2006), "Enforcement and Its Impact on the Cost of Equity and Liquidity of the Market." Available at SSRN: https://ssrn.com/abstract=952698.

100 CNN (1999), "Insider Trading Lurks," May 14, 1999.

101 Sommar, J. (2001). "Feds bust Mexico-US insider trading ring," *New York Post*, May 9, 2001.

102 Zambrana (2008), "Sanciones por uso de informacion privilegiada aumentan a nivel mundial." Economia y negocios, July 23, 2008.

103 BMV (1999), "Corporate Governance Code for Mexico," www.ecgi.org/codes/documents/m exico_code_en.pdf.

104 Martinez, J.M. (2007), "Telmex, con la mayor multa de la CNBV," Expansion, July 2, 2007.

105 Davis, M. (2018), "Insider-trading paradise: Where no one goes to jail," *Bloomberg*, March 22, 2018.

106 Murray, C. (2017), "Mexichem, Aeromexico board members fined in Mexico for insider trading." Reuters, October 24, 2017.

107 Davis, M. (2018), "Insider-trading paradise: Where no one goes to jail," *Bloomberg*, March 22, 2018.

108 Bris, A. (2005).

109 www.janasansadaya.org/page.php?id=173&lang=en, last checked March 12, 2019.

110 Vines, S. (1997).

111 Wordie, J. (2017).

112 Smart, A. (2018).

113 Lam, L. (2014).

114 Heidenheimer, A.J. and Johnston, M. (eds). (2001).

115 ICAC.org (2018).

116 Tsang, S. (2007).

117 Transparency International (2018).

118 Lee-Jones, K. (2018).

119 The World Bank Group (2018).

120 World Justice Project (2018).
121 Political and Economic Risk Consultancy, Ltd. (PERC) (2018).
122 ICAC.org.hk (2018).
123 Cheung, Simpson, and Cheung (2018).
124 Lau, C. (2017).
125 ICAC.org.hk (2018).
126 CPAS.ICAC.hk (2018).
127 Ibid.
128 Ibid.
129 Convoy Global Holdings Ltd. (2017).
130 Bloomberg.com (2018).
131 Ng, E. (2017).
132 Yiu, E. (2017).
133 Ng, E. and Yi, E. (2017).
134 hkbedc.icac.hk (2018).
135 "Gee Dor Dor's Space Adventure" Cartoon Movie (2014).
136 Poon Kam-ying and Pearl Poon (n.d.).
137 UNCTAD (2017).
138 World Federation of Stock Markets (2017).
139 UNCTAD (2017).
140 Lucas, R. (1988), "On the Mechanics of Economic Development," *Journal of Monetary Economics* 22, 3–42.
141 Fischer, S. (2003), "The Importance of Financial Markets in Economic Growth," Citigroup.
142 Wurgler (2000).
143 Levine (2005).
144 Wright (2002).
145 Guiso et al. (2002).
146 Thiel (2001).
147 The description of the Chinese banking system is based on Bris and Cheung (2017).
148 This is the latest information available pending the release of 2016 data by the China Banking Regulatory Commission.
149 www.ibef.org/industry/banking-india.aspx.
150 Yoo (2005) and Khan (2014).
151 Reserve Bank of India, "Social Controls, the Nationalisation of Banks and the era of bank expansion—1968 to 1985." Retrieved January 12, 2015.
152 www.worldatlas.com/articles/which-are-the-leading-banks-in-india.html.
153 https://qz.com/india/1020168/the-rbi-is-worried-about-three-big-problems-in-indias-banking-sector/.
154 www.livemint.com/Opinion/nioD0s2ZNJSsXxh2Nges4N/How-bad-are-our-public-sector-banks-Here-are-some-vital-sta.html.
155 See www.novartis.com/sites/www.novartis.com/files/alcon-20f-filing-2018.pdf, last checked March 14, 2019.
156 University of Helsinki Research: www.helsinki.fi/en/news/nordic-welfare-news/heikki-hiilamo-disappointing-results-from-the-finnish-basic-income-experiment, last accessed March 14, 2019.
157 To see the results of the experiment, check Kela's website at www.kela.fi/web/en/news-archive/-/asset_publisher/lN08GY2nIrZo/content/preliminary-results-of-the-basic-income-experiment-self-perceived-wellbeing-improved-during-the-first-year-no-effects-on-employment.
158 The Heritage Foundation (2019), Index of Economic Freedom, The Heritage Foundation, Washington, DC.
159 Murphy (1999).
160 Ibid.
161 Khaddar (2001).
162 Murphy (1999).
163 The Associated Press (1984), Curfew Imposed Across Tunisia As Riots Spread, *The New York Times*.

164 Times Wire Services (1987), Longtime Tunisian Leader Deposed by Prime Minister, *Los Angeles Times*.
165 World Bank (2004) .
166 The Boston Consulting Group (2010).
167 BBC (2011), Tunisia: President Zine al-Abidine Ben Ali forced out.
168 BBC (2011), Tunisian PM Mohammed Ghannouchi resigns over protests.
169 Kottoor, N. (2014), Tunisia 2.0—from revolution to republic, BBC.
170 Reuters (2014)
171 Cuesta et al. (2015).
172 Ibid.
173 Györi and Soares (2018).
174 Györi and Soares (2018).
175 Cuesta et al. (2015).
176 Ibid.
177 IMF (2014).
178 Cuesta et al. (2015).
179 IMF (2017).
180 Reuters (2014), Tunisia govt raises fuel prices, fourth hike this year, Reuters.
181 Anon. (2019), Price Rankings by Country of Loaf of Fresh White Bread (500g) (Markets), Numbeo.com.
182 Meighan (2019).
183 Ibid.
184 IMF (2014).
185 The World Bank (2014).
186 Amara, T. and Laessing, U. (2018), Tunisia will increase aid for poor in response to protests, Reuters.
187 Anon. (2019), Cost of Living in Tunis, numbeo.com.
188 Cuesta et al. (2015).
189 Meighan (2019)
190 Anon. (2019), Cost of Living in Tunis, numbeo.com.
191 Anon. (2019), Gasoline prices around the world, 28-Jan-2019, GlobalPetrpPrices.com.
192 Loukil (2017).
193 World Bank (2018a)
194 OECD (2018)
195 World Bank (2018b)
196 Luscombe (2012), Oman Protectorate, Britishempire.co.uk.
197 Bauer, P. (2018), Jebel Akhdar War, Brittanica (Encyclopaedia Brittanica, London).
198 Shamsunahar (2018).
199 Luscombe, S. (2012), Oman Protectorate, Britishempire.co.uk.
200 Shamsunahar (2018).
201 Anon. (2000), Happy and rich in an Omani toytown, *The Economist*.
202 The World Trade Organization (2000), WTO's General Council approves accession of Oman.
203 CIA (2019)
204 The World Bank (1994).
205 Ibid.
206 Krane and Monaldi (2017).
207 Ibid.
208 Times News Service (2017), Oman slashes subsidies by more than OMR500 million in a single year, *Times of Oman*.
209 World Bank (2018)
210 Hasan, Syed Haitham (2018), Budget 2018: A helping hand for Oman, *Times of Oman*.
211 *Oman Daily Observer* (2017), Omani citizens to get subsidised fuel.
212 Times News Service (2019), More than 300,000 register for fuel subsidy system in Oman, *Times of Oman*.
213 *Gulf Business* (2018), Oman officials discuss removal of electricity subsidies, *Gulf Business*.
214 Times News Service (2019), Oman's budget 2019: Strong and fair, *Times of Oman*.
215 LoveMoney Staff (2018), Most expensive and cheapest countries to buy gas in 2018, MSN.

216 www.dynamic-ews.com/Tariffs/Electricity%20Tariffs/Oman.pdf, last accessed January 10, 2019.
217 Anon. (2019), Cost of Living in Muscat, numbeo.com.
218 The World Bank (1994).
219 Al Shueili (2014).
220 *Muscat Daily* (2016), Study demonstrates possibility to reduce residential water demand by increasing price—Oman, *Muscat Daily News*.
221 Anon. (2018), Water Challenges in Oman—Fanack Water.
222 Al Shueili, Ali Abdullah Mohamed (2014), Financial sustainability of the water sector in the Sultanate of Oman, Loughborough University Institutional Repository.
223 *Muscat Daily* (2016), Oman subsidy spending to fall 64%, says World Bank, *Muscat Daily News*.
224 Ibid.
225 Kotagama et al. (2012).
226 Al Mukrashi, F. (2015), Oman cuts subsidy spending by 48% in 2015, *Gulf News*.
227 *Muscat Daily* (2016), Study demonstrates possibility to reduce residential water demand by increasing price—Oman, *Muscat Daily News*.
228 Anon. (2019), Cost of Living in Muscat, numbeo.com.
229 The World Bank (2018b).
230 Ibid.
231 Dudley, D. (2018), Oman Told By IMF It Needs To Make "Substantial" Reforms To Its Economy, *Forbes*.
232 Ibid.
233 Moerenhout (2018).
234 Fergusson, N., Milken Institute Global Summit April 2012.
235 Although the two provinces share identical pronunciation, the extra "a" in Shaanxi indicates a slightly different tone, typically indiscernible to a non-native ear.
236 The four ancient capitals in China are Xi'an, Beijing, Nanjing, and Luoyang.
237 Shaanxi borders with Shanxi, Henan, Hubei, Sichuan, Gansu, Ningxia, and Inner Mongolia.
238 The erosion particularly affects the area north of the Qin Mountains where officials planted more trees, extended irrigation networks, and increased usage of agricultural terraces.
239 In China, most farmland is measured in mu; 1 mu = 0.06 hectares.
240 A Communist Party policy that aims to end rural poverty and double the impoverished farmer's income to $1,200 by 2020.
241 The four major specialized banks in China, known as the Big Four, are Agricultural Bank of China (ABC), Bank of China (BOC), Construction Bank of China (CCB), and Industrial and Commercial Bank of China (ICBC).
242 Corporate Social Responsibility Report, Agricultural Bank of China Limited, 2015.
243 The rural population in China counted 577 million people at the end of 2017.
244 Adam Smith was an 18th-century Scottish philosopher and a pioneer of political economy who wrote *An Inquiry into the Nature and Causes of the Wealth of Nations*.
245 *Arab News*, March 29, 2011.
246 A report by the kingdom's General Directorate of Traffic stated in 2011 that an average of 17 Saudi Arabian residents die on the country's roads each day. The World Health Organization published a study showing that Saudi Arabia has the world's highest number of deaths from road accidents, now the country's principal cause of death in adult males aged 16–36. The study also showed that 6,485 people had died and more than 36,000 were injured in over 485,000 traffic accidents during 2008 and 2009.
247 After the 2003 rule, local taxi companies asked the government to provide 7,000 Saudi drivers through the JCCI (Jeddah Chamber of Commerce and Industry) to comply with Saudization rules but only 17 names were given, of which only two showed up (*Arab News*).
248 Abdul Latif Jameel Community Initiatives Annual Report 2011.
249 Since 2002, more than 2,209 young males have benefitted from this program.
250 The group owns three Daihatsu dealerships in Germany.
251 www.alj.com.
252 Alsharif, A. Saudi should free woman driver-rights group. Reuters, May 24, 2011.
253 This section is based on: Business Monitor International. Competitive Landscape, Passenger Vehicles—Saudi Arabia, Q4 2011. October 17, 2011.

254 Source: Statista, last checked February 25, 2019.

255 www.alj.com.

256 Porter, M. (2011), Creating shared value. *Harvard Business Review*, January–February.

257 ALJCI (2011), Annual report.

258 Zain, M. (2008), A Beacon of Corporate Social Responsibility: Abdul Latif Jameel Co. Dinar Standard, May 28.

259 Bab Rizq Jameel offers them interest-free and fee-free financing starting from SR 10,000 to a maximum of SR 150,000 with a repayment period that can extend up to four years. Projects financed by Bab Rizq Jameel cover a wide range of industries from service to industrial to production. The goal is to support job creation for young males and females by developing new projects or expanding existing ones.

260 This is more difficult than it seems in a country like KSA, where many situations that are considered normal under Western standards, are not appropriate.

261 ALJI (2011) Annual report.

262 Founded by Profs. Abhijit Banerjee, Esther Duflo, and Sendhil Mullainathan at the MIT Department of Economics.

263 www.povertyactionlag.org.

264 Hensiek, S., Worthly.com. "Five of The Largest U.S. Monopolies in History," https://worthly .com/business/largest-monopolies-in-the-us/ accessed March 18, 2019.

265 The Learning Network (*NY Times*) (May 15, 2012), "May 15, 1911 | Supreme Court Orders Standard Oil to Be Broken Up." https://learning.blogs.nytimes.com/2012/05/15/may-15-1911 -supreme-court-orders-standard-oil-to-be-broken-up/, accessed March 19, 2019.

266 Koenen, J. (February 2, 2018), "The invincible duopoly of Airbus and Boeing." https://www.han delsblatt.com/today/companies/closed-market-the-invincible-duopoly-of-airbus-and-boei ng/23580956.html?ticket=ST-2198004-T0XBeMp0nGtPBoLKGu6Y-ap6, accessed March 19, 2019.

267 Economics Online UK. www.economicsonline.co.uk/Business_economics/Oligopoly.html, accessed March 19, 2019.

268 Dohmen, F. and Hawrenek, D. (July 27, 2017), "Collusion Between Germany's Biggest Carmakers," www.spiegel.de/international/germany/the-cartel-collusion-between-germany -s-biggest-carmakers-a-1159471.html, accessed March 19, 2019.

269 Villasanta, A. (February 7, 2019). "Disney, Fox Layoffs: 10,000 May Lose Jobs After Merger," www.ibtimes.com/disney-fox-layoffs-10000-may-lose-jobs-after-merger-2760642, accessed March 19, 2019.

270 IBM. "Volkswagen's world-class procurement strategy produces breakthrough productivity gains," www.redbooks.ibm.com/additional_materials/SG247466/Volkswagen_World-class _procurement_strategy.pdf, accessed March 19, 2019.

271 Zaks, D. (February 19, 2019), "'Swindon's finished': UK town in shock over Honda plant closure." https://phys.org/news/2019-02-swindon-finished-uk-town-honda.html, accessed March 19, 2019.

272 Kennedy, R. (February 19, 2019), EuroNews. https://www.euronews.com/2019/02/19/what -are-the-real-reasons-honda-is-closing-its-factory-in-swindon-euronews-answers, accessed March 19, 2019.

273 Furukawa, K. (February 20, 2019), Nikkei.com. "Honda plant closure causes ripple effect through UK supply chain." https://asia.nikkei.com/Business/Companies/Honda-plant-closu re-causes-ripple-effect-through-UK-supply-chain, accessed March 19, 2019.

274 https://en.wikipedia.org/wiki/Ford_Germany. Also Opel.

275 Szymkowski, S. (January 11, 2019), "Cadillac Tipped To Challenge Tesla And Become Lead Electric Car Brand." GMAuthority.com.

276 Source: http://koreajoongangdaily.joins.com/news/article/article.aspx?aid=3046059, March 26, 2018.

277 Source: www.cfr.org/backgrounder/south-koreas-chaebol-challenge, May 4, 2018.

278 Source: www.bloomberg.com/quicktake/republic-samsung, updated October 5, 2018.

279 Source: www.nytimes.com/2017/02/17/business/south-korea-chaebol-samsung.html, February 17, 2017.

280 Source: www.cfr.org/backgrounder/south-koreas-chaebol-challenge, May 4, 2018.

281 Source: www.bloomberg.com/quicktake/republic-samsung, updated October 5, 2018.

282 Source: www.cfr.org/backgrounder/south-koreas-chaebol-challenge, May 4, 2018.

283 Source: www.nytimes.com/2017/02/17/business/south-korea-chaebol-samsung.html, February 17, 2017.

284 Source: www.cfr.org/backgrounder/south-koreas-chaebol-challenge, May 4, 2018.

285 Source: www.ft.com/content/88a7bcac-e70c-11e4-afb7-00144feab7de.

286 Source: www.bloomberg.com/quicktake/republic-samsung, updated October 5, 2018.

287 Source: https://asia.nikkei.com/Politics/South-Korea-grapples-with-cycle-of-corruption-and-pardons, February 17, 2017.

288 Sources: www.lifewire.com/history-of-samsung-818809, updated September 4, 2018; www.cfr.org/backgrounder/south-koreas-chaebol-challenge, May 4, 2018.

289 Sources: www.fundinguniverse.com/company-histories/hyundai-group-history/; www.nytimes.com/2001/03/22/business/chung-ju-yung-85-founder-of-the-hyundai-group-dies.html, March 22, 2001.

290 Sources: www.sk.co.kr/en/about/history.jsp#ctrlArea; https://blogs.wsj.com/briefly/2015/07/31/5-questions-about-sk-group/, July 31, 2015.

291 Sources: https://asia.nikkei.com/Companies/LG-Electronics-Inc, last updated February 27, 2019; www.lgcorp.com/about/history.dev.

292 Source: www.koreatimes.co.kr/www/opinion/2018/12/633_209282.html, July 13, 2017.

293 Source: http://koreajoongangdaily.joins.com/news/article/article.aspx?aid=3046059, March 26, 2018.

294 Source: www.koreatimes.co.kr/www/news/opinon/2013/01/298_129378.html, January 24, 2013.

295 Source: www.ft.com/content/7af74400-3b06-11e3-a7ec-00144feab7de, November 6, 2013.

296 Source: www.koreaherald.com/view.php?ud=20180405000687, April 5, 2018.

297 Source: https://zenkimchi.com/commentary/koreas-e-mart-supermarket-policy-hurt/, May 25, 2017.

298 Source: www.forbes.com/sites/elaineramirez/2017/05/31/5-promises-that-south-koreas-new-president-made-to-startups/#206261836444, May 31, 2017.

299 www.ft.com/content/815ab38c-bae4-11e8-8274-55b72926558f, November 5, 2018.

300 www.ft.com/content/1ff86f26-ee06-11e8-89c8-d36339d835c0, November 28, 2018.

301 Source: www.ft.com/content/1ff86f26-ee06-11e8-89c8-d36339d835c0, November 28, 2018.

302 http://english.hani.co.kr/arti/english_edition/e_national/854031.html, July 19, 2018.

303 Source: www.mss.go.kr/site/eng/main.do.

304 Source: www.ft.com/content/815ab38c-bae4-11e8-8274-55b72926558f, November 5, 2018.

305 https://thediplomat.com/2018/08/moons-economic-policies-face-their-first-major-hurdle/, August 23, 2018.

306 www.ft.com/content/53f5cb4c-e3f3-11e8-a6e5-792428919cee, November 9, 2018.

307 Walters, L. "Timor-Leste is on hip travellers' must-visit lists, but it needs to sort the basics." Stuff.co.nz. www.stuff.co.nz/travel/destinations/asia/106452007/timorleste-is-on-hip-travellers-mustvisit-lists-but-it-needs-to-sort-the-basics, accessed January 9, 2019.

308 Smit, W. and Soares, M. (2016).

309 USAID.gov. "Timor-Leste," www.usaid.gov/timor-leste/democracy-human-rights-and-governance, accessed January 9, 2019.

310 Rajalingam, G. (2017).

311 Ibid.

312 EITI.org. "Who We Are." https://eiti.org/who-we-are, accessed January 8, 2019.

313 Smit, W., and Soares, M. (2016).

314 Timor-Leste.gov. "Beyond EITI: Timor-Leste a model of transparency," http://timor-leste.gov.tl/?p=5582&n=1&lang=en (published August 29, 2011), accessed January 9, 2019.

315 Timor-Leste.gov. "Timor-Leste—a Transparency Model," http://timor-leste.gov.tl/?p=4962&n=1&lang=en (published May 3, 2011), accessed January 9, 2019.

316 Budgettransparency.gov.tl. "Transparency Portal gets officially launched by Prime Minister," www.budgettransparency.gov.tl/publicArticle/showNewsArticle/4;jsessionid=8300E712ADA6392D9EA671B42A7D5CC8, accessed January 9, 2019.

317 Paksi, J.A. (2013).

318 Eprocurement.gov.tl. www.eprocurement.gov.tl/publicPage/showPage/1;jsessionid=584C97803D0E7B83B7176949A0585DF9, accessed January 9, 2019.

319 Governmentresults.gov.tl. http://governmentresults.gov.tl/publicResults/index, accessed January 9, 2019.

320 USAID (2018).

321 Lechela, Ntaoleng, "Five banks ranked among SA's strongest brands." Fin24.com. (May 24, 2018), www.fin24.com/Companies/Financial-Services/five-banks-ranked-among-sas-strongest-brands-20180524, accessed January 11, 2019.

322 IMD World Competitiveness Report 2018.

323 BusinessTech.co.za. "16 things businesses hate about South Africa" (October 8, 2016). https://businesstech.co.za/news/government/138875/16-things-businesses-hate-about-south-africa/, accessed January 12, 2019.

324 Kingston, M., "How to rebuild trust and integrity in South Africa." WEF Forum. (June 27, 2018), www.weforum.org/agenda/2018/06/how-to-rebuild-trust-and-integrity-in-south-africa/, accessed January 11, 2019).

325 Ibid.

326 National Government of South Africa, Department: Communications, https://nationalgovernment.co.za/units/view/393/department-communications-doc, accessed January 12, 2019.

327 *Mail & Guardian*, "What was Thabo Mbeki and Essop Pahad's role in the rise of the Guptas?" (April 24, 2017), https://mg.co.za/article/2017-04-24-what-was-thabo-mbeki-and-essop-pahads-role-in-the-rise-of-the-guptas, accessed January 12, 2019.

328 BrandSouthAfrica.com. www.brandsouthafrica.com/, accessed January 12, 2019.

329 National Government of South Africa, "16 Days of Activism," www.gov.za/16DaysofActivism2018, accessed January 12, 2019.

330 Ibid.

331 BrandSouthAfrica.com. www.brandsouthafrica.com/, accessed January 12, 2019.

332 BrandSouthAfrica.com. "10 Things to Know about Banyana Banyana," www.brandsouthafrica.com/people-culture/sport/10-things-to-know-about-banyana-banyana, accessed January 12, 2019.

333 GlobalSouthAfricans.com. http://globalsouthafricans.com/about.html, accessed January 12, 2019.

334 Ruth, R.A. (November 7, 2017), "Why Thailand Takes Pride in the Vietnam War" (Editorial). *New York Times*. www.nytimes.com/2017/11/07/opinion/thailand-vietnam-war.html, accessed January 17, 2019.

335 EIU.com digital. "Democracy Index 2016—The Economist Intelligence Unit," www.eiu.com. www.eiu.com/public/topical_report.aspx?campaignid=DemocracyIndex2016, accessed January 17, 2019.

336 Yabiladi.com (2015).

337 Fuller, T., "With King in declining health, future of monarchy in Thailand is uncertain," (September 21, 2015). www.todayonline.com/world/asia/king-declining-health-future-monarchy-thailand-uncertain?singlepage=true, accessed January 17, 2019.

338 Barooah, J. (2012), "Thai Buddhist Temple, Wat Rong Khun, Built With Images Of Superman, Neo From The Matrix." *The Huffington Post*. www.huffingtonpost.com/2012/04/26/thai-buddhist-temple-wat-rong-khun_n_1447032.html?ec_carp=4014962788798399158, accessed January 17, 2019.

339 Lines, L. (2015).

340 Prachatai English. "Junta to purge Pattaya of prostitution," (February 22, 2017). https://prachatai.com/english/node/6942, accessed January 17, 2019.

341 TAT (2019).

342 TAT News (archived).

343 Ibid.

344 Sritama, S. (2017).

345 Burton, M., "Bangkok's First-Ever Michelin Guide Is Here," (December 6, 2017). Eater.com. www.eater.com/2017/12/6/16741494/bangkok-first-michelin-guide-stars, accessed January 17, 2019.

346 Turner, R. (2015).

347 UNWTO (2019).

348 Wikipedia (2019).

349 TAT News (2019).

350 BBC, January 6, 2014. www.bbc.com/news/magazine-25548060, last checked March 12, 2019.

REFERENCES

Aakvik, A., Salvanes, K.G., and Vaage, K. (2010). Measuring Heterogeneity in the Returns to Education in Norway Using Educational Reforms. *European Economic Review*, 54 (4), 483–500

Aho, E., Pitkänen, K. & Sahlberg, P. (2006). *Policy Development and Reform Principles of Basic and Secondary Education in Finland since 1968*. Washington, DC: World Bank, Education Working Paper Series 2.

Angrist, J., & Krueger A. (1991). Does Compulsory Schooling Attendance Affect Schooling and Earnings? *Quarterly Journal of Economics*, 106(4), 979–1014.

Antikainen, A. & Luukkainen, A. (2008). Twenty-Five Years of Education Reform Initiatives in Finland. In *Manuscript for a book on Globalization and Education*, available at http://www .oppi.uef.fi/~anti/publ/uudet/twenty_five_years.pdf

Ben-Hur, S., Bris A., Caballero J., & Pistis M.. (2020). *The Drivers of the International Mobility of Managers and Executives: Evidence from OECD Countries*,IMD Working Paper.

Biesta, G. (2015). Freeing Teaching from Learning: Opening up Existential Possibilities in Educational Relationships. *Studies in Philosophy and Education*, 34(3), 229–243.

Biesta, G. (2017). *The Rediscovery of Teaching*. London: Routledge.

Bloomberg.com. Company Overview of Perfect Team Group Limited. https://www.bloomberg.com /research/stocks/private/snapshot.asp?privcapid=108748692 (Accessed 26 December 2018).

Bris, A. (2005), Do Insider Trading Laws Work?. *European Financial Management*, 11, 267–312.

Bris A. & Cheung Stephanie. (2017), Promoting Inclusive Finance: Agricultural Bank of China," IMD Business School case IMD-7-1923.

Cheung, Simpson. & Cheung, Tony. (21 June 2018). No Harm Done, Says Scandal-Hit Ex-Chief of ICAC Timothy Tong. *South China Moring Post*.

Clark, N.L., & Worger, W.H. (2016). *South Africa: The Rise and Fall of Apartheid*. London: Routledge.

Convoy Global Holdings Ltd. *Notes to the Condensed Consolidated Financial Statements*. Interim Report (2017). Page 30.

CPAS.ICAC.hk. (n.d.a). Anti-Corruption Programme: A Guide for Listed Companies. https://cp as.icac.hk/UPloadImages/InfoFile/cate_43/2018/da04fabe-65d6-45f3-8377-f80ef87978ef.pd f (Accessed 26 December 2018).

CPAS.ICAC.hk. (n.d.b). Sample Code of Conduct for Managers and Staff of Kindergartens. https:/ /cpas.icac.hk/UPloadImages/InfoFile/cate_43/2016/ac8f9b49-6fa6-4c8b-aaf0-fce72bc722a9 .pdf (Accessed 23 December 2018).

Cropley, A. (2004). Creativity as a Social Phenomenon. In M. Fryer, (Ed.), *Creativity and Cultural Diversity* (pp.13–23). England: Creativity Centre Educational Trust Press.

Cuesta, José, El-Lahga AbdelRahmen, & Ibarra Gabriel Lara. (2015). *The Socioeconomic Impacts of Energy Reform in Tunisia*. World Bank Group.

Data.worldbank.org. (2019). Government Expenditure Per Student, Primary (% of GDP per capita) | Data. [online] Available at: https://data.worldbank.org/indicator/SE.XPD.PRIM.PC. ZS?locations=FI (Accessed 1 Mar. 2019).

Dolton, P., & Marcenaro-Gutierrez O. (2011), Teachers' Pay and Pupil Performance. *CentrePiece Magazine*. Centre for Economic Performance, Autumn, 20–22.

Duchesne, S., & McMaugh, A. (2018). *Educational psychology for learning and teaching*. Cengage AU.

Esquivel, G. (1995). Comment and Reflection. *Educational Psychology Review*, 7, 215–218. doi:10.1007/BF02212496

Gal, S. (2019). The Best and Worst Countries to be a Teacher, based on Salary. [online] *Pulse.com .gh*. Available at: https://www.pulse.com.gh/bi/strategy/the-best-and-worst-countries-to-be -a-teacher-based-on-salary/p7d6kwh (Accessed 1 Mar. 2019).

"Gee Dor Dor's Space Adventure" Cartoon Movie. https://www.youtube.com/watch?v=wbo8h1xr i38 (Accessed 27 December 2018).

Guiso, L., Sapienza, P., & Zingales, L. (2002). Does Local Financial Development Matter?. National Bureau of Economic Research Working Paper No. 8922.

Györi, Mario, & Soares Fabio Veras. (2018). *Universal Social Protection in Tunisia: Comparing the Effectiveness and Cost-Efficiency of Food and Energy Subsidies with a Proposed Universal Child Allowance Programme.* International Policy Centre for Inclusive Growth.

Hanushek, E.A., & Woessmann, L. (2015). The Economic Impact of Educational Quality. *Handbook of International Development and Education,* 6–19.

Harmon, C., Walker, I., & Westergaard-Nielsen, N.C. (2003). *Education and Earnings in Europe—A Cross Country Analysis of Returns to Education.* Cheltenham , UK: Edward Elgar Publishing, UK Publication Hardback.

Heidenheimer, Arnold J., & Michael Johnston (eds). (September 17, 2001). *Political Corruption: Concepts and Contexts,* 3rd Edition. Transaction Publishing.

Hofstetter, R. (2012). La Suisse et l'enseignement aux XIXe-XXe siècles. Le prototype d'une « fédération d'États enseignants » ?. *Histoire de l'éducation,* 2(2), 59–80.

Hong Kong Business Ethics Development Centre. Defrauding by Giving False Information. http://www.hkbedc.icac.hk/english/publications/case_studies.php?industry=9 (Accessed 26 December 2018)

ICAC.org.hk. (n.d.a). (Accessed 21 December 2018).

ICAC.org.uk. (n.d.b). Guide to Reporting Corruption. https://www.icac.org.hk/en/rc/guide/index .html (Accessed 24 December 2018).

International Monetary Fund (IMF). (2014). *Subsidy Reform in the Middle East and North Africa: Recent Progress and Challenges Ahead.* Washington, DC: Middle East and Central Asia Department, International Monetary Fund.

IMF. (2019), *If Not Now, When? Energy Price Reform in Arab Countries.* Rabat, Morocco: International Monetary Fund.

Investopedia. (2019). What Country Spends the Most on Education? [online] Available at: https ://www.investopedia.com/ask/answers/020915/what-country-spends-most-education.asp (Accessed 1 Mar. 2019).

Kam-ying Poon, & Pearl Poon. (n.d.). Outstanding Security Guard Election. https://me.icac.hk/i cac/ebook2015/story/home/en/home_en_pdf.pdf (Accessed 27 December 2018).

Karpowicz, I., C. Góes, & M. Garcia-Escribano, (2018). Filling the Gap: Infrastructure Investment in Brazil. *Journal of Infrastructure, Policy and Development,* 2(1).

Khaddar, Moncef M. (2001). Tunisia. in Joel Krieger (ed), *The Oxford Companion to Politics of the World,* 2nd edition. Oxford: Oxford University Press.

Kotagama, H, Boughanmi H, Zekri S, & Prathapar S. (2012). Food Security as a Public Good: Oman's Prospects. *Sri Lankan Journal of Agricultural Economics,* 10, 61.

Krane, Jim, & Francisco J. Monaldi. (2017). *Oil Prices, Political Instability, and Energy Subsidy Reform in MENA Oil Exporters.* Houston, TX: Center for Energy Studies.

Lam, Lana. (15 February 2014). Forty Years Since Its Creation, How the ICAC Cleaned up Corruption in Hong Kong. *South China Morning Post.*

Lau, Chris. (03 November 2017). *A Timeline of Former Hong Kong leader Donald Tsang's Legal Journey.* South China Morning Press.

Lee-Jones, Krista. (13 June 2018). *Best Practices in Addressing Police-Related Corruption.* Transparency International.

Levine Ross (2005). Finance and Growth: Theory and Evidence. In Philippe Aghion and Steven N. Durlauf (eds), *Handbook of Economic Growth,* 1, chapter 12, 865–934

Lines, Lisa (July 2015). Prostitution in Thailand: Representations in fiction and narrative non-fiction." *Journal of International Women's Studies,* 16 (3), 86–100. https://vc.bridgew.edu/jiws /vol16/iss3/7/ (Accessed 17 January 2019).

Loukil, S. (2017). Economic Challenges and Opportunities after the Revolution in Tunisia: Inflation and Exchange Rate. *Journal of Global Economics* 5, 17.

Marsh, S. (2014). How the Job of a Teacher Compares around the World. [online] Guardian. Available at: https://www.theguardian.com/teacher-network/teacher-blog/2014/sep/05/how-the-job-of-a-teacher-compares-around-the-world (Accessed 1 Mar. 2019).

Meighan, Brendan. (2019). *What Tunisia and Sudan Can Learn From Egypt on Subsidy Reform.* Washington, DC: Carnegie Endowment For International Peace.

Moerenhout, Tom. (2018). *Energy Pricing Reforms in the Gulf: A Trend but Not (yet) a Norm.* Geneva, Switzerland: Global Subsidies Initiative, International Institute for Sustainable Development.

Moraes, T., & Ferrer, J. (2010). *Brazil Infrastructure.* Working Papers. Washington, DC: George Washington University.

Murphy, Emma. (1999). *Economic And Political Change In Tunisia.* London : Palgrave Macmillan.

Ng, Eric. (29 December 2017). Timeline: How Convoy Morphed from MPF Adviser to Focus of Hong Kong's Biggest Graft Probe. *South China Morning Post.*

Ng, Eric, & Yiu, Enoch. (29 December 2017). Explainer: "Who's Who in the Tangled Web of the Convoy Enigma." *South China Morning Post.*

O'Cadiz, P. (2018). *Education and Democracy: Paulo Freire, Social Movements, and Educational Reform in São Paulo.* London: Routledge.

Organization of Cooperation Economic Development . (2010). Finland: Slow and Steady Reform for Consistently High Results..

Oral, G. (2006). Creativity of Turkish Prospective Teachers. *Creativity Research Journal*, 18, 65–73. doi:10.1207/s15326934crj1801_8

Paananen, M., Kumpulainen, K., & Lipponen, L. (2015). Quality Drift within a Narrative of Investment in Early Childhood Education. *European Early Childhood Education Research Journal*, 23(5), 690–705.

Paksi, Jose Angel. (September 2013). A Critical Analysis of the Impact of Foreign Aid in Timor-Leste. Universitat Jaume I working paper.http://repositori.uji.es/xmlui/bitstream/handle/10234/74447/TFM_Arie%20Paksi.pdf (Accessed 9 January 2019).

Political and Economic Risk Consultancy, Ltd. (PERC). Perceptions of Corruption in Asia, the US and Australia in 2018. http://www.asiarisk.com/subscribe/exsum1.pdf. (Accessed 23 December 2018).

Popkova, E.G., Chechina, O.S., & Abramov, S.A. (2015). Problem of the Human Capital Quality Reducing in Conditions of Educational Unification. *Mediterranean Journal of Social Sciences*, 6(3 S6), 95.

Pratt, S.M., Imbody, S.M., Wolf, L.D., & Patterson, A.L. (2017). Co-planning in Co-teaching: A Practical Solution. *Intervention in School and Clinic*, 52(4), 243–249.

Psacharopoulos, G., & Patrinos, H.A. (2004). Returns to Investment in Education: A Further Update. *Education Economics*, 12(2), 111–134.

Rajalingam, Gobie. (9 August 2017). Timor-Leste Prepares for New Government and Opportunities for Tourist Economy. *Asia Foundation.* https://asiafoundation.org/2017/08/09/timor-leste-prepares-new-government-opportunities-tourist-economy/ (Accessed 8 January 2019).

Risku, M. (2014). A Historical Insight on Finnish Education Policy from 1944 to 2011. *Italian Journal of Sociology of Education*, 6(2), 36–68

Routti, J., & Ylä-Anttila, P. (2006). *Finland as a Knowledge Economy. Elements of Success and Lessons Learned.* Washington, DC: World Bank.

Rushe, D. (2018). The US Spends More on Education than other Countries. Why Is It Falling Behind? [online] Guardian. Available at: https://www.theguardian.com/us-news/2018/sep/07/us-education-spending-finland-south-korea (Accessed 1 Mar. 2019).

Sahlberg, P. (2009). *A Short History of Educational Reform in Finland.* In *Educational Reform in Europe: History, Culture, and Ideology*, Information Age Publishing, pp. 1–24.

Schwartzman, S., Pinheiro, R., & Pillay, P. (Eds.). (2015). *Higher Education in the BRICS Countries: Investigating the Pact between Higher Education and Society* (Vol. 44). Springer.

Shamsunahar, Imran. (2018). *The Dhofar War and the Myth of 'Localized' Conflicts, RealClearDefense*, available at https://www.realcleardefense.com/articles/2018/01/12/the _dhofar_war_and_the_myth_of_localized_conflicts_112890.html

Shay, S. (2017). Educational Investment towards the Ideal Future: South Africa's Strategic Choices. *South African Journal of Science*, 113(1–2), 1–6.

Smart, Alan. (April 2018). The Unbearable Discretion of Street-Level Bureaucrats Corruption and Collusion in Hong Kong. Current Anthropology, 59.

Smit, Willem, and Soares, Manuel. (30 October 2016). *Resistir e Vencer: Branding Timor-Leste*. Asia School of Business.

Sritama, Suchat (29 November 2017). Michelin Guide Set to Hit Thai Tables." https://www.ban gkokpost.com/business/tourism-and-transport/1368711/michelin-guide-set-to-hit-thai-ta bles (Accessed 17 January 2019).

TAT News. (n.d.a). *Bangkok Ranked in Top Ten List of Global Cities for Dining and Shopping in MasterCard Index 2018*. https://www.tatnews.org/2019/01/bangkok-ranked-in-top-ten-list -of-global-cities-for-dining-and-shopping-in-mastercard-index-2018/ (Accessed 17 January 2019).

TAT—Tourismthailand.org. (n.d.). https://www.tourismthailand.org/About-Thailand/About-TA T (Accessed 17 January 2019).

The Boston Consulting Group. (2010). *The African Challengers: Global Competitors Emerge from the Overlooked Continent*. Focus, Boston Consulting Group.

The World Bank. (1994). *Sultanate of Oman Sustainable Growth and Economic Diversification*. Washington, DC: World Bank.

The World Bank. (2004). *Republic of Tunisia*. Washington, DC: Country Assistance Evaluation, The World Bank.

The World Bank. (2006). *Policy Development and Reform Principles of Basic and Secondary Education in Finland since 1968*. The World Bank.

The World Bank. (2014). *Unleashing the Potential of Agriculture to Boost Growth in Interior Regions*. Washington, DC: The World Bank.

The World Bank. (2018a). *International Bank for Reconstruction and Development Program Document for a Proposed Loan in the Amount of Euro 413.4 Million (Equivalent to Usd500 Million) to the Republic of Tunisia for the Investment, Competitiveness and Inclusion Development Policy Financing*. Washington, DC: World Bank.

The World Bank. (2018b). *Oman*. Washington, DC: World Bank.

The World Bank. (2019). Subsidies and other Transfers (% of Expense) | Data. Data.worldbank.org.

The World Bank Group. (n.d.). The Worldwide Governance Indicators. http://info.worldbank.org /governance/wgi/index.aspx#home. (Accessed 23 December 2018).

Thiel Michael. (2001). *Finance and Economic Growth: A Review of Theory and the Available Evidence*. European Union, Directorate General for Economic and Financial Affairs, working paper.

Transparency International. (2018) https://www.transparency.org/en , (Accessed 23 December 2018).

Trostel, P., Walker, I., and Woolley, P. (2002). Estimates of the economic return to schooling for 28 countries. *Journal of Labor Economics*, 9(1), 1–16.

Tsang, Steve. (August 15, 2007). *A Modern History of Hong Kong*. I.B.Tauris.

Turner, Rochelle (2015). Travel & Tourism, Economic Impact 2015, Thailand. London: World Travel & Tourism Council (WTTC). http://www.iberglobal.com/files/2016/thailand_tour ism.pdf (Accessed 17 January 2019).

UN World Tourism Organization (UNWTO). (2014). UNWTO Tourism Highlights. Madrid: UN World Tourism Organization (UNWTO). https://www.e-unwto.org/doi/pdf/10.18111/9789 284416226 (Accessed 17 January 2019).

Vines, Stephen. (14 November 1997). Hong Kong: A corrupt police force haunted by its criminal record. Indeopendent.co.uk.

Walker, P. (2014).OECD report: are larger school class sizes a good thing? [online] Guardian. Available at: https://www.theguardian.com/education/2014/sep/09/school-class-sizes-good-thing-oecd-report (Accessed 1 Mar. 2019).

Wikipedia, Tourism in Thailand. https://en.wikipedia.org/wiki/Tourism_in_Thailand (Accessed 17 January 2019).

Willams-Grut, O. (2016). The 11 best school systems in the world. [online] Available at: https://www.independent.co.uk/news/education/11-best-school-systems-in-the-world-a7425391.html (Accessed 1 Mar. 2019).

Wilson, A. (2005). *Creativity in Primary Education: Theory and Practice (achieving QTS Cross-Curricular Strand)*. Learning Matters Ltd.

Wordie, Jason. (28 April 2017). Hong Kong's history of gifts and bribes, from waiter's tip to comprador's commission." *South China Morning Post*.

World Justice Project. The WJP Rule of Law Index 2017–2018. https://worldjusticeproject.org/our-work/wjp-rule-law-index/wjp-rule-law-index-2017%E2%80%932018 (Accessed 23 December 2018).

Wright, R.E. (2002). The Wealth of Nations Rediscovered: Integration and Expansion in American Financial Markets, 1780–1850. Cambridge University Press, Cambridge, UK.

Wurgler, Jeffrey. (2000). Financial Markets and the Allocation of Capital. *Journal of Financial Economics* 58, 187–214.

Yabiladi.com. (n.d.) Democracy Index 2015: Democracy in an age of anxiety. *The Economist Intelligence Unit*. (Retrieved 26 January 2017).

Yiu, Enoch. (7 December 2017). Executives of Hong Kong Financial Services Firm Convoy under Investigation by Graft Watchdog. South China Morning Post.

Yoo Tae Hwan (2005), Indian Banking Sector Reforms: Review and Prospects. *International Area Studies Review*, 8(2), 167–189.

Part 5
Being competitive in the 21st century

53. INTRODUCTION

In a recent blog post, Dani Rodrik stipulates that "we live in a world of astonishing inequality."[1] Whether this analysis is conducted at the inter- or intra-country level is relatively unimportant, as examples of health, income, racial, social, and wealth inequality are omnipresent around the globe, irrespective of geography. The usual culprits behind this dynamic—namely the pursuit of hyper-globalization, the reduction in corporate and progressive taxation, the de-institutionalization of labor markets and the dismantling of the welfare state, the advantage given to companies and corporate profits—often appear to be rooted in economic ideas that are associated with neoliberal agendas. Based on the doctrines of leading economists such as Friedrich Hayek and Milton Friedman, these policies of market fundamentalism have essentially created the widespread association of economics with the incapacity to achieve large-scale social reforms. More often than not, economics as a discipline has therefore been viewed as the source of the policies that have not only created but also exacerbated the inequalities we see today. And competitiveness and its advocates—international organizations as well as academic institutions such as the Institute for Management Development (IMD) itself—are partly to blame.

However, well-renowned academic economists have recently joined forces to create a movement countering this stigmatization of economics as a discipline inert and unreactive to social inequality. Officially titled "Economics for Inclusive Prosperity" (EfIP), this movement aims to convey how true economic reasoning can be conducive to the creation of a more equal economy and society. Based on purely original content, the innovative policy briefs published have a far-reaching aim: providing a coherent overall vision for economic policy that offers genuine alternatives to market fundamentalism. This vision moves away from the prioritization of reaching a competitive equilibrium, which tends to distribute too much weight to the "average," or so-called middle class. This new approach to policymaking via academically approved economics is well resumed by the authors who claim that they "strive to achieve a whole that is greater than the sum of the parts."

Essentially, inclusive prosperity aims to promote the values of democratic rule and social efficiency by suggesting proposals which tackle societal asymmetries through the balancing and redistribution of power for economic ends. While pure economic efficiency in the textbook sense is put aside, inclusive prosperity offers a refreshing view on how desirable outcomes can be obtained for all stakeholders. The approach is very holistic, also taking into consideration non-pecuniary sources of well-being such as health and political rights as well as addressing problems of collective action such as environmental degradation. With 10 policy briefs currently published on their website, the academic economists of the EfIP have already made recommendations across a wide variety of topics, ranging from labor markets to international trade and finance.

According to the authors, only a restricted number of actors substantially contribute to the current economic debate surrounding policymaking in the political sphere (strongly US-based analysis). On the one hand, we have conservatives who have shown the tendency to justify their preferred policy agendas through vague economic reasoning, while on the other, we have liberals who have increasingly been depicted as insensitive to the economic requirements of a prosperous economy. The only other major actors monopolizing the debate around economic policy are think tanks, who often assign priority to economic growth and push forward the existence of an inevitable efficiency/equality trade-off. In this regard, the introduction of inclusive prosperity as a notion that is independent of politicians' agenda is a welcome and innovative disruption to the status quo.

Do competitive economies converge toward inclusive prosperity?

This is an intriguing and legitimate question as the nuances that separate both concepts are small, yet not void of meaningful interpretation. Although competitiveness and inclusive prosperity share similar values that strive for the sustainable creation of wealth—and hence a reduction in disparity—through economics, achieving the former does not necessarily imply the latter. In recent years, we ourselves have moved from a concept of competitiveness merely based on achieving high productivity levels, to incorporating prosperity, social fairness, individual rights, and quality of life as final goals of policy. Productivity is only the anchor, the intermediate variable through which economies create wealth that must then be shared among citizens in pursuit of happiness and a meaningful life.

Firstly, it is important to point out that the vast majority of indicators used by the proponents of inclusive prosperity to measure inequality and disparity are not new. Their innovative policy proposals tackle issues that are generally well known, and the indicators from which they base their analyses are relatively common, ranging from issues such as taxation levels, government efficiency measures, public and private sector reform, as well as evaluations of financial practices. As such, their analysis of Pareto inefficiencies is based on factors which are already being measured by a multitude of other actors. Following this line of thinking, the work undertaken by the World Competitiveness Center in regrouping more than 300 economic indicators into one easily interpretable ranking provides an extremely useful analytical tool that is compatible with the concerns voiced by inclusive prosperity advocates. The way data from a diverse range of international and national sources is computed allows academics, economists, politicians, and other public officials to accurately pinpoint the sources of national inequalities. Broadly speaking, both competitiveness studies and inclusive prosperity aim to promote economies and policies that generate wealth across all sections of the population. Whereas the competitiveness ranking allows for a facilitated visualization of an economy's strengths and weaknesses, from which policy outlines can be formulated, the notion of the EfIP relies more heavily on the proactive delivery of solutions to issues framed as a hinderance to inclusivity.

However, there are some considerations which speak against the complete convergence of inclusive economic policy recommendations with competitiveness calculations. For instance, although the broad topic areas addressed in the policies are extremely similar to our competitiveness pillars—such as the roles of taxation, government and business efficiency, finance and infrastructure on growth, for example—the fundamental difference lies in the way the indicators are interpreted. Whereas the IMD rankings consider the ontology of competitiveness as stable and rooted in utilitarian economic logic (i.e., being more competitive is better), the EfIP authors challenge the very essence of this neoliberal reasoning (i.e., more competitive policies may not always lead to the most socially desirable outcomes). A concrete example of this can be found in the measure of taxation. Following the reasoning that lower corporate tax rates attract foreign companies and therefore increase investments in the domestic economy, the World Competitiveness Ranking positively interprets reductions in the former. However, the policy brief by Gabriel Zucman treating the same subject matter employs the opposing rhetoric. It warns against the dangerous consequences of the race to the bottom in corporate tax rates, arguing that it could ultimately create a large-scale global public deficit as a result of considerable losses in tax revenue.

The general trend, however, does indicate that countries performing better in the competitiveness ranking do in fact have more inclusive societies. This is partly due to the fact that the ranking is structured in a way that directly accounts for inequalities as a negative trait to economic development. The very definition of competitiveness as the sustainable creation of value implies that the wealth generated must not contribute to a detrimental advance in non-pecuniary objectives such as access to education or healthcare. Competitiveness is often regarded as a key driver of economic growth, and the challenge faced by numerous governments today is ensuring that this growth is inclusive in its reach. The two notions of competitiveness and inclusiveness are not mutually exclusive, however they are self-reinforcing. A good example of this is the United States, where the Black and Latino communities comprise 42 percent of the country's population, but only produce around 4 percent of national gross domestic product (GDP) and a mere 1 percent of job growth. Given that these two communities currently experience some of the highest growth rates in terms of startup generation, a greater inclusion of these individuals in the national economy would considerably increase the country's competitive potential.

Fundamentally, the ability to highlight national economic weaknesses through tools such as the very concept of competitiveness, along with the willingness to implement concepts such as economic inclusive prosperity, provides crucial synergies that ensure future improvements in competitiveness are targeted and accomplished in ways that guarantee the inclusiveness of future economic growth. These coordinated efforts ought to be mirrored on the public–private divide, whereby private investments and know-how should be carefully associated with government intervention to foster a more innovative and dynamic economy. The resulting productivity boost and job creation should provide the keys to achieving growth that is inclusive, cohesive, and sustainable. In other words: future prosperity is synonymous with competitive inclusivity!

Consequently, this part of the book describes the specific aspects of competitiveness that will become more relevant for societies of the 21st century. I start by emphasizing the importance of institutional factors in fostering innovation. The role of the individual skills in innovation, as well as the traits and practices that lead to successful innovation are most often the focus of our discussions with our participants in executive programs. However, individual talent is only one of the legs on which the innovation table stands. The other two are the availability of capital—fundamentally provided by the state—and the existence of educational institutions that centralize early innovation efforts. The role of the state in innovation has been widely and masterly discussed by Professor Mariana Mazzucato in *The Entrepreneurial State*.[2] I will therefore focus on the importance of universities and talent management and how there is a direct correlation between the innovativeness of a country and the quality of its secondary and tertiary education. The United States (and Silicon Valley) comes straight to mind, but I write extensively about the innovation ecosystems in Israel and several Eastern European countries. Israel is one of the most important information technology (IT) hubs in the world today and this is a result of governmental policies that have encouraged innovation starting in the most important universities of the country. Today, Slovenia, Lithuania, Ukraine, and Hungary exemplify the ability to be outstanding in innovation because of talent excellence. Of course, in most of these countries, a lack of capital and insufficient funding in subsequent stages of corporate development prevent societies from fully benefitting from innovation, because their ideas usually end up in foreign hands. In recent years, this trend has been exacerbated, certainly helped by the monopolistic power earned by digital platforms such as Google and Amazon. Microsoft buying Skype; Apple's acquisition of Shazam; Google acquiring AIMatter from Belarus and its technology; and Tencent taking over Supercell are only a few examples of innovation that travels to financially stronger countries. The key to a successful innovation ecosystem is then the optimal combination of ideas, usually generated out of educational institutions, and state financial support (the "entrepreneurial state") to make sure that those innovations remain in the country and create jobs there.

Subsequently, I emphasize the role of technology and digital transformation in fostering prosperity. I am positively impressed every time we take our client companies on discovery expeditions to Singapore and Estonia, two countries that any senior executive must see if he or she wants to understand what it truly means to live a digital life. In Estonia, some of the poster children of corporate development there (Skype, TransferWise, Nortal) have been born out of the emphasis that public policy has placed on technology as a unique differentiator of the economy. I also consider Turkey as a growing IT hub bridging Eastern Europe and the Middle East. Business and country competitiveness will not be possible in the coming decades without digital competitiveness.

The competitiveness agenda has already been set for the coming years, and it has been agreed by most world governments and formalized in the 14 Sustainable Development Goals (SDGs). These are the best proof that country success and inclusive prosperity will grow hand in hand. I want to emphasize though, that the SDGs are not only a public sector agenda. Indeed, goal #14 calls for the implementation of public–private partnership to develop the goals, and I discuss several business models that are currently showing the way ahead. We at the IMD World Competitiveness Center are also working to incorporate those criteria into our rankings. Particularly, inclusive prosperity and competitiveness both require gender balance, so I describe the efforts that an already competitive country such as Norway has made to break gender roles and improve equality with its quota system.

I will conclude this part by analyzing the changing role of public policy in developing 21st-century societies. I strongly believe that governments are nowadays more important than ever. Through several examples of market failures (from Peru to Hong Kong and

Nepal), I discuss the types of government interventions necessary to avoid generating corruption and bureaucracy. I also spend a few pages describing what the education systems should promote in the future, in light of the changing labor markets and the need for new skills and a more flexible workforce. I have already written extensively about this in my previous book (*Flex or Fail*, jointly with Robby Mol and Tony Felton[3]), so this part is an addition to that book.

Finally, I pay attention to two important challenges of the next decades: how to curtail income inequality while preserving the competitiveness of nations, and what is the role of democracies given that, as I have shown in Part 3, benevolent dictators fare better in terms of formulating and executing national strategies.

54. THE ROLE OF UNIVERSITIES IN INNOVATION ECOSYSTEMS

The brothers Auguste and Louis Lumière probably count among the most prominent and best-known French individuals and certainly two inventors who changed the world for good. Born in Besançon in 1862 and 1864, respectively, to a non-conformist father, the siblings were forced to flee eastern France in 1870 due to the looming threat of a Prussian invasion. Resettling in Lyon, their father was adamant that the family-owned photography business could only survive if his sons pursued further education. Closely monitored throughout their schooling, they eventually graduated as engineers from La Martinière: the largest polytechnic school in the city and one of France's leading institutions at the time.

Focusing on their education while simultaneously immersing themselves in the day-to-day realities of their father's photographic plate industry turned out to be a winning investment. Indeed, by their thirties, the Lumière brothers had revolutionized the industry and had become among the first filmmakers in history. They were responsible for over 170 patents in the field of cinematography and imagery development and are, to this day, among the rare French nationals to be honored in Hollywood's Walk of Fame for their contribution to modern cinema. What explains such a spectacular success story and how did the Lumière brothers manage to transform an entire industry without completely disrupting its existing technology?

Family interests and exposure to the field

First, it is important to acknowledge their father's influence as well as their constant immersion in his world of photography. Louis, for example, began experimenting with his father's photography equipment from a very early age. In 1881, as a 17-year-old teenager, it was Louis who developed instant photography through the dry plate process known as blue label or "*étiquette bleue*." This invention brought fame and financial stability to the family business, even allowing them to purchase a new factory near Monplaisir in the suburbs of Lyon.[4] By 1894, the Lumières were producing up to 15 million plates per year and business was thriving.

That same year, their father, Antoine, attended an exhibition of Thomas Edison's kinetoscope in Paris, a revolutionary machine which allowed people to view a moving sequence of photographs capturing the effect of movement. Given a sample length of film by one of the concessionaires, Antoine Lumière was immediately convinced of the incredible potential behind the technology and lost no time in presenting it to his two sons. Although the kinetoscope was patented, he urged Auguste and Louis to temporarily interrupt their research on autochrome color plates to work on developing a way to replicate the motion pictures. His grand idea was to address one of the kinetoscope's biggest weaknesses—its individualistic use—by projecting the moving images onto a screen for simultaneous viewing.

Won over by the economic potential of the idea and spurred on by their father, the brothers started working on prototypes in the winter of 1894. They eventually created the "Cinematograph Lumière," whose key innovation was the mechanism through which the film was transported through the camera device. It was inspired by the intermittent movement of their mother's sewing machine, allowing for a stop-and-go motion that enabled the device to undertake three functions at once: record, develop, and project motion pictures.[5]

Industry-specific knowledge and positive spillovers

La Martinière undoubtedly played a crucial role in developing the innovative capacities of the Lumière brothers and a brief look at the school's history, structure, and pedagogic approach certainly unveils some interesting takeaways with regard to the role of academic institutions and centers of excellence in driving innovation. Set up in 1827 by the city of Lyon through the generous funding of General Claude Martin, La Martinière had unique traits which quickly brought it to the forefront of Lyon's industrial prowess. Promoting an academic curriculum adapted to the needs of local infant industries, the school strongly emphasized the importance of chemistry in industrialization processes. Charles-Henry Tabareau played a crucial role in developing this unique pedagogic approach, which was heavily industry driven. His background as an engineering student at a polytechnic influenced his work, and throughout the 19th century, La Martinière continued to produce Lyon's most prominent industrial and commercial leaders. The school quickly gained popularity and started attracting an ever-increasing number of students as well as foreign delegations interested in the promotion of industrial knowledge.[6]

The Lumière brothers publicly admitted their pride in being part of the Martinière student body and it is a combination of their natural interest in photography and the skills and knowledge acquired in chemical engineering at the school which lay the groundwork for their success. Without completely reinventing the industry, the brothers were able to use the competences obtained during their two years at the school to understand which products had the potential to commercialize well. Inspired by the work of other engineers in the field, Auguste and Louis intelligently built on and improved some of the ideas circulating around them. The most infamous example is their 1895 patent of the Cinématographe Lumière, which was an improved version of Léon Bouly's 1892 cinematograph. They also patented several other processes leading up to their final film camera product, including the film perforation mechanism that advanced the images through the projector. The brothers saw film as a novelty and decided to withdraw from the business 10 years later in 1905, determining that they did not have enough industry-specific knowledge to further develop its potential. This was a clever strategic move as they went on to develop the first photographic color process known as the Lumière Autochrome a few years later.

The smart career decisions undertaken by Auguste and Louis as well as their ability to objectively analyze the market situation of their inventions can partly be attributed to the very industry-based approach of the learning they were offered at La Martinière. The environment to which they were exposed during those two years gave them the competitive edge that their father lacked, to develop the business through innovation. Surrounded by some of France's leading engineers and driven by the innovative spirit of the polytechnic and Lyon's industry, the Lumière brothers had numerous sources of inspiration around them. This notion of being part of an "innovation hub" is often promoted by modern centers of excellence as one of the key drivers behind modern growth. Schools such as Lausanne's EPFL or Zurich's ETH are perfect examples of this, gathering some of the world's most prominent scientists and engineers to equip them with the knowledge needed to create synergies between the extremely demanding technical side of technological innovation and the more pragmatic and profit-oriented world of business and industry. As such, centers of excellence in education play an undeniable role in developing innovative capacity—and this independently of the quality of a country's overall education system.

Wealth, education, and exposure: The key drivers behind innovation?

Today, innovation is widely accepted as one of the main drivers behind economic growth, partly explaining why numerous governments relentlessly encourage policies that foster and stimulate such an outcome. The spectrum of these policies tends to vary considerably from very direct measures such as tax cuts for companies engaging in research and development (R&D) to more long-term and indirect pathways such as educational subsidies, predominantly in STEM (science, technology, engineering, and mathematics). Their effectiveness remains unclear, however, as we continue to know relatively little about the factors that truly induce individuals and companies to become innovators. Ongoing academic literature and discussion on the matter frequently bring up knowledge, education, and an indifference to risk as key drivers.

Often forgotten in this conversation, however, is the tangible role played by a trait frequently observed among both entrepreneurs and inventors: their access to financial capital—whether through family wealth, inheritance, or networks resulting in financial stability. Though many people attribute risk-taking behavior as a commendable prerequisite for innovative thinking, it is usually the very access to a stable financial situation that allows innovators to take these necessary risks. Indeed, it appears easier to engage in creative problem-solving when the financial safety net is guaranteed, allowing for individuals to take risks without compromising their future livelihoods. A 2013 paper by Berkley economists Levine and Rubinstein delves into this question and analyzes the traits of American entrepreneurs, finding that a large majority of them are white, male, and highly educated.[7] As such, the ability to innovate should be considered a privilege that is not accessible to all in the general population. Indeed, barriers to entry are often very high and around 81 percent of entrepreneurs never get access to a bank loan in the United States. The average funding of USD 30,000 required to start a firm falls under the USD 100,000 mark, which represents the point at which banks realistically believe a loan can be made profitable.[8] This considerable barrier to capital has undeniable consequences for individuals who do not benefit from a social status that allows them to raise the necessary capital through their own means.

These trends are confirmed in a recent study by five Harvard, MIT, and LSE researchers who analyzed the lives of more than 1 million inventors in the United States using a new de-identified database linking patent records to tax and school district records.[9] Their research produces some extremely interesting results with regard to innovation. First, large disparities in innovation rates by socioeconomic class, race, and gender are apparent. According to their study, children whose parents are in the top 1 percent of the income bracket are 10 times more likely to file a patent than children whose parents are in the bottom 50 percent of the income distribution. The racial gap is analogous: white children are three times more likely to become inventors than black children at all income levels. Similarly, only 18 percent of current inventors are female, and although the gender gap is gradually shrinking over time, it would take an estimated 118 years to reach gender parity in innovation at the current rate. The study further stipulates that very little of the observed innovation gap is explained by differences in ability—as measured by test scores in early childhood. In fact, children at the top of their third-grade math class are only more likely to become inventors if their families are in the top 10 percent of income earners. As for the high-scoring kids from poorer or minority families, they remain extremely unlikely to invent and file a patent. As the authors put it, "Becoming an inventor in America relies upon two things: excelling in mathematics and science and having a rich family."[10]

A second notable finding is the fact that exposure to innovation substantially increases the chances of being innovative. The research found that children who grew up in areas with more inventors were not only more likely to register patents, but also did so in fields similar to the ones to which they were exposed. For instance, kids who were raised in Silicon Valley were especially prone to achieving patents in computer technology, whereas children from Minneapolis—where the manufacturing of medical devices is abundant—were far more likely to develop inventions in the medical sector. Similarly, children whose parents hold patents in a certain field are more likely to file a patent in the exact same field. Interestingly, exposure to innovation also occurs in a gender-specific way. Women are therefore more likely to invent in a given field if they grew up in an environment where female inventors were active in that field, whereas growing up around male inventors has little or no impact on their propensity to innovate.

This may help to explain why women, minorities, and children from low-income families tend to experience significantly lower rates of innovation, as their level of exposure through their families and neighborhoods are likely to be much lower than that of the more affluent. The study predicts that if these groups were to invent at the same rate as white men from the top 20 percent of the income bracket, the rate of innovation in America would quadruple. In terms of policy implication, the researchers argue that the obtained conclusions—that familial wealth and not aptitude is the biggest lacking ingredient for those groups—should encourage governments and local authorities to target their spending more accurately. For instance, pair young girls with innovative female mentors and support low-income children who excel at math and science!

Of course, these factors—access to finance and education, and exposure to innovation—are driven by national institutions and policies. To innovate, or more precisely to nurture innovators, a country requires policies that optimize the interaction among the three pillars of what I call the *innovation ecosystem*: access to finance, education, and talent, and an innovative mindset through collaboration.

Why is education important to innovation? In his famous book *Outliers*, Malcolm Gladwell points out that "achievement is talent plus preparation" and instantly popularizes the 10,000-hour rule, according to which a master has spent 10,000 hours polishing the skill to achieve excellence. Further, Gladwell emphasizes this point in the following way: "The closer psychologists look at the careers of the gifted, the smaller the role innate talent seems to play and the bigger the role preparation seems to play."[11] The more humankind progresses in knowledge development, the more relevant this idea becomes.

Natural talent is no longer enough. Nobody is born a world-class pianist or an elite athlete; any ability blossoms if continuously trained toward perfection.

Jeff Bezos, chief executive officer (CEO) and founder of Amazon, tops the *Forbes'* 2018 list of the world's most innovative leaders.[12] After graduating from Princeton University, he worked in telecommunications, banking, and finance before starting Amazon. His experiences ranged from international sales to product development; however, it is important that most of the companies he worked for were either startups or very young enterprises. So, by the time Bezos founded Amazon he had extensive knowledge about startups. Princeton University can boast many other alumni known across the globe, including Malcolm Forbes, Alan Turing, Michael Porter, and F. Scott Fitzgerald.[13]

Bezos' closest competitor on the *Forbes'* list is the product architect of Tesla and founder of SpaceX, Elon Musk. The serial technology entrepreneur is a University of Pennsylvania graduate who dropped a promising academic career in favor of running his business. By the time Tesla released the first successful electric car in 2008, Musk had 13 years' experience as an entrepreneur.

For more examples, we should look no further than to Google, which was born from a PhD thesis. Larry Page, who obtained his bachelor's degree from the University of Michigan and a master's degree from Stanford, was researching the anatomy of the internet at Stanford. The article that was to be a part of his PhD thesis laid the foundation for the most powerful search engine in the world.[14] Stanford, as long as we're mentioning it, is actually known to be the alma mater of the founders and co-founders of the largest number of startups in the world. Besides Google, the university has seen the birth of Netflix, Nike, and Gap, to name just a few.[15]

Still does not sound compelling enough? Probably, natural talent will make its way without any education. After all, we have all heard that Mark Zuckerberg and Bill Gates were Harvard dropouts, while Steve Jobs spent only one semester at Reed College before leaving it.[16] However, all of them spent days and nights working on developing and perfecting their projects, acquiring the skills necessary for success, and gaining the experience needed to succeed. For example, Zuckerberg started coding while he was in middle school and was known as a "programming prodigy" upon his arrival at Harvard.[17]

So, that's it? Anyone who works hard and preferably graduates from a college is destined to become a great innovator? Naturally, this would be a simplification. Practice and hard work are a necessary but not a sufficient condition. Innovation needs talent the same way that success does. The combination of talent and practice explains why Switzerland is a fintech center, German technology is the best, Estonia is leading the global digital innovation, and Lithuania is rapidly becoming a blockchain innovation hub.[18]

Universities are usually the seed of innovation. I already mentioned that Stanford is the global leader in the production of startups; however, other universities are not lagging far behind. Facebook and Microsoft are probably the most obvious examples of a company born in Harvard dorm rooms, while in total Harvard is the alma mater of 1,310 entrepreneurs.[19] We do not have to look far for more companies started in colleges. Michael Dell was a student at the University of Texas in Austin when he founded Dell. Dropbox was born in MIT, WordPress at the University of Houston, Reddit at the University of Virginia. How big is the impact after all? Big enough for us to care. For example, the combined economic effect of MIT alumni–founded companies and their ecosystems would be roughly equal to the 17th largest economy of the world.[20] Probably, this works only in the United States? Not really. For example, Skype was developed by a graduate of Uppsala University (Sweden). Obviously, there is something at universities that fosters innovation. What is so special at universities to make them conducive to innovation? Traditionally, universities combine two activities, teaching and research, and both play their role in the process.

How does university research drive innovation?

Doing research essentially means searching for something new, something not known or not existent yet. So is innovation. According to the president of Universities UK, Professor Dame Janet Beer, "Universities really do transform lives. The technology we use every day, the medicines that save lives, the teachers who inspire—all come from UK universities and the important work being done by academics up and down the country."[21] This is true not only in the UK but also anywhere else in the world. But how does research result in practically implemented innovation? In a multitude of ways. For example, companies oftentimes monitor the published research, directly partner with research institutions, or employ established scientists.[22] Researchers themselves may start a business stemming from their research. More recent trends in the business–academia collaboration include locating R&D departments close to research centers, directly financing PhD and post-doctorate-level research, sustaining long-term recurring relationships rather than one-off projects, and extending the range of prospective universities.[23] Over the last decade, industry funding for university research exceeded USD 4.2 billion per year, growing by more than 5.5 percent annually.[24] Sometimes, a research field develops so rapidly that it creates a whole industry around it. An example is the studies on aging, surrounded by numerous social and traditional enterprises targeting older generations.[25]

Teaching and innovation

Teaching is no less (and probably even more) important for nourishing innovation than research is. Most often, the companies born in a university fall into two categories: either they are an outcome of a course, or the founders select their classes to foster the development of an already existing project.[26] What do those classes look like? Let us take a closer look at several examples.

At Harvard Business School, students are offered the Field Immersion Experiences for Leadership Development (FIELD) course. Based on the case studies conducive to the development of a founder's mindset, the class can be complemented by FieldX, where students have to carry out an actual business project.[27]

Most MIT companies started with the New Enterprises course, designed and taught by a serial entrepreneur, Bill Aulet. The course description promises that students will become entrepreneurs in the classroom.[28] Princeton University offers the High-Tech Entrepreneurship course designed in a similar way. Taught by Christopher Kuenne, a successful serial entrepreneur himself, the course makes students create a "venture" that they will have to pitch to "investors" as a final exam.[29] In general, hands-on entrepreneurship teaching is gaining popularity. Another example is the Startup Studio class at Cornell Tech, in which students develop, prototype, test, and pitch a project that can be presented at the university's startup awards and eventually be financed.[30]

Stanford is offering extensive rounded support that ranges from the startup incubator Y Combinator to the d.school initiative. Y Combinator offers financing, fund-raising, product development guidance, and meetings with potential investors during the three-month program. The incubator can boast launching Reddit, DropBox, and AirBNB among other companies.[31] At the d.school, students are offered more than 30 classes aimed at taking a fresh look around and creatively addressing existing inefficiencies. While the school positions itself as centered on design, University Innovation is among its programs and "launching new organizations" is on the school's impact list.[32]

Innovation demands constant change and, apparently, the universities grasp the rules of this game quickly. Hackathons, entrepreneurship classes, incubators, and serial entrepreneurs in professors' seats are taking the place of fundamental science and library halls. Universities are innovating and reinventing themselves to pave the way for the new startups that will be known across the globe.

Israel: the startup nation

> It was the most unbelievable place to grow up. I was with my friends from morning till night. We ate in the same dining hall, we drove to the same school, and then we all did our homework together, or we didn't do our homework together. It was awesome.[33]

This is how Adam Neumann, the founder of WeWork, describes his experience of growing up in a kibbutz (collective communities of Israel). Spending his early years this way clearly left a footprint on his personality and likely inspired the future second most-valuable US startup.[34]

Kibbutzim are one of the factors behind the innovative success of Israel. Their residents, who moved to Israel from 130 countries, were initially working in agriculture and living in a very special social structure. They shared everything—from food and clothes to sleeping places; their children were taken care of by the community and lived in separate dormitories. This was a large-scale social experiment that forged creative thinking and risk-taking skills in its participants. Shared economy and search for novelty were at the heart of kibbutzim and gradually turned into the capacity to innovate.[35]

Neumann is not a unique player in the shared economy market. The shared economy took a capitalism twist and is booming in Israel. GetTaxi offers ride-sharing services, OurCrowd invests in startups mainly through crowdfunding, EatWith connects tourists with locals for authentic dining experiences, and WeWork rents out coworking spaces.[36] The shared working space market itself is on the rise in Israel. If, in 2014, less than 16,000 square meters were offered in the country by WeWork, Regus, and Mindspace combined, in 2018, Regus and WeWork alone provide more than 60,000 square meters, and at least 32 new coworking companies have entered the market over those years.[37] What is happening in the country that it needs so many shared working spaces? The answer is—startups.

Israel, once referred to as "the land of milk and honey," is nowadays known as a "leading innovation center" or the "startup nation."[38] According to the World Economic Forum (WEF), the country's innovation ecosystem is among the 10 global leaders,[39] while Bloomberg ranks Israel as the fifth most innovative country in the world.[40] From 2000 to 2015, more than 10,000 companies were started in Israel and half are still going.[41] Further, according to Israel's innovation authority, the country enjoys the largest number of startups per capita in the world and is home to more than 2,000 startups, 3,000 small and medium enterprises, 30 growth companies, and 50 large companies.[42] Among the well-known innovative products developed by Israeli entrepreneurs are IP Telephony, drip-irrigation technology, and ICQ messenger.[43] Israel can also boast 18 unicorns valued at over USD 1 billion, the founders of which have connections with the country.[44]

What is behind this tremendous success? How can a country with less than 10 million population and 70 years' history, surrounded by Arabic countries hostile to it, be such an important player on the innovations scene? In brief, Israel learned to turn challenges into opportunities. How did it manage that?

Innovation ecosystem in Israel

According to Delloite, the main features of the Israeli innovative ecosystem are strong R&D capabilities, state and investment support, a flexible and creative economy, a strong and well-developed venture capital (VC) market, and an educated and skilled work-force.[45] This list looks like a standard textbook example, a "recipe" for innovation. As in any good recipe, the spices are what make the difference. In Israel, likely the unique mix of "spices" is made up of government support, mandatory military service, the culture, and, ultimately, the people. Let us take a closer look at the role of those factors.

Government support plays an important role in the ecosystem. Israel can boast the world's highest ratio of R&D investments compared to GDP—about 5 percent.[46] The country has a government body in charge of fostering innovation—the Israel Innovation Authority (previously known as the Office of Chief Scientist).[47] The agency runs several programs aimed at harnessing innovation; for example, the Technological Incubators Program launched in 1991. One of its early goals was to provide financing to well-edu-cated immigrants from the former USSR to start their business. Since then, the program has turned into 24 incubators, the majority of which are now privately owned. Their main targets are high-risk, early-stage technological projects. These ventures are incubated for two years and receive grant financing covering up to 85 percent of the budget, which is to be repaid after the company generates a cash flow. The program is not involved in any management activity and, in general, leaves it up to the market to decide on the most promising startups and successful technologies. What it actually aims at is mitigat-ing the risks of the projects' early stages, thus increasing their survival chances at the early stages. The results speak for themselves—more than 1,500 ventures were incubated, 60 percent of them raised USD 3.5 billion in private investments, and 40 percent of them are still working.[48]

Two years after the start of the Technological Incubators Program, Israel's government launched Yozma, "the most successful and original program in Israel's relatively long history of innovation policy."[49] At its launch, Yozma provided USD 80 million in invest-ments to 10 investment funds in exchange for a 40 percent share in them. The funds were allowed to buy out the share of the state at a reduced price within five years. Besides, the program insured 80 percent of the downside risk for the funds. Finally, Yozma estab-lished a fund of its own to invest USD 20 million directly into small businesses, and out of 15 ventures it invested in, 9 ran an initial public offering (IPO) or were acquired.[50]

Yozma facilitated the development of the venture capital industry in Israel along-side financing, promising Israeli startups at the early stage to help them enter the mar-kets. Thanks to the program, the share of venture capital investments increased from USD 58 million to USD 3.3 billion, and currently the share of private equity capital to GDP in Israel is the second largest in the world after the United States.[51]

Another factor of Israel's innovation success is the mandatory military service for all citizens. First and foremost, the army has highly selective elite units, where the recruits work on complex, demanding projects as early as age 18. The stakes are high—essentially, human lives. Thus, young adults are immersed in a demanding environment, tackling hard-to-solve problems and bearing the full responsibility for them. Sounds like a very entrepreneurial experience, doesn't it?[52] The military needs were behind many machine learning and big data disruptive technologies that were successfully turned into businesses; for example, providing consumer analytics. Former recruits often use the skills and knowledge developed for the army to start innovative businesses or develop disruptive products. For example, Gil Shwed was involved in the military project to secure classified networks and developed a firewall. This is how CheckPoint, one of the largest cybersecurity companies in the world, started.[53]

Michael Porter, a renowned Harvard Business School professor, argues that the concentration of interrelated institutions forms innovation-fostering clusters, and this is precisely what happened in Israel.[54] In the relatively small territory, there are 9 universities, 32 colleges,[55] more than 350 multinational R&D centers, several thousand startups, more than 70 venture capital funds, and several hundred startup accelerators,[56] in addition to the military bases. Multinational companies, such as Tata, Kodak, CitiBank, and others choose Israel as the location for their innovation centers.[57] Nowadays, more than 250 companies, including 80 enterprises on the Fortune 500 list, host R&D labs in Israel.[58] Not surprisingly, technological companies tend to locate their offices in geographical proximity to the army facilities to benefit from the spillover effects that arise there. This creates an ecosystem in which people work together in tight connection with the army, startups, academia, VC funds, research, and development.[59]

Another crucially important factor is that the people in Israel are very interconnected. We already talked about kibbutzim and their unique way of ultimately sharing lives, but there is more to it. Mandatory military service forges a lifelong friendship, which naturally intersects with the social circles developed in schools, neighborhoods, and universities; people naturally cooperate and exchange ideas. A very special talent profile, an entrepreneurial lifestyle, natural adoption, and the development of technological solutions stem from this interconnected ecosystem. It is a cornerstone of Israeli culture—a strong sense of community, mutual support, and belief in each other.[60]

Another shared national trait is "chutzpah"—originally referred to as overconfidence, it is now understood as the courage to change and improve the status quo. This is what makes Israel more proactive and risk-tolerant. At the same time, the culture takes failures as lessons and urges continued efforts and persistence, leading to eventual success. Israeli innovation success is not an outcome of innate talents or magical blessings; it is the result of hard work, persistence, overall support, and optimism.[61]

Israel cannot boast a large territory or natural resources, which, together with its geopolitical situation, limits the opportunities for industrial development. What could be its competitive edge then? Israel opted to invest in people and education.[62]

The role of universities

Israel is one of the most educated societies in the world, enjoying the highest number of engineers and scientists per capita in the world.[63] According to the Organization for Economic Cooperation and Development (OECD), 46 percent of adults in Israel have a university degree,[64] while half have a STEM major.[65] The country is known for high-quality education and one of the highest numbers of university degrees and scientific publications per capita.[66]

Still, not every well-educated society excels in innovation. What makes Israeli universities special? First and foremost, they are very active in research. A third of the state R&D expenditure is directed to universities. No surprise that Tel Aviv University, Weizmann

Institute, and Technion are at the top of the list of patent applicants in the United States. But this is only where the story starts. Israeli universities excel at bringing the outcomes of their research into practice through their own technology transfer companies.[67] The success stories range from biotechnologies to a device that automatically removes dog waste.[68] To make it even more impressive, for example, the total research budget of MIT is USD 1.5 billion, twice the combined research budget of all Israeli universities. The income MIT receives from the commercialization of its research, on the other hand, is comparable to that of Technion.[69]

The concept of technology transfer was introduced at the University of Wisconsin but started to blossom in Israel.[70] How does it work? For example, the Hebrew University of Jerusalem has run the technology transfer company Yissum for more than half a century. One of the three oldest in the world, the company has more than 9,000 patents and more than a hundred spinoffs. It runs two types of activities: it connects researchers with big industry players like Intel and Google and creates on average 10 new ventures per year. Examples include Mobileye—the developer of visual technology for the advanced driver assistance system, now a part of Intel, the value of which exceeded USD 9 billion in 2016. The company receives 3–5 percent in royalties from commercialized products and enjoys equity and investments from industry players. The whole ecosystem of the university is aligned with Yissum. On the one hand, the patent portfolios of researchers are the basis for promotions, thus fostering the commercialization of research. On the other hand, Yissum enhances the quality of research. Researchers and laboratories receive 60 percent of the company's revenues, which allows them to open 300 new jobs annually.[71]

Teaching is also on par with research in creating new ventures. All leading Israeli universities offer degrees as well as short-term courses in innovation and entrepreneurship. Besides theoretical studies, they equip students with hands-on knowledge and networks to start a new venture. Moreover, Amnon Dekel, the managing director of the Hebrew University Innovation and Entrepreneurship Center, has as a priority teaching each and every student something about innovation from day one. He firmly believes that innovation and entrepreneurship are skills that can be taught and learned.[72] The students themselves find the courses in entrepreneurship very useful. They highly praise not only the knowledge of economics but also the skills to identify needs and particularly the networking opportunities. Dror Matalon, chairman and co-founder of InovyTec, met his partner at such a class. The two were actually working for Shin Bet—Israel's security agency—but did not know each other before they started the entrepreneurship studies at Ben Gurion University of the Negev.[73] In 2017, the company secured USD 3 million in investments from Vincent Medical Holdings, China, in exchange for 15 percent of the equity. The contract has opened the Chinese market for InovyTec.[74]

Instead of a conclusion

Zack Weisfeld is in charge of setting up Microsoft accelerators across the globe and he knows a thing or two about innovations. David Yin, a *Forbes* contributor, once asked him what was so different about Israel. Weisfeld's answer was "the banana story." Here is how Yin recalls it. Once, the head of an American company decided to create a banana straightening machine. Presumably, it is easier to slice straight bananas. The big boss calls American and Israeli developers to create the device. The American developer drafts a work plan, hires external consultants, and after several years produces a fancy USD 2,000 device. In turn, the developer from Israel also agrees to develop the device. He invites his childhood friends from the kibbutz who grow bananas. A couple of weeks later, the developer presents the big boss with a USD 13 device that works 60 percent of the time and straightens bananas perfectly. This is what Israeli innovation is all about: bootstrapping, networking, and providing a creative solution as fast and as cheap as possible.[75]

Eastern Europe

Ballpoint pen, Rubik's Cube, Insulin, soft contact lenses, sugar cubes—these are just a few of the inventions that have come from Eastern Europe. The legacy of the Communist Eastern Bloc—developed human capital and a high level of education—is what such countries as Hungary, the Czech Republic, Poland, Ukraine, and Bulgaria are famous for. The region regularly excels on the various ranks of educational achievements in mathematics and science. Almost half of the finalists of Google's programming competition Code Jam in 2018 were from Eastern Europe.[76] In addition, teams from Eastern Europe consistently take first place in the prestigious ACM International Collegiate Programming Contest.[77] At the same time, companies in the United States find it challenging to hire good programmers, which results in a wave of "acqu-hires"—acquisitions done with the purpose of accessing the skilled team of developers. Such strategies offer companies a competitive advantage by combining cheaper (and often higher skilled) talent from Eastern Europe with the opportunities in North America and Western Europe. However, Eastern Europe is more than just an outsourcing hub. Recent years have seen the rise of startups from Central and Eastern Europe (CEE), including AVG and Avast from the Czech Republic; Filestube developed in Poland; Vector, BitDefender, and Soft32 born in Romania; Ustream, Prezi, IndexTools, and LogMeIn from Hungary;[78] and Grammarly, TripMyDream, Petcude, and many others developed in Ukraine.[79] Common among these businesses is developing features that bigger brands would like to have—and are ready to pay for. Examples include the 30-day battery life Vector smartwatch, acquired by Fitbit for USD 15 million,[80] or Ukraine-born Looksery, which became a part of Snapchat for USD 150 million because of the filters that let you photoshop your face during a video call.[81]

These countries do not have many resources; they just lived through the vulnerable transition period after the collapse of the Soviet Union. Their levels of economic development and standard of living are still quite different from those in Western Europe and some of them are still living through turbulent times—for example, Ukraine. What is behind these success stories then? Education. The post-Soviet education system did not change much and is still very much about teaching mathematics, natural science, and engineering—those skills were of great value in the former Soviet Union.[82] In Poland alone, some 40,000 graduates major in IT and successfully secure employment anywhere across the globe, from Singapore to Silicon Valley.[83] The state clearly recognizes the talent-pool potential and is willing to support it; for example, with plans to turn universities into innovation hubs to facilitate the development of new ventures, similar to the way it is done in the UK.[84] And there is indeed a lot to build on—some of the oldest universities in the world are located in the region, such as the University of Prague in the Czech Republic and Jagiellonian University in Poland, both dating back to the 14th century.[85] All countries in the region are following their own—fascinating and exciting—development paths. We invite you to join us in discovering what is happening in Ukraine and Hungary, the countries not covered much in the English-language literature.

Ukraine—The Secret Tech Hub

Who was Igor Sikorsky? Probably, an easier question would be, "Who was Sergei Korolev?" The former was the designer of the first helicopter, the latter, the scientific star of the Soviet space program and the scientist behind the "First man in space" project. Both were graduates of Kiev Polytechnic Institute in Ukraine. The strong educational system inherited from the Soviet past is still in high demand among the youth—80 percent of 19- to 25-year-old Ukraine citizens are obtaining tertiary degrees. Common for the post-Soviet education system, the education largely focuses on STEM subjects—this is where between 90,000[86] and 150,000,[87] depending on the estimate, skillful Ukrainian IT developers and programmers come from. No surprise that the country's information and communications technology (ICT) sector exported USD 2.5 billion in 2015, according to some estimates,[88] which makes it the country's third largest exporting sector.[89] This talent pool is growing at a tremendous rate—every year it is joined by 36,000 new graduates with IT-related degrees. Ukrainians love to study and continue upgrading their skills even after graduation by taking up classes in artificial intelligence (AI), big data, blockchain, and the Internet of Things (IoT). No surprise that the IT industry in Ukraine is forecast to reach USD 5.7 billion by 2020.[90] Coupled with relatively low wages and vibrant social communities, this talent pool makes Ukraine the perfect outsourcing hub for US and EU companies. The annual output of IT outsourcing increased five times from 2011 to 2015[91] despite the political instability in the country that started late in 2013. For example, Elance, formerly one of the leading freelancing websites and currently a part of Upwork, mentioned Ukraine among the three best places to find people with advanced skills.[92] Sounds remarkable, doesn't it?

But Ukraine is not an outsourcing hub. Or, at least, not only an outsourcing hub. We already mentioned the augmented reality startup Looksery that was acquired by Snapchat. Other examples include doorbell firm Ring, sold to Amazon for USD 1 billion.[93] Other stories of funding success include Grammarly that raised USD 110 million in May 2018; BitFury, which secured USD 30 million; and Petcube, which received USD 10 million.[94] These companies are not unique. Amid political and economic instability, 44 Ukrainian startups (or those founded by Ukrainians) secured USD 264 million of investment in 2017, a 3-fold increase compared to 2016.[95] Universities play their role here, and some of them are extending support to new ventures. For example, students from KPI and Taras Shevchenko National University of Kyiv are the founders of at least 80 enterprises based on data from Crunchbase. Other universities supporting alumni startups include Dnipropetrovsk National University, Kyiv National Economic University, and the National University of Kharkiv.[96] Besides, the country has seen the birth of 60 fintech startups since 2015—58 percent of the total number of companies in the sector.[97]

The most remarkable story is probably the one of Monobank—a mobile application offering payment services, micro-loans, and deposits. The company went live in November 2017 and less than a year later the number of Monobank's clients exceeded half a million.[98] More than 3,000 new users join daily—a clear sign that the country is ready for fintech.[99]

The founders of Monobank—Dima Dubilet, Misha Rogalskiy, and Oleg Gorolhovsky—worked together for the country's largest bank, PrivatBank. After leaving the company in

2016, they analyzed the banking industry in Ukraine and decided that there was plenty of room for the development of online banking. Dubilet recalls how they came up with the idea:

> We wanted to reduce the hassle of physically dealing with the bank—no one likes to deal with their bank in person unless it is to check their pay, so we decided interaction with your bank should be hassle-free and fun and not something that you postpone all the time.[100]

Becoming a Monobank client is as simple as downloading the app and sending a photo of your passport over it. A courier will then deliver the credit card to you as Ukrainian law does not allow bank cards to be sent by post. After activating the card, you can make ATM withdrawals and transfers to family and friends through the app. Monobank has no physical offices, which significantly reduces its costs and allows the company to offer interest rates 10–15 percent lower than those of their competitors, with up to a 62-day grace period, which is 50 percent longer than any other bank in Ukraine offers.[101]

According to Dubilet, the success of Monobank is only partly the outcome of its unique competitive advantage. The other significant success factor was... the photo of the cat.[102] The gist is this: shortly before launching Monobank, Dubilet posted a photo of his new backpack with his pet cat inside. The picture went viral and Monobank decided to use it in its early advertisement campaign. It issued a series of stickers for computers and laptops with the picture that eventually turned into a collectible.[103]

This was not the only extravagant idea of the company. All of us dream of being paid for working out at least once in our lives. Monobank offers such an opportunity with its "sport deposit savings account" with an initial interest rate of 17 percent, which, however, falls to 15 percent if the user fails to walk 10,000 steps daily for more than three days during the deposit term.[104]

The team is planning to expand outside Ukrainian borders—Dubilet was recently awarded an Exceptional Talent UK visa, so the team is planning to launch in the United Kingdom before 2020.[105]

In addition to the more traditional fintech initiatives, many things are happening on the Ukrainian cryptocurrency scene. This is true also almost literally. Once, a statue of Lenin stood in the center of Kyiv, which was quite typical for any Soviet Union city. The monument was eventually removed during the protests in 2013—the destiny shared by many statues of Lenin—but the plinth remained. However, recently, a new monument was "erected" there, to some extent. Using an augmented reality app, one can see the person who symbolizes the anonymous creator of Bitcoin, Satoshi Nakamoto. After the protests of 2013, the change of government, and the long war in the eastern regions of the country, the Ukrainian hryvnia abruptly collapsed against the US dollar and never managed to recover. Still, thousands of Ukrainian developers were hired by outsourcing companies from the West, and many others are working as freelancers with a greater or lesser extent of visibility. Hard to imagine a more fruitful soil for the rise of cryptocurrencies. The average salary in Ukraine is roughly USD 300. The daily trading of crypto coins in the country amounts to USD 1.9 million. There are more than 25 crypto coins in circulation and it is quite simple to use them for offline payments; for example, one of the sellers in Kyiv's central farmers' market accepts 11 cryptocurrencies in payment. Luxury cars, once the symbol of power affordable only to the oligarchs, are now seen on the streets of the Ukrainian capital driven by those who made wealth in cryptocurrencies.[106] In 2014, buying bitcoins for cash at 5,000 ATMs was as easy as withdrawing money or executing any other transaction. This passion for bitcoins is easily explained by the country's political and economic situation—the population was simply using cryptocurrencies as a hedge against inflation and the weak and unstable hryvnia. Ukraine is the first regulated market to offer bitcoin futures.[107]

Although the success stories are spectacular, and the level of courage is admirable, Ukraine is just at the beginning of its journey to becoming an innovation hub of Eastern Europe. Are there other candidates for this title in the region?

Hungary—The New Sweden?

Hungary has a broad and systematic approach to innovation. According to the country's startups database,[108] there are 141 new ventures in the country, which is quite impressive given a population of fewer than 10 million people. Crunchbase reports even higher numbers—523 registered companies. The diversity in terms of the choice of industry is also incredible. IoCamper offers the solution that turns any van into a motorhome,[109] Turbine AI aims at treating tumor diseases with the help of artificial intelligence,[110] and Seon is assisting online businesses to reduce fraud.[111] But probably the most well-known success story from Hungary is the interactive presentation tool, Prezi.

Prezi was founded in Budapest in 2009 by Peter Arvai, Peter Halacsy, and Adam Somlai-Fisher. Somlai-Fisher had the idea for such a presentation tool and actually coded the first version. Back in 2009, Budapest was a weird place to start a venture—there was no ecosystem, no successful entrepreneurs, and essentially nothing of what nowadays is expected from a startup hub. Prezi was among those who laid the first bricks of what evolved into a vibrant startup scene. Nowadays, the company runs two offices—in Budapest and San Francisco—and can boast more than 45 million users across the globe and 55,000 new registrations daily.[112]

Budapest has also experienced a dramatic change over the last decade to the extent that it is ranked the #1 destination to launch a business after Brexit,[113] for which there are plenty of reasons. Nowadays, Budapest boasts a talent pool of educated engineers, mentors eager to extend support, people with great ideas, notwithstanding its location in the heart of Europe, and the simplicity of issuing visas. It is easy to build a diverse team here.[114]

Prezi, in collaboration with Ustream, LogMeIn, and NNG, launched Bridge Budapest—an entrepreneurship-promoting non-governmental organization (NGO).[115] The market correctly interpreted the move and now Budapest is attracting international angels and ventures, building business accelerators and offering a variety of funding options. The government has supported the move by offering a 9 percent corporate tax, the lowest in the European Union (EU), and an "early stage" status that provides startups with the opportunity to reduce their corporate tax base. Coworking spaces and incubators are being opened all over the city and the Central European University is dedicating significant effort to facilitating the creation and expansion of new enterprises.[116]

In general, public policy was to a great extent behind the development of entrepreneurship and innovation in Hungary in general, and in the country's educational system in particular. On the one hand, the educational system in Hungary is rather traditional, rigid, and still bears the features of the Soviet influence. While this is good in terms of fundamental approaches to teaching and relatively strong STEM subjects, the rigidity itself somewhat impedes the innovation process. On the other hand, departments and faculties at the universities have a great deal of autonomy, allowing entrepreneurship and innovation clusters to be built around them. There are also several central technology transfer offices in place that support the commercialization of research. Interestingly, Peter Halacsy from Prezi was a university researcher prior to joining the company.[117] Students are becoming increasingly more interested in starting up their ventures and the universities are responding to those demands by offering more entrepreneurship and innovation courses. Still, so far, education in Hungary is very much technology oriented, which offers a competitive advantage of highly skilled graduates in engineering but to some extent misses the opportunities of promoting entrepreneurship in a broader sense.[118]

> I think Hungary has everything that Sweden has. We wanted to inspire people to start their own businesses, and we wanted to share our stories to show that you can build a company from Hungary too. For us today, Hungary seems to have the most vibrant startup scene in Europe.
>
> *Peter Arvai, CEO of Prezi[119]*

Innovating across the globe

We started this chapter with a discussion of the role of education in innovations. Whenever we saw an example of an innovative country, be it as established an innovator as Israel, or just a beginner such as Ukraine, the universities and education are the most frequent factors. This is true across the globe: innovative hubs center around universities. In the United States, those are Stanford and UC Berkeley in Silicon Valley and Harvard and MIT in Boston. In Great Britain, those are obviously Oxford and Cambridge as well as many others located in and around London. Northern Europe is famous for its geographical innovation clusters with examples of the innovation ecosystem in Aalto in Finland, and the incubators in Stockholm and Uppsala in Sweden. Switzerland is another well-known innovation center with an exceptional number of high-level universities given the country's size. ETH Zurich, University of Geneva, Swiss Federal Institute of Technology Lausanne, and University of Basel are just a few examples. Probably, this is true only for Western culture, right? Not really. Singapore, South Korea, and Hong Kong are perfect examples of innovation hubs in Asia, while the National University of Singapore, Seoul National University, and Hong Kong University of Science and Technology are globally recognized brands. Innovation and education go hand in hand anywhere in the world, so it seems high time to start applying the 10,000 hours rule and... innovate.

55. COMPETITIVENESS THROUGH TECHNOLOGY

In today's competitiveness landscape, the digital component of an economy is becoming increasingly important, affecting not only how businesses function but also how countries perform and evolve in the future. In fact, once all economies move from the manufacturing sector to that of services and eventually technology, it is extremely likely that the latter will play a pivotal role in determining global competitiveness trends. There is little doubt that, over the next decade, technology will become one of the leading differentiating factors between low- and high-performing nations. In this era of digital transformation, the role of government and regulation will therefore be paramount in providing the guidelines of a country's future success.

It is true that governments around the world are currently investing heavily in enhancing their digital economy in order to augment value creation and prosperity in their countries. While the pursuit of technological improvement is an essential and necessary condition for the future well-being of a nation, it is not sufficient. Digital technology needs not only to be implemented, but also to be explored in order to achieve two important goals: first, to improve efficiency, and second, to enhance both the range as well as the quality of services provided to citizens and businesses alike. In order for the decision-makers in both the public and private sectors of an economy to address this rapid transformation, it needs to be quantified and accounted for.

To capture these elements and determine the readiness and adaptability of countries to technological disruption, the World Competitiveness Center has—since 2017—proposed a framework which can be used to assess the ability of countries to facilitate the digital transformations of companies. The World Digital Competitiveness Ranking (WDCR) analyzes the extent to which a country adopts and explores new digital technologies leading to transformations in government practices, business models, and society in general. The underlying assumption behind the research is the notion that digital technologies are not possible if

- Talent is not available.
- The country lacks digital infrastructure.
- Cultural/social barriers prevent the penetration of new technology-based business models.

These three factors which hinder digital growth offer a strong hint as to what constitutes the pillars of digital competitiveness. First, knowledge and talent. This captures the know-how necessary to discover, understand, and build new technologies and is represented by criteria such as the availability of talent in a country, the level and quality of the education system and traineeship, as well as the production of scientific knowledge. Second is infrastructure and the technology environment. This looks at the overall context enabling the development of digital technologies and is measured by notions such as how supportive the regulatory environment is or whether an economy provides capital for investments in technology. Last, attitude and future readiness. This pillar analyzes and reflects on a country's preparedness to exploit digital transformations and is calculated by taking into consideration factors such as the level of agility exhibited in the country as well as the level of integration of digital technologies within the economy.

The following section will explore in more depth the pillars of digital competitiveness mentioned above. It will offer some interesting insights collected from the good and not so good students around the globe on the matter and build on these examples to provide a holistic overview of the subject.

Digital knowledge and talent

First and foremost, a country must invest in its digital education to guarantee a future stream of talent in the field. This can not only be achieved through specific technology-driven programs but can also be obtained via a general investment in the quality of the education system and a redefinition of the national curriculum. To effectively manage and expand the digital economy, or so the argument goes, it is imperative to have a large pool of "techies." That is, students who are active in the so-called STEM disciplines: science, technology, engineering, and mathematics. There are, however, an increasing number of actors advocating the need for complementary skill sets located outside this spectrum. Within this logic, the arts and social sciences play a crucial role in enhancing the technical components of technological innovation with the creativity needed to effectively develop innovative solutions. Even though it is very important for an economy to have competent and knowledgeable members, concentrating on math or science may not be the only path to success. Additional competencies that reflect an open attitude or the ability to integrate different experiences are also very important. In short, the humanities have not yet become irrelevant!

Perhaps not surprisingly, the most digitally advanced countries are also the ones with the best education systems. However, more than simply analyzing statistics such as the PISA test scores of a nation's average 15 year old, it is more relevant to understand how digital talent is acquired. Where is this knowledge taught? How is it integrated into other fields? Interestingly, some studies have shown that exposing young children to too many technological tools in their earlier years of education might be counterproductive as it impedes their ability to focus—often distracted by the technologies themselves, such as tablets. For this reason, countries like Hong Kong have excelled in adapting their education system in accordance with age, gradually introducing digital technologies as schooling progresses, with the ultimate peak reached at university level. In Nordic countries, especially Finland and Denmark, digital agility is taught at a younger age through the integration of technologies in the classroom. However, to ensure a smooth transition and dampen the risks described above, such countries have invested considerably in providing education professionals with the necessary support to help them transition to the increased use of electronic devices in their work.

Another important aspect which helps countries maintain a large pool of digitally able individuals is the setting up of information technology hubs within their tertiary education systems to attract foreign talents. This is the case in Switzerland, for example, whose federal polytechnic schools (EPFL and ETH in Lausanne and Zürich) have both been listed in the global top 10 for ICT education and continually attract some of the most talented IT graduates from across the globe. The rationale behind this is the following: highly skilled migrants bring with them an enhanced level of adaptation and flexibility; or they rapidly integrate into the existent high level of adaptation in their host economy. This enhanced level of flexibility potentially spills over to the aggregate unit of the firm itself. Thus, highly skilled migrants are also associated with high levels of business agility. In sum, flows of highly skilled labor strengthen an economy by contributing, among other things, to a higher degree of flexibility and resilience.

Digital infrastructure and technology environment

The second pillar is digital infrastructure and is concerned with determining how well countries are equipped are to further develop their digital technologies. Although the analysis could be undertaken on a macro-level at the national scale, it can also be useful to narrow its scope to include certain recent developments in the field, such as the emergence of smart city projects. Increasingly popular in recent years, smart cities are anchored in the belief that technologies can and should be used to increase citizens' quality of life by providing better and more reliable data from which policymakers and the public can draw conclusions regarding future developments. According to the European

Parliament, a smart city is defined as one which seeks to "address public issues via ICT-based solutions built on a multi-stakeholder, municipally-based partnership. These solutions are developed and refined through Smart City initiatives, either as discrete projects or (more usually) as a network of overlapping activities." The emphasis here is set on technology's role in meeting the real-time demand of the public.

Similarly, this analysis can be transposed onto the WCC's Digital Competitiveness Rankings: although technology is useful per se, its use must meet the needs of the economy and its degree of development. For instance, it would make very little sense for a country like Venezuela to engage in large-scale investments in digital infrastructure when this issue area is at the bottom of the population's current priority list. Although it can be seen as a long-term investment in the promotion of a greater quality of life, public spending on digital infrastructure may be highly ineffective in countries where the very penetration of technological items is poor. Likewise, private investment in digital infrastructure may not generate profitable results in countries that are experiencing unstable political environments or are engaged in armed conflicts. In such contexts, developing digital infrastructure is, in fact, counterproductive in the sense that it can generate outcomes which are damaging for the economy.

Attitudes to technology and future readiness

To fully understand the impact of this pillar on the digital competitiveness of countries, it is important to distinguish between individual and corporate attitudes to technology, which both have an impact on an economy's capacity to absorb and employ digital innovation. At the individual level, the ease with which one can adapt to new environments and become accustomed to new technologies provides an indication of the capacity to successfully adapt to changes within professions. The Adaptive Attitudes sub-factor of the IMD Digital Competitiveness Ranking quantifies this ability. Similarly, the flexibility and resilience that a firm exhibits toward disruptive changes brought about by new technology, and thus the competence and ability to adapt at a business level, is reflected in the Business Agility sub-factor of the same ranking.

A typical example of a country whose population persistently demonstrates negative attitudes to technology is Switzerland, as depicted by its poor ranking in the e-participation and e-commerce indicators. Although the arrival of Twint has facilitated cashless payments across the country in the last couple of years, Swiss citizens have clearly demonstrated a reticence in moving away from their beloved (and very colorful) banknotes. Similarly, contactless payments have only just become the norm with regional cantonal banks, and Raiffeisen Bank recently included the Vpay function on its debit cards. This stands in stark contrast to countries like the United Kingdom, where the population has become so accustomed to the cashless economy that holding cash nowadays represents more of a burden than anything else! A quick trip to buy groceries in a local corner shop in London is all that is needed to realize the extent to which this has become true. In this regard, the average Swiss person's willingness and ability to absorb digital and technological disruptions are less than those of a British person. Such knowledge can have an influence on the investment decisions of some companies that wish to remain very agile and require/demand that their staff members remain open to changes within the global business environment.

Corporate attitudes to technology, or what we call business agility, play a similar role in promoting or hindering an economy's ability to absorb technological change. Generally speaking, there appears to be underlying country effects (both cultural and historical) which impact the national business agility of certain states. In Italy, for example, where respect for traditional and familial entrepreneurial methods is high, the probability of witnessing a countrywide shift toward modern production methods is not as likely as in Estonia, a country that has decided to undergo a dramatic and existential national shift toward modernity as a way of achieving stable economic growth in a difficult post-Soviet environment. In essence, it can be argued that all other things being equal (*ceteris paribus*, as economists like to say), companies in certain countries are predisposed to be more agile than their foreign counterparts due to factors such as the national business environment or the country's historical legacy. Again, this could play an important role in the future business decisions of corporations looking to settle in countries where the local economy and surrounding businesses demonstrate a willingness to incorporate new ideas.

Why and how is it all relevant?

Technological innovation, particularly digital, has undeniably been a key enabler of global socioeconomic development in recent years. Through channels such as enhanced productivity, technological transformations have gradually altered societies in such profound ways that they have required a paradigm shift at the organizational, institutional, and even structural level. Organizations are now increasingly aware that they need to recognize, foresee, and strategically plan for the challenges and opportunities brought about by the emergence of new technologies, while institutions have started focusing on their openness and flexibility to technological adaptation by readjusting relevant rules, regulations, norms, and beliefs. Structurally, economies have been required to accommodate the necessary research, production, market, and demand conditions that encourage and foster innovation to allow for the development of new products, the emergence of new markets, and the entry of new actors into relevant technology-driven sectors.

As such, technological transformations have led to major disruptions in the workings of government, business, and society at large. Since disruptions are, by definition, something that cannot be accounted for; decision-makers in all the aforementioned fields have been confronted with the challenge of accommodating such drastic changes and turning them into opportunities. The WCC's Digital Competitiveness Ranking reflects these considerations and suggests that economies which exhibit high levels of adaptability and agility are better placed to face these abrupt adjustments. A prerequisite, so to speak, for exhibiting these characteristics is the stock of knowledge and technological competencies available in a country. Providing decision-makers with a comprehensive overview of these factors, the WDCR aims to give decision-makers worldwide the necessary tools to identify and build upon their economy's strengths while simultaneously encouraging them to improve upon their weaknesses.

With technologies playing an ever-increasing role in the world, it is interesting to see whether we will observe a gradual shift toward a redefinition of competitiveness to one more closely tied to digital capacities. Will countries such as Sweden, Finland, Israel, Estonia, Slovenia, and Croatia—which all perform better in the digital ranking—catch up in IMD's Competitiveness Ranking in the coming years?

One thing remains for certain, however: as the nature of competitiveness changes, so too must the ways of measuring it.

ITC development in Turkey

Economic and social development in Turkey has undergone significant transformations, shaping the economic environment with political changes, the increased role of globalization, and profound reforms. Turkey has maintained long-term reforms challenged by the economic environment from the 1950s to modern days. Industrialization became the main economic policy target in the post-World War II period from the 1950s to the 1980s. Industrial development in Turkey was not only determined by rapid modernization of Turkey's economy but also by a long-planned objective, implemented by relevant policy and institutional developments. The key features of Turkey's industrialization were observed by government-guided policies, including import substitution and a protectionist economic doctrine. From the 1980s onward, Turkey's economic doctrine moved from protectionism to trade and investment liberalization, promoting the country's openness and integration into global economic schemes. An export-oriented growth model, designed to replace import substitution policies and support local exporters, determined Turkey's economic performance, securing a 6 percent growth rate on average. The 1990s were marked by economic turbulence in Turkey with the most notable foreign investment crisis, which led to a sharp decrease in capital inflows and the borrowing ability of the government. However, since the 2000s, Turkey has demonstrated a profound economic performance and achieved sustainable economic growth. A strong economic and social development performance resulted in the implementation of relevant economic and social policies and was reflected in Turkey's macroeconomic stability. Macroeconomic and fiscal stability resulted in increases in employment and income. Key policy objectives, focused on income inequality, regional development, and poverty, significantly improved social aspects in Turkey in recent years. During the same period, Turkey rapidly urbanized, increasing its openness to foreign trade and finances, and reforming its trade and financial regulations according to the standards of the EU. Additionally, the development activities in the early 2000s and economic stability minimized the effects of the 2008 financial crisis, with minor economic stagnation, and the economy was able to recover fast, demonstrating a moderate economic growth since the 2010s.

Some economists define Turkey as a newly industrialized country; however, Turkey faces challenges typical for emerging economies, including human development, income inequality, and institutional development. Lack of institutional development is reflected in Turkey's unequal labor market, rising income inequality, and corruption. Challenges in institutional development affect a country's competitiveness, placing Turkey in 46th position according to the IMD's Competitiveness Ranking.

Despite Turkey's development and institutional challenges and its low level of competitiveness, it has achieved significant progress in developing modern industrial areas and increasing the role of technology and communication in social and business life.

Particularly, the information and communications technology sector has been developed rapidly during the past years. The ICT sector in Turkey was worth USD 32 billion in 2017. The ICT industry has the fastest growth rates, at around 18 percent, compared to 2016 and is estimated to reach 10–15 percent growth rates on a yearly basis. Additionally, Turkey achieved significant progress in developing a large and competitive consumer electronics and home appliances sector with leading positions in the European market.

The ICT sector development did not accrue at once but has been developed alongside the industrial development, relevant economic policies, and business culture transformations in Turkey. As its main investor, Turkey's government plays an essential role in the development of the ICT sector. The ICT sector's success is based on a combination of various factors, starting with the socioeconomic development policy in Turkey that resulted in the country's economic development and modernization. However, it can be noted that the demographic composition of Turkey and business culture modernization played an equally important part.

Business sector modernization, which is heavily dependent on digitalization, has increased rapidly in recent years, gaining its momentum from trending digitalization, access to the internet, and use of social media by Turkey's businesses. Turkey's business sector appears more advanced in the early stages of digitalization compared to other European and OECD member states. Consequently, a broad digitalization is expected to improve overall economic performance, including financial and fiscal transparency, increasing the private sector's productivity. Digitalization is mainly an endogenously driven business component aimed at increasing accessibility and productivity. Additionally, the insertion of digital aspects in the private and public sectors is strongly encouraged by Turkey's government. The digital transformation is guided by governmental agencies as part of the implementation of the economic development policy. At the institutional level, digitalization as a part of business modernization is reflected in the socioeconomic modernization policies, including the Ministry of Economic Development's establishment of a Department of Fourth Industrialization.

Increasing digitalization in Turkey stimulates the development of the ICT sector where the communications infrastructure and internet accessibility are an essential aspect. Turkey has a leading position in Europe in terms of businesses' use of websites and social media. Another major component in the development of the ICT sector is a result of the government's economic development policy in Turkey, where the ICT sector is freely open to foreign investors, including mobile telecom and other communication technologies. Additionally, Turkey has largely benefited from its demographical composition; a large proportion of its young and middle-aged populations participate more actively in ICT sector development vis-à-vis similar OECD and European countries. Turkey's young population is relatively more open to using technology in business and social life. The rapid development of the ICT sector in Turkey is observed by a large interest in engineering and IT professional education; in particular, the number of graduates with ICT-related qualifications has increased rapidly in recent years. Educational preferences and demographic composition are reflected in the availability of IT and engineering skills, where Turkey has a leading position among other similar countries.

The drivers of the development of the ICT sector in Turkey have increased the value of the ICT market, bringing investors and stimulating local startups, accumulating USD 14.5 billion in foreign direct investment from 2005 to 2015. ICT deployment policy and openness to foreign investors gradually formed a competitive market which is aimed at becoming a significant IT hub in the near future. Turkey is used as a management hub by world ICT giants such as Intel, Huawei, Microsoft, and Ericsson.

The biggest participants of the ICT sector are represented by communication technology companies including Turk TeleKom, Turkcell, and Vodafone, grossing over USD 15 billion in revenue combined. Complementary to the ICT sector development, the IT sector has been greatly developed in recent years, including various unicorn IT companies and an increasing number of promising IT startups. The success factors of IT companies in Turkey are a result of a competitive domestic market, skilled labor, and investment inflows. For example, Turkey-based e-commerce company Trendyol, founded in 2009, managed to gain a leading position in Turkey's IT market with a market share of 16 million consumers, and received USD 750 million in investments from the Chinese Alibaba Corporation. Significant investments in Turkey's IT startups has been frequently observed in recent years, including Yemeksepeti, an online food delivery platform which was acquired by Delivery Hero for USD 590 million. Insider, another IT startup founded in 2012 in Turkey, received USD 11 million from Sequoia, the company that specializes in online marketing and business optimization. A leading company in the field of electronic document management systems, CBKSoft Software, gained attention and was eventually merged with InfoFort, a major player in and provider of digital solutions in the Middle East and Africa. The successful example of CBKSoft represents the potential and growing demand of Turkey's IT market reflected in the business sector's modernization and digitalization.

The development and recent success of Turkey's ICT sector are a result of combined policy implementations including Turkey's past efforts at industrialization and recent institutional transformations aimed at modernizing the business sector. In this regard, Turkey has benefited greatly from the developing ICT sector—being competitive and attractive to investors.

The ICT sector is also a significant contributor in Turkey's foreign trade balance, accumulating USD 15 billion in foreign trade. Additionally, Turkey's government has stimulated the export of the ICT sector by implementing a 50 percent export revenue tax reduction on ICT products and services policy.

Estonia

Estonia, a small Baltic republic with a population of just 1.3 million, has been hailed as the most technologically advanced nation on earth. And this does not merely mean that every citizen has a smartphone. In Estonia, advanced digital technology is woven into the very fabric of the nation. Thanks to X-Road, an online tool that coordinates multiple data repositories and document registries, the essential tasks of voting, filling out tax returns, and signing documents are all done online. X-Road provides all Estonians, including ordinary citizens, organizations, and government officials, with easy access to the data they need to do business and get licenses, permits, and other documents that in other countries would take days, weeks, or even months.

Despite its small population, the World Bank considers Estonia a high-income economy. According to the International Monetary Fund (IMF), in 2016 the GDP (PPP) per capita of the country was USD 29,312. The American CIA's *World Factbook* puts the figure higher, at USD 31,800.[120] Because of its robust growth, alongside Lithuania and Latvia, Estonia has often been described as a Baltic Tiger. As a reflection of its continued economic stability, on January 1, 2011, Estonia adopted the euro and became the 17th eurozone member state.

Estonian citizens are provided with free education, universal healthcare, and the longest-paid maternity leave in the 36-member Organization for Economic Co-Operation and Development.

With a low ratio of government debt to GDP, a flat-rate income tax, free trade policies, a balanced budget, low public debt, innovative e-services, a competitive commercial banking sector, and widespread mobile-based services, Estonia has become an island of prosperity and stability in the Baltic region. In fact, as a member of the eurozone, the North Atlantic Treaty Organization (NATO), and the European Union, of all Nordic states, Estonia is the most integrated into Western European organizations.

Estonian businesses

TransferWise

If you've ever traveled to a foreign country, you've encountered the challenge of changing your currency into the currency of the place you happen to be at that moment.

If you're carrying dollars while in Beijing, you have to exchange them for renminbi.

When carrying euros in Brazil, you need to change them to Brazilian reals.

To make the change, you go to someone who has a supply of both kinds of money—the one you have and the one you want. This broker is usually a bank or some other money-changer. Because no one works for free, the exchange will cost you a fee.

At your own bank—assuming it has a branch or an ATM in the country you're visiting—the fees for currency exchange are likely to be from 1 to 3 percent. Out-of-network ATMs are an option, but on top of a possible foreign transaction fee, you could be required to pay an additional surcharge to your bank and the ATM owner. If you go to a kiosk in the airport, you're probably going to pay the highest rates.

It is bad enough if you're a tourist, but if you're working in a foreign country and getting paid in the currency of your employer in another country, then constantly paying currency exchange fees can quickly become tiresome and expensive.

In January 2011, two Estonian workers found themselves in just this situation: paying to convert their paychecks into another currency. This bothered them, and they wanted to find a solution.

Taavet Hinrikus worked for Skype, the internet video conferencing service. (He happened to be their first employee.) A citizen of Estonia, he worked in London and was paid by Skype in euros. His problem was that he needed to pay his bills in English pounds, and making constant currency exchanges was expensive. As Hinrikus told Gabriella from *London Loves Business*, "I was losing 5 percent of the money each time I moved it."[121]

Meanwhile, his friend Kristo Käärmann, a financial consultant, was living in London as an expat. At the time, he was being paid in pounds, but still had a mortgage back home in Estonia, which required payment in euros. He, too, was constantly paying exchange fees.

Traditionally, the reason you've needed a middleman to change your money is that you didn't know anyone who had the currency you needed, so you went to a trusted middleman, like a bank. But Hinrikus and Käärmann realized that each had what the other needed—Hinrikus had euros and wanted pounds, while Käärmann had pounds and wanted euros. They also had something that most strangers do not have, which is *trust*. They trusted each other, which meant that any exchange between them didn't require third-party verification.

They devised an amazingly simple scheme: After checking the daily currency exchange rates, Hinrikus would deposit euros into Käärmann's bank account, while Käärmann would deposit an equivalent value of pounds into the bank account of Hinrikus. Each got what they needed, and at no cost.

They wondered if their system could be scaled up in size to work between strangers who had no reason to trust each other.

What they came up with closely resembles the ancient *hawala* system of money transfer that's still used around the world, especially in the Middle East, India, and North Africa. In the *hawala* system, money never crosses borders. A customer walks into an office in, say, Riyadh, and wants to send funds home to Islamabad. After the *hawala* agent in Riyadh has received payment plus a small fee, he notifies the broker in Islamabad that the recipient is owed the funds. The funds come directly from the broker in Islamabad—there is no "transfer" in the way Western banks would do it. Later, the two offices reconcile their books. The system is based on trust; the broker in Islamabad knows that the broker in Riyadh is an honest and trusted member of the network.

The TransferWise system is a bit more complicated, but it is based on the same concept that money does not move anywhere; it is taken in and paid out from local pools of cash. TransferWise maintains a network of bank accounts in Europe, the United States, Canada, Asia-Pacific, and Latin America. When a customer puts money into a TransferWise account in, say, London, the recipient is paid from the local TransferWise account in their city—say, Jakarta. Meanwhile, the TransferWise bank account in Jakarta is replenished by the funds added to it by local Indonesians who want to send funds to other places. The idea is that all 300 (as of this writing) local TransferWise bank accounts are continuously "topped up" by people depositing their money to be credited to a recipient somewhere else. When the system is working steadily, money that's deposited in one local office is simply rerouted to a local recipient who's being sent a similar amount by someone overseas, making it a peer-to-peer service.

To be fair, TransferWise has not eliminated the middleman. It has simply become a *more efficient* middleman than the established system of sending money from one bank to another, across borders. There are fewer steps involved, and fewer steps mean lower costs.

Like the *hawala* system, TransferWise requires the sender to pay a small service fee. The example given on the TransferWise website is if you send GBP 1,000 from the UK to someone who wants euros, then the TransferWise fee is 0.35 percent of the amount that's converted plus GBP 0.80, which totals GBP 4.29. Therefore, the amount that's converted is GBP 995.71, which (on the day we accessed the TransferWise website) was EUR 1,099.26.[122]

It is definitely cheaper than bank transfers—but exactly how much cheaper is open to debate. In May 2016, TransferWise's claim that the customer saved "up to 90 percent against banks" was questioned by the Advertising Standards Authority (ASA), which said the claim couldn't be verified. In its defense, TransferWise said it had commissioned an independent third party to conduct "mystery shopping exercises" to compare the cost of TransferWise's service with those of its competitors.[123]

Regardless of the bottom-line savings, it is clear that TransferWise is doing something right, and both investors and the marketplace are responding. TransferWise customers send well over USD 1 billion each month using the service. Those little fees add up—by September 2018, the company's revenues had reached USD 151 million.[124] The company has received funding from a wide variety of venture firms and individual investors, including PayPal co-founder Max Levchin, former Betfair CEO David Yu, Wonga.com co-founder Errol Damelin, and Sir Richard Branson.[125]

TransferWise is a good example of how the spirit of technology innovation in Estonia has led to the development of an innovative cash transfer architecture that threatens to disrupt the old entrenched system.

Skype

In addition to being one of the co-founders of TransferWise, Taavet Hinrikus also participated in the early development of a service that disrupted international communications.

To understand Skype, imagine the world of the 20th century—not that long ago! Let's say you had relatives in Italy, or China, or any foreign country. One day, the television news reports a terrible earthquake in the country where your relatives live. Then, it is reported that the earthquake struck the very *town* where your relatives live. How would you know if your relatives were alive or dead? How would you be able to *see* them, in real time, and make that reassuring visual connection?

Before Skype, you could try to make contact via long-distance telephone. But that was a hit or miss proposition. With Skype, you could log onto your computer or smartphone, open the free app, and establish a real-time video link with your loved one. What's more, your video visit cost you *nothing*. (If you're old enough, you will remember the exorbitant price you had to pay for making a "long-distance" phone call.)

How about a business conference with your colleagues on a different continent? Or a guest appearance from your home office on a national cable news program? Before Skype, such connections were only possible with sophisticated and expensive satellite hookups. With Skype, they became ubiquitous.

The story of Skype began in 2003, when Niklas Zennström, from Sweden, and Janus Friis, from Denmark, collaborated with three software engineers from Estonia: Ahti Heinla (chief technical architect, and a graduate of the University of Tartu), Priit Kasesalu (who studied at Tallinn University of Technology), and Jaan Tallinn (also a graduate of the University of Tartu). (A few years later, the same core group of Zennström, Kasesalu, and Friis collaborated on the music file-sharing application Kazaa, which made its debut in November 2006.)

The first public beta version of Skype was released on August 29, 2003. The service was a peer-to-peer voice over internet protocol (VoIP) client that allowed its users to place voice calls and send text messages to other users of Skype.[126] Basically, the Skype software converted voice signals into data, sent that data over the internet from the host computer, and then restored the audio on the receiving computer.

It permitted voice calls from PC to PC and little else. It was developed by Kazaa, which had begun as a peer-to-peer file-sharing application and then subsequently a legal music subscription service. Your ability to download the app for free and make some free calls made Skype a "freemium" service, which means that you could use the basic service at no cost. Freemium is a two-tiered user acquisition model that introduces users to a free tier with basic functionality, and then offers a premium tier with additional features for which they need to pay.

On Skype, paid services that generate the majority of Skype's revenue include voice messaging, calling landline/mobile phones from Skype (formerly called SkypeOut), and allowing landline/mobile phones to call Skype (formerly called SkypeIn and now Skype Number).

With the release of the Beta 2.0 version in 2005, the service grew exponentially. That same year, eBay acquired Skype for USD 2.5 billion. A streaming video service known as Joost was rolled out, which proved unsuccessful. In May 2006, the company introduced Skypecasts, which allowed users to host conversations with up to 100 participants. The concept resembled a video chat room under the control of the host, who determined who could speak. As Rob Whent wrote for Itbusiness.ca, "The innovation forever changed what we wear in front of the computer. One hundred and thirty-six years after Alexander Graham Bell patented the telephone, he could finally see what Watson was wearing!"[127]

In early 2008, with eBay not seeing the expected revenues, conflict between eBay and Skype management teams steadily increased. Continuing upheavals in management personnel culminated in the departure of Friis and Zennström. In February, Josh Silverman became CEO, and pushed the company more in the direction of video calls. Features including Skype Find and Skypecast were abandoned.

In 2009, Skype 4.1 was launched, introducing a screen-sharing feature. This version also used Boingo, a pay-per-use service, offering wireless internet access through access points. The program would eventually be dubbed Skype Wi-Fi Access.[128]

By the next year, Skype 4.1 was firmly embedded in Mac, Windows, and Linux. The next step was to make the service work on mobile devices including Android, iPhone, and iPad. The first iterations for mobile permitted only voice calls. In December 2010, Skype introduced video calls to iPhone users. Six months later, in June 2011, the same access was given to Android.

In May 2011, Skype was bought by Microsoft. The price was USD 8.5 billion. By this time, the platform had progressed to Version 5.3, which included group video calls and Facebook integration. Unfortunately, at this time, Microsoft chose to install its own leadership team, which effectively ended the involvement of the pioneering Estonian entrepreneurs who had created the system eight years earlier.

But the original architects of the system had laid a secure foundation for growth. In November 2012, the service took another big step forward when Microsoft announced that it was discarding its proprietary Messenger service and making Skype the primary Microsoft messaging service. This brought a significant increase in Skype usage.

Today, Skype is still part of Microsoft. The basic video calling service is still free. Its headquarters are in Luxembourg, with offices now in Tallinn, Tartu, Stockholm, London, Palo Alto, Prague, and Redmond, Washington (home of parent corporation Microsoft). The app has been downloaded one billion times. It has three hundred million monthly active users and 4.9 million daily users, who spend an average of 3 billion minutes per day on the site.[129] It has a broad base of appeal among young adults; as of January 2018, when sorted by age group, WeAreFlint.co.uk found that 51 percent of internet users aged 18–24 used the telecommunications application software.[130] Because Skype is a division of Microsoft, no data is available on its revenues—but if we know anything about Microsoft, it is that the company wouldn't keep a money loser around very long!

With the visionary contributions of its three programmers from Estonia, Skype has come a very long way since its humble beginnings in 2003.

Nortal

In Ülemiste City, Tallinn, Estonia, there is a plain rectangular building constructed of stone bricks. With its tall, 24-paned windows and lack of ornamentation, it looks like a 19th-century mill or factory—functional, timeless, and sturdy. But when you step inside, you enter a space with a soaring atrium, sleek interior balconies, a big exposed spiral staircase, and an ornate antique billiard table ready for the next player.

This surprising blend of old and new is the headquarters of Nortal, a tech company with a big social mission. Founded at the turn of the century in 2000, the company strives to "build a seamless society that stands on three pillars—enterprise, e-health, and e-government."[131] In each of these three areas, the company has helped very influential customers achieve strategic change and build better experiences. Indeed, Nortal has been at the forefront of Estonia's breathtaking transformation into a global leader in building a national digital identity.

Originally founded as Webmedia by three men in Tartu, Estonia, the company quickly grew into a renowned authority on e-government strategy and solutions. (With typical Estonian modesty, Nortal does not lionize or promote its founders; they are not named on the company's website.) In 2008, Deloitte & Touche ranked Webmedia among the 30 fastest-growing companies in Central and Eastern Europe, and among the 500 fastest-growing technology companies in the Europe, Middle East, and Africa (EMEA) region.

In 2012, the company changed its name to Nortal, which stands for Nordic talent ("Nor-Tal"). Its 2017 revenues were EUR 48.3 million. With offices in Germany, Lithuania, Serbia, Oman, Dubai, and the United States, Nortal has a working presence in 10 countries across four regions: Europe, the Middle East, Africa, and North America.

Employing more than 800 professionals from different fields, the company is passionate about making life easier for others. It is involved in a dizzying array of projects—the company says there are currently 150 around the globe. Here are just a few:

- For the nation of Oman, the company built a new business register. Today, in less than three minutes, you can register a company in Oman. As a result, Oman's rating went up 127 places in the World Bank's rankings of ease of doing business.
- Also in Oman, Nortal created a holistic technical solution to help Oman implement a value-added tax (VAT). According to Andres Raieste, head of public finance management at Nortal, the solution helps ensure effective collection of the tax with minimum administrative burden and costs, while creating user-friendly services for all taxpayers and a fair business environment.
- Nortal helped Neste, a Finnish oil refining and marketing company, achieve 15 years of problem-free production. The partnership came about as a result of a hackathon that Neste held in spring 2017. "Neste is exceptional among hackathon organizers in that it has continued active system development based on the ideas presented in the event, specifically with one of the participating teams," said Nortal's project manager Juha Virko, who participated in Neste's hackathon.[132]
- Their solutions have helped John Deere Forestry save a million euros annually, and their production efficiency has gone up more than 80 percent.
- The company assisted Nigeria in setting up a single treasury account for the country, called the Government Integrated Financial Management Information System (GIFMIS), allowing the African nation to save more than EUR 7.5 billion. During the project, Nortal employees, while in the process of sorting and organizing Nigeria's public finances, discovered that the national budget was written down in books of graph paper. Some government officials had never even used a computer, much less worked with sophisticated IT systems. Even worse, 60,000 non-existent phantom employees were on the nation's payroll, and there were even fictitious government agencies dipping into the government bank account.

   Nortal's website noted that "a number of reputable international companies have recently announced that they are considering doing business in Nigeria. One such company is TransferWise, a company with an Estonian background, which resumed provision of their services to Nigerians this autumn."[133]
- In 2011, Nortal played a pivotal role in Estonia's population and housing census. For the first time in the history of Estonian censuses, Statistics Estonia—the controlling agency—used an e-census. The digital system enabled residents of Estonia

and those who were temporarily staying abroad to submit their census data electronically. Those few Estonians who were not digitally connected could still submit their information through a face-to-face interview.

In October 2018, Nortal announced plans to expand its presence in North America through the acquisition of Seattle-area startup Dev9, a cloud services firm focusing on building continuous delivery features for clients and showing them how to automate and streamline parts of the process, allowing them to ship code more quickly.

A year earlier, after signing an e-commerce project deal with a large telecom company, Nortal had opened an office in Seattle. With the Dev9 acquisition, the company planned to merge its Seattle operation of roughly 20 people with the 70-person Dev9 team to form a combined group.

In a statement, Nortal President Oleg Shvaikovsky said, "This merger enriches our offerings, in the U.S and globally, by enhancing our existing data-driven technology capabilities and adding significant depth to cloud modernization."[134]

TransferWise, Skype, and Nortal are just three examples of the spirit of technological and social innovation that, in the words of *Wired* magazine, has made Estonia "the most advanced digital society in the world."[135]

The historical legacy of the country

Estonia under the Soviet Union

The current economic, social, and political vitality of this small Baltic nation is all the more remarkable in light of its history from August 6, 1940 until August 20, 1991, when Estonia was a satellite state under the Soviet Union and, briefly, Germany.

World War II found Estonia caught between two massive warring nations—the Soviet Union and Nazi Germany. Following the Molotov–Ribbentrop Pact between Germany and the Soviet Union in 1939, the latter occupied Estonia, and quickly imposed a brutal regime. Tens of thousands of people, including most of the country's leading politicians and military officers, were arrested. Many were executed, while others were shipped to Gulag prison camps in Russia, from where very few returned. Under the pretext of mobilization into the Soviet army, 32,100 Estonian men were forcibly relocated to Russia, where nearly half died of hunger, cold, and overwork while serving in the so-called "labor battalions." Estonian Jews, too, were deported to Siberia.

When Germany attacked the Soviet Union, life in Estonia only became worse. During its retreat in 1941, the Red Army destroyed most industrial constructions, power plants, vehicles, and even cattle. During the evacuation, millions of dollars' worth of goods were taken from Estonia to Russia.

When the Germans seized Estonia, they made it a part of the German-occupied "*Ostland*"—the civilian occupation regime composed of the Baltic states (Estonia, Latvia, and Lithuania), the northeastern part of Poland, and the west part of the Belarusian SSR. Like the Soviets before them, the Germans looted the country to supply their war effort, and they also unleashed the Holocaust in Estonia, during which they murdered tens of thousands of people including ethnic Estonians, Estonian Jews, Estonian Gypsies, Estonian Russians, Soviet prisoners of war, Jews from other countries, and others.

When the German war effort collapsed in 1944, the Soviet Union retook Estonia. After reoccupation, the Soviet nationalization policy of 1940 was reimposed, as well as the collectivization of farms. Officially called the Estonian Soviet Socialist Republic, Estonia had no political or economic independence from the Soviet Union. It became, in effect, a colony of the much larger state, which systematically eliminated the last vestiges of Estonian self-governance.

Economic structures were deliberately destroyed, and new production structures were constructed only to satisfy the interests of the Soviet Union. Former European trading partners were cut off and the Estonian economy was focused squarely on trade with the colonial power.

Estonian banks and accounts were nationalized. Industrial machinery was dismantled and shipped to other Soviet territories. Estonian environmental resources were stripped, and employment and migration policies were engineered to assimilate the native population.

It was the goal of the Soviet Union to, over time, fully absorb Estonia into the USSR, and to dilute and eventually erase all remaining traces of Estonian national culture and identity. During the Brezhnev era of the late 1970s, as the Russian language was beginning to be taught in Estonian elementary schools, Estonians from all walks of life were growing increasingly worried about the threat of cultural Russification to the Estonian language and national identity.

By the dawn of the Gorbachev era in 1985, concern over the cultural survival of the Estonian people had reached a critical point. But as *perestroika* emerged in the Soviet Union, Estonian nationalism could be more safely expressed. The republic's Supreme Soviet—its Soviet-approved parliament—emerged as an authentic regional lawmaking body. In 1988, this relatively conservative legislature passed an early declaration of sovereignty, followed the next year by a law on economic independence, which was confirmed by the Supreme Soviet of the USSR that November. A law making Estonian the official language was adopted, along with local and republic election laws stipulating residency requirements for voting and candidacy.

Independence and restoration of parliamentary government

A peaceful restoration of independence came on August 20, 1991, when the Estonian parliament issued a declaration of independence from the Soviet Union. On September 6, the Supreme Soviet of the USSR recognized the independence of Estonia, which was quickly followed by widespread international recognition of the newly independent Republic of Estonia.

The language of independence was carefully chosen. Instead of "declaring" independence from the Soviet Union, which would imply that Estonia had never before been independent, the declaration "confirmed" Estonia as a state independent of the Soviet Union, and willing to re-establish diplomatic relations of its own accord. Estonians wanted the world to understand that the nation was merely resuming its normal national affairs that had been interrupted in 1939, when the Soviets had taken over.

On June 28, 1992, the fourth and current Constitution of the Republic of Estonia was adopted by referendum. This document re-established the parliamentary government with a president as chief of state and with a government headed by a prime minister.

The highest organ of state authority is the Riigikogu, the nation's unicameral legislative body. All-important state-related questions pass through the Riigikogu. In addition to approving legislation, the Riigikogu appoints high officials, including the prime minister and chief justice of the Supreme Court, and elects the president. According to the

1992 constitution, the Riigikogu has 101 members. Citizens of Estonia who are at least 21 years of age and eligible to vote may stand for election to the parliament of Estonia. Those who are at least 18 years of age and not convicted of a criminal offense have the right to participate in the voting for the parliament of Estonia.

Elected in free elections for four-year terms according to the principle of proportional representation, members of the Riigikogu convene within the historic Toompea Castle complex, an ancient stronghold in use since at least the ninth century. Located atop Toompea Hill in the central part of Tallinn, the building in which the Riigikogu meets was designed by architects Eugen Habermann and Herbert Johanson and completed in 1922. While its exterior is traditional in appearance, the interior is Expressionist in style, making it the world's only Expressionist parliament building. Indeed, if you're accustomed to seeing the typical monochromatic, neo-classical, or Gothic interiors of national legislative chambers, the exuberant Session Room of the Riigigoku will be a startling sight.

As the official government website describes it:

The color scheme of the Session Hall is also typical of Expressionism: lemon yellow ceiling, ultramarine blue walls, and rust brown sides of the window and door openings decorated with the zigzag motif. The cold yellow tone of the ceiling was balanced by the warm yellow tones in the lower part of the room. The warm tones were created by the wooden parquetry floor and light birch veneer furniture. The furniture was enlivened by contrasting black details and the dark blue Manchester plush of the seats, which harmonized with the rows of black balls above the press boxes.[136]

Elected by the Riigikogu or a special electoral body for a five-year term, the president of the Republic of Estonia is the head of state. A ceremonial figurehead with no executive power, he or she is obliged to suspend his or her membership in any political party for the term in office and hold no other elected or appointed office.

The president can be re-elected any number of times, but not more than twice consecutively. As of this writing, the current president is Kersti Kaljulaid, elected by parliament on October 3, 2016, becoming the first woman and, at age 46 when elected, the youngest person to ever hold the position.

The president's many duties include calling for regular or extraordinary elections of the Riigikogu, promulgating laws and signing the instruments of ratification, nominating the candidate for the post of prime minister, and nominating the chairman of the Supreme Court.

The prime minister is the head of government. After appropriate consultations with the parliamentary factions, he or she is nominated by the president and then confirmed by parliament.

Since the prime minister must maintain the confidence of parliament in order to remain in office, by convention, he or she is the leader of the majority party. While general elections to the Riigikogu are held at least every four years, no term limits are imposed on the office of prime minister.

The significance and power of the prime minister often depend on the position of the party led by the prime minister in relation to the minority or coalition parties, and on how much influence the prime minister possesses within his or her own party. If the prime minister has a strong position within his or her party, and the government includes a majority of representatives of that party, he or she can enjoy considerable authority. In all crucial national questions, however, the final word rests with the Riigikogu as the legislative power.

The day-to-day affairs of government are managed by various ministries, each of which is headed by a minister. Ministries are further divided into departments, divisions, and bureaus. The Supreme Court—the Riigikohus—reviews rulings of other courts and acts as a constitutional court.

Elections in Estonia

The idea of having electronic voting in Estonia gained popularity in 2001 with the "e-minded" coalition government. In 2005, with its pilot project for the municipal elections, Estonia became the first nation to hold legally binding general elections over the internet. Out of 1,059,292 eligible voters, 9,317, or 1.9 percent, voted online.[137] Estonians call it "i-voting," and it is described by the government thusly:

> Internet voting, or i-voting, is a system that allows voters to cast their ballots from any internet-connected computer anywhere in the world. Completely unrelated to the electronic voting systems used elsewhere, which involve costly and problematic machinery, the Estonian solution is simple, elegant and secure.

> During a designated pre-voting period, the voter logs onto the system using an ID-card or Mobile-ID and casts a ballot. The voter's identity is removed from the ballot before it reaches the National Electoral Commission for counting, thereby ensuring anonymity.

> With any method of remote voting, including traditional postal ballots, the possibility of votes being forced or bought is a concern. Estonia's solution is to allow voters to log on and vote as many times as they want during the pre-voting period. Since each vote cancels the last, a voter always has the option of changing his or her vote later.[138]

In 2005, the electronic voting system withstood the test of a real-life election and was declared a success by Estonian election officials.

In another world first, the Estonian parliamentary election in 2007 also used internet voting.

In the 2017 local municipal elections, which are the most recent elections, 186,034 people used i-voting. This means that roughly 31.7 percent of participating voters gave their vote over the internet. The last parliamentary elections were held in Estonia on March 3, 2019.

Estonia is rightfully proud to note that the digital infrastructure required for i-voting has been developed by Estonian companies. As e-Estonia.com noted, the systems and applications necessary for e-governance have been provided by the following Estonian companies:

- Cybernetica (i-voting, TIVI).
- Nortal Digital (business register).
- Ericsson (government cloud).
- OpenNode (government cloud).
- Telia (government cloud).

- State Infocommunication Foundation (government cloud).
- Dell EMC (government cloud).

In fact, Estonia has begun exporting its IT expertise. As e-Estonia.com notes,

> Today, Estonia has shared its e-governance journey with sixty governments and exported its solutions to over 130 countries around the world. The Estonian IT sector and ambitious startup community (known affectionately as the Estonian Mafia) dare to create innovative e-services that change the world, from Skype to e-Residency. In fact, Estonia is one of the top countries that has the most startups per capita established than anywhere else in Europe!"[139]

Political parties

Currently, six political parties hold seats in the Riigikogu. They are reported in Table 5.1. Founded in 1994 by Siim Kallas, who had been president of the Bank of Estonia and previously uninvolved in politics, the Estonian Reform Party is the most economically liberal in the political landscape of Estonia. The party supports a 0 percent corporate tax on re-invested income and lower income tax rates and wants to eliminate the dividend tax. While the party attracts votes from all demographics, it is supported predominantly by young and well-educated urban professionals who live in the cities. Its voter profile is significantly younger than average, well-educated, and with higher incomes.

Active since 1991, the Estonian Center Party claims that its goal is the formation of a strong middle class in Estonia. It tends to be economically liberal yet socially conservative; for example, the party has suggested that Estonia should consider re-establishing criminal punishments for the possession of even small amounts of illegal substances,

Table 5.1 Political Parties in Estonian Parliament, 2008

Party	Original Name	Ideology	Riigikogu Members (2018)
Estonian Reform Party	Eesti Reformierakond	Classical Liberalism	30
Estonian Centre Party	Eesti Keskerakond	Centrism	25
Social Democratic Party	Sotsiaaldemokraatlik Erakond	Social Democracy	14
Pro Patria	Isamaa	National Conservatism/ Christian Democracy	11
Free Party	Eesti Vabaerakond	Liberal Conservatism	6
Conservative People's Party of Estonia	Eesti Konservatiivne Rahvaerakond	National Conservatism / Estonian Nationalism	7

Source: Riigikogu.

and its stance on same-sex marriage, which is traditionally supported by social liberals, is unclear. The party is often described as populist and has become the most popular party among Russians in Estonia, being supported by up to 75 percent of ethnic non-Estonians.

The prime minister as of 2008, Jüri Ratas, is a member of the Center Party. The former mayor of Tallinn, he was elected prime minister in 2016.

In 1990, during the perestroika era, the Social Democratic Party was formed as Estonia's social-democratic movements merged. Generally, social democracy is a political, social, and economic ideology that supports economic and social interventions to promote social justice within the framework of a liberal democratic polity and capitalist economy. Social democrats tend to view government intervention favorably, and support measures for income redistribution, regulation of the economy in the general interest, and welfare state provisions. It has been identified with the Nordic Model, which refers to the economic and social policies common to the Nordic countries (Denmark, Finland, Norway, Iceland, Greenland, the Faroe Islands, and Sweden). While based on the economic foundations of free market capitalism, it is typified by a comprehensive welfare state and collective bargaining at the national level with a high percentage of the workforce unionized.

Pro Patria is a conservative political party founded on June 4, 2006, when two conservative parties, Pro Patria Union and Res Publica Party, merged.

The party's website enunciates its platform, which in this Google translation includes:

A strong family is the foundation of society, based on respect for ancestors and intergenerational integration. The marriage between a husband and a woman must be protected under the Constitution.

The ultimate goal of the Estonian state is to ensure the preservation of Estonian nationality, language and culture. Independent democratic parliamentary nation of Estonia is our only option.

Our economic policy cornerstone is a free market economy based on entrepreneurship, private property, fair competition, stable finances, low taxes and minimal national regulation. A successful economy relies on innovative (and science-based) technological solutions.[140]

The Estonian Free Party was founded in 2014 and holds the center-right position. The party advocates raising personal income tax while raising the non-taxable basic exemption to support the poorer majority of taxpayers. It supports increased taxes on alcohol, tobacco, and confectionery.

On social issues, the Estonian Free Party has declared its opposition to the law recognizing same-sex unions in Estonia, claiming the law needs to be revised and possibly also split into multiple regulations. In regard to the European migrant crisis, the party opposes compulsory EU-wide migrant quotas and advocates that the number of refugees to be admitted needs to be determined through negotiations. In November 2018, the party voted against Estonia joining the UN Global Compact for Migration.

The most conservative of Estonia's major parties, the Conservative People's Party of Estonia was founded in March 2012 with the platform of ensuring the survival of Estonian ethnicity. Many of its policies are directed toward preserving Estonian families, reducing emigration of Estonians, and preventing immigration from nations outside of the European Union. It also wishes to implement Swiss-style direct democracy, with the direct election of the president and other government officials.

For the Conservative People's Party of Estonia, the preservation of Estonian national identity and the dangers of Islamic immigration are top priorities. As party chair Mart Helme wrote:

The government intends to confirm at the UN General Assembly, one week after, Estonia's accession to the United Nations Migration Treaty and will make Estonia a long-term plan for importing Islamist terrorism. There is still time to rethink and not open the doors of our country for mass immigration and the accompanying Islamist terrorism."[141]

With its return to independence in 1991, Estonians could have sunk into internal squabbling, sought to become dependent on a strong neighboring nation, or otherwise chosen a course of mere survival rather than exceptional achievement. But the political system has produced a range of parties, each offering its own vision for the future; and together they compete at the polls before assembling in the Riigikogu to make the laws that will move Estonia into a bright future.

56. GENDER BALANCE AND GROWTH

"We need to resist the tyranny of low expectations. We need to open our eyes to the inequality that remains. We won't unlock the full potential of the workplace until we see how far from equality we really are."—Sheryl Sandberg, COO of Facebook, founder of LeanIn.org, and author of *Lean In: Women, Work, and the Will to Lead.*

The harsh reality of the global economy is that no one country in the world has closed its gender gap although the "economies that provide the necessary framework for sustainable value creation are exhibiting lower levels of gender inequality." Some Nordic countries are getting close as reported in the World Economic Forum's Global Gender Gap Report 2018. Iceland has closed over 85 percent of the gender gap, followed by Norway (83.5 percent), Sweden, and Finland (82.2 percent); yet worldwide, only 68 percent of the gender gap has been closed.

In academic terms, 68 percent would translate to a C+, a far cry from excelling at what the United Nations deemed a sustainable goal to be achieved by 2030. There is just over a decade until the UN's deadline, yet the Gender Gap Report prediction is that at the rate we are going it will take 108 years to achieve overall gender parity and 202 years to reach full equity in the world's workforce. In a world where female leaders sit at the helm of multinational corporations and govern significant economies, the overall reality entering 2019 is of a global economy that still discounts, misuses, and underpays half of the world's potential talent.

It needs to be recognized, as Maya Angelou so eloquently put it, that "diversity makes for a rich tapestry, and we must understand that all the threads of the tapestry are equal in value." Gender inequality weakens both economic and social progress. More initiative must be taken, and quickly, to address gender inequality to, in the words of the UN, "achieve a better and more sustainable future for all" by 2030.

The timing is especially crucial as humanity stands on the cusp of the digital revolution, wherein the lines that divide humans and technology blur and broad societal and economic transformation is already beginning in response. The digital revolution holds remarkable promise with the advancement of artificial intelligences, machine learning, and blockchain, concepts that were unimaginable at the advent of the first Industrial Revolution. This technological evolution brings with it a demand for those elements that make us human: our capacity for creativity, skill development, and resourcefulness. Alongside technology-driven fields should be more demand for jobs that machines cannot do, jobs that depend on human traits, attributes often credited to women such as empathy, sympathy, and compassion.

The majority of jobs in the new economy are going to have a technology component. With the speed of technological advancement, it is impossible to conceive the exact skill sets that will be required, especially in industries that have yet to be developed. However, what is known is that women represent half of the world's population, thus women also represent half of the world's potentiality. Women need to understand the skills required to excel in this new economic frontier. Gender equality is crucial to the framework of a global economy that is both viable and prosperous and comes down to the realization that together we are stronger. As Christine Lagarde, managing director of the International Monetary Fund stated in her 2013 "A New Global Economy for a New Generation" speech, "When women do better, economies do better."

While Lagarde's statement reflects a broadly recognized sentiment, the truth is that the global economy is increasingly shaped by technologies that could further exacerbate gender inequality. The 2018 Global Gender Gap Report, which indexes 149 countries, shows that gender gaps are already emerging in the field of AI. A collaborative study between LinkedIn and the World Economic Forum shows that only 22 percent of global AI professionals are women. If these gaps are not remedied, then it will only serve to worsen the gender divide in economic participation as we progress further into the digital economy. This rift also flags other weaknesses in the economic fabric, such as the lack of diverse talent in developing these technologies and shortages of qualified labor due to barriers against half of the population.

In a time when skills such as empathy and dexterity are of increased importance, it is not a sound strategy to disregard half of the population's ability to contribute talent to the world economy. It is vital that the number of women working in AI, at all levels, from research and development, to sales, to the creation of startups, is balanced with that of their male counterparts. That balance brings with it the promise of greater ingenuity, collaboration, and innovation.

Unbalanced

We're unbalanced. No matter the call for reform, the quotas, the protests, and #MeToo movements, the record numbers of women seeking office and banging against (sometimes shattering) glass ceilings, and the progress that's being made, it is still a male-centric world. This is especially true in the domains that will be most influential in the digital world, that of research and development and economics.

The IMD World Competitiveness Center reports that by almost every global benchmark, from the political arena to education, women are more economically excluded than men. Many countries and institutions have come to understand that when capable people hold business, government, or research positions, regardless of their gender, the greatest outcomes are realized.

Women face institutionalized inequalities such as wage gaps, greater unpaid work burdens, deterrents, and discrimination based on societal and cultural gender role norms, and lack of quality work and educational opportunities. This disparity is especially overt when examining global data surrounding both research and development and women holding executive positions and board seats. While most economies showed improvement between 2008 and 2015, with the most improved awards going to the countries of Estonia and Kazakhstan, there is still much work to be done. Studies indicate that women currently hold a mere 34 percent of managerial positions, and this number drops significantly to only 7 percent in Egypt, Saudi Arabia, Yemen, and Pakistan.

The lack of women in managerial positions, positions that coincide with higher incomes, translates into a significant global wage gap between genders. According to the World Economic Forum, the global pay disparity between men and women is so large and the pace of change so slow, it will take 202 years to close the wage gap. This is only slightly more hopeful than the 2017 prediction of 217 years. The WEF findings show that, globally, women earn 63 percent of what men do on average. There is not one country in the world where women and men are equal earners. Iceland is making strides, including making the gender pay gap illegal as of 2018. The Icelandic law requires companies with 25 or more employees to show evidence that they pay men and women equally for the same work. It is too soon to tell if this measure will bridge the gap. What will help to close the wage gap worldwide is more women working in what have been traditionally male-dominated professions and vice versa. With a digital economy on the horizon that means focusing on technology fields, research, and design.

The rapper, Notorious B.I.G., observed that with *Mo Money* came *Mo Problems*. Well, concerning research and design, *mo money* means fewer female researchers, signifying more problems with closing the gender gap. In the digital economy, when research and design in the technology fields will be paramount, this does not bode well for decreasing parity. Studies show that the more competitive the economy, the fewer female researchers it employs. The reason for this may be that in economies that really need researchers, the availability of skilled female researchers is too low. This could be because of cultural or societal pressures that discourage them from pursuing that type of work, or because of low expectations for future employment because they are female. It's also possible that research and development pathways have traditionally not been appropriately marketed and therefore not as enticing for girls, or that girls haven't been as informed of their options when pursuing education to foster careers in science and technology. As Marie Curie said, "You cannot hope to build a better world without improving the individuals." Clear educational and career pathways need to be designated for both males and females to follow in research and development.

Part of the remedy to this shortfall is the relatively new push for STEM educational pathways especially focused on tempting young women to pursue traditionally male-dominated disciplines. By changing the narrative, it is hoped that more young women will step foot on the STEM path. Research and development correlate with women's contribution to the economic realm as well. With more industry focus on technology, financial participation and wages become increasingly linked to jobs in STEM disciplines. It becomes increasingly important that women not only take entry-level jobs but also see that they can rise to the top and potentially steer companies focused on research and development. That means seeing female directors in those positions on boards today.

In a comparison between 2008 and 2016, the number of women participating on corporate boards has increased worldwide except in Hungary, Indonesia, and the Philippines. With the percentage of female board members in the 10 most competitive economies at almost 21 percent, there is still a long way to go to reach equality. This may be because of quota laws, both voluntary and sanctioned, that have been instituted in many European countries, or voluntary equality efforts such as the 30% Club in the UK.

The 30% Club was launched in 2010 in the UK and has now spread to 11 other countries including the United States, Canada, South and East Africa, and Italy. The 30% Club

> aims to develop a diverse pool of talent for all businesses through the efforts of its Chair and CEO members who are committed to better gender balance at all levels of their organizations. Business leadership is key to our mission, taking the issue beyond a specialist diversity effort and into mainstream talent management.

Whatever the reason, whether mandated or voluntary, there is a stronger representation of women on board seats, even while there is still a great inadequacy of parity in upper managerial and middle management positions.

What women bring to the board table

> "When we listen and celebrate what is both common and different, we become a wiser, more inclusive, and better organization."—Pat Wadors, Head of HR at LinkedIn

Women who have a seat at the boardroom table are still far less in number than their male counterparts. Boardroom diversity is on the rise. According to MSCI's research that indexes over 2,600 companies globally, women held 17.3 percent of directorships in 2017, which is up from 15.8 percent in 2016. One study found that countries with specific quotas, and non-compliance penalties (such as Norway, Iceland, Finland, and Sweden), had nearly twice the average percentage of women participating on boards (about 34 percent) than countries without those laws.

The numbers have risen when direct action against the disparities in representation and wages has been taken. Other than the fact that women have a right to be there, the question remains why should women be seated at the boardroom table? One reason is that more female leadership translates into more role models for young women, which is of the utmost importance if parity is to be achieved. More than that, there is the underpinning belief that the presence of women on corporate boards can affect the governance of companies in substantial ways, lessening groupthink mentality. As an unnamed female corporate board member said, "When you make a decision, whatever that decision is, whether it's about an acquisition, whether it's about anything, [being a woman] just makes you more sensitive to everyone that's involved; ... their healthcare, their retirement, all their benefits."

But one woman is not enough. Research has found that it takes three or more women on a board to create a "*critical mass*" which can lead to better financial performance. Reaching this critical mass changes boardroom dynamics significantly, increasing the opportunity for women to have a voice, for their ideas to be heard, and for ideas to generate from that particular diversity.

It is become widely known that having female leadership increases creativity by broadening contributing perspectives when decision-making. Evidence supports that women are present at more meetings and are more apt to be allocated supervision of sub-committees than men. This leads boards with more female directors to be potentially more involved in decision-making as the board voice is heard at the committee level. Boards that have women at the table oversee companies with fewer instances of bribery and fraud. Boards with more female members seem more aligned with shareholder interests, invest more in research and design, and overall have lower volatility. Women have traditionally been seen as more empathetic and better listeners than their male counterparts, which may also contribute to board culture and happier shareholders.

Shareholders are happiest when company returns are high. Multiple studies show that corporations that employ more women in senior positions are more profitable than their competitors. My own research, together with Maryam Zargari from the IMD World Competitiveness Center, shows that companies with female CEOs enjoy stock returns that are 15 percent higher on average than for companies run by men.[142]

Among the United Nation's Sustainable Goals is not only the *Achievement of Gender Equality* but the call to *Promote Economic and Sustainable Growth* that encompasses inclusive working environments and closing the wage gap between men and women. Policy initiatives such as board quotas are striving to fast-forward gender parity, but the question remains, are these initiatives working?

Case study: Norway

On December 21, 1879, Norwegian playwright Henrik Ibsen's *A Doll's House* premiered to whispers of scandal in Copenhagen, Denmark.

> *HELMER:* But this is disgraceful. Is this the way you neglect your most sacred duties?
> *NORA:* What do you consider is my most sacred duty?
> *HELMER:* Do I have to tell you that? Is not it your duty to your husband and children?
> *NORA:* have another duty, just as sacred.
> *HELMER:* You can't have. What duty do you mean?
> *NORA:* My duty to myself.[143]

The play was a mirror held up to the society of its time, examining a woman's fate in a male-dominated world. Ibsen stated of its theme that "a woman cannot be herself in modern society," as it is "an exclusively male society, with laws made by men and with prosecutors and judges who assess feminine conduct from a masculine standpoint."[144] Ibsen was reflecting the first inklings of change rippling through Norwegian society. In 1886, the first recommendation to alter the constitution so that women would be permitted to vote was made. Twenty-seven years later, on June 11, 1913, women were granted that right. That same year, American suffragettes were fighting for the vote, and Norwegian women rallied to their cause, marching in a parade in New York City. Since then, Norway has become an exporter in the commodity of gender equality.

In 2013, 100 years after the vote was obtained, Norway used it to elect Erna Solberg to lead the parliament as prime minister, but she wasn't the first female prime minister of Norway. Gro Harlem Brundtland, the youngest person and the first woman to hold the office, had already served three terms starting in 1981. Brundtland's appointed government, made up of 8 women and 10 men, was the first significant progress toward closing the gender gap that had been made since 1913.

Norway has worked hard to create a society of equality. Norway has a monarch, King Harald V; however, the power sits with the democratically elected parliament. His wife, Queen Sonja, a self-proclaimed feminist, talented photographer, and graphic artist, appears very concerned with women's issues. In the cabinet currently, 7 of 18 members are women including Siv Jensen, acting Minister of Finance, and 69 of the 169 parliament representatives (41 percent) are women. It says a great deal about the culture of a country when women hold such influential positions, acting as role models for younger generations. It is no wonder that Norway is now a leader on the gender-equality front. According to the 2018 Global Gender Gap Report, of the 149 countries tracked, Norway sits in second place, only slightly behind Iceland, having closed 83.5 percent of its overall gender gap.

Norwegian policy does not just talk the talk, so to speak. Norway has actively taken measures to ensure and enforce gender equity in the economic and political spheres through stringent gender equality policy. In 1978, the Norwegian parliament implemented the Gender Equality Act, which underwent revision in 2013. The act aimed to foster the position of women by mandating equal opportunities in the facets of education, employment, and cultural and professional advancement.

Informal gender quotas have been in place in Norway since Brundtland first came to power in the 1980s. The political process to move toward more formalized gender quotas began in 1999 with a government motion tendered by the Minister for Gender Equality, Valgerd Svarstad Haugland, who asked for an amendment to the Equal Status Act of 1978. Before the last vote on the bill, the Minister of Trade and Industry said that he was "sick and tired of the male dominance of business life." Sadly, not everyone shared his viewpoint. After much controversy and discussion surrounding the issue and amid shareholder protests, in 2003 a board quota amendment was added to Norway's Companies Act. The goal of the amendment was to increase women's representation in corporate positions of power and decrease gender disparity in earnings. The bill reads as follows:

> The Companies Act (as amended in 2003): §§ 6–11a. Requirement of representation of both genders on the board.2 (1) In the boards of publicly listed … companies both genders should be represented, as follows: 1. Where there are two or three board members, both genders should be represented. 2. Where there are four or five board members, both genders should be represented with at least two members each. 3. Where there are six to eight board members, both genders should be represented with at least three members each. 4. Where there are nine or more members of the board, each gender should be represented with at least 40 per cent each. 5. Rules 1 to 4 also apply to the election of deputy members.

At first, the amendment was to be a voluntary initiative with the hope that corporate Norway would view the progress as positive. However, after seeing little to no improvement in female board representation, in 2006, Norway was the first country to pass a gender quota law requiring all publicly listed companies to have a minimum 40/60 gender balance on their boards, which was fully enforced by 2008. Mandatory legislation was a way to compel an equitable culture with the hope that if equity were in place at the top, then it would trickle down through the management levels. "We see that we have made great progress on gender equality, but that female representation in society is shaped like a pyramid," says Siri Terjesen, a professor at the Kogod School of Business at the American University in Washington, DC, and an adjunct professor at the Norwegian School of Economics in Bergen.

> Women are well represented in the educational system and the labor force, but at the top of the power hierarchy, they are still surprisingly poorly represented. It is the strict enforcement of sanctions that is the key to understanding Norway's success with gender quotas for boards.

When faced with gender quotas in 2003, companies could choose to avoid both conforming and sanctions and change their status from public to private. Unfortunately, a significant number of companies (217) did decide to change their status to private between 2003 and 2005. Between 2005 and when the quota law was in full effect, the public to private boat-jumpers increased, leaving only 179 on board by 2008. If companies do not uphold the gender quota requirements in Norway, then they face harsh sanctions in the form of financial consequences, being delisted from the stock index, and dissolved by the courts. Norway, according to Terjesen, has a culture of politicians keeping their word, so publicly listed companies have complained, yet complied. To date, no companies have faced sanctions.

Aftermath

Many feared imminent disasters when the quota law was laid down. Forced regulation of gender composition would lead to tokenism, recruitment based on gender, not knowledge, skill, or experience. This less-competent leadership would ultimately destroy the company and was a form of discrimination against more competent men. Women would cause financial ruin. While quotas have not been the catastrophe that many people had dreaded, they have also underachieved in doing what the government had pledged they would do.

Overall, although male to female board composition has vastly transformed since the advent of the quotas, we are still a far cry from achieving an old girls' club of sorts. A gender hierarchy still exists within the boards with only 5 percent of board chairs being women. Many female directors sit on multiple boards as well. These women, disparagingly nicknamed "*golden skirts*," seem to have benefited the most from the quotas by accumulating directorships in bulk and reaping the corresponding wages and experience. "Before the quota, there were all these women who were banging their heads against a glass ceiling, and suddenly they are being offered all of these non-executive roles," says Elin Hurvenes, head of the Professional Boards Forum in Oslo. "But now headhunters are starting to look to the boards and pick up women for executive jobs."

Eli Sætersmoen, the current CEO of Cryogenetics AS, has made her golden skirt designation work for her while sitting on multiple boards since 2000. She currently sits on three boards and chairs one according to her LinkedIn profile. Sætersmoen is an example of how quotas broke the glass ceiling. She had been a portfolio director of a non-executive board and was persuaded back to management. Sætersmoen says that "the reason I was able to get the job was that, through the board experience I had, I developed a very good, solid network."

Equality has mostly failed to trickle down to even the upper and middle corporate echelons, as was the hope when quota policies were put in place. Only 2 percent of directors and CEOs of Oslo stock exchange–listed companies, and 10 percent of top management, are women. The equality struggle is still very real.

As women's place in AI and research has already been touched on, let's turn our attention to the biotechnology companies listed on the Oslo stock exchange and see how they fare concerning board and management equality. After a public search, four biotech company names surfaced: Targovax, BerGenBio, and Nordic Nanovector are all companies focused on biotechnology that fights cancer, while Biotec Pharmacon's work is focused on immune-modulating compounds.

The three biotech companies that focus on cancer research also have very similar board of director configurations. Targovax has eight board members split fifty-fifty by gender, but with a male chairing. Nordic Nanovector has seven board members, three of whom are female, and a male chair. BerGenBio has six board members, four male and two female, and you probably saw this coming—a male chair. Biotec Pharmacon stands alone with a female chair and a female majority with three of five board members being women.

However, Biotec does not rate so highly in managerial team parity with a team that is composed entirely of men. The BerGenBio management team consisting of nine members boasts only two women, and they just joined the company in 2015 and 2018. Targovax has a male-dominated management team as well with four of six leaders being men. Nordic Nonovector boasts a nine-person management team with the majority, six members, being female. All four companies have male CEOs.

Although every study seems to conclude that the positive, and for that matter adverse, effects of gender quotas are primarily inconclusive, it may just be the old adage that time will tell. It has only been 10 years, after all, since full implementation. When asked in a recent interview if gender quotas are still a necessity today, Helga Hernes, former State Secretary in the Ministry of Foreign Affairs, known as "the mother of state feminism," former leader of the gender equality committee, and Labor Party politician, replied,

> We should always be women conscious. Nowadays it is particularly discouraging that women have so little power and influence in the private sector. It is very interesting that we have a society in which gender equality has been achieved on so many areas, and yet the business and financial world is almost completely dominated by men.

So, that's a yes?

Change is hard, and sometimes a hard push is needed instead of an encouraging nudge. The negative sanctions imposed by Norway created a sense of urgency, and it worked, to a degree, by balancing the boards. Study results illustrate that those female board members have an extensive and valuable impact on the structure and workings of the boards on which they sit. This evidence didn't prove that quota policy in any way improves firm function on average.

Board quotas worked to balance the playing field for some, to raise awareness and get decision-makers talking, and forced a re-examination of corporate culture. Perhaps, though, board quotas are not the answer in the long run and should not become permanent fixtures.

The European Commission has been trying to jump on the gender quota bandwagon, advocating for gender quotas similar to Norway's to be mandatory across the EU, with the requirement that 40 percent of non-executive directors be female. Companies that fail to meet that requirement will have to prioritize female candidates over men as board seats become available. Countries such as Spain (which adopted quotas in 2007), and Belgium, France, Italy, and the Netherlands (which all adopted quota policy in 2011) have some of the highest percentages of female directors in the EU. While initiatives taken in these countries have translated into an increase of women in board positions, the gender gaps remain in middle management similar to those viewed in Norway.

Abenomics

Japan's former Prime Minister Shinzo Abe worked to reform Japan's economy, fostering more equality. These reforms have been nicknamed *Abenomics* or *womenomics*. Ten years ago, Japan ranked 80th on the WEF's Gender Gap Report. In 2017, it ranked 114th and rose to 110th out of 149 countries in 2018. Female employment numbers have increased in Japan, and in 2018, 68.4 percent of women were part of the workforce. However, the number of women holding legislative, senior official, and managerial positions is appalling at only 13.2 percent, ranking Japan 129th out of the 149 countries. So, the quantity of work is not the issue; however, the quality is.

In 2015, Japan, under Abe's leadership, made it a law that companies employing more than 301 people had to set targets for increased female management and make public their results. There are no non-compliance penalties to coincide with the law. If you look at the data from the 2014 WEF Gender Gap Report, the year before the law's establishment, it shows that 64 percent of women participated in the workforce and that of those, 11 percent held legislative, senior official, and managerial positions. So, three years after the law's implementation, there is only a 4.4 percent increase in women in the overall workforce and just a 2.2 percent jump in women obtaining those coveted power positions.

In 2016, the government, having seen that it perhaps bit off more than the corporate world could chew when it declared that by 2020 they would fill 30 percent of senior positions in both the public and private sectors with women, reassessed the targets. The new, seemingly more realistic goals of having 7 percent female leadership in senior government positions and 15 percent female management in private companies were set. It's been two years, halfway to the 2020 deadline, and little progress has been made.

Glass floors

In 2012, Sheryl Sandberg became the first woman elected to Facebook's board of directors. An impressive accomplishment, Sandberg herself, however, realizes that the bar to recognizing equity is still low. A report on Women in the Workplace by McKinsey in 2018 showed that men viewed having 1 in 10 senior leaders as female was "well represented" in power positions in the United States. More upsetting is that "a third of women agree."[145] Sheryl Sandberg and president of LeanIn.Org, Rachel Thomas, responded to the report saying, "When so many people see a leadership team that's only 10 percent women—who, let's remember, are half the population—and think, 'That's good enough,' it is a sign that we're too comfortable with the status quo."[146] As the tennis player, Billie Jean King, once said, "Everyone thinks women should be thrilled when we get crumbs, and I want women to have the cake, the icing, and the cherry on top too."[147] Women need to believe that they have the potential to obtain the cake, cherry and all. If they do not see potential in an industry or a company, then to pursue a career down those avenues is futile.

The problem that the Norway case study illuminates, and the problem with board quotas in general, is that female representation at the top does not translate to female representation in the lower rungs of organizations. Instead of starting from the bottom and working up, board quotas are trying to problem-solve at the top and hoping it will cascade downwards. Companies need to start from the bottom and change hiring and promotion policies at entry and management levels to ensure real progress is made.

The problem, it seems, is with corporate culture overall, and that is where attention needs to be placed. A re-evaluation is required that addresses hiring practices, mentorship, communications, and advancement potential. It is not enough to merely attract diverse candidates, because if the company culture does not support them, they won't stay. Nor is tokenism in hiring the answer if real change is to be implemented. A focus on creating genuinely inclusive cultures is imperative where women are not only hired, but are also able to hold decision-making positions and help to steer the company.

Aileen Lee, a co-founder of Bay Area–based Cowboy Ventures, said at a technology conference, "We have to make tech and tech-driven companies more equitable for women and people of color and people who are different—people who didn't go to Harvard and Stanford, people who didn't grow up with privilege." When later asked about how leaders in technology companies can inform change, Lee responded that "founders and CEOs should be purposeful with who they hire and the company cultures they build." That those in decision-making positions need to

> pay attention not just to the numbers of who you're hiring, but the culture—the quality of conversations, who's going to lunch with whom. Paying attention to whether everyone in your company feels like they have an equal chance of being successful, regardless of what level or function they are in, I think, is really important.

It's the little things that can make a huge difference. As Lee pointed out, the conversations are meaningful. So too is the language used. Comparative research, conducted in Canada, studied reactions to job postings for the same jobs. When the job postings used stereotypically male language, women found the advertised jobs less appealing. When questioned, the women said they felt that they were capable of doing the job but took the language to mean that the workplace would be male dominated and therefore they wouldn't belong in it. Perhaps, moving forward, more attention needs to be paid to culture, not quotas.

57. SUSTAINABILITY: PUTTING PEOPLE FIRST

"The collective 'we' are dumbfounded that people still drive drunk," said Helen Mirren, the "notoriously frank and uncensored British"[148] actress, to start a 2016 Anheuser-Busch InBev (AB InBev) Budweiser Super Bowl commercial. The commercial, set in a pub, with Mirren staged behind a burger and a bottle of beer, delivered an amusing verbal smackdown of people who drink too much and drive. The star-powered advertisement was part of InBev's media campaign to negate the misuse of alcohol and advocate for smart, responsible drinking globally. Premiering it during the Super Bowl, now known for big-budget, star-studded commercials as much as for the athletic championship, was a sound strategy. AB InBev's marketing agenda was more profound than merely combating the lousy media that alcohol gets from people's poor choices. It's part of their mission to support the United Nation's Sustainable Development Goals and make the world a better place for everyone.

This is not the first, and indeed not the most controversial, marketing campaign to indirectly address one of the UN's Sustainable Development Goals. Gillette, a Procter & Gamble company, stirred up significant controversy with the *We Believe: The Best Men Can Be* advertisement that attacked bullying, harassment, and male "boys will be boys" stereotypes, saying there is "no going back" after the societal shift brought about by the #MeToo movement and the conversations that ensued. The commercial encourages a re-examination of the attitudes and behavior that have long been silenced in society, calling for a change because the "boys watching today will be the men of tomorrow."[149]

Dove Men + Care, a Unilever company, recently released the *Dear Future Dads* campaign that is "championing paternity for Dads everywhere." The commercial tugs at the heartstrings as fathers relay how much having a child has meant to them and has changed them. Some of the dads well up with emotion. One father in the commercial says that young children "need time with both their parents"; another dad adds, "Do whatever you can to take time off."[150] Both the Dove and Gillette campaigns discussed different topics, and neither was really about the company's product apart from the logos used. However, both defied stereotypes in advertising and both were combating social norms concerning women, which is a crucial factor in the implementation of the SDGs. The paternity leave commercial is not just enforcing the notion of gender equality or promoting good parenting, it speaks to a broader issue about women's place in the workforce and is a message that, if given serious consideration, would help to close the wage gap. Both Unilever and Procter & Gamble have made their goals concerning the SDGs clear. They are both constructing, much like AB InBev, sustainable and competitive business models that work to their benefit, as well as to the benefit of the world.

Setting the sustainable development goals

In New York City in 2015, 193 United Nations member states voted unanimously in favor of adopting 17 SDGs to be achieved by 2030. Each of the 17 goals has specific targets, totaling 169 therein, tracked by 232 indicators of progress. The goals, ranging from Quality Education to Zero Hunger to Sustainable Cities and Communities, are an imperative call to action for all countries to work together for a peaceful and prosperous world.[151]

The SDGs started their incubation at the 2012 United Nations Conference on Sustainable Development in Rio de Janeiro, where it was mandated that an open group be created to come up with a draft agenda to establish sustainable goals past 2015. The group, which consisted of representatives from 70 countries, held many discussions taking into account mass feedback that included national consultations and mass survey feedback from citizens that had them prioritize the areas that they wanted the goals to address. The working group created a draft with its 17 SDG suggestions. The SDG draft was presented in 2014, and after fine-tuning the wording of the goals and targets, the document was finalized in 2015. The goals came from a globally shared realization that there were crucial economic, political, and environmental issues facing humanity that required urgent action. The recognition of these issues and their urgency was not new to the UN.[152]

In 2000, the UN launched the Millennium Development Goals (MDGs), which were an aggressive attack on poverty, disease, and extreme hunger among other correlating issues that plagued developing countries. Between 2000 and 2015, the MDGs compelled advancements in many vital areas, such as clean water and sanitation access, the battle against diseases such as HIV/AIDS, malaria, and tuberculosis, and improved maternal health.[153]

The SDGs were born from the lessons learned through establishing and driving the MDGs. Even with much progress made, the MDGs were not fully realized. Many people believed the MDGs to be too narrow of vision, driving change but doing little to address the underlying issues causing the problems.[154] Also, the MDGs, although not explicitly stated, focused on the needs of developing countries that were to be improved through financial assistance from wealthier nations. Thus, a relationship between countries built on charity was created, further increasing power imbalances. The SDGs were not developed because all the MDG boxes were checked, and the MDG initiatives were not forgotten in light of a shinier new set of goals. Instead, the MDGs became entwined within the other areas that needed improvement and rebranded as the SDGs. At the basis of the SDGs is the idea that nations, whether developed or developing, work together to create a sustainable world. The power imbalance then shifts, becoming that of co-creators, and a relationship built on collaboration begins. While the MDGs were about the rich helping the poor, the SDGs are accepting that every country in the world needs to do better, that no one country is perfect.[155] Now, three years into the SDGs, there is recognition that tackling the SDGs is a process and that states can look to each other for ideas and guidance in approaches that are successful.

In 2015, most nations were pleased with the created goals; however, a small collective of member states was not as enthusiastic. The United Kingdom and Japan were among the collective of naysayers. Some nations found some of the goals uncomfortable, especially those concerning the environment. For some, it was just the belief that 17 goals were too many to implement. David Cameron, former British prime minister, said he wanted 12 goals at most; 10 would have been even better. He did not state which goals he wanted removed. The UN Secretary General's special adviser, Amina Mohammed, said that it was difficult to narrow the list to 17; making further reductions would be strongly opposed.[156] However, the consensus overall was that 17 goals that target foundational issues such as gender equality and good governance are better than fewer goals that ignore those areas (which the MDGs mainly did).

The 17 SDGs are interconnected; if a change is affected in one, then it impacts the others, both positively and negatively. For example, reaching gender equality means closing the wage gap, more women in positions of power, and more women participating across industries. Gender parity, ultimately, helps to eliminate poverty and will help economies to flourish. The first and foremost goal, to end poverty, stands on its own, but it is also a thread that runs through each of the other 16 goals. The goals, which are set to transform the world by 2030, are not about short-term impact.[157] They are about creating a better, safer future and helping the planet to sustain its inhabitants for another 2,000 years. They represent a paradigm shift away from the capitalist view of corporate and government spheres that exploit each other for different gains toward a partnership for the greater good, and therefore stronger economies.

The SDGs' ambitious foci affect all of humanity and are greater than the sum of their 17 parts. Globalization must be an inclusive force that does not leave behind a subset of citizens or countries. The SDGs have directed a clear path on which to progress. If corporations, governments, and citizens look to the SDGs for guidance, then moving toward corporate and state sustainability is possible. The goals illuminate the need for governments, industry, and citizens to work together and look beyond borders.[158] As Helen Keller said, "Alone we can do so little, together we can do so much."[159]

There's still a long and bumpy road ahead

The progress toward achieving the SDGs is uneven and, overarchingly, far too slow. Francesca Perucci, chief of the Statistical Services Branch at the UN Statistics Division, stated, "Almost all areas where you see progress, if you look at the rate, or the pace of progress, it is never sufficient to meet the targets."[160] A frightening thought when you consider millions of lives and meeting basic human needs are what is at stake. Inequality, pockets of poverty, and rapid urbanization are some of the factors challenging countries' attempts to achieve the SDGs. Conflict and climate change are both contributing factors leading to increased populations facing hunger and forced displacement. In fact, conflict is one of the primary drivers of food insecurity in 18 countries[161] and, "for the first time in more than a decade, there are now approximately 38 million more hungry people in the world, rising from 777 million in 2015 to 815 million in 2016."[162] Conflict and climate change are also hindering work toward universal access to water and sanitation.

According to John McArthur, senior fellow at the Brookings Institution and senior advisor to the UN Foundation, some targets are on track, while others, especially newer "frontier issues," are lagging.[163] The goals that have roots in the MDGs, like health and well-being (SDG3), have multiple targets that are on track to reach more than half of the lofty UN goals. The focus on AIDS, infectious diseases, and malaria has an excellent ecosystem of actors in place among academics, institutions, and companies, and although they haven't yet reached the goals, they have a clear vision of what they are doing and have established markers for progress. Because the underlying concerns of SDG3 have been issues for an extended period, and because the MDGs gave them a kick-start, they now have a sense of momentum and organization. As McArthur says, they have in place a "machinery in terms of thinking about these things."[164]

Contrast that to newer goals, such as SDG14 Life Below Water, which lack the pre-established processes and partnerships; therefore, developing the necessary framework is slow.[165] There is a considerable need in addressing SDG14, as the focus is on 70 percent of the planet. Strict rules already govern what happens on the water in terms of shipping and such, but there is not an effective system in place to protect what is beneath the water's surface. The marine conservation and protection aspects are new. With such a vast geographical expanse in question, the very nature of the goal's subject matter mandates global cooperation.

Other SDGs, such as education, are caught somewhere in the middle. Education was part of the MDGs and while much progress has been made in getting children into educational settings, the full machinery of thinking and organizing around what they are learning and how best to prepare the next generation for the new economy is not yet in place. Some targets, like extreme poverty and child mortality, are on track to reach more than halfway to the determined goal by 2030.[166] The proportion of the world's workers living on less than USD 1.90 per person a day has fallen from 26.9 percent in 2000 to 9.2 percent in 2017, while the under-five mortality rate dropped by almost 50 percent in the least developed countries.[167] Other SDG targets, such as childhood obesity and air pollution, are moving in the opposite direction. The 2018 UN SDG Report found that 38 million children under age five are obese, while 9 out of 10 people residing in cities breathe polluted air.[168]

Three years in and countries haven't yet figured out how to achieve all of the goals, but they are starting to think through how to organize themselves around the SDGs. Federal governments realize that the SDGs are a "complex task that no single actor can do."[169]

Governments are looking for a variety of players, outside of their institution, who will be critical to their country achieving sustainability. Every year, the UN has a summer check-in where ministers from the SDG Compact give status updates about what their nation has achieved concerning the SDGs. In September 2019, the check-in is supposed to come from the presidents and prime ministers, the top echelon of government. The 2019 check-in will provide an opportunity to crystalize what we, as a global community, are not doing well enough. António Guterres, Secretary-General of the United Nations, says that we must "narrow the gaps. Bridge the divides. Rebuild trust by bringing people together around common goals. Unity is our path. Our future depends on it."[170]

SDG17 partnerships for the goals

Of the 17 goals, it is easily arguable that the final, Partnerships for the Goals, is the most critical:

> A successful sustainable development agenda requires partnerships between gov-ernments, the private sector, and civil society. These inclusive partnerships built upon principles and values, a shared vision, and shared goals that place people and the planet at the center, are needed at the global, regional, national, and local level.[171]

Without partnerships among governments, companies, communities, citizens, educa-tors, and financers, these goals will not be reached by 2030, or for many years beyond. António Guterres, Secretary-General of the United Nations, stated, "Since there can be no poverty eradication without generation of wealth, we should further promote the UN Global Compact, highlighting the benefits of corporate responsibility."[172] Strong partner-ships drive better business, which in turn creates a competitive national economy.

The competitiveness of states is vital to future prosperity and a sustainable economy. According to our definition at the IMD World Competitiveness Center, "Competitiveness is the extent to which a country is able to foster an environment in which enterprises can generate sustainable value."[173] Fostering a country's competitive environment coincides with the initiatives laid out by the UN. The 17 goals work at establishing sustainable pros-perity for all of humanity which would, in turn, strengthen the world economy.

Competitiveness as a definition has evolved as the economy has changed. It is no longer merely the idea that to be competitive means to be profitable. In the current economy, competitiveness is related to the notion of *inclusive growth*.[174] Inclusive growth evaluates how countries can achieve growth while simultaneously balancing socio-environmental outcomes. Competitiveness needs to be a collaboration among compa-nies, industries, and nations. Relationships between private and public stakeholders can increase, or decrease, the overall competitiveness of the company, industry, or country.[175] For example, a company becomes more profitable by adopting a new manufacturing process. However, its new manufacturing process is highly pollutive. The result is then that the overall competitiveness of the country in which the company manufactures will be negatively affected because of environmental and health concerns stemming from the pollutants. Socioeconomic and environmental factors must be managed alongside profitability to achieve prosperity and sustainability in both the short and long term. This consideration of factors outside of sheer profit is sustainable competitiveness and is based on the idea that being competitive today should be obtained without conceding the chance of competitiveness tomorrow.[176,177] Sustainable competitiveness needs to be the penultimate objective of corporate and national development, especially in the new business landscape.

The new business landscape is characterized by both unprecedented risk and opportunity. There is a growing certainty among progressive stakeholders that companies can't merely be concerned with short-term profits because there are so many factors that can hurt their long-term prosperity, such as social unrest and natural disasters. Consideration of both the risks and opportunities leads to sustainable and competitive business practices and is the foundation for sustainable and competitive countries. Working toward the SDGs requires mass collaboration. World leaders, corporations, and small businesses alike, civil society, educators, investors, and individual citizens all need to come together to evoke change and thrive. If all of the parts of the sum thrive, then the sum itself thrives and increases its competitiveness.[178]

In 2000, Kofi Annan, then UN Secretary-General, created the United Nations Global Compact. The Compact was to "give a human face to the global market."[179] When the Compact was founded, corporate sustainability was only a principle on the periphery of the business world. Now, the idea to unite profit and responsibility is central. The UN Global Compact is the "largest global network of sustainable companies—with 9,300 businesses in 165 countries committed to uphold UN values and principles in how they operate."[180]

Of 1,000 CEOs surveyed by the UN Global Compact, 87 percent agreed that the SDGs "provide an essential opportunity for business to rethink approaches to sustainable value creation."[181] The SDGs are a shared approach to success among the UN, governments, civil society, and corporations. These partnerships are essential to the success of innovative, sustainable, and competitive companies. Justin Perrettson, chair of the ICC Commission on Environment and Energy, illustrates that by saying,

> The SDGs provide a strategic framework for government, business, and civil society to help frame the contexts of many key challenges and opportunities facing the world over the coming decades, highlighted through the 2030 Agenda. In seeking to maximize their positive contributions, public-private partnerships for the SDGs can enable those who engage in leveraging their strengths, learn from their unusual collaborations, and create additional value that can be measured in terms of positive socioeconomic and environmental impacts.[182]

So far, the advancement of SDG17 has been slow. In a time of advancing protectionism and inequality, there seems to be an ever-increasing number of obstacles in building private–public global partnerships. For example, in 2017, 102 states were implementing national statistical plans.[183] Sub-Saharan Africa was in the lead, with 31 countries implementing such projects; however, only three received full funding.[184] The net official development assistance (ODA) in 2017 totaled USD 146.6 billion, which was a decrease of 0.6 percent from 2016. The ODA as a portion of a donor's gross national income remained low, at 0.31 percent,[185] falling short of what is required to guarantee that countries in developing regions are adequately equipped to implement and monitor their development agendas.

As former Beatle George Harrison sang, "But it is gonna take money/A whole lot of spending money/It is going to take plenty of money/To do it right child."[186] It all comes down to money. The SDGs are huge initiatives and to implement them properly requires money, large sums of money. Public resources are not sufficient; private investment is a must. However, to cough up funds in support of the SDGs and revolutionize their business models, companies need to see the direct benefit to them, in increases in competitiveness and chances for economic growth. Corporations are not charities; after all, they are money-making components of a capitalist system.

Partners in inclusive capitalism

The current form of capitalism is driving a greater wedge between the haves and the have-nots, leaving subsets of people and countries behind and placing the planet under severe strain. A call for more inclusive capitalism has been made, one that aligns itself with the SDGs. Businesses can help drive a reboot of the current system, creating more sustainable business models and contributing to a more sustainable world. Many forward-thinking industry leaders have partnered to serve both their bottom line and the SDGs. Companies that have adopted the SDGs as best practices are numerous, spanning all industries. Of those, the companies that are prioritizing SDG17 and striving for innovative partnerships are seeing the most significant rewards. Innovative partnerships like:

> Nestlé, in collaboration with the Swiss Agency for Development and Cooperation, is engaging with Vietnamese coffee farmers to create better irrigation and water management (SDG6). In Switzerland, Nestlé integrated the ECO-Broye program, a combination of environmental conservation and a commitment to work closely with local farmers and stakeholders (SDG15).[187]
> General Electric, along with J.P. Morgan and the UK government, are working together to repair Iraq's power grid. The public–private partnership should get electricity to millions of homes and businesses in Iraq (SDG11).[188]
> Timberland partnered with startup Thread to launch a line of boots, shirts, and backpacks made entirely from plastic waste; the Haitian government enabled it. This partnership has generated more than USD 16,000 in local revenue while eliminating pesticides and water usage (SDG15).[189]

What follows is a small sampling of businesses whose initiatives are in line with multiple SDGs. Across these examples are companies thinking outside of the boardroom and across borders. The cases highlight the correlation between the goals and that working toward one really means working toward many.

Syngenta is a Swiss agricultural company that offers crop solutions that make better use of resources. They aim to help feed the world, sustainably. Their mandate is rooted in environmental and societal sustainability. Syngenta is actively working toward a multitude of SDGs. They have clear targets set for SDGs 1, 2, 3, 8, 12, 13, 15, and 17, much of which is rooted in their Good Growth Plan. The Good Growth Plan is creating answers to how to deal with the growing population, impoverished farmers, and eroding farmland. The goal is to improve agricultural sustainability and Syngenta's business through six commitments to be achieved by 2020: make crops more efficient, rescue more farmland, help biodiversity flourish, empower smallholders, help people stay safe, and look after every worker. To find solutions, Syngenta is working with governments, NGOs, and growers. Through private–public partnerships, they are strengthening the agricultural industry and building sustainable nations, while contributing to a sustainable economy, because it does not matter how profitable a company is if the population of workers or the population of the country that governs the company is not able to feed itself.[190]

Siemens, which provides ingenuity for life across finance, healthcare, mobility, energy, and software, among other sectors, is working toward many SDGs. From diversity to decarbonization, its mandate to be competitive both now and in the future is clear. Here are some of the SDGs that Siemens is working toward, and how. Towards Quality Education (SDG4), it has created youth education programs to combat the skilled worker shortage in engineering. Siemens has created over 30 learning programs and 3 interactive games. The materials are available online for free. This program has increased interest in STEM, which encourages youth to explore STEM fields as future career pathways, thereby encouraging a solid foundation of future industry talent. Safe Water Enterprises focuses on Clean Water and Sanitation (SDG6) and is providing safe drinking water to communities while creating hundreds of jobs in East Africa. Also, Siemens is actively managing its water consumption so as not to impact local water resources negatively.

Toward SDG15, Siemens contributes to biodiversity protection in Brazil through the Ecological Trail, where its employees raise awareness by teaching environmental topics to 3,500 children. For Partnerships (SDG17), Siemens collaborates with LO3 to facilitate peer-to-peer transactions by using blockchain to share PV solar energy credits, which are reinvested in renewable energy. Also, Germany's Federal Ministry for Economic Cooperation and Development has signed an alliance to support occupational training for over 5,500 Egyptian youth over the next four years. Focusing on SDG7, Siemens aims to be carbon neutral by 2030 and has so far reduced its CO_2 emissions by 25 percent, while 100 percent of green energy powers 60 percent of its German sites. The company is forecast to save more than EUR 20 million annually from 2020 onward by using energy-efficient projects. That's good for the planet and the shareholders' pockets.[191,192]

Telefónica, a Spanish telecommunications company whose mission "is to make our world more human by connecting lives," also wants to make the environment better for the people it is connecting. Concerning Sustainable Communities (SDG11), Telefónica's digital solutions, which optimize traffic planning and public transit, reduced its CO_2 emissions by more than 230,000 tons. Telefónica reuses or recycles more than 96 percent of its electronic waste (SDG12) and has continued collaborations with the Inter-American Development Bank to protect the distribution of environmentally sound technologies to rural communities in Latin America (SDG17). In partnership with the United Nations International Children's Emergency Fund (UNICEF), Telefónica has implemented multiple big data projects which mitigate health emergencies. For example, in Mexico, Telefónica partnered with the government to tackle the spread of the H1N1 influenza. Toward SDG7, Telefónica has embraced green energy, running on 79 percent renewable energy in Spain, 95 percent in the UK, and 100 percent in Germany. Between 2015 and 2016, it lowered its global emissions by 22 percent, successfully cutting over 68,000 tons of CO_2. Turning to green energy sources saved Telefónica EUR 22 million in one year. Saving the planet was also good business.[193,194]

The Anheuser-Busch InBev case

As we strive to bring people together to build a better world, we at Anheuser-Busch are dedicated to reducing our carbon emissions. Helping to grow the renewable

energy market is not only good for the environment, it is a strategic business move as we strive for long-term sustainability. Now more than ever, we are excited to lead our company's global effort toward a renewable future.[195]
— Anheuser-Busch's president and CEO, João Castro Neves

Ab InBev is the world's largest beer brewer and, as such, wishes to be a powerful force for good. It has articulated core principles that drive its business model. The principles are

a healthier world, where every experience with beer is a positive one, for lives well lived; a cleaner world, where natural resources are accessible and safe for all; and, a growing world, where everyone has the opportunity to improve their livelihood.[196]

To work toward a healthier world, as a corporation, AB InBev elected to approach the global health agenda through its core operations promoting societal, as well as economic, objectives. AB InBev took into account the SDGs, as well as other global health targets, in developing initiatives to position the company as "a private-sector model working innovatively across sectors to support global health objectives."[197]

One of AB InBev's global targets on which it is focusing a great deal of effort is the call to reduce deaths and injuries from road traffic accidents (SDG target 3.6). Hence, the anti-drinking and driving campaign featuring Mirren. AB InBev is 1 of 16 members of Together for Safer Roads, a private sector coalition. Together for Safer Roads is advised by an expert panel that guides them on how their companies can initiate more global road safety. The alliance works in partnership with city governments to tackle specific road safety challenges. Each of the 16 companies brings its knowledge specialty, technology, and data into the coalition.[198]

The coalition has demonstrated AB InBev's potential for impact on global priorities. The positive experience that the company continues to have as part of the coalition has increased internal corporate support to develop a new initiative focused on another SDG target, the reduction of harmful alcohol use, globally (SDG target 3.5). As part of this initiative, AB InBev made a 10-year commitment to be the global champion for this target through its Global Smart Drinking Goals.

In 2015, AB InBev launched the Global Smart Drinking Goals, which is a set of initiatives focused on altering social norms, customer behavior, and business practices to reduce the harmful use of alcohol worldwide. The four collaborative and evolving goals that are evidence based were constructed in partnership with public health officials and require the collaboration of public health bodies, civil society, and governments to be fully realized. AB InBev has taken the World Health Organization's desire to reduce the harmful use of alcohol and the United Nations' SDG3 to ensure healthy lives and promote well-being for all and applied them to its own best practices. The four Global Smart Drinking goals are as follows:

Goal 1: Reduce the harmful use of alcohol by at least 10 percent in six cities by the end of 2020. Implement the best practices globally by the end of 2025.
Goal 2: Invest USD 1 billion across our markets in dedicated social marketing campaigns and related programs by the end of 2025.
Goal 3: Ensure no- or lower-alcohol beer products represent at least 20 percent of AB InBev's global beer volume by the end of 2025.

Goal 4: Place a guidance label on all of our beer products in all of our markets by the end of 2020. Increase alcohol health literacy by the end of 2025.[199]

As stated in the AB InBev Annual Report (2016):

> We are building a company to last. Not just for a decade. However, for the next 100 years. We are committed to helping farmers, retailers, entrepreneurs, and communities thrive. Through our brands—and our investment in communities—we will make our company an essential part of our consumers' lives for generations to come and achieve our Dream of bringing people together for a better world.[200]

Another of AB's goals is to reduce carbon emissions and develop the green energy market. In 2017, Anheuser-Busch reached a power purchase agreement with Enel Green Power concerning wind energy. The wind energy purchased would be equal to the power of half of its total purchased electricity in one year and substantially reduce emissions from its operations. AB InBev, Anheuser-Busch's parent company, has declared a commitment to securing 100 percent of its purchased electricity from renewable sources by 2025. This pledge is in keeping with its commitment to the SDGs and is reflective of SDG7 and SDG13. In fact, in 2018, AB's best-selling Budweiser beer revealed a renewable energy symbol to showcase its commitment to brewing using 100 percent renewable electricity.[201]

Stella Artois, a beer brand under AB InBev's umbrella, began a partnership with Water.org under the branding "Buy a Lady a Drink." This effort directly targets SDG6, and since its inception in 2015, more than 1.7 million people have gained access to clean water as a result of the partnership. The partnership's goal is to provide access to safe water for 3.5 million people in the developing world by 2020. On the surface, this appears to be just about water, but as the "Buy a Lady a Drink" marketing indicates, it's also about gender equality. According to Water.org, globally women "spend a combined 200 million hours collecting water every day for their families. That's 200 million hours they could spend caring for their families, generating income and making other contributions to their communities."[202] The partnership is about more than raising awareness about the water crisis; it is about ensuring clean water accessibility and supporting the women who spend so much of their time collecting water, perhaps freeing them to be able to pursue different roles. Instead of paying it forward, Stella Artois is "Pouring it Forward."[203]

AB InBev believes so strongly in the SDGs that by 2025, it has high targets in developing smart agriculture (SmartBarley),[204] water stewardship (Corona X Parley),[205] circular packaging (packaging either made of recycled content or is returnable), and climate action.[206] As a company, AB InBev is not satisfied with what it has achieved; it is driven to push to be better and wants to urge others to be better too with the 100+ Accelerator.

AB InBev's 100+ Accelerator initiative is "mobilizing the world's brightest minds to solve some of the most pressing global sustainability issues." AB InBev is actively looking for "partners who can deliver breakthrough advancements in water stewardship, farmer productivity, product upcycling, responsible sourcing, green logistics, and more."[207] The 100+ Accelerator is open to applications. Those who are successful will receive funding and mentorship. As Tony Milikin, AB InBev's chief sustainability & procurement officer states, "It is incumbent on global businesses to play a bigger role in creating a better world for all." He goes on to say that at AB InBev we have a long-term vision to build a company to last for the next 100+ years, which relies on driving sustainability across our business. Our approach is rooted in the communities where we live and work, and we are well positioned to support entrepreneurs who are tackling local challenges. Through the 100+ Accelerator, innovators will benefit from our resources, experience, and global reach to speed their progress and scale.[208]

Through all of its initiatives, AB InBev has recognized that "In addition to galvanizing the power of our own programs and colleagues, we must build meaningful partnerships with state and local governments, civil society, research institutions, NGOs, and other businesses."[209] It is with this visionary approach to business sustainability and partnership that AB InBev has become the top brewer in the world.

Unilever's value chain

Business cannot thrive in the long term unless the world makes progress towards the SDGs. For us, that means applying an SDG lens to every aspect of strategy: appointing the right leaders, innovating to create sustainable solutions, marketing products and services that inspire consumers to make sustainable choices, and using the goals to guide leadership development and women's empowerment at every level.[210]

—Paul Polman, former CEO of Unilever, and chairman,
International Chamber of Commerce

Unilever believes that business should serve society and that a more inclusive form of capitalism is required, that it is not possible to sustain business success in a world suffering from poverty, hunger, and climate change. Human progress and business progress coincide, and that is why Unilever is committed to working toward the SDGs.[211]

Unilever has been part of the SDGs before their inception, as former CEO Paul Polman served on the UN's High-Level Panel of Eminent Persons in 2012 when discussions began to focus on the development of a post-2015 agenda. Since that time, Unilever has been a business leader in bringing other international corporations on board to drive positive change, coordinating the development of the Post-2015 Business Manifesto (2014) and co-founding the Business & Sustainable Development Commission (2016), which culminated in the launch of a seminal report, Better Business, Better World (2017). Unilever has "long recognized that the only acceptable business model for Unilever is one in which the planet and society thrive."[212]

Unilever's commitment to sustainable business practices began in 2010, years before the SDGs' development, when it launched the Unilever Sustainable Living Plan (USLP). The USLP was its blueprint for sustainable growth developed in response to both the challenges and opportunities of a world constrained of resources and unequal in many ways. Unilever's USLP also happens to be well-aligned with the SDGs. Unilever believes that its scale and influence can help advance its sustainable priorities, as well as the SDGs, globally, while simultaneously recognizing that it is a money-making enterprise and not a charity.

By using our resources as a business to address issues such as nutrition, sanitation, hygiene, and climate change, we are delivering short-term and long-term benefits for shareholders as well as society. We're convinced that achieving the SDGs will be good for the global economy, and for business in general. The opportunities that this transformation creates will be enormous—market opportunities of up to USD 12 trillion a year, and up to 380 million new jobs by 2030, according to the Business & Sustainable Development Commission.[213]

Unilever is a leading consumer goods company, making and selling approximately 400 brands. Each day, 2.5 billion people, spanning 190 countries, use Unilever products. With that level of scale and reach, Unilever is making progress across many of the SDGs through its USLP. Here are some of the ways it is working toward achieving the SDGs while being a highly profitable and competitive global corporation.[214]

- Unilever has committed to becoming carbon positive (SDG7) across all of its operations, from research and development labs to data centers, from corporate offices to manufacturing and distribution, by 2030. It is already meeting 33.6 percent of its energy needs with renewable sources.
- Unilever has put in place multiple recycling programs (SDG11), such as the Community Waste Bank in Indonesia, to get recycling into areas with limited infrastructure.
- Unilever also has a Sustainable Living Plan in place to help 1 billion people improve their health and hygiene, and prevent disease, through using Unilever products.
- Unilever has committed to resource optimization (SDG12), having already cut CO_2 emissions from energy by 47 percent, water abstraction by 39 percent, and total waste disposal by 98 percent per ton of production.
- Unilever's Sustainable Agriculture Program (SDG15) promotes better working conditions and livelihoods for farmers, as well as developing sustainable practices for soil and water management and creating biodiversity.
- In partnership with WPP, IPG, UN Women, Facebook, Google, Mars, Microsoft, and J&J, Unilever launched the Unstereotype Alliance to eliminate gender stereotypes from advertising. Hence its *Dear Future Dads* commercial campaign championing paternity leave.[215]

These are just some of Unilever's best practices and initiatives; there are more. However, Unilever's focus on partnerships may be its most important, because Unilever realizes that SDG17 is the key to making progress across all other SDGs. Rebecca Marmot, global vice president, advocacy and partnerships, explains that Unilever is

Already working with a wide range of partners, including NGOs, governments and other businesses, and exploring innovative approaches that drive progress towards the SDGs. For example, TRANSFORM, our partnership with the UK government's DFID, brings private sector creativity and a public-private finance model to bear on persistent developmental challenges. By aiming to enable 100 million people in sub-Saharan Africa and Asia to gain access to products and services that have been shown to improve health, livelihoods, the environment, or well-being, it addresses a wide range of SDGs. These interconnections can be found throughout our work. For instance, empowering women in our value chain by challenging gender norms and unlocking women's personal and economic potential is a key strategic priority for us. Our efforts directly address gender equality (SDG5), as well as other SDGs such as alleviating poverty (SDG1) and hunger (SDG2), good health and well-being (SDG3), and decent work and economic growth (SDG8).[216]

As Marmot points out, "Transformational change requires transformational partnerships. That means new ways of doing business—not just for us, but for everyone who wants to see the vision of the SDGs become a reality."[217] We are all stakeholders in the SDGs, from business to government to citizens, and we each have a role to play and a contribution to make. That is why partnerships is, in itself, one of the SDGs, because without the goal of collaborating, none of the other SDGs can be reached.

Toward a sustainable future

SDGs are a guide for companies to engage with stakeholders on how to create sustainable business strategies that can change both business models and the communities wherein the businesses operate. By making goals that align with the SDGs, both a company and a state's economy can make a buck and a difference. The SDGs drive companies, and economies, to be more competitive—and that's a good thing.

To achieve the SDGs by 2030, action needs to be taken now. Corporations need to be looking at their path and partnerships, envisioning how their products, services, and operations can support the planet and humanity. It is no longer enough for companies to look at short-term profits because there are so many outside forces that can damage long-term gains. It is also a mistake for companies to focus solely on innovation and technology to be competitive in the new economy. To achieve lasting sustainability, companies need to take on responsibilities in fundamental areas like the environment, and human rights and labor. It is time for local businesses to address global concerns, as the new economy ushers in a new era of responsible business practices.[218]

Companies face challenges addressed by the SDGs, such as diminishing natural resources, lack of qualified talent, and weak financial markets, that cap their potential growth. By harnessing the opportunities outlined by the SDGs, companies are ultimately helping themselves to grow. As Unilever's SDG commitment states:

Companies have a once-in-a-lifetime opportunity to embrace the SDGs as a driver of business growth. If they fail to get behind system change and the kind of inclusive capitalism laid out by the UN Sustainable Development Goals, the costs and uncertainty of doing business will swell. On the other hand, if a critical mass of companies joins the movement for system change, it will create an unstoppable force.[219]

John W.H. Denton, AO Secretary General, International Chamber of Commerce, calls all stakeholders to action. Denton says,

The world is at a crossroad and the stakes are high—we are facing rising trade tensions and increasing protectionist measures; extreme poverty is far from being abolished and the cleavages between rich and poor are widening; there is unprecedented migration, by necessity rather than by choice; and we are at risk of irreversible global warming and biological degradation. We must act swiftly and collectively.[220]

Notice Denton's use of "we"; it is only by working together to advance the SDGs, by finding new and innovative partnerships, that we can become the unstoppable force moving toward a sustainable future.

58. PUBLIC POLICY TO RESOLVE MARKET FAILURES

Seat belts in Peru

My first trip to Peru was on a family trip to visit Lake Titicaca, the Amazon rainforest, Machu Picchu, and Cuzco. It was an amazing experience, especially after getting rid of the altitude shock and adapting to the new (and stunning) Peruvian cuisine. To move around, we rented a car and, having driven before in Cairo, Mumbai, and around the Arc de Triomphe in Paris, neither the traffic nor the roads were particularly shocking. Quite the opposite, the roads were fine given the hostile orography and the lack of public transportation alternatives to the car, in a country that hosts millions of tourists every year. If anything, sometimes it seemed a miracle to be able to pass a bus in the opposite direction on the narrow roads that took us to Aguascalientes on our way to Machu Picchu.

It was during my second trip, this time a business trip with a colleague to discuss the competitiveness of Peru in Centrum Business School, that I found out something shocking about the country. Not once, but every time we took a taxi, the driver would turn to us and (in Spanish) ask us to fasten our seat belts. It became such a habit that we ended up doing it without warning. Never before did this happen to me—that the driver orders the passenger to wear a seat belt. Not even in Switzerland. It is a common conception that countries that have high rates of compliance and rule of law are developed countries that historically have had an outstanding economic, political, and social status. In fact, there is a strong correlation between GDP per capita and the World Bank's Rule of Law index. But there is a notable exception: in Peru, 85 percent of drivers use a seat belt.[221]

Figure 5.1 illustrates the exceptionality of Peru.[222] In economically developed countries (the Netherlands, for instance), most people use a seat belt (almost 100 percent). In India, by contrast, less than 30 percent of the population wear it. The reason is quite intuitive. Low GDP per capita implies poor infrastructure, which in turn reduces the marginal benefit of wearing a seat belt (which protects against frontal collisions,[223] but not if your car falls off a cliff). Besides, with better roads, speed increases, so fatal collisions are higher, and therefore the cost of not wearing a seat belt increases in high GDP countries.

An additional reason why economic development is negatively related to seat belt use is that implementing road safety measures is not a priority in a developing country. Its low budget tends to be allocated to more urgent issues such as social plans, welfare, international debt payments, and other expenses that prevent it from allocating resources to specific areas not deemed urgent, such as effective transit programs, education, and enforcement. Interestingly, as the Peruvian economy has been strengthening over the last two decades, the Ministry of Transportation and Communications (MCT) has also increased its budget every year for the last 10 years. In 2018, it was USD 4,224,574 (14,240,405 Soles vs 2,612,000 Soles in 2008).[224] The MTC is in charge of the National Road Safety Council (CNSV), whose main task is to

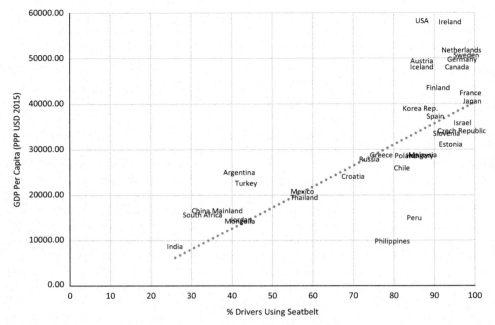

Figure 5.1 Seat Belt Wearing Rate and Economic Development in 2016

Source: World Health Organization and IMD World Competitiveness Center.

improve road safety conditions, formulate and develop studies and projects, as well as carry out campaigns to promote compliance with traffic regulations among the Peruvian population.

Most underdeveloped countries consider the money they spend each year on road safety as an expense within their budget, when in fact it is proven to be an investment. An investment that, if not paid due attention, will bring negative consequences to the economy of any country, especially to economically emerging countries such as Peru. According to a new study by the World Bank, if a government manages to reduce the number of traffic accidents, this will have a positive effect on its economy in the long term. This study shows how those countries that do not invest in road safety could lose between 7 and 22 percent of GDP per capita over a period of 24 years.[225] And in this sense, Peru has been taking the right steps.

The implementation of an effective program regarding the use of seat belts by the Peruvian government is part of a more extensive road safety program that includes a clear understanding of the traffic laws, an efficient institution that enforces them, and appropriate road safety education in all areas of the population. The creation of two agencies (The National Road Safety Council and the Health Strategy of Peru, exclusively dedicated to dealing with road safety in all regions of the country) has been a fundamental measure to improve compliance with traffic regulations in the country.

The National Road Safety Council was created on June 13, 2001. It is an institution under the MTC whose principles are based on "concerted action aimed at improving road safety conditions in the country."[226] In order to contribute to the improvement of road safety conditions at the national level, the CNSV will provide each region with technical assistance and conduct a review, approval, and follow-up of the progress of the road safety plans.

It is very important to emphasize that for the Government of Peru, road safety is not only about ordering traffic and fining offenders (as it is in many countries of Latin America), but it is also officially a public health issue, much in line with those programs adopted by developed countries, such as Canada, which the Peruvian government took as role models. That is the reason why the Ministry of Health of Peru (MINSA), in 2004, created the National Healthcare Traffic Accident Strategy (ESNAT), in response to the growing number of injuries, deaths, and disabilities caused by traffic accidents.

Through these institutions, the government has carried out important promotional campaigns to encourage the population's compliance with traffic regulations. Through continuous advertising campaigns in all media (television, street posters, social networks), the government has promoted public awareness specifically in relation to the use of seat belts.

In February 2015, the Ministry of Transportation and Communications along with the CNSV launched a nationwide campaign seeking to reinforce driving habits, placing special emphasis on the use of seat belts. Informative materials were given to approximately 40,00 people. A survey subsequently conducted found that the vast majority of Peruvians were already using them.

Successful policy, is it not? As we all know, the use of seat belts is not driven only by knowledge of its benefits. If this were the case, it would not be mandatory to use them. In some countries (for instance, the United States) it is not mandatory for motorbike riders to wear a helmet. The reason is that individual freedom is more important than safety, and individuals will do what they think is best when only their lives are at stake. Why is the use of seat belts mandatory instead, when the same individual liberties can be put on the scale? Because not wearing a helmet harms no one but the person making the choice, while seat belts are an issue of public policy. Therefore, it cannot be left to individual choice, and governments must enforce rules to ensure safety.

Enforcement

According to a study conducted by the United States' National Highway Transportation Safety Administration (NHTSA), increasing fines for not wearing a seat belt is associated with an increase of nearly 4 percent in observed seat belt use.[227] As in many other countries in the world, a 2001 Supreme Decree[228] established the official regulations regarding the use of seat belts in Peru and designated that their use in all vehicles traveling through the national territory is mandatory. The National Police of Peru, through its traffic police branch, supervises compliance with traffic regulations and road safety; its function is to control and direct the normal development of traffic and to report potential infractions of National Traffic regulations to the authorities.[229] The National Traffic Regulations establish that the non-use of a seat belt by all passengers in a vehicle is a serious infraction, with sanctions amounting to 288 Soles (USD 85) and 20 points on the driver's license.[230] If a driver accumulates 100 or more points over 24 months, the license will be suspended for 6 months. If the license has been suspended once and the driver reaccumulates 100 points, the license will be suspended for one year. The third time the driver accumulates 100 points in the span of 24 months, the license will be permanently canceled and the individual will not be able to drive ever again.[231] In 2014, the USD 85 fine increased to 336 Peruvian Soles (USD 100), with the same number of points.[232]

Table 5.2 is a comparative table of the fines for not wearing a seat belt in the most important countries in South America as well as different developed countries from different parts of the world. Clearly, Peru has both the highest percentage of adherence to using seat belts in Latin America as well as one of the most severe sanctions for not using them worldwide (higher than in Switzerland!!!). And the numbers shown do not take into account purchasing power, because if they did, Peru would be the worst country in the world to be caught not wearing a seat belt!

Policies work: good regulation, education, and enforcement measures guarantee success. An interesting additional feature of Peruvian regulation is that the driver is—unlike Spain, for instance—responsible for all his or her passengers. I should not have been surprised when taxi drivers in Lima checked our seat belt use before starting the route every single time. They were well educated and were aware of the consequences of a violation, and they acted rationally.

Table 5.2 Fines for Seat Belt Violations Several Sources[233].

Country	Fine for Not Wearing a Seat Belt	Seat Belt Use (% of passengers)
Australia	USD 386—4 demerit points	97
Belgium	USD 50—Withdrawal of license if repeated	92
Canada	USD 146—2 demerit points	95
Colombia	USD 91—Not available	64
France	USD 154—3 demerit points	98
Germany	USD 30—None	98
Italy	USD 91—5 demerit points	62
Norway	USD 171—Not specified	98
Paraguay	USD 42—3 demerit points	No data available
Peru	USD **100–20 demerit points**	**85**
Russia	USD 16—Not specified	66
Switzerland	USD 60—Not specified	94
United Kingdom	Up to USD 632—3 demerit points	95
United States	Ranges from USD 15 to USD 235 depending on state	90
Uruguay	USD 50—Not available	63

The unintended consequences of enforcement: corruption

The problem is that sometimes good regulation increases the benefits of corruption. That is what happened in Peru, and in the next section we will explain why. Let us start by saying that the National Police of Peru has a very bad reputation in terms of its corruptibility, and this is something recognized both by the population and by the Anticorruption Observatory of the police itself. A 2013 report by the Anticorruption Observatory of the National Police of Peru detailed that "traffic bribery has become part of urban life in Lima," and confirmed a high level of both acceptance of and request for bribes by the police forces.

Figure 5.2 shows the level of registered bribery attempts by both police officers and citizens; of course, we can assume that most bribes remain unreported, so the actual figures slip by the official reports. Nevertheless, it seems that police corruption is widespread as revealed by a national household survey conducted by the National Institute of Statistics and Informatics of Peru in 2018, and shown in Figure 5.3.[234] With a big difference, the National Police of Peru is the most cited for asking to pay or feeling obligated to pay a bribe.[235]

When it comes to the enforcement of regulations, police corruption is not the only problem. Offenders also have a simple way to avoid paying fines: to appeal and wait. The contested fines cannot be reclaimed by authorities and after four years they prescribe. The problem is not in the imposition of fines but in the collection. This function corresponds with the tax administration service (SAT) of the Municipality of Lima. It is this institution that is affected by the different tricks used by offenders to avoid payment.[236] The following is an excerpt taken from an RPP News report on this subject:

'The administrator has 3 months to go to the administrative litigation of the Judiciary and that may take more than the 4 years it takes to prescribe,' says Luis

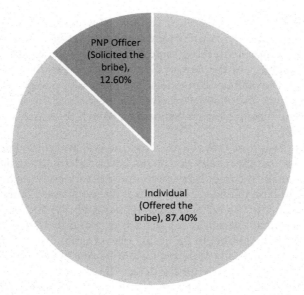

Figure 5.2 Traffic Bribes in Metropolitan Lima according to Offender

Source: Anticorruption Observatory of the Lima Police.

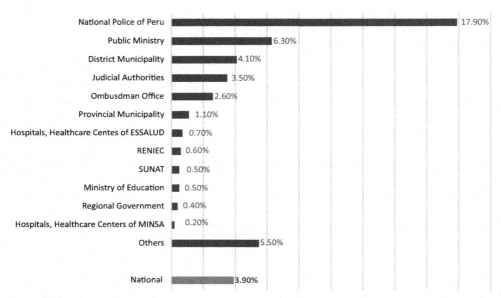

Figure 5.3 National Survey on Corruption Perception

Source: National Institute of Statistics and Informatics of Peru (INEI).

> Quispe Candia, director of the NGO Luz Ámbar. If we add to this an expert lawyer to delay, we have the perfect combination to perpetuate impunity. While the ballot is contested, the sanction remains pending and the SAT cannot use coercive means to collect. For example, they will not be able to seize bank accounts or request the capture of the car.

In 2017, 15,010 infractions were recorded in Lima of which 96,044 were paid. In 2018, between January and June, 3,525 fines were imposed and 46,357 were canceled. Why more fines are paid in Lima than those imposed per year has a legal explanation: as this type of sanction is subject to the Law of General Administrative Procedure (Law No 27444), under which the offender can extend the process of payment through a *recurso* (challenge). That is, once the offender receives notification of the sanction, the fine can be appealed in several instances. Even debtors can stretch the process so much that their infraction prescribes.[237]

With this in mind, suppose that you are a corrupt police agent in Peru. Without regulation mandating the use of seat belts, you do not have any bargaining power. But imagine that the authorities make it compulsory and impose severe fines (including the removal of your driving license) on offenders. The law is now giving you a fantastic tool to extort citizens. Because suddenly you are entitled to demand a bribe and, more importantly, a bribe becomes an optimal alternative for the driver. Not only that, the more severe the fine, the higher the optimal bribe. In Peru, since the sanction is USD 100 plus 20 points, a corrupt police officer can easily request a USD 100 bribe (and even higher), which will be accepted as a cheaper alternative for the driver. This is indeed what has been happening. Police corruption is not any more rampant than before, but Peruvian drivers are in strict compliance with the law, not because the law is tougher, but because the bribe is too expensive!!! Note, however, that regulation itself is the major driver of a corrupt behavior.

The Peruvian seat belt case shows two important features of public policy: sometimes we need regulation because individuals will not behave in an optimal way, even if they behave rationally to maximize their personal gains. This is what we will call a *market failure* in the next section. When preventing market failures, however, governments can in turn spur more corruption. Therefore, when rules are to be enforced, they have to be carefully considered and take into account the institutional and social environment in order to avoid creating a problem where there was none initially.

You may also be wondering what the solution to corrupt police should be. Remember Chapter 46 and our discussion of corruption: only good enforcement, combined with educating the population, works. Regulation by itself is not enough and—as shown here—it may even have counterproductive and unintended consequences.

Governments and market failures

At some point in our lives, we have experienced rushing to the store to pick up a product we need, only to be told that the item is out of stock. The choices we face are either to wait until the item is back in stock or get a similar item that is currently in stock. However, the overarching question we ask ourselves here is—why does not the store supply sufficient product to meet the demand in the market? The answer to this question is "market failure." Market failure is occasioned when consumer demand for certain products is not met by the supply of the same products in the market. Therefore, each time the market fails to offer an efficient allocation of resources, the situation results in a market failure. In Peru, the costs of wearing a seat belt (waste of time, inconvenience) are greater than its benefits (preventing a potential death), and yet many drivers do not use it, so the regulator needs to intervene.

Broadly, market failure is defined as an inefficient distribution of goods and services in the free market resulting in an economic situation that affects both businesses and customers. This concept underscores the fact that the driving factors behind rational behavior for the individual do not ensure that there will be rational outcomes for the group. Each individual makes decisions that are beneficial and correct to meet self-interests, but, in many cases, such decisions prove to be detrimental to the group. In conventional microeconomics, this situation is referred to as a "steady state of disequilibrium," where the quantity of product or services supplied to the market is not equal to the quantity demanded.

Typically, the view of rational behavior in regard to economic need is positive. However, rational behavior driven by individual decisions does not always augur well with the needs of the group. In this case, the group ends up worse off than if it had not acted in perfectly rational self-interest. The group either faces a surge in costs or a decline in benefits. Although this issue seems simple, it can be easily misidentified and can be misleading as well.

The overall perception of the market failure concept is that it refers to inherent market imperfections within the market economy, but this is not the case. There can be market failure in government activities as well.[238] For example, special interest groups can achieve massive concessions from the government through their lobbying for small costs on everyone else in the market economy through tools such as the imposition of tariffs. However, when each small group complies with this dynamic and imposes its costs, the whole group ends up suffering more than it would have without lobbying. Additionally, it is crucial to establish that not every outcome emanating from market activities can be categorized as a market failure. It does not mean that in the event of a market failure, private market players cannot solve the underlying challenge. However, not all market failures have direct potential solutions, even through extra public awareness or prudent regulation. Let me consider some examples.

The Hong Kong market failure—housing crisis

According to a 2018 article in the *South China Morning Post* by Mike Rowse, the housing sector in Hong Kong is trending toward a marked decline in the size of a flat and a sharp surge in the price or cost to purchase or rent such a flat.[239] Rowse argues that the surge in the number of non-permanent residents purchasing property in Hong Kong has driven the cost of housing to stratospheric and obviously unaffordable levels for a majority of permanent residents in Hong Kong. This has led to a massive surge in the clamor for government intervention in regulating the number of non-permanent residents purchasing property in Hong Kong, as well as establishing a legal and regulatory minimum flat size—ideally not less than 700 sq ft.[240]

This situation in Hong Kong highlights both the benefits and the downside of capitalism. On the one hand, the forces of demand and supply are determining and regulating the markets. In this case, the demand for flats is high compared to the supply. As a result, the costs are going up significantly even as the size of the flats are getting smaller and smaller. On the other hand, the people who are suffering are those who the Hong Kong authorities have a duty to protect. Therefore, this issue assumes moral (social) and economic stripes within Hong Kong. For example, under the protection of welfare laws, a farm animal in Europe is assured of a bigger living space than a resident living in Hong Kong!

Therefore, this is a market failure because the demand for typical-sized flats at affordable prices is scarcely available to Hong Kong's permanent residents. The shortage has been occasioned by an influx of non-permanent residents in Hong Kong who have a significantly high purchasing capacity compared to local residents. Therefore, the market is not providing the products that the market is demanding.

Market failure of the Chinese healthcare sector

The concept of market failure in the Chinese context is complicated compared to some of the nations in the West. This is because although the Chinese economy has a somewhat free market, its operations are still heavily influenced by the Chinese state through state-owned enterprises (SOEs) and direct control by the ruling authorities. This creates a blurred line between market failure and government failure in the Chinese context. This issue is also seen in several countries that have not fully liberalized economically across Asia, Africa, and South America.

According to an article appearing on the *Asia Sentinel* website by Peter Fuhrman and Dr Yansong Wang (2017), the Chinese healthcare sector is facing an increasing incidence of Alzheimer's disease cases.[241] It is the fastest growing disorder in China and is ultimately fatal. As of 2017, China had at least 9.5 million diagnosed cases of Alzheimer's, with an equivalent number of people undiagnosed. Estimates also show that by 2030, China will be experiencing a massive acceleration in new Alzheimer's cases.

The dynamic of this disorder in China is pervasive because Alzheimer's is a major disease with one of the greatest mismatches between the number of patients who need care and the amount of specialized care available. Comparatively, the United States has about 50 percent less Alzheimer's patients than China; however, the United States has *73,000 beds in specialist Alzheimer's treatment centers.*[242] China has less than 200 beds dedicated to Alzheimer's patients. In the United States, the care for Alzheimer's patients is an impressive USD 250 billion industry, while in China it has not gotten off the ground.

The mismatch in China is emblematic of the strain that the Chinese healthcare sector is facing as it attempts to reform and restructure to meet the surging demand and the dynamic needs of a modern population. The Chinese healthcare industry is seeking to improve its quality of care overall, with a focus on infectious and acute diseases such as asthma, cancer, and hepatitis. In the process, the focus on diseases such as Alzheimer's has not been improved because it is not a top priority for the healthcare companies, investors, or the government. This is a clear market failure. While the Chinese government in collaboration with the private sector and SOEs has made significant investments in old age care, a huge chunk of this investment has been diverted to building and selling apartments in retirement communities. There has been no focus on old age challenges or care such as building specialist centers for Alzheimer's disease.

Need for government intervention

The examples above show that governments play a significant role in correcting the market when it fails. The private sector also has a massive role to play in this process by ensuring that it does not resort to unfair and anti-competitive practices. In this regard, correcting market failure improves social welfare. Intervention is necessary because a failing economy has a significant impact on the rest of the country and its overall economy.[243] Additionally, government intervention is crucial because of the globalized nature of an economy, where a fall in one country market might have a ripple effect on others.

How market failures lead to corruption

A paper published in 2000 by MIT Professors Daron Acemoglu and Thierry Verdier (A&V) titled "The Choice between Market Failures and Corruption,"[244] has been the foundation for many analyses of market failures across the world and some of the approaches that have been adopted to correct them. They argue that the prevailing understanding in the market is that the government, as a corrective force, can play a massive role in rectifying market failures and establishing them on the straight and narrow. However, the reality is that many governments have significant failures which are hard to reconcile with a corrective role when markets fail. According to Acemoglu and Verdier, the overarching conditions that influence the role of government in correcting or intervening in markets when they fail include:[245]

- Government is often driven by information gathered by bureaucrats that can then be used in implementing policies.
- At least one of the agents belonging to the government's bureaucracy is corruptible.
- Government bureaucrats display some form of heterogeneity.

These three conditions indicate that government intervention in markets is likely to create corruption opportunities and a corruption culture, including the misallocation of resources and rents for public officials. The chance of corruption makes the government bigger with new officers trying to curtail it. This does not mean that government intervention is always negative.[246] The article highlights the high probability that such corruption might occur and thus fails to help in correcting the markets, and instead plunges them into even more chaos. In many cases, the government might be trying to tax some activities in the market while not doing the same for others, with the aim of addressing the market failures. The study highlights the fact that optimal government intervention can be beneficial, although the likelihood of such optima conditions is significantly minuscule.[247]

The public sector and the government have a significant susceptibility to corruption. As a result, the intervention of the government in the private sector in the event of a market failure puts the markets at risk of developing a corruption culture, or a spillover effect from the inefficiencies and corruption in the government. In this case, the proportion of the population that is willing to take part in corrupted transactions is crucial in determining the overall attitude of the country toward corruption.[248] If many people are unwilling to be corrupt, then the susceptibility to the vice reduces significantly, while the opposite is true. In many emerging economies and developing countries, the level of susceptibility to corruption is significantly high. This highlights the challenge facing Peru, for instance, when choosing between market failure/dysfunction or government corruption. In many cases, there is no middle ground.

China

A good example of government intervention is China. The role of the government in the operation of some of its major multinational organizations or dominant firms within the domestic Chinese market is massive, as underscored by its ownership.[249] Most of the major businesses in China in important sectors are state owned. This gives the Chinese government a determining role in the country's corporate sector. In the summer of 2015, the Chinese government intervened in its markets to fix the instability that resulted from the stock market crash. The crash came about because the Chinese economy was slowing down.[250] Most of China's major businesses were experiencing significantly slow growth. This set off a panic and massive speculation that increased the volatility in the market. The Chinese government's intervention was aimed at preventing a crisis in investor confidence, which could have set off even higher panicky sell-offs and create heightened adverse effects on the country's economy.[251] The Chinese government stepped in and bought the shares to stabilize the markets, restore confidence, and thus avert a crisis.

Government intervention in such a manner has faced massive criticism from the West, especially targeting the Chinese government's role in giving most of its core multinational corporations advantages in the competitive world that are not available to other privately owned businesses. Additionally, the Chinese government has been accused of interfering in lowering the value of its currency, the Renminbi, to maintain an export advantage against some of its major trade partners, such as the EU and the United States. Therefore, China is an example of the intervention of government in markets that has been significantly effective in establishing a dominant economy in the world, maintaining growth at sustainable levels, maintaining its currency at beneficial levels, and establishing a market environment that encourages growth and avoids massive risks that might adversely affect the rest of the economy.

The Chinese government has also played a significant role in enforcing anti-monopoly policies. Such regulation is driven by the understanding that monopolies are bad for establishing a competitive environment and thus bad for consumers as a whole.[252] The Anti-Monopoly Law gives the Chinese authorities the power to regulate markets and intervene in cases where companies are deemed to be in violation of this law and the regulatory aspects accompanying it as it operates in the Chinese market.[253] The impact has been massive fines, to the tune of millions of dollars, paid by companies judged to be engaged in unfair, anti-competitive monopolistic pricing. Other companies have had to lower their pricing to avoid investigation.

India

Another example of government intervention in market failure is India's anti-pollution policies led by Prime Minister Narendra Modi.[254] More than 50 percent of all the rivers in India are polluted because massive quantities of industrial and municipal waste are discharged into them daily. On top of this, India faces a massive air pollution problem emanating from crop burning, coal-fired power plants, vehicles burning diesel fuel, and domestic cooking with firewood.

The surge in pollution in India has come from the 25 years in which the country has experienced massive economic growth and development achieved by an increasing portion of the population, which has in turn modernized their lifestyles, leading to an increase in waste and thus pollution of the environment.[255] The prime minister has prioritized cleaning the Ganges—the major river that also has sociocultural uses for Hindus—in his government's mandate, making it a key policy goal.

However, Prime Minister Modi believes that there is a need for a collective approach to fighting pollution. This is because even though the government can do its fair share, the effective control of pollution can only be achieved if the people transform their lifestyles and thus the rest of the corporate sector, the chief polluters, will follow suit.[256] In a Reuters article written by Neha Dasgupta and Mayank Bhardwaj in 2018 titled "Deadly Political Calculations: Why India Is Not Fixing Its Toxic Smog Problem," the authors assess the bleak situation that India is facing with pollution and the expected health consequences.[257] The challenge is disproportionately affecting the middle class and the poor, especially in India's rapidly growing urban centers. Despite the government's efforts to intervene in this area where the market has failed, the results are not demonstrably better.[258] The issue here is that the Modi government, on the one hand, is encouraging the industrialization of India because it is creating jobs and value for the country. On the other hand, the rapid growth and industrialization process has created a massive environmental challenge. The conflict here is severe for Modi and thus affects the effective intervention of the government.

Much of the pollution is coming from the industrial sector, which employs many Indian citizens, contributes significantly to national revenue, and plays a massive role in the national GDP and India's competitiveness on a global stage. However, climate change and massive pollution are two issues that point to a market failure. Much of industry has no motivation to reduce its carbon footprint or prevent adverse pollution.[259] Therefore, government intervention is required to establish a standard regulatory framework that seeks to prevent pollution and contribute toward the fight against global warming by insisting on sustainable approaches in the business sector. The failure of the Indian government to arrest the runaway pollution in the country underscores the cracks in government intervention that are massively susceptible to corruption and thus maintaining the status quo.

Nepal

In Nepal, more than 70 percent of the country's population works in the agricultural sector. This translates to around 38 percent of its GDP. However, food production in the country is not sufficient to meet demand. As a result, more than 50 percent of Nepal's population is undernourished.[260] Moreover, almost 50 percent of all the children in the country below the age of five are chronically malnourished, which has been shown to result in lifelong damage to the functioning of the individual affected.[261]

The Nepali government has thus declared food security a national priority and has intervened in the markets in collaboration with international organizations such as the United States Agency for International Development (USAID) to launch programs aimed at increasing agricultural productivity and boosting the incomes of smallholder farmers in the country.[262] The government has managed to scale up the productivity of its agricultural sector and so increased people's prosperity.[263]

Mexico

According to Reuters, and as reported by Public Radio International (PRI),[264] 89 people died in a powerful explosion at a gasoline pipeline in central Mexico. A pipeline punctured by fuel thieves on January 2019 occasioned the explosion.

PRI reported that many of the relatives of the deceased and people in the local community indicated that a severe fuel shortage was the driving factor behind people risking their lives to fill plastic containers from the leak.

The shortage has been heightened by the focus of President Andrés Manuel López Obrador on fighting corruption in Mexico as a whole, and specifically his focus on streamlining the Pemex supply chain. The focus of the Obrador administration is to reduce or eliminate the siphoning of fuel by thieves from Pemex's extensive pipeline network, which has led to tremendous losses for the company annually.

The Mexican government announced its intervention measures in the gas crisis facing the country, where growing fuel theft meant increased inefficiencies in the supply chain and thus the government was not getting its full value. This intervention was meant to reduce the thefts and thus destroy the black-market channels of selling fuel in Mexico.[265]

The Resulting shortage

Although operating illegally, the thieves fulfill a massive need in the country's energy value chain. Therefore, removing or disrupting the operations of the Mexican black market in fuel was bound to affect the typical operations by blocking an ironically important channel of distributing fuel throughout Mexican society.

The Obrador government underestimated the dependence that the black market has created within Mexican society. By sealing all the loopholes for theft, the government unleashed a severe shortage of fuel in the country, causing people to risk their lives to siphon fuel from pipes punctured by thieves.[266]

According to Reuters, President Obrador insists that this regulatory approach and intervention will not stop, and that the siphoning is costing the economy billions of dollars. The president has also increased his focus on the use of distribution trucks. However, this shift has led to gigantic logistical challenges such as delivery delays and long lines at gas stations.[267] This means that this move is causing an artificial shortage in the market because of the inefficiency of the new approach.

Corruption and inefficiency in the Mexican fuel sector

However, the involvement of the government in Pemex has been blamed for the establishment of organized corruption and criminal cartels that seek to tap Mexico's sprawling and growing motor industry—the sixth largest in the world. The Mexican government's lack of attention or its lack of will to fight back, allowed these criminal organizations to embed across Mexican society until President Obrador sought to disentangle them from the energy sector of the country and starve them out of existence by sealing all available loopholes.[268] Reuters also reports that most of the stealing is done with the complicity of some of the employees and higher-ups within Pemex. Therefore, the fuel stolen from Pemex often ends up in the hands of the retailers that sell gasoline and diesel from Pemex through legal means.

This indicates that the government, Pemex, and the fuel black market have established a structure through which they can coexist. The relationships, especially in the pre-Obrador regimes, were geared toward individual benefit. This established a culture of corruption within Pemex, which in turn permeated throughout its supply chain in a manner that allowed more and more organized gangs to siphon fuel from the system.[269] The Obrador approach to fighting corruption and the resulting shortage indicate that the efforts are bearing fruit. It means that more and more thieves are finding it hard to puncture pipes and siphon fuel into the black market.

Part of the reason behind the escalation in fuel theft in Mexico in recent years has been the uptick in the fight against drug cartels. This has provoked many ex-drug dealers into looking for alternative means of making money. Thus, Mexico's network of pipes has become a target for these organized crime gangs across the country. Currently, President Obrador's aim to fight corruption, streamline Pemex, and stabilize oil prices in the country has not got off to a great start.[270] His intervention appears to be causing harm to the supply of oil into the market, which is heightening a market failure, and driving the desperation behind the explosion.

The downside to the fight against corruption

The corruption culture within the fuel sector in Mexico has been the norm for many years. In a way, it represents the overall structure, and many Mexicans have adapted to this operational model. Therefore, the Obrador administration's intervention in the market was a significant shock to the system that has disrupted the "typical" supply system, causing massive suffering to consumers. For example, the pricing policy of black-market fuel and its availability to drivers in the community serve to facilitate major daily activities.[271] However, by sealing off this option in the fuel supply chain, although justified, it is having several negative effects on the daily operations of the community. The shortage, and the subsequent desperation to risk lives in filling plastic containers with spilled fuel, underscore this issue.

The market intervention here, on the one hand, has been effective in significantly reducing the cases of fuel theft from Pemex. On the other hand, it has led to inconvenience, inefficiency, and hardship to consumers in accessing fuel. Additionally, this challenge has exposed some of the most glaring weaknesses in the entire energy sector in Mexico.[272] This is especially the case for its reliance on imports of refined fuels. Primarily, the problem has been Pemex's inability to operate at the expected levels to meet demand. The driving forces of such underperformance have been serial underinvestment, deferred maintenance, and frequent accidents, such as deadly explosions that have occasioned stoppages that cost the company billions of dollars.

This chapter highlights the need for government interaction in failing markets. This need is borne out of the understanding that in a capitalist world, the interest of businesses is not necessarily consistent with those of the people and the rest of the country at all times. In the event that there is convergence between the interests of the business sector and those of the country and its people, then the synergy can be tapped to enhance development and growth. On the other hand, when there is divergence in interest, the resulting scenario is a market failure. For example, the cost of housing shoots through the roof and beyond the affordability of a massive chunk of the population, or pollution and emissions surge so that a business can turn a profit. In such cases, the involvement of the government as a regulator or arbiter on the side of the people can be crucial to even the odds.

However, the risk of corruption increases significantly in such interventions, especially in nations that are highly susceptible to corrupt behavior by players in the public sector. In this case, if the number of people willing to conduct corrupt business is more than those unwilling, then government intervention in markets establishes a high risk of not only spreading the corrupt culture but also allowing it to embed itself into the typical ways of doing things. High levels of corruption can be seen mostly in African countries that have not fully liberalized their economic structures, in Brazil, and in other nations in South Africa and Asia. The most effective government intervention so far has been the Chinese economy, which has used its ability to intervene to the advantage of its economy.

Which type of government interventions are the best/worst?

Government intervention results from the inability of markets to allocate resources properly. Governments use to that end taxes, regulation, and subsidies. Additionally, government interventions can be promoted by the government with the aim to promote overall economic fairness and social welfare. This is one of the most widely appreciated and understood drivers of government intervention across the world. For example, breaking down monopolies as well as regulating negative externalities such as pollution is a well-traveled path of government intervention.[273] National security or national unity can also be used as the driving forces behind government intervention.

Maximizing social welfare

As an intervention factor, governments must protect the public from the excesses of the business sector. In a typical free market, businesses are left to operate freely and only respond to the basic laws as well as the forces of demand and supply. However, in a capitalist world, businesses can operate beyond their means, take too much risk, and thus risk the entire economy of a country and the world.[274] This can be seen by the subprime mortgage crisis in the United States that led to the Great Recession of 2008.

Therefore, government intervention here is aimed at ensuring that businesses operate in a realm that not only meets the core targets but is also sustainable and does not expose the entire economy to unwarranted risks. The example of governmental intervention here is the Chinese government's 2015 passing of the Anti-Monopoly Law, which aims to ensure that no single business is too big to pose a threat to national security or the well-being of the rest of the economy.[275] So far, this approach has been effective in maintaining

Chinese growth at sustainable levels and thus preventing its economy from overheating and exposing itself and the rest of the world to a serious bust or recession.

The understanding is that without regulation, businesses can produce a massive number of negative externalities that are not without consequences. This will lead to a decline in resources, an anti-competitive environment favoring monopolies and dominant players, stifled innovation, and reduced trade and the wide array of benefits it brings to the market and society.

Through regulation, government intervention can also address core issues such as pollution and climate change. In this case, organizations are forced to work within a regulatory framework that governs a business' impact on the environment. This aspect is mentioned in the India example above. However, the Indian experiment in intervening in the failed market to fight pollution was partly unsuccessful.[276] Pollution is a social as well as an economic challenge. Therefore, the Indian government's approach should have adopted a socioeconomic approach, by getting the communities involved and investing emotionally in the fight against pollution. This will tie the profitability and the brand of the business with its carbon footprint and pollution as well. As a result, it will not make sense for the businesses not to be onboard the venture to reduce pollution and its impact on the health of the local people, especially in India's bustling and fast-expanding urban areas.

Socioeconomic factors

Intervention in the markets for the benefit of some of the most exposed people in an economy is a widely and significantly popular approach across the world. The best welfare structures are in the Nordic countries, which have adopted an economy that is regarded as fair and equal. In the United States, although social welfare is significant, the inequality in the country is significant too.

Other interventions include setting the minimum wage for employees in certain sectors as applied in Finland and Switzerland. Many businesses argue that a minimum wage has a negative impact on the business sector, especially when exposed to the impact of globalization and competitors coming from low-cost countries such as Mexico and South East Asia nations.[277] However, the intervention here is focused on protecting workers and ensuring that they can earn a decent living from their jobs.

The worst approaches to government intervention

Fundamentally, government intervention should come in regulatory form, while allowing private businesses to operate in liberalized and free markets where the ultimate forces involved are demand and supply. However, the use of nationalization as a method of intervention can be detrimental to the short- and long-term well-being of the free enterprise and the economy.

For example, the role of the government in the ownership of Petrobras—Brazil's national oil company—exposed the company to massive cases of corruption involving the company's executives, top honchos in the Brazilian government, and foreign investors. Such exposure is significantly reduced when the company is operating as a private entity with shareholders in a free competitive market.[278]

It should be noted that nationalization does not always mean failure or massive corruption; take, for example, Saudi Aramco, Saudi Arabia's national oil company and one of the most valuable companies in the world. However, moving vibrant assets from the private sector and exposing them to the inefficiencies and corruption of the public sector establishes a massive foundation for failure and significant mismanagement. For example, the ascent to power of Hugo Chávez in Venezuela, leading what was once considered one of the most competitive economies in the world, was followed by a spree of nationalization of major companies and businesses in the country. What followed was a marked fall of a promising economy into one of the poorest and most mismanaged countries in the world under Chavez's beleaguered successor, President Nicolás Maduro.

Hence, the best approach to government intervention in a marketing failure is to establish a platform that supports businesses to grow and expand while sustaining a modicum of fairness, protecting consumers, and minimizing the risk such businesses pose. There will always be risk; economies develop because of the enthusiasm and innovation of the private sector. Stifling such innovation is not in the best interest of a country or its people. However, allowing a *laissez-faire* environment might mean that businesses will bite off more than they can chew.[279]

59. EDUCATION FOR THE 21ST CENTURY

In 1980, country music superstar Dolly Parton sang

> Workin' 9 to 5, what a way to make a livin'/Barely gettin' by, it's all takin' and no givin'/They just use your mind and you never get the credit/It's enough to drive you crazy if you let it/9 to 5, yeah they got you where they want you/There's a better life, and you dream about it, don't you?[280]

Even 30 years ago, Parton had a vision of a better work environment than the structured 9:00 to 5:00. To her, this was an antiquated model wherein only those on the top rungs had a voice. It was challenging to fight your way up through the many layers of management toward the top. The picture she paints is dismal—work takes, but what does it give, aside from a living wage? The digital economy is allowing for a new business structure that promises employees more freedom. A shift in the concept of work will see jobs become project based, with remote and freelance work blossoming, and humans will be allowed to focus on work of creativity and substance, while productive jobs such as positions in sales, manufacturing, and administration will become increasingly autonomous.

To paint a day in the life of an employed individual 50 years from now looks very different from painting a current typical workday, even with so many changes to workplace structures and approaches already occurring. We can see the beginnings of the promise of what is to come; however, like anything, institutional change is slow under the weight of skepticism and fearful resistance.

Ladders collapse into Lattice

Long gone are the days of starting at the bottom of a company's corporate ladder and climbing one rung at a time over a 50-year career until retirement, where you exit with a piece of cake, a handshake, and perhaps a nice watch to cap off a lifetime of dedicated servitude. Denise Morrison, former CEO of Campbell Soup Company, makes it clear when she says that "I describe my career path as a zigzag, not a ladder with a straight trajectory up. I've jumped the curve to seek new experiences."[281]

Nowadays, a person changes jobs an average of 12 times during his or her career.[282] The majority of workers spend five years, or less, in each job, with the median employee tenure being 4.3 years for men and 4.0 years for women.[283] The world of work is changing. The future reality of employment means that the next generation of workers will likely hold multiple jobs simultaneously, but those jobs will look much different than current models. Also, instead of moving up the traditional corporate ladder, employees will instead move laterally across a *corporate lattice*[284] or grid model, tapping into new networks and gaining new insights and experiences. This corporate lattice allows for fewer managerial layers, more creativity and innovation, and more career flexibility.

The model of a corporate ladder dates to the Industrial Revolution, where business models held a strict hierarchy, and standardization was the pinnacle of optimized performance. As Cathy Benko, co-author of *The Corporate Lattice*, says

> But we don't live in an industrial age, we live in a digital age. And if you look at all the shifts taking place, one [of the biggest] is the composition of the workforce, which is far more diverse in every way."[285]

Career paths are becoming more fluid, following what Morrison called a "*zigzag*." Benko believes that the lattice model offers more opportunity for success. Benko goes on to say that

> in the ladder model, you're looking in one direction, which is up. In the lattice organization you can find growth by doing different roles, so you have new experiences, you acquire new skills, you tap into new networks. The world is less predictable than it was in the industrial age, so you stay relevant by acquiring a portfolio of transferable skills.[286]

The metaphor of climbing a ladder only to find it propped against the wrong wall or wrong building has been echoed since the advent of the corporate ladder by authors Allen Raine, Monk Thomas Merton, and Stephen R. Covey in his book *The 7 Habits of Highly Effective People*. Working within a lattice structure, there is less chance of climbing toward the wrong wall. This ties into the idea that in the future of work, people will busy themselves with self-fulfilling employment instead of just menial labor. Lattice allows for tangents of learning and exploration.

The concept of the corporate lattice structure is not new; however, as we progress further into the new economy, its concept becomes tantamount to how work is structured. Cloud technologies allow for global collaboration by providing a linked network of data between people. The future of work will be more like a people cloud with a focus on accessing assets instead of owning them. Talent will be shared globally, enabled by technology. Networks will link us in innovative ways we've never imagined. Technologies will allow for freedom in workspaces and connect talent from anywhere in the world to where there is need. Those who will be the most successful in the future workplace will be those who are disruptive to the norm, people who can reimagine systems, are adaptive problem-solvers, collaborate for solutions, are resilient, and who are, above all, creative thinkers.

In 1930, a year into the economic crisis caused by the stock market crash on Wall Street, John Maynard Keynes dreamed of a 15-hour work week in the essay *Economic Possibilities for Our Grandchildren*.[287] The remainder of the "work" week, he posited, would be spent pursuing our own passions, pleasures, and projects. We aren't there yet, but maybe in the future we will be.

The fall of the 9 to 5

The day in the life of a worker in 50 years begins with waking up, not by an alarm blaring from your smartphone, but to the rousing smell of coffee, sunlight coming in your window from a curtain being drawn back, and a gentle stirring massage or vibration from your mattress. All of this is courtesy of the Internet of Things in your smart home. You wake up well-rested because a sleep sensor has made sure not to wake you during a round of rapid eye movement (REM) sleep, but instead when your sleep cycle brings you closest to the surface of sleep. Your voice assistant (the Siri of tomorrow) will brief you on your projects for the day as your closet offers you weather-appropriate clothing options. If your morning wake-up routine has been this altered, then it reasons that your day of work will be similarly transformed.

There is going to be a fundamental shift in the concept of work. We will move away from productive tasks that compensate us based on our productivity because productivity will be generated by automated machines. Humans will perform tasks that do not generate revenue, and we will not get paid for them in the same way as we do now. Jobs will therefore be self-fulfilling and not economically profitable and there will be fewer of them. Talent assets will be a global commodity and employees will be hired based on task necessities. With the freedoms that technology offers, increasingly people will work remotely on many of these tasks and not be governed by employers that reside in their city, let alone their country. The working environment will greatly alter with less physical, brick-and-mortar office spaces and an increase in shared multipurpose spaces. We will live longer. Globally, life expectancy at birth has increased by six years since 1990.[288] Correspondingly, the age of retirement is on the rise and by 2028 will be 67 for both men and women in the UK,[289] up from 65 and 62, respectively. Rising retirement ages mean that multiple generations will be participating in the workforce. This also means that the volume of people in the workforce will increase, while the number of jobs will decrease.

In the future world of work there will be fewer "*cubicle zombies*,"[290] jobs will be more self-fulfilling, and there will be less of what author David Graeber calls "*bullshit jobs*." "A bullshit job is one that even the person doing it secretly believes need not, or should not, exist,"[291] a job that is "as if someone were out there making up pointless jobs just for the sake of keeping us all working."[292]Graeber claims that productive jobs have become increasingly automated, yet the result, instead of more free time, has been the creation of a multitude of meaningless jobs. As Graeber illustrates:

> Rather than allowing a massive reduction of working hours to free the world's population to pursue their own projects, pleasures, visions, and ideas, we have seen the ballooning of not even so much of the 'service' sector as of the administrative sector, up to and including the creation of whole new industries like financial services or telemarketing, or the unprecedented expansion of sectors like corporate law, academic and health administration, human resources, and public relations. And these numbers do not even reflect on all those people whose job is to provide

administrative, technical, or security support for these industries, or for that matter the whole host of ancillary industries (dog-washers, all-night pizza delivery) that only exist because everyone else is spending so much of their time working in all the other ones.[293]

Technology will take jobs, especially many of the "bullshit" jobs. But it will create space for new jobs and place more value on emotive and creative occupations that machines can't perform. Self-fulfilling careers in arts, therapy, counseling, spiritual services, and even personal training will flourish. There will be a paradigm shift surrounding the definition of "job" and our income will no longer be earned from simply "working."

In my book *Flex or Fail*, written with Tony Felton and Robby Mol, we anticipate what we call the "seven sources of income." In the future, jobs will not be represented by a position in a hierarchy or a title, but by a series of tasks, which, even if not necessarily productive, provide self-fulfillment for the individual. Besides, those sources of income may not necessarily result from what we today call a "job." For instance, today, technology platforms—some of them using blockchain—allow us to monetize our social capital by doing a web search or posting a message. The collaborative economy also implies that we will share our properties but will be compensated in return, adding a new source of income to our labor income. Perhaps upcoming basic income schemes will compensate individuals for tasks that are today considered social and charitable services, such as attention to the elderly, belonging to a book club, and volunteering in the local homeless shelter. The speed at which we will change our jobs, and their short duration, together with a future working life where we will combine several jobs/tasks in a single day, requires very different skills that our education systems are still not ready to provide.

The question now becomes, how do we prepare a workforce to be successful in jobs that haven't taken shape yet? It comes down to teaching a skill set and developing one's adaptability quotient.

Adaptability

First there came the stressed importance of intelligence quotient (IQ), the score associated with someone's human intelligence. Much educational onus has been placed on the concept of IQ, if not the actual test. The traditional educational model trained students to memorize, through lecture, reading, and rote memorization a sort of encyclopedic knowledge of the world that would make them knowledgeable employees. One of the most notable creations of the Enlightenment was the Encyclopedia, a book created by the greatest thinkers of the time that aimed to encapsulate humankind's collective knowledge. In *We Did Not Live Entirely in Vain* (1764), Diderot, one of the editors and primary contributors to the encyclopedia, stated:

> I think that our work is on a level with our century, and that is something. The most enlightened man will find in it ideas that were unfamiliar to him and facts he did not know. If only general education could advance at such a rapid rate that twenty years from now there would be, out of a thousand of our pages, scarcely a single line that was not popular knowledge![294]

It seems that education is still playing chase. Now, technology, specifically the internet, is our encyclopedia. We are no longer reliant on factual memorization or scrolling through indexes to locate answers to our questions. With the advent of the internet, we began to shift away from IQ or encyclopedic educational models.

Then, in the 1990s, emotional quotient (EQ), or emotional intelligence, emerged alongside a more technology-rich business model. Emotional quotient is developing empathetic understanding, understanding our own emotions and the emotions of others, and using that emotional intelligence to guide our own thinking and behavior and better adapt in a variety of situations. Now, in the digital economy, the educational trend is teaching toward the adaptability quotient (AQ). AQ is measuring how able one is to adapt and thrive in an ever-changing environment—which is what business in the digital economy is. In *Adapt or Die*, AQ is defined as "the ability to adjust course, product, service, and strategy in response to unanticipated changes in the market."[295] The skills that increase your AQ are being collaborative, globally minded, receptive, and creative.

In Begumpet, India, there is one of the best high schools in the world, if you consider long-term graduate success in the fields of business and technology. Hyderabad Public School (HPS), a private school, is the alma mater of some of the most influential business people on earth, including Microsoft CEO Satya Nadella, Adobe CEO Shantanu Narayen, and Mastercard CEO Ajay Banga. The school's website states, "HPS has a unique academic philosophy. We train students to make a difference in whatever they do and leave their footprints on the sands of time."[296] The school's mandate reflects traits of global mindedness and innovation. Satya Nadella said of his education, "I think more than anything else, it gave us the freedom to think, learn, and pursue bold dreams."[297]

The reality is that you can teach coding and math, knowledge is "Google-able," and you can learn through practical demonstrations on YouTube or through massive open online courses (MOOCs). The expanse of knowledge is available at our fingertips. What can't be garnered from the internet is the capacity for AQ skills. While technology makes collaboration and being globally minded easier, technology in itself can't teach or develop those skills.

Implications for a Robust 21st-century education system

Ten years ago, John W. Gardner, former US Secretary of Health, Education, and Welfare, said that "much education today is monumentally ineffective. All too often we are giving young people cut flowers when we should be teaching them to grow their own plants."[298] Plants are the equivalent of encyclopedic knowledge and outdated processes; the gardening of plants is fostering creativity, adaptability, and innovation. "What we make with our minds is of growing importance economically; the way we generate new and creative ideas is the focus of educational and economic think tanks across the globe."[299] Globalization and technology have created an ever-changing world. It is easy for an employee to pick up company or product information. What is hard to find is an adaptive and creative employee. "Employers say that they want people who can think creatively, who can innovate, who can communicate well, work in teams and are adaptable and self-confident."[300] The first Industrial Revolution shaped our educational system of today. Now factories have given way to creative industries or intellectual property centers. This already huge, and continuously growing, sector includes, but is not limited to: advertising, arts, architecture, crafts, design, computer services, gaming, writing, publishing, architecture, fashion, and patents from science and technology. Factory "mentality," creating task or career-specific individuals, is an outdated notion. Yet, globally, it is still largely the way the institution of education is structured. "We live in a world that's shaped by ideas, beliefs, and values of human imagination and culture."[301] We are building a new, global community. We are joining communities together and creating sub-communities. We are socially reorganizing through technology. How we share, express, talk, think, and learn are all part of that shift. We can't hold on to our old ways of educating out of some tired sense of nostalgia. We must imagine, create, and innovate our educational model.

There is a famous line from the movie *Jaws* (1975): "You're going to need a bigger boat." That was a gross understatement. What they really needed (based on the shape of the sinking vessel and the death count at the end of the movie) was an indestructible, fully armed, shark-killing machine. But, as one of those didn't exist in their world at that time, they went with the only equipment that they knew, a larger fishing boat, harpoons, and guns, and they did their best. Modern education isn't quite as daunting as a gigantic, blood-hungry killer shark—but often, like Chief Brody, I think we are in need of a "bigger boat."

To maintain the transportation analogy, our current pedagogical model is much like a classic car. We've added new headlights, given it a new paint job, put in airbags, better rims—basically "suped" it up. But, underneath, it is the same old car. What we need to do is blow up the car and get a new mode of transportation. British author, creativity and education advocate Sir Ken Robinson, is in agreement, only his phrasing lacks the explosives. Robinson states, "Current systems of education were not designed to meet the challenges we now face. They were developed to meet the needs of a former age. Reform is not enough: they need to be transformed."[302] Part of that transformation needs to be a push toward educational methodology that fosters creativity, empathy, collaboration, and communication skills—the skill set that autonomous technologies can't offer humanity. The most difficult of those skills to teach and develop is creativity, even though we are born creative beings.

Lev Vygotsky, whose work shaped the social constructivist educational theory, examined child psychology and the place of imagination and creativity in human development and learning. Vygotsky saw imagination as a high functioning mental skill that begins at a young age with child's play and develops into creativity. Anything that requires seeing through, seeing beyond, or constructing something new relies heavily on imagination. He claimed,

> With the help of fantasy not only artistic works are created but also all scientific inventions, all technical constructions. Fantasy is one of the manifestations of human creative activity, and specifically in adolescence, converging with thinking in concepts, it receives a broader development in this objective aspect.[303]

Fantasy and imagination are at the root of all invention, no matter what area, scientific, technological, or otherwise. Vygotsky believed that creativity was in all of us as children, taking different forms as we develop. "The old adage that child's play is imagination in action must be reversed; we can say that imagination in adolescents and schoolchildren is play without action."[304] To Vygotsky, the imagination was part of the thought process that takes shape through social interactions while we are young, and matures, as we mature, for use in creative problem-solving in arts or sciences when we are adults.[305]

Creativity relies on critical judgment and is fueled by intuition and imagination. Robinson identifies three related areas that build, each off of the other: imagination, creativity, and innovation. He defines imagination as "the process of bringing to mind things that are not present to our senses; creativity, which is the process of developing original ideas that have value' and innovation, which is the process of putting new ideas into practice."[306] This process of "being creative" is at the root of future educational pedagogy. Yet, in the majority of current educational models, creativity has been stifled since kindergarten—as Sir Ken Robinson boldly pointed out in his noteworthy TED talk,[307] by processing them through an outdated factory of education routed in the requirements of the Industrial Revolution. A creative educational model that better focuses on AQ skills is needed to foster learners who will be successful in the workplaces of tomorrow and contribute to the digital economy.

A creative educational model harkens back to a Renaissance approach to creating a school curriculum that builds well-rounded, great thinkers, not merely great knowers. Think of Leonardo da Vinci, who designed flying machines, dabbled in biology, and painted the Mona Lisa. Even in modern society, I would argue that he would excel because he was a great thinker and highly adaptable. Students need STEM classes—this involves computer science that delves into programming, robotics, and artificial intelligence. However, the way that these courses have been traditionally structured also needs to change, moving away from being memorization and task-oriented driven, to real-world, problem-based, student-centered, collaborative learning models that focus on creative thinking and adaptability. More value must be placed on the arts, with studies in

Image 5.1 Singapore, Skills to Jobs. Photo taken by the author

theater, music, visual art and design, and dance. These courses develop creativity, adaptability, communication, and social skills, as well as increased collaboration skills. There are also strong links between math and music, and empathy and theater, for example, which demonstrate that arts strengthen all learning. Arts also help in developing global mindedness and a cultural mindset. Philosophy courses which are, right now, almost invisible in secondary schools, need to be reinstated to inspire reflection and debate, and, yes, hopefully thinking as well. Socrates and his subsequent generations of followers, including Plato and Aristophanes, learned through conversation, discussions in what I would equate to our modern communities of practice. They were lifelong learners who continually developed a more progressive understanding through conversation communities. It seems that this is where we need to be heading in modern education. We need to work toward "advancing the conversation of humankind,"[308] like Socrates attempted so long ago, only now the communities and conversations are taking place globally and online. With STEM, arts, and philosophy grounding the school curriculum, we will create lifelong learners, creative thinkers who are adaptable, able to collaborate, and are globally minded. Citizens who are ready to rise to the challenges that rapid technology adoption ushers in.

As children, we are naturally ensconced in wonder. We question everything, see the world in interesting ways, and our imagination and creativity are integral to our development. As Spanish painter Picasso said, "Every child is an artist. The problem is how to remain an artist once we grow up."[309] Or, as Robinson stated, "we don't grow into creativity; we grow out of it."[310] So, it is not a matter of teaching learners how to be creative, it is about allowing them to hold on to that intrinsic quality, to nurture and develop it. Creativity is a way of thinking and seeing that allows for flexibility and adaptability when approaching new situations. Ideally, "adaptive expertise"[311] is the developmental goal. It doesn't matter in which area of expertise the learner focuses, the goal is to have them master adaptability and creative thinking so that they can meet whatever external demands may be made of them. Being creative, innovative, globally minded, and empathetic are skills that allow for the adaptability required to find success in the new economy.

60. COMPETITIVENESS AND INCOME INEQUALITY

Thomas Piketty's *Capital in the Twenty-First Century* generated a lot of attention in 2013, in his study of income inequality in the developed world since the 1800s. Although the long-term trend in inequality is far from being uniform, Piketty shows that since 1980, inequality has undoubtedly increased, at least in Europe and the United States. In the latter, for instance, the top 1 percent of households took in 22.5 percent of income in 2012; in 1979, they only got 10 percent. Inequality is unfair and undesirable: unfair because wealth and income no longer reward hard work or talent. In *Success and Luck: Good Fortune and the Myth of Meritocracy*, Cornell University economist Robert H. Frank argues that people's fate is mostly determined by geopolitical factors (the country where one is born or lives) and luck.

As a result of economic monopolies, certain individuals enjoy excessive rents and this leads to significant income inequalities. In very unequal societies, the lower class is also the less educated and therefore does not have access to high-skill jobs, nor contributes to productivity increases in the country overall. Finally, inherited wealth reduces incentives for both the rich and the poor.

My colleague José Caballero from the IMD World Competitiveness Center has extensively investigated the relationship between income inequality and competitiveness. His analyses have shown[312] that inequality is usually the cost of competitiveness improvements. When countries lack an efficient social safety net (as in Western Europe), wealth accumulation by the rich does not yield any benefit for the poor. However, innovation-driven economic growth requires rents to be captured by a minority and therefore those countries that start from a lower level of economic development (low- or low-middle-income economies) often witness that improvements in competitiveness are associated with increases in inequality.

Accepting that inequality *within* countries has increased worldwide in the last 20 years, the question is to what extent economic development has made world economies converge or diverge in terms of income. In *The Great Escape: Health, Wealth, and the Origins of Inequality*, a marvelous book by Angus Deaton, the 2014 Nobel Prize Winner in Economics shows that the world has experienced the most progress in the last years in terms of differences between rich and poor countries. Such progress has been caused in part by the amazing improvement in living conditions in the two most populated countries in the world, India and China.

Social disparities then refer to differences in income among countries. Remember how in Table 2.1 we show that, in 2017, the ratio in GDP per capita between the richest country (Qatar, USD 116,936) and the poorest (Central African Republic, USD 661) is 176 times. In 1960, GDP per capita in the richest country (Bermuda) was 175 times that of the poorest (Myanmar).

Figure 5.4 shows the difference in GDP per capita between the richest and the poorest country in the World Competitiveness Yearbook between 1995 and 2018. These countries are different every year: in 1994, the poorest country in our sample is India; but in 2017,

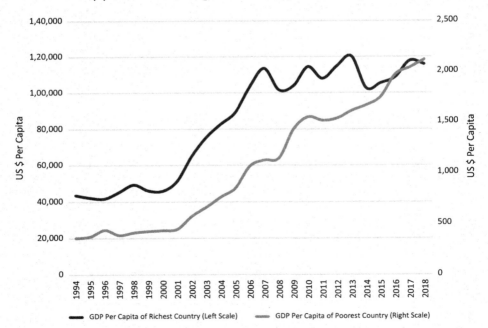

— GDP Per Capita of Richest Country (Left Scale)   — GDP Per Capita of Poorest Country (Right Scale)

Figure 5.4 GDP per capita in the Richest and the Poorest Country in the IMD World Competitiveness Rankings 1994–2008

Source: IMD World Competitiveness Center.

Venezuela is the poorest. Similarly, Switzerland is the richest country in terms of GDP per capita in 1994, while the ranking is topped by Luxembourg in 2018.

Two observations are noteworthy from Figure 5.4. First, both rich and poor countries have improved their wealth levels in the last 25 years. Second, while the poorest country in our ranking has been improving since 2008, the wealth of the richest countries has plateaued. Consequently, the 2008 financial crisis has initiated a period when social disparities in the world have declined.

The relative increase in prosperity in poorer countries is more visible in Figure 5.5, where GDP per capita in the richest and poorest countries is plotted, but as an index, with 1994 as the base year. While the wealth of the poorest countries has increased 6-fold, the wealth of the richest countries has increased three times.

Gross domestic product is dependent on the structure of the productive system in an economy, so comparisons across countries may be hiding differences in productivity and technology development. Can we find the same pattern of social disparities when we look at actual compensation levels? The answer is yes. However, there are interesting twists in the data. In Figure 5.6, we report data on hourly compensation in the manufacturing sector in the best- and worst-paying countries. Because of absolute differences between the two, we report the worst-paying country in the right-hand-side scale. In the best-paying country, salaries in manufacturing increase 1.8 times between 1994 and 2018 (from USD 27 to USD 50); in the worst-paying country, they increase 5.5 times (from USD 0.19 to USD 1.02 per hour). In these countries, there has been a significant increase mainly after 2004. In contrast, salaries in the best-paying countries have decreased between 2007 and 2018.

One can also look at the remuneration of the CEO. CEO salaries in the best-paying countries have multiplied by 3.4 between 1995 and 2017 (from about USD 266,000 to USD 900,000). In contrast, in the worst-paying countries they have reduced by half (down from USD 38,000 in 1995 to USD 28,000 in 2017). In consequence, the gap between CEOs

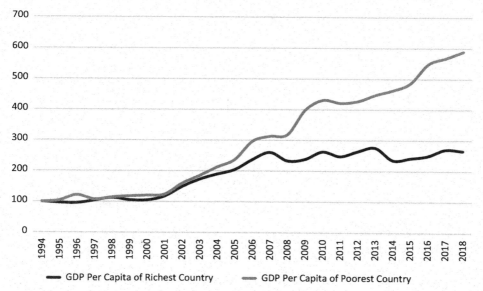

Figure 5.5 GDP per capita index in the Richest and the Poorest Country in the IMD World Competitiveness Rankings 1994–2008

Source: IMD World Competitiveness Center.

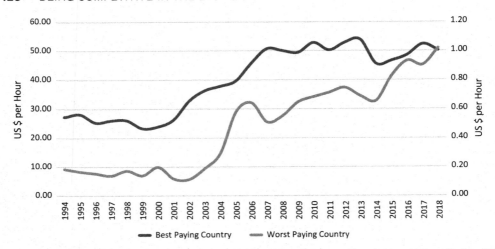

Figure 5.6 Total Hourly Compensation in Manufacturing (Wages + Supplemental Benefits) in US Dollars

Source: IMD World Competitiveness Center.

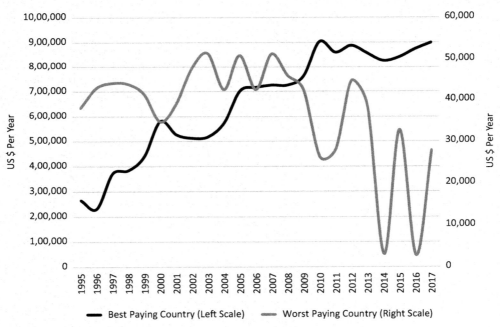

Figure 5.7 CEO Pay. Total Base Salary plus Bonuses and Long-Term Incentives

Source: IMD World Competitiveness Center.

in poor and rich countries has widened significantly: salary difference has increased five times in that period.

In conclusion, despite significant social disparities among countries, the world has become less unequal between 1995 and 2018. The income gap among countries has reduced in the last years both because the financial crisis has impacted rich countries negatively, and because poorer countries have continued developing. Income differences have widened particularly due to the performance of extreme countries, especially the richest countries, whose wealth per capita has improved at astonishing rates. We also observe social disparities have been larger across income groups and across countries: differences in CEO salaries between best- and worst-paying countries have increased 5-fold in the last 25 years. Similarly, the gap in salaries in the manufacturing sector has widened, even if one takes into account the impact of the 2008 financial crisis.

Neoclassical economists have always argued that economic inequality is not just the price of growth and development, but a key incentive for maximizing social and economic outputs. The efficiency–equity trade-off is one of the foundations and dilemmas of neoclassical economic theory, arguing that there is a trade-off between increasing productive efficiency and reducing distributive equity. Involuntary redistribution, through taxes or public expenditure or other means, may discourage economic actors from seeking their maximum production possibility frontier. However, the 2008 financial crisis, and the consequent global economic recession and European debt crisis, have placed income inequality in front of politicians, journalists, and academic economists as public dissatisfaction represented in various social movements and street protests taking place all over the world. Piketty's breakthrough book *Capital in the Twenty-First Century* suggests that disparities in the distribution of wealth reached or exceeded the Victorian era and the gilded age inequality levels of the 19th century. A research paper published by Oxfam found that the richest 1 percent owns more than half of the world's wealth.[313] Concentrations of wealth in the hands of a few families or individuals carry great societal problems. Even from a pure economic theory lens, huge disparities in income distribution will significantly reduce consumption as a result of limiting the ability of the majority to consume and the excessive saving rates of the wealthy. This will reduce economic multipliers and slow economic growth rates. Political consequences are also substantial. Huge economic disparities fuel public dissatisfaction leading to political instability or diminishing democratic practices by restraining people's ability to lobby and influence political institutions. In addition, several examples now support the poverty-trap dilemma and economic inequality sustains such status quo, leaving a narrow—or closed—window for low-income families and their children to climb the class structure.

Kuznets (1955) was one of the pioneering economists to establish the idea that economic development may inherently increase levels of income inequality in the early stages of development. However, he hypothesized that as economies develop, market forces will reduce the economic inequality of society. Kuznets' observations and his optimistic predictions were hastily adopted by policymakers and political institutions, ignoring that Kuznets relied on very narrow data to build his hypothesis covering only the United States, the United Kingdom, and Germany for a period from 1880 to 1948, where he also overlooked the effect of the two world wars on income distribution and the Great Depression. He stated himself that his paper "is perhaps 5 percent empirical information and 95 percent speculation, some of it possibly tainted by wishful thinking."

Since the 1970s, several academic studies have emerged based on cross-country data supporting Kuznets' hypothesis—low- and high-income economies were found to have low inequality levels, while middle-income economies had higher ones.[314] (Yet, none of these studies followed Kuznets' own inquiry by analyzing the historical evolution of income inequality of a specific economy through different stages of economic development.) On the other hand, many other academics have found no evidence for Kuznets' conclusion when observing changes in income distribution and the statistical correlation between growth and inequality in a number of economies.[315] Overall, the relationship between competitiveness or economic development and income inequality remains greatly disputed. One potential assertion is that income inequality is the price to pay for competitiveness: as countries develop, they need to raise the income of the wealthiest 1 percent, as they are the innovators and main driving force for economic growth. Another hypothesis is that since low-income countries are also the more unequal, prosperity increases tend to benefit the lower 90 percent more than the top 1 percent. The remainder of this chapter discusses recent trends, perceptions, and debates on wealth and income inequality, namely in Chile, Switzerland, China, and the Middle East, and sheds light on current proposed solutions to income inequality tax reforms and universal basic income.

Case Studies

Chile: how did bachelet's educational reform try to curtail income inequality?

"Chile has only one great adversary: inequality. And only together we will be able to defeat it," said Michelle Bachelet to the crowd celebrating her outside the presidential palace in Santiago de Chile in March 2014 after being sworn in as Chile's president for a second term.[316] She became the first woman president of Chile when she held her first term in office from 2006 to 2010, where she achieved remarkable social and economic reforms, marked by focusing on women's rights and improved healthcare services.

Daniel Hojman, associate professor of economics at the University of Chile, explained for the *World Politics Review* the long history of wealth and income inequality in Chile, as in most Latin American countries, and Bachelet's policies to address inequality.[317] Until the first half of the 20th century, land and wealth were highly concentrated in the hands of a few elites, and the Chilean economy relied on the extraction of natural resources, the early stage of industrialization, and cheap low-skilled labor. Redistribution policies, the nationalization of natural resources, and land reforms were adopted in the late 1950s, but the military coup of 1973 that brought Pinochet to power halted these redistribution processes. Income distribution data shows that during the Pinochet regime, income inequality reached its highest recorded level in the 1980s, driven by extensive privatization of the public sector that led to concentrated ownership of major industries, alongside weakened labor institutions and reduced social expenditures.

Chile's economy experienced remarkable growth for almost three decades after Pinochet's regime and the restoration of democracy. The economy tripled in size and the poverty rate drastically decreased with effective social protection policies. However, income inequality remains quite high even though it has slightly declined since 1990. Even as access to healthcare and education services has improved, a market-oriented approach to education and pensions and, to some extent, healthcare services as well, has caused the quality of these fundamental services to be considerably different across socioeconomic groups. Generally, a small minority have access to good-quality services while the vast majority of the population is left with low-quality services, making inequity a severe challenge for Chile's economic and political order.

Michelle Bachelet ended her second four-year presidential term in March 2018. Her education reforms came after a period of student-led protests demanding fundamental action on the extreme disparities in income and education structures. During her second term, Bachelet's ambitious reform agenda to reduce the high levels of inequality was faced with strong resistance. Nevertheless, she succeeded in introducing free university education for low-income students, strengthening labor unions, decriminalizing abortion, and establishing the Ministry of Women and Gender Equality. She implemented tax reforms, imposing higher taxes on top incomes and corporations to finance the new social reforms. The new tax reforms were intended to ensure that 75 percent of the growth in tax revenue would come from the richest 0.1 percent. Such policies harmed investment and affected growth rates, which dropped to an average of 1.7 percent in 2013–2017 compared to 5 percent in the prior 20 years, yet it is clear that these reforms were inevitable in response to student protests demanding an end to the damaging disparities in income and education.

Bachelet's strategy tried to increase public expenditure on education to reach 2 percent of GDP, with almost half of this expenditure going to improving the quality of public schools serving more than 90 percent of school students. The strategy sought to increase teachers' salaries, improve hiring procedures, and provide ongoing training, in addition to expanding financial aid for students of low-income households. Bachelet banned for-profit primary and secondary schools. Before Bachelet's education reforms, Chile had one of the most socioeconomically unequal education systems in the world, with subsidized voucher-based private schools allowed to charge high fees and set their own criteria for selecting students. At the university level, her policies could not meet her promise of "free university for all," but granted free tuition for students of families from the 60 percent lowest incomes group. Yet, these reforms are not without limitations: there are increasing concerns over the quality of the education at the university level, with many experts suggesting that large investment should have targeted university education better than school level.[318] According to the Standardized World Income Inequality Database (SWIID) computed by Harvard University, Chile's Gini coefficient on income (pre-tax and transfers) rose from 49.1 in 1968 to 51.4 in 2015, whereas the Gini coefficient on disposable income (after tax and transfers) stayed relatively unchanged from 44.6 in 1968 to 44.9 in 2015. While it is impossible to see Bachelet's education reforms reflected in income distribution in the short term, we shall expect fundamental changes in the socioeconomic structure of Chile, if the new conservative president Sebastián Piñera does not reverse these reforms.

Switzerland: minimum guaranteed income, the 12:1 referendum

In less than five years, Swiss voters have overwhelmingly voted against redistribution proposals aimed at introducing a cap on top executives' salaries and providing a minimum guaranteed basic income for everyone.

The first referendum in 2013 on the "1:12 initiative for fair pay" proposed to limit top executives' pay to 12 times their lowliest employees' salaries. Almost two-thirds of voters rejected the proposal, with a margin of 66 to 34 percent. The initiative was proposed by the youth wing of the Social Democrats (JUSO). The rationale behind this proposal was that no one should earn in one month what the lowest-paid employees earn in a year.

Opponents of the proposal highlighted the threat imposed by a cap on executive pay on the competitiveness of the economy, warning that it would discourage employees and limit the capability of firms to hire high-skilled staff. They argued also that the proposal would negatively affect social security contributions and tax returns. It seems that "the

Swiss people have clearly decided that it is not up to the state to have a say on pay," Reuters quoted Valentin Vogt, the president of the Swiss Association of Employers.[319]

Despite the referendum results, David Roth, president of JUSO, declared that

> Of course we are disappointed. But I also believe that we have an achievement nonetheless. A year ago, opponents were defending high salaries. Today, no one is doing that. No one in Swiss politics would dare say that million-dollar salaries are justified.[320]

The pay debate in Switzerland was fueled earlier in 2013 by the high pay of 72 million Swiss franc for former Novartis chairman Daniel Vasella, to make sure he would not work for other competitors. A referendum held early in 2013 to give a veto to shareholders on compensations to new and outgoing managers and ban golden handshakes and parachutes was overwhelmingly supported by the public. It is considered the strictest control on executive pay in an advanced economy, where Swiss voters supported the proposal by nearly 68 percent against 32 percent.

Moreover, Switzerland was the first country to have a referendum on universal basic income. It was clear from the beginning that most Swiss politicians were not in favor of the proposal as no parliamentary party supported it. However, the referendum took place after advocates for the basic income initiative succeeded in collecting more than 100,000 signatures, making it eligible for public vote under the Swiss popular initiative system. The organizers of the initiative started calling for the referendum in April 2012, aiming to introduce an unconditional guaranteed basic income as a constitutional right. In less than six months, the petition collected 42,000 signatures and around 70,000 signatures in one year. By October 2013, a referendum on basic income was constitutionally binding as 130,000 citizens had signed the petition, exceeding the legal requirements for a minimum of 100,000 signatures in 18 months. Although the initiative did not indicate a specific amount for the proposed basic income, supporters suggested a minimum of 2,500 Swiss francs a month for every adult, whether working or not, and 625 Swiss francs for each child, to compensate the high cost of living in Switzerland. According to the European digital news outlet, The Local, the Swiss federal government estimated that introducing a guaranteed basic income would have cost 208 billion Swiss francs a year, and would require tax revenues to increase by more than 153 billion Swiss francs, with the remaining 55 billion Swiss francs being financed from expenditures on social insurance and assistance.

The petition supporters were concerned with the increasing inequalities in wages and the rapid automation in production that limits the available jobs for workers. The BBC quoted a campaigner for Basic Income Switzerland, Che Wagner, arguing that basic income is not pay for nothing. "In Switzerland over 50 percent of total work that is done is unpaid. It is care work, it is at home, [and] it is in different communities, so that work would be more valued with a basic income."[321] On the other side, Luzi Stamm, a member of parliament for the right-wing Swiss People's Party, told the BBC, "If Switzerland were an island, the answer is yes. But with open borders, it's a total impossibility, especially for Switzerland, with a high living standard."[322] He argued that "if you would offer every individual a Swiss amount of money, you would have billions of people who would try to move into Switzerland." The proposal was remarkably rejected by Swiss voters in 2016, with nearly 77 percent of the voters refusing the initiative, and only 23 percent supporting it.

Yet, the idea of a guaranteed basic income in Switzerland has not entirely expired. In June 2018, the small town of Rheinau in the area of Zurich conducted an experiment by introducing a universal basic income scheme.[323] Under this project, more than half of the town's 1,300 residents would receive 2,500 Swiss francs, while the Swiss film-maker Rebecca Panian intended to document the one-year experiment and produce a documentary on the experiment. The project was initially funded by crowdfunding and donations from several institutions with an estimated cost of 3 million to 5 million Swiss francs. However, the filmmaker failed to raise the money.

Switzerland positions itself as a unique business-friendly economy that protects competitiveness while maintaining low levels of class disparity and a strongly stable social and economic order. Income inequality remains relatively stable in Switzerland, and that may explain the public disfavor for new radical redistribution policies. According to the SWIID, the pre-tax and transfers Gini coefficient slightly increased from 40 in 1980 to 41.3 in 2015, while after tax and transfers Gini coefficient declined from 31.5 to 29.2 over the same period, reflecting strong welfare and redistribution policies adopted by one of the wealthiest economies in the world. In the country, the ratio of the share of the top 20 percent against the share of the bottom 20 percent was 38.2 in 2015, before tax and transfers.[324] This means that the top 20 percent earned more than 38 times the bottom 20 percent of earners. However, this ratio drops to only 4.8 percent after tax and welfare redistributive transfers, raising the income share of the bottom 20 percent to 7.8 percent, up from only 1.2 percent pre-tax and transfers, while the income share of the upper 20 percent earners decreased from 44.5 to 37.2 percent. Meanwhile, the income share of the middle 60 percent stayed relatively unchanged, with 54.3 percent before redistribution and 55 percent after redistribution.

China, inequality is becoming rampant, but is it a problem?

China's economic growth has no historic precedent, yet it is not without caveats. The country moved from underdevelopment with a history of a famine crisis, to become the second-largest economy in less than 50 years, and the economy is still growing faster than any other big economy.[325] Before the economic reforms of 1978, China was among the poorest countries in the world, with real GDP per capita equivalents only 3 percent of the United States' and 40 percent of Brazil's GDP per capita in 1960. By 2017, China's GDP per capita was almost 15 percent of the United States' and 90 percent of Brazil's GDP per capita. The World Bank (2018a) data shows that in the last 40 years, China experienced remarkable, relatively stable, explosive growth rates with an average of 9.5 percent from 1978 to 2017.

According to the World Bank,[326] recent estimates of poverty rates witnessed an impressive decline under both international and national poverty rate standards. The poverty headcount ratio at the national poverty line fell from 17.2 percent in 2010 to 3.1 percent in 2017. Using international standards (incomes of USD 1.9 per day), the percentage of poor people in China fell from 66.6 percent in 1990 to just 0.7 percent in 2015.[327]

Unfortunately, widespread corruption and unreported incomes are major obstacles to measuring income and wealth levels in China. The World Bank argues that China's economic growth benefited the lower-income population as well as the total population. It estimates that the average consumption growth of the bottom 40 percent has been higher than the average consumption growth of the total population by 1.7 percent.

The World Bank argues that there has been a drop in the level of income inequality with the Gini coefficient showing a decline from 49.1 in 2008 to 46.5 in 2016, suggesting that China's economic growth promoted shared prosperity and welfare gains for all the country.[328] However, this enthusiastic claim is being questioned by many observers. Since the start of the economic reforms in 1978, many economists and policymakers have highlighted the impact of China's rapid economic growth on income inequality. In recent years, there has been growing interest in the extreme levels of income inequality in China, with the *Financial Times* calling "China income inequality among the world's worst,"[329] and Bloomberg warning that "China is racing to the top in income inequality."[330]

A more historical income and wealth inequality data than that reported by the World Bank signals the increasing levels of inequality in China in the last four decades. The SWIID data shows that pre-tax and transfers Gini coefficient rose from 32.5 in 1978 to 46 in 2015, and after tax and transfers Gini coefficient rose from 29.6 to 40.2 in the same period. The World Inequality Database (WID) reports that the income share of the top 1 percent jumped from only 6.3 percent in 1978 to nearly 14 percent in 2015, and the income share of the top 10 percent from 27.2 percent to more than 41 percent. Over the same period, the income share of the bottom 50 percent fell from 27 percent to less than 15 percent. This took place even during the period 2005–2015, when the government sought to actively tackle corruption and income inequalities by promoting a "harmonious society" at the 2005 National People's Congress.[331] Increasing disparities have been the result of wealth accumulation at the top. The WID estimates that by the end of 2015, the top 1 percent owned approximately 30 percent of total wealth in China, a huge increase from 1995, when they held only 15.8 percent of the nation's wealth. And this trend gets even grayer when observing the evolution of the wealth share of the top 10 percent, which rose from nearly 41 percent in 1995 to more than two-thirds of the nation's wealth by the end of 2015.[332]

In a recent article published by the IMF, Sonali Jain-Chandra points out that income inequality in China was not an inescapable consequence of economic development, showing that inequality in education is one of the major factors for the tremendous growth in income and wealth gaps.[333] Differences in education are even worse when comparing rural to urban areas, with very low educational attainment in rural areas enforced by the hukou system, restricting migration to urban areas, which also affected wage inequality between rural and urban areas. Jain-Chandra also argues that rapid industrialization and skill-biased technological change widened the wage gap between skilled and unskilled labor. And while the government has introduced some measures to control the level of income inequality, such as increasing the minimum wage, removing agricultural taxes, increasing social protection expenditures in rural areas, and raising the taxable income bracket on several occasions, these policies are insufficient to stop the rise in inequality if they are not linked to additional structural changes on personal income and consumption taxes.

One can argue that increasing inequality was an unavoidable price for the impressive high economic growth rates. However, there is growing literature warning that high levels of inequality are real threats for sustainable growth as well as social stability.[334] Widening income inequality may deter investment in health and education services that are also essential for sustainable growth[335] and may reduce public support for growth-enhancing policies while making populist policies more favorable by the majority and risking political stability.[336]

Income and wealth inequality in the Middle East

Wealth and income distribution remains a fierce topic of debate in almost all the countries in the Middle East, being without doubt one of the causes of the 2010–2011 uprisings. However, conventional measurements of income inequality, like the Gini coefficient based on household surveys reported by the World Bank, estimate very low inequality levels by international standards, suggesting the Middle East to be among the most egalitarian regions. For instance, the latest available Gini coefficient for Palestine is 33.7 in 2016; 31.8 for Egypt in 2015; 32.6 for Mauritania in 2014; 29.5 for Iraq in 2012; and 27.6 for Algeria in 2011.[337]

Unfortunately, current available information at the national level is inadequate to make reliable estimates of the top income shares in the Middle East, because household income and expenditure surveys almost systematically underestimate top incomes, because of top coding or inaccurate responding by top income households, making fiscal data much more reliable than self-reported surveys.[338] The Global Wealth Report of the Credit Suisse Research Institute remains a reliable and available source for the distribution of wealth. Credit Suisse estimates put Egypt among the top 12 countries with high levels of wealth inequality in the world, and one of the nine countries that witnessed extreme growth of wealth inequality. According to the data,[339] the wealth share of the top 10 percent in Egypt increased from 61 percent in 2000 to more than 73 percent in 2014, and from 31 percent in 2000 to 48 percent in 2014 for the top 1 percent.[340]

A recent report by the World Inequality Lab, led by Thomas Piketty, has classified the Middle East region as the most unequal region in the world in economic inequality. The "World Inequality Report 2018" suggested that income inequality in the Middle East, including Turkey and Iran, is higher than Brazil and South Africa, the two countries considered the most economically unequal.[341] The report measured inequality among all the citizens of the region.

Therefore, in 2016, the income share of the top 10 percent in the Middle East was above 64 percent, compared to 37 percent in Western Europe, 47 percent in the United States, and 55 percent in Brazil, making it the world's most unequal region.[342,343]

Income inequality in the region is widening within countries as well as between countries. The World Inequality Report 2018 attributes economic inequalities between countries in the Middle East to the concentrated ownership of oil in small areas in the region. As a result, the income share of the oil-rich countries in the Gulf was nearly 42 percent of the region's income despite accounting for only 15 percent of the region's population. Income inequality within individual nations in the region is a result of multiple historic and persistent factors, such as concentrated political and, as a result, economic power in small entrenched elites, failed economic policies, rooted corruption, weak rule of law, and flawed or non-existent income tax systems. In addition to these factors, non-rich oil countries like Tunisia, Morocco, and Egypt experience a widening income gap between urban and rural areas, with rapid urbanization and moderate industrialization, in addition to government investment in infrastructure favoring urban areas, all of which has a significant influence on the distribution of national income. Inequality within Middle Eastern countries is also alarming and is not only related to oil. The income share of the top 1 percent in Lebanon earned 2.4 percent of the nation's income in 2016, which is higher than the share of the top 1 percent in oil-rich Kuwait, which is 17.7 percent.[344] The region is currently doomed by civil conflicts, authoritarianism, sectarianism, and religious extremism; the threat caused by economic inequality cannot be ignored or underestimated as an irrelevant factor in the current political situation in the Middle East.

Current proposed solutions to income inequality

Universal basic income

Universal basic income, also called basic income guarantee or basic living stipend, is an unconditional set of money transfers from the state to all the citizens or residents of a country or a region to cover their basic living needs such as food, housing, and clothing, irrespective of their level of income or employment status. Universal basic income is considered by some advocates as a logical policy for inclusive welfare on the principle of social solidarity. This minimum income can be very helpful in reducing poverty and income inequality among the population and provide security and flexibility for people to find appropriate jobs and support those who are negatively affected by automation. Universal basic income is attracting an increasing number of advocates in the 21st century and is becoming one of the most discussed ideas in the economic and political debate on poverty and income inequality driven by socioeconomic and technological changes.

The idea can be traced back to the 16th century when Thomas More published *Utopia* in 1516 and has been revisited by many scholars and politicians including Thomas Paine, Charles Fourier, Abraham Lincoln, Henry George, Bertrand Russell, Franklin Roosevelt, and Tony Atkinson.[345] The idea is no longer a radical leftist proposal, and advocates for universal basic income now come from different ideological backgrounds. The idea is now adopted by both left- and right-wing thinkers as a way to eliminate or reduce poverty and inequality and as a more sufficient mechanism to replace the current welfare system. Most of the current debate has started to shift from just opposing the idea to focus more on the specific type of money transfer, its mechanism, and whether it should be an unconditional transfer, job guarantees, or a negative income tax.[346]

Some supporters of universal basic income argue that unconditional basic income is important for peoples' freedom and allows people to do what they want and freely choose their occupations.[347] The unconditionality of universal income guarantees that people are not forced to spend all their time doing the bidding of others simply to provide basic necessities for themselves and their families.[348] Basic income is also a powerful tool to promote gender equality, as it recognizes unpaid domestic work and guarantees minimum financial independence for women.[349] Immigration is fiercely incorporated in basic income debates. In Norway, for instance, many opponents of basic income fear including outsiders or immigrants in the proposed schemes.[350]

A similar argument was found in Switzerland during the previous referendum on guaranteed income as mentioned earlier. The major argument against basic income is that it will encourage people to be lazy and not seek employment, which will have a negative effect on tax revenue, and thus less funds for public expenditure and even for basic income itself.

Some experiments have been carried out on universal basic income. It has been experimented in Alaska in the United States through the Alaska Permanent Dividend Fund. Two of the most recent experiments took place in Canada and Finland, and both were canceled for different reasons. In Ontario, Canada, the Liberal government in office at the time launched a three-year pilot in three cities in July 2017: Hamilton, Thunder Bay, and Lindsay. The pilot targeted 4,000 participants from those currently unemployed with no or low income, thus making it more similar to the existing welfare system in Canada than actual universal basic income. Participants received monthly payments and it was planned to assess whether or not the scheme had provided stability and positive changes in these cities. The budget set for the pilot was CAD 150 million. Participants who were single were to receive up to CAD 16,989 while couples were to receive CAD 24,027, in addition to child or disability benefits if applicable. However, the experiment was canceled after only one year in July 2018 by the newly elected Conservative government, citing it was unsustainable, though no sufficient data was provided to support such a claim.[351] Another two-year pilot program was launched by the Finnish government in January 2017, targeting 2,000 participants. The pilot was the first government-backed universal basic income experiment in Europe. Participants received EUR 560 irrespective of their employment status and were not obliged to seek or accept employment. Furthermore, cash transfers continued with the same amount even if a participant took a new job. However, the Finnish government refused a request in April 2018 from Kela (Finland's social security agency) to extend and expand the program. Olli Kangas, one of the experts working on the pilot, told the Finnish public broadcaster YLE that "two years is too short a period to be able to draw extensive conclusions from such a big experiment. We should have had extra time and more money to achieve reliable results."[352]

The case for basic income has to be made anyway, taking into account that, in the future, it is very likely that automation and technology will eliminate many jobs. Therefore, the issue of whether basic income disincentivizes people to work is, in my opinion, irrelevant when it comes to satisfying the primary needs of individuals who do not have any alternative to not working. Of course, there are very few cases of universal incomes deterring people from seeking jobs even when these were available, but the necessity of universal income in the coming years will be such that its benefits will massively outweigh its costs.

For me, the key issue is how to finance these schemes. The Swiss referendum in 2013 on a popular initiative for a minimum guaranteed income was rejected by the Swiss population primarily on the grounds that such a system would be financed by taxes—very few justified their "no" on the bad incentives argument. And I can clearly see why. In the very moment that the government raises taxes in order to fund a universal income scheme, it becomes an inefficient intermediary between the productive economy and individuals. Instead, I advocate for a system that in the future will finance basic incomes through private sector initiatives. I will not call these necessarily "social responsibility." Instead, firms will get a license to operate by customers from the communities where they live only if they return their increasing profitability to people. Think about the extreme in which a company does not need to employ anybody because it is fully automated. All profits revert to capital, but at the same time the need to preserve a customer base requires that individuals earn money somehow. So, it will be in the economic interest of the company to finance the private sector—schools, hospitals, salaries for self-fulfilling yet not productive activities. There is no need for a government to force such transfers through taxes—it is already optimal for a company to do so.

Tax policy

In addition to financing public expenditure needed for health, education, and public services as well as infrastructure, all of which play a role in increasing social equity, tax policy is also a crucial tool for redistribution through money transfers and social welfare programs. However, as Alan Carter, the head of the International Tax Dialogue Secretariat, and Stephen Matthews, from the OECD Center for Tax Policy and Administration, suggest, the effects of taxation on income distribution must be seen as a trade-off between growth and equity. Most advanced economies have well-functioning tax regimes with average tax revenues reaching 35 percent of GDP.[353]

Taxation is effective to correct market failures that may have contributed to an unequal distribution of income. Individual and corporate income taxes are mainly driven by concerns about equity.[354] Progressive tax systems are seen to be more effective for redistribution, where high tax rates are imposed on high-income households and large corporations compared to low-income households. The distribution of after-tax income is more equal than income before taxes. This contributes to less unequal after-tax income distribution; as top earners pay higher tax rates, high-income households tend to have a slightly lower share in total income after-tax, while the share of low earners increases.[355] This is also apparent when comparing pre- to post-tax Gini coefficients in most countries, especially in Scandinavia, some Western Europe countries, and Canada.

In *Capital in the 21st Century*, Thomas Piketty goes on to suggest a global progressive tax on individual net wealth as the optimum current solution for mitigating the increasing rise in unequal income distribution. Piketty argues that income tax does not cover the rise in the value of wealth and property, which is a typical phenomenon in all economies, and falls outside the tax system. A global progressive tax on wealth will require international cooperation, and while that seems difficult, Piketty argues that it is still feasible. As the United States and the European Union account for nearly half of the world output, they can coordinate and lead the efforts for a global registry of financial assets and impose sanctions on tax havens that refuse to cooperate. Worldwide, the number of developed countries with a wealth tax has shrunk from 12 in 1994 to 4—France, Spain, Norway, and Switzerland."[356] Supporters of tax on wealth stress the fact that wealth inequality is far higher than income inequality in almost the entire world, and that the return on capital (or wealth) is usually higher than the average growth of the economy; thus, tax on wealth tries to tackle the roots of inequality rather than just mitigating its effects. The OECD has concluded that

> wealth accumulation operates in a self-reinforcing way and is likely to increase in the absence of taxation. High earners are able to save more, meaning that they are able to invest more and ultimately accumulate more wealth. Moreover, investment returns tend to increase with wealth."[357]

61. HOW CAN DEMOCRACIES EXCEL?

In 2016, only 4.5 percent of the world population lived in a fully democratic country, according to *The Economist* Intelligence Unit's Democracy Index. About 45 percent of people lived in flawed democracies, while 33 percent of people were subjects of authoritarian regimes.

Some of us have been brought up under the accepted wisdom that, starting with the ancient Greeks, democracy is the best system in the world. Indeed, among the top 10 most competitive economies in the IMD World Competitiveness Rankings of 2018, only three economies (Hong Kong, Singapore, and the United Arab Emirates) are not full democracies. Yet, the data shows that today the world is less, not more, democratic than it was 10 years ago; additionally, the countries whose competitiveness has improved the most in that period are non-democratic. And these—Singapore, the UAE—are the role models for many public sector officials.

In *Against Democracy*, Professor Jason Brennan from Georgetown University has highlighted the ignorance of voters as one of the major pitfalls of modern democracies.[358] He classifies voters into three categories. Hobbits are those who do not bother to learn about politics, and therefore vote in full ignorance. A second class are hooligans, those who follow their own party with the devotion of a sports fan, and who therefore adhere to a certain party irrespective of both past performance and future plans. Finally, a significant minority of people behave rationally, gather data, and vote with full information—the vulcans. Unfortunately, and because of the dominance of hobbits and hooligans, democratic outcomes are not only not representative of the majority's true views, but also wrong and damaging to the common good.

You can, in fact, argue that when massive demonstrations in the United States were opposing a recently elected president, people were protesting against a dictatorship of hobbits and hooligans.

Brennan convincingly argues that true democracy, where all affected by a political choice are involved in the decision-making process, does not exist anywhere. In fact, there is no reason why only citizens above 18 years of age vote. Moreover, since the outcome of the presidential election in the United States affects all citizens in the world somehow, we all should vote. In the extreme, detracting future generations from the right to vote today (by the obvious reason that they do not exist yet) is unfair when it comes to deciding about pension systems, for instance.

The Brexit vote may have been a rational decision by well-informed individuals, but it is certainly restricting the future opportunities of many UK citizens who will be unable to access a larger European market—and nobody has asked them.

There are other problems with democracy: importantly, democratic outcomes can usually be wrong outcomes. Nobody will criticize the legitimacy of the result of the Colombian referendum regarding the so-called "peace agreement" with the FARC. But the "No" vote has contradicted the original endorsement of Pope Francis himself, who under the Catholic infallibility dogma is preserved from the possibility of error.

I would also add that democracy is a very slow decision-making process. The Swiss system is best in terms of popular participation and representation, and decisions are accepted because direct democracy is implemented everywhere. However, agreements take time, sometimes too long. A good example is the CEVA (Cornavin-Eux-Vives-Annemasse) rail line in Geneva, a 16-kilometer line designed to connect downtown Geneva with France. The project was completed on December 2019. However, the original project dates to 1850, and its construction originally began in 1912! Such a massive delay has been caused by the difficulty in winning the consensus of all involved stakeholders.

Interestingly, we thought for ages that democracy is by nature redistributive, and therefore protects the lower class against the excesses of any ruling minority. However, such premise was recently proven wrong by Professor Daron Acemoglu and his coauthors, who, in a large longitudinal study of more than 100 countries,[359] showed that democracy does not seem to have any significant effect on income inequality. On the contrary, inequality tends to increase after democratization processes when the economy has already undergone significant structural transformation, when there is high land inequality, and when the gap between the middle and poor classes is small.

Therefore, we can only claim the triumph of democracy if we acknowledge the problems of any of the alternatives. Dictatorships (and epistocracies to a lesser extent) rely on a somewhat random allocation of political leaders. Countries can be lucky to end up with a *good dictator* (the UAE, Singapore, and even this is questionable) with noble intentions and selfless policies; but this is rarely the case (North Korea, Equatorial Guinea), and most times dictators are not accountable to the common good (China, Saudi Arabia).

Alternatives to democracy are in principle more corrupted systems. And this is because the supporting group of a democratic leader has to be larger by nature, and therefore more difficult to please. This group is what Bruce Bueno de Mesquita and Alastair Smith call the essentials,[360] the winning coalition. In any political system—they claim—there are three important political groups to consider: the interchangeables or nominal electorate, which includes any person with some say in choosing the leader (in a democracy, those who can vote); the influential or real electorate, who are the ones who truly select the leader (in a democracy, those who actually vote); and the essentials, whose support truly matters (in a democracy, those who vote for the winning candidate). The less democratic a system is, the smaller the latter group, and therefore the more corrupted because the system needs to ensure the financial satisfaction of only this group. Alas, the 10 most corrupted economies in the IMD World Competitiveness Ranking of 2018 are indeed democratic countries.

I personally like to live in a democratic country. Yet, I do not think that I feel academically legitimated to recommend any country, especially a new country, to follow this path. Especially when one takes into account the outcomes of some of the democratic processes of the last years.

NOTES

1 https://growthpolicy.org/inequality/economics-for-inclusive-prosperity.
2 Mazzucato (2015).
3 Bris et al. (2019).
4 www.institut-lumiere.org/musee/les-freres-lumiere-et-leurs-inventions/breve-histoire.html.
5 Pruitt (October 3, 2014).
6 www.lamartinierediderot.fr/historique.php.
7 Levine, R. and Rubinstein, Y. (2013), "Smart and illicit: who becomes an entrepreneur, and do they earn more?" National Bureau of Economic research, Cambridge MA. Working Paper 19276.
8 Jacob, L. (July 25, 2018), "3 Trends That Prevent Entrepreneurs from Accessing Capital," Kauffman Foundation.
9 Bell, A., Chetty, R., Jaravel, X., Pektova, N., and Van Reenen, J. (2017), "Who Becomes an Inventor in America? The Importance of Exposure to Innovation," The Equality of Opportunity Project.
10 https://voxeu.org/article/how-exposure-innovation-influences-who-becomes-inventor.
11 Gladwell (2008).
12 Allen (2018).
13 Princeton University (2019).
14 Google Tech Talk (2009).
15 Nathani (2018).
16 Cox (2017); Isaacson (2013).
17 Vargas (2010).
18 A.A.K. (2013); Wallen (2018a).
19 Nathani (2018).
20 Roberts and Eesley (2009).
21 Armstrong (2018).
22 Satell (2016).
23 Lutchen (2018).
24 Jahanian (2018).
25 Cohen (2018).

26 Bartlett (2018).
27 Frei (2019).
28 MIT (2019).
29 Princeton University (2019).
30 Cornell Tech (2019).
31 Y Combinator (2019).
32 Stanford School (2019).
33 Leibovitz (2015).
34 Dodds (2018).
35 Israel Ministry of Foreign Affairs (2019).
36 Paz-Frankel (2017).
37 Levy (2018).
38 Israel Ministry of Foreign Affairs (2019).
39 Schwab (2018).
40 Coy (2018).
41 Yin (2016).
42 As cited by Paz-Frankel (2016).
43 Israeli Foreign Trade Administration at the Ministry of Economy (2019).
44 Cai (2018).
45 Deloitte Israel (2019).
46 Israeli Foreign Trade Administration at the Ministry of Economy (2019).
47 Yin (2017).
48 Yin (2017).
49 OECD (2010a).
50 Yin (2017).
51 Yin (2017).
52 Mitchell (2016).
53 Yin (2016).
54 Yin (2016).
55 Study in Israel (2019).
56 Kite-Powell (2018).
57 Deloitte Israel (2019).
58 Yin (2016).
59 Yin (2016).
60 Yin (2017).
61 Yin (2017).
62 Yin (2016).
63 Deloitte Israel (2019).
64 OECD (2014).
65 Yin (2016).
66 Yin (2016).
67 Yin (2016).
68 Yissum (2019).
69 Klein Leichman (2018).
70 Klein Leichman (2018).
71 Yin (2016).
72 Solomon (2018).
73 Solomon (2016).
74 Solomon (2017).
75 Yin (2017).
76 Code Jam—Google's Coding Competitions (2018).
77 ACM ICPC World Finals (2018).
78 Szabo (2013).
79 Pavlova (2018).
80 Rogowski (2013).
81 Sheremeta (2015).
82 Jezard (2017).

83 Flinders (2014).
84 Jezard (2017).
85 Rogowski (2013).
86 Aridi (2017).
87 Sung Kim (2018).
88 Aridi (2017).
89 Sung Kim (2018).
90 Tkach (2018).
91 Borys (2018).
92 Satell (2014).
93 Adams (2018).
94 Wallen (2018b).
95 AVentures Capital (2018).
96 The World Bank Group (2017).
97 Wallen (2018).
98 Monobank.biz (2018).
99 Wallen (2018a).
100 Wallen (2018a).
101 Wallen (2018a).
102 Source: Dubilet's Facebook page: https://m.facebook.com/dubilet/posts/picfp.762053551/
?photo_id=10155270527008552&mds=%2Fphotos%2Fviewer%2F%3Fphotoset_token%3D
picfp.762053551%26photo%3D10155270527008552%26profileid%3D762053551%26source
%3D69%26refid%3D17%26cached_data%3Dfalse%26ftid&mdf=1,
103 Wallen (2018a).
104 Monobank (2018).
105 Wallen (2018b).
106 Kinstler (2018).
107 Carnes (2017).
108 http://startups.hu/.
109 Szedlacsek (2018).
110 Lajtai-Szabó (2019).
111 Kennedy (2019).
112 Coleman (2014).
113 Watts (2019).
114 Coleman (2014).
115 Coleman (2014).
116 Coleman (2019).
117 Coleman (2014).
118 OECD/EU (2017).
119 Coleman (2014).
120 CIA (2019), Middle East: Oman—The World Factbook—Central Intelligence Agency, Cia
.gov.
121 https://londonlovesbusiness.com/qa-taavet-hinrikus-co-founder-of-transferwise-which-has
-landed-1-3-million-funding/.
122 https://transferwise.com/pricing/gbp-to-eur.
123 https://www.businessinsider.com/transferwise-ad-banned-by-asa-2016-5?r=UK&IR=T.
124 https://www.forbes.com/sites/jeffkauflin/2018/09/09/heres-how-transferwise-has-nearly
-quadrupled-revenue-in-two-years-reaching-151-million/#22ff7b32c69d.
125 https://angel.co/transferwise.
126 Baset, S.A. and Schulzrinne, H., "An Analysis of the Skype Peer-to-Peer Internet Telephony
Protocol," https://arxiv.org/pdf/cs/0412017v1.pdf.
127 A brief history of Skype, www.itbusiness.ca/blog/a-brief-history-of-skype/20750.
128 www.dsp.co.uk/history-of-skype.
129 https://expandedramblings.com/index.php/skype-statistics/.
130 https://weareflint.co.uk/main-findings-social-media-demographics-uk-usa-2018.
131 https://nortal.com/us/about-us/.

132 www.neste.com/neste-and-nortal-develop-demo-cutting-edge-sustainability-portal-raw
-material-suppliers.
133 https://nortal.com/us/blog/nigeria_missing_billions/.
134 GeekWire,   www.geekwire.com/2018/nortal-acquire-cloud-modernization-startup-dev9-
will-expand-seattle-area-footprint/.
135 Wired, www.wired.co.uk/article/estonia-e-resident.
136 Riigikogu.ee (2018).
137 Vitt et al. (2006).
138 E-Estonia.com (2018a).
139 Ibid.
140 ISAMAA.ee (2018).
141 EKRE.ee (2018).
142 Bris, A. and Zargari, M. (2020), When Do CEOs Matter? A Global Study on the Value of
Leadership, IMD Working Paper.
143 Ibsen (2014).
144 Ibid.
145 www.mckinsey.com/featured-insights/gender-equality/women-in-the-workplace-2018.
146 https://thriveglobal.com/stories/sheryl-sandberg-we-need-to-resist-the-tyranny-of-low
-expectations/, last accessed December 9, 2019.
147 www.wusa9.com/article/news/nation-world/us-womens-team-players-have-options-after
-setback-in-court/507-73948cca-c694-4b3b-9366-632f07e285c7#:~:text=King%2C%20wh
o%20was%20calling%20for,cherry%20on%20top%2C%20too.%E2%80%9D,   last   accessed
December 9, 2019.
148 Marketing, "Cause" (2016), Budweiser #GiveADamn Campaign: "Helen Mirren" Ad (Super
Bowl, 2016), YouTube.
149 Gillette (2019), "We Believe: The Best Men Can Be" | Gillette (Short Film), YouTube.
150 dovemencareuk (2018), "Dear Future Dads," YouTube.
151 Anon., "Background of the Sustainable Development Goals," UNDP.
152 Ibid.
153 Anon., "United Nations Millennium Development Goals," United Nations.
154 Ford, L. (2015), "Sustainable Development Goals: All You Need to Know," *The Guardian*.
155 Goldberg, M.L. (2018), Podcast: "How Much Progress Are We Making Towards the
Sustainable Development Goals?" UN Dispatch.
156 Ford, L. (2015), "Sustainable Development Goals: All You Need to Know," *The Guardian*.
157 Anon.,   "About   the   Sustainable   Development   Goals—United   Nations   Sustainable
Development," United Nations.
158 Anon. (2017), "Making Global Goals Local Business," Publication Making Global Goals
Local Business, United Nations Global Compact.
159 Garson, "Alone We Can Do So Little. Together We Can Do So Much," Quote Investigator.
160 Lieberman, A. (2018), "SDGs Show Slow Progress, Not on Track to Reach 2030 Targets," UN
reports, Safety & Security Manager | Devex.
161 Anon., "Overview—SDG Indicators," United Nations.
162 Anon., "The Sustainable Development Goals Report 2018," | Multimedia Library—United
Nations Department of Economic and Social Affairs, United Nations.
163 Goldberg, M.L. (2018), Podcast: "How Much Progress Are We Making Towards the
Sustainable Development Goals?" UN Dispatch.
164 Ibid.
165 Ibid.
166 Ibid.
167 Anon., "The Sustainable Development Goals Report" 2018 | Multimedia Library—United
Nations Department of Economic and Social Affairs, United Nations.
168 Ibid.
169 Goldberg, M.L. (2018), Podcast: "How Much Progress Are We Making Towards the
Sustainable Development Goals?" UN Dispatch.
170 Anon. (2018), "Secretary-General's Video Message: An Alert For The World," Secretary-
General, United Nations.

171 Anon., "About the Sustainable Development Goals—United Nations Sustainable Development," United Nations.

172 Anon., "Vision statement," António Guterres.

173 Anon., "World Competitiveness Center Mission—IMD Executive Education," IMD Business School, International Institute for Management Development.

174 Anon., "Defining Sustainable Competitiveness, Global Competitiveness Index 2017–2018."

175 Andreoni, V. and Miola, A. (2016), "Competitiveness and Sustainable Development Goals," Rep. Competitiveness and Sustainable Development Goals, European Union.

176 Anon., "Defining Sustainable Competitiveness, Global Competitiveness Index 2017–2018."

177 Andreoni, V. and Miola, A. (2016), "Competitiveness and Sustainable Development Goals," Rep. Competitiveness and Sustainable Development Goals, European Union.

178 Ibid.

179 Anon. (2015), "All Grown Up? The UN Global Compact at 15," Safety & Security Manager | Devex.

180 Anon. (2017), "Making Global Goals Local Business," Publication Making Global Goals Local Business, United Nations Global Compact.

181 Ibid.

182 Anon. (2018), "Business Action for Sustainable and Resilient Societies," Publication Business Action for Sustainable and Resilient Societies, International Chamber of Commerce.

183 Anon., "The Sustainable Development Goals Report 2018," | Multimedia Library—United Nations Department of Economic and Social Affairs, United Nations.

184 Ibid.

185 Ibid.

186 Anon., George Harrison (1987), "Got My Mind Set on You," Genius Media Group Inc.

187 Anon. (2018), "Business Action for Sustainable and Resilient Societies," Publication Business Action for Sustainable and Resilient Societies, International Chamber of Commerce.

188 Ibid.

189 Ibid.

190 Anon., "Accelerating Progress of the UN SDGs," Syngenta.

191 Anon., "Sustainability," siemens.com.

192 Anon. (2018), "Business Action for Sustainable and Resilient Societies," Publication Business Action for Sustainable and Resilient Societies, International Chamber of Commerce.

193 Ibid.

194 Anon., "The Sustainable Development Goals," Telefónica.

195 Anheuser-Busch and Enel Green Power (2017), "Anheuser-Busch and Enel Green Power Announce Renewable Energy Partnership," PR Newswire.

196 Anon. (2017), "2016 Better World Report," AB InBev.

197 Ibid.

198 Anon., "Member," TogetherForSaferRoads.

199 Anon., "Smart Drinking Goals, Who We Are," AB InBev.

200 Anon. (2017), "2016 Better World Report," AB InBev.

201 Anon., "How We Are Supporting the UN Global Goals, Who We Are," AB InBev.

202 Anon., "Water Charity for Safe Water & Sanitation," Water.org.

203 Anon., "Water," Stella Artois.

204 Anon., "Smart Agriculture," Who We Are, AB InBev.

205 Parley (2017), "Corona x Parley: 100 Islands Protected by 2020."

206 Anon. (2017), "2016 Better World Report," AB InBev.

207 Anon., "Sustainability," Who We Are | AB InBev.

208 Ibid.

209 Anon., "How We Are Supporting the UN Global Goals," Who We Are, AB InBev.

210 Anon. (2018), "Business Action for Sustainable and Resilient Societies," Publication Business Action for Sustainable and Resilient Societies, International Chamber of Commerce.

211 Anon., "UN Sustainable Development Goals," Unilever global company website.

212 Ibid.

213 Ibid.

214 Ibid.

215 Anon. (2018), "Business Action for Sustainable and Resilient Societies," Publication Business Action for Sustainable and Resilient Societies, International Chamber of Commerce.

216 Anon., "UN Sustainable Development Goals," Unilever global company website.

217 Ibid.

218 Anon. (2017), "Making Global Goals Local Business," Publication Making Global Goals Local Business, United Nations Global Compact.

219 Anon., "UN Sustainable Development Goals," Unilever global company website.

220 Anon. (2018), "Business Action for Sustainable and Resilient Societies," Publication Business Action for Sustainable and Resilient Societies, International Chamber of Commerce.

221 World Health Organization, figure from 2016. It is worth noting that in 2014, Peru had a seat belt compliance of 58.2 percent.

222 Source: World Health Organization and IMD World Competitiveness Center.

223 On August 13, 1959, the first series of automobiles fitted with three-point seat belts were made at a Volvo factory in Sweden. It was a revolutionary day for the safety of millions of people around the world thanks to the invention of an engineer named Nils Bohlin. Since then, this practical invention has saved more than 1 million lives worldwide. It's such a timeless and effective way to prevent fatal injuries among the occupants of a vehicle that, to this day, it's included in virtually every car that makes its way onto the streets and roads of every country in the world. According to World Health Organization (WHO) statistics, wearing a seat belt will reduce the risk of fatality among front-seat passengers by 40–50 percent in the event of a car accident.

224 MTC (2018), "Vision of Development of the Road Infrastructure," Edmer Trujillo Mori.

225 World Bank (2017), "The High Toll of Traffic Injuries: Unacceptable and Preventable."

226 Principles defended by the CNSC—official website.

227 National Highway Traffic Safety Administration (2010), "Strategies to Increase Seat Belt Use: An Analysis of Levels of Fines and the Type of Law," James L. Nichols, A. Scott Tippetts, James C. Fell, Amy Auld-Owens, Connie H. Wiliszowski, Philip W. Haseltine, and Angela Eichelberger.

228 MTC – National Transit Regulations Supreme Decree No. 033-2001-MTC.

229 Ibid.

230 Ibid.

231 Government of Peru (2018), "Driver's License System for Points," official website.

232 MTC—National Traffic Regulations—Supreme Decree No. 003-2014-MTC.

233 With the exception of Peru, the percentages were taken from the last study carried out by the WHO in 2014, which is the latest worldwide seat belt rate conducted by this organization. Sanctions are current as of 2018. Price of fines in their national currency: Peru S 332; Argentina $ 1.300; Brazil R 195; Chile $ 69.000; Colombia $ 300.000; Paraguay PYG 255.00; Uruguay $1.625; Australia AUD 550; Belgium €50; Canada CAD200; Germany € 30; Italy €81; Norway K1500; Russia ₽1000; Switzerland CHF60; UK £500.

234 The contrast with Chile is striking here. The Chilean police ("Carabineros") is considered one of the most reliable institutions in the country.

235 There are also plenty of videos taken by Peruvian citizens and made public that show a high level of corruptibility on the part of the traffic police at the time of carrying out the traffic infractions:

- Policewoman bribe: https://www.youtube.com/watch?v=89HY7Cgf0pY.
- Policewoman is taped when she asked a driver for a bribe for drunk driving: https://www.youtube.com/watch?v=LBAXqd3qE3s.
- Policeman asking a taxi driver for a bribe to delete ballots: https://www.youtube.com/watch?v=19wo1AOwx4c.
- Police recorded asking for a bribe: https://www.youtube.com/watch?v=OHJoJP_lpgg.
- Police receiving a bribe: https://www.youtube.com/watch?v=uwEOHSZp4JU.
- Police collect bribe from Spanish tourist: https://www.youtube.com/watch?v=DEAJcj5Voj4.

236 Josefina Miró Quesada (2018), *El Comercio* newspaper.

237 Ana Bazo Reisman (2018), RPP News.

238 Dimitrova-Grajzl et al. (2012).

239 *South China Morning Post* (2018), "Two quick ways to fix Hong Kong's housing market failure." [online] Available at: www.scmp.com/comment/insight-opinion/hong-kong/article/2163297/free-market-failure-hongkongers-need-government.

240 Ibid.

241 *Asia Sentinel* (2017), "China's Greatest Market Failure and Greatest Healthcare Opportunity," www.asiasentinel.com/society/china-alzheimers-disease-failure-opportunity/.

242 Ibid.
243 Aidt, T.S. (2003), "Economic Analysis of Corruption: A Survey," *The Economic Journal* 113 (491): F632–F652.
244 Acemoglu and Verdier (2000).
245 Ibid.
246 Ibid.
247 Ibid.
248 Rudolfová, J.V.M., "Government Failure and Corruption."
249 *Investment Week* (2015), "Lessons from an A-Share Bubble," www.investmentweek.co.uk/investment-week/analysis/2427415/is-china-downturn-really-a-social-crisis-caused-by-naive-investors.
250 Ibid.
251 Ibid.
252 East Asia Forum, (2014), "The Reign or Reining in of Chinese Monopolies," www.eastasiaforum.org/2014/12/16/the-reign-or-reining-in-of-chinese-monopolies/.
253 Ibid.
254 Burke, J. (2015), "Half of India's Rivers Are Polluted, Says Government Report," *The Guardian*. www.theguardian.com/world/2015/apr/07/half-india-rivers-polluted-new-government-report.
255 Ibid.
256 Ibid.
257 Dasgupta, N. and Bhardwaj, M. (2019), "Deadly Political Calculations: Why India Isn't Fixing Its Toxic," Reuters, www.reuters.com/article/us-india-pollution-politics-insight/deadly-political-calculations-why-india-isnt-fixing-its-toxic-smog-problem-idUSKCN1NB215.
258 Ibid.
259 Ibid.
260 USAID.gov. (2019), "Agriculture and Food Security," www.usaid.gov/nepal/agriculture-and-food-security.
261 Ibid.
262 Ibid.
263 Ibid.
264 Public Radio International (2019), "Mexico's gas crisis, explained," www.pri.org/stories/2019-01-21/mexicos-gas-crisis-explained.
265 Ibid.
266 OilPrice.com (2019), "Mexico's Oil Crisis: Pirates, Cartels, and Corruption," https://oilprice.com/Energy/Energy-General/Mexicos-Oil-Crisis-Pirates-Cartels-And-Corruption.html.
267 Ibid.
268 Forbes.com. (2019), "Observing Effective Controls in Mexico's Rapidly Transforming Energy Sector," www.forbes.com/sites/riskmap/2018/06/11/risk-and-reform-observing-effective-controls-in-mexicos-rapidly-transforming-energy-sector/#1d412e297476.
269 Reuters.com (2019), "Special Report: As Mexico Oil Sector Sputters, Crime and Violence...." www.reuters.com/article/us-mexico-oil-violence-specialreport/special-report-as-mexico-oil-sector-sputters-crime-and-violence-rattle-industry-towns-idUSKBN1JO1U7.
270 Ibid.
271 Bliss, B. (2019), "Mexico Corruption Report," Business Anti-Corruption Portal, www.business-anti-corruption.com/country-profiles/mexico/.
272 www.dw.com (2019), "New Mexican President Lopez Obrador Promises Oil Sector Clean-Up," www.dw.com/en/new-mexican-president-lopez-obrador-promises-oil-sector-clean-up/a-44513214.
273 Bourne, R. "How 'Market Failure' Arguments Lead to Misguided Policy."
274 Vogel, S.K. (2018), *Freer Markets, More Rules: Regulatory Reform in Advanced Industrial Countries*. Cornell University Press.
275 Frieden, J.A. (2018), *Modern Political Economy and Latin America: Theory and Policy*, Routledge.
276 Buckley, P.J. (2018), "Internalisation Theory and Outward Direct Investment by Emerging Market Multinationals," *Management International Review* 58(2): 195–224.

277 Li, J., Xia, J., and Zajac, E.J. (2018), "On the Duality of Political and Economic Stakeholder Influence on Firm Innovation Performance: Theory and Evidence from Chinese Firms," *Strategic Management Journal* 39(1): 193–216.
278 Grubb, M. and Newbery, D. (2018), "UK Electricity Market Reform and the Energy Transition: Emerging Lessons," *The Energy Journal* 39(6).
279 Stiglitz, J. (2018), Evaluation in a World of Complexity and Information Failures. In *Evaluation and Poverty Reduction* (pp. 39–48). Routledge.
280 Anon. (1980), Dolly Parton, "9 to 5," Genius Media Group Inc.
281 Anon. (2014), Denise Morrison, "Integrating Work and Life, Metadata Librarian, Blizzard Entertainment Vault Team."
282 Anon. (2017), "News Release," Bureau of Labor Statistics, U.S. Department of Labor.
283 Anon. (2018), "Employee Tenure Summary," U.S. Bureau of Labor Statistics.
284 Benko et al. (2011).
285 Ibid.
286 Ibid.
287 Keynes (2009).
288 Fox, K. and O'Connor, J. (2015), "Five Ways Work Will Change in the Future," *The Guardian*.
289 Ibid.
290 Anon. (2018), "Bullshit Jobs and the Yoke of Managerial Feudalism," *The Economist*.
291 Ibid.
292 Anon. (2013), "On the Phenomenon of Bullshit Jobs: A Work Rant," *STRIKE!* magazine.
293 Ibid.
294 Rogers (2011).
295 Anon. "Adapt or Die Whitepaper," ForbesBooks.
296 Anon. Hyderabad Public School, Begumpet.
297 Hess, A. (2018), "How One High School Produced the CEOs of Microsoft, Adobe and Mastercard," CNBC.
298 Gardner and Rose (2009).
299 Davis, S. (2007), "Drama, Engagement, and Creativity."
300 Robinson (2011).
301 Ibid.
302 Ibid.
303 Smolucha and Smolucha (1986).
304 Ibid.
305 Ibid.
306 Robinson (2011).
307 Robinson, K. (2006), "Do Schools Kill Creativity?" TED talk.
308 Harasim (2012).
309 Hughes (1973).
310 Robinson (2011).
311 Bransford et al. (2004).
312 Caballero (2016).
313 Fuentes-Nieva and Galasso (2014).
314 Paukert (2007); Ahluwalia (1976a and 1976b); Saith (1983); Papenek and Kyn (1986); Campano and Salvatore (1988); Ram (1988); Bourguignon and Morrison (1990).
315 Deininger and Squire (1996 and 1998); Higgins and Williamson (1999); Savvidesa and Stengos (2000); and Barro (2000).
316 https://ara.reuters.com/article/topNews/idARL2N0M80YY20140311, last accessed December 2, 2019.
317 www.worldpoliticsreview.com/trend-lines/22154/how-chile-s-bachelet-tried-to-tackle-in equality-and-why-it-s-still-a-problem, last accessed December 3, 2020.
318 fSeiler, B. and Raderstorf, B., "Michelle Bachelet's Underappreciated Legacy in Chile," March 2018, *Americas Quarterly*, www.americasquarterly.org/article/michelle-bachelets-underap preciated-legacy-in-chile/, last accessed December 3, 2020.
319 Reuters, November 24, 2013.
320 Reuters, November 24, 2013.

321 BBC, June 5, 2016.

322 Ibid.

323 www.thelocal.ch/20180606/swiss-town-set-for-universal-basic-income-experiment-rheinau, last accessed December 5, 2020.

324 https://lenews.ch/2018/01/26/income-inequality-in-switzerland-remains-stable-after-redistribution/, last accessed December 4, 2020.

325 Zhu, (2012).

326 World Bank (2018b).

327 And under the lower-middle income class poverty line of USD 3.2 a day, poverty rate fell from 90.1 percent in 1990 to 7 percent in 2015, and under the upper-middle income class poverty line of USD 5.5 a day, it fell from 98.3 percent in 1990 to 27.2 percent in 2015.

328 World Bank (2018b).

329 *Financial Times*, January 14, 2016.

330 Bloomberg, October 23, 2018.

331 Kanbur et al. (2017).

332 SWIID (2018); Alvaredo et al. (2018).

333 Jain-Chandra (2018).

334 Easterly (2007); Berg and Ostry (2011); Piketty (2014); Ostry et al. (2014); Dabla-Norris et al. (2015).

335 Galor and Zeira (1993); Banerjee and Newman (1993).

336 Alesina and Rodrik (1994); Alesina and Perotti (1996); Perotti (1996); and Benabou (2000).

337 When analyzing income inequality in Egypt, Verme et al. (2014) and Bibi and Nabli (2010) do not question the reliability of the income inequality measurements, and suggest that the gap between conventional inequality measurement (Gini coefficient) and the publicly perceived rise in inequality is driven by other social factors related to the perception of inequality rather than the actual increase in the disparity of income. These astonishing figures have been termed the "Arab inequality puzzle" (Ianchovichina et al., 2015).

338 Alvaredo and Piketty (2014) and Van Der Weide et al. (2017). Hlasny and Verme (2016) found that the Gini coefficient of Egypt estimated by household surveys is significantly and consistently underestimated due to unit non-responses after correcting for top incomes biases. In line with that, Van Der Weide et al. (2017) suggest that conventional measurements of income inequality that rely only on household surveys are inconsistent as they underestimate the level of inequality within the country. They construct an adjusted Gini coefficient for urban Egypt after correcting for the missing upper tail data, using available data on real estate prices to estimate the upper tail of the income distribution and combine it with the household survey to estimate the bottom shares of income distribution. Their adjusted Gini index for urban Egypt increases to 52 compared to 39 as per the conventional measurement.

339 Credit Suisse (2014).

340 Based on this data, Osama (2018: 23) calculated the average annual growth in the wealth of the top 1 percent in Egypt to be 7 percent and for the top income decile to be 5 percent between 2000 and 2014, at a time when the average annual growth rate of GDP per capita was only 2 percent.

341 http://wir2018.wid.world, last accessed November 23, 2019.

342 Alvaredo et al. (2018).

343 Assouad et al. (2018) combined recently available tax data, with the standard used household surveys in addition to fiscal data and national accounts to provide new estimates for the distribution of income in the region. They estimated that the income share of the top 10 percent earners as a percentage of the total pre-tax national income in the Middle East was above 60 percent in 2016, with relatively stable levels of inequality since 1980. Moreover, the WID shows the income share of the top 1 percent to slightly decline in the last three and half decades, from nearly 31 percent in 1980 to above 26 percent in 2015, yet it was still the second highest income share below only Latin America. Alvaredo et al. (2018) suggest that the severity of the income and wealth gap in the Middle East threatens the presence of a broad "middle class." These fears are quite legitimate as the WID reports that the middle 40 percent earners in the Middle East receive only 29.5 percent of the total national income, compared to 43 percent in Europe, 33.4 percent in Sub-Saharan Africa, and 32.4 percent in Latin America. Similarly, a drastic trend appears in the share of the bottom 50 percent earners, who received

only 9 percent of the total national income of the region, way below the 19.2 percent recorded in Europe, and 12.2 percent in Sub-Saharan Africa and Latin America. Overall, the data shows that from 1990 to 2016, the top 10 percent earners in the Middle East gained more than 60 percent of the region's income on average, whereas the bottom 50 percent were left with less than 10 percent of the regional income.

344 Alvaredo et al. (2018).
345 Klein (2016).
346 Chohan (2017).
347 Widerquist (2013) and Van Parijs (2000).
348 Sheahen (2012).
349 McKay (2001).
350 Bay and Pedersen (2006).
351 Kassam (2017, 2018).
352 Henley (2018).
353 Carter and Matthews (2012).
354 Burman (2013: 563).
355 Sammartino (2017).
356 Farrell (2018).
357 OECD (2018).
358 Brennan (2016).
359 Acemoglu et al. (2015)
360 Bueno de Mesquita and Smith (2012)

REFERENCES

Acemoglu, Daron, and James A. Robinson (2012), *Why Nations Fail: The Origins of Power, Prosperity, and Poverty* (New York: Crown Publishing Group).

Acemoglu, Daron, and Thierry Verdier, (2000), "The Choice between Market Failures and Corruption," *American Economic Review* 90(1): 194–211.

Acemoglu Daron, Suresh Naidu, Pascual Restrepo, and James A. Robinson (2015), Chapter 21 – Democracy, Redistribution and Inequality, in *Handbook of Income Distribution* vol. 2, pp 1885–1966.

Adams, Susan (2018), "The Exclusive Inside Story of Ring: From 'Shark Tank' Reject to Amazon's Latest Acquisition," Forbes.com.

Ahluwalia, Montek S. (1976a), "Income Distribution and Development: Some Stylized Facts," *American Economic Review* 66(2): 128–135.

Ahluwalia, Montek S. (1976b), "Inequality, Poverty and Development," *Journal of Development Economics* 3(3): 307–342.

Alesina, Alberto, and Dani Rodrik (1994), "Distributive politics and economic growth," *Quarterly Journal of Economics*, 109(2): 465–490.

Alesina, Alberto, and Roberto Perotti (1996)," Income Distribution, Political Instability, and Investment," *European Economic Review* 40(6): 1203–1228.

Allen, Frederick E. (2018), "The World's Most Innovative Leaders," Forbes.com.

Alvaredo, Facundo, and Thomas Piketty (2014), "Measuring Top Incomes and Inequality in the Middle East: Data Limitations and Illustration with the Case of Egypt," Economic Research Forum.

Alvaredo, Facundo., Chancel Lucas, Thomas Piketty, Emmanuel Saez, and Gabriel Zucman, (2018), "World Inequality Database," https://wid.world/.

Aridi, Anwar (2017), *Can Ukraine Transform Itself into An Innovation-Driven Economy?" Private Sector Development*, World Bank.

Armstrong, Paul (2018), "These Are The UK's Top University Breakthroughs," Forbes.com.

Association for Computing Machinery (2018), "Moscow State University Team Wins World Finals of ACM International Collegiate Programming Contest," https://www.acm.org/media -center/2018/april/icpc-2018.

Assouad, Lydia, Lucas Chancel, and Marc Morgan (2018), "Extreme Inequality: Evidence from Brazil, India, the Middle East, and South Africa," in AEA Papers and Proceedings, vol. 108, 119–23.

AVentures Capital (2018), "Ukrainian Startup Investment Grew Threefold in 2017," *The European Trade Association for Business Angels, Seed Funds and Early Stage Market Players*.

Banerjee, Abhijit V., and Andrew F. Newman (1993), "Occupational Choice and the Process of Development," *Journal of Political Economy* 101(2): 274–298.

Barro, Robert J. (2000), "Inequality and Growth in a Panel of Countries," *Journal of Economic Growth* 5(1): 5–32.

Bartlett, Natalie (2018), "Want to Find the Next Big Startup? Try These Top University Courses," Forbes.com.

BBC (2016), "Switzerland's Voters Reject Basic Income Plan," https://www.bbc.com/news/world -europe-36454060.

Benabou, Roland (2000), "Unequal Societies: Income Distribution and the Social Contract," *American Economic Review*, 90(1): 96–129.

Benko, Cathy, Molly Anderson, and Susanne Vickberg (2011), The Corporate Lattice: Achieving High Performance in the Changing World (Boston: Deloitte).

Berg, Andrew G., and Jonathan D. Ostry (2011), *Inequality and Unsustainable Growth: Two Sides of the Same Coin?* (International Monetary Fund).

Bibi, Sami, and Mustapha Nabli (2010), "Equity and Inequality in the Arab Region," in Economic Research Forum.

Borys, Christian (2018), "Ukraine's economic secret: 'Engineering is in our DNA," *BBC News*.

Bourguignon, Francois, and Christian Morrison (1990), "Income Distribution, Development and Foreign Trade: Across Sectional Analysis," *European Economic Review* 34(6): 1113–1132.

Bransford, John D. et al. (2004), *How People Learn: Brain, Mind, Experience, and School* (Washington, DC: National Academy Press).

Brennan, Jason (2016), *Against Democracy* (New Jersey: Princeton University Press, 304 pp).

Bris, A, Robby Mol, and Tony Felton (2019), *Flex or Fail: The Future of Jobs and Pay* (Amsterdam).

Bueno de Mesquita, Bruce, and Alastair Smith (2012), *The Dictator's Handbook: Why Bad Behavior is Almost Always Good Politics, Public Affairs*, 352 pp.

Burman, Leonard E. (2013), "Taxes and Inequality," *Tax Law Review* 66(4): 563–592.

Caballero, José (2016), Competitiveness and Social Disparitiesö A Contribution Toward the Debate," IMD World Competitiveness Center.

Cai, Edmund (2018), "Israeli Unicorns: These 18 Companies Are Valued At Over $1B," *Israeli Innovation News*.

Campano, Fred, and Dominick Salvatore (1988), "Economic Development, Income Inequality and Kuznets' U-shaped Hypothesis," *Journal of Policy Modeling* 10(2): 265–280.

Carnes Ben (2017), "Ukraine Is Silently Leading A Digital Currency Revolution," Forbes.com.

Carter, Alan, and Stephen Matthews (2012), "How Tax Can Reduce Inequality," *OECD Observer*, http://oecdobserver.org/news/fullstory.php/aid/3782/How:tax_can_reduce_inequality.html.

Central Intelligence Agency (2018), :World Factbook—Estonia," https://www.cia.gov/library/pu blications/the-world-factbook/geos/en.html (Accessed December 16, 2018).

Chohan, Usman W. (2017), "Universal Basic Income: A Review," *SSRN Electronic Journal*, https:// ssrn.com/abstract=3013634.

Cohen, Pinchas (2018), "How Universities Drive Innovation in Aging," Forbes.com.

Coleman, Alison (2014), "How Prezi Helped Turn Budapest Into Europe's Newest Startup Hub," Forbes.com.

Coleman, Alison (2019), "Why Budapest Is The 'Go To' City For Entrepreneurs," Forbes.com.

"Collaborative Environments for Innovation: Successful Experiences from Switzerland and India," (n.d.), International Journal of Production Research 47(17).

Commonwealth of Australia (2007), Bhutanese Community Profile, https://www.dss.gov.au/si tes/default/files/documents/11_2013/community-profile-bhutan.pdf (Accessed August 23, 2017).

Cornell Tech (2019), "Startup Studio."

Cox, Josie (2017), "Mark Zuckerberg Has Finally Got a Degree from Harvard 12 Years after Dropping Out," *The Independent*.

Coy, Peter (2018), "The Bloomberg Innovation Index," Bloomberg.com.

Dabla-Norris, Era, Kalpana Kochhar, Nujin Suphaphiphat, Frantisek Ricka, and Evridiki Tsounta (2015), *Causes and Consequences of Income Inequality: A Global Perspective* (International Monetary Fund).

Deaton, Angus (2015), *The Great Escape: Health, Wealth, and the Origins of Inequality* (New Jersey: Princeton University Press, 376 pp).

Deininger, Klaus, and Lyn Squire (1998), "New Ways of Looking at Old Issues: Inequality and Growth," *Journal of Development Economics* 57(2): 259–287.

Deloitte (2019), "The Israeli Technological Eco-system."

Department Working Papers, No. 838, http://dx.doi.org/10.1787/5kgj3l0wr4q6-en.

Dimitrova-Grajzl, V., P. Grajzl, and A.J. Guse, (2012), "Trust, Perceptions of Corruption, and Demand for Regulation: Evidence from Post-Socialist Countries," *The Journal of Socio-Economics* 41(3): 292–303.

Dodds, Laurence (2018), "Wework Valued at $42 Billion after Massive New Cash Injection from Softbank," *The Telegraph*.

Easterly, W. (2007), "Inequality Does Cause Underdevelopment: Insights from A New Instrument," *Journal of Development Economics* 84(2): 755–776.

Education, C.s. (2015), *l'éducation en Suisse: Rapport 2014*.

E-Estonia.com (2018a), "E-Governance," https://e-estonia.com/solutions/e-governance/i-voting/ (Accessed Dec. 16, 2018).

E-Estonia.com, (2018b), "IT Sector Competences," https://e-estonia.com/it-sector/ (Accessed Dec. 16, 2018).

EKRE.ee, (2018), "Chairman of the Estonian Conservative People's Party," https://www.ekre.ee/ esimees/ (Accessed Dec. 16, 2018).

"Electoral Service Affairs Commission: Guideline of Hong Kong election," (n.d.), at https://www .eac.gov.hk.

Farrell, Sean (2018), "Use Inheritance Tax to Tackle Inequality of Wealth, Says OECD," *The Guardian*, https://www.theguardian.com/inequality/2018/apr/12/use-inheritance-tax-to-t ackle-inequality-of-wealth-says-oecd.

Flinders, Karl (2014), "What Can Poland's STEM Culture Teach the UK?" Computerweekly.com.

Forbes. Ukraine (2016), *FinHub Global: как превратить идеи в работающий бизнес и почему финансовые инновации не обходятся без украинских специалистов (FinHub Global: how to transform ideas into working business and why financial innovations need Ukrainian experts.)*, Forbes.net.ua.

Galor, Oded, and Joseph Zeira (1993), "Income Distribution and Macroeconomics," *Review of Economic Studies* 60(1): 35–52.

Gardner, John W, and Pat Rose (2009), "Much Education Today Is Monumentally Ineffective. All Too Often We Are Giving Young People Cut Flowers When We Should Be Teaching Them to Grow Their Own Plants," *Journal of Advertising Education* 13(2).

Gladwell, Malcolm (2008), *Outliers: The Story of Success* (New York: Hachette Audio).

Google (2018), *Google's Coding Competitions – Code Jam, Hash Code and Kick Start*.

Harasim, Linda M. (2012), *Learning Theory and Online Technology* (New York: Routledge).

Henley, Jon (2018), "Finland to End Basic Income Trial after Two Years," *The Guardian*, https://ww w.theguardian.com/world/2018/apr/23/finland-to-end-basic-income-trial-after-two-years.

Higgins, Matthew, and Jeffrey G. Williamson (1999), "Explaining Inequality the World Round: Cohort Size, Kuznets Curves, and Openness," National Bureau of Economic Research Working Paper No.7224.

Hughes, Robert (1973), Art: "Pablo Picasso: The Painter as Proteus," *Time*.

Huguenin, Jean-Marc (2015), "Determinants of School Efficiency: The Case of Primary Schools in the State of Geneva, Switzerland," *International Journal of Educational Management* 29(5): 539–562.

Ibsen, Henrik (2014), *A Doll House, CreateSpace*, 68 pages.

Isaacson, Walter (2013), *Steve Jobs* (New York: Simon & Schuster).

ISAMAA.ee (2018), "Basic Principles of the World View of the Parish Party," https://isamaa.ee/ir li-maailmavaate-aluspohimotted/ (Accessed Dec. 16, 2018).

Israel Ministry of Foreign Affairs (2019), Mfa.gov.il.

Jahanian, Farnam (2018), *4 Ways Universities are Driving Innovation* (Cologny, Geneva: World Economic Forum).

Jain-Chandra, Sonali (2018), "Chart of the Week: Inequality in China," *IMF Blog*, https://blogs.i mf.org/2018/09/20/chart-of-the-week-inequality-in-china/.

Jezard, Adam (2017), *Eastern Europe became a Hot-Bed for Tech Start-Ups. This is How It Did It* (Cologny, Geneva: World Economic Forum).

Kanbur Ravi, Yue Wang, and Xiaobo Zhang (2017), "The Great Chinese Inequality Turnaround," VoxEU.org.

Kassam, Ashifa (2017), "Ontario Plans to Launch Universal Basic Income Trial Run This Summer," *The Guardian*, https://www.theguardian.com/world/2017/apr/24/canada-basic-income-trial -ontario-summer.

Kassam, Ashifa (2018), "Ontario's New Conservative Government to End Basic Income Experiment," *The Guardian*, https://www.theguardian.com/world/2018/aug/01/ontarios-new-conservative-government-to-end-basic-income-experiment.

Kennedy, John (2019), "10 brilliant start-ups from Budapest to watch," *Silicon Republic*.

Keynes, John Maynard (2009), *Essays in Persuasion* (New York: Classic House Books).

Kinstler, Linda (2018), "'Bitcoin and Guns, That's the Only Way to Save This Country,'" Bloomberg .com.

Kite-Powell, Jennifer (2018), "Why This New Innovation Hub In Israel Decided To Welcome Startups And Enterprises," Forbes.com.

Klein Leichman, Abigail (2018), "Why Israel Rocks at Commercializing Academic Innovations," Israel21c.

Kuznets, Simon. (1955), "Economic Growth and Income Inequality," *American Economic Review* 45(1): 1–28.

Lajtai-Szabó, Gergely (2019), "The Most Promising Hungarian Startups of 2018," *Daily News Hungary*.

Leibovitz, Liel (2015), "For WeWork's Adam Neumann, It's about Finding a Way to 'Change the World,'" *Creator by WeWork*.

Levy, Dotan (2018), "In Frenzied Israeli Coworking Market, Smaller Competitors Drop Out," *CTECH*, https://www.calcalistech.com/ctech/articles/0,7340,L-3739434,00.html.

Lutchen, Kenneth R. (2018), "Why Companies and Universities Should Forge Long-Term Collaborations," *Harvard Business Review*.

Maddison, Angus (2007), *Contours of the World Economy 1–2030 AD: Essays in Macro-Economic History* (Oxford: Oxford University Press), 427 pp.

Madise, Ülle, Pritt Vinkel, and Epp Maaten (2006), "Internet Voting at the Elections of Local Government Councils on October 2005: Report," Estonian National Electoral Committee.

MarketWatch (n.d.), "Giant Manufacturing Co. Ltd.," https://www.marketwatch.com/investing/ stock/9921/profile.

Marti, Simon (2017), "Switzerland's Apprenticeship System: A Source of Inspiration," Techniques.

Mazzucato, Mariana (2015), *The Entrepreneurial State: Debunking Public vs. Private Sector Myths*, Revised Edition (New York: Public Affairs).

McClellan, Doug (2008), "For A-Team Bikes Are Mission Possible," *Bicycle Retailer*, https://www.bicycleretailer.com/international/2008/05/02/team-bikes-are-mission-possible#.XBARB9tKiUk.

McKay, Ailsa (2001), "Rethinking Work and Income Maintenance Policy: Promoting Gender Equality Through a Citizens' Basic Income," *Feminist Economics* 7(1): 97–118.

Meltzer, Joshua P. (2016), *Taiwan's Economic Opportunities and Challenges and the Importance of the Trans-Pacific Partnership* (Brookings Institution).

Mihály Fazekas, S.F. (2013), *A Skills beyond School review of Switzerland* (OECD Publishing).

Ministry of Education (2011), "Technological and Vocational Education in Taiwan."

Mitchell, Julian (2016), "Startup Nation: This Israeli Company Uses Military Principles To Build Scalable Businesses," Forbes.com.

MomentumBiking.com (n.d.), "Giant Bicycles," https://www.momentum-biking.com/global/about-us.

Monobank.biz (2018), "Развитие Монобанка | omono — Все о Монобанке, (Development of Monobank | omono — All about Monobank)" Monobank.biz.

Morton, Michael Quentin (2016), *Keepers of the Golden Shore: A History of the United Arab.*

Muehlemann, Samuel (2016), Making Apprenticeships Profitable for Firms and

Myrna Flores, et al. (2009), "Universities As Key Enablers to Develop New".

Nathani, Komal (2018), "Stanford is the Top Producer of Startups in the World," Entrepreneur.

News (2018), "Income Inequality in Switzerland Remains Stable after Redistribution," https://lenews.ch/2018/01/26/income-inequality-in-switzerland-remains-stable-after-redistribution/.

OECD (2003), *Reviews of National Policies for Education - Tertiary Education in Switzerland* (Paris: OECD Publication Service).

OECD (2010a), *Finland: Slow and Steady Reform for Consistently High Results* (Paris: OECD Publication Service).

OECD (2010b), "SMEs, Entrepreneurship and Innovation," http://www.oecd.org/cfe/smesentrepreneurshipandinnovation.htm.

OECD (2017), "Supporting Entrepreneurship and Innovation in Higher Education in Hungary," http://www.oecd.org/industry/supporting-entrepreneurship-and-innovation-in-higher-education-in-hungary-9789264273344-en.htm.

OECD (2018), "The Role and Design of Net Wealth Taxes in the OECD," https://doi.org/10.1787/9789264290303-en.

Oecdbetterlifeindex.org (2017), "How's Life?" http://www.oecdbetterlifeindex.org/ (Accessed Aug. 16, 2017).

Once in A Lifetime Journey (2017), "18 Surprising facts about Bhutan," https://www.onceinalifetimejourney.com/once-in-a-lifetime-journeys/asia/18-surprising-facts-about-bhutan/ (Accessed Aug. 23, 2017).

Oral, Gunsell (2006), "Creativity of Turkish Prospective Teachers," *Creativity Research Journal* 18(1): 65–73, https://www.tandfonline.com/doi/abs/10.1207/s15326934crj1801_8.

Ostry, Jonathan D., Andrew Berg, and Charalambos G. Tsangarides (2014), *Redistribution, Inequality, and Growth* (International Monetary Fund).

Oxfam International (2014), *Working for the Few: Political Capture and Economic Inequality.*

Papenek, Gustav F., and Oldrich Kyn (1986), "The Effect on Income Distribution of Development, the Growth Rate and Economic Strategy," *Journal of Development Economics* 23(1): 55–65.

Parliament of Estonia (2018), "Session Hall of the Riigikogu," https://www.riigikogu.ee/en/visit-us/toompea-castle/session-hall-of-the-riigikogu/. (Accessed Dec. 16, 2018).

Paukert, F. (2007), "La répartition du revenu adifférents niveaux de developpement: Quelques aspects concrets," *Revue Internationale du Travail* 108, 103–134.

Paz-Frankel, Einat (2016), "Israel Is 2nd Most Innovative Country," *Israeli Innovation News*.

Paz-Frankel, Einat (2017), "Israeli Office-Sharing Startups Are Changing the Way We Work, Expanding Globally," *Israeli Innovation News*.

Perotti, Roberto (1996), "Growth, Income Distribution, and Democracy: What the Data Say," *Journal of Economic Growth* 1(2): 149–187.

Piketty, Thomas (2014), *Capital in the 21st Century* (Cambridge, MA: Belknap Press).

Planning Tank (2017), "Gross National Happiness (GNH) Index," https://planningtank.com/development-planning/gross-national-happiness-gnh-index (Accessed Aug. 17, 2017).

Psacharopoulos, George and Harry Anthony Patrinos (2004), "Returns to Investment in Education: A Further Update," *Education Economics* 12(2): 111–134.

Publique, C. S. (2007), *Accord intercantonal sur l'harmonisation de la scolarié obigatoire (concordat HarmoS)*.

Quora (2017), "Why Isn't Bhutan the Happiest Country as Per the Latest World Happiness Report by the UN? https://www.quora.com/Why-isnt-Bhutan-the-happiest-country-as-per-the-latest-world-happiness-report-by-the-UN (Accessed Aug. 17, 2017).

Ragusa, Frank, and Nathaniel Barzideh (2014), "Abenomics and Japanese Monetary Policy: A Path to Economic and Ethical Recovery," Wharton Research Scholars, University of Pennsylvania.

Ram, Rati. (1988), "Economic Development and Inequality: An Overlooked Regression Constraint," *Economic Development and Cultural Change* 43(2): 425–434.

Ratcliffe, Alison (2016), "'Secret' Giant is World's Biggest Bicycle Manufacturer and Still Growing," *Supply Management*, https://www.cips.org.

Redding, Gordon (1995), *The Spirit of Chinese Capitalism* (Berlin: de Gruyter).

Roberts, Edward B., and Charles E. Eesley (2009), "Entrepreneurial Impact: The Role of MIT," *The Foundation of Entrepreneurship*.

Robinson, James A. (2009), "Industrial Policy And Development: A Political Economy Perspective," in World Bank ABCDE Conference.

Robinson, Ken (2011), *Out of Our Minds: Learning to Be Creative* (Chichester, UK: Capstone).

Robinson, Sir Ken (2006), "Do Schools Kill Creativity?" *TED Talk*.

Rogers, Perry McAdow (2011), *Aspects of Western Civilization: Problems and Sources in History* (Boston: Prentice Hall).

Rogowski, Mikolaj (2013), *Harnessing Central and Eastern Europe's innovative potential* (World Intellectual Property Organization).

Saith, Ashwani (1983), "Development and Distribution: A Critique of the Cross-Country U-Hypothesis," *Journal of Development Economics* 13(3): 367–382.

Sammartino, Frank (2017), "Taxes and Income Inequality," Tax Policy Centre, Urban Institute and Brookings Institution, https://www.taxpolicycenter.org/publications/taxes-and-income-inequality/full.

Satell, Greg (2014), "Could Ukraine Be The Next Silicon Valley?" Forbes.com.

Satell, Greg (2016), "Innovative Companies Get Their Best Ideas from Academic Research — Here's How They Do It," *Harvard Business Review*.

Savvidesa, Andreas, and Thanasis Stengos (2000), "Income Inequality and Economic Development: Evidence from the Threshold Regression Model," *Economics Letters* 69(2): 207–212.

Schwab, Klaus (2018), "Competitiveness Rankings," The Global Competitiveness Report 2018.

Sheahen, Allan. (2012), *Basic Income Guarantee: Your Right to Economic Security* (New York: Palgrave Macmillan).

Sheremeta, Bozhena (2015), "Snapchat Buys Looksery in Reported $150 Million Deal, Making it Biggest Acquisition of Ukraine Tech Player," *Kyiv Post*.

Singapore Management University (2013), *The Singapore Constitution: A Brief Introduction* (Singapore: SMU Student Publications).

Smolucha,, Larry, and Francine C. Smolucha (1986), "L.S. Vygotsky's Theory of Creative Imagination," in 94th Annual Convention of the American Psychological Association.

Solomon, Shoshanna (2016), "In Nod to Startup Nation, Ivory Towers Foster Entrepreneurs," Timesofisrael.com.

Solomon, Shoshanna (2017), "Israel's Inovytec Gets $3m Boost from China's Vincent," Timesofisrael .com.

Solomon, Shoshanna (2018), "In New Vision for Hebrew University, All Students Will Study Entrepreneurship," Timesofisrael.com.

Solt, Frederick (2016), "The Standardized World Income Inequality Database," *Social Science Quarterly* 97(5): 1267–1281.

Stanford d.school (2019), Stanford d.school, Stanford d.school.

Statistics Times (2017), "List of Countries by GDP (Nominal)," http://statisticstimes.com/eco nomy/countries-by-gdp.php (Accessed Aug. 23, 2017).

Studwell Joe (2013), *How Asia Works* (London: Profile Books).

StudyCountry (2017), "Religious Beliefs and Spirituality in Bhutan," http://www.studycountry.c om/guide/BT-religion.htm (Accessed Aug. 16, 2017).

Sung Kim, John (2018), "Ukraine Is the Best Kept Secret in California's Startup Scene," Forbes.com.

Szabo, Balazs (2013), "How Central Eastern Europe Is Transforming from Outsourcing to A Real Tech Hub," Forbes.com.

Takada, Masahiro (1999), *Japan's Economic Miracle: Underlying Factors and Strategies for the Growth* (New York).

Tessin, C. i. (2010), *Plan d'étude Romand*. Retrieved from tessin, C. i. (2010), Plan d'étude Romand. https://www.plandetudes.ch/web/guest/PG2-fg Neuchatel: Secrétariat général de la CIIP.

"The Basic Law of Hong Kong," at https://www.gov.hk.

The Economist (2013), "How did Estonia become a leader in technology?"

The Economist (2018), "Steering Chile Away from the Middle-Income Trap," https://www.eco nomist.com/the-americas/2018/09/29/steering-chile-away-from-the-middle-income-trap.

The Economist Intelligence Unit (2018), "Creating Innovation Ecosystems in Eastern Europe."

The Local (2016), "Swiss to Vote on Guaranteed Income for All," https://www.thelocal.ch/201601 27/swiss-to-vote-on-guaranteed-income-for-all.

The Local (2018), "Swiss Town Set for Universal Basic Income Experiment," https://www.thelocal .ch/20180606/swiss-town-set-for-universal-basic-income-experiment-rheinau.

The World Bank (1996), "A New Dataset Measuring Income Inequality."

The World Bank (2006), Policy Development and Reform Principles of Basic and Secondary Education in Finland since 1968.

The World Bank (2015), "Inequality, uprisings, and conflict in the Arab World."

The World Bank (2016), "Top Incomes and the Measurement of Inequality in Egypt," *World Bank Economic Review*, 32(2).

The World Bank Group (2017), *Innovation and Entrepreneurship Ecosystem Diagnostic* (Ukraine: The World Bank Group).

Times Higher Education (2017), *World University Rankings 2016–2017*.

Tkach, Igor (2018), "A Practical Guide to Building Productive Offshore Development Teams in Ukraine," Forbes.com.

Tourism Council of Bhutan (2017), "Plants and Animals," http://www.tourism.gov.bt/about-bhu tan/flora-fauna (Accessed Aug. 16, 2017).

van der Weide, Roy, Christoph Lakner, and Elena Ianchovichina (2017), "Is inequality Underestimated in Egypt? Evidence from House Prices," *Review of Income and Wealth* 64(1).

Van Parijs, Philippe (2000), "Basic Income for Allm," *Boston Review*, http://bostonreview.net/a rchives/BR25.5/vanparijs.html.

Vargas, Jose Antonio (2010), "The Face of Facebook," *New Yorker*, September

Verme, Paolo, Branko Milanovic, Sherine Al-Shawarby, Sahar El Tawila, May Gadallah, and Ali El-Majeed (2014), *Inside Inequality in the Arab Republic of Egypt: Facts and Perceptions Across People, Time, and Space* (Washington, DC: World Bank Publications). http://visionofhuman ity.org/indexes/global-peace-index/ (Accessed Aug. 23, 2017).

Wallen, Joe (2018a), "How Has Lithuania Become One of Europe's Most Exciting Fintech Hotspots?" Forbes.com.

Wallen, Joe (2018b), "Monobank Leads the Expeditious Emergence of Ukraine's Fintech Sector," Forbes.com.

Watts, Julia (2019), "The Top 10 European cities for Start-ups to Launch in after Brexit," Startups .co.uk.

Widerquist, Karl (2013), *Independence, Propertylessness, and Basic Income: A Theory of Freedom As the Power to Say No* (New York: Palmgrave Macmillan).

World Happiness Report (2017), "Frequently Asked Questions," http://worldhappiness.report/faq/.

World Health Organization (2017), "Suicide Rates per 100 000 Population," http://www.who.int/g ho/mental_health/suicide_rates/en/ (Accessed Aug. 17, 2017).

Yin, David (2016), "Secrets To Israel's Innovative Edge," Forbes.com.

Yin, David (2017), "What Makes Israel's Innovation Ecosystem So Successful," Forbes.com.

Zhu, Xiaodong, "Understanding China's Growth: Past, Present, and Future," *Journal of Economic Perspectives* 26(4): 103–124.

Conclusion

Arturo Bris

The crisis of 2020 will certainly go down in history as the most serious of the last hundred years, and it will remain in the memory of several generations. Falls in production, wages, employment, and prosperity are massive in every country in the world, from China and the United States to Finland, Mexico, Switzerland, and Namibia. In a perverse sequence of supply and demand shocks, our economies are today in cardiac arrest from which most countries will recover, although with side effects that will remain for years.

Most of this book was written in the pre-pandemic era. In the years following the Global Financial Crisis of 2008, there has been a growing mistrust in governments and an increasing conviction that public policy is either an obstacle to economic prosperity, or a passive agent not responding diligently enough to crises. This is not surprising given the poor policies that followed the fall of Lehman Brothers and the subsequent recession that extended everywhere. Increases in income inequality, more and more countries submitting to non-democratic systems, the loss of jobs, the fragmentation of societies, and a negative attitude toward immigration have been the result of the crisis. The most important symptom, however, is that our economic and political systems did not guarantee people's prosperity and the competitiveness of nations.

62. WALLS

By the time the first cases of Covid-19 were publicized in China, our world was divided at different levels and with varying degrees of conflict. We had built walls that were keeping people separated. The first wall was generational. In the next years, the world is going to witness the biggest wealth transfer in human history, from baby boomers and Generation X to millennials. Our kids are taking over and their demands and ideas are

457

completely different from ours. I consider my cohort (I come from Gen-X) as the first generation in history that can be considered a "learning" generation. Traditionally, people learn from their parents, and educate their children. In contrast, Generation X has learned from their parents, but we are now learning from—not teaching—our children. This is because they do not have much to learn from us: we have grown up with the idea that jobs are for life; that many of our jobs are *bullshit jobs*.[1] We have considered earning an income as our way to achieve a decent quality of life, and we have learned to use technology and adapted to it, because there were no computers when we were at school.

Instead, our children are preparing themselves to perform tasks, not jobs. And for them, self-fulfillment (and not income) is paramount. This is because *shit jobs* (jobs that nobody wants to do) are going to be taken over by machines and technology. Technology that they have not learned, because they were born with it, they are its sons and daughters. A new generation that, in contrast to our individualism, values collectivism and the social good much more than we do. That is why we have Greta Thunberg and why more and more members of the younger generations are vegan, environmentally aware, politically active, and more tolerant to others than us 20th-century bigots.

In addition to a wall between generations, there is a wall erected between genders. The #MeToo movement started in 2017 and it has increased our awareness about the big gap between men and women in terms of sociopolitical rights, pay, and access to education. Part 5 of the book addressed this in detail, with my conclusion being that much more needs to be done, by both companies and governments.

Of course, in a world of growing income inequality, the barrier between the rich and poor is higher than ever. But as much as inequality has grown within countries, it is also worrisome that social disparities between rich and poor countries are also larger now than 10 years ago. In search of a better life, many people from developing economies and poor nations are leaving their homes, and poverty has caused one of the biggest exoduses in human history. In the most developed countries, the reaction has often been very negative toward immigrants, resulting in increasing populism and nationalism.

The environmental wall that separates societies is less visible. In principle, there should not be any disagreement with the notion that the preservation of our world and its resources requires immediate attention, and that we have gone too far with fossil fuels, pollution, and overexploitation of natural resources. However, political agendas and corporate interests are at odds with each other, and many are demanding a complete overhaul of our economic system in order to make sustainability our priority, instead of tax revenues and profits.

In the early 2000s, I used to think that globalization could be the countervailing force against some of the dividing walls mentioned above, but in the post-2008 era there has been a noticeable period of deglobalization. Protectionism and trade wars have surprisingly become the solution to a prisoner's dilemma-like conflict between economic powers. And I say surprisingly because, from the beginning of our work 30 years ago, we have defended that openness and international trade create a win-win situation for countries. When China and the United States moved toward more protectionism, there was no other route for other economies (the European Union, Latin America, South East Asia, Australia, etc.) to respond in the same way. However, in a trade war there are no winners, only losers.

Indeed, the US–China trade war is a race for technological dominance. Technology has been another separating factor in our societies. The United Nations Commission for Trade and Development (UNCTAD) has shown that the geography of the digital economy is concentrated in two countries, the United States and China. These two countries account for 75 percent of the patents related to blockchain technology, 50 percent of the global spending on the Internet of Things (IoT), and more than 75 percent of the cloud computing market. Besides, 90 percent of the market capitalization of the 70 largest digital platforms is traded in either US or Chinese stock markets.[2]

Finally, because governments and inefficient policies contributed to the global financial crisis and because the same governments were unable to help people in its aftermath, our political systems are also in crisis. Leadership has moved from the public to the private sector, with many of the big changes happening in our world in recent years being initiated by corporate leaders, social influencers, and non-governmental organizations. With democracy in crisis, populism has grown. But although populist solutions may be appealing, they do not solve our most crucial problems.

63. SOME WALLS ARE PSYCHOLOGICAL, OTHERS REQUIRE POLICY

Initially, a certain degree of personal responsibility should be demanded to take down these walls. Individual attitudes toward immigration and gender issues, as well as individual actions to protect the environment should help change our societies. But individuals and private initiative cannot do it all. Some walls require governmental policies, very often coordinated internationally.

The first claim in this book is that now, more than ever, governments are important. To make our democracies more effective, we need to implement processes that empower people and reduce corruption and inefficiencies. The fight against income inequality (as I showed in Part 5 of the book) requires responses, either through universal income schemes, or through more egalitarian fiscal policies. Immigration can be tackled from the top down by opening borders and accepting foreign labor, as this is a way to improve the competitiveness of domestic talent.

But this is not all. I am strongly convinced that the environmental protection race that we have started requires the intervention of governments. Companies and individuals by themselves cannot be responsible for a sustainable world. In a recent event in Copenhagen, the chief executive officer (CEO) of one of the largest companies in Denmark was questioned by the audience regarding the firm's environmental policy. The CEO's response was that, unless governance rules changed, he could not undertake measures that would cost the company 1 percent of its profit margin, and probably 5 percent of its stock market value—he and his executive team would be fired by the board. Therefore, in order to support a country's business infrastructure, firms need public policy to allow them to be profitable and sustainable. The extended idea that sustainability results only from exploiting win-win opportunities for customers and society is, in my opinion, flawed.

In a digital economy, knowledge and talent are key assets for a country. That is why I pay so much attention to education in this book. The most successful countries are those with good education systems. The causality goes in both directions: it is easy enough for Singapore and Finland to invest in education, compared to Ghana and Brazil. At the same time, the best investment a country can make is its people. And it is shocking how many countries—a few examples are described in the book—bypass the opportunities provided by a positive economic cycle, and do not reform and boost their education systems. Education and infrastructure are the most important responsibilities of a competitiveness-driven government. And both require long-term policies, social consensus, and stability of policies that go beyond one generation.

I am not claiming that we need more regulation, nor should my recommendations be taken as a defense of planning economies, like those that characterized Europe and Asia after World War II. We need better, not more regulation, and we should praise regulators in the aftermath of the 2008 crisis for giving us rules that better protect customers and shareholders. The world is a better place thanks to Basel III, the European Shareholders Rights Directive, and the Dodd–Frank Wall Street Reform and Consumer Protection Act, for example. Additionally, the capitalist system has changed, and the new business ecosystem involves the government, either as a financier or as an active agent that provides firms with a license to operate. Such systems were analyzed in Part 4 of the book. Once the public and private sectors interact, the resulting model is fairer and more efficient: the government guarantees a level playing field, facilitates business with a friendly environment and invests in infrastructure and education; the private sector is responsible for creating jobs and paying high salaries.

The second message of the book is that national governments should embrace competitiveness and prosperity as the main objective of their country's strategy. Competitiveness is a key performance indicator (KPI), and its value drivers are education, infrastructure, technology, rule of law, efficient capital markets, transparent governments, good regulation, natural resources, values, and culture. When these value drivers combine into a productive economic system, jobs are created, taxes are collected, the government can invest, and the country attracts foreign capital and talent, which ultimately generates prosperity and enhances quality of life. I have provided a tool to measure the success of countries.

64. WHAT THE PANDEMIC HAS TAUGHT US

Finally, let me finish this book with some lessons learned in the first six months of 2020.

The pandemic has taught us, firstly, that a country's gross domestic product (GDP) is the economy's thermometer, but not its medicine. I want to say that when the Organization for Cooperation and Development (OECD) estimated in its last economic outlook that the world economy will fall, in the best case, by 6 percent in 2020, we all understand the magnitude of the crisis and can estimate its impact on our lives. But these figures do little to guide our governments on the best solution to remedy the crisis. The fact that the United States will contract by 7.3 percent while the Spanish economy will shrink by 11.1 percent does not mean that Spain and the United States should apply the same solutions.

What, then, are the right policies that we need? The ultimate goal should not be to return to positive growth figures, but to generate prosperity, consumption, economic activity, employment, and a decent quality of life. In short, competitiveness.

In the post-pandemic world, we need to spur the creation of value for society through employment and productivity, without leaving anyone behind. Only by understanding that desirable policies are those that put the individual, and businesses (large, but also small and medium), at the center of attention, will we end this decade with a higher quality of life than we began.

We have learned from the 2020 crisis that monetary policy measures that help the financial system are useless if they are not translated into more credit for households and the non-financial sector. We have understood that aiding companies in dire straits is not compatible with these firms using the funds received to buy back shares or pay dividends. We also know that direct subsidies to individuals do not work if they only increase household savings rates.

Effective policies—competitiveness policies—must be aimed, as an ultimate goal, at increasing productivity, raising wages and expenditure, and thus state revenues through taxes. The state has to manage the public finances so that both the costs and the benefits of public spending are fairly distributed, promoting sustainability and environmental protection. The priority of public policy is to manage the short term, without forgetting that infrastructures and health and education systems are key to ensuring a country's long-term prosperity. Governments must improve the efficiency of the public sector by eliminating bureaucracy and fighting corruption. At the same time, the private sector needs to implement corporate governance rules that promote transparency and transform economies through technology and innovation. And all this must be done with the understanding that job creation is a task for the private sector, not the public sector; that the necessary social consensus must be generated so that everyone assumes the personal and economic cost of a perverse crisis and an onerous recovery.

NOTES

1 Graeber, David (2018), *Bullshit Jobs: A Theory*, Simon & Schuster, pp. 368.
2 UNCTAD Digital Economy Report 2019.

Index

463

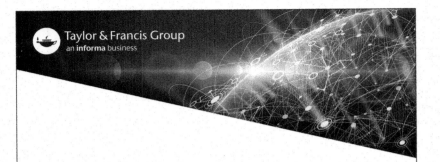